FIRES IN THE IN-BASKET

FIRES IN THE IN-BASKET

The ABC's of the State Department

JOHN P. LEACACOS

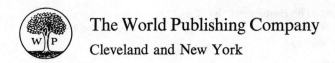 The World Publishing Company
Cleveland and New York

Published by The World Publishing Company
2231 West 110th Street, Cleveland, Ohio 44102
Published simultaneously in Canada by
Nelson, Foster & Scott Ltd.

First Printing 1968

ACKNOWLEDGMENTS

The poem "The Bureaucrat" by Katie Louchheim is from
With or Without Roses, Doubleday, © 1966. Reprinted by
permission.

The definition of the gyroscope is from *The Random
House Dictionary of the English Language.* © Copyright
1966, 1967 by Random House, Inc. Reprinted by
permission.

The quotation by J. R. Wiggins, editor of the *Washington
Post,* is from an article entitled "President, Press, Dissent
and War." Reprinted by permission.

CONTENTS

For

Velia

and

Peter

PREFACE

ONE OF THE AMUSING SIDE-lights of doing this primer has been the reaction among friends in the State Department. Some thought it was to be a snow job; others, a hatchet job. I hope it is an authentic job. It proposes to give some indication of the way in which the State Department is supposed to function; the way in which it actually functions; and the way in which it should function, according to the more progressive and realistic minds in it.

Regrettably, there will be no merry rattling of skeletons in this work. I have not been the beneficiary of any revelations from on high. Consequently, it has been catch as catch can to parse history in motion, even at the periphery.

Like most of my colleagues, I would like to know 99.99 per cent of what really goes on, who said what to whom, what did they mean by it, what did they really intend to do, and what the results were—good or bad. In short, the facts. Yet, facts crumble and disappear in the swirls of history.

So, better still, the technicalities. These one can try to clothe with the steamy spoor of human beings and their motivations, to evoke a hint of even diplomacy's raw richness, or, at least, to attain some texture of veri-similitude and a sprinkle of the gold dust that rubs off reality and gives weight to the narration. Its shimmer, alas, may turn out to be only the melting sparkle on the mist of appearances. In any event, a modicum of insurance is needed against the risk of being led down the garden path by predigested conclusions or the disclosures from the edge of which slips out a self-serving interest.

I must record a series of off-stage effects in the course of my inquiries: a mockery of Proust, a shadow of Kafka, an echo of the Duc de Saint-Simon, a wisp of Orwell, and, while ruminating among the classic diplomatic types, a vision of Henry Adams *en gelée*. The full scenario needs the talents of a Namier-Tocqueville, perhaps with a slight assist from Al Capp.

To the scores of individuals, high and low, in and out of government, who have been helpful and patient in the preparation of this essay, my appreciation and obeisance.

J. P. L.

January 24, 1968
Arlington, Virginia

CHAPTER I

CRITICISM: Noises from the Mob

FROM THE BIRTH OF THE Republic until today, the conduct of United States foreign policy has been under intermittent attack. The State Department, more specifically, has been under constant and mounting criticism for the last twenty years. It has been a lightning rod for the nation's fears and hopes—agonizings over failed aspirations, messianic frothings, and feelings of global claustrophobia, as time and space in this age of traumatic passage are foreshortened to bring the tumult and violence of the outside world before our eyes and ears.

The historic American pendulation between daydreams of heaven-on-earth and nightdreams of Puritan hellfire was sharpened by the casualties of four major wars in the last fifty years. The vast uncertainties of the nuclear epoch have engendered subcutaneous sensitivity to alarums. The popular condition is inflamed by the crescendo of developments in the baffling rationales of the undeclared Vietnam war. The anxiety and unease are exacerbated by the antiwar demonstrations and the flatulent exaggerations that some youth of the 1960's affect. This youthful segment of the population—more than half under thirty, the average American male being only twenty-six—is the volatile and unformed backdrop against which high policy is played.

Today the State Department has become the perennial scapegoat for the imported ills beyond our national control. All manners of men and stylists of expression feel licensed to participate in the game of pinpricking the American diplomat. Once it used to be that every man was a self-proclaimed expert on women, liquor, religion, and food. Today, thanks to the millions who have fought and traveled overseas, every man-jack is now also an expert on foreign affairs—with his latest off-the-cuff opinion buttressed by snatches from blurred newspaper headlines, half-tidbits from radio, and photoflashes from TV.

The lounge-chair diplomat has succeeded the arm-chair strategist and the Monday-morning quarterback. The vogue of spy novels, movies, and TV serials, not to mention the comic strips, promotes the familiarity that sniffs and snorts at the U.S. diplomat. The barroom broadsides are orchestrated on a somewhat higher level in university halls. Ganglions of academic intellectuals shoot fusillades at the State Department's lack of unspecified creativity and imaginativeness. The fervid protests obscure the professors' absent-mindedness about the realities, complexities, and absurdities of the American political system of checks, double-checks, and stalemates. Adding to the verbal carnage are atavistic resentments from the valley-minds of the peasant-immigrant nationality groups.

Nor has the nation's business community befriended the reputation of the State Department. The middle-class and middle-management businessmen have no experience of the class oppression which the immigrants remember and which foreign policy must take into account indirectly. The prosperous merchant or manufacturer rarely has a clue as to what it means to live in misery and build up the potential of political explosiveness with which American diplomacy may later have to cope.

Like the conservative currents, the nation's liberal leanings, too, are reflected in views of the State Department. The liberal critique stems from attitudes of open-handed reasonableness to compromise; in America there is so much that can be divvied up generously. The natives take it for granted that terms will be honored by both sides, a phenomenon not necessarily axiomatic in the rest of the world.

Bedeviled by visionaries of past utopias on the right and of future panaceas on the left, the State Department with its own defensiveness does little to uphold its fair name. A clutter of clichés obfuscates the ingenuous: The State Department has no constituents like the vested interests that flock around the Department of Agriculture; no resources such as those the Department of Interior can provide in forest preserves, petroleum, and minerals; and no products such as those the gargantuan Department of Defense can generate through multimillion-dollar procurement contracts. Small wonder the State Department sometimes acts like a masochistic Joan of Arc or, at other times, like a furtive Typhoid Mary.

In another way the Department is the victim of a delayed shock reaction. Americans are first mystified and then indignant at tales of perfidious diplomatic practices by foreigners. The sense of outrage is transposed to American diplomats suspected of practicing the same dark arts of duplicity. Unable to vent their wrath on the distant foreigners and their devious practices, the citizens take it out on their fellows closer to home.

The abuse runs from the trite to the malicious. The Department was a "bowl of jelly" to President Kennedy, a "fudge factory" to former Under Secretary George W. Ball, a "taffy-pull" to Under Secretary Nicholas deB. Katzenbach, and a rack of poached eggheads to others. Foreign ambassadors in Washington have called it a "good rescue squad"—but no hospital for world ills.

Others recall that the British muddled through their foreign policy; the Americans keep theirs in the deep-freeze, or blast off all over the place. Many Congressmen profess to believe the Department is practically moribund. A Capitol Hill wit charged, "There wasn't enough current in the State Department to keep a glow worm from going blind." Another wag claimed that the mills of the gods grind slowly, but they probably grind a damned sight faster than those of the Department of State. Press pundits pick lint off everything the State Department does. Even Secretary of State Dean Rusk, when mildly assailed for some characteristic bureaucratic pokiness in the Department, threw up his hands, shrugged his shoulders, and said with a wry grin, "You know how the State Department is. . . ."

Consistently the critic tends to think of the State Department and its supposedly sinister core, the Foreign Service, as much more powerful entities than they are. The corporate indictment is that "THEY" failed to protect us against the strangers who would assault this happy land.

It is an old and tired canard. More than a century and a half ago, in 1798, Congressman John Nicholas of Virginia began the denigration. "What could be benefitted by any sort of compact these foreign agents [our own diplomats] could frame for us," he said. In 1859, Congressman Benjamin W. Stanton of Ohio asseverated, "I know of no other area of public service that is more emphatically useless than the diplomatic service —none in the world."

Seventy years ago, Secretary of State John Hay thought the State Department was "an antiquated, feeble organization influenced by precedents and routine inherited from another century, remote from the public gaze and indifferent to it." In 1905, advisers to Secretary of State Elihu Root were "horrified at the pitifully inadequate State Department organization for conduct of foreign affairs." Both President Wilson and Secretary of State William Jennings Bryan distrusted the Department as being "too slow moving and conservative."

In 1918, a State Department veteran rated Department personnel "terribly weak and utterly incapable." At the end of World War II, a Department special consultant said, "The point has been reached where there can be no question concerning the widespread dissatisfaction regarding the State Department as an institution."

At the same time, the New York Times ripped the foreign policy conducted by the State Department as "inept, hesitant and equivocating." A seedbed of the noxious atmosphere surrounding the Department was the nationalistic xenophobia of Depression days. When economic disaster hit the nation, concurrently, liquidation of war debts by America's allies from

World War I stopped with the Hoover moratorium on intergovernmental payments in 1931. Popular discontent was visited upon the allies. The ultimate victim again became the Department—for "protecting" foreign interests. To the lexicon of opprobrium at that time were added the adjectives "amateurish," "constipated," and "unreliable."

The isolationism of the 1920's and the neutralism of the 1930's splintered into two contending camps on the eve of World War II: America Firsters and those who believed that the rise of Nazi Germany made it imperative for the United States to re-enter the world scene. The 150-year-old debate between isolationists and interventionists was to shatter on the rocks of reality. Unavoidably, the State Department was caught in the tug of war. It caught flak from both sides. In 1942, a book entitled *The Riddle of the State Department,* by Robert Bendiner, charged the Department with favoring appeasement and representing the so-called Eastern Establishment.

With the war's end there was a free-for-all. Experts attacked foreign policy decisions. Ethnic blocs and Republicans were indignant at the "sell-out" of Eastern Europe at Yalta. The manner in which the nation was apparently losing the peace after winning the war exasperated the citizens. The witch-hunt atmosphere began with the first accusation of Communist cliques in the State Department. The nadir was reached in 1953 when U.S. Senator Joseph R. McCarthy of Wisconsin, opposing the confirmation of Charles ("Chip") Bohlen as Ambassador to the Soviet Union, cried in Congress: "Where statesmen should have been working for us, traitors and their dupes connived against us. Where patriots should have fought, cowards fled the enemy or joined its camp."

Faggots for burning the State Department were piling up at the stake. Bitter Zionists denounced the Department as pro-Arab and ready to let Jewish refugees in the new state of Israel be massacred by the Arab armies. The Department was the butt of pro-Israel Americans in the Suez crisis of 1956 and in the Arab-Israeli war in 1967.

George Kennan, former Counselor of the State Department, wrote in the McCarthy period: "The Foreign Service has been weakened beyond real hope of recovery. The Service has become the helpless object of discouragement and defamation by outside critics; hemmed in and suffocated by competing services and demoralized by security agents. The Eisenhower Administration has inherited not a going professional service, but an administrative ruin."

Gerald W. Johnson said shortly after, in the *New Republic*: "It has become dangerous, if not suicidal, for an official of the State Department to show any sign of intelligence, for the men who have dominated the scene in the past year and a half, intelligence, being utterly alien, is a threat."

Nonetheless, R. W. Scott McLeod, the late Security Chief of the State Department, pressed the attack. He said, "U.S. diplomats imitate the dress, accent, mannerisms and even the thinking of foreigners." McLeod was virtually quoting U.S. Senator William E. Robertson of New York, who, in 1885, had said, "This diplomatic service is working our ruin by creating a desire for foreign customs and follies."

Former Under Secretary Ball had an explanation for the hysteria of McCarthyism: that it had been bred in the disillusionment of the American people after the war, when, in the wake of heroic valor and astronomical expenditure, they had demobilized the mighty armies and fleets, only to find the new villain of Soviet Communism appearing to foil their dreams of peace and fair weather.

Whereas in prewar years the Department had been criticized for being too conservative, in postwar years it was more often raked over the coals for being too liberal. The right wing thought that the new internationalism— Clare Boothe Luce tagged it "globaloney"—neglected the nation's vital interests. Pressure groups with narrow interests belabored the Department for advocacy of foreign aid and of the necessity to help other nations, including Communist countries like Yugoslavia and Poland. The anti-foreign-aid wave rose to a new climax over military aid and the charge that such aid begat U.S. military involvements, as in Vietnam. Revived were the stale epithets of earlier years—cookie pushers, striped-pants boys, tea drinkers, messenger boys in white spats, and the rest of the tedious aspersions.

Secretary of State John Foster Dulles indirectly added his bit to the tarnished repute of the Department by scare phrases like "massive retalia-tion" and "agonizing reappraisal." Dulles' publicized posture of ignoring the Department by keeping foreign policy in his vest pocket further lessened respect for the institution.

The miasma surrounding State was not mitigated by coinage of "brink-manship," attributed to Dulles and, ironically, so advertised by his own allies in the Luce publications. The Department stood silent and defense-less. It could have made a case for public understanding of the concept behind the misbegotten word, along the lines which this writer obtained from the diplomatic pros and published in the Cleveland *Plain Dealer* in November 1952, before the term was invented. The lead of the article said: "New policies for overcoming the Soviet Russian threat, clearly sig-naled as the prime task of President-elect Dwight D. Eisenhower, will have to be positive enough to exert real pressure on the Kremlin, but in so doing will force the United States to take constant calculated risks of starting World War III."

Further verbal mayhem upon the State Department, the repercussions of which are still being felt today, was inflicted by the nation's principal official, in charge of foreign policy and all else, President John F. Kennedy. As a Congressman, Kennedy had been neither impressed nor amused by the caliber of the Foreign Service officers he had met on trips abroad. He felt that they knew neither the language nor the customs of the countries to which they were assigned and spent too much time at tennis and cocktails. President Kennedy's anger with the CIA and collateral slow burn at the State Department after the Bay of Pigs fiasco increased his impatience with bureaucratic counselors who had ill-advised him or had sat on their hands while the Cuban exiles' invasion fell into the swamps of despair.

Kennedy was quoted time and again as being clearly irked at the State Department's lack of ideas; as saying that he and his staff, above all, McGeorge Bundy, could get more work done in one day in the White House than the State Department could in six months and that giving instructions to the State Department was like dropping notes into the dead-letter box.

The President's irritation at the traditional lethargy of the Department was heightened by his belief that his decisions were never executed or that their implementation was changed in a manner which negated the policy he wanted to pursue. Kennedy's distaste for the State Department was inherited by former associates who continued to bemoan the lack of ideas at State and its failure to re-examine the basic premises of American foreign policy, and it was shared by traditional liberals like U.S. Senator Joseph S. Clark of Pennsylvania, who found continual evidence of the "frozen *status quo* outlook of our foreign policy."

The Kennedy years sparked a spate of journalistic autopsies, inquiries with such titles as "What's Wrong with the State Department?," "The Trouble with the State Department," "The Soul Searching of the State Department," "Disarray at State," "Foggy Bottomology," "State Department Turmoil and Turnover," "Is the State Department Losing Us the Cold War?," "Latest Troubles in the State Department," and "Reorganization at State."

Under the Johnson administration, criticism of the State Department as such has been somewhat sidetracked in favor of wholesale assault on the conduct of the Vietnam war by the President, the Secretary of State, and the Secretary of Defense, sparking an apparent revulsion toward neoisolationism. There were anguished afterthoughts in the U.S. Senate Foreign Relations Committee and lamentations concerning the self-righteous obsession and overcommitment of U.S. power endemic in State Department policies.

When not taking aim at Vietnam, the pugilists of journalism zeroed in on the crisis of the Foreign Service, the tardiness in filling key positions at

State and at overseas embassies, the managerial confusion, and the old refrain of bureaucratic inertia.

What amazed and depressed the observer was the pure ignorance and insular self-absorption mirrored in the popular criticism, a condition which in past periods of history has been an indicator of incipient decline of nations to second-rate status.

Nothing so portentous is soon in store because of the sheer spill-over vitality of the American nation. But the indictment can be made that the lack of education and information evident in American citizenry is down-right appalling. Much of the criticism is vacuous because of failure to comprehend fundamental considerations in the role of the State Department. The nation is heir to the debris of World War II and corollary con-flicts like the Korean and Vietnam wars. The late *New York Herald Tribune,* on November 30, 1945, spoke to the point: "There is a tangled legacy from all sorts of conflicting policies and personalities being administered by an equal tangle of conflicting agencies and authorities. The United States cannot indefinitely leave these foreign policies to the accidental interplay of the brilliant amateur, the opinionated eccentric and the bureaucratic intriguer."

The period of the sharpest criticism of the State Department coincides with the years of greatest foreign affairs activity in American history— Berlin, Cuba, Vietnam, the Congo and Communist China, their seismic tidal waves still in train. In less than one generation the State Department has sailed from a comparatively stagnant sidewater full thrust into the whirlpool of clashing world interests, rather like Nehru's India after the Chinese Communist attack of 1962. For almost 150 years the Republic practically had no need for a foreign policy. Today it must take account of 123 centers of national sovereignty in the world, nations whose foreign policies weave a spider web of restraints around the superpower of the modern United States.

The President, the Congress, and the Supreme Court can unite to enact, execute, and enforce a piece of legislation for the citizens of the United States. The State Department deals with that part of our affairs which it cannot control. As Secretary of State Dean Rusk likes to say, "They don't click their heels and salute when we show up." McGeorge Bundy made the same point to this writer at the very beginning of the Kennedy administra-tion: "We can control events in the United States; but do we control them outside the United States?"

The truism of diplomacy that is most difficult to appreciate, however, is that the most polished practitioners, acknowledged wise men, confess that they cannot see clearly, or know precisely, what is in the future. Yet the principal work of the State Department is exactly that—an exercise in the future. Constantly peering into the fog of the unknown entails, in the understatement of the century, a considerable degree of uncertainty. This underlying configuration drives the tidy minds of the fashionable systems analysts close to desperation. They confess that what actually happens is full of fantastic surprises. They neatly create categories of unpredictable events, only to have the boiling water of life shatter their antiseptic concepts.

The State Department is likewise made fretful and frustrated by the unforeseeable. The irritation of the ordinary citizen begins to become understandable. The locale of foreign events is remote, its subject matter intricate and hard to explain. The temper of the times is that of an adversary climate, overladen with fears of possible dangers and potential foes, of mysterious secrets which are never explained, even after the need for secrecy to conceal their temporary sensitivity has passed. Cankers of unanswered questions remain in the mind. Doubts burgeon about the credibility of all statements, which in their official plenitude will duly be made public only twenty or twenty-five years hence. Forced into awareness of the relevance of foreign affairs to his personal fate, the citizen indulges in verbal potshots. He usually looks at an incident in isolation, not at the circumambient situation.

He vents his wrath directly on the State Department when it says "no" to pet projects and narrow economic interests. He is ready to get rid of a problem, but he does not consider the stake the nation may have in it or how it will meet the subsequent consequences of impetuous recommendations. His pragmatic antecedents create a "solve it" complex, as if it were as easily done as said. He confuses tactics with strategy, and vice versa. He cries for compromise in negotiations, failing to recall that it takes two to make a compromise and that the most skilled negotiator fails when the other side shows no willingness to discuss acceptable solutions. Sovereign countries have minds of their own and cannot be forced to cooperate if they do not so wish, even when they are wrong.

The deepest dissatisfaction with the State Department's behavior lies perhaps in the Department's apparent flouting of the ingrained pragmatism of the American people. The popular impulse is often that of the master mechanic, Mr. Fix-It, the do-it-now man. It assumes that piecemeal pragmatics can clear the decks and let us all go home or to the movies. Formal American scholarly assumptions in vogue predicate that human activities are measurable, if not curable. While the outside world whirls along in its own indeterministic way, American intellectuals appear to concentrate on the operational immediate, leaving the future's blueprints for the next generation.

The patent conclusion to all this is that before the State Department is reformed, where it needs precise reforms, the education of the American people needs reform. There are enough books at least for the massive educational job required. The Library of Congress has nearly 3 million books, among its total of nearly 14 million volumes and pamphlets, that touch on foreign affairs. More than 55,000 titles contain the word "international." The State Department library, founded in 1789 and endowed with 18,000 volumes of Thomas Jefferson, has more than 575,000 volumes covering all areas of the world and their peoples, and it is strong in diplomatic history, international, political, and economic developments and in social and cultural trends among the developing nations. In short, the information is there.

The instruction of the 200 million Americans who theoretically keep the State Department under constant scrutiny must start perforce in the secondary schools if the citizens are to arrive at a detailed appreciation of the State Department's role in foreign policy. In the end, the Department can only be what the people want it to be, by knowing what it should be, to fulfill their legitimate aspirations.

A sampling of popular civics texts in high schools shows a depressing minimum of desultory attention paid to the State Department. One or two pages here; four or five casual mentions there; in others, no mention at all; and one text with only a solitary paragraph on the Department. The civics curriculum in secondary education, with rare exceptions, is the weakest sector among the so-called social sciences. Courses in history at the college level, save for the top universities, are likewise spotty and thin. Too many students know only about surface appearances, confirmed largely by what they have seen on TV the night before. Current-events test scores of college students show no real rise in the level of basic information about the world or the Department's role. Obviously, such scant impressions left upon adolescents linger on to become the flimsy structure of adult reference. It is not the alien outside world alone which is creating all these foreign policy difficulties. There is also what Pogo says in the comic strip, "We have met the enemy and they is us."

CHAPTER II

FOREIGN AFFAIRS SPECTRUM: Half the Government

THE STATE DEPARTMENT professes to be the sole agency of the United States Government that serves the totality of United States interests. In the long run, its claim appears just. By delegation from the President of the United States, the State Department is the command pinnacle of the foreign affairs community that spreads across virtually half the United States Government. The Department lives by osmosis. It constantly feels the pulse and temperature of a global atmosphere that impinges on it at a thousand points, creating pressures and chain reactions as often as not accidental, as well as concerted. It can legitimately declare itself to be the nation's first line of defense, since the primary causes of war are almost always results of foreign policy conflicts or failures.

The Department is the first executive agency established under the Constitution in 1789 and thus the senior agency of the United States Government. Compared with foreign ministries of practically all other nations around the world, the State Department must literally have a global outlook. Affairs of most other foreign ministries are almost parochial by comparison. From its pinnacle—the question is whether it is a hollow pinnacle—the Department is both an umpire and a participant in the perpetual argument between Hobbes and Plato, between the raw, and sometimes evil, world of nature and the ideal order of human values. But, as indignant Congressmen frequently complain, "Don't those people in Foggy Bottom realize that foreign affairs is bigger than the State Department?" Indeed it is. The fact remains that the Department, in its least aspect, is the political arm of foreign policy, with ramifications uncountable. Thus, when asked why he chose to accept the post of Under Secretary of State rather than continue as a full Cabinet member in the role of Attorney General, Under Secretary Katzenbach said, "Compared with foreign affairs, everything else is marbles."

The foreign affairs community, which the State Department is accused of complacently discounting, is so huge and complex that it resembles a Rube Goldberg-Krazy Kat contraption, housed in an enormous skyscraper on rollers. How to get this vast monstrosity, with all its parts and inhabitants (the latter estimated at nearly 200,000, both at headquarters and in the field), to move in the right direction, let alone change its course in a hurry, is the nation's most baffling problem in today's perilous world.

The State Department leads the foreign affairs community in overseeing an imperium of United States territory that crosses the international date line into the eastern reaches of the Pacific, stretches west nearly halfway around the world to the Virgin Islands, and reaches nearly half the distance from Pole to Pole, from Point Barrow in Northern Alaska south to American Samoa.

The world that the State Department and its allied federal agencies oversee through the medium of diplomatic relations encompasses no longer one nation, France, as in 1789. Today there are, at the latest 1967 count, 123 nations, 63 of which were created since 1943, midpoint in World War II. It is a world with which the United States is inextricably tied by 4,599 treaties and executive agreements, of which 42 are mutual defense treaties, 4 of these being regional defense alliances. It is a world in which the United States is bound by membership in seventy-one international organizations and by participation in some fifty international operating programs. Hardly a day goes by that the State Department is not represented at a meeting in some part of the world. The regular annual schedule of international conferences includes more than 600, of which barely 125 may be reported in the press. A two-year span of such conferences comprises more than all the conferences the United States had attended in the entire period from the American Revolution to Pearl Harbor. It is a world and an era, moreover, in which the United States, only the fourth most populous nation and only the third largest in area, has spent more than $105 billion in aiding the outside world since World War II.

The most illuminating fact, however, is that of the seventy-five departments, agencies, and other independent units serving the President of the United States, fully one third are heavily engaged in foreign affairs. At least half are directly engaged in a substantial way, and practically every federal agency today has an international division. The narrow kernel of the foreign affairs community under the State Department comprises State, the Agency for International Development, the United States Information Agency, the Peace Corps, and the United States Arms Control and Disarmament Agency.

On a wider compass, the foreign affairs spectrum takes in the Defense Department, the Central Intelligence Agency, and economic agencies such as the Agriculture Department, the Commerce Department, and, with today's emphasis on social conditions as breeders of revolutions, the Department of Health, Education and Welfare. As many as forty-two agencies have operating responsibilities abroad. The U.S. Embassy at Bonn has had thirty-six agency representatives; London, thirty-five.

As might be expected, the Defense Department has the largest overseas representation attached to U.S. embassies—more than 10,000. This does not include nearly 100,000 Americans employed by the Defense Department in connection with organized commands, and it excludes strictly combat units like the more than half million members of the armed forces operating in and around Vietnam. The State Department's overseas representation proper is only 14 per cent, or about 7,000 Americans, of its total of nearly 26,000 employees—15,301 Americans and 10,477 foreign local nationals. This is more than six times the total number of employees State had at the end of World War II.

The Defense Department aside, the largest number of agency representatives attached to U.S. embassies overseas is that of the Central Intelligence Agency; the Department of Agriculture ranks second, and the Department of Commerce third.

In the foreign affairs community, practically every participant, except State, has immediate operational motivations for carrying out its particular programs. This is a built-in advantage to operating agencies which at least have specific choices to argue about. State, on the other hand, sometimes appears to have the investment bankers' syndrome, or that of a holding company supervising a string of other corporations from its eyrie on the sixty-fourth floor. And, like bankers, the gentlemen of State sometimes present the appearance of either knowing how it all should come out on the lower levels or of disregarding mundane operational trifles as being basically of no account, as long as the mystique of high policy is properly enshrined.

The State Department's deceptive mask of nonchalance quickly drops when it gets down to money, as it does with the rest of us. The Department's $406 million requested budget for 1968, trimmed to $404 million by the President and cut down in late 1967 to between $382 million and $386 million by Congress, is still the smallest proposed appropriation of all Government departments. State, however, has a direct or indirect foreign policy voice in the disposition of $8 billion of other departments' money for foreign expenditures. Its own comparatively tiny budget today is nevertheless of an astronomical magnitude compared with the Department's first budget, in 1789—$5,950—and eight times the size of its budget at the end of World War II.

A breakdown of the State Department's budget indicates its responsibilities. Nearly $214 million were requested for the direct administration of foreign affairs, principally salaries and expenses. Another $100 million go as contributions to international organizations. Missions to these organizations take nearly $4 million to run. Just going to the international conferences of these international organizations costs $32 million. Three international commissions—Mexican, Canadian, and fisheries—take over $15 million. The big plum in the State Department budget, in years past almost sacrosanct, is the $50 million allotted to educational and cultural exchange activities.

Having no substantial resources of its own, the Department must almost always call on some other agency to obtain the tools to do the necessary jobs. These may involve anything from the details of wholesale or retail foreign aid to arrangements for the placing of Peace Corps missions or for the passage or stationing of armed forces and space-tracking stations, and the sale and distribution of U.S. surplus farm goods and surplus arms.

An analysis of the utilization of State Department human resources discloses that manpower employed in service functions, that is, mechanical and clerical, accounts for 30 per cent of the total State Department personnel. Administration and logistic functions, or support functions, take 40 per cent. Supervisory functions, or the theoretical overseeing of policy requirements in the carrying out of missions by embassies and other agencies, take 10 per cent of State's manpower. Substantive functions, such as exchange programs or other actions designed directly to influence events around the world, take 20 per cent. Management analysts calculate that only 5 per cent deals with the classic niceties of diplomatic negotiation.

Patently, there is a certain basic illogic when one looks at this array of functions and the division of the State Department into five geographical compartments to run U.S. foreign policy in the world. In comparison with the expenditures of the Defense Department, with its $75 billion budget, State's are 200 times as small. Thus, the mystery how the comparatively miniscule State Department senior staff can presume to advise on, or construct, the political strategy which governs the deployment of the Defense Department's 3,300,000 armed forces, its 23 missile squadrons with 1,050 ICBM's, its 600 strategic bombers, and its 37 submarines armed with 502 Polaris missiles. In this thermonuclear age, when the giant power of the United States is self-inhibited, circumscribed by world conditions, it is simply a marvel that any effective working relationship between State and Defense is achieved at all. As Samuel Johnson said to Boswell about the dog's walking on his hind legs, "It may not be done well, but you are surprised to find it done at all."

The Department's regular pittance of nearly $400 million is augmented by its authorized handling of another $200 million. Half of this goes for voluntary special contributions to international organizations from foreign aid funds, over and above the $100 million in assessed contributions to international organizations. The other $100 million come from reimbursement by the other overseas agencies for support services from State. To play around with on the side, there is also a cash kitty of $4 billion worth of foreign currencies owned by the United States. However, almost $2 billion of these currencies are in declared excess, hence, mostly useless. This latter sum derives from eleven countries which have been major recipients of United States aid. For this aid they set aside huge amounts of their own local currencies for use as counterpart funds. India has so many rupees for U.S. use that, at the current rate of expenditure, they will not be exhausted for twenty years; Poland's zlotys, for sixty-one years; and Yugoslavia's dinars, for twenty-five years.

State's employment of other people's millions, in a sense, gives the Department officers a certain expense-account psychology, the feeling of largesse and spacious handling of monies which are not necessarily theirs but over which they posit the high-toned policy formulations of the Department of State.

Despite all these extra pennies and the big wad of $8 billion about which the Department has a say-so, State is a piker financially. The Department of Agriculture has a nest egg of $6 billion; Health, Education and Welfare, nearly $12 billion; Treasury, $15 billion; NASA, more than $5 billion—and let us not forget the Veterans Administration, with $6 billion. These other agencies have specific functions prescribed for them and policies which, with a minimum of efficiency, they can more or less realize.

But the State Department has to achieve United States national objectives only by making them acceptable to other sovereign governments. In short, State has at least one strike on itself before it starts dealing with the foreigners. It chalks up the second strike in dealing with its fellow Americans: for, its alleged authority in directing policy notwithstanding, the actual monies to carry out specific objectives are appropriated to other agencies. Thus immediately begins the friction that stems from splintered responsibility and power rivalries: who will use the funds and the manpower and resources this money represents to achieve what objectives and in whose special manner?

The multiplicity of foreign affairs agencies on the domestic front and the increasingly multilateral aspects of relations on the foreign front have compounded the confusion. The jurisdictional disputes within the Government have tended to be melded into compromises acceptable to the principal barons of the bureaucracy. So much so, in fact, that it can possibly be said that a fourth power of Government is growing up. The federative power of key agencies, assigned to major projects with huge resources, creates a self-adjudicated consensus which may in effect present a *fait accompli* to the

Chief Executive. It may not be at all what he really wanted in the first place but what the mastodon of bureaucracy imposed on him.

In 1961, President Kennedy, all for briskness, order, and excellence, in a personal letter, told all U.S. ambassadors that they, as personal representatives of the President, were to be in complete charge in their respective countries and to supervise and coordinate operations of all U.S. agencies. This directive, in the hands of a strong ambassador, did begin to create a semblance of order and coherence in X country's affairs. But, as far as the United States Government was concerned, the rule did not apply at the Washington end.

General Maxwell D. Taylor, Kennedy's personal military adviser, was profoundly impressed by the disclosure that the ball had fallen between the outfielders in the Cuban Bay of Pigs fiasco. As a result, a special group of top officials was created to watch over all matters of counterinsurgency, and in particular not to let the Central Intelligence Agency get out of hand again. Taylor came to the conclusion that the special group—CI (for counterinsurgency)—was in reality only an ex post facto stopgap. A much wider span of control was needed in Washington to supervise, coordinate, and direct combined U.S. efforts toward agreed-upon U.S. objectives.

Taylor's impressions were strongly reinforced by his experience as U.S. Ambassador in Saigon. He came to the conclusion that the crucial spot for an effective synthesis of actions to put foreign policies into practical effect was at the level of the Under Secretary of State. This was close enough to the operating bureaucratic echelons to ensure their compliance with decisions taken. A short-lived precedent had occurred when Douglas Dillon was Under Secretary, in 1958–1960, and had had the authority and decisiveness to try to mesh foreign policy with economic- and military-aid factors.

Taylor was backed by U.S. Ambassador to Japan U. Alexis Johnson, who had been Taylor's colleague in Saigon and then Deputy Under Secretary for Political Affairs. The Taylor-Johnson campaign was climaxed on March 4, 1966, when President Johnson promulgated NSAM-341, a National Security Council Action memorandum. This created the Senior Interdepartmental Group, composed of the Under Secretary of State, as Chairman, the Deputy Secretary of Defense, the Administrator of AID, the Director of USIA, the Chairman of the Joint Chiefs of Staff, the Director of CIA, and the Special Assistant to the President on National Security Affairs. When subjects in their competence came up, representatives of Agriculture, Treasury, HEW, the Disarmament Agency, and any other agency that felt it had a voice to be heard could attend the meetings. SIG, as the Senior Interdepartmental Group came to be abbreviated, was to be the forum where differences in the Washington high command could be continually adjusted, compromised, and—here is an unusual word in government —decided.

SIG is potentially the most significant conception created for bringing key executive officials to the most important sector of the nation's business— foreign affairs—since the United States fell heir to the game of global scrabble in 1945. But, as the other agencies with foreign affairs interests have been expanding overseas, the State Department's Foreign Service, its operational core, has been constricting. Therefore, if State is to control this multiagency menagerie of lions and tigers, and sort out the apples and oranges in resources, it must staff out the instruments of control and make certain that they are high-class enough to ride herd on the problem.

By late 1967, more than a year after its creation, the State SIG operation was still only a barely fleshed skeleton. Whether State ever does operate SIG successfully or not, there is one fundamental fact that the other federal agencies are now discovering in the lush fields of foreign affairs: to get permanent and legal agreements in diplomatic relations with other nations, these powerful agencies, willy-nilly, have to resort to the State Department. For State has the last word to the outside world, though very often it is a very tardy word.

From its first meeting, on March 8, 1966, in its first year SIG met four times the first month, once in April, three times in May, twice in June, twice in July, once in September, and it met once in January and once in February 1967, for a total of fifteen meetings. No major decisions were reached.

The SIG system has a corollary in the IRG's, or Interdepartmental Regional Groups. These are headed by the Assistant Secretaries of State's five geographical divisions and composed of key members of corresponding bureaus in the other agencies. In little over a year, the Middle East IRG met forty times; the Far East IRG, twenty times; the Latin American IRG, forty-one times; the European IRG, eight times; and the African IRG, twenty times. These IRG's theoretically thrashed out differences, and those they could not thrash out were kicked upstairs to the SIG.

Typical items on the SIG agenda were Middle East arms aid, European payments other than those affecting the balance of payments, and the Indonesian question. In effect, SIG was organized to clear the interagency foreign affairs underbrush and to handle medium-sized problems, it was hoped before they grew into full-sized headaches. Agencies that objected to SIG decisions, which, in theory, the Under Secretary of State was fully empowered to make on his own, could always appeal to the President on major issues. But in the first year of the SIG's treading water, many important foreign policy problems were not dealt with at all, though the original directive required such problems to receive "full, prompt and systematic consideration." Nor, in the first year and a half, did SIG make, as the directive explicitly asked, any surveys of "the areas and the issues to which the U.S. Government applies its resources"; in short, fix world operational priorities as to importance of areas, programs, and available funds.

SIG theoretically took over responsibilities of the special group (CI) which involved close attention to the symptoms of counterinsurgency or subversive activities in the restless underdeveloped world. Ideally, with foresight, effective preventive action could be taken in good time, before a condition ripened to the state of rottenness that invites insurgency.

Again, theoretically, the idea was to shape SIG as the instrument through which would be applied the latest governmental tool in fashion, the Planning-Programming-Budgeting-System, or PPBS. This is the pet project of the Bureau of the Budget, which is attempting to establish the systems-analysis approach all across the Government and especially the foreign affairs community. PPBS was the creation of Charles J. Hitch, the first comptroller of the Defense Department under former Defense Secretary Robert S. McNamara. There it had notable success in rationalizing the cost-effectiveness and use of the mass manpower and bulk material that the Defense Department deals in. But it has never been applied to the varying combinations of nuts and bananas, apples and oranges, the contrasting ingredients and intangibles that make up the State Department's foreign affairs stock in trade.

The conglomeration of agencies and the search for effective means to direct and utilize them came after twenty years of intensive United States involvement in the world. This period of time had seen unprecedented prosperity in the United States, with 1967's estimated gross national product, in constant dollars, of $664.6 billion, more than double the GNP of $309.9 billion in 1947, when the Cold War began. Compared with the prewar era of 1939, when World War II started in Europe and the United States was still neutralist-isolationist, the depressed economy had a gross national product, in constant dollars, of only $209.4 billion, three times less than in 1967.

This was the period in which the United States learned once and for all that it could no longer depend on the illusion of security given by the width of the Atlantic Ocean. Even a hundred years ago the Atlantic could have been bridged by navies in days, but, in recent decades, by bombers in hours and, today, by intercontinental ballistic missiles in minutes. As far back as 1875 the British Earl of Derby wrote that American statesmen were just beginning to understand that the basic security of the United States centered, like England's, on a balance of power in the Eurasian land mass that traversed from France on the Atlantic, in the west, to Siberian Russia on the Pacific, in the east.

It was a period, too, that saw the breakup of the world order after two global wars. Nationalism was rampant in two thirds of the globe as ancient peoples felt the imperative need to command their own destinies and to restore the dignity of their heritage. Soviet Russia and assorted Communists were resurgent in the thrust of vitality born from the sufferings and challenges they had mastered in the war against Hitler's Germany. The period ran from the time of Stalin's refusal to cooperate with the West in the Marshall Plan to Khrushchev's attempt to outflank the West through the third world of emerging nations, an attempt which fizzled to failure in the Cuban nuclear crisis. It was also a period which saw the United States' own realization that the Cold War policy of containment had become a colander.

But from the second phase emerged a third, wherein wars of anticolonialist independence were transmuted by Communist ideological electrolysis into wars of national liberation. The Russians, understanding their limitations in applying their massive power at distant points of the earth, had begun to search the seas for avenues of movement, to create their own airlift capabilities. They even began to appreciate American military doctrines of flexible response and not all-out war. In brief, the United States, learning the hard way to deal specifically within the limits of the possible because the world was not its oyster after all, now watched its major enemy of two decades, the Soviet Union, perhaps discovering the same moderate road. The United States was still uncertain whether its new potential major enemy of the next decades, Communist China, would yet discover these same modern fundamentals. The United States was certain that the myriad new nations, insisting on leading their own lives, alone or preferably in new regional groupings, would be increasingly impatient at all outside bridles, halters, or reins. This is the world that the State Department deals with today, case by case, as each pops up, out of the fires in the in-basket.

CHAPTER III

THE MASS MEDIA:
Sieve, Mirror, or Mirage

THE PRESS, MEANING NEWS-
papers, magazines, radio, and television, is a window, screen, mirror, or
prism, through which the American people learn about the acts and rationales of the State Department in foreign policy and form their own conclusions or illusions. The reports of the press form the premises of the intellectual framework within which the so-called facts of the matter are to be
considered. The press reports, in addition, outline the political skeleton
under the corpus of fact, with further implications, inferences, overtones,
impressions, atmospherics, and undertones.

The facts, or even the errors—recalling Oswald Spengler's truism that
error can be as universally propagated as truth—are transmuted into motivations of political will, impulses of energy; in short, into elements of
power. Therefore, conflicts are bound to arise over what is decided, interpreted, utilized, manipulated, organized, or exploited, and by whom, to
develop a pattern and a design for a political impression to be conveyed
in order to further objectives of an administration. Patently, there is a
lot of clutter and confusion in the press and foreign policy.

All aspects of international problems are *ipso facto* interrelated via the
mass media because they are all verbalized or visualized in an instantaneous
or apparently continuous image. Press reports of foreign affairs illustrate
vividly that foreign policy is fundamentally indivisible. The setting of the
logical premises of a foreign policy argument by the officials and the press
inquiries and editorial selection of facts by the reporters create the tension
from which the shadowy lineaments of truth may eventually begin to
emerge.

Like so many other things in the modern State Department, public affairs in the current sense was born in 1944, during World War II, a
major recognition of the continuing importance of public relations in foreign policy. Today, the Bureau of Public Affairs is a component of State
Department bureaucracy, with 144 persons and a $2.5 million budget. The

heart of its operation is the News Division, under the Assistant Secretary for Public Affairs. Every day, with infrequent exceptions, the News Division gives an on-the-record briefing for those of its more than five hundred accredited correspondents from thirty-four countries who wish to attend. The briefing, which rates second only to that of the White House Press Secretary, normally occurs between noon and 12:30 P.M. and is variously attended by between twenty-five and fifty correspondents. It is the place and the time for the United States Government to place its views concerning foreign events squarely on the record for all the world to hear, through the medium of an Official Spokesman. Illustrative were the working methods of such an official public voice, Robert J. McCloskey, Director of the News Division and also Deputy Assistant Secretary of State for Public Affairs.

McCloskey did not go on the firing line unprepared. The whole Bureau of Public Affairs, in effect, acted as legman to backstop the Spokesman. From 6:30 to 8:30 in the morning, subordinates in the News Division read all the available metropolitan morning papers and the night's news tickers, and then prepared a summary of events about which correspondents at the noon briefing might ask questions. These events and the possible questions were passed on to the five geographical bureaus of the State Department and other offices of competence to obtain guidance on the way in which the anticipated questions should be answered. Usually each Bureau replied by, first, stating the question; second, offering a report of the pertinent facts; third, giving official recommendations on how much of this basic information should be made known and on the manner and limitations within which the question should be answered.

Often the Foreign Service officers or operating Bureau officials do not wish to talk about the matter at all, or they want to give a bare minimum of an answer or dismiss the probable query with a "No comment." McCloskey, on his own responsibility, frequently challenged a ruling of the geographical bureau and, in a pinch, took the matter up directly with Secretary of State Rusk. He was a sophisticated enough bureaucrat not to carry a fight to the Secretary without being sure of his ground and, of course, he had to accept any adverse ruling the Secretary might give. Normally, however, crucial questions were already cleared in advance by the Assistant Secretary for Public Affairs, McCloskey's bureaucratic superior.

Yet, as a result of the muddle in press relations resulting from the U-2 cover story in 1960, no State Department public affairs official today will go to the press with a report if he feels he is being lied to by higher authorities. Foreign Service officers on public affairs duty felt, in the end, that it was easier to tell the truth, though perhaps not all of it.

Prepared with his answers, which had been thrashed out at an 11:30 A.M. meeting, McCloskey proceeded to the den of press lions to make his announcements, if any, and to submit himself to the questions, most of which, as indicated, had been anticipated. McCloskey talked on the record. Occasionally he stopped his on-the-record discourse to go "on background." This meant that he was not to be directly quoted, but his background explanation helped put his on-the-record answers into clearer perspective. However, he went "background" as little as possible. Being completely vulnerable when he makes on-the-record statements, the Spokesman must be alert to, and aware of, the implications of everything he says. To illustrate: the Japanese lead the State Department press corps in the number of accredited correspondents, with twenty-seven. The Germans come next, with twenty-six. The British, who used to be first, are third, with twenty-five. The Spokesman is wary of the Japanese contingent, among others, because its members are not only very smart but also highly competitive for the exclusive angle. They or other foreign nationals may wish, for their own purposes, to prosecute points further than the Spokesman can even discreetly do for his own U.S. Government. As a result of his instructions, of telephone calls around the Department, of the final just-before-the-battle meeting, and of his own scanning of fifty to seventy-five of the latest cablegrams, McCloskey entered the press briefing armed usually to answer at least six or seven questions from the press. More often than not, he was asked about only one or two of them, and frequently only one topic dominated the half-hour or forty-five minute question period.

By virtue of his constant exposure, McCloskey developed a feel for the line of press questioning, which generally veered away from what the officials may have thought of as the major aspects of the day. In his press briefings, McCloskey never went "off the record," which means "not for publication." Principally, this was because of the presence of Communist correspondents, representatives of the Russian TASS and Eastern European news agencies—Polish, Hungarian, and Czech—who obviously have a more direct interest in asking questions for propaganda purposes.

But this was not the end for McCloskey. Through the day he may have received as many as thirty telephone calls. When he went home, he may have received between half a dozen and a dozen more, sometimes at 2:00 or 3:00 A.M. if a foreign crisis exploded overseas. None of the State Department Public Officers, in the experience of most correspondents, try to subvert or lie in their explanations to the press. It is their job, however, to put the best face possible on their information, to put the right spin on it, a normal function of government press officers. McCloskey was very careful about the way he allowed himself to be quoted. He gave away no gold nuggets of news, but he leveled with correspondents to give them the correct interpretation, the authentic backdrop to the news, as officials saw it. He definitely did not try to mislead newsmen, and he attempted to steer them away from freak interpretations that, as far as he knew, were off the beam.

Urbane and savvy as McCloskey might have appeared, the path of all official spokesmen is full of sand traps. The greatest single danger is getting caught in the scrimmage of correspondents' questions by being a shade too eager to be helpful. The temptation then is to overstate an answer, to go beyond the letter of instructions by as little as a millimeter during a hot crisis briefing. In the 1967 Arab-Israeli war, McCloskey caused a national political uproar which took President Johnson and Secretary Rusk to calm down. Asked about the United States position in the war, McCloskey replied, "We are neutral—" and then added, "in thought, word, and deed." No senior had instructed him to use those exact words. McCloskey was also a devout Catholic. The words "thought, word, and deed" were in many of the prayers he had been familiar with since childhood. The words issued spontaneously, almost like an unconscious gloss. The moral for spokesmen: Stick to your knitting and let someone else do the embroidery.

The State Department news officials have strict practical priorities about their jobs with the press. The number one clients are the American wire services—the Associated Press and United Press International. The AP claims nearly 7,000 outlets, including 1,236 daily newspapers, 2,924 broadcast stations, and foreign clients. The UPI has nearly 6,000. Between them, they service 2,000 U.S. newspapers and more than 7,000 radio and TV stations. The wire services are the State Department's first line of offense and defense in news handling. Tickers of the AP and UPI are clicking away twenty-four hours a day in the News Division. An Agence France Presse ticker also serves the European Bureau. Carbon copies go to all the major bureaus and senior officials. The News Division is geared to give immediate service to the heads of the two State Department bureaus for wire services, who most recently were John Hightower of the AP and Stewart Hensley of UPI. Both services require immediate replies to their questions, if possible, because they are on deadlines around the clock.

The wire services, in turn, perform an indispensable function for the State Department. Their reports from around the earth are put on the wire as fast as possible, and thus for a very large part of the time precede receipt of the official reports from embassies abroad. Four more news tickers are on the seventh floor for the top executives, three on the sixth floor for the Assistant Secretaries, and two on the fifth floor.

Secretary Rusk recognizes the primacy of the wire services as an instrument of communications by making sure they get the facts first whenever a major crisis occurs. When the emergency airlift with U.S. planes and Belgian paratroopers for the rescue of the refugees at Stanleyville in the Congo was made in early 1964, Rusk ordered communications from the plane to be funneled directly into the State Department Operations Center.

From there former Under Secretary George W. Ball ran the items personally down the hall to Rusk's office, where the Secretary handed them to Hightower and Hensley. Rusk had called them at midnight to come from their homes.

Though the wire services get the official story first in most cases, the State Department has a heightened sense of the importance of radio and television because of the immediacy of these media. The Department knows that recent surveys show that as many as 58 per cent of the American people get their news through audio-visual means. Timing of news releases for afternoon and morning papers on an alternate basis has been discarded because of the constant need to take advantage of the electronic media's ubiquity. It is also recognized that the Department can make news directly on its own through the appearance of State's key officials on Sunday television programs. State obtains not only sizable audiences on these Sunday shows but frequently a double return in Monday morning's newspapers after effective appearances on NBC's "Meet the Press," CBS's "Face the Nation," or ABC's "Issues and Answers." Secretary Rusk went on radio-TV at least ten times in 1966 at critical times. The news officials are not blind to TV's handicaps—compressing a story to the point of transparent thinness because of the incredible brevity of time on the air and the consequent tendency to needle a story out of focus to make it register as more important and dramatic than it really is.

The third priority among the clientele of the State Department News Division goes to the metropolitan newspapers that cover the Department regularly and in depth. The first-line papers include only the *New York Times,* the *Washington Post,* the *Washington Star,* and, in the last year or two, perhaps the *Los Angeles Times.* The newspapers, particularly the *Post* and the *Times,* offer the advantage of considerable space and afford the Department an opportunity of obtaining a balanced news report, a luxury which it cannot afford to ignore.

The *New York Times* and, in recent years, the *Washington Post* provide another function—that of unofficial Government house organs in which all officials can note what their fellows are saying and doing and get a reading of what appears most important. Over a hundred foreign embassies in Washington similarly may receive an impression of what are the current concerns of the U.S. Government. Through the Paris edition of the now-combined *New York Herald Tribune, Washington Post,* and *New York Times,* news of Washington is carried direct to ministries in foreign capitals. Inevitably, these newspapers profit by being used informally as the channels for unofficial government-to-government communication; for example, their reporters gain freer access to the powers that be in diplomatic officialdom.

A secondary layer of important papers, such as the *Chicago Sun Times,* the *Chicago Tribune,* the *Chicago Daily News,* the *St. Louis Post-Dispatch,* the *Baltimore Sun,* and the *Christian Science Monitor,* are accorded a degree of privileged status by the Department for their regular coverage of foreign news and for their circulation, power, and so-called prestige, real or assumed.

Last but not least in importance come the great mass-circulation news and picture weeklies—*Time, Newsweek, U.S. News and World Report, Life,* and *Look*—which deserve, in the State Department view, special treatment because of their mass audiences and the emphasis they can place on desired aspects of foreign policy.

At the bottom of the list comes the so-called provincial press—the papers of Boston, Cleveland, Kansas City, New Orleans, and everywhere else. The quality of the attention bestowed on these newspaper representatives is in direct ratio to the Department's respect for and acknowledgment of individual reportorial caliber and to the newspapers' presumed level of regional political weight and traditional repute, which ebb and flow with people's memories. Apropos, Averell Harriman once told this writer, "Sure, I remember the *Plain Dealer* when I was a black Republican and the *Plain Dealer* was considered the *Manchester Guardian* of the United States" (when the *Guardian* was at the zenith of its fame).

Sometimes it seems that officials spend most of their time reacting to news from abroad. "If I could only spend as much time originating information as I do catching up with the commentary," McCloskey used to say with a sigh. This is evident from the distribution of the time zones around the world. The news cycle seems to end in Washington, which becomes the end-of-the-day catchall for world news. From Washington, for example, Saigon is twelve hours in the future, that is, tomorrow, and thirteen hours ahead, on daylight saving time. In effect, this makes officials respond today to what already happened "tomorrow" but whose news was received here "today." Like a dog chasing its tail, theoretically one can never catch up with it. In making news the Department constantly has to keep in mind these time zones and what news may create repercussions where. Every Washington official statement thus has multiple audiences who will take it in different ways and at variant times of the day.

The situation becomes further complicated when the news run is thin here in the United States. The correspondent, under pressure to find something to write about, grabs an iffy or tangential story arriving from a European capital several hours earlier. Department news officials, as a consequence, tend to weigh all statements because the same words must satisfy all men, potential enemies as well as uneasy allies.

The news officials do receive some breaks, however. Monday is normally an easy day. The better-rated correspondents who regularly cover the Department are usually off on Monday, so they are not around to needle officials. It is a good day to surface news which the Department wants to get out and which can be published without too much notice taken of it. Tuesday, Wednesday, and Thursday are busy days. The peak of the week seems to come on Thursdays, when the news run is usually very brisk. Friday is a light day again, as the week tapers off. State Department employees, except for a very few top officials, do not work on Saturday. This is a good day to get out news that can be played up in the Sunday papers, when the news run is traditionally weak.

Everybody, press and officials, gets a break in December. From the twentieth through the Christmas holidays, the Department seems to shut down. Many officials use the time to take their leaves. In fact, December appears to be the quietest month of the year. Crises around the world are usually tapering off, and others not starting up. In the last ten years, not a single major world crisis started in December, as indicated by the topics chronicled in the *New York Times* index.

But even when there is no news, it doesn't mean that the Bureau of Public Affairs does not have other problems. In 1967 there were thirty-two Public Affairs Advisers scattered around the Department in the different geographical and functional bureaus. These officers are not under the control of the Bureau of Public Affairs. Key bureau operators tend to direct their own news policies. Raymond A. Hare, former Assistant Secretary of State for Near East and South Asian Affairs, used to cable press instructions to his ambassadorial domains without consulting the Bureau of Public Affairs. In 1967, Assistant Secretary of State for East Asian and Pacific Affairs William Bundy likewise sent his far-flung embassies news guidance telegrams—with twenty-two clearances from other operating bureaus and agencies, but none from State's Bureau of Public Affairs.

Although the Bureau is the official liaison channel for State Department policy guidance to the U.S. Information Agency, the detailed guidance to USIA more often comes from the public affairs advisers of the geographical operating bureaus. The specific Bureau of Public Affairs complaint is that these officers reflect the influence of their immediate operational superiors, who may prefer to stop or distort the outflow of news rather than follow the bidding of the Bureau by releasing the more or less unvarnished news.

In Washington, moreover, it is virtually impossible to cover foreign affairs without covering both the State Department and the White House. It follows, then, that State Department news officials keep a weather eye on the White House as they speak to the diplomatic press, since the President's attention may be drawn to some explanation in the noonday briefing transscript that does not quite coincide with the views he might like to have had expressed. Needless to say, White House thunderbolts do strike, but much less frequently than one might think.

One of the least known responsibilities of State Department public affairs officials is keeping bloopers out of the news or turning off programmed happenings that suddenly surface from the bureaucratic deep. Such booboos could very well make the United States look silly, not only to the general American public but also to the disenchanted eyes of the outside world. Rather than let goofs get by and afterward have to think up cover stories to shroud the absurdities, State keeps a constant watch for "wafflebirds" before they screech into the public air.

At the time of the Manila Conference, in October 1966, there was a flurry of activity to call off an underground nuclear test that had been scheduled for the same time by the Atomic Energy Commission. The risk in this particular case was that the test was of the type that might vent, that is, break the surface of the earth and allow some radioactivity to escape into the air. Unfavorable propaganda repercussions were the last thing public affairs officials wanted when the President was making his Far Eastern foray. State succeeded in having the AEC test canceled. It was rescheduled two months later.

Another time, a year or so earlier, by sheer coincidence the Bolivian desk officer answered a call from a man whose name was that of a fellow-worker in the State Department. It was also the name of a correspondent—one who was calling from the State Department Press Room downstairs. In talking to the presumed friend, the desk officer gave a detailed analysis of the political situation in Bolivia, with realistic asides as to the probable sad fate of the current regime in that country. The next day, when the story hit the front page of the *New York Times,* with sources directly attributed to the State Department, it looked as if the Department were engaged in psychological warfare to turn out the administration of a friendly country. Naturally there was a tiny-tot flap, which in the end subsided like most similar tragicomedies in a thimble.

In another instance, a junior White House functionary, bug-eyed and bushy-tailed to please the Big Boss, routed a cable to Far Eastern embassies right after the Manila Conference. He asked them to supply material for possible publicity on the "Americanization of Asia" that "should" result from the trip of President Johnson to the area. This infantilism was quickly scorched to death by heated replies from outraged ambassadors in the area. Needless to say, the promising author of that hapless essay is no longer in residence.

Politically appointed officials ingenuously admit that their priorities in the consideration of the effect of news are, first, what good or ill it does the

President, and, second, what the fallout is on the image of the Secretary of State. The repute of the State Department itself is third.

A characteristic incident causing international repercussions that fizzled out into "just one of those things" occurred in 1966, when a U.S. Air Force plane flew off course in France and overflew Pierlatte, a classified French nuclear installation. It transpired that the pilot had indeed filed his flight plan, a standard operating procedure, but the particular Air Force installation which would have routinely notified the French on the day in question was under physical repair. An alternate flight tower notified the French, but through other than the usual channels. The flak persisted for two weeks before the simple facts proved everybody innocent.

The touchy occurrence that alarms news officials is anything which even remotely skirts intelligence activities. In October 1966, Vladimir Kazan-Komarek, an American of Czech origin, was arrested in Prague when the Soviet Aeroflot plane in which he was a passenger to Moscow made an unscheduled stop in the Czech capital. At the airport Czech authorities arrested Kazan-Komarek for alleged subversive activities during the late 1940's, in the depths of the Cold War. The State Department news officials had to know right away what the pitch was. The first call was to Richard Helms, Director of the Central Intelligence Agency, with one question, "Is he one of ours?" He was not. Kazan-Komarek was later freed and returned to the United States.

The biggest flaps of all occur when anything tricky pops up in a war, for example, in Vietnam. There was the famous flap over the bombing of Hanoi in the winter of 1966. The State Department simply could not get the necessary information fast enough from the Defense Department to give sensible answers. Harried Defense Department news officials stuck to their creed, "Let's get all the facts first," instead of shooting from the hip merely because the importunate press demanded immediate reactions.

The panic button was almost pushed again, in December 1966, when the presence of North Korean pilots in North Vietnam became known. News officials were immediately sensitive to the possibility that the American public would be alarmed that the war was expanding by significant reinforcements of Communist forces to the Hanoi cause. The story broke in Paris via the *Washington Post* Foreign Service. Immediately, Department officials alerted George Christian, the White House Press Secretary, down at the LBJ ranch, and Secretary of State Rusk and Defense Secretary McNamara. Defense Department news officials worked under strict orders from State. The policy decision was not to make any official announcement of the presence of North Korean pilots in North Vietnam. That would constitute "rocketry" and highlight the disclosure. The ploy was that any queries would be answered "affirmatively." The presence of from twenty-

five to fifty North Korean pilots in North Vietnam duly made page one in
the metropolitan press the next day, but it was reported in proper context
and perspective. Whereupon the news officials sighed in relief.

The postscript is almost as interesting as the original news emergency of
the moment. The State Department had actually known of the presence of
North Korean pilots in North Vietnam for at least six weeks, or since
around November 1, 1966. The public affairs officials learned of it only
after four weeks. They had spent the last two weeks of these arguing with
the Far Eastern Bureau, which felt there was no need for unnecessary
alarm until verification was obtained. Others thought release of the news
might embarrass Ambassador Llewellyn Thompson, who was just leaving
for Moscow for his second tour of duty there. Thompson needed no
untoward incidents to mar the atmospherics of his reception at a delicate
moment, a moment, it later developed, when the United States was attempting to start negotiations with Hanoi to stop the fighting in Vietnam.

To the brood of enterprising and competitive newsmen who cover the
State Department, this backroom chiff-chaff was something to laugh about
between major spot developments or portentous explanations of high policy.
In general, the State Department press corps is the most responsible
group of reporters in Washington. They take pains to understand the fine
points of diplomacy. Rare would be the reporter, if any at all, who would
deliberately blow the whistle on serious diplomatic negotiations in which
the nation is engaged. State newsmen are neither factionalists nor pundits.
But, like all of us, they are subject to human fallibilities.

The foreign affairs reporters tend to write for themselves. Their close
trade working relationships create a somewhat incestuous daisy chain, since
all read each other's newspapers to brief themselves on what is being
discussed in the public prints, to be better loaded for bear when they bait
the officials. Some develop the Walter Mitty complex, as if they were actual
directors of foreign policy and knew all the answers. This trait was lam-
pooned by former Secretary of State Dean Acheson, who said that the
New York Times was the only newspaper which maintained two Secretaries of State—James Reston in Washington and Cyrus Sulzberger overseas. In any event, the *New York Times* representatives who cover the
State Department, armored with assurance in a high-class tradition of
foreign coverage, are an extremely able group, intelligent, energetic, and
competitive. They are especially rivals among themselves, to see who can
crack the invaluable space on page one which will hit the public in the
eyeball. The *New York Times* reporters seem to identify themselves more
with the State Department than any other group. But it is rather in an
adversary relationship, as if they, the gentlemen of the *New York Times,*
and the seigneurs of the State Department were jointly responsible for the

success or failure of foreign policies. Indeed, it is one of the most edifying spectacles in Washington to contemplate a covey of *New York Times* correspondents, all with pipe in hand, arrayed like so many owls, out on a limb of the tree of knowledge.

The tone of the State Department press is very serious, almost laboriously so, as if all the weight of the world were on the shoulders of reporters, like so many adolescent Atlases. Yet even this mythological phalanx of stalwarts and the other more mortal correspondents suffer from a basic conflict in the news-gathering occupation. As reporters, most of them are looking for a story. Each piece of information the reporter gets is valuable only if he can get it into a newspaper; otherwise, it is of no value for his practical purpose of the moment. Therefore, reporters look for decisive stories, dramatic stories, funny stories, scandalous stories. The difficulty is that State Department news does not come in such tidy and entrancing categories.

More basic perhaps is the gap between the way in which foreign policy is articulated and the manner in which it is conducted. There is insufficient recognition by the working press of the limited objectives placed before an official, the limited machinery he must work with, and even at times the limited capacities of the officials themselves. A reporter asks, "What's new?" or "What has happened?" The operating official asks, "What is there to do to take advantage of what has happened, to remedy any unbalance to U.S. interests created by what happened, or to initiate a diversion by making something happen in another direction?" In short, the reporter and the official are looking at two different things, or at least at the same thing from two almost diametrically opposed viewpoints.

Thus, the reporter almost automatically and immediately must plunge into the interpretative field. He tends to the short-range view. He appears to interpret each move in diplomatic affairs as a change in policy, though it might actually be a change in tactics. Like the participants themselves, he is baffled by what is essentially the blind man's bluff of diplomacy. He tries to make it more concrete than it really is, thereby building up, despite the best will in the world, a fabricated abstraction that may or may not be consonant with the realities. The reporter unconsciously tends to vocalize in elaborate charades, or symbolic language. When his interpretative articles suggest that there is a review of foreign policy under way, the unvoiced assumption is that it is probably time for a change from past policies. Or, when he indulges in the largesse of mass psychologizing, saying, for example, that certain nations don't understand each other because of their own internal philosophies, he may be manufacturing a myth which covers the fact that the nations in question have basically different national vital interests. Such kindergarten-variety double-dome "think" pieces are clothed in abstraction instead of fact, and help to put the cotton wool around complex subjects. Such press "interpretatives" give excuses to the lazier official brains to fall back on the foam mattress of ideology as their own cover for obtuseness or inaction.

Coupled with the vague and ambiguous nature of the subject matter that the correspondents must deal with in the State Department is the fact that, like those of all foreign ministries in the world, the officials are constantly and necessarily involved in public or semipublic discourses with one purpose—to justify the official performance before the home public and world opinion.

Constant scepticism therefore is the hallmark of an alert State Department correspondent. To those who have been foreign correspondents abroad, in Russia or in the Middle East, or even among the smooth triple-tonguers in London, Paris, and Rome, or the transcendentalists and political pettifoggers in Bonn, it is useful sometimes to treat the United States as a foreign country. It helps gain a fractional degree of objectivity. Official ministries everywhere cannot help attempting to sell their bill of goods. It may be the real bill of fare. It may be dressed up for advertising. It may be controversial, argumentative, or even slickly sophistical. But in the nature of things, there will always be the superimposed context of the official who sets down the syllogism from which the reporter will often draw the corollary the official would like him to draw.

From time to time, the built-in chaos of foreign news becomes insupportable and a *crise de confiance* occurs. Vehement charges of news management and credibility on the press side clash with bitter complaints of prejudiced reporting and distortions from the official quarters. The discreet State Department, of course, is never as vocal or pointed in its critical remarks as when the same battles unfold in the more political milieu of the White House. Footless explorations between correspondents and officials ensue, with eventual truces for better treatment of the press, etc. Officials go on a binge of "keeping the press happy." This, in itself, is a delusion, which quickly becomes evident when the next crisis occurs. The vital self-interests of the officials, in their duty as representatives of an elected national administration, crash into the self-proclaimed right to know of the press correspondents about the stories they cannot obtain.

From the official point of view, there is a sincere effort to persuade the correspondents that they should try to "educate" the public—a word which means develop, cultivate, train, or persuade. This the more austere minds of the press quickly translate into "propagandize." What the correspondents want, first and last, is information. They want an acknowledgment that the legitimacy of information is the fundamental need of a democracy, so that people may learn the facts and the explanations, without advance doctoring, and make up their minds for themselves. Crisis news, whose sudden impact offers little time to explain, since most crises are unforeseen, generates abrasive attitudes. But, by and large, the State Department correspondents and the officials get on remarkably well.

The public affairs officials have a shrewd sense of the importance and value of most of the correspondents, of their commercial and political weight, particularly in relation to the effectiveness of their medium as an instrumentality for the State Department. The officials know who is reliable and who unreliable, who is thorough and who superficial. The Department keeps classified files on many correspondents because obviously in a Department of such great sensitivity to national security interests, it would be folly not to do so. All other foreign ministries keep dossiers on correspondents in much more elaborate form than the United States State Department does.

When former Assistant Secretary of State for Public Affairs Carl McCardle accompanied Secretary of State Dulles to the Berlin Conference in 1954, he boasted that he had brought "his boys" along from Washington. McCardle voiced the suspicion that many American correspondents abroad were unreliable or possibly infected by the fellow travelers and Communists with whom they were unavoidably in contact. This was in the heyday of the McCarthy era.

Officials criticize the correspondents for billboard writing, that is, over-simplification; for onion-skin-deep reporting; for warped impressions given by tendentious headlines; for dubious angles inserted to jazz up the lead or the first paragraph of a story. The correspondents know—most editors usually do not—that they cannot cover the State Department on the fly between editions, as one would a running story in Congress or in a police station. State Department news is usually an evolving story which has to be steeped like tea until it is mature enough and the time comes to write it.

For their part, officials do not necessarily know that correspondents have to fight internal handicaps in their own medium. The necessity for brevity curtails adequate explanations of the significance of events, which is the primary purpose of most State Department coverage. There is the never-ending chore of the wire service reporters, from whom 98 per cent of the nation's newspapers derive their foreign news and interpretation. In the late afternoon these newsmen must write a night lead for the morning papers, and later that evening they must write an overnight lead for the first edition of the afternoon papers the next day and a day lead for the principal editions of the afternoon papers on that day. And, if there has been no real new development since the original story, the reporter must still rewrite or rephrase any fine crumb of a new fact he can find or offer a new facet of interpretation in order to merchandise the story as if it were brand new. This is so the multiple outlets he serves may believe they are receiving "fresh" news. The "specials" or individual newspapers, on the other hand, constantly face the question of limited space, the demands of editors for brighter and sharper features that attract attention (but give less information), and the sinister brilliance of overburdened copy desks, which change words, or write in words, for their own occult reasons.

Another circumstance which erodes the effectiveness of the State Department correspondent in covering foreign affairs is the "competition" of chiefs of Washington bureaus. In defense of their own importance and status in being theoretically privy to all the important news in the capital of the nation, the bureau chiefs insert themselves into foreign affairs coverage. Too often it is with scant preparation and understanding. Further, since 75 per cent of the American newspapers have no representatives in Washington, the prestige of the nearly 1,500 working newsmen in Washington is all the more enhanced if they can have a say-so about such a priority topic as foreign affairs. It does not matter where the originating source may be found—the State Department, the White House, or the Congress. As a consequence of this proliferation of experts, there frequently develops a chasing of will o' the wisps in Washington coverage of foreign affairs— shreds, fragments, rumors, and dust. All these must be duly run down, eliminated, or, in the trade jargon, "knocked down" by the professionals. This feverish and thankless activity complicates and confuses their normal work. But it remains an inescapable obligation. Some of the amateurs' rumors might be true.

An obvious source of news is the press conferences of Secretary Rusk. In 1966 he held fourteen, but in the first nine months of 1967 only four. As everybody knows, Rusk had never been a headline grabber. Indeed, the Secretary hated headlines. He had a deep aversion to translating emotional words into diplomatic verbiage, though he himself had a quiet fame among diplomatic colleagues as a graphic phrase-maker in private. Too vivid words were dangerous: there was too much inflammable tinder around. Therefore, a dull public image for a Secretary of State was fire insurance, Rusk believed.

Secretary Dulles appeared to derive considerable merriment at the ease with which he could mystify his interlocutors. Though a preacher's son, Rusk deliberately eschewed the use of the rostrum as a pulpit. Essentially, he had too direct an approach to matters of high policy to copy the deliberately histrionic style of Dulles, whose friend and co-worker he had been. Whereas Dulles was a great headline writer, Rusk deplored slogans. Dulles used to play tag with the press, and, Houdini-like, he almost always slipped out of its clutches. Rusk, after his first press conference, was physically shaken by the experience. He was temporarily distressed at the persistently sharp questioning. Afterward he would ask senior correspondents, "How did I do this time?" Whereas Dulles evoked grudging admiration by his counterpoint in black-and-white, the Rusk performance drew press deprecation as "plausible but not convincing."

Though he found press conferences personally uncomfortable for a long time, given his shy nature, Rusk faced up to their necessity like a soldier. He spent an intensive hour with public affairs officials and key advisers to prepare for them. Reviewing facts and policies on at least fifty possible questions, he was surprised to find on the actual firing line that perhaps only three matters dominated the half-hour press conference, with perhaps one or two secondary questions edged in.

Rusk and his senior executives were amazed to note in the transcript of press conferences that as much as 80 or 90 per cent of the questions focused on the future. Very few reporters indeed asked about the past and about what actually happened. The officials shrewdly noted that with the new multiplicity of by-lines or signatures by star correspondents, questions tended to get more and more specialized. It indicated the desire of the newsman for a private spin-out. It put a premium on the special angle he must produce for a unique column with which to compete against his rivals on the morrow.

Yet, the State Department correspondents' emphasis on the future is not idly speculative, but on the same wave length of the reality that the officials themselves face. In the continuing conflict between the officials' working viewpoint and the press' spectator or analysts' viewpoint, the official is thinking of coordinating actions, while the correspondent is focusing on learning intentions. But both are looking toward what comes next.

In the crossplay between the future-to-be and the actuality-in-process occurs the major occupational hazard that State Department officials suffer, namely, the leak. The regularity and recurrence of leaks in the State Department raise official tempers periodically, though, on assessment, the net damage more often than not turns out to be insignificant. But the moment a leak escapes, a sweatbox atmosphere of artificial crisis is created, sometimes leaving officials tense and irritable for days. Possible sources are tracked down. Lesser minions are drawn and quartered. Not rarely, State's security office, or SY, is called in to find where the press miscreant obtained the leaked story.

A leak is an unauthorized disclosure of information which is inopportune politically, embarrassing bureaucratically, possibly injurious in the domestic American political scene, or conceivably damaging to U.S. national interests and relations with other sovereign states. A leak may be wholly true, partly true; a trace of truth may be in it, and the rest false, fabricated, or speculative. But the net effect is that, though a crumb of the truth has escaped, it's a big enough crumb to induce the outside world and interested hostile observers to try to bake a whole cake with it. Leaks often turn out to be tornadoes in a teacup. Leaks have plagued the State Department since the beginning of the Republic and the administration of President George Washington, when the terms of the Anglo-American trade treaty were leaked to the press from the Senate. Today, with constant briefing of Congress by the State Department, plugging leaks becomes virtually impossible.

There are well-known leaks from the top when high officials launch trial balloons or slip out well-disguised canards about rivals. The State Department itself leaks officially but privately to a major metropolitan newspaper, whose reporter believes that he just got a story; however, all other reporters, left out of the deal, consider it to have been a leak pure and simple. Some higher officials have become knowledgeable enough about leaks to be able to make shrewd guesses as to how they came about. There is the affable official who likes to be known as a good guy with the press and spills like a sieve. There is the clever reporter who approaches a junior officer and hornswoggles him: the reporter pretends to know the whole story and draws the facts out of the poor innocent. There is the hotshot reporter who browbeats a lesser functionary into revealing things he shouldn't. There are leaks from the Pentagon which have foreign policy repercussions, like the famous leak on the cancellation of the Skybolt missile for Britain. Its chain of consequences to a degree influenced Charles de Gaulle's veto of Britain's entry into the European Common Market in January 1963. Officials ruefully recall that the leak happened in December 1962, the day before the *New York Times* went on strike for several months. There are officials with large vanities, easily massaged with adroit flattery. Or the baby-face look of a conniving reporter elicits enough telltale strands of information to reconstruct the concealed story, which then becomes the leak.

There are two varieties of ordinary leaks: the in-the-shop tragicomedy or the out-in-the-world straight farce. In November 1966, for an example of the former, there was "premature disclosure" of the decision made for the supply of food grains to India. President Johnson had been mulling it over for four months in an attempt to get other nations to join a food aid consortium. Most citizens couldn't have been less interested, but some two dozen officials in Washington thought it was the end of the world for a couple of days.

There was the ludicrous series of German leaks during the Berlin crisis which used to drive normally self-possessed former Deputy Under Secretary of State for Political Affairs Foy D. Kohler out of his mind when he was Assistant Secretary for European Affairs in the early 1960's. News of discussions between the United States and Germany would invariably hit the fan from the leaky faucets in Bonn. German political parties constantly intrigued against each other, and leaking the plans of others to the U.S. press was the handiest weapon within reach.

A negative factor in leaks is that it forces premature governmental action before all the arrangements are operationally in readiness. This gives time to the opposition to pull strings and to create pressures to stop the proposed plans that have been leaked. There are also debatable leaks during delicate diplomatic negotiations where the national interests may become vulnerable, as in the so-called peace feelers to Hanoi about ending the Vietnam war, prompting one wit to remark: "Never was so much secret diplomacy so publicly discussed."

The most serious objection to leaks, other than that of irresponsibly disclosing information during secret negotiations, are two: one is the complaint of the systems-analysis school, which claims that the options of the officials, usually meaning the President, are foreclosed if a leak shows his hand. Options theoretically mean a spread of alternatives which gives the President a choice of actions, a wider latitude to do that which he must do. This sometimes turns out to be a shell game. The options may be an array of possible excuses to take no action. Or stopping leaks may be a foreclosure of reasonable alternatives of policy to argue about, examine, discuss, and clarify. The second, and probably the most valid, objection to the leak has to do with the manner in which it affects the competence and confidence of a political leader. He may feel that his immediate circle of loyalties is made smaller and smaller by leaks from so-called confidantes. Leaks reduce, negate, or constrict the feeling of being completely frank, trusting, and protected within the officially loyal circle.

In the long run there have been very few leaks which seriously affected the course of history. Despite recriminations, breast beatings, and attendant uproar, any administration or Department of State that has a sound plan and operating procedure can proceed to do whatever it should do, leaks or no leaks.

As a matter of fact, officials underrate the acuity of correspondents in believing there is always sleight of hand in obtaining officially illicit information. Sometimes correspondents who offended official mores by publishing leaks are given "The Treatment." Their telephone calls are not answered. Secretaries are snippy. The merely officious become downright obnoxious. The culprits are ignored, not invited to special briefings, and even castigated publicly in official displeasures. What happens in many cases is simply the result of initiative, with some luck, on the part of the correspondent. Good reporters will pick up bits and pieces from not one but three or four or five or six sources. Not infrequently they come up with a surprisingly accurate story of a supposedly secret operation, the publication of which makes the official's hair stand on end and prompts a call for the cops.

To cite a routine example, this writer once figured out how former Soviet Premier Nikita Khrushchev was to be restricted physically to Manhattan on his spectacular visit to the United Nations in 1960. By talking around to about ten or twelve sources, he was able to disclose the story a full day before the official announcement. If an experienced reporter knows the process of foreign policy formulation, he can triangulate his grid points, calculate at what point a decision ought to be made, cross-hatch his findings, then move in for the kill and the story. At times the process of plumbing the official mind veers curiously close to an eerie feeling of being engaged in counterespionage against one's own government.

The experience of any first-class correspondent is that the man who asks the right questions at the right time gets the news, if he has taken the trouble to estimate the practical probabilities of the situation. The reward is the big star-spangled prize called an "exclusive" in the trade, a "scoop" in the movies, and a leak by the officials. What is essential is the relationship between the reporter and the State Department official or Foreign Service officer. The reporter theoretically knows nothing about confidential official business, the official theoretically knows everything. How the two interact depends in the long run more on the official than on the reporter. The official represents an institution which has been continuously in existence for some 180 years. The official must develop a realistic sense of values concerning the press and information as part of his working tradition. It isn't yet quite so.

Career Foreign Service officers, for the most part, apparently need a basic new orientation about the press to overcome their traditionally repressive attitudes about information. Almost every middle-to-senior-level Foreign Service officer has had his fingers burned at one time or another by talking with reporters, an experience which makes many officers twice as leery. The press is separated into good guys and bad guys; those you can trust and talk to fairly frankly and those you had better steer clear and be wary of. Some senior officers are subtle and slippery. Others smother the reporter in a marshmallow flow of platitudes merchandised as beatitudes. Or, if a conversation gets close to the bone, officials sometimes decline to be explicit but become argumentative to enforce acceptance of their authorized version as the gospel. This tends to equate Department "positions" with truth, whatever "truth" may be.

A major area which Foreign Service officers with excessive piety claim as "privileged," that is, cannot be talked about, is information from other countries. This is classed as "sensitive." In the early 1967 federal grand jury investigation in Washington into the bombings of six Yugoslav missions in the United States and Canada, hardly a single State Department official would give a reporter the time of day or the merest background of facts concerning possible currents among anti-Tito Yugoslavs in the United States. Many officials just do not trust the press. As one said, "Maybe I can trust them not to write it, but can I trust them not to speak it?" Another feels talking to the press is like Russian roulette, one wrong word and "you're cooked." Some officers adopt a condescending tone to the press, as if instructing morons.

Bitterness aroused by the Vietnam war has indurated the prejudices of not a few officials who privately go so far as to say they "despise" the press as being "irritating and irresponsible." A harassed official said, "The press deludes itself if it thinks we are here to make their job easier. We will fight them if necessary. We have a job to do." Other critics charge that the press does not do its homework before interviews and press conferences and asks irrelevant or contentious questions.

Newly appointed officials from civilian life not infrequently are much worse than career Foreign Service officers. Some new officials seem to believe they are the sole proprietors of the public's business and hold a monopoly of expertise on how to deal with the press. Their line is that officials are better judges of what the public ought to know than the press is, ignoring the State Department's need of public support for its policies.

The State Department nevertheless tries to provide considerable information by means of briefings or "backgrounders" for "guidance," basically expositions for reporters who have had no time to do their homework. Such convocations include ambassadors home for consultation, Assistant Secretaries of State whose areas are in crisis, or high seventh-floor officials. These unnamed sources give the lowdown on countries in the news, present the United States view on the antiballistic missile, or explain what may be the latest interpretation of the Sino-Soviet conflict or the background of Vietnam policies. Secretary of State Rusk gives occasional backgrounders which turn out to be rather mass affairs of some twenty-five to thirty-five correspondents, sometimes including news agency chiefs from allied countries like Britain, France, and West Germany. The Secretary is listed as having had five backgrounders on key subjects in 1966. Frequently, when he is not too pressed with urgent matters, he holds more intimate backgrounders late on Friday afternoons in an eighth-floor State Department salon. Of these, there were seventeen in the first three quarters of 1967. A bar offers free whisky. The atmosphere is clubby, relaxed, a bit sleepy. Neither the Secretary nor other personalities are ever identified by name or position and no attribution may be laid to them. The practice has been to indicate the sources by various tag phrases, such as, "U.S. sources," "official sources," "authoritative sources." This last usage, it seems, has spread to

Moscow. There, in the spring of 1965, Leonid Zamyatin, chief of the News Division in the Soviet Foreign Ministry, talking about a Geneva Conference of the Laos type as a possible exit from the Vietnam war for the United States, said to this writer, "You can use 'authoritative sources,' just like in Washington."

The important background conferences are almost always "deep, deep background." This means that the correspondents write it on their own, according to the so-called Lindley rule, named for Ernest K. Lindley, a former contributing editor of *Newsweek* and later a special assistant to Rusk. This means writing it as if one were personally the originator of the great thoughts. Anybody who reads the Washington or New York press carefully on a Saturday or a Sunday will frequently note the similarity of a spate of articles adverting to current issues, all written more or less along the same lines. This after all was the purpose of the anonymous official's backgrounder.

At times, however, the correspondents fail to get the background message. Former Assistant Secretary of State for Inter-American Affairs Lincoln Gordon, when he was Ambassador to Brazil, gave a detailed analysis "on the background" of why he thought former President Goulart of Brazil would be deposed by a coup. Gordon issued this warning at least four months before Goulart fell. Yet when Goulart was overthrown, everybody was taken by surprise. Hardly anyone bothered to write about the situation Gordon had predicted. When there is a real flap and backgrounders might be useful to illuminate the emergency, they are hard to arrange. Everybody buttons his lip until the heat is off.

In the spring of 1966, when the Buddhists ran riot in South Vietnam, many officials in the Department, and indeed some in the White House, were alarmed, depressed, and even panicky. There was a feeling that the game was lost, that the United States would have to scuttle out of Vietnam. The press, more or less, reflected the same view, with rare exceptions. No official laid it on the line, in contrast to the 1962 Cuban nuclear crisis, when the State Department press corps was briefed on developments at least three times a day.

Obviously, some subjects are much too sensitive for backgrounders of any kind. The best the correspondents can obtain are oblique hints and nuanced nudges, if they ask careful questions in the correct area of official concern. The criterion of caution applies foremost to United States relations with the Soviet Union, the only major potential antagonist of the United States by virtue of the thermonuclear destruction Russia can visit upon America, and vice versa. The truce of deterrence of the last decade may possibly be lapsing into a phase of overlapping mutuality, as the diplomats phrase it, where common interests between the United States and Soviet

Russia allow for some give-and-take. The U.S. interest is to keep bilateral relations with Russia as far as possible outside any context of confrontation in Vietnam. The State Department goes to considerable lengths to keep matters as smooth as possible with the Russians. It naturally does not talk about it for fear of stirring to wrath the cold warriors of Congress.

In the last year the State Department has tried to do all it could do, within the limits of vital national objectives, to enhance this feeling of mutuality between Russians and Americans. The trend toward such tentative consensus began when Soviet Premier Alexei Kosygin offered to mediate the Indian–Pakistani war at Tashkent in 1965. There were arguments within the Department as to whether the Russians should be allowed to score points as peacemakers. Once the decision was made to let the Russians try their hand at responsible and constructive peacemaking, U.S. officials privately gave the Russians the benefit of their experience with the Indians and the Pakistanis over the last decade. The Russians came to know the pitfalls and problems of Kashmir and other prickly points which they would have to deal with at Tashkent.

At the Russians' request, the Americans as unobtrusively as possible de-emphasized the ineffectiveness of the Soviet-supplied missiles in North Vietnam. Otherwise there would be pressure by Hanoi to demand more modern and accurate weapons systems from the Soviets. The Russians were against overdoing public discussion of West German difficulties in the nonproliferation discussions that had been in train the preceding year. They asked the Americans to play down that aspect in their analyses of the situation for the U.S. press. On the issue of the antiballistic missiles, the State Department feared that the more the press talked about the ABM, the more the Russians would get skittish and not agree to such talks. Officials wished that the subject would drop out of the public prints for at least a few weeks while they did business behind closed doors in the Kremlin. It did not develop that way. The Department's view was that the Russians had acted with restraint in Vietnam and in the Middle East, by and large. Officials tried to persuade the press to see the relationship of the two superpowers in this light. The only difficulty was that other international bystanders were not so self-abnegating. They had their own fish to fry. In these situations, the leak became an official weapon of other governments with which to attempt to obtain marginal leverage in any negotiations between Americans and Russians. This necessitated further convoluted interpretations by the State Department public affairs officials. It was unavoidable when the French, the British, the West Germans, or the Communist Chinese dropped their particular porcelain on the sidewalk, in order to make themselves heard as nations that must still be taken into account and not be left out in the cold by the two world superpowers.

Despite all the difficulties inherent in the nature of the business and the mutual brickbats, of officials taking reporters for saps and reporters taking officials for dopes, the overriding fact remained that the U.S. State Department was the largest collection of brains most easily available in Washington. They could be picked over almost at will by enterprising reporters. Foreign correspondents from other countries are amazed at the ease of access to most State officials and the general availability of ordinary technicians in the diplomatic vineyard. There is absolutely no comparison for a similar open-door policy to the press anywhere else in the world, "free" or otherwise. In the final analysis, mutual respect and trust between officials and reporters are the only basis for responsible coverage and interpretation of foreign news.

CHAPTER IV

ROUTINE: Organization of Confusion

MUCH LIKE FOREIGN POLICY itself, the Department of State, on "C" Street at Twenty-second Street Northwest, is a paradox in many respects. The exterior of Indiana limestone and Minnesota and Texas granite is strictly no-nonsense semiutilitarian. The interior ranges from a softly efficient modernism in its conference rooms on the ground floor to a dessicated sumptuousness in its reception rooms on the top, or eighth, floor. Over its nearly twelve acres and five miles of corridors, touches of surrealist symbolism mingle with corner-drugstore camaraderie in the cafeterias, whose customers imbibe nearly two million cups of coffee a year. The polished and slippery synthetic tiles in the corridors can be a menace even to diplomats with an Indian-guide tread. In the summer, a continuous line of ceiling air vents sympathetically hisses cool air on fevered brows. The only area which seems to lack this benediction of modern technology is the seventh-floor reception rooms of the Secretary of State, where, despite continuous tinkering with the air-conditioning, the climatological atmosphere remains rather stale and airless.

The clinical neatness of the halls, however, is deceptive. For more than 7,000 persons are industriously engaged in taking care of the interests of the United States, with 123 national clients around the earth, by means of United States representatives in 276 overseas posts. In the Department of State is the Great Seal of the United States, the official symbol of the nation's sovereignty. Its aureole sheds a glow of self-importance on the denizens of the vast structure, who are punctiliously proud to declare themselves employees of the United States Department of State.

As Secretary Rusk likes to repeat, "Eighty-five per cent of the work of the Department is routine." It is done quietly, with unadvertised efficiency and with more or less dispatch, ungracious rumors to the contrary notwithstanding. Basically, this largest part of the Department's duties is simply that of carrying on the business of the United States in the society of nations, participating in the international polity of manifold mechanisms whereby states exchange goods, monies, ideas, and people.

The State Department's bureaucracy has standard operating procedures, normally effective in handling this routine and main grist of its mill. Most bureaucracies operate most effectively when they can cite precedents. They are most comfortable in the predictability of what they expect to happen in the routine administration of international courtesies, conveniences, and contractual obligations. In fact, it is quite remarkable how the bread-and-butter chores of the august Department of State get executed despite the headline crises and political lightnings which may be afflicting the Department's leaders on the seventh floor. These, most of the time, are unaware of what goes on on the lower floors. This normal work goes on even when the seventh floor is missing several top officers, as happened in late 1966, when there were three vacancies below the level of the Secretary of State. Work progresses even better when one of Washington's occasional blizzards stops all traffic. Snow does not keep the dedicated clerks and lesser officers from coming in to handle the essential papers in their in-baskets, without having too many senior bosses breathing down their necks.

Today junior officers make decisions that before World War II were the province of the Secretary of State, such as deciding when ambassadors should come home for consultation or sending out and coordinating notes to fifty or more nations, notifying them of policy determinations in the Vietnam war. The underlying reason for all this ubiquitous activity, of course, is that the United States world presence is today so all-pervasive. The nation must marshal an Argus-eyed organization that is able ceaselessly to monitor, to preserve, and to protect this American presence anywhere and everywhere in the world where Americans see fit to go or to do business. It is the extreme ramifications of this new but natural development that in late years raised critical charges that the United States was attempting to "police" the world.

The beehive activity of the Department is reflected in its telegraph branch, which handles about 4,000 messages a day, incoming and outgoing, a total of about 15 million words a month. Approximately 55 per cent of the State Department cable traffic is classified, which means not for unauthorized or public inspection. In January 1967, a slower month than usual, 44,817 cables were received and sent. This is almost five times the number sent in January 1944, during World War II. There are over 300 overseas telephone calls to and from Washington a day. The Department leases about a hundred international lines between the United States and foreign countries for teletype messages. The telegraph branch is a nerve center not only of the State Department but of the entire United States Government. Varying numbers of its cable copies go to every existing U.S. agency, depending on the subject matter and the need to know. This means roughly sixty departments and agencies. Major distribution points are Defense, CIA, the White House, AID, USIA, AEC, Commerce, Treasury, and Agriculture. Until 1966 the Department burned six and a half thousand pounds of classified papers a day. Since then, a newly installed automated system has been pulping and macerating the paper for faster burning.

The Department's burst of activity coincides with the space age and the end of the Eisenhower administration. Passport issuances since 1960 have almost doubled, as did visa issuances after passage of the 1965 revised immigration law. Almost 140,000 commercial reports are made a year. Seventeen U.S. embassies have been opened in new countries since 1960. Yet, with all this hustle and bustle, the total number of persons on the payroll since 1960 has increased by less than 3 per cent.

The Department handles 19 million pieces of mail a year. Seventy diplomatic couriers fly on fifty-seven airlines throughout the world and chalk up over 130,000 travel miles a year. Ordinary Department mail flies on eighty-eight airlines, while 43,000 pouches, weighing 2 million pounds, sail by surface transportation to overseas posts.

The Language Service Division makes official translations of 20,000 pages of diplomatic documents in fifty foreign languages every year and translates 5,000 pages from English into forty-two languages. It screens 50,000 letters in foreign languages originally addressed to the White House.

The State Department makes loans to destitute Americans abroad who want to come home. By 1966 it had made such loans to 35,080 persons, for a total of $13,482,170. Seventy-four per cent of the loans have been repaid.

State is a big real-estate holder, owning $250 million worth in 1,400 buildings in 180 foreign cities, together with 2,900 houses and apartments for its officers and personnel abroad.

The State Department foreign policy apparatus that the citizenry is most concerned with, however, is concentrated in its five geographical bureaus. These are the heart of the Department's executive direction and policy formulation in Washington, a headquarters operation which costs $16 million a year. The five bureaus—European, African, Inter-American, Near Eastern and South Asian, and East Asian and Pacific Affairs—do not quite correspond to all the continents of the globe. In the nature of today's world, the activities of the five bureaus inevitably cut across, impinge upon, or penetrate into the interests of one another, giving rise to several favorite saws of senior officers: "It is not possible to divide the indivisible," "Every problem merges into every other," and "There is always an illogical residue which is like life itself."

The geographical bureaus are the line commands for direct conduct of United States foreign policy in their respective areas. A Department metaphor terms the Assistant Secretaries of State "Executive Vice Presidents for the world." The Assistant Secretaries have surprising autonomy and leeway in their special areas. It is only when the bone and gristle become too much to cope with that the problem is kicked upstairs, or grabbed by the seventh-floor executives, or sent all the way up to the White House.

The geographical bureaus were established in 1909 as the most important innovation in the State Department structure since before the Civil War. The Assistant Secretary of State in each area is the first level of actual policy making. But routine problems can become prickly very fast. Officials desiring to solve them apply for the authorization of State Department Circular 175, which is a document that must be signed on the Under Secretary level to give authority to lower officials to begin negotiating an issue on behalf of the United States.

In the State Department vernacular the idea is to solve the problem with a "minimum of breakage." This brings us to the second layer of difficulties. The theory is to keep the ship of state floating on an even keel in foreign waters, or to prevent situations from developing to the point where they may become imminently critical. This avowed purpose of soft-peddling or deflecting a possible crisis underlies many of the estimated thirty-five meetings a day which take place in the State Department. The meetings range from formal gatherings of established committees to informal conclaves talking over specific problems.

For beyond the normal work of handling run-of-the-mine contacts and complications between nations there is the larger role of the diplomatic tradition to maintain the balance of power between states. The object is to insure that no one nation or group of nations obtain such preponderance of strength as to affect, impede, or bar this nation's free access to normal converse with other nations. And still beyond that, in this era of nuclear-tipped missiles and sudden-death threats of final confrontations over cumulative disagreements, there is the ultimate question of physical survival. All three factors have to be kept constantly in mind in considerations of foreign policy problems today.

Each bureau has two general responsibilities: first, to take action for initiating a piece of paper that contains a policy recommendation concerning problems in its area; and, second, to "clear" it, that is, to obtain the concurrence of any of the other four bureaus that may have an interest conflicting or collateral in the problem. In the current wide-ranging foreign affairs community of the Government, clearance is also needed with other interested departments. The procedure is elaborate and time-consuming. Indeed, the gantlet may have to be run more than once if major changes are made in the process. But the substance, when all the *i*'s are dotted and the *t*'s crossed, may be somewhat unsubstantial. For the very nature of diplomacy depends on a vision that is bound to be cloudy and on other people's attitudes, which more frequently than not are uncertain. Nevertheless, the Assistant Secretary has the duty of isolating the problem, defining it, making studies of it, reaching decisions as to the best way to handle it, and making plans to put that decision into effect. He then executes the decision as far as he is able through the agency of the State Department, but most often with other agencies. Lastly, he must take up the problem with the foreigners themselves, who may be friendly, semifriendly, indifferent, suspicious, or downright hostile.

It is this policy formulation process upon which criticism of the State Department's performance is usually based. To begin with, the Assistant Secretary, as the chief policy maker for his area, has a staff who are his bureaucrats. An institutional hallmark of a bureaucrat is his insistence on looking at the problem "in the round." The bureaucracy is the organized memory of a department. It does not have many new ideas, but it seems to have a loquacious inclination to remember all the past ideas. This tends to make a bureaucracy crawl like a centipede with snowshoes on. Where policy makers are prone to think big, bureaucrats are habituated to talk of the little items. Since there is usually no end to the problem, which comes from the shaggy reality of life in the outer world, the making of policy becomes a continuous, nonstop process. The resulting compromise of living together between policy makers and bureaucrats, whose job is to thresh out the proposals advanced, is to settle for middle-range objectives and to play a variation on tactics, though professedly not abandoning the objectives.

A standard bureaucratic gambit, ostensibly not devoid of common sense, is to take each issue "on its merits." The phrase, however, at once begs the question, because these so-called merits, the very essence of the matter, are what can be, and often are, arguable. This open-ended approach encourages foggy temporizing or short-range policy. This word—"policy"— seems to be used a million times a day in the Department and in the outside world with reference to the State Department. Yet, there is actually no such thing as a United States foreign policy as a whole. There is a network of policies. There are prime, secondary, and tertiary policies. No two foreign service officers or State Department officials define policy in the same way. Policy is, to some, an expression of an intent to pursue a certain pattern of attitudes and behavior, with consequent actions, in order to attain implicit or explicit goals. Or, a policy may be a decision expressed in plans of actions—or no-actions—in order to maintain, as well as to arrive at, predetermined objectives or conditions that are favorable to

United States interests. Most references to policy are abstract, but specifics are the key to policy matters. Specifics may be peripheral, and miss the point. Or late in application, and miss the boat. Or the detail itself may become the policy. This may generate further lines of action that may proceed under their own momentum but whose implications are not spelled out, with unforeseen results, as in the dispatch of troops to an area, with no idea when one will get them out after one puts them in. Secretary Dulles, speaking of troops dispatched to Lebanon in 1958, said: "Getting them in is not the point; how far they should go, and getting them out, is the big problem."

Veteran Foreign Service officers in the field bitingly remark that all the State Department's elaborate plans are at bottom procedural. In the end their success or failure will depend upon the man on the spot to put them into effect. In the final analysis, the work of diplomacy turns out to be a matter of persuasion. The degree of implementing American foreign policy hinges on the State Department's ability to influence foreign governments— over which the United States has no control—in contrast to the work of other U.S. Government departments, which can carry out national legislation by their own executive and physical means within the territory of the United States. Charles Burton Marshall, former State Department policy planner, summed it up neatly: "The foreign policy of the United States is a course of action undertaken by the authorities of the United States in pursuit of national objectives beyond the stand of jurisdiction of the United States."

The Bureau of European Affairs is the classic geographical office of the State Department. Its origins go back to the creation of the Department itself in 1789, when its first and only client was France, the young nation's sole ally. It still considers itself the prestige bureau, where the best qualified officers and most cultivated gentlemen naturally find their proper level. Its field of activity contains the glamor capitals of history—London, Paris, Rome—and also one world capital of the opposition, Moscow. The Bureau's western area has nearly 270 million of the world's best educated and most highly skilled people, nearly $20 billion in gold reserves, and record production of steel, coal, chemicals, machinery, and autos, in short, a global powerhouse of $545.6 billion gross national product at 1966 current rates.

The twenty-six countries of Europe and the five dependencies and territories—all the latter in the Western Hemisphere, by the way—put out the biggest gross national product of any group of countries in the world outside of the United States. The Bureau has nearly 250 officers in the Washington headquarters and nearly 1,400 abroad, the largest number in any one area. It spends more money than any other bureau on its requirements, $37 million a year. To show how far time has run, in 1930 there were only 29 officers in the European Bureau and 578 overseas. The Bureau's ambassadors were such stars of the established diplomatic school as David K. E. Bruce, Ambassador to London; Charles E. Bohlen, Ambassador to Paris until 1968; and Llewellyn E. Thompson, Ambassador to Moscow.

The European Bureau is predominantly Anglophile. The last major Francophile was the Bureau's former Assistant Secretary William R. Tyler, who was quietly extricated under the anti-Gaullist regime of former Under Secretary Ball and sent to be Ambassador to the Netherlands. Just as the fact that a vast majority of Americans are of European ancestry gives primary importance to the European Bureau, so does the equally obvious fact that the United States was once a colony of the British Crown, and for nearly 150 years basically dependent on the power of the British Empire on the seven seas for its security.

Working relations with the British have been continuous and intimate all through the history of the United States, from border arrangements concerning the Empire's Canadian possessions to cooperative but sometimes conflicting interests in Panama and South America. Diplomats of both countries understand each other almost instinctively.

The reduced state of Britain notwithstanding, the British manner of upper-crust poise and man-to-man ease sparks an appreciative response in most senior State Department policy makers. The bread of mutual good feeling is buttered by the agglomeration of Rhodes scholars in the Washington area. In 1967 there were 105 in the District of Columbia itself, another 14 in Maryland, and 39 in the Virginia suburbs. They included such luminaries as Secretary of State Rusk, Under Secretary Katzenbach, Director of Intelligence Thomas L. Hughes, key State collaborators like House Majority Leader Carl Albert, and, in the White House, the former key State Department policy planner, Walt W. Rostow.

Since World War II, the British Embassy in Washington has been the highest diplomatic overseas post of the British Foreign Office and consistently staffed with top-drawer men. Some have been intimates of American Presidents, like Ambassador Sir David Ormsby-Gore, now Lord Harlech, with President Kennedy. Within the limitations and distortions produced by their effortless rhetoric, the British liked to picture their relationship to the Americans as that of the wise and cultivated ancient Greeks of Pericles to the powerful but unpolished Romans of the Caesars. The Americans admired the refreshing British intellectual honesty concerning their world role today, as was expressed by the Plowden Report of a few years ago on the reorganization of the British diplomatic service. It said, "Our economic resources as a whole are now less adequate than once they were to serve as a lever for exerting influence or pressure overseas. We have accepted the fact that we no longer have within our control the economic resources of the worldwide empire."

This acknowledgment was even more pointed in a remark of Lord Strang, the former British Permanent Under Secretary of State, who said, "We must recognize the effect on Britain's power of her relinquishment of control in many strategic areas of the world since 1945. No longer can we deploy military and strategic resources, such as the Indian Army, with which we once effectively controlled the whole area outside the trade route from Malta to the Far East and Australia." But, the proud report added, "We do not have to be content to be relegated to a minor role in the world, therefore we must make the best possible use of the diplomacy of persuasion."

In the practical field, the State Department's relationships with the Foreign Office, indeed, the entire U.S. Government's relationships with the British Government, are far more numerous than those with any other country in the world. Disputes between the two countries in the political field are minor. The United States recognized that the British people were opposed to U.S. policy in Vietnam, while the British Government loyally defended its support of U.S. policy despite the political handicaps of doing so. The British in this era are more or less subservient to United States interests, as West Germany used to be during the depths of the Cold War. This intimate understanding of each other's interests and motivations can be expected to remain despite the erosion of what the British for many years fondly called their "special relationship" with the United States.

The paling mythology of the Anglo-American "special relationship" is publicly acknowledged by the British Conservatives, privately admitted by the ruling British Laborites, and openly derided by influential high priests of the American Establishment like former Secretary Dean Acheson. It has not prevented all British Governments from capitalizing on it as a bargaining counter with other nations, such as France or Germany. But no British Government will officially concede that its independent nuclear deterrent is merely the last vestige of British nationalistic pride and at best a possible hole card for eventual contribution to a European nuclear force.

Heavily in hock to the United States, the British pay off with intangibles, in the nature of advice, good offices, the friend-of-the-court drill. There are innumerable intertwined contacts with U.S. interests in finance, Soviet relations, the Middle East, the African area of their former colonies, and collateral Commonwealth influence, such as it is, with Canada, Pakistan and India, and East of Suez. There the thinning British power is now committed to only 1971 to stand by the United States in maintaining lines of communication on Indian Ocean island way stations in the event of world conflict over Vietnam or Communist China or more upheavals in the vast area. Because of this intimate British connection, the European Bureau sets itself up as a major clearance point and/or roadblock with the other geographical bureaus of the Department.

The European Bureau's involvement with British relations in the last twenty years is a virtual history of the progressive evacuation of British responsibility, namely, Britain's diminishing ability to marshal funds and forces in world affairs. It started with the British turnover of accountability for Greece in 1947, when that passionate land of ancient liberty and democracy was threatened with Communist rebellion.

The practice of the United States' picking up the check has continued consistently, accelerated by the huge British expenditures outflow of $4.7 billion, more than it has earned, in the decade preceding 1967. Almost the entire sum was made up by United States loans, in combination in 1965 with a European consortium, to save the pound sterling from devaluation, which, notwithstanding, took place in late 1967. This was a matter of more than incidental self-interest to the United States because of contagious effects on the dollar, since the American balance of payments likewise had been in deficit for almost the same ten years.

These major problems become more or less academic for Assistant Secretaries of State for European Affairs, however. When issues escalate to this size, they are first grabbed by the Department's Under Secretary or his political deputy, and then by the White House, which frequently turns to top outside talent like John J. McCloy, former U.S. High Commissioner in Germany. The Bureau similarly reverts to an indeterminate staff role at first in the eventual question of Britain's seeking acceptance as a member of the European Economic Community or Common Market, until basic national considerations and attitudes have been sorted out in White House councils. The pertinent regional offices of the European Bureau—NATO and Atlantic political-military affairs, and OECD, European Community and Atlantic political-economic affairs—can then start feeding in their ideas. But once more there is a catch to this theoretical line command: Just as former Under Secretary George Ball called the tune almost exclusively in these areas, this next time the new Under Secretary for Political Affairs, Eugene Rostow, leads the Department orchestra.

Rust in the glitter of the European Bureau's repute in the past decade can be traced almost exclusively to its French syndrome—frustration, exasperation, and virtual impotence in dealing with the phenomenon of the French. In this case it meant almost exclusively Charles de Gaulle, President of France. President Franklin D. Roosevelt's animosity toward De Gaulle's porcupine tactics in World War II appears to have been mild irritation compared to latter-day anti-De Gaulle feeling in the State Department. The functionaries' resentment seemed to parallel the degree to which De Gaulle achieved success in restoring French national integrity and pride.

Squabbles with the French have not been new in the love affair which diplomats of the two countries have conducted since France became the first ally of the new American nation in 1778. There was the famous case of the Citizen Genet interfering in American affairs in the days of the French Revolution. There was near-war with France during the Napoleonic period and friction over American rights and freedom of the seas. French refusal to pay World War I debts to the United States for war supplies had an 1834 precedent. President Andrew Jackson threatened action for non-payment of $12 million in maritime indemnities. Jackson said he had waited twenty-five years for France to acknowledge a just debt, but, he declared, he would not wait twenty-five years to be repaid. Some sixty years ago, French Ambassador Jules Jusserand was an intimate adviser to President Theodore Roosevelt. French diplomacy consistently has been prickly in particulars, as witness Anglo-French argumentation during the disarmament discussions of the 1920's as to which came first, disarmament or security, the same argument which has pingponged back and forth between Americans and Soviets in the last fifteen years.

The France that the European Bureau deals with today is only one twentieth of its pre-World War II empire of 4.8 million square miles and 110 million population. Since 1940, France has granted independence under duress, that is, revolt in some notable cases—Indochina, Algeria, Tunisia, Morocco—to twenty-four former territories, and it has returned ceded areas to India and China. A large measure of American diplomacy's failure to cope with the French problem may be laid to a combination of an attitude of anachronism, for example, a frozen idea of French weakness and a rather insensitive appreciation of France's necessity to restore faith in herself after the humiliation and vicissitudes of twenty years of colonial war and internal political factionalism.

The decade since De Gaulle's return to power in 1957 was marked by fitful attention paid by the Eisenhower administration, indecisiveness during the Kennedy administration, and plain waiting it out by the Johnson administration. The time perhaps may be approaching when—with an aging De Gaulle and his political heritage in doubt, a new coalescing of left-wing forces, and new economic preoccupations in the Common Market—France again may become a proper subject for normal consideration by normal diplomats of the European Bureau.

Leaving aside the overriding global problem of the Soviet Union whose issues quickly hie themselves to the seventh, executive, floor and thence to the White House, the biggest single customer of the European Bureau is

West Germany. To the U.S. Embassy in Bonn are attached over 800 Americans, though only one fourth of them belong to the State Department itself. Germany has been a problem to the State Department for more than half a century. Martin Hillenbrandt, now Ambassador to Hungary and a top Germany expert of the State Department, said in 1961, when Nikita Khrushchev threatened Berlin: "Let's face it. The German problem has been in the deep freeze for ten years." Nothing could be done about Germany because of Russian intransigence concerning the reunification of Germany.

By 1967, eighteen years after the creation of the Federal German Republic, the West Germans were becoming independent in a manner never experienced by Americans accustomed to having their blithe way in Germany since the occupation started in 1945. A young German diplomat in the Washington Embassy said: "We feel that we are just beginning to create the first German foreign policy since before the first World War," that is, 1914. The younger German diplomats felt that most State Department officials in the United States and in the Foreign Service were still conditioned to having their say-so without question in dealing with German officials and that very few treated the Germans as psychological equals, but rather as junior Americans. For almost two decades the United States had been a sounding board for German politicians, who paid visits to the White House to score points for benefit of their political futures back in West Germany. German political parties copied American styles of political campaigning, particularly John F. Kennedy's "New Frontier" electoral tactics. The Germans quickly caught on to the pattern of Washington lobbying. They hired the bumbling but shrewd Julius Klein to gild the lily on matters which the U.S. Government was freely amiable in accommodating the Germans without a go-between.

There is little on the record of State Department foresight in recognizing in good time the politico-economic conditions which would bring German-American relations in the early months of 1967 to the crisis stage. This concerned German refusal to continue paying funds to offset the upkeep of U.S. forces in Germany, in order to relieve the continued strain on the U.S. balance of payments. Actually, the first steps to face this coming German problem were taken by the U.S. Treasury, not by the State Department. As early as 1961, former Treasury Secretary Douglas Dillon twisted the German arm to persuade them to buy surplus U.S. military equipment and to pay for it in advance, to boot, in order to ease the persistent U.S. payments deficit. Dillon knew that there would come a time when the German goose would not lay any more golden eggs. As early as 1964, Dillon recommended a new approach. Dillon then predicted that the United States would sooner than later have to face the necessity of withdrawing as many as two divisions from Germany. His words came partially true in April 1967, when 35,000 American soldiers were officially scheduled to leave Germany. The troops' announced departure was accompanied by the promise that they would be rushed back inside of two weeks in case of an emergency. The 1963 big U.S.-German trial airlift of rushing combat troops across the ocean had resulted in a considerable gap between the military equipment and supplies arriving simultaneously with the manpower.

Financial difficulties, which forced the Germans to put their back up against American demands, were ironically a product of American advice in framing the West German constitution in 1949. In order to ensure that no strongly centralized government could again become authoritarian and take the road of a Kaiser and a Hitler, a large measure of the revenue-raising power was given to the Laender, or states. Later, the German economic boom forced the comparatively meek German workers to demand a share of the apparently perpetual prosperity. The late Chancellor Konrad Adenauer raised social security benefits progressively to satisfy labor. The restricted federal budget was unable to support the increased social security charges, forcing the Germans to plead budgetary necessity for cutting down their offset expenses. The German budget dilemma reached a climax in the summer of 1967, when Chancellor Kurt Kiesinger proposed slashing West German defense forces, the core of European contributions to NATO. In sum, the Americans had taken the Germans for granted a mite too long. U.S. staff work had expended itself on minutiae of German internal politics or proclaimed large ambiguities about the German role in a unified Europe. In this latter connection arose the problem of Germany's sharing control over nuclear armaments through the multilateral nuclear force. This would have been a force of several nations, including Germany, and would have had the use of U.S. nuclear arms under certain conditions. This conception took almost seven years to falter into abortion. But all the while it kept the Germans in a state of frustrated suspense, not to say anxiety.

U.S. handling or nonhandling of German affairs may be noted in the Bonn Republic's policy of eventual reconciliation with the Eastern European Communist states. These had suffered most from Nazi Germany and actively feared a rearmed, reunited, and revanchist Germany which once more could become a threat to their national existence. Chancellor Adenauer had had as his first objective reconciliation with the ancient German enemy in the west, France. But he definitely had in mind a similar approach to initiate new relations and amicable relations with Germany's eastern neighbors.

In May 1955, after the restoration of German sovereignty to the Federal

Republic in Bonn and adhesion to the NATO alliance in Paris, Adenauer gave this writer, a foreign correspondent at that time, a written interview, answering questions concerning his intentions for reconciliation with Poland and the other satellites, which Adenauer said he favored. The Chancellor made it a condition that his answers, placed in the hands of the German Embassy in Paris, be released and published under a Bonn dateline as soon as his plane, then leaving Paris, had landed in Bonn within the hour. As it happened, Adenauer's companion aboard the plane was Walter Hallstein, author of the Hallstein Doctrine, that is, the doctrine that no German diplomatic relations should be maintained with countries that recognized the German Democratic Republic, or East Germany.

On the half-hour trip Hallstein sold Adenauer off the interview. It was not until 1962 that the first notes for a possible reconciliation with the Eastern Communist states began to be sounded by Bonn and trade missions began operating in Eastern Europe. It was not until 1967, under Chancellor Kiesinger, that a proclaimed policy of peaceful new relations with Communist countries of Europe was established, in short, twelve years after Adenauer's original intentions. There is little record of U.S. diplomatic interest or advice at the time to further this policy, which, at the very least, might have hastened the development of desired events. The Department's lack of effectiveness in initiating new policies with regard to Germany can be attributed to two factors. First, there was a lack of high-level interest in attempting the apparently impossible after U.S. experiences with the Russians at the conferences of 1954, 1955, and 1959. Second, there was a lack of recommendations originating on the lower, or European Bureau, level, because the atmosphere was not conducive to a bureaucrat's sticking his neck out on an issue which, to all intents and purposes, was dead.

In contrast to that absence of specific new ideas on Germany, the work of the State Department's Berlin Task Force in 1961 stands out in sharp relief, despite an initial stumble. This was the slowness in answering the Soviet *aide-mémoire* of June 4, 1961. The reply was made by July 17, 1961, after a forty-three-day delay, a pace which infuriated President Kennedy. But once on top of its assignment, the Berlin Task Force, under Assistant Secretary Foy D. Kohler and with the authority of the President solidly behind it, had a remarkably successful record to the very end. It met, countered, and faced down the Soviet threat until the crisis faded out at the end of 1961.

Only one decision of the Task Force was ever appealed to Kennedy: a contingency plan on the way to meet a possible East German move physically to stop U.S. convoys in proceeding from Western Germany to Berlin on the Autobahn. The Task Force recommended a showdown right then and there if the East Germans as much as lifted a finger to stop an

American vehicle. Kennedy vetoed it in favor of prudence. The risk he accepted was that of the Communists possibly winning via their so-called salami tactics of piling up minor precedents to create a policy against Allied vital interests.

The most constructive lesson about the way in which the State Department operates on a great issue of primary European-American importance is NATO. This historic alliance was created under the leadership of Secretary Acheson in 1949. After De Gaulle's notification of his withdrawal from the NATO organization in March 1966, NATO was saved by the same Dean Acheson, called in by President Johnson to do the salvage job. In contrast to the brilliant activity of the great period in Truman's administration, Acheson, calling upon the specialists of the European Bureau for plans and ideas, was astounded to find that "the memoranda that came up were not good enough to throw into the wastebasket." Acheson was forced to create the whole plan of saving NATO from the effects of the French decision practically by himself. As one of his 1966 collaborators put it: "Acheson had not only superb diplomatic expertise and perspective, but above all else he had the driving purpose to accomplish his mission of saving the Atlantic Alliance."

Like Germany, NATO had been kept in a frozen *status quo* by the chill of the Cold War from 1957 to 1967, when Acheson engineered its long overdue reform. In that decade there was, at first incipient and then endemic, European unease at NATO's adequacy for the nuclear age. Europe was reluctant to raise larger conventional armies without first having a voice in nuclear decisions. "We made a hundred mistakes," McGeorge Bundy said of that period in Congressional testimony. One was possibly made in April 1962, during the Kennedy administration. General Gaston Lavaud, the French Chief of Staff, led a mission to Washington to shop for advanced equipment for the French atomic program. The U.S. nonchalantly treated Lavaud as a mere visitor, instead of using his visit as an opportunity to reopen practical talks with De Gaulle. By then the specter of nuclear proliferation was already causing anxiety in the Kennedy administration. State's policy operators did not feel inclined to pick up the French hint, just as, four years earlier, during the Eisenhower administration, De Gaulle had not seen fit to pick up the American suggestion of global strategy discussions with him, because, as the French said, the suggested talks would have been "limited" to Africa, whereas, the Americans said, Africa would have been only a "start." State's European experts discounted the bitterness of the French feeling of affront at the apparent United States intention to maintain a special atomic relationship with Britain but not with France. French atomic ambitions predated De Gaulle. So did French proposals for closer technological relations, a further bid ignored by the Americans at the time, in 1957, and confronted for the first time ten years later, in 1967.

It was within this deteriorating atmosphere that the MLF, or multi-lateral nuclear force, got its formal birth, in 1963, as an entirely legitimate device to meet the problem of providing nuclear participation to the have-not NATO nations. The Kennedy administration had waited for more than a year for the Europeans to draw up a plan of their own. This the Europeans failed to do. Thus the ball was back in the Americans' court. MLF's principal objective was to head off the Germans from being driven into an eventual demand for their own national nuclear power. But somehow, in the next three years, the ends became confused with the means. The MLF battle inside the U.S. Government became as heated as the theological arguments at the schools of Paris during the Middle Ages over how many angels could sit on the head of a pin. MLF, ostensibly created to solve the crucial problem of what would become a new NATO, became the tail that wagged the dog. Former Under Secretary Ball, with whom MLF was a raging passion, confessed after MLF was laid to rest that perhaps he had committed errors in tactics. Whatever he did, Ball did with a flair and a drive that overwhelmed at least all bureaucratic foes.

A curiosity of the MLF affair is that the whole battle was fought almost exclusively outside the U.S. Foreign Service. Ball was a political appointee and his three principal aides were career Civil Service officers, all holding the top government grade of GS–18. These were then Deputy Assistant Secretary of State for European Affairs, J. Robert Schaetzel, Deputy Chairman of the Policy Planning Council Henry D. Owen, and Ball's special assistant, George S. Springsteen, Jr. Also brain-trusting for Ball were, from the outside, Robert B. Bowie, Director of the Center for International Studies at Harvard University and later the Department's Counselor, and, on the inside, Walt W. Rostow, then the Policy Council's Chairman, a post which Bowie had held under Secretary Dulles, and Gerard C. Smith, still another former Dulles policy chief, brought in especially for the MLF drive. Significantly, Bowie had been the energizer for the U.S.-sponsored European Defense Community, or EDC, also a multinational force, which died a-borning in 1954. Ball's obsessive vision of Atlantic unity gave him a tremendous advantage over the regular nitpicking bureaucrats, who did not know how to get where they did not know they wanted to go. The Department's Foreign Service senior officers stayed above the battle. They freely agreed with the ultimate objective, but also observed that the Russians had a point in one of their favorite sayings, "Some problems have to get ripe for a solution." Ball, in the end, won over everybody in a classic campaign of bureaucracy—everybody that is, but the White House. Noting this fact, the West Germans, for whose benefit the whole exercise had been

organized, finally cooled on MLF themselves. MLF achieved for the
United States at least the useful purpose of dampening German ardor for
military nucleonics. Putting the epitaph on the arduous but vain effort,
Secretary Rusk said: "At least we had an idea; nobody else had anything."

The NATO crisis that the MLF had temporarily muffled came in late
February 1966, when De Gaulle announced that he was withdrawing all
French participation and personnel from NATO and asked that foreign
troops, that is, American, be withdrawn from the soil of France. U.S.
intelligence was forecasting a French notice of withdrawal from the Atlantic
Alliance treaty but not pointing up sharply enough the possibility of
France's leaving the NATO organization. Generalized planning for the
transfer of U.S. military supplies had been undertaken in 1965. But when
Acheson came on the scene in mid-March 1966, no State Department
studies of the military-political implications were on hand. European Bureau experts had provided fascinating conversations on NATO and De
Gaulle; however, these turned out to be pointless, because there was no
specific situation which the experts could sink their teeth into and make
specific plans for.

Starting virtually with a clean slate, Acheson turned in a textbook performance in recasting U.S. NATO policy in five months, from March to
July 1966. The first thing he did was draw up a working plan for himself:
what was there to know about NATO; the big and little issues raised by
the French decision; pipelines; legal and technical details. His second step
was an exhaustive study of all items and an indication of what could
possibly be done about each of them. By late April, Acheson had defined
the problems and outlined them in his first memorandum to President
Johnson. He then met with the President to discuss the direction in which
the solutions might go in the U.S. national interest. Acheson's next step
was a double one. First, he recognized that NATO as then constituted was
indeed out of date and did not fit the needs of today. Its Korean War–born
regulations had long since become rigid and obstructive, as the French had
repeatedly pointed out. The organization needed reform and updating.
Second, new measures were imperative to compensate for the negative
effects of the French withdrawal and to seize the opportunity for putting
into practice recommendations which French negativism had prevented in
the past. Acheson suggested the original idea of using NATO as an instrument for promoting détente and better East-West relations. His impetus
resulted in President Johnson's speech in October 1966 about peaceful
engagement between East and West, a major U.S. policy initiative.

Acheson also suggested a new multilateral approach to sterilize the
problem of the balance of payments concerning military expenditures in
NATO. He had in mind the constant irritant of the offset dispute with the

West Germans which finally came to crisis in December 1966, during the visit of former Chancellor Ludwig Erhard to Washington. But President Johnson was not disposed to grasp this nettle in the summer of 1966. Acheson further proposed continuous and organized contacts on the nuclear issue within NATO, a plan which resulted in the formation of the Nuclear Advisory Group. A hard-minded character himself, Acheson was all for pillorying the French and for dragging out evacuation discussions, in which precise compensation would be demanded from the French for the expense to which they were putting NATO in moving the military headquarters to Brussels and for moving the logistical network. Milder measures—merely getting out quickly and quietly—were preferred by the European Bureau of the State Department. The President ruled against any punitive or vindictive response to De Gaulle. His instruction was, "Be out on time, and take everybody but him [De Gaulle]." The evacuation of NATO from France, the thrift-minded President recalled later, cost only $150 million. "The generals thought it would cost $1 billion."

If the European Bureau classes itself at the top, the African Bureau admits with chagrin that it is at the bottom of the heap in priorities in the State Department. Not, however, that it considers itself by any means the least important. Indeed, in the prospect of the future, Africa, as long ago as 1948, was called the "Asia of tomorrow." The African Bureau is the crucial organ of the State Department for dealing with this area. It symbolizes the crux of the racial conflict pock-marking the world today, the differentiation of color that divides the races and leaves a smoldering bed of bitter embers that flames up so frequently and will continue to do so for years to come. But when all that is said, the African Bureau still has the bottom rating in the State Department. It is pilloried from without as having "no policy." It is patronized from within as being inexperienced, inept, and disorganized or "too committed," that is, overeager. It handles fifty-two countries, forty of which were independent by 1968. Twelve areas still had colonial status, including three tiny Spanish enclaves. The continent contained a population of over 270 million, divided into 2,000 tribes; 82 per cent of the inhabitants, speaking more than 800 languages or dialects, were illiterate; and the gross national product in 1965 was only $40 billion. One fourth of that GNP was that of South Africa alone, the bête noire of all black Africa.

Youth marks the personnel of the African Bureau. Youth makes its officers less hidebound and more willing to take a chance on new ideas. But at the same time youth makes more mistakes because of lack of experience. When a midgrade officer in the Bureau has a hassle over an internal dispute with a senior officer of, say, the European Bureau, both handling equivalent jobs theoretically, the usual result is a rout of the African Bureau as far as its version of the U.S. national interest is concerned.

The Bureau has been growing steadily since it was organized in 1958. Today it has 187 officers in Washington and 1,085 in its overseas posts, at a total investment of $18 million in the State Department budget. Despite the scant attention initially paid to the Bureau by the seventh, executive, floor, the Department is slowly developing an awareness of Africa. This is so particularly as Africa adversely affects U.S. national interests around the world, including NATO and the Middle East, and U.S. concern for repercussions of the Sino-Soviet rivalry. Up to now, the basic United States policy in Africa has been to keep an American presence and a continuing influence, in order to deny a place to Communist pressures. Preoccupation of the senior officers with Vietnam and other U.S. crisis areas led them to discount Bureau warnings, right up to the day before, that Rhodesia would declare its unilateral independence in 1966. In fact, it had been extremely difficult for the Bureau to get any kind of a hearing at all on the seventh floor. In 1964, when the island of Zanzibar threw out its Sultan and Arab ruling class and joined Tanganyika to form the new state of Tanzania, President Johnson was so startled as to ask in the State Department: "Who looks after Africa over there?" When informed that none of the senior officers did, he placed the then Under Secretary of State for Political Affairs, W. Averell Harriman, in charge. Harriman was a short-lived champion because he became a roving ambassador and had his attention shifted almost entirely to Vietnam.

Only in May 1967 did the Bureau get a sort of helping left-hand status when Under Secretary Katzenbach embarked on a three-week tour of eleven African countries. His aim was to learn at first hand about the endemic problems of a continent that had few resources, was extremely backward, had little local agriculture to provide food, received low prices for its chief exports—raw materials—and had differing colonial heritages from the British and the French. The Bureau was further slighted by having its crises, such as the recurrent ones in the Congo, from 1960 to 1964 and again in 1967, snatched out of its hands. Special task forces, senior executives, or the Bureau for International Organizations took on the operating responsibility. In brief, the African Bureau was left with all the tedious, trivial work, which it had to perform with inadequate means, while the glory of "solving" major African problems consistently fell to outsiders.

The Bureau oversees a locale with numerous petty wars which belatedly began to ring alarm bells inside the Department and produce nightmare visions of little "Vietnams" in Kenya, Somalia, Angola, Ethiopia, Nigeria, not to mention the Congo again, and most recently of all, Southwest Africa.

The United Nations, where Africans are the single largest bloc, talked wildly of forcing well-armed South Africa to give up the mandate of the territory given it by the League of Nations forty-seven years ago. A series of coups—in Ghana, Nigeria, Uganda, and Upper Volta, to mention a few—further made political galvanometers quiver.

Time and again the African Bureau has clashed with the European Bureau over whether U.S. policy is to support Africa for the Africans or, as the European Bureau demanded, to restrain its ardor in favor of the Metropole, or Metropolitan Europe, the former colonial overlords of the African colonies whose substantial economic interests continue in Africa.

The African Bureau has had to accept the policy that British influence in Africa should still have precedence in dealing with African problems in formerly British Africa, despite the fact that the British had fewer and fewer resources in funds and manpower to do the job. The African Bureau had to bear the brunt of the wide misunderstanding in Africa of United States support of Britain in Africa in the case of Rhodesia's rebellion against the British Crown. The rebellion was based on the domination of a miniscule white minority of some 200,000 against the overwhelming black majority of 4 million in the British territory. African lack of information about United States policies in Africa has been matched by ignorance among the American people concerning the new foreign policy horizons opened by the African problem. It was only in May 1966 that President Johnson made the first presidential address ever devoted exclusively to the subject of Africa. President Kennedy, in 1961, had instituted a new African policy, such as it was, of more sympathetic attention to African concerns, particularly dramatized by the numerous visits to Africa of former Michigan Governor and Assistant Secretary of State for African Affairs, G. Mennen ("Soapy") Williams.

In more recent times the United States stand on Rhodesia injected itself into American politics through private organizations, mostly pro-African but more recently anti-Negro also. An example of the latter is the recently organized American-Southern Council, which upbraided the Department of State and the Johnson administration for committing the United States to United Nations policies. Such attempts to interfere in the affairs of South Africa might lead to an escalation of the crisis between black Africans and South Africans, a development that could result in United States participation in a United Nations attempt to take Southwest Africa by force.

The Bureau's enforced middle-of-the-road policy, or even right-of-center policy, has unavoidably gone against the grain of the dominant militant or left-of-center African states. These tended to flirt with the Communist world in frustration at not being given special consideration by the United States. Even the latest American diplomatic strategem of regionalism, that is, considering the problems of areas rather than those of a single country, had been taken with ill grace by some Africans. President Sekou Touré of Guinea told Under Secretary Katzenbach in Conakry, during the first visit of a top State Department officer to Africa, that regionalism smacked of "neocolonialism" and a depreciation of individual countries' national sovereignties. The Sekou Touré encounter came as a bit of a shock to the new Under Secretary. Katzenbach, in his innocence, thought he would have a private meeting. Instead, he found himself in a typical African "palavar." Sekou Touré had all his cabinet and senior party officials around him. The Katzenbach entourage, traveling correspondents and all, became, perforce and per Conakry protocol, the visiting Americans' side of the bleachers.

In any event, Africa is changing, just as things have changed in Ouagadougou, in Upper Volta, where perhaps two messages a day used to be received while more recently 63,000 words a month have been sent out. But beyond its own ferment, the major impact of Africa has been upon the Africans' ancestral brothers, the Negroes of the United States. The American Negroes played a significant role in stimulating and shaping African nationalism in the thirty-six African states becoming independent since the climactic 1960 session of the General Assembly of the United Nations when seventeen colonies became new states and former Soviet Premier Nikita Khrushchev seized the opportunity of riding the decolonizing tide. There began a procession of African Prime Ministers and leaders to Washington, where they were received with great flair and sympathy by President Kennedy. As the Negroes of America watched their black brothers from Africa taking salutes and receiving honors of state, they were proud of their race, but they also thought why couldn't they, the American Negroes, also be received with similar courtesies and honors.

As American Negro encouragement of African nationalism paid off, African independence in turn encouraged the civil rights movement in the United States. The trend continues as polls indicate that an increasing number of American Negroes are again identifying themselves with Africa. An indicative 1967 fashion layout in *Ebony* magazine, depicting the life of the affluent Negro society in the United States, promoted African styles, that is, Negro hair in its natural kinky state, whereas, before, Negroes tried to copy white people's straight hair.

The Negroes of Africa watch the United States closely, as does the rest of the colored world in Asia, to see how American society allows, encourages, or discourages the American Negro to come of age. Secretary Rusk, taking note of this fact, said: "The biggest single burden that we carry in our foreign policy of the 1960's is the problem of racial discrimination here at home. There is just no question about it." Rusk's remarks are a variant of a statement made by W. E. B. DuBois some seventy years ago: "The problem of the twentieth century is a problem of the color line—relations of the darker to the lighter areas of man in Asia, in Africa, in America and in the islands of the seas."

The United States domestic problem of civil rights thus equates itself with the global problem of racial equality. Former Deputy Assistant Secretary J. Wayne Fredericks, whose idealism for Africa on behalf of United States national interests might be said to surpass even that of George Ball for Atlantic unity, recalled the conclusion reached by Gunnar Myrdal some twenty years ago. Myrdal pointed out that America's handling of the Negro problem would be either "a liability or an opportunity" and that the United States could add immense "spiritual" resources to its financial and military might if it demonstrated the actual brotherhood of man in a true democracy by solving the Negro problem. This combination of national security interests with domestic political pressures, symbolized by the 20 million U.S. Negro minority, is the framework within which the African Bureau always has to work.

Before the African Bureau was created, the lowest level, according to internal State Department ratings, was held by the Bureau of Inter-American Affairs, that is, the Latin American Bureau. The two bureaus had some points of contact through Castro's Cuba, where there is a not inconsiderable Negro strain in the population. The Latin American Bureau likewise did not have an effective framework and direction until the birth of the Alliance for Progress in March 1961. The Alliance did not burst full blown from the brain of the New Frontier. It was built on the sound foundation of the Act of Bogotá of October 1960, six months earlier. Both Bureaus had in common big, emotional send-offs. Just as the Alliance for Progress took about three years to get off the ground, the African Bureau's so-called new policy is still in somewhat the same stage of more or less treading water. But, unlike the African Bureau, where decisions on such matters as Portuguese Africa would be taken out of its hands by the European Bureau or its thinking on Rhodesia would be heavily influenced by what the Near East and South Asian Bureau thought was the weight of Egypt's views, the Latin American Bureau has had probably more autonomy than any other bureau in the State Department. Its Assistant Secretary of State could with more justice be called "Secretary of State for Latin America" than his four peers for their respective areas.

Latin America has played a continuous role in U.S. diplomatic history since Simón Bolívar raised the banner of revolt in South America in 1815. Even before the 1823 Monroe Doctrine of President James Monroe, Secretary of State Henry Clay three years earlier was proposing a League of Freedom for the Americas. In 1826, Clay sent an urgent request to the Congress for funds to hire more help because of the great increase of work required by the recognition of seven new states in Latin America. President Franklin Pierce and Secretary of State William L. Marcy were eager to purchase Cuba from Spain in 1855. In 1870 a major reorganization of the State Department occurred with the formation of the second diplomatic bureau. The impelling reason was the need for an extra office to handle the seventeen Latin American countries which had attained independence by that time. President James Garfield's Secretary of State, James G. Blaine, created Pan-Americanism as it is known today, though the same term had been used first by Bolívar in Latin America. Secretary of State Henry L. Stimson, under President Herbert Hoover, originated the "Good Neighbor" policy and stressed nonintervention. President Franklin Delano Roosevelt expropriated the "Good Neighbor" policy and made a big deal of it before World War II. After the United States entered the war, there was so much purchasing for profitable supplying of the American war effort that there was no need for fancy slogans.

Then came the postwar decade and renewed American indifference to Latin America as the United States poured its single-minded energies into the Cold War. The near-lynching of then Vice President Richard M. Nixon in Bogotá in 1959 shocked the Eisenhower administration into belated review of the teeming, boiling continent south of the border. The success of the October 1960 Bogotá Conference was almost exclusively the work of Under Secretary of State Douglas Dillon, who said: "The inspiration for much of my thinking on Latin America came from the Buenos Aires Conference in August 1957 which was a real eye-opener for me." Dillon had been shocked at the rigidity and restrictiveness of U.S. attitudes toward Latin America which, Dillon felt, had already begun to change by 1953. By coincidence, in late March 1960, Dillon and this writer were having lunch in his office in the State Department when, discussing the problem of Latin America and the need for a massive shot in the arm for the Latin American economy, the writer remarked that money alone would do no good unless it were given under an "umbrella of social justice." That casual remark had a peripheral effect on Dillon and eventually helped to contribute a modest molecule to his approach. Dillon got the Department's Policy Planning Council quickly to draw up the Bogotá plan, which was adopted formally by the National Security Council in June 1960. A request by President Eisenhower to Congress to authorize $500 million to start the program was honored by the Congress promptly, so that Dillon was able to go to Bogotá with a pledge of assured funds in hand.

Just as newly elected administrations frequently take over the policies or programs of the old team and dress them up in new clothes, the Kennedy administration took over both the Bogotá plan and the Special Fund for Social Development of the Inter-American Bank, another Dillon creation in 1959, when it launched the Alliance for Progress in 1961. The attendant massive propaganda was needled in on the theory that it would create emotional attachment for the Alliance and a momentum that would help it surge to success. The only trouble with the idea was the often repeated point that any true and lasting mystique for the Alliance would have to come eventually from the Latin Americans themselves, as former Assistant Secretary for Inter-American Affairs Lincoln Gordon said. After the euphoria of anticipation had dissipated, the cynical reaction to the Alliance was that it was merely a counter to the zealous energy of the Castro revolution in Cuba and its threat to undermine and crumble the established order in Latin America. This ruling order had persisted almost intact for three centuries, or from the time of the feudal Spanish colonies, the Bolívar revolution notwithstanding.

The new Johnson administration's Assistant Secretary for Latin America, Thomas C. Mann, who was criticized as being an unsympathetic technician, was able to put substance on the New Frontier rhetoric and knock together a solid foundation for the Alliance for Progress by 1964.

Six years and nearly $5 billion later, at the 1967 Punta del Este Summit Conference of American Presidents, the Alliance for Progress reached the ground floor and was ready to build upward. The superstructure envisioned at Punta del Este was a continental Latin American common market which would take eighteen years to create and to which the United States pledged billions of dollars to keep the pump primed. Already a miniscule experiment in that line had taken place in five Central American countries, which had created a common market in 1960 and seen their intrazonal trade jump five times, to $155 million in 1966, 90 per cent of the commerce in the free trade category.

The continent's nearly 240 million people, with a gross national product of only $91 billion, still had far to go. The 1966 growth rate of 4.5 per cent was barely keeping ahead of the population rate of 2.9 per cent, the highest birthrate in the world. The financial investment problem was bad enough in Latin America, which was expected to provide $80 billion of the $100 billion investment termed necessary for the ten-year period from 1961 to 1971. There was a host of other problems blocking the path to progress. Resistance of the ruling classes had been underestimated. American diplomats had forgotten the lessons of Italy and the authoritarian traditions of the Mediterranean seeping into and hardening in the upper-crust controlling families of South America. While a Milan millionaire would entertain a guest with twenty liveried servants wearing white gloves, it was not uncommon for the great houses of the Latinos in the Western Hemisphere to have fifty such servants, as in pre-Castro Havana or in Peru even in 1967. The rich were not about to give up the perquisite of four centuries for the mere asking by the rabble.

There was too much push for short-range effects, straining inadequate administrative machinery, so that there was not enough trained personnel to keep pace with the plans. Inflation was appalling: jumps of between 40 and 80 per cent a year were not uncommon; in Brazil the rise was 120 per cent one year. Deflation, when tried, put the brake on growth and left the jobless still without income, generating or continuing a climate of political unrest. Contrasts in income and literacy, like the geographical distances, were immense. Mighty mountains and dense jungles sundered the nations. Food-to-eat agriculture was scant. Chile had to spend $150 million a year to import potatoes from distant Poland.

The ferment of self-generated peaceful revolution nevertheless had begun to penetrate the top levels as well as the articulate new middle classes. Even the military, once derided as decorative doormen of banana republics, had visions of national pride and civic reforms. Nearly everybody agreed that economic progress meant not only industrial investment but also grass-root agriculture and education, above all. It meant retail aid, that is, developing market networks in the rural regions for small industries so that the historically poverty-stricken peasants and Indians of the hinterlands could join in raising themselves by their bootstraps. The menace of Castro Communism had receded because of the bombast-without-action of Castro himself and Cuban entanglement in the Sino-Soviet conflict. Castro openly attacked Soviet policy, which was promoting popular fronts with democratic elements in Latin America rather than espousing flagrant guerrilla action, as Castro wished.

As is evident, a very large portion of the work of the Latin American Bureau is economic, possibly as much as 80 per cent. The Bureau's effectiveness in handling complex political-economic factors can be attributed in part to an experiment in the State Department, pioneered by the Latin American Bureau under former Assistant Secretary Mann. Regular political officers of the Bureau were placed "back to back" with the parallel economic officers of the Agency for International Development. The integrated State and AID personnel worked side by side as a team, reducing, in effect, Bureau clearances for their programs and policies. Its efficacy depended, however, on first-class personnel, always hard to come by. Assisting substantially the work of the Bureau was the creation of CIAP, the inter-American coordinating committee for the Alliance for Progress, modeled on the Organization for European Economic Cooperation (OEEC), which had coordinated the Marshall Plan in Europe. The first

American representative on CIAP was Walt Rostow, the economic historian who simultaneously held the post of Chairman of the Department's Policy Planning Council and who lent enthusiasm and vision to help energize CIAP as the political motor of Latin American cooperation.

The Bureau in 1965 had 1,260 officers overseas and 173 in Washington, at a total cost of nearly $20 million. It had come quite a long way since 1930, when there were only 22 officers in Washington and 312 in Latin America. The Bureau internally had matured considerably since the first days of the Kennedy administration, when it was considered not quite as inventive, able, or forceful as it ought to have been. It had angered President Kennedy after the Bay of Pigs disaster in 1961, when, asked for recommendations on what the new policy should be to recover ground lost after the calamity, the Bureau dawdled for four days, forcing Kennedy to go to Roger Hilsman, Director of the Bureau of Intelligence and Research, who came up with what the President wanted in twenty-four hours.

In the last decade, the Bureau has been the beneficiary of relatively firm support from both Republicans and Democrats. Republican friendliness stemmed from the deep interest taken in Latin America by President Eisenhower by osmosis from his brother, Milton. The idealism inspired by President Kennedy, who felt that Latin America was perhaps more crucial to the United States than any other region of the world because it was physically contiguous, almost a continental exurbia, raised Latin America to near top priority. Last but not least, sustained support came from President Johnson, who from youth had been in intimate contact with Mexican voters in Texas and who deeply sympathized with conditions in Mexico across the Rio Grande. Johnson felt that Latin American problems were the same that he had faced in the arid and poverty-ridden areas of west Texas in his youth. The Bureau is no longer a dumping ground for mediocrities of the Foreign Service whose presence the highly intelligent Latinos resented. It has had very capable Ambassadors like John H. Crimmins in the Dominican Republic, Fulton Freeman in Mexico, Douglas Henderson in Bolivia, John Jones, an old pro, in Peru, and Edwin Martin, a former Assistant Secretary of State, in Argentina.

With the obvious exceptions of the crises over Cuba in 1962, Panama in 1964, and the Dominican Republic in 1965, the Bureau has been remarkably free from top-level interference but for one grievance—military aid. The Bureau suffered, on the one hand, from the political backflak of the Vietnam war when dissenting voices in Congress charged that U.S. military aid to South Vietnam had overcommitted the U.S. to a point of active intervention in that war. More detrimental to the Bureau's domestic relations was the fact that twelve nations, since the Alliance for Progress was organized, had fallen under dictatorship or military rule, causing Congressional tempers to wear thin. This was an apparent retrogression to 1954, when twelve of the twenty Latin American republics were ruled by generals or colonels. Military aid brought the Bureau its first serious interagency hassle in 1966, with none other than the redoubtable Robert S. McNamara. The Bureau felt that the seventh, executive, floor of the State Department had left it in the lurch over the Bureau's insistence that modest military aid be continued to the Latin American republics, instead of being cut off entirely as Defense had apparently desired to do at first, perhaps wanting to demonstrate that in at least one area of the world the Defense Department was pacifist.

U.S. military aid to Latin America was started in 1950. All told, in seventeen years it had amounted to about $700 million. At first the aid was provided as part of Cold War strategy for defense of the Hemisphere and the Panama Canal. In recent times, 90 per cent of it had been for internal security purposes. The Pentagon first maintained that provision of military aid was unnecessary because the Latin American countries had no real cause to fight one another. Moreover, providing military aid would stimulate an artificial arms race and take precious funds away from the economic sector so woefully in need of the money. Pentagon ire was particularly aroused when countries like Argentina, Brazil, Chile, and Peru purchased modern jet fighter bombers with their own funds instead of investing the cash in their own economies. Former Assistant Secretary Gordon characterized the arms purchase as an "arms crawl." He maintained that the Latin American armed forces needed a modicum of modern equipment to keep up a minimum of technical pride in their profession rather than be allowed to become restless and look for political adventures. Gordon's plea for a compromise, while accepting some limitation of arms purchases, cooled off in Under Secretary Katzenbach's office while the efficient Defense Department bureaucracy sent out orders to its military missions in Latin America to announce an early closeout to U.S. military aid. The amount involved for fiscal 1967 was a mere $72 million and $55 million for 1968. The whole Latin American region got barely 7 per cent of the total U.S. military assistance program for the entire world.

CHAPTER V

CRISES: Clutching at the Uncontrollable

IF THE RULE OF THUMB IS that 85 per cent of the work of the State Department is routine or normal, 15 per cent of it is exceptional or abnormal. Perhaps 5 per cent of the 15 is especially exceptional, verging on critical. One per cent is in the crisis area, where a sleepy slip can fling the world into the atomic apocalypse. World events, small and large, shower upon the Department's attention like electrons pulsing through a cyclotron. More specifically, as former Under Secretary Ball said, "At any given time there are perhaps eight to ten trouble spots around the world where the Department is trying to bring together two friendly nations engaged in a bitter local dispute." Or, as Secretary Rusk said, "Every time you go to sleep, two thirds of the world is awake and up to some mischief." The headline incidents that escalate into crises are there for all to see. A seedbed of war-born troubles ushered in the postwar period. New fractious states emerged from the debris of colonialism. Coups crackled like Chinese firecrackers on three continents. Crises occurred when so-called United States foreign policy plans broke down through erosion. Or radical change in circumstances took place. Or foreign nations deliberately upset normal international patterns. Or new nations' aspirations and movements began to grate and clash with those of more settled societies. The Department's operational stance, therefore, is consistently fixed at some practical point of immediate urgency in the inbasket: to avert or to stop, and even possibly and hopefully to solve, some immediate irritant which is boiling close to the overflow point.

Yet, a large percentage of United States foreign policy problems can have no satisfactory short-term solutions. Hence, waffling, ambiguity, and fuzziness are frequently desirable in the diplomatic process of moving issues from the front burner to the back burner, to the steam table, to the cooling shelf, where eventually they may be handled without second-degree burns and with equity and possibly even reason. The difficulty is always that, in the flux and muddle of the transitional movement, United States diplomats must be constantly on guard not to get stuck in a tactical situation that could freeze, despite their best efforts, into a permanent disadvantage for the United States. What it comes down to, all the static about preplanning and contingency alternatives notwithstanding, is that the players at the controls of power must stay loose at the plate. All bets are off at the moment of crisis as far as theoretical considerations are concerned. What counts right then and there is what pitch is coming across the batter's box. Regrettably, the pitches are not from one pitcher alone, but, in the unortho- dox rules of the power game, from perhaps two or three or more potentially hostile or directly aggressive opposing pitchers. Thus, the crisis situation again emphasizes the element of the unknown, the uncertainty regarding the intentions of others and the contrast between the illusive calm of ordinary routine events and the icy hysteria which can grip men of reason in the maelstrom of great and uncontrollable events.

Compared with the Department's routine lubrication of normal world contacts, the crisis area deals with disruptions in the balance of power which theoretically makes the normal world contacts possible. Closer to the point, the threat of destruction of the balance of power becomes crucial or fissionable when it involves political-military factors. These, given modern world conditions of basic instability, present a problem like that of juggling nitroglycerin. The least insensitive touch can blow up the whole horizon. Moreover, the newest element in world diplomacy is that of the tremendous technological acceleration of time, space, events, and human desires and frustrations. The fragile mosaic can explode into violent action with infinitesimal provocation at a terrifying rate of propulsion. The simple geometrical accommodation of the past balance of powers is disappearing. The movement of nations today seems often more like that of ice floes, affected by deep currents, diverse and unfathomable, from whose conflu- ence or collision the icepacks on the surface smash and crash and up-end against each other in nihilistic unreason.

It was this new and chilling consideration of the new Mach-X speeds, specifically that of the ICBM, that prompted President Kennedy to dump the slow-moving machinery for top-level decisions, symbolized by the National Security Council apparatus under President Eisenhower. Kennedy went to the other extreme of improvising whenever a case arose, with the instrument of on-the-spot task forces tailored to the concrete situation. Kennedy used to immerse himself completely in every step of the short-cut enterprises. As a politician of superb caliber, Kennedy could differentiate between the shadow and substance of power. He knew that, at the naked end of possible confrontation, foreign policy becomes again power politics at its rawest and roughest. The brutal imposition of one's will must be weighed icily in order to protect one's vital interests or to gamble for great gains. The process involves decisions that must be taken possibly in seconds and minutes, no longer in days and weeks. Yet, despite a competent staff inspired by the brilliance of McGeorge Bundy, President Kennedy could not devise and execute foreign policy by himself.

This brings us to the place in the State Department where theoretically the command of operations is supposed to lie, in the Executive Secretariat, as the arm of the Secretary of State. The question before the house is whether the Executive Secretariat ultimately is a message center or a command post. That, in turn, depends on who is occupying the highest post in the Department, that of Secretary of State, and how he wants to use the facilities of the Executive Secretariat.

The Executive Secretariat is the operational gearbox of the Department of State. It is the immediate operating staff of the Office of the Secretary and costs the U.S. Government nearly $700,000 a year. As the functional staff agent of the Secretary, the Secretariat is also his crisis foreman. It nursemaids the geographical bureaus' communications to and from the Secretary, except when problems of utmost urgency are taken out of the hands of the geographical area by the Secretary. But if the Assistant Secretary is a forceful enough personality and has good enough rapport with the Secretary to have effective and frequent contact with him, the Assistant Secretary can become a powerhouse in his own right. The Secretariat is a creature born of necessity in World War II, when Secretary of State Edward R. Stettinius established the first joint secretariat, in December 1944. In 1949, however, the Hoover Commission noted that the Secretariat still needed rejiggering to "divest the Secretary from the pressures of day-to-day business." This is what the present Secretariat tries to do by insuring that memoranda of recommended actions come up to the head man in proper form, that the memos have been cleared of possible objections, or have been contributed to by other responsible bureaus in the Department and in other federal agencies with overseas interests.

The Secretariat allots and spreads the top-level business among key subordinates of the Secretary. These are the Under Secretary, the Under Secretary for Political Affairs, and his deputy. This is done to allow time for the Secretary himself to be free of everything but the most urgent and pressing demands, and particularly to be available at an instant's notice to consult with and advise the President of the United States. In the process, a constant shuffling and reshuffling of priorities for the Secretary's attention is under way. Determinations must be made as to what matters of real necessity must get through to him because it will be of vital interest to the White House. Among a batch of priority documents, what may have been on top as the number one item at 9 A.M. may have receded several positions by noon, as papers are bumped by even more urgent items. To save the Secretary time, a special assistant underlines key words and phrases in green ink, although the color has no particular significance. The Executive Secretary and his elite staff of approximately 110 officers inevitably provoke considerable irritation and frustration on the six floors below. The Secretariat sends back documents that have not been properly staffed out, with all the necessary slices of national interest adequately proportioned. Lower-level officials are annoyed at not being able to reach the Secretary, not only via their memoranda but especially in person, because of the Secretariat's guard over the Secretary's precious time, the most valuable commodity he has.

In the current attempt at ordering the priorities in time and content for the four top officers of the Department, Executive Secretary Benjamin H. Read arranges every morning at 8:45 intelligence briefings for Secretary of State Rusk, Under Secretary of State Katzenbach, Under Secretary for Political Affairs Eugene V. Rostow (Walt Rostow's brother), Deputy Political Under Secretary Kohler, and his successor, Charles E. Bohlen. Formerly, there used to be three staff meetings a week, presided over by the Secretary and attended by all Assistant Secretaries and other important officials. This was cut down to one large meeting a week. The Secretary also holds a small daily staff meeting at 9:15 with his immediate seventh-floor advisers.

Besides coordinating the activities of eleven bureaus of the Department, namely, Public Affairs, African Affairs, Inter-American Affairs, East Asian and Pacific Affairs, European Affairs, Near Eastern and South Asian Affairs, Economic Affairs, Educational and Cultural Affairs, Intelligence and Research, International Organization Affairs, and Security and Consular Affairs, the Executive Secretariat serves as a channel for communications to and from the seventh floor for approximately fifteen other organizational units which do not have bureau status. These include the Policy Planning Council, the Office of Congressional Relations, and the Legal Adviser.

Riding herd on twenty-two of the subordinate units are ten middle-grade line officers, who are the immediate link for fast communications from downstairs to the top floor. Among five officers, one has nine units, including the hot ones of the Near East and Far East; the second one has only four, but these encompass the many problems of Europe; the third has six, which include the United Nations and the press; the fourth has five, including Africa; and the fifth has only four, but these include Latin America and AID. Given the absolute dependence of the Department of State upon the wishes and even the whims of the President, the crucial function of the Secretariat is to serve as the official channel between the

Department of State and the White House. Decisions taken at the informal Executive Committee meetings of the President, the Secretary of State, the Secretary of Defense, and the Special Assistant for National Security Affairs at the Tuesday White House luncheon sessions on the Vietnam war and other critical issues generate a flow of at least a dozen follow-up actions. These are communicated to the State Department through the Executive Secretariat. There are four other Department channels to the White House: the Protocol Office, for diplomatic ceremonial, particularly for visiting chiefs of state and heads of government; the office of John Macy, Director of the U.S. Civil Service Commission, for Presidential appointments in the diplomatic field; the office of the Deputy Under Secretary for Administration, to the Bureau of the Budget and on to the President, for administration and management and financial affairs; and the office of the Assistant Secretary for Congressional Relations, to the White House liaison office for the Senate and House of Representatives on legislation and foreign policy matters in which the Congress has an absorbing interest.

The Secretariat has still other duties which range from the delicate to the prosaic. When former Under Secretary Ball retired, a notice was sent out that "the Under Secretary will be in his office, Room 7220, from 3:30 P.M. to 4:30 P.M., September 30, 1966, and would be pleased to receive personnel of the Department who may wish to bid him good-bye." Clerks, janitors, elevator operators relish such good-byes to the brass. Another duty is handling the vast influx of staff studies received in the Department. For 1966, these totalled 19,378, or 1,615 a month, or 54 a day, figured on a seven-day week. All sooner or later are funneled to one of the four principal officers on the seventh floor, with the Executive Secretary culling thirty of the current and choice for the Secretary of State's bedtime reading.

The imperative function of the Secretariat, however, is, on the one hand, to keep an especially alert eye on the torrent of incoming items and to flag those which demand action and immediate attention of the Secretary and, on the other, to pass on the result of this scrutiny to the attention of the President and his staff, to relevant bureaus, to the field embassies, and to the other agencies of the Government, particularly Defense and CIA, which also attempt to maintain an instant awareness of world actions and problems flashing to the surface. Patently, this entails a vast and intricate screening process for the average of 2,000 cables coming in and another 1,000 cables going out. This allows the Secretary personally to read from beginning to end about eight to ten cables on the average, but sometimes up to twenty-four cables a day, plus summaries of another 100 to 200 important cables, or even summaries of summaries of cables. The Secretary may personally initial from one to two dozen outgoing cables and indirectly influence the framing of another two dozen a day. He may pass on to the President two or three cables of the highest importance.

Though Secretary Rusk may direct his meticulous attention to comparatively few cables a day, incoming and outgoing, he scans as many as he can with incredible rapidity. He particularly keeps close tab on the news agency wires, riffling through yards of news-ticker copy like a housewife running ribbon through her hands. If the news looks hot or ominous, Rusk leaves his office, turns right a few steps down the inner blue-carpeted corridor, hits the bar on a locked door with the butt of his hand, and proceeds twenty steps down the Number Five corridor on the seventh floor, to a right-hand door into the Operations Center, where he can see the news coming in directly from the hot spots across the world.

The Operations Center is the eyes and ears of the State Department, its heartbeat in this nuclear age. Given the comparatively microscopic amount of time allowed, the first necessity is for instant and reliable communications. The communications must be such that they can be technically adjusted to any demand of time and space all over the globe, in order to furnish the very latest information for the quickest possible decision necessary. Rusk's purposeful and brisk walk to the Operations Center may be occasioned by something like the Greek crisis of April 1967, when a military coup overthrew the civilian government, although the fact that something was afoot had been spotted weeks before by State's Intelligence Bureau. Or a possible "sudden-death crisis" like that generated by Egypt's Gamal Abdel Nasser in the Gulf of Aqaba in May 1967. Both illustrate the State Department practice that when the fissionable issue reaches the critical mass, and is on the road to explosion, the problem is kicked upstairs and the top team has to take over. Inevitably, when the curtain goes up on one of these dramas and the laymen are separated from the professionals, an observer instinctively wonders how the top team will do and what kind of mentality, training, plans, and outlook they bring to the deadly game that unfolds.

In theory and in practice there are all kinds of policies and plans covering almost all situations which might arise. In the main, policy is a sense of direction, an attitude of mind under the auspices of which long-run decisions have been made for long-range objectives. Ideally, the subordinate sets of specific decisions will all tend in the same direction. The aim is to suffuse the short-term decisions with the sense of purpose implicit in the long-range attitude. When all this is said and done, there is still a world of difference between the reality of operations and the opinions, judgments, and conclusions of outside analysis and commentators who do not have the official operational responsibility for bringing policies and plans to pass. Even the official staff papers written under the classic headings of "Problem," "Facts Bearing on the Problem," "Considerations," "Conclusions," "Recommendations," and "Action to Be Taken" do not seem adequate when the chips are down. Contingency plans invariably turn out to be slightly different from the new, immediate fact of the living moment. Thus, a wholesale shifting of the patterns of prethinking and of the resources to be assigned becomes necessary. For example, the case of the Berlin Wall was anticipated, but not at all in the manner in which it actually took place. Nor was its speed of execution predicted or its political purpose divined to dry up West Berlin into a stagnant and insignificant backwater, like Trieste in Italy.

The key ingredient for emergency diplomacy appears to be a multifaceted versatility in all aspects of the political, military, economic, and psychological factors that enter into the equation. It is a versatility which does not arrive all at once, full-bodied and mature, but has to be a combination of experience, training, and native talent. The many variable factors have been instinctively checked off by the subconscious, in a manner of speaking, and are at hand to be tapped by the conscious and alert officer as he cross-slices the crisis to find the all-essential element. The pilot of a U.S. Air Force B-52 bomber, for example, has to go through at least six major check stages before he takes off. This requires at least 122 check-off items, with another 262 extra ones under certain conditions, for a total of thirty-six pages of printed directions. Yet an airplane, complex as it is, is still finite. With care and precision, all the check points can be covered, and all unexpected crises and breakdowns can be overcome by the airman's skill and instincts, guided by experience.

Operational orders for military movements are even more complex because of the vast number of heterogeneous units which must be marshaled and commanded into a unity. An operations order for an army corps, the primary document which makes the units move, may have from twenty-five to thirty annexes and run as long as 200 pages. The order would have annexes for intelligence, fire support, a road movement table, barrier plan, and signal annex. An accompanying administrative order would include sections for personnel estimate, logistical estimate, quartermaster annex, medical annex, and engineer annex, totaling fifty-four pages. A similar check list of foreign policy is possible, except for the fact that foreign policy is made up of partly known and mostly unknown factors and intangibles. It applies more to the process of thinking by the responsible officer than to a textbook solution, which it would be fatal to impose on an actual situation.

Secretary Rusk emphasized this difference between theory and practice in a speech in September 1965, before the American Political Science Association. The main point that Rusk, in his ever-pragmatic style, stressed was, "What is the question?" In short, how "to identify accurately the question which has to be answered" and "the point to settle." Even a cursory foreign policy check list included at least sixty or seventy points to consider, or rather points that should be automatically or instinctively kept in mind. Check points might include: Who raised the question? Is it something for the United States to worry about? Does it involve the objectives or interests of other countries? What specific countries? In what measure? Does the United States need to take any specific action? Is it covered by existing Congressional legislation? Or would the administration have to go to Congress? Given the political complexion of the nation at the moment in question, could the administration get the new legislation? Are U.S. actions to be public or secret? If public, must the press be prepared? Or, if secret, can the secrecy be justified for real or valid reasons? Or is the secrecy merely for the convenience of the bureaucracy? Finally, can the responsible official concerned deliver the results needed, in contrast with those who only have to talk about it?

The officers of the Executive Secretariat who are picked to handle the Operations Center crisis controls for the Department of State make up five four-man teams, which work round-the-clock shifts, with four teams rotating and one stand-by. Five military officers, one on each team, are also assigned to the Operations Center, while five State Department men perform similar functions in the National Military Command Center in the Pentagon. Six special machines take off the cream of the priority messages that pour into the Department from all over the world. The traffic pattern varies. At one hour, at 3 A.M., for instance, Washington time, Europe is not quite awake, the Far East is not quite ready to send, and South America is sleeping. Friday is a heavy day and Monday a light one. The in-rush tapers off after midnight, the radio waves stilling between one and three o'clock. Operations Center Watch Teams have a sign above a blackboard, called the "menu board," which says, "Today's crisis." From time to time, there is more than one crisis going on simultaneously, like Laos and Cyprus in 1964, Berlin and the Dominican Republic in 1965, Indonesia and India-Pakistan in 1965, not to mention Vietnam and the Middle East in 1967. During 1964, the Center handled four crises simultaneously: the Congo, Bolivia, Cyprus, and Vietnam. Crisis is defined in each instance as urgent action demanded by an instantaneous torrent of events. While the six special machines are extracting scat readings from the mass cable influx in the Operations Center on the seventh floor, some twenty-six teletype machines are clicking away in the Department's main Communications Center on the sixth floor.

The Operations Center is plastered with maps which outline the exact situation on the ground in all parts of the world; they are immediately covered when visitors enter. Sometimes, when an event occurs in some far-away place, there is a rush to the maps to find out where the erupting country is located. The officers monitor about seventy-five telephones in Department offices of key officials in order to intercept important calls. On file are the private and unlisted numbers of all senior officials who might have to be alerted. Five scrambler phones—there are seventy in the whole Department, most of them rarely used—are kept constantly clear and secure for immediate communication with crisis agencies that, like the State Department, have a role in overseas operations. The Watch Teams keep a comprehensive log of the precise times of receipt of certain cables and the alerting of responsible Department officers. If a series of cables spells a crisis, a systematic chronology is kept of everything that comes in and of the replies that go out as action directives to the field embassies. The officers develop a sixth sense in perceiving the imminence of a crisis by shadings of urgency in the tone of the cables, which at a certain point begin to be punctuated by emergency telephone calls from the area. Operations Center lines are cut into the global military communications network of the United States. Thus, when a major crisis, such as the Buddhist crisis in Vietnam in March 1965, develops, there is instant communication with Saigon through military satellites in the sky. On those tense nights, Secretary Rusk was talking with Ambassador Henry Cabot Lodge on one phone and Secretary of Defense McNamara with Lieutenant General Lewis W. Walt, the U.S. Marine Corps Commander at Danang, on another. An extra phone, nearby, was available for personal communication with the President, if necessary.

Since it was organized in 1961, during the Berlin crisis, the Center has served as the cutting edge of State Department reactions to the challenging events which were assailing it from the outside world. Communications since then, and up to 1967, have been improved to the point that a cable can arrive from an embassy to the State Department in three minutes. Counting all the mechanics of handling, the cable would be in the hands of the responsible action officer in less than a half hour. When the chips were down on at least two occasions, the Operations Center was able to perform a complete cycle of diplomatic activity within seven minutes.

In the first instance, a Berlin Autobahn convoy incident in the fall of 1963 happened to coincide with a visit of Soviet Foreign Minister Andrei Gromyko to Washington. A Russian officer on the Autobahn passed on to a U.S. officer a remark which the American was smart enough to realize contained a significant change in the usual formula. From his jeep radio he was able to send the word back into West Germany. From there it went at once to the State Department. The message was rushed to Secretary Rusk, who was able to alert the President of the changes in circumstances within seven minutes of their occurrence, and before Gromyko arrived at the White House.

The second case occurred on January 4, 1967, when a MACE-A air-to-air missile, without a warhead, misfired at the Eglin Air Force Base in Florida and ran away, out of control, streaking toward Cuba. With the nightmare of the Cuban nuclear crisis in mind, the State Department was able to get immediate information on the exact location and fall of the missile into the sea. It called the Swiss Embassy, which was acting as caretaker of United States interests in Cuba, to pass the word to the Castro Government. Then, Secretary Rusk called Soviet Ambassador Anatoliy Dobrynin to inform him of the mishap and its fortunate ending—again all within the unbelievable time of seven minutes.

Illustrative of the in-rush of cables during a crisis is the log on the military coup in Greece in April 1967. The first word was flashed in at 8:45 P.M. on April 20. By 3 P.M. on April 21, eighteen hours later, at least fifty cables had come into the Department, giving a blow-by-blow description of the sequence of events. Obviously, there is no typical average load of cable traffic, volume being dictated by events. However, the importance of active areas can be indicated by the number of incoming cablegrams from selected spots. In a little over nine months, from July 1966 through April 1967, 17,756 cables were received from Saigon; 10,709 from Paris, where a close watch was naturally kept on President de Gaulle; 7,191 from New Delhi, with its grave problems of famine and fears of Pakistan and Communist China; 2,784 from Kinshasa, the former Leopoldville, capital of the former Belgian Congo, but 4,361 from Lagos, capital of Nigeria, with coups and revolts stirring; only 3,982 from Moscow, where words are kept to a minimum and actions speak louder; 5,216 from Rio de Janeiro in the vast country of Brazil; and only 2,479 from Cairo, where the Aqaba crisis was to explode within weeks. On the average in 1967, from 1,800 to 1,900 cables were received a day and from 1,000 to 1,100 sent out, a total of 3,000 cables in traffic. The average length of each message was about 200 words, or 600,000 words a day, running to over 15 million words a month —three times the average of 5 million words a month in 1954 but less than the 20 million words a month expected by 1969.

When the load of cables pours in, the key matter is the processing. Teletype machines flick the messages in at 100 words a minute, with instantaneous coding at the sending end and instantaneous decoding at the receiving end. The intricate processing routine starts with logging or time-clocking the received message, next stripping it of communications jargon, re-editing the flow of the language to recognizable English, and retyping it. Then the message analyst takes over and decides what the main subject is in order to determine which officials would be interested in receiving the cable. The distribution of incoming cables is based primarily on the end-user, his operating responsibility, his "need to know" in order to act, or his need to be at least aware of the contents. Thus, incoming cables with topics of wide interest may go to as many as 300 persons, while an outgoing cable, say to Berlin, may have a dozen extra informational addresses.

Necessarily, the cables have a communications classification. This starts at the bottom with "routine," which means telegrams which are not of sufficient urgency to justify a higher precedence but which still must be delivered without delay; it climbs to "priority," which is the highest precedence assigned to telegrams requiring speedy delivery; and then goes to "immediate," designating urgent telegrams involving situations with important foreign policy implications where immediate attention is mandatory. Such "immediate" telegrams are processed upon receipt, and responsible officials are notified promptly regardless of the time of day or night. The top designation is "flash," used only for the most urgent action telegrams containing information vitally affecting the country's foreign relations and requiring instant attention by the addressee. These "flash" telegrams are processed immediately upon receipt and the responsible officials are again notified at once, regardless of the time of day or night. State Department instructions caution that "flash" telegrams should be used "extremely sparingly and brevity is mandatory."

Further, there is for security purposes the classification of the contents of a cable, beginning again at the bottom with "limited official use" and moving up to "confidential," "secret," and "top secret." Several more esoteric labels exist, but their names themselves are classified and available to the general run of officials only on a "need-to-know" basis. Further specialized classifications deal mostly with technology or matters relating to nuclear developments, where the classification made popular in spy novels as "Q" clearance is a U.S. Atomic Energy Commission designation.

Security classifications, however, are not the essential elements in the transmission and distribution of State Department cablegrams. Of the 44,817 cables received and sent during January 1967, 36,029 had "routine" precedence. Eight incoming and seven outgoing cables were "flash" for a total of 15; 1,178 incoming and 600 outgoing cables were "immediate," for a total of 1,778; and 4,349 incoming and 2,636 outgoing cables were "priority," for a total of 6,985. The "flash" cables take anywhere from five to ten minutes to deliver from time of receipt; "immediate," less than an hour; "priority," from one hour to perhaps three hours; and "routine," from three hours to eight hours.

Thus, there is classification for security or secrecy; a system of precedence for urgency in delivery of cables; and, lastly, what is generally not known, a system of classification for the distribution of cables, particularly where it affects highly sensitive information which is operational at that very moment and when current activity could be seriously impaired by premature disclosure.

The designations in this system are, from top to bottom, "NODIS," that is, "no distribution," and often also tagged for "Eyes Only"; "EXDIS," or "exclusive distribution"; "LIMDIS," or "limited distribution"; and the bottom category, "GENDIS," or "general distribution." Practically, the distribution is governed by the Secretary or his designated proxy at the moment, to keep the contents of such cables tightly held and reserved, so that "NODIS" may go to possibly three or four or five officials, though from eight to ten copies may have been run off; "EXDIS" may go to ten or fifteen; "LIMDIS," to thirty or forty; and "GENDIS," to as many as eighty or a hundred. In the calendar year 1966, of 330,977 incoming and 219,804 outgoing telegrams, 10,081 incoming and 3,454 outgoing were "LIMDIS." The figures on the number of "EXDIS" and "NODIS" cables are classified, that is, secret or not available for public information. The "NODIS," or most restricted category, is also a collateral protection device to decision-making. Too many, or inept, cooks could spoil the broth. The Hanoi "peace feeler" cables are frequently, but not always, in the "NODIS" class.

Although President Johnson is frequently charged with excessive preoccupation with secrecy, President Kennedy had the same concern with keeping official matters close to his vest. During the limited nuclear test ban treaty negotiations in Moscow in the summer of 1963, Kennedy gave orders that "Eyes-Only" cables from Ambassador Averell Harriman, who led the negotiation team, should be distributed only to six people besides himself and National Security Assistant McGeorge Bundy. These were Secretary Rusk; Under Secretary Ball; William Foster, Director of the United States Disarmament Agency; Defense Secretary McNamara; John McCone, Director of the Central Intelligence Agency; and Llewellyn E. Thompson, the Soviet Affairs Adviser. Though such "NODIS" messages are frequently sent in the clear, and though the test ban negotiations were a mutually profitable short cut to share the loss of atmospheric testing, untimely disclosure of U.S. activities might well have upset the mood of the Russians and have made accord more difficult to achieve.

The 100-word-a-minute rate, with instantaneous coding and decoding, was a significant advance from former times, when the process took forty-eight hours, later cut to six hours. But even 100 words a minute are too slow in this electronic age. A study was made in September 1963 to establish the most advanced systems communications through computers. A contract was signed with the International Telephone & Telegraph Corporation for $3,200,000, the largest single contract ever entered into by the

State Department, to produce the most modern system possible with to-day's art. The new computer system began functioning in May 1967. It is on the fifth floor of the State Department and will eventually displace the sixth-floor Communications Center. It is a unique and unprecedented set-up duplicated nowhere in the world, as far as is known. It features special TV devices with 21-inch screens, instead of conventional teletype machines for receiving telegrams from overseas. The analysts read the message on TV tubes instead of scanning it on tape or on teletype printer rolls. This major improvement will eventually allow the computerized system to achieve the dizzying speed of 1,200 lines a minute in reception. A circuit scanner will permit an automatic check every two minutes on the transmission quality of the circuits to world-wide points and on other devices which can pour messages into the computer at the rate of 1,000 words a minute.

For the first year's rent of $612,000 paid to ITT, the Department was able to own a system whereby no United States embassy in the world was farther away than one relay station of the ten which the Department operates around the globe, including London, Paris, Bonn, Athens, Cyprus, Asmara, and Manila, with the principal American relay point being Brandywine, Virginia, near Washington. The computer will not only expedite the speed of transmission and reception but it will be programmed to perform the logging of the cables received and sent and the checking of captions and addresses, classification, and the destination of distribution. The system will have duplicate electronic files, capable of storing 50 million words each and so set up that they can return file information within two seconds. The system will eventually have a triple fall-back in reserve power so that it can go between sixty and ninety days with a full load. The quarters in which it is housed have been built like a submarine, so that one cannot open one door without closing the opposite door. Technically, this new Automated Terminal and Relay Station is described as an ITT 7300 Model 11 Automatic Data Exchange (ADX) Communications Switching System, including various subsystems and other specialized equipment.

Yet, despite this marvel of modern technology, the human brain at its best can at times bring to bear its intuitions from the depths of its sub-conscious even more quickly. The question remains, therefore, of how more or less ordinary human beings can use the computer aids to handle the crises generated by other human beings as a result of their needs, passions, frustrations, ambitions, and power drives. How do instant communications and computer easements help predict when the frozen crisis of the Middle East will erupt into a shooting crisis, as occurred in May–June 1967? In some still invisible future, diplomacy might profit from the science of cryogenics, whose most notable characteristic is the eccentric behavior of matter in deep cold, to explain how a frozen crisis becomes a hot crisis. But in the end it will still be people who will make the analysis and the decisions.

As far as the Middle East is concerned, the Department's Bureau of Near East and South Asian Affairs, the fourth of the Department's five geographical bureaus, had never entirely by itself handled a crisis of the Middle East, the crossroads of the world and Biblical birthplace of man. When a crunch came, the Bureau provided staff work for the major operators on the seventh floor or for the White House. Though State's other bureaus rate the Middle East outfit as workmanlike and precise in its handling of paper work, the Bureau has been cursed from the beginning by three apparently insoluble problems: the Arab-Israeli conflict (wars in 1948, 1956, 1967), the India-Pakistan impasse over Kashmir (war in 1966), and the Cyprus dispute between Greeks, Turks, and Cypriots (war in 1964 and near war in 1967). It has had diplomats whose principal preoccupation was quietly to put things back as they had been before, instead of originating any ideas, policies, or programs which might have met the need to repair the basic fissures of the area. Until fairly recently, the Bureau had been staffed mainly by traditionalist officers who, like fluent dilettantes, could talk about classical Arabic literature and history. Comparatively few had much firsthand knowledge of the current social and economic ferment in the Arab world. In the other area of its responsibilities, India and Pakistan, cliques developed of pro-India adherents, sentimentalist derivatives from the Mother India era of the 1920's, or Pakistani admirers who were smitten by that nation's soldierly qualities and felt the nostalgic pull of Kipling's Kim and romantic traditions of the Khyber Pass and Northwest Frontier.

The Bureau's status essentially was an accurate reflection of the nation's slow realization of its responsibilities in this critical area of the world. In 1930 the Bureau took in not only the Near East and South Asia but all of Africa, an area from the Dardanelles to the gates of Burma. It encompassed one fifth of the world's population, with only 9 officers in Washington and 97 overseas, for only six countries. By contrast, in recent years 647 officers, 106 in Washington and 541 abroad, look after American interests in twenty countries, at a budgetary cost of approximately $15 million. Though the African part was lopped off in 1958 and made a separate geographical bureau, the Bureau is still a schizophrenic monstrosity. It has the vast subcontinent of India, with its more than 500 million inhabitants, at one end and the Middle East, the Arab countries principally, and Israel, plus Iran, Turkey, and Greece at the other end. The Bureau today oversees an area that has 35 per cent of the world's population, one third of the world's oil production, and 68 per cent of the world's oil reserves. A tiny oil-rich country like Kuwait owns $4 billion in gold reserves, and India has a $100 per capita annual income. The eastern, or India-Pakistan, side of the Bureau usually moves more like a glacier, whereas the western, or Middle Eastern part, more often runs like rapids.

United States policy in the Middle East has seemed more like a follower of events than an advance guide. On the one hand, U.S. policy is pictured as keeping control of the momentum of forces in the Middle East; on the other, as shakily maintaining a precarious peace. Among United States world priorities of the recent past, the number one position has been the Vietnam war; the second, the Soviet Union; the third, Communist China; the fourth, the NATO alliance; and only the fifth, the Middle East, with Africa bringing up the rear. In the world power blocs, there were evident disintegration and erosion in the Western alliance around the United States, and likewise in the Eastern alliance around Soviet Russia. This promoted a tentative link of interest between the two superpowers in the Far East, based on fear of the Chinese Communist threat. It left the Middle East as a sort of happy hunting ground for both. Besides the strange bedfellows in the Bureau, there is the further anomaly of the exclusion of other Arab states from the Bureau's range of responsibility. These include Libya, Tunisia, Algeria, and Morocco, which are under the African Bureau. Before a concentrated intellectual unity can be devoted to the problems of the Middle East, a radical shift may be necessary to move Greece and Cyprus into Europe and to divide the Bureau into two new bureaus. One for South Asia might include Turkey, Iran, Afghanistan, Pakistan, India, etc., while the other bureau would take the Middle East proper, plus the Arab countries of the Mediterranean and North Africa, and, unavoidably, Israel.

The lowest common denominator of the foreign policy which the Middle East Bureau is charged with formulating and executing is expressed in the bromide of "retaining the United States position in the Arab lands, based on strategic considerations of the area as a crossroads, and essential rights of overflight to get to other parts of the world, and the vast amounts of oil beneath the sands of the desert," while the other half of the policy is to defend Israel, or rather, not to allow Israel to be annihilated as a nation.

Yet between Arab-Israeli wars, United States policy, as carried out by the Bureau, has been an alternation of frenetic action or sterile no-action, while on the seventh-floor executive level the Middle East was in latter years largely overlooked. The last operating Assistant Secretary, Phillips Talbot, became Ambassador to Greece in September 1965. A clearly interim appointment brought in Raymond A. Hare, a career professional, able, intelligent, shrewd, a sound man to have in a tight corner, but otherwise committed by conviction to keeping things peaceful in the Middle East. Hare held the office a year, despite his express wish to retire. So, for six months there was only an Acting Assistant Secretary, until Lucius D.

Battle took office in April 1967, barely in time to confront the Arab-Israeli war in June of that year. In effect, there was no active operating leadership of the Near East and South Asian Bureau for over a year and a half. Even in the Department's Policy Planning Council there was no member designated to think profound thoughts about the Middle East for at least nine months, and for a time it appeared that the Middle East was deemed not important enough to need a planning specialist.

The sense of purpose which at least characterized the other four geographical bureaus in the Department appeared absent in the Middle East Bureau. The Bureau developed a reputation in the Department as being rather cliquish. Its key officers were described, on the eve of the 1967 Arab-Israeli crisis, as "talented but tired," dispirited, with a sense of "What's the use?" as constant tension, without release, drained their initiative. Outside experts were regarded more or less as amateurs, despite their professional status in the scholarly or business worlds. The Bureau's staff in the past had presented a classic example of closing ranks under attack. This tactic was the psychological pattern termed "printing" by the behaviorist school. It mysteriously prompts a new policy maker to defend the established position immediately upon his appointment to the office which is the repository of past decisions. Successive bureaucratic generations argue on behalf of what their predecessors have done or failed to do. The line of accepted doctrine is carried down from former officeholders to later officeholders, without a basic examination of the premises which new circumstances have made untenable and anachronistic. A fundamental factor in this closed-end intellectual attitude had been the failure to grasp the concrete realities of the sociological, economic, and political changes that had occurred in the Middle East area, the wastebasket of history and the cemetery of civilizations. There was inadequate reporting from the field and, therefore, a lack of facts of current revelance upon which to generate new policies realistic to the situation and of practical value in protecting the interests of the United States.

The core of the information required differed from the stereotyped textbook categories. It should have dealt most concretely with the internal politics and new power classes of the developing countries. The old habit prevalent in the Foreign Service in the immediate postwar period in Europe was to deal only with governments, not with peoples and the opposition. This outdated style persisted much longer in the Middle East. There was no effective, or sufficient, appreciation of the emerging new elite. Despite the best will and efforts of United States Information Agency propaganda, no profitable conduits existed into the veins of the populace of these countries as they shifted their own social bases in creating new nations and societies. For instance, there was little apprehension of the significance of the creation in Iran of 100,000 newly educated persons, almost half of whom had studied in the United States, and of the effect this new factor would have on Iranian national politics. The old, easy techniques of dealing with the upper classes, also endemic in Latin America before the Alliance for Progress, are fast disappearing, or in process of disappearing, in the Middle East. In short, the conventional wisdom of past United States policies in this area no longer applied. The new paradox indicated that so-called underdeveloped states of the Middle East were in actuality perhaps a third, or a quarter, of the way to development and therefore bound to give infinitely more trouble in their growing pains than the primitive types, as in Africa, which had to start from near zero.

The aridity of Middle East policy was dramatized at the outbreak of the Israeli-Arab war of 1967. In the traditional safe pattern of bureaucracy, it was felt that initial recourse could be had to the precedent of the 1956 Suez crisis in the United Nations to talk out or mitigate the Arab-Israeli exacerbations which were at the brink of hostilities. But, again, lack of an intimate apperception of Middle East psychology overlooked the new circumstances that already had modified precedents. The Israeli used the cover of expected protracted negotiations in the United Nations to give themselves public moral credit for patience, masking their own highly skillful preparations for surprise and pre-emptive striking of the enemy at a moment most propitious for their own fortunes of war. When the actual crisis of combat arrived, the Bureau was reduced to the status of *fonctionaires* and the making of decisions was immediately taken over by the Secretary of State and the President. A special presidential executive committee, whose executive secretary was McGeorge Bundy, wielded the real levers of power and commanded the Bureau machinery through an interdepartmental Control Group to execute such functions as it had capabilities for. Yet this new Balkans of the world in the Middle East, where over 100,000 clashes between Arab and Jew had been reported to the United Nations from 1949 up to the June 1967 war, still retained elements of rationality, hopefully to be nurtured and utilized at the wise discretion of the great powers, the United States and the Soviet Union. The Soviet-American confrontations of the 1950's in Europe, and their near peripheral confrontations of the 1960's in Asia, may be in process of transference to the Middle East for the 1970's. The mix of rapidly growing Arab populations and the real though slow growth of technical practices possibly one day will build the way toward a new regional framework that can include all states, Arab and Israeli, coexisting peacefully in a comity of commerce, if not yet of understanding.

The acceptance of the Soviet Union as a responsible partner in the Middle East was envisaged by some as the only practical alternative to the development of nuclear weapons by Israel, or even by Egypt. Given the historically volatile nature of the Middle East, the United States, as a responsible imperial power, had no choice other than to create a reasonable and realistic policy that could accommodate the interests of all, including its own. If the United States intent was to accelerate the process of history in thawing out the Cold War, as had been started in Europe, the stated objectives of the past in the Middle East, that is, to prevent the Soviet Union from dominating the area, would have to be drastically modified in a fresh evaluation of the way in which the Soviet Union could be included in the area. But this would have to be done without allowing Soviet presence to sow festering seeds of conflict leading to general war, yet still permit the nations on the ground to develop most effectively.

Be that as it may in the so-called long view, the most hopeful new fact about the Middle East Bureau arose out of the fire and destruction of the six-day Israeli-Arab war. The trial-by-proxy combat brought to life, as it often does with human beings in a showdown, all the best qualities of the highly trained experts in the Bureau. The personnel were sparked additionally by the leadership of a top-drawer new Assistant Secretary of State, Lucius D. Battle. His vigor, common sense, and down-to-earth manner helped drive away the stale air of the desert mystique that had suffocated the Bureau for much too long. Battle had been in and out of the Government several times, civil servant as well as a Foreign Service officer, and though an accepted Establishment figure, he was definitely not stuffy about it. He never let superior rank become an overawing obstacle to getting a job done. He always knew he could return to the "outside," a fact which helped freshen his independence. Battle came to Washington from the hot spot of the Middle East, the U.S. ambassadorship to Cairo. He had barely been confirmed in April 1967 when the Greek *coup d'état* occurred, and not many days later two U.S. consular officials were imprisoned in Yemen. Again, after only a few weeks, in May, the Middle East started to boil ominously.

Naturally Battle was aware of the open-ended chances for trouble in the Middle East from his two years and more in Cairo. Danger spots included Yemen, Libya, and Palestine. Arab-Israeli friction had been smoldering since the November 1966 border fight with Jordan, and since March 1967, with Syria. Any of the three could blow the gaff. Instead, Gamal Abdel Nasser, President of the United Arab Republic, suddenly asked the United Nations Emergency Force to withdraw from the Gaza Strip. Nasser, habituated to the late UN Secretary-General Dag Hammarskjold's slow and careful style, was as surprised as the rest of the world when UN Secretary-General U Thant of Burma, with indecent haste, immediately ordered withdrawal of UNEF from Gaza and also from Sheikh al Sharm, guarding the Strait of Tiran. UNEF's presence there had guaranteed free access for

Israeli-bound shipping through the Gulf of Aqaba to the port of Elath. Contingency plans were fashioned for a test run of allied shipping to Elath, but they never got off the ground by the time the war started.

U Thant's precipitate action, without consultations or delay, was laid to his resentment against the United States for the American lack of response to halting the bombing of North Vietnam and ending the Vietnam war. The sudden Israeli attack brought Battle, unshaven, to his office at 3:30 A.M. and made a single-minded team out of his Bureau. Alfred A. Atherton, Jr., the country director for Arab-Israeli affairs, moved into the Operations Center to head a task force which became the spearhead of U.S. operations, getting the cables first and acting as the end-man to fan out instructions to the field. Officers slept in their offices for several days.

Tensions mounted day by day through the six-day war. Pressure was nonstop during the "flap," diplomatic jargon for crisis. Telephones rang continually. Battle fielded the calls as best he could, ran up to his Operations Center team and back countless times, snapped out answers to officers who poked their heads in the door with the latest urgent problem, read incoming cables, and approved or wrote outgoing instructions.

In between he had top priority appointments. Here is the Battle calendar for Wednesday, June 7, 1967, the day after the driving Israeli forces, routing the Egyptians, had turned their destructive attention to Jordan:

9:00 A.M. — Congressional briefing
10:00 A.M. — Staff meeting
12 noon — National Security Council meeting with President Johnson
2:30 P.M. — Iraqi Ambassador Nasir Hani
3:00 P.M. — Yemen Ambassador Abdul Aziz Al Futaih
3:30 P.M. — Turkish Ambassador Melih Esenbel
4:00 P.M. — Syrian Charge d'Affaires A. Galeb Kayali
5:00 P.M. — Control Group meeting with Under Secretary Eugene Rostow
6:30 P.M. — White House meeting
8:00 P.M. — Staff meeting

But the end of hostilities did not spell "finis." The cease-fire had to be negotiated at the United Nations, involving scores of cables to foreign offices to bring pressures on the UN delegations and to endeavor to make the United States position understood.

Sage old Ray Hare had a timely story about the climactic 1967 war. Hare said that watching the Middle East was like watching a wheel go round and round the same old trail. Watching it so intently, one was apt to become hypnotized by the sameness—so that one might miss a jerk in the wheel, which could indicate the pattern was about to change. In June 1967, the Middle East wheel jerked.

The moral was that the 1967 Arab-Israeli war was not just another deadly repetition of past conflicts. It was the end of an era of twenty years. It was time to call it quits, to make a true peace, and to end the state of belligerency which had remained an excuse and a still-burning fuse to ignite future shooting. The Soviet Union had been persuaded by President Johnson, in a letter to Soviet Premier Alexei Kosygin in the latter part of May 1967, before the war started, that neither of the two great powers should ever enter into a collision course on the account of third parties. The Glassboro, New Jersey, summit in June 1967, between Johnson and Kosygin, confirmed this parallel decision to agree not to disagree with force.

It was all too evident after the shooting stopped that the Soviets were determined to maintain their new position in the Middle East and to continue to keep the area in ferment as a club against the conservative regimes still in power there. The first major interagency study made in years of Soviet moves in the Middle East had disclosed in March 1967 that Russia was actively engaging itself in practically every country, except Israel, between the Mediterranean and the Indian Ocean. The lynch-pin of the concerted Soviet drive, climaxing 200-year-old Russian aspirations for the warm seas, was Egypt. The Soviet-supplied armed might of Egypt, left a shambles, was written off as virtually a total loss by the Soviets. Substantial Soviet replacement of destroyed armor and equipment likewise was written off in advance. No other choice was open for the sake of Soviet prestige. What did impel the Russians to take a second look, however, was the economic bill of damages presented for payment by Egypt. Its economy already in sad shape before the 1967 war, Egypt now had to be supplied with a minimum of $125 million worth of grain a year for an indefinite future, as well as other supplies or scarce foreign exchange to make up for the loss of $225 million in Suez Canal revenues. The Egyptians had rendered the canal unusable. Nearly $100 million income was lost because of the absence of tourists. The $500 million—heavier even than the $300 million annual subsidy Russia paid to support Castro's Cuba after the 1962 crisis—was a stiff price to pay for Nasser's follies.

The Egyptian revolutionist of 1952 had aged and soured in the fifteen years to 1967. The death of Nehru, together with the fall of Sukarno in Indonesia and Nkrumah in Ghana, Nasser's fellow leaders of the so-called third world, left him low in mood and suspicious of "imperialist plots" supposedly planning his own overthrow. His attempts to intervene on behalf of the Congo rebels had fizzled, his Yemen adventure had run into the sand, and he had needlessly and outrageously offended the United States. Though not a Communist, Nasser's social-economic thinking had been strongly influenced by the socialist doctrines of his crony, Marshal Tito of Yugoslavia. Like an arrested adolescent, full of insecurities and blown-up pride, Nasser carried a log on his shoulder and could never quite believe that the American democratic system of government was just what it seemed on the surface. He made a big show of inviting prominent Americans, who he thought were the "real" powers, to see him privately. Among them were former World Bank President Eugene Black, former Chase Manhattan Bank Chairman of the Board John J. McCloy, former Treasury Secretary Robert Anderson, and Representative Democratic Congressman Wayne Hays of Ohio, whom Nasser liked because Hays had been affectionate with Nasser's daughter on Hays' first visit to the Nasser home. At the same time that Nasser allowed Egyptian mobs to attack and burn U.S. Embassy buildings and made ferocious anti-American speeches, shouting, "Let them jump into the sea!" Nasser, in subsequent interviews with U.S. diplomats, would bring his face to within three inches of the American Ambassador's face and declare, with utmost seriousness: "Pay no attention to the speeches. Watch what I do." The absurdity was that Nasser's speeches frequently were "answers" to some American Congressman's pro-Israeli outburst on Capitol Hill or to some U.S. mayor's political speech to voters.

The solution of the Arab-Israeli conflict clearly was going to be a long, drawn-out affair. President Johnson had laid down the principles of U.S. policy early. These were: Mutual recognition of the political independence and territorial integrity of all countries in the area, encompassing recognized boundaries and other arrangements, including disengagement and withdrawal of forces, that will give them security against terror, destruction and war; freedom of innocent maritime passage; just and equitable solution of the refugee problem; registration and limitation of arms shipments into the area; and recognition of the right of all sovereign nations to exist in peace and security.

This time, as far as the Middle East Bureau under Battle was concerned, the situation was to be looked at as an opportunity, not as a depressing excuse to sit on one's hands hopelessly. The war, in a sense, had offered the Bureau a new opening similar to that which the Alliance for Progress had given the Latin American Bureau in 1961. The Middle East Bureau was coming of age and into the modern world.

The top-rated outfit in the State Department in recent years has been the Bureau of East Asian and Pacific Affairs, the fifth and last of the geographical bureaus. Its growth and importance have paralleled the rising gigantic shadow of Communist China on world affairs, a shadow ringed in 1967 with the radiation of its fast-developing thermonuclear threat. The Bureau became critical with the deepening commitment of the United States in the Vietnam war since 1961 and its massive intensification since 1965, when the U.S. bombing of North Vietnam was begun. The Bureau's 731 officers, 143 in Washington and 588 abroad, formulate and carry out U.S. policy for the entire Far East and Vietnam, though in South Vietnam there is a large additional Foreign Service, AID, and Defense Department civilian contingent, besides the more than half a million U.S. armed forces. The Bureau's growth in strategic relevance may be measured in terms of its staffing in 1930, when only 11 officers in Washington and 163 abroad oversaw United States interests. The area, excluding China, in 1967 had a total gross national product of $120 billion, of which, however, Japan itself produced $85 billion.

Though the total Far East area covered by State Department representatives has a total population of 375 million, no direct account is taken of the vast mainland of Communist China and its estimated 750 million people because the United States has no diplomatic relations with Communist China, hence, no reason to include it in official statistics. Despite the fact that the U.S. Government has literally reams and reams of detailed intelligence information about Chinese Communist activities inside China from its Consulate-General in Hong Kong, a large gap exists concerning Chinese power politics at any one moment, a lack of information the Peking Chinese apparently share, since there are yet no clear results in the long and bitter struggle ensuing from Mao Tse-tung's so-called cultural revolution.

The Bureau's staff operates at a fast pace because of the demands of the Vietnam war and collateral requirements in adjacent sensitive areas like Indonesia, Laos, Thailand, and Japan. Everyone constantly has to keep in mind the potentialities and practical scope of Communist Chinese actions and reactions. The Bureau has had a galaxy of ambassadorial stars in the field, officers like U. Alexis Johnson in Japan and Ellsworth Bunker in Vietnam and comers like William H. Sullivan in Laos and Marshall Green in Indonesia. All are acknowledged first-class operators who have had opportunity to shine under the stresses of wars and revolutions. This roster, with incentives for swift and cogent decisions under urgent conditions, can be constructively compared with the battery of United States envoys who operated in the Middle East during the frozen crisis of that area until it exploded in the Arab-Israeli war of 1967: Chester Bowles in India (who was also tagged the "president of the Indian Chamber of Commerce"); Armin Meyer in Iran; Robert Strong in Iraq; Dwight Porter in Lebanon; Jack Jernegen in Algeria; Hermann Eilts, a graduate of the Middle East "factory" in the U.S. Embassy in London, in Saudi Arabia; Parker Hart in Turkey; and Ray Hare, who had been in Egypt and Turkey and was Assistant Secretary for the Middle East on an interim basis. All were classed as excellent men. But they had had scant opportunity to flash because of the gray and insoluble aspect of their problems and the intermittent neglect which their regions had had to suffer, compared with the top-level sustained attention which the Far East had been receiving from the President and the Secretary of State in recent years. Yet, even during its peak period of high repute and intensive operation, the Far East Bureau was more or less carrying out instructions rather than initiating fundamental policy. For the particular characteristic of the Vietnam operations has been that the supreme desk officer has been the President himself, with the Secretary of State as the Vietnam desk officer in the State Department, and the Defense Secretary as the Vietnam desk officer in the Defense Department. Under President Kennedy a special Vietnam task force operated out of the White House, and only after his death did it move as a special unit into the State Department. It was taken over by the Far East shop in late 1964, its chief function being that of keeping minute tabs on the war and politics in South Vietnam and sending out detailed instructions based on the decisions made by the President and the Secretaries of State and Defense.

The widespread and acrid debate about, and considerable opposition to, the Vietnam war in the United States, particularly since 1965, has been historically passionate, distorted, and unavoidable. There were debates of a similar nature, though never on such a popular basis, in European societies during the nineteenth century over the right of intervention in aid of oppressed societies, as in Greece in 1821 and in Hungary in 1848. President Theodore Roosevelt in 1905 opposed "crusades of liberation." He felt they would never be popularly supported by willingness to perform the task required to carry out the so-called mission of freedom. Given its high-level panoply, the Vietnam war never had the benefit, ideally at least, of intensive participation from the start and from the ground up by the responsible Far East Bureau. Alexis Johnson, when he was Deputy Under Secretary for Political Affairs, then Deputy Ambassador in Saigon and again Deputy Under Secretary, confessed that there had been an initial error of judgment on Vietnam in not appreciating the Viet Cong danger as such in 1961, and particularly in underrating Vietnam in favor of Laos at that time.

This writer recalls talking to Theodore Sorensen, Special Counsel to President Kennedy, within the first two weeks after the inauguration in 1961. Asked what were the administration's foreign policy priorities, Sorensen said flatly, "Laos." In reply to the question, "What about Viet Nam?" he repeated "Laos." But within a few weeks, by March 1961, the Kennedy administration, in alarm, had begun to meet the problem of Vietnam and faced the possibility of heavily augmenting United States military advisers in South Vietnam as a result of a special task force report on Vietnam by Walt Rostow. In that same period President Kennedy was quoted as crying out, "[President] Eisenhower briefed me about everything—but Vietnam." Assistant Secretary William Bundy recalled that, when he had headed the

International Security Affairs Division in the Defense Department, not enough attention had been paid to Vietnam in those early days, for the problem was considered mainly a military one of dispatching aid and advisers. In August 1967, in a speech, Bundy admitted that "serious mistakes" had been made in U.S. policy in the past. The spring of 1961 had been crucial for President Kennedy, with the tragedy of the Bay of Pigs on April 17 and the fears of a Communist takeover in Laos, though in the same period the President had demonstrated his cool courage in the face of the Communist challenge by ordering 5,000 marines to embark on transports at Okinawa to sail to Thailand for possible action in Laos. This fact was not lost on then Soviet Premier Nikita Khrushchev, who said to Kennedy three times in their June 1961 meeting in Vienna, "You did something about Laos, didn't you?"

The Laos crisis, a cease-fire having resulted from Kennedy's threat to commit United States troops, passed to the diplomatic bargaining table at the Geneva Conference in April 1961. Secretary of State Rusk had gone over to give instructions to seek a diplomatic solution, as President Kennedy had directed. Rusk went directly from his plane to a meeting. It was pointed out to him that, with the Berlin crisis simultaneously heating up and in the aftermath of the Bay of Pigs, an American appearance of being too eager to settle the Laos crisis might prompt the overconfident Soviets into a grave miscalculation. As a result, Rusk changed his instructions from Kennedy. He sent a cable to the President, stating that he would seek a diplomatic solution but not preclude a resort to arms in corridor talk, in order at least to give the Russians pause.

Yet, there was still no universally clear realization that the importance of Laos lay in that it was the back door to Vietnam, a much more strategic and rich territory open to Communist expropriation by direct or indirect aggression and internal subversion. In fact, the North Vietnamese by May 1961 were already violating the Laos Accords by using the Ho Chi Minh Trail to infiltrate trained cadres and supplies into South Vietnam. That same May, President Kennedy finally did order United States forces into Thailand, up to the Mekong River, on the border of Laos. He instructed Harriman to tell the late Soviet Deputy Foreign Minister G. M. Pushkin at Geneva that he had better make his North Vietnamese allies behave, or "we'll have a real war in Vietnam." A month later, in June 1961, Walt Rostow told the President that the sources of infiltration had to be stopped and the safe-haven advantage of an unattacked sanctuary denied to the Communists before the situation further eroded.

Though the Laos settlement was envisaged as a deal of concessions by the United States, it turned out much better than anyone had a right to expect. The so-called neutralist, Souvanna Phouma, proved to be a far stronger character than anticipated in the Western definition of neutralists. Agonizing in the White House persisted over the burgeoning crisis in South Vietnam and its practical relation to the United States commitment in that country. Still, it was not until the Viet Cong attacked and temporarily held the capital of Phuoc Thanh Province, fifty-five miles from Saigon, on September 18, 1961, that the fire bells began to ring at the White House. A few weeks later, in October, the Rostow-Taylor mission was sent to make an on-the-spot evaluation in South Vietnam and recommendations for United States policy. The latter included a big increase in aid and military advisers, but also insistence on social reforms by the Diem Government. The reforms never materialized. But no prior conditions for aid had been laid down either.

From the start the programs of the United States in South Vietnam operated under two handicaps: the ambiguities and ambivalence of policy and the failure to use integrated command machinery in Washington. Operations were run by a White House staff that, though of high intelligence, was not particularly experienced in recognizing the built-in complexities and drag of bureaucratic machinery as applied to the chaos of politico-military operations on exotic shores. Yet a model existed in the interagency task force on Berlin, which consisted of picked operating personnel and was backed with full presidential authority and which in the end resolved all but the most difficult issues, which were appealed to the President only as the last resort. A result of the haphazard early handling of the Vietnam war was that decisions appeared ragged, with loose ends, giving rise to loose talk, confusion, and friction on the lower levels. The Vietnam conflict coursed up and down until the fall of 1964, when this writer remarked to a high Defense Department official that the Mekong River Delta had the "smell of the Red River Delta," an evocation of the time when, in 1952, the writer had been in Hanoi and the Communist Viet Minh had begun to turn the tide against the French. After February 1965, when the bombing of North Vietnam was begun, and June 1965, when the first United States combat action took place, through 1967, negotiations to settle the undeclared war between the United States and North Vietnam reached an impasse. The character and extent of the United States vital interest and commitment to South Vietnam became more and more the crux of the argument in wide-ranging discussions, analyses, argumentation, and diatribes in the popular press, among intellectuals, in Congress, and within the Government.

As far back as 1945, President Franklin Delano Roosevelt, inspired in part by family stories of his Aunt Sara Delano Roosevelt concerning the mistreatment of the natives by French feudal interests in Indo-China, spoke of placing Indo-China under the United Nations, as its first trusteeship, and evicting the French. President Truman had initialed the first military aid supply agreements to the French as an ally after the end of World War II. President Eisenhower increased that aid at the urging of Secretary Dulles, whose stubborn belief had been to hold South Vietnam at all costs as a barrier against expansion of the rampant North Vietnamese Communists in 1954. Dulles had wanted to intervene on behalf of the French at the battle of Dien Bien Phu, on the advice of Admiral Arthur Radford, Chairman of the Joint Chiefs of Staff. Radford, however, never had time to present his clinching arguments to President Eisenhower because he failed to get from the French military in Indo-China agreement on command arrangements for the planned United States air strike against the encircling Viet Minh forces around Dien Bien Phu. The French had demanded that the U.S. planes be placed under their operational command, an arrangement which Radford could not permit. South Vietnam, despite initial and relatively large-scale United States aid in 1954–1956, slid into apparent neglect as the United States became absorbed in the Suez crisis of 1956, the crashing impact of the Soviet Sputnik in 1957, the Lebanon-Iraq crisis of 1958, and Eisenhower's initiative for a détente with the Soviet Union in 1959.

Yet, even with the pull of other momentous issues, Laos was high on President Eisenhower's agenda for his Camp David discussion with Khrushchev in September 1959, when the North Vietnam-backed Pathet Lao were starting to make major gains.

That same autumn, Deputy Assistant Secretary of State John M. Steeves, later Director General of the Foreign Service, wrote a prophetic analysis in which he delineated the necessity for a clear decision about Southeast Asia. Either the United States had to come to a fix to support independent regimes in the area or it should declare the area as not one of vital interest to the United States—but, Steeves pointed out, at the risk at a later date of a major war in South Vietnam.

In this period, South Vietnam went its own way while the military assistance group, under Lieutenant General Sam Williams, trained the South Vietnamese army in the South Korean pattern for a frontal conventional war instead of the guerrilla war that was to come. The South Vietnamese army of that time was virtually a mercenary legion for Ngo Dinh Diem, President of South Vietnam, as indicated by its pay scale, which in 1957 was fifteen times that of the Philippine Army, U.S. foreign aid inspectors discovered. The crisis opening up for the United States and President Kennedy in South Vietnam in 1961 was therefore no mere sudden or passing foreign policy affair but already a crisis rooted in, and watered by, the attitudes, action, and programs of three Presidents before JFK.

Whatever his criticism of the handling of real problems on the spot, no senior U.S. Foreign Service officer of professional qualifications has failed to observe that the United States commitment to South Vietnam existed since the very beginning, in 1954, when Dulles engaged the honor, word, and prestige of his nation. By 1963, with expansion of U.S. aid and advisers, the commitment had become almost irrevocable. Foreign Service officers pinpoint the conviction that Vietnam had always been a "critical" United States interest, not merely a "prestige" interest, though a minority argued otherwise, and all agreed that the point became academic when the chips were down. The question of whether the United States could ever have withdrawn its commitment to South Vietnam was even less arguable. It could have bowed out in 1954 and allowed North Vietnam to take over the South, facing the risk of Communist domination of Southeast Asia, in the hope that Ho Chi Minh would have become an Asiatic Tito on the Communist periphery of China and would loosen his ties with Peking, as the Eastern European countries were to do with the Soviet Union after 1956. The United States could also have folded its tent and stolen away at the end of 1964. The Vietnamese situation had grown so bad by then that there were simply no grounds for political settlement; the United States just had no leverage. South Vietnam would have slid under the Communist aegis within three weeks to three months if the United States had done nothing more at all at that trembling moment. The Hanoi offer for negotiations in late 1964 was strictly on Hanoi terms. Within the State Department and the White House the outcome in the fall of 1964 was in full view, and the question of whether the United States should jump in with both feet or allow South Vietnam to fall to pieces was already being discussed, the presidential campaign's electoral verbalisms notwithstanding.

There had been the possibility that the United States could have withdrawn with honor from Vietnam up to 1956 and 1957, which appear to be the last years in which President Diem of South Vietnam still had the opportunity to become an unchallenged leader of an underdeveloped country in the modern tradition. Diem, in effect, outmaneuvered the United States into allowing him to renege on the Geneva pledge for the 1956 election on reunification of North and South. The Diem ploy on the reunification elections could have been countered by saying, "yes, but," and imposing conditions. The United States had enough leverage at that time to pressure Diem into hastening the progress which had been initiated under the first impact of American aid. But it failed to seize the opportunity. The years from 1957 to 1960 were the lost years.

A rare practical opportunity for the United States honorably to mitigate or alter the basic Vietnamese situation arose after the Cuban nuclear crisis, when U.S. prestige was riding high following its victory in the near-nuclear showdown with the Soviet Union. On November 28, 1962, Anastas Mikoyan, the Deputy Soviet Premier, after a visit to Fidel Castro in Havana, went to see President Kennedy. It was strongly recommended to

Kennedy that the President use his diplomatic advantage to tell Mikoyan to make Hanoi stop its violation of the 1962 Geneva agreements and to cease supporting the Pathet Lao in Laos and the Viet Cong in South Vietnam. Otherwise, Soviet Russia and the United States would have a much worse affair in Vietnam than the recently concluded diplomatic fencing match over Cuba. Kennedy did not raise the subject with Mikoyan.

Given the actualities on the ground, the administration arguments, whether President Kennedy's or President Johnson's, and regardless of their monotonous repetition, remained consistently valid, particularly in view of volatile world uncertainties, such as were exposed in the 1967 Middle East crisis. Withdrawing from South Vietnam at such a late date would have seriously undercut United States diplomatic credit everywhere in the world at a fragile moment. Similarly, the Joint Chiefs of Staff thesis had substantial weight: that a successful Communist war of national liberation in Vietnam would encourage more such wars of national liberation and less effective resistance to them, in at least half a dozen places around the world. Conversely, the shibboleth, born of the Korean war, that United States armies must not get mired on the mainland of Asia overlooked geopolitical fundamentals: that the United States action strategy is based on naval power on the oceans and massive airlift in the skies and over the islands, while the ICBM power is a last-resort insurance deterrent. The potentially hostile continental land masses frequently terminate in strategic peninsulas which, in friendly hands, can serve as insurance barriers to contain hostile spearheads of expansion against the key island aggregations and sea lanes vital to freedom of United States movements around the globe. South Korea, South Vietnam, the Horn of Africa, Greece, Norway, and even South Africa are examples of such strategic real estate, in the military view.

If earlier Vietnam policy had been marked by too little and too late, delays, and rather aimless conferences, later Vietnam policy, that is, from 1965 on, was characterized by the disorganization attendant upon such a swift and massive influx of United States troops and material. By late 1967, the United States commitments, economic, political, and military, had begun to mesh. Operators on the spot felt that the vast programs in progress were splendid in outline but might have been much more efficacious had they been launched five years earlier, or in 1962. Secretary Rusk so argued inside White House councils in 1961: that the United States should throw in massive resources and combat troops at once, and crush the rebellion before it got entrenched. Rusk mused in retrospect at Canberra, in July 1966, that if the United States had realized after the June 1961 Vienna conference between Kennedy and Khrushchev that there would be no favorable consequences with regard to the Vietnam crisis, that then would have been the moment to pour in power for Saigon and President Diem. But there was no organizational setup to move in troops and aid as fast as such a decisive act required.

The most melancholy aspect of the Vietnamese war has been America's interminable reluctance to come to grips with it. As long ago as 1953, Edwin O. Reischauer, the noted authority on Japan and former United States Ambassador there, pointed to the problems of Asia and coming Vietnamese troubles as an aftermath of Korea. In a similar vein, this writer cabled a dispatch from the Indo-China conference in Geneva in May 1954 to the Cleveland *Plain Dealer* saying: "The Indo-China war actually means that the gigantic problem of Asia has suddenly been dumped into the laps of the American people at a moment when they were least ready for it."

Even more depressing to recall is a dispatch cabled in June 1954 from Paris: "The gravest peril of a general clash between the Russo-Chinese Communist bloc and the free world lies in a mutual misunderstanding of what the word 'war' means."

The dispatch went on to describe the wars of liberation which President Kennedy had become exercised about after reading Khrushchev's speech on the subject to the December 1960 Soviet World Congress of Communist Parties. The *Plain Dealer* cable said:

The Reds believe a war of liberation or an "anti-colonial war" is a legitimate and internal affair subject to no outsider's "imperialist" meddling. The "popular" side of "just civil wars" can legitimately claim Red logistical aid and advice.

Unfortunately, the facts of the transitional period now underway in Asia appear to support the Communist thesis. The Communists managed to take on "nationalist-revolutionary-anti-colonial" coloration early and efficiently, or actually seize leadership of originally authentic national movements.

On this base of attacking "discredited" regimes, the Communists find fair sailing for three further sound techniques.

Systematized guerrilla warfare comes first. It's designed as a dispersed but pervasive, long-range but non-stop pin-pricking the "enemy" to death. It is eminently suited to underdeveloped countries with poor communications and age-old feudal grudges.

The next Communist weapon is perhaps the most effective of all. It is to make every move with a political aim in mind. This means impressing the foe with the fatalistic idea of his ultimate defeat because the foe is in the "wrong." To get political points across when they deem it necessary, the Reds throw tactical common sense to the winds and sacrifice thousands.

The third technique is the transfer of their fighting cadres to Red Party politics. Trained, disciplined and obedient in war, the new soldier-politician provides the same unquestioning single-mindedness in peace. The Russians, the Chinese, and now the Indo-China Viet Minh are veterans of this new technique in power politics.

Historically, Vietnam has had a series of three wars. The first, from 1945 to 1954, culminated in the creation of North Vietnam. The second round lasted from 1959 to 1963, ending with the murders of President Diem and of President Kennedy. In 1964 the war was left to the special task force and the Far East Bureau, and it slacked off without dominant control from the top because of the presidential elections. The third Vietnam war began in 1965 and was going on in 1968. Former Under Secretary Ball, in 1961, arguing against involvement in South Vietnam, had warned President Kennedy that the increase of military advisers to Saigon from 666 (to 16,000-plus) would eventually escalate inexorably to 300,000 in five years. Ball was nearly 200,000 off. He was the only consistent opponent of the Vietnam war inside the administration. He did not want to get in in 1961, and he wanted to get out in 1964. For three years, Ball sent out critical memos at least once a week. He defended the official policy in public, however.

The only persistent fight in the Kennedy administration against what appeared to be the predominantly military approach in Vietnam was made by Assistant Secretary Roger Hilsman, against former Defense Secretary McNamara and the Pentagon military establishment. Hilsman maintained that the only way to wage the war was to concentrate on a counterinsurgency or antiguerrilla campaign in the South. By this he meant not only ceaseless and concerted patrol actions against the Viet Cong, but parallel economic and political measures to make the countryside secure and resistant to Viet Cong infiltrations. It was not until five years later again, by late 1967, that a realistically organized approach to "pacification" was at least devised for the first time under the spur of Robert Komer, President Johnson's special aide for civilian operations in Vietnam. But the question of halting outside infiltration had not been fully faced in Hilsman's time.

Walt Rostow also had had a guerrilla approach in mind—guerrilla warfare through air power. President Kennedy personally cleared Rostow's speech to the Fort Bragg, North Carolina, Special Forces (Green Beret) training center in April 1961, when Rostow first advocated a policy to deny a guerrilla sanctuary to an enemy and to "seek out and engage the ultimate sources of aggression." This was the first official hint of the eventual policy of bombing the infiltration routes and led to the heavy air raids on North Vietnam.

But the piecemeal, almost apologetic, bombing pattern that developed from 1965 to 1967 shredded all systematic plans, between pressures from the Joint Chiefs of Staff and political expediencies to cushion Congressional reactions, but, even more importantly, from the stubborn facts of logistics.

Postbombing speculations, stated with varying degrees of guesswork concerning the theoretical role of Rostow as a prime mover in the North

Vietnam bombing policy, were largely irrelevant, given the actualities. The first of these was that President Johnson, of all political leaders, was given neither to snap judgments nor to single-source consultation. The second was perhaps a failure in ideal strategic procedure. The original issue in the councils of war was whether to bomb North Vietnam or not to bomb. The immediate corollary, if the decision was to bomb, was not to play at war but to apply the fullest power possible, short of the nuclear, to attain desired political objectives. Testimony released in Congress in late 1967 indicated that the U.S. military desired to bomb all-out and to mine the Port of Haiphong at the very start in early 1965. With hindsight, the generals and admirals charged that the slow gradualism of the bombing and its public discussion placed the Soviet Union under public pressure to do something about aid to its "fellow socialist state." Worse, it gave the Communist side sufficient time to emplace antiaircraft defenses in depth, defenses greater than any encountered in World War II.

Three raw facts of life, two of them not fully realized or expected, intervened, however. The first was a double miscalculation. White House councils staked their hopes on the belief that a normal enemy, seeing the incoming bombs as a warning, would have enough sense to come to terms, which would have been largely in their favor, since the United States bombing was a clear desperation measure to stave off collapse in South Vietnam. There were long-range pledges expressed in President Johnson's speech of April 1965, in Baltimore. There were no long, detailed advance plans of any practical value for South Vietnam, except to hang on and not allow the embattled nation to go completely Communist by default. South Vietnam's independence, even a nonaligned independence, was the primary consideration. But Hanoi did not scare easily in 1965. Perhaps the North Vietnamese were too unsophisticated to realize they were getting beat. Nor did Hanoi grasp the opportunity of winning at that time at the conference table what it was clearly going to be more difficult to gain at a negotiation in 1968 or later.

There was as early as December 1964 and January 1965 an even greater restraining factor against the proposition of a sudden massive bombing of North Vietnam. This was the U.S. administration's fear that a mighty show of force would indeed alarm Communist China and the Soviet Union into critical reaction. China could move mass troops in support of Hanoi on the pattern of the Yalu in North Korea in 1950. With 1962 in mind, Russia could feel a renewed U.S. nuclear challenge to the existence of the Communist world. Both were, and are, cautionary factors in Vietnam war policy still.

Johnson used to grumble in those days that if he had followed the generals' advice, he would be in war with Russia tomorrow morning.

Rusk, a year after the bombing, used to say that if anyone had told him a year earlier that the United States could have gotten away with as much as it had in the air war, he would have been rather sceptical.

But on the ground, the practicalities were the true limiting factor. As a 1965 participant in the councils of a strategy said, you don't mash a button electronically and start a war. There was no early effective bombing in the desired classic war plans sense. There were only three bases for jet bombers. There was a great insufficiency of expert pilots, trained to the pinpoint accuracy required for hitting selected targets in the midst of civilian populations.

Arguments arose regularly at the Tuesday White House meetings over U.S. Air Force claims of promised performance. They aroused particularly in the precisely functioning mind of McNamara considerable scepticism about the efficacy of bombing plans. General Earle G. Wheeler, Chairman of the Joint Chiefs of Staff, was the normal conveyor of proposed bombing plans to the White House when a new phase was to be opened or when the new phase was discussed by the National Security Council in full session. As the final target officer, Johnson was as rough as sandpaper on his military counselors. At meetings where General "Bus" Wheeler came along without a fellow Joint Chief and could not personally vouch for a proposed detail, Johnson would pick up the phone right then and there and call the Joint Chief responsible and say, in effect, Bus here tells me you say you can put this stuff right on target. Now are you sure, General, you can put it exactly where it is supposed to go and not go blasting half of China? Johnson's highly graphic and pointed vernacular had impact. The generals understood cavalry language and got the point. One didn't get fancy with The Boss. Johnson had a right to be a little piqued on certain occasions. After one early 1967 air raid on the oil depots in North Vietnam, the proposed policy for which had been well aired in the American press, it was found by reconnaissance that the oil had been moved and the tanks were empty.

In South Vietnam, in any event, Hilsman's ultimate failure, on his limited operational level, was that of not being able to deal with President Diem, who by that time had become completely obdurate and deaf to American pleas for administrative and political reforms. When, in desperation, the Kennedy administration did not stop the coup that overthrew and killed Diem, though he had been offered sanctuary in the U.S. Embassy, a United States policy debacle ensued. For six weeks after Diem's death, the Washington planners were disoriented and in disarray. Diem's death destroyed the real and effective power infrastructure that Diem had created and the anti-Communist leadership figure his existence symbolized. Into this vacuum the Communists moved at once with speed and success, amazed with unbelief at the sacrifice of Diem by the Americans. President Johnson later felt that permitting the destruction of Diem had been the big mistake of U.S. policy in the early Vietnam war.

In retrospect, 1963 was the "make or break" year for the Kennedy administration in Vietnam. The impact of American aid by the summer of 1962 had begun to show results. In early 1963 there were indications that Hanoi was having second thoughts about, and slowing down, its support of the Viet Cong. Hanoi's intervention in South Vietnam had started with the creation of the National Liberation Front in December 1960, following the resolution of the North Vietnamese Lao Dong (Communist) Party in September 1960 to "liberate the South." Renewed Diem intransigence and his repression of Buddhist demonstrations distracted the administration from following through with its pressure on Saigon to clean up the Viet Cong. President Kennedy on several occasions, in 1963 in particular, made the point, with not too well-concealed impatience, that it was "their war" and that it was "up to the South Vietnamese to win it."

The interpretation has been made that Kennedy's reluctance fully to engage the American nation in South Vietnam could be construed as an unwitting signal to Hanoi, or was so taken by the Communists, that the United States would not intervene in South Vietnam. Such a possible Communist interpretation would have been similar to that which they made of former Secretary of State Acheson's definition of the United States Pacific defense perimeter, in a January 1950 speech, which omitted South Korea and purportedly encouraged the North Koreans to attack that nation in June 1950. In any case, Hanoi could see opportunity in the combination of the disappearance of Diem, the temptation opened by the civil disturbances and Buddhist riots, and the mixture of seeming American indecisiveness and conventional static military strategy carried out by U.S. General Paul Harkins, Chief of the United States Military Assistance Mission in Saigon. Harkins' original appointment had envisaged him as a theater commander for Southeast Asia, a job which Harkins apparently expected momentarily to open up. His attitude downgraded South Vietnam to a secondary front. All these factors encouraged the North Vietnamese to begin sending larger organized units southward in a growing infiltration in 1964.

The Hanoi influx of men, supplies, and direction nearly took over the country when President Johnson, almost at the last minute, decided to intervene in force to deny the Communists the winning of the whole nation on the cheap. In 1965 the North Vietnamese doubled their infiltration of organized units over 1964, and again in 1966 they further increased the tempo of organized infiltration. By 1967 there were approximately 100,000 North Vietnamese regular troops in South Vietnam. This was over and above at least 192,000 native and local Viet Cong guerrillas, full-time hard-core units, part-time marauders, and picked political cadres and logistical teams. The superbly organized network was ostensibly under the National Liberation Front but militarily under the top command direction of the People's Revolutionary Party of South Vietnam, and with direct links to the Defense Ministry in Hanoi.

As 1968 opened, both sides, Allied and Communist, were still impaled on their frozen negotiating points, despite at least three hundred so-called peace-feeler contacts, that is, messages, suggestions, specifics, and pure nonsense, from primary, secondary, and tertiary sources, in a cable file described as at least a foot and a half thick.

In an autopsy of the era, the most glaring United States failing had been overrating the capabilities of its allies in South Vietnam and underestimating those of the Viet Cong and North Vietnamese opposition. Finally, observation indicates that when the chips are down in a major crisis like Vietnam, the geographical State Department bureau of purported responsibility, the Far East Bureau in this case, plays a derivative and secondary role, but an inescapably necessary one in fitting all the nuts and bolts into place if it can. The Bureau turned necessity into a virtue by developing into a crack coordinating agency that meshed the Washington directives into understandable coherence for the Saigon Embassy. It shifted with professional smoothness from serving as a "holding" operation under Leonard Unger, the first chief of the Vietnam working group at the start of the so-called Americanized war of 1965, to Philip Habib, who was clearly heading by 1967 a "forward" operation. The Bureau's efficiency and dispatch, after very rough experiences, set a precedent in sustained State Department operations.

CHAPTER VI

THE SECRETARY OF STATE: Premier Paladin of the Presidency

THE FIFTY-FOURTH SECRE-
tary of State of the United States of America, the Honorable Dean Rusk of
Georgia, had good reason to smile his Mona Lisa smile in 1968. He had
been in office longer than any other Secretary except Cordell Hull, who had
a record of twelve years. From the start, Rusk had been ceaselessly battered
by crisis after crisis: Laos, Cuba, Berlin, the Congo, Vietnam in 1961;
Vietnam, Berlin, Communist China, and Cuba in 1962; Vietnam and the
Congo in 1963; Vietnam, the India-Pakistan war, the bombing of North
Vietnam, and the Dominican Republic in 1965; Vietnam in 1966 and 1967,
plus the sudden shock of the Middle East crisis in 1967; and still Vietnam
in 1968. He had suffered and survived a double round of malignities. The
first came from his associates and the press in the early days of the Kennedy
administration, particularly after the Bay of Pigs disaster, when the State
Department, possibly with some measure of justification, was made one of
the scapegoats for the errors of the federal bureaucracy and Rusk, as its
appointed head, received his share of blame for the state of the Department
and his failure to do something about it right away, or preferably the day
before.

The second round of opprobrium to be visited upon Rusk came with
the heightened passions of the country in consequence of the United States
bombing of North Vietnam and the massive United States military intervention in South Vietnam in 1965. Rusk became the lightning rod that
initially drew the hottest fire away from the President. He thus became the
instant target of all the Vietnam opposition, led jointly by United States
Senator J. William Fulbright and his fellow doves on the Senate Foreign
Relations Committee and by a very large section of the nation's academic
intellectuals. The Secretary of State historically becomes the number one
controversial figure in crises. He is an easier prey for those critics who feel
the President might be too big game for them.

Rusk had been damned with faint praise as possessing at least eighteen of the twenty qualifications for an ideal Secretary of State, including stamina, good relations with Congress, capacity for articulate exposition, first-class mental equipment, Southern birth, personal interest in military affairs, infinite capacity for small talk and for speeches and ceremonials, mastery of the nomenclature of foreign policy, gentlemanly comportment and courtliness, a sense of history, pride of office, and his individual concept of the role of the Secretary of State as standing at the right hand of the President, indeed as the President's absolute and personal servant, in Rusk's own credo.

Kennedy administration detractors heaped left-handed compliments upon Rusk, describing him as silken and tough, cool, controlled, committed, conscientious, dispassionate, realistic, honorable, talented, diffident, concise, diligent, persuasive, prudent, durable, forebearing to a fault, gentle, gracious, amiable, quiet, cautious, highly intelligent, well-informed, bland, logical, terse, low-key. Kennedy insisted to outsiders that Rusk was the President's principal adviser and agent in foreign policy, not the bright starlets of his White House entourage. On the other hand, the assertions of the Kennedy circle that JFK would not have retained Rusk as Secretary of State if the President had won the 1964 elections also appear plausible. Characteristically, Rusk never for a moment thought of resigning, despite the public panning by Kennedy's friends.

Theodore Sorensen, President Kennedy's Special Counsel, related that Rusk objected to discussing serious matters of state with persons who did not have operational responsibilities. Arthur Schlesinger, the Kennedy era's court historian, likewise complained that Rusk did not condescend to engage in argumentation with the White House circle on matters of high policy. The malice of those first years of Rusk's penance served up as canapés on the Georgetown cocktail circuit further tidbits: Rusk had left no imprint on the State Department; no single public utterance of major moment could be attributed to Rusk. Rusk gave a rare tart rejoinder: that he never did talk secrets in front of the White House staff because he knew they would then no longer be secrets. Further, that he, Rusk, unlike others, would never write his memoirs.

More to the heart of the argument was Rusk's conception of the role of the Secretary of State as the principal staff officer to the Presidency in foreign affairs. Rusk was keenly aware that he might be the navigator but could never be the captain of the ship of state in foreign affairs. This fundamental conviction was buttressed by Rusk's interpretation of the character of the American constitutional system. He never forgot that the President was the President and Chief Executive. But he remembered as well that the Constitution included the Congress as a co-equal and that the American system would be unable to work unless the executive and legislative branches were in tandem, at least at critical times. Rusk thought of himself as the President's executant, at best. He would never dream of taking a position in advance of the President or of circumscribing or pre-empting the President's right of eminent domain over foreign relations, nor did he feel resentful of the President's writ.

Rusk regarded the Secretary of State as the custodian of the commitments of the United States in foreign policy, commitments that have been duly ratified by the United States Senate. Perforce, he had to appear as a symbol of the state and retain a certain graven image, magisterial and taciturn, to portray this continuity of United States policy. In consequence, a certain Roman *gravitas* was esthetically appropriate to Rusk, and by its very nature prohibited the liberty of sounding off as flippantly and casually as other luminaries with fewer legally authorized responsibilities than those a Secretary of State is forced to accept.

President Kennedy's own understanding of human nature led him to appreciate greatly Rusk's stalwart solidity at the time of the 1961 challenge of Berlin by Khrushchev. JFK marveled at Rusk's patience and surface imperturbability under the sting and goad of press criticisms and the cruel gossip about him handed around the Kennedy circle. In his turn, Rusk was more than loyal to President Kennedy. In the days of gloom following the Bay of Pigs debacle, it was Rusk who demonstrated an unexpected intensity of passion by crying out, "We have to save this man," meaning President Kennedy, from the consequences of the errors of judgment on Cuba. After President Kennedy's death, Rusk said, in tribute, that the President had been "an extraordinary and incandescent man who shall be forever young," a phrasing of poetic succinctness which exemplified Rusk's style of concise and taut ellipsis of speech in private talk.

It was fitting, recalling those earlier days of sniping by the rhetoricians of presidential power, that Rusk, a deeply religious man, cited as his favorite Psalm in the Bible the Ninety-first, whose second verse says, "I will say of the Lord, He is my refuge, and my fortress: my God; in him will I trust," and the third verse, "Surely he shall deliver thee from the snare of the fowler, and from the noisome pestilence." Also, the Twenty-third Psalm, "The Lord is my shepherd," gave solace to Rusk. Besides the bright lights personally near the President, there was the ring of prestigious names in the State Department: Chester Bowles, Adlai Stevenson, Averell Harriman, Mennen Williams, Adolf Berle. All were direct personal political appointments of the President. In the light of one of General George Marshall's sayings, "Be careful not to be made a prisoner of your own appointments," Rusk, in effect, was a double captive of Kennedy's choice, since, despite his title and responsibility, in personal prestige and popular status he rated a poor third. Small wonder then that, surrounded by such galaxies of potentially ambitious rivals, Rusk put his guard up, and with utter self-discipline maintained the reserve and aloofness he is frequently charged with. Those were the days when Rusk impressed upon his immediate staff the need to keep in "low silhouette." Going out of town to make a speech, he was greeted at the airport with the news of a major foreign affairs event. An aide suggested that the Secretary make a comment about it and so gain some publicity, whereupon Rusk shook his head and said, "The play is to be inconspicuous."

As the minuet of power progressed and some of the dancers fell out of grace or receded into indifference from the throne, Rusk began to show evidence of having made two basic decisions with regard to the occupancy of his office. The first was the determination to survive the handicaps of the Washington ambiance and entourage so that he could be on hand to perform his duty, as he saw it, to be able to advise the President of the United States to the best of his abilities.

This was the era in which Rusk's associates criticized him for not conveying his thoughts to them, a criticism that continued to be voiced in the Department. Rusk believed, like General Marshall, that ideas should flow from the bottom up. He reiterated that he had never penalized a subordinate for overreaching his authority, and that the horizon was there for him to grasp who could reach it. Rusk encouraged dissent and vigorous debate among his subordinates while an issue was under discussion. Hearing once that a Foreign Service Institute instructor had advised a class of entering Foreign Service officers "not to stick your neck out," Rusk sought out the same class and lectured the members on the virtues of not being "yes-men," pointing to the roster of brilliant U.S. diplomats who had never been afraid to speak their piece. But, Rusk added gently, dissent was due before decision, and loyalty after, even though one had been personally opposed to the views accepted officially in the end. The only other honorable alternative, in Rusk's view, was to resign.

Rusk was suspected of having adopted Machiavellism in order to survive, tagged a "Protestant Jesuit" because of his subtleties, circumlocutions, and gnomic generalities, and indirectly assailed as a "leftist" by John Birch Society members. Nevertheless, he did endure and did give his private counsel for the President's ears alone, with a passionate love of country and deep sense of duty that brought to mind the marmoreal public figures of the eighteenth and nineteenth centuries. Rusk had some quiet stratagems of his own in order to live and fight another day. He had a policy of purposeful procrastination, when necessary. He took no-action, a deliberate decision, especially when he felt that the opposing party did not have sufficient strength to put a project through. The 1967 civil war in Nigeria, for instance, was a no-action decision, though Rusk knew that

Communist Czechoslovakia and Russia had supplied planes to the Nigerian Federal Government, meaning that the estimate of Nigeria becoming "another Vietnam" was weighed and discounted, at least for the moment.

Rusk was an expert in-fighter in the bureaucratic clinches when it counted. He could be scathing about the chorus of carping cries for ideas, initiatives, imagination, flexibility, and creativeness by replying that "an idea is not a policy" and that "to transform an idea into policy is frequently an exhausting and frustrating process." He might become furious under provocation, but he would bottle up his resentment. Unlike John Foster Dulles, who was also held unapproachable, Rusk never indulged in give-and-take, preferring not to expose his flanks in too-familiar discourse, even in private. Like President Johnson, Rusk had a style of giving the other fellow enough rope (a) to swing with it or (b) to hang himself. The second denouement took care of not a few of Rusk's political problems in time. Rusk shared with Johnson the technique of allowing the erosion of the normal political climate to wear down his enemies or rivals, while he quietly and imperceptibly kept on moving in the direction of his own considered desire.

As Rusk grew by forced feeding in the first two years of the Kennedy administration, learning which levers and buttons to push in the power apparatus, he made his second major personal decision, a measurement of the limitations of his possibilities. He had so much to do, and so little time to do it in. He had to set his own priorities, determine what was important to himself, in order to be in that state of preparation and readiness to advise the President on those matters, and only those matters, which were of vital and overriding national concern, to be decided by the President alone. To Rusk such an operating philosophy meant primarily three things: First, constant awareness of all issues, and at least a recognition vocabulary of the basic facts involved. Second, concentration on the top critical items which affected the President—Soviet-American relations, Chinese-American relations, nonproliferation, the food-population problem, which he ranked second only to the nuclear danger in gravity, and, third and constantly, the Vietnam war, after the United States intervention in 1965. A result of this personal policy was a tendency for Rusk to over-focus on the problems of the day, the fires in the in-basket, because those were the questions the President, Congress, and the press would ask about. He thus made himself the State Department's chief desk officer for Vietnam, starting in the spring of 1964, when President Johnson ordered him to go to see that trouble spot at first hand. This was the first time that Rusk had been in Saigon, after three years of consciously allowing McNamara to be in charge of Vietnam policy, by default. This was because, as Rusk thought at that time, Vietnam was essentially a military problem to be handled by the military, whose superior was theoretically the Secretary of Defense.

Rusk's selection of priorities left on the sidelines three major matters for which he had been widely criticized. The first was management and administration of the State Department. The second was the choice of personnel for key posts, though Rusk had more of a voice in this field under President Johnson than he had had under President Kennedy. The third was encouraging long-range policy planning and prospects. Rusk's mind focused on operational particulars; he did not deem theoretical planning relevant to the immediate moment, however much he appreciated intellectually the import of the long look, as was evident in speeches about his own long-term ideals.

President Kennedy wanted Rusk to throw his weight around and make an impact on the Department, on his colleagues, and on any would-be rivals. Rusk did not do so for his own good reasons of style and temperament. Whatever might have been his fate had President Kennedy survived, Secretary Rusk came into his own under President Johnson. Though President Johnson personally at times might prefer the hidden-ball plunge to the broken-field running of President Kennedy, he reinvested Rusk as the only authorized official channel for high foreign policy between the State Department and the White House. Moreover, and without indulging in photographic phrenology, it might be noted that at least half a dozen candid snapshots of Rusk with the President reveal an openness, a new warmth, and an expressiveness of countenance which were never quite visible in pictures of Rusk taken with President Kennedy.

This apparent closeness of Rusk to President Johnson reached a sort of public climax at the June 1967 Glassboro, New Jersey, summit conference between President Johnson and Soviet Premier Alexei Kosygin. At the Sunday meeting, Mrs. Johnson, the President's wife, and his daughter Lynda leaned over to Rusk for familiar pecks on the cheek, an indication of the fondly familiar Southern style with which both the President and Rusk are at home. There is no picture, as far as is known, of Jacqueline Kennedy kissing Rusk in public. Rusk's compatibility with President Johnson was no new thing. The Secretary personally briefed Lyndon Johnson regularly when Johnson was Vice President. At a meeting of the National Security Council in August 1963, when Rusk was in the chair, in the absence of President Kennedy, he took the unprecedented step of calling on the Vice President for his views on Vietnam. Johnson had usually been an interested but silent spectator at NSC meetings.

Instead of being, as was charged, a "shadow head" of the State Department during the Kennedy administration, Rusk, under Johnson, was "absolute boss" when he was directly interested in an issue, senior colleagues unreservedly testified. The White House staff question became:

Has Dean Rusk seen and approved this? In his later, easier comportment, Rusk no longer minded discussing—but not arguing—issues in the proper official circles of competent responsibility. Yet he never rendered his net judgment in large meetings. He still exercised the right to take up certain matters of high importance and sensitivity directly and solely with the President, in person and in private. For that matter, so had Secretary Dulles, who, associates said, "felt no reason to expose himself to a vast melange of people on matters for which he had specified responsibility." Therefore, Dulles had often met President Eisenhower alone, after other interlocutors had left, to discuss his views.

Secretary Rusk, in brief, ceased being an outsider of sorts in the Kennedy administration and became definitely an insider in the Johnson administration. President Johnson, like President Kennedy before him, was impressed by Rusk's great mastery of detail, swift getting to the point, and avoidance of trivia, the latter likewise a trait of Rusk's professional ideal, General Marshall. Both Presidents admired Rusk's courage and judgment. Johnson was impressed by Rusk's calmness and solidity in a crisis when, despite the current of arguments which seemed to be drawing to a definite conclusion, Rusk would intervene and say, "Now just a minute." As did Kennedy, Johnson wanted Rusk to get mad and fight, though persons present at such discussions reported that Rusk just sat there and laughed. Also like Johnson, Rusk had a major preoccupation—fearing that the foreign world might mistake the veiled and understated strength of the United States for weakness. In a word, Rusk hated for either the United States or himself to be taken for a patsy.

By 1967, Rusk had progressed so far in Johnson's esteem that the President frequently told visitors a story of what the President's cabinet thought about Rusk and McNamara, the President's other doughty principal officer. If the eleven cabinet members, the President, and the Vice President were all voting on the question of who had the best judgment of any man in the room, there would be twelve votes for Rusk. If the thirteen men present were voting on who was the greatest organizing genius in the room, there would be thirteen votes for McNamara.

From his subdued but never submerged years as Secretary of State, Rusk emerged with no bitterness. He liked to recall from his military days, "Enlisted men have morale problems; not officers." Rusk was an exemplar of that definition of the art of government which said, the problem is to keep power technically and deserve it morally. Rusk survived a roster of at least nineteen aspiring successors and a press commentary which had been patronizing and perfunctory when it was not deprecatory. At the same time, Rusk was surprised and delighted in early 1967 at receiving over 50,000 letters, 85 per cent of which were in approbation, from ordinary citizens for his championship of the United States commitment in Vietnam. He also received requests for at least 5,000 photographs, which his office duly sent out.

In retrospect, he had had an active twenty years since March 1947, when General Marshall brought Colonel Dean Rusk over from the War Department to become the Assistant Chief of the State Department's Division of International Security Affairs. On that day Rusk had been within twenty minutes of having been sworn in as a regular Army officer. He had been slated to become the United States Army's authority on international law. At State, Rusk progressed to become the first Assistant Secretary for International Organizations Affairs, that is, United Nations affairs, and in 1949 he became Deputy Under Secretary of State for Political Affairs, an assignment which consisted in large measure of fighting the Pentagon under Defense Secretary Louis Johnson. In the Korean war, Rusk was asked by Secretary Acheson to take on the trouble-shooting job of Assistant Secretary of State for the Far East, from which Rusk resigned in 1952 to become President of the Rockefeller Foundation.

A veteran professional, Rusk was not one to suffer fools gladly, if he had the choice. He developed his own verbal shorthand for handling time-wasters, a sort of dissembling by a double-cover of clichés. The familiars, in any event, learned to translate. A choice Rusk response to a certain type of proposition was, "I'll turn it over in my mind." The witless eventually found out that Rusk meant, "You are rather an oaf, and wasting my time." But the outer language was invariably courteous and courtly. His immediate aides had to be fast and accurate and speak to the point, or else. . . . Associates marveled at his incredible ability to sum up a complex situation in four minutes flat. His enormous background of expertise allowed Rusk instinctively to coordinate multiple ramifications and to see the spectrum of a problem at a glance. Switching from the crisis in X country to repercussions in Y countries, Rusk was famous in the trade for his rapid synthesis of all possible angles as he made his exposition and recommendations to the President. But in the process, he tried to do too much himself, iron man though he might be, and did not delegate enough priority tasks to his senior colleagues, let alone attempt to monitor their activities, shortfalls, or overreaches.

For a man in the public eye, it was remarkable how the enigma of the Rusk personality baffled and confounded most onlookers. The negative critics still employed such epithets as "a man without a shadow," "impervious," "colorless," "pedestrian," "a loner," and "a prisoner of his own experience" (referring to the World War II China-Burma-India theater and the Korean War), while friendly analysts cited his iron self-control and self-discipline, integrity and character, self-confidence and eloquence, loyalty, incisiveness, and steadfast solidity. Foreign embassies in Washington ranged in their opinions from high respect to sheer admiration, employing such tag lines as "prudent but not timid," "a man of talent, heart, and guts," and "humane, friendly, and sincere." Foreign diplomats testified that Rusk remembered their names, positions, and the contexts of their employment and background, the lowly as well as the high-level, and that he appeared to make a warmer impression on foreigners than he did on his own American colleagues, whom he was accused of keeping at arm's length.

Rusk's candid admission that he modeled himself, as far as possible, on his great former boss as Secretary of State, General Marshall, raised quizzical eyebrows among the sceptics. Rusk admired Marshall's great sense of public duty; his calmness in the midst of crisis; his high standards of performance, which he insisted upon in himself and in his colleagues; his concern for accuracy of detail and the role of precision in diplomacy; and his belief that a man in high office cannot afford to have close or intimate friends or confidantes because friendship and human weakness might get in the way of performing one's impartial duty for the public good and because the personal bias of friendship might influence what should be impersonal standards of public service.

Like Marshall, Rusk disliked windy theorizing. He liked to quote a favorite saying of Marshall's, "Don't ask me to agree on principle. That only means you have not agreed amongst yourselves yet." Rusk liked short, sharp memoranda, what he called "snippets" of information, and ideas of basic character, rather than long, involved, and prolix position papers. Rusk's wife, Virginia, said once that "only small things ever irritate Dean, petty annoyances like taking the short cut that turns out to be the longest way around." The well-masked Rusk irritation sometimes applied to diplomatic colleagues who went around the mulberry bush to explain what they could have done in one tenth the time.

Rusk insisted that it paid to be extremely polite to everyone in the routine of diplomacy, despite the strains and provocations, since underneath, he said, "This is a job that requires ice water in your veins"; that one had to "wait it out," particularly the "awful lot of spinnings of the spider that goes on in this business." Rusk saw much of diplomacy as an "exercise in tedium to talk the inflammation out of the problem," even though in the process there was a lot of pointless chatter. Rusk detested what the French call *"blague solennel,"* or solemn humbug, a characterization which some detractors applied to Rusk's speeches, though to him they were simple statements of fact based on implicit faith in an old-fashioned, pious patriotism redolent of the nineteenth-century atmosphere in which he was reared. Instructively, among his illustrious predecessors, besides Marshall, Rusk most admired Jefferson, John Quincy Adams, and Acheson.

Rusk's very fast and prodigious pace of work sometimes made him appear impatient with colleagues or visitors who spoke or worked or thought very slowly and wandered all over left field during State Department briefings. An apocryphal story has it that Rusk, in the China-India-Burma theater during World War II, learned from a Negro Army sergeant that there is sometimes only one way to talk to a mule: hit him square between the eyes with a two-by-four. Anecdotes of Rusk's deliberately losing his temper and thus verbally smiting his opponent, however, are rare. As was said, the State Department itself was not Rusk's personal top priority. The Secretary's priorities appeared to have been, first, the President and his immediate desires; second, the top operations problems of the current crisis; third, public opinion as reflected in the press, radio, and TV and in the vast inflow of letters from the public; fourth, Congressional opinion; fifth, Rusk's need to be aware, at least, of everything that was going on in the world; and only sixth and last, the routine of the State Department itself. To the experts who came to brief him he sometimes seemed a benign Buddha expressing an amiable scepticism. He insisted that "the State Department policy officers must give an expert his place—but also keep him in it."

Rusk, in his person, was the sharp edge of State Department policy on the major issues of the day, whenever he chose to be. As a polished professional, he was coolly ruthless with subordinates who presented problems to him if they had committed the fatal fault of leaving out what, in his opinion, was the crucial element calling for decision. Time and again, after having patiently listened to an exposition which had been requested for the purpose of making recommendations, he would patiently ask, "And what is it that you want me to do?" He was persistently trying to bring down generalizations to the specific actions necessary at that tactical moment. His succinct manner of expression had certain folkloristic overtones, frequently harking back to his rural experiences as a youth, as when he told Soviet Foreign Minister Andrei Gromyko, in rejecting seeming Russian concessions for the ill-defined Allied rights of access to Berlin, "That would be buying the same horse twice." Or in another rural metaphor, in reference to the United States' not objecting to the Soviet offer of mediation between India and Pakistan at Tashkent in 1965, Rusk said, "They have been biting at our feet the last seventeen years; let them bite at theirs for a change." The metaphorical reference was to hogs.

In intimate converse Rusk had been known to dispose of a picayunish or nonsensical approach to a subject by uttering one four-letter word. Rusk was rated a tough-rough type in negotiations, receiving the epithet from some subordinates as "a combination Metternich-Molotov." Given the inescapable presidential primacy, Rusk had yet to undertake a make-or-break negotiation with a major adversary like the Russians strictly on his own. He had always been, as he would wish, under the remote-control guidance of Presidents Kennedy or Johnson in negotiations over Laos, Berlin, and the Cuban missile crisis, and with the Latin Americans at Punta del Este, in this period of the piecemeal peace.

A compulsive worker, the Secretary concentrated on what he could do, to the exclusion of everything else. He would not waste time on matters that he felt he could do nothing about. This was unlike his former alter ego, Under Secretary George Ball, whose tremendous energy drove him all over the place, taking on all kinds of sticky assignments, which Ball would expound in sweeping generalizations, to the Secretary's mild amusement. Ball's boundless thrust, power of intellect, and infinite good intentions were bound to come to little or nothing in such thorny matters as solving the Kashmir dispute between India and Pakistan, mediating the Cyprus conflict between the Greeks and the Turks, or resolving with Portugal the dilemma between independence for Angola and NATO needs for the Azores Islands way station. But Rusk did not stop Ball from the good old college try, which in the final analysis at least was helpful if not conclusive.

In 1967 the Secretary initiated an informal meeting of his own "Joint Chiefs of Staff," meaning himself, Under Secretary Katzenbach, Under Secretary for Political Affairs Eugene Rostow, and Deputy Under Secretary for Political Affairs Foy Kohler. The four would meet at 6:30 P.M. for a drink in Rusk's office, where they would rehash the worries of the day and indicate a path and an approach for the morrow. Unfortunately, half the time Rusk was not there. He was at the White House, for when the President calls, the State Department swings like a yo-yo at the end of the President's telephone line. Or Rusk was meeting Congressmen and Senators on Capitol Hill, or he was out of the country. As of April 14, 1967, Rusk had traveled a total of 726,200 miles, 527,210 of them in foreign travel to thirty-eight countries and 198,990 in domestic travel, by far more than any other Secretary in history. By January 1968, his total mileage rose to 783,000.

Sipping Scotch at his desk on late afternoons, with his coat off and draped over his chair, Rusk tried to do as much office work as possible alone, making himself go through with it whether he liked it or not, such as the chore of signing letters, a responsibility which he was reluctant to delegate to anyone else. If a letter had his name on it, he wanted to see it and, if necessary, to sign it. His aides let him sign about ten letters a day. Or key functionaries might have had to see him before an important meeting. Rusk would riffle through a twenty-page memorandum, but actually read only the covering memo on top and ask two simple questions: "What's new in this?" and "What should we expect from this meeting?" and close the subject. His staff tried to schedule his first visitor at ten A.M. and one every half-hour thereafter until lunch at one o'clock, the appointment schedule resuming at three. When he felt the world was crowding him a bit inside the State Department, Rusk retired to an Operations Center conference room and sealed himself off from all visitors, and only the President himself could reach him.

Rusk did more listening than talking to his visitors. He made a point of granting requests frequently for visits from foreign ambassadors accredited to Washington in order to help ensure that the United States envoys abroad would likewise be received by the foreign ministers of the countries to which they were accredited. In his conversations with outsiders, Rusk was a classic diplomat of tradition, particularly in speech. The conditional mood seemed to be one of the preferred grammatical forms in the literature of diplomacy. Rusk was a devotee of this style, frequently using locutions like "one would attach . . ." or "I would expect . . ." or, in the phrase that would make State Department press correspondents groan amiably at press conferences, "I would suppose. . . ." The more persons there were in his audience, the more closely he followed his self-imposed policy of "biting the tongue."

In essence, there was no State Department position on an issue until the Secretary himself took a position. The alternately mystifying and infuriating aspect of Rusk's style resulted from his own deliberate reasons: he frequently avoided taking a position. Yet, if he had taken one, he would wrap it up and deliver the message in a cogent vernacular, if among friendlies, or in a precise or deliberately obfuscating formulation, as he deemed wise, among others. In any event, it was in these private sessions that Rusk's real stature emerged unobtrusively and impelled such respect as to lead foreigners to have rated him as the "wisest" of the President's advisers. To the foreign pros, the most satisfying element of the Rusk encounters was that he did not present United States successes as triumphs of good over evil in the world, nor did he exaggerate defeats or setbacks as the end of the world. Rusk's use of understatement had a double-barreled effect when he coolly outlined a specific course of probable American action. Listening thus once to a dispassionate Rusk discourse, a visiting foreign minister rose in alarm and said, "You scare me." Rusk replied, "Well, I did not intend to soothe you."

Rusk applied his oblique humor sometimes to himself, his powerful shoulders shaking in suppressed merriment as if he were satirizing himself.

Rusk's face indeed recalled those of Brueghel (Pieter the Elder), the great sixteenth-century Flemish artist whose brush evoked the poignant grotesqueries of the human countenance. When Rusk bid the Operations Center, "Happy New Year" on December 31, 1966, he added: "Do me a favor: please sweep 1966 under the rug. I've had enough of it." Or his remark to a certain United States Ambassador from a Latin American country at one of the Punta del Este meetings a few years ago. The American Ambassador kept on addressing Secretary Rusk as, "Mr. Dulles." Finally, Rusk asked mildly, "How long does it take for the pouch to reach you?" that is, the diplomatic pouch with official messages from Washington. Or when some flatterer compared Rusk with John Quincey Adams, who was both President and Secretary of State, Rusk replied with a lop-sided grin, "Yes, he was bald, too."

The periodic refrain about Secretary Rusk's reserve and deep-seated defensiveness of mind from time to time succeeded in provoking a comment from Rusk. He stressed that the essence of the diplomatic business was to speak before you think. He told one interviewer: "Sure I get mad, but it's part of my job not to let people know when I'm angry and when I'm not. It's deliberate. It's not that I don't have feelings." Rusk felt the sting of the intellectual upmanship of the Eastern Seaboard academic establishment, which appeared to look down on the attainments of back-water colleges like Davidson College in North Carolina, which Rusk and his father attended, though Davidson is known as "the poor man's Princeton." In private asides, Rusk sometimes deprecated the cant of the eastern intellectuals and their self-conscious accent of assumed superiority. Neither did Rusk believe that the eastern foreign policy establishment, as exemplified by the lordly pretenses of the Council on Foreign Relations in New York, was quite as important and influential in the formulation of United States policy as it thought it was.

Beyond the snap judgments of the metropolitan press in creating the myth of Rusk as a glorified common man was the now-departed world of pre-World War I Americana. In terms of the era of his youth, Rusk was a virtual Horatio Alger of the high bureaucracy, a man from the ante-bellum atmosphere of the twentieth century, who had a visceral faith in America and literally believed the words of the Declaration of Independence that "these truths" are held "to be self-evident." He was a boy who did live on the other side of the railroad tracks, who sat around the ice plant across the railroad tracks watching them make ice while sucking on a sliver of ice, who got a thrill out of the firehouse around the corner and the "wonderful horses pulling the pumping wagons in the middle of night . . . the firemen shoveling coal into the blazing fire to get the pumps started," who, like urban urchins anywhere, foraged around the city dump to "find all sorts of things with which one could make almost anything one could imagine," who up to the sixth grade used to go to school barefoot in the springtime and got into his share of fights just like any other kid, and who when he was only six, heard the famous William Jennings Bryan and Billy Sunday orate in full voice.

To city slickers it might be rather incomprehensible to have Rusk say, as he did in an unprecedented interview over WSB-TV in Atlanta, Georgia, in 1965: "So we had a very stimulating environment in which to live in those days. There was always adventure, always something to fire the imagination."

Rusk's family beginnings were as impecunious gentry in the red-clay countryside of Georgia's Cherokee County amid the rednecks straight out of *Tobacco Road*. The Rusks came over from northern Ireland at the end of the eighteenth century. Dean Rusk's father, Robert Hath Rusk, was first a minister and then a cotton farmer, before ill health drove him to the city to become a mailman in Atlanta. The rural Neanderthals of Georgia must have induced the original psychology of caution and mistrust in Rusk as well as compassion for the lot of the poor Negroes of those days, subject to abuse, exploitation, and lynchings, impressions which lingered in the adult Rusk to make him a fervid believer in the sanctity not of civil rights alone, but of human rights for all races. In that boyhood time Rusk's father built his two-room cottage with his own hands, causing Rusk to remark in later years, "We had to fight for everything we had," and to have sparked the father's advice to the boy, "Pray as if it were up to God; work as if it were up to you."

These old-fashioned attributes of Rusk were startling to the wordly wits of Washington who did not know the consistency of his upbringing. During the period of isolationist America, Rusk, the young debator, espoused the cause of the League of Nations. As a youth, still in high school, he thought of becoming a minister, but had his interests turned to wider fields under the influence of Lord Bryce's *American Commonwealth*. As a boy, even at twelve years of age, he had his eye fixed on becoming a Rhodes scholar, which he finally did in 1931, taking Modern Greats at Oxford, that is, philosophy, economics, and politics. He was a normal American youth—a word which seems out of date and context among the beatniks, hippies, and eccentrics of today—who went through both the junior and senior activities of "Christian Endeavor," was president of the Y.M.C.A., a Lieutenant Colonel in the R.O.T.C., Phi Beta Kappa, and a star center on the varsity basketball team at college, scoring 300 points in three years, the last of the "midget centers," at six-foot-one. One of his teachers, Dr. Preston F. Epp, said that Rusk was "one of those rare persons who seem to have been born mature and confidently adequate to meet any situation which might confront them. I have not met more than five such students in forty-five years of teaching."

The WSB Atlanta interview remains the unique disclosure of Rusk's mainsprings. The quotations which follow speak for themselves.

"Religious dedication," Rusk said, "was a very important part in our own family. We were pretty faithful at Sunday school and midweek prayer meetings. One concentrated a good deal on the Bible, memorizing the Psalms and the shorter Catechism and all those things, because on Sundays there wasn't much else that was proper and so we had a considerable amount of home life built around the church religion when I was young. We did commit a good deal of the Bible to memory and one of the ways to do that is, of course, to read it a lot more than once until you have it under control." Rusk added later, "The Bible is still an important part of the order of things as far as I am concerned."

For a long time the Rusk children never got to see the Sunday funnies until Monday, though, to their annoyance, their neighborhood pals could come over and read them.

From his father Rusk received certain fundamental traits. As Rusk himself said, "a sense of the importance of the difference between right and wrong was something that was before us all the time. There was also a sense of propriety, a sense of constitutional order, a sense of each playing his part in the general scheme of things with a good deal of faith and hope and confidence and a passionate interest in education."

Besides absorbing the precepts of his presbyterial-minister father, Rusk felt deeply the influence of his mother, Elizabeth Frances Clotfelter Rusk. His mother, Rusk said, was "a beautiful woman. They used to call her the best looking girl in Rockdale County. She was a very hard-working woman as any wife of a family in poor circumstances in those days would be. She made most of our clothes. We did our own washing, of course. I have on my front porch now [in Washington] the black wash pot under which I built up hundreds of fires to fire up the family wash. She was interested in music, and had gone to normal school, had done some teaching and strongly reinforced my father's interest in books and learning. I was most fortunate in my family environment there."

The Rusk family's composure under strain was an outstanding characteristic; Rusk said: "We were a rather quiet family without expressing our emotions under any circumstances. This was part of the reticence, perhaps it goes with Calvinism, perhaps it comes from the Scotch-Irish; perhaps it comes with the tough battle of the soil—the family had to wrest a living out of a not-too-productive soil in Cherokee County. There was a certain reticence in the tradition of our families that carried on into our own."

There was a story about Rusk's grandmother's funeral and, though the custom in the South was that the departed were mourned rather loudly, in the Rusks' instance there was no wailing at the bar. Rusk said, "This is not only part of the reticence, it is the general view that God had these things in charge." Rusk confirmed as correct what another member of the Rusk family had said: "We feel it inside."

In the Atlanta interview Rusk said that one of the legends about him, as he himself had thought, was that he had been delivered by a veterinarian. He added: "My sister [Margaret] knows all these things and keeps the record straight and reminded me that I was delivered by Dr. Woodfield of Woodstock, Georgia, so that it wasn't quite as bizarre as I had supposed."

Miss Margaret Rusk, the family authority on the Rusk genealogy, related that the Rusks had emigrated to the United States in the eighteenth century from Londonerry in northern Ireland, while the family origin on the mother's, or Clotfelter, side was a mixture of Scotch, German, and Dutch.

Rusk gets along very well with the Africans, Asians, and Latinos, but is said not to be particularly *simpático* with the continentals of western Europe. He gets along best with the British and their ingratiating manner of making a foreigner feel at home, taking him into the club. Rusk's empathy with the underdeveloped peoples has a direct relevance to his belief that changes and rapid improvements can occur in a democracy. He recalled:

If one goes back fifty years, Cherokee County is what we would call an underdeveloped part of the world. There was very little public health, there was only limited medical care, and very little advanced agricultural technique. I've seen many villages in rural areas in other parts of the world. It is very seldom when you can find one today where typhoid fever is just a part of the environment as it was for us in the beginning there in Cherokee County, where education is so primitive, where the school [which Rusk attended] had exterior walls which were all open with only canvas screens to be pulled up when it rained and we were in the open air, therefore, throughout the year, throughout the winter. This was a tremendous experience which we all very much enjoyed. In the winter time we were enclosed in big woolen sacks that were pulled around you. You brought your hot brick with you in the morning, put it in the bottom of the sack and about every two hours there would be a brief break and you would have hot chocolate.

I have been able to see in my own lifetime how that primitive environment had been revolutionized with education, with technology, with county agents and with electricity, all that helping to take the load off the backs of the people who live there. And when I see this happening in one lifetime, I disregard those who say that underdeveloped countries will need two or three hundred years to develop because I know it isn't true because I have seen it with my own eyes.

As a concomitant to such progress, Rusk told a Reinhart College (Georgia) homecoming that civil rights were a necessary adjunct of foreign policy. He said: "I have felt all my life that the dignity of the individual is at the very heart of our political system in our country, that Constitutional rights are fundamental and, without them, nothing else is very much worthwhile. In the long run, the more I have traveled around the world, the more important these things have become to me."

This special characteristic of embodying in his own person the strains of American history runs all through the Rusk pattern. He could cite both his grandfathers, who fought in the Civil War, and his great-grandmother, who was born in 1776, as echoes of high dramas in the history of the Republic. To his critics, the Rusk philosophy in his speeches seemed a thin translation of the rubrics of civics textbooks. Rusk's deep-seated beliefs are more often to be found in his short and pithy off-the-cuff remarks at occasional events, where his style has been described even by iconoclasts as brilliant, always relevant, and remarkably apt to the event which he had been called upon to celebrate.

Rusk was constantly interested in youth, although to the youth of many metropolitan centers he was a figure to hang in effigy because of the Vietnam war. He repeatedly pointed out that half of the American people do not remember World War II and the events leading up to it. It was particularly challenging to him to meet the questions of youth in an open give-and-take. Small-college audiences were visibly impressed, not only by the scope of Rusk's professionalism but also by the romantic overtones with which he painted the future of the world sprouting from the seeds of the past. Rusk constantly called for a dialogue and mutual respect between the young and the old. He recalled a remark of a preacher he had heard during his boyhood: "Remember when you point your finger at someone else, there are three fingers pointed at yourself."

Rusk's style of plain and unpretentious love of country, as well as his casual and collected approach to discussing the complex fate of the world, came as a surprise to youthful audiences who questioned how he managed to look so composed in the midst of the tornadoes. Rusk replied: "I've lived through a lot of these crises, so I tend not to get excited as a lot of people do. My wife accuses me of having a capacity for accepting the inevitable. I have never known what the alternative is."

Press correspondents who covered Rusk's speeches away from the great cities were frankly mystified at Rusk's ability, despite the hecklers outside, to command the attention of young college audiences. Rusk's knack seemed to lie in picturing the sweep of coming great events and in his direct injunction to the young that it was their responsibility to take charge of the chain of reactions arising out of the disintegration of the colonial empires of the past, the collapse of white global supremacy, the new age of science and technology, the concept of world order, and the rethinking of the usefulness of war as an instrument of national policies. It was a picture of a committed teacher whose words were suffused with the emotion of conviction attempting to make an impression on the unformulated uncertainties of youth.

The Rusk principles of foreign policy as expressed in staff-written speeches are neither numerous nor sensational; they are even deliberately bald and banal, if you will. This exasperates those who would like to learn Rusk's specific intentions. Yet, these same professional colleagues paradoxically admitted that Rusk was an expert in the nuances and procedures of diplomacy, with a high degree of operational relevance, and tactically imaginative. Rusk joked that foreign ministers as a trade union had a recurring responsibility to try to solve issues without the use of military force, and to find "some space" inside the tightly coiling interstices of intensifying crises "for diplomacy." This sentiment he expressed during the Cuban nuclear missile crisis, when he felt that the blockade was preferable as giving "room" to find diplomatic openings.

In the end, the critique seemed to come down to a basic philosophy of operations: whether one rode the ship of state on the currents of the times, trying only to keep it afloat and right side up, or whether one should attempt to ride the currents of history, and pull and push the craft so the ship could take advantage of existing currents. In short, the argument was between the activists' and the passivists' interpretations of history. Rusk appeared to have his own interpretation, that, whenever he could, he preferred to nudge the course of world history, to direct it little by little to where he thought it ought to go, or to resist it when it seemed to be pushing him where he did not wish to go. Rusk's concrete actions were a matter of timing and tactics of the moment, though Rusk had plenty of long-range guidelines. He pointed out, first of all, that foreign policy, in the most profound sense, was built into the nature of the nation, and that most such policy was taken for granted and not articulated. For example, no foreign nation ever doubts that when the United States Government makes an agreement it intends to keep it. From this followed a cardinal Rusk precept: a deep belief in reciprocity. Likewise, the United States preferred peaceful solutions to those of violence, a view which sprang from Rusk's deepest conviction that the survival of the human race was no longer a figure of speech but the number one operational problem for every government in the world.

From such grave concerns followed the corollary that Rusk opposed the football-stadium psychology of public diplomacy, as pressured by mass media communications, which demand to know how each move developed and who won or lost on the play. This, to Rusk, was completely secondary to how the story came out in the end. In a sense, Rusk appeared to believe that foreign policy is a sort of organizational exercise to set the world in order, and to defy those who upset it. Rusk was not of the temperament to give the world order a wholesale shaking, and thus he resisted what he considered premature attempts of his own colleagues to launch initiatives whose ends could not be foreseen. Even more, Rusk resisted attempts at alterations of the world order by foreign powers. Rusk constantly was amazed at faint hearts in the American establishment who failed to remember how close to disaster or defeat the nation would have been time and again, had it not been for steadfast courage and faith in itself. He recalled 1942, before the invasion of North Africa, when the fortunes of the Allies were at their lowest ebb; or the winter of 1948 in Berlin, when the airlift was in doubt; or 1947 in Greece, when the Communist guerrillas were only thirty miles from Athens; or 1948, when the Communist Huks were in the suburbs of Manila. This resistance to foreign encroachment, instead of quick accommodation, exposed Rusk to the charge of what the French call *"flottement"* and *"immobilisme,"* a "do-nothing" policy. Rusk insisted that when the chips were down, on interests vital to the United States, negotiations were simply not in order. The United States did not negotiate on Berlin in 1961, nor on Cuba in 1962, nor on Greece in 1947. He deplored the notion that when critical problems arose, the tendency was hastily to divide the problem, a procedure which he defined as an agreement to participate in Communist salami tactics of crowding, crowding while gaining objectives a slice at a time.

In the overriding necessity of the human race today to organize the peace, whether it be a new balance of power or an idealistic turn toward world government, Rusk insisted that what he called "the forces of consent" must prevail, so that any new arrangements would be self-enforcing. To allow the "forces of coercion" to win out would mean that the defeated party thus coerced would retain a built-in irredentism in its national objectives, a harbinger of woe for a future date.

To arrive at his conception of a world of independent states, run by the consent of the governed, Rusk cited five general desiderata for United States foreign policy as part of a continued process: One, deterring aggression at any level, to keep changes in the world order from falling prey to violence. Two, developing closer relations between the United States and western Europe and Japan, as the growing power of the Far East. Three, helping the underdeveloped countries survive their independence in conformity with their own needs. Four, assisting the world community to multiply normal contacts and activities wherever possible. And five, encouraging, promoting, and achieving as much measure of disarmament as possible through the nonproliferation treaty, nuclear test ban, control of the ABM and ICBM defensive and offensive missile systems. On the surface, these objectives might be termed an updating of Lord Palmerston's nineteenth-century Concert of Europe.

But there was yet more. Rusk fervently believed that the dynamics of the United States experience were a revolutionary explosive force, that the experimentation which has taken place, and is taking place, in the United States since the American Revolution, its constant probing, is a living formula that can be matched by none of the ideological revolutions of the past. Rusk had faith that the American people have allies all over the world, and in places least expected, and that this common effort of the American republic moves with the flow of history, because the aspirations of all peoples are basically the same in trying to attain and enjoy the fruits of civilization and peaceful human intercourse.

CHAPTER VII

THE PRESIDENT:
The Nation's Gyroscope

A USEFUL INDICATOR OF THE function of the President in foreign policy may be noted in the dictionary definition of a gyroscope:

An apparatus consisting of a rotating wheel so mounted that its axis can turn freely in certain, or all, directions, and capable of maintaining the same absolute direction in space in spite of the movements of the mountings and surrounding parts. Its motion is based upon the principle that a body rotating rapidly on an axis will tend to resist a disturbing change or torque (twisting movement) by rotating slowly in the direction perpendicular to that of the disturbance.*

A number of examples come to mind in application of this gyroscopic metaphor to the function of a President in keeping the nation on the level and progressing in the direction in which the national will, as symbolized in the person and the institution of the Presidency, may direct, given the political climate and circumstances of foreign turbidity as limiting factors.

The Constitution of the United States in no place explicitly states that the President has direction of foreign policy. His powers are directly implied by the definition in Article II, Section 2, Paragraph 2, in which he is empowered to make treaties and to appoint ambassadors, with the advice and consent of the Senate; and Paragraph 3 of the same Section, which instructs the President to receive ambassadors. In no place in the Article concerning the Presidency is the word "foreign" stated, though the word "foreign" appears three times in Article I, dealing with the Congress: in Section 8, Paragraph 3, empowering the Congress to regulate commerce with foreign states; in Paragraph 5, empowering the Congress to regulate the value of foreign coins, that is, in relation to United States coinage; and in Section 10, Paragraph 3, prohibiting any state from making agreements

* From *The Random House Dictionary of the English Language*. © Copyright 1966, 1967 by Random House, Inc. Reprinted by permission.

with a foreign power. Once more "foreign" is mentioned in the Constitution, in Article III, Section 2, Paragraph 1, dealing with the judiciary, in which the courts are authorized to declare on treaties and cases affecting ambassadors and cases between citizens of states and foreign states. As it develops, the executive authority as expressly stated in the Constitution is ambiguously divided and, in actuality, the responsibility is more or less shared in matters which by inference deal with foreign affairs.

Over and above these specific citations, the President, as a symbol of the national sovereignty and the Chief Executive of an independent nation, becomes the residual depository of all the possible powers that accrue to an independent and sovereign nation, and, again by inference, any power not specifically denied is inherently in the possession of the President, to exercise as far as his reach can stretch, or as political conditions in the Congress may restrain him. In short, the sky is the limit theoretically, save for the concrete configuration of the practical moment.

The President of the United States has been called the "highest temporal power on earth." He has been compared to a medieval monarch, almost absolute in time of war and in normal times a combination of king and prime minister. In the ultimate instance, the power of the President is the power to act. In many instances of foreign policy, moreover, Presidents act first and rationalize later. With the spawning of the nuclear age, the concentration of authority in the President spotlights the imperative necessity of acting almost immediately, or within hours and minutes, at the imminence of possible thermonuclear threats that can mushroom into crises from minor conflicts in any place in the world. Whereas once the isolated character of such happenings meant little or nothing, today a faraway incident may converge with several other factors and become the spark to ignite unstable elements of latent hostility into fission in racing fractions of time. This imposes upon the President the necessity to move with utmost celerity and, hence, specifically implies that he must have the power so to act. The axiom that foreign policy and defense policy today are indivisible means that the policy that the President has to determine is a national security policy and that the presidential power to decide can in no wise be delegated. Whenever the issue is truly important, the President himself must get into it personally. He alone must set the priorities among rival claims for his attention and make the final judgment on which issue is the overriding one to decide or to choose among alternative courses of action.

As Secretary Rusk wrote concerning the Presidency in the June 1960 *Foreign Affairs Quarterly* before the Kennedy election:

> The President is clearly in charge of foreign policy. This is not only a Constitutional responsibility: it is a political necessity, for it is he who mobilizes political support in the country and in the Congress. In brief, the President

is the Chief Executive of everything, but of foreign policy above all. He has the total responsibility for the amalgam of domestic and foreign policy as it relates to the nation at large, and the same total responsibility for the nation as it relates to the world at large.

Illustrative of the cardinal importance of foreign policy in the early days of the Republic is the fact that six Secretaries of State became President— Thomas Jefferson, James Madison, James Monroe, John Quincy Adams, Martin Van Buren, and James Buchanan. In more recent times, the almost overwhelming surge of foreign affairs as a dominant concern of the Presidency is evident from the record—FDR with World War II and the UN; Truman with the aftermath of the war and Potsdam, the atom bomb over Hiroshima, Azerbaijan, Greek and Turkish aid, the Truman Doctrine, the Marshall Plan, Point IV, and Korea, not to mention the Palestine war and emergence of the state of Israel. With President Eisenhower, there were the Lebanon-Iraq crisis, Quemoy-Matsu, the Suez and Hungarian crises, the ultimatum over Berlin, the Khrushchev visit, and the 1960 summit collapse over the U-2 incident. With President Kennedy, there were the continuing Berlin crisis, the Cuban nuclear crisis, the Chinese attack on India, the nuclear test ban, Laos, Vietnam, and the beginnings of the NATO crisis. And with President Johnson, there were again Vietnam, the Dominican Republic crisis, Laos, Thailand, Indonesia, the NATO crisis, the Middle East, and, not to be forgotten, the Indo-Paskistani war and Cyprus. In every case in the last two decades, every major foreign affairs crisis skyrocketed from the State Department to the White House level to become the personal concern of the President.

While there hardly has been a President of the United States who has not left an imprint of some character on United States foreign policy, strong Presidents have invariably tended to act as their own Secretaries of State, from President Washington on down to President Johnson today. President Jefferson was responsible for the first major commercial treaty, that with Britain, and he personally handled the vexing question of impressment of American seamen by the British Navy. President Andrew Jackson acted personally by seizing French property in an attempt to force France to pay its debt to the United States, an early instance which showed that the President was absolutely supreme whenever he wished to assume specific direction of a situation. In the 1880's, Secretary of State James G. Blaine said, "Foreign affairs, in their inception and management, are exclusively executive, and nothing decisive can be done in that field except with the President's personal knowledge and official approval."

There was the notoriously strong foreign policy stance of President Theodore Roosevelt in building the Panama Canal. President Woodrow Wilson handled the Versailles Peace Treaty with minimum assistance from the State Department. President Franklin Delano Roosevelt was the extreme example of a President taking over the role of Secretary of State when he felt so inclined, pulling the rug out from beneath the State Department in whatever initiatives it took, not even inviting the State Department to participate in his momentous conferences abroad at Casablanca, Cairo, Tehran, and Yalta, and in the end prohibiting the State Department from attempting to plan for the peace. Even in the halcyon days of the State Department under Secretary Acheson, President Truman was strong-minded enough to assert that there could be no delegations of authority by the President for decisions of state and that "a President must use whatever power the Constitution does not expressly deny him in helping to meet the issues of foreign policy."

The Secretary of State, in bare truth, is a creature of the President's whim. He is neither more nor less than the President allows him to be. Since every President views the Secretary of State and the State Department in his own individual way, every change of administration has to alter the pitch of the propellers before the giant aircraft of state can take off into the foreign air. Rusk described the Secretary of State's job as that of flying a four-motor plane, whose four engines are the Secretary's relationship with the President, the Congress, the Department, and the press and public. Johnson made it a 707-jet, but in the 1967 days of Vietnam emotions he felt that everybody was hitting him, shoving a needle into him, making it difficult for him to fly the plane.

The Secretary of State's role had been defined by Rusk as that of "the President's chief adviser, his chief arm in formulating and carrying out foreign policy. The Secretary must do his best to see to it that the President's views on policy are impressed on the whole administration. This is not done by issuing directives but by keeping in close touch with all departments—Defense, Commerce, Treasury—whose work has bearings on foreign policy."

The Secretary must reflect at all times the views of the President, particularly if he is a strong President with strong views, as almost all Presidents in this century have been. The Secretary's subordinate but cardinal role in relation to the President creates several built-in conflicts in the Secretary's functions as the principal presidential adviser, manager of a huge bureaucracy, head negotiator, principal expositor of foreign affairs policy to the citizens, and leading advocate of administration foreign policy to Congress. Rusk, however, at no time ever thought of himself as an alter ego to the President in foreign policy. At the same time the special relationship of the Secretary to the President impelled Rusk, as it had Secretary Dulles with Eisenhower, to keep his personal counsels to the President direct, private, and personal, and, if need be, out of earshot of the White House staff.

For the organization of professional Foreign Service officers under the Secretary, the dependence on the President necessitates a constant shifting of gears to keep in speed with every new President, in order to be able to function effectively, while lesser bureaucrats of the Department tend to use this never-cut umbilical cord as an excuse to sit on their hands and pass the buck to the White House. In press coverage of foreign policy, covering the State Department exclusively cannot fail to result in incomplete or distorted reportage. Therefore, it is automatic for all correspondents who aspire to complete understanding of a foreign policy situation to cover both the State Department and the White House, so as to give a true picture of United States initiatives or reactions to foreign events.

Every President operates in the field of foreign policy according to his unique character, personality, experience, and style. Whether publicly vague as in Eisenhower or bright as in Kennedy, style, however, is for the birds when it comes down to the hard, vital issues of national interest and substance.

Eisenhower, in the election campaign of President Kennedy, was identified as presiding over a do-nothing and static administration, a canard that has persisted. Yet, as a foreign policy leader at least, Eisenhower has been sold short for too long. Eminent subordinates still in the diplomatic business attest that he conducted National Security Council meetings seriously and effectively and arrived at sensible conclusions. There was little doubt in the Eisenhower administration that the President had all the reins in his hands and could pull them whenever he desired to, and actually did so. Eisenhower took full personal command of U.S. foreign policy in April 1959, when cancer forced Secretary Dulles to resign. Eisenhower could play the role of Commander-in-Chief, the man in top charge, to perfection, from the habits of wartime. He was able to handle his military brass when it came to a showdown better than President Kennedy or President Johnson could, even with the help of McNamara. The seeming inarticulate incoherence of the Eisenhower press conferences did not distract those who knew him from the hard fact that Eisenhower's instincts and foreign policy judgments were first-class. The partisan depreciation of Eisenhower overlooks his 1945 London Guild Hall speech, when he called for European unity, a worthy forerunner of President Kennedy's speech in July 1963 on Atlantic unity; his 1953 speech before the United Nations on atoms-for-peace; his revolutionary open-skies proposal at the 1955 Geneva Summit Conference; and his 1954 decision not to intervene in Indo-China.

A vivid example of the Eisenhower foresight was expressed to this writer in an interview with Eisenhower when he was Commander-in-Chief at SHAPE in Paris in November 1951. He had just returned from the

United States, where he had gone to testify for NATO appropriations before the Congress and had contemporaneously been tendered presidential bids by both the Democratic and Republican parties. Eisenhower's public relations officers at SHAPE decreed that no politics were to be discussed with General Eisenhower. So, Eisenhower, his legs stretched comfortably on the coffee table, amiably discussed what the foreign policy of a President ought to be, while the U.S. Army Brigadier General-escort officer also present played a nervous tattoo on the arms of his chair. Eisenhower at that time defined coexistence at least two years before the term was coined by Soviet Premier Malenkov in Moscow. The United States, Eisenhower said, would build up to a military parity from the U.S. nadir at the outset of the Korean war in 1950. The Free World would win in the end because of the ineffectiveness of the Communist system to meet the pressing needs of the world's humanity.

Eisenhower had more personal advance experience in the nuts and bolts of national security policy, that is, the mix of foreign policy and defense strategy, than any other President, before or since, thanks to his World War II and postwar background. From organizing NATO, he drew the conclusion that his European job had been 70 per cent political and 30 per cent military. He learned from his European tours of duty that the office of the Presidency in this nuclear and global age of foreign policy needed an efficient presidential agency to coordinate an administration's myriad activities in the foreign field. This was his rationale for placing so much trust in the structure of the National Security Council, which, in a measure, was a partial copy of what the Europeans had been using for a long time, that is, the Office of the Presidency of the Council, a fairly elaborate office serving only the Prime Minister or Chief Executive of a nation. In Europe, Eisenhower learned further that the legislative and executive branches of government had been at loggerheads for decades, with the legislative eroding the powers of the executive. The opposite trend had been evident in the United States since the FDR administration. Eisenhower moved to fight and beat the Bricker Amendment by one vote in 1954, when it threatened the powers of the Presidency. The Bricker Amendment would patently have constricted the President's scope in foreign affairs. Eisenhower was the leader in the battle for creation of the European Defense Community, on the sound grounds that the EDC would create a political community to supervise military affairs, whereas the later MLF, or multilateral nuclear force, would only aspire to that end eventually. Eisenhower had the guts to give a clear "yes" or "no" during the heat of grave issues. He denied the U.S. military permission to atom-bomb Communist China during the 1958 Quemoy-Matsu crisis. He agreed to replace the rebel planes which had been destroyed in the anti-Communist guerrilla attempt to take over Guatemala in June 1954, rather than see the effort collapse. Politically and ethically, the Eisenhower character was reflected in two other incidents: When he overruled his subordinates and took full responsibility for knowledge of the U-2 flight over Russia in May 1960, because the simple fact was that he had authorized the flights four years before. Eisenhower knew for two full years from his U-2 flight reports the truth about the so-called missile gap, which the Democratic Party was beating to death against the Republicans in the 1960 campaign and which, as McNamara said in his first press conference, never existed. But Eisenhower never disclosed his secret knowledge, even for his party's benefit.

A Soviet commentator said in 1967 that "seizing power is poetry, but running a country is prose. Mao Tse-tung's trouble is that he persisted in being a poet." In a wild analogy, the same remark might be applied to Eisenhower's successor, President Kennedy, a man of catalytic charm and the casual air of a prince. President Kennedy's advent on the national scene created a sense of spaciousness, shot through with imaginative possibilities and hopes of an iridescent future. He broke the mold of the postwar reigning classes and brought exhilaration to his participating cohorts. The Kennedy air of gallantry and wry mannerism suffused with a nascent radiance the liberated dreams of Americans who felt that perhaps the moment had truly come when buried desires could be spun into living realizations. But as life eroded illusions, the brio of the beginning tended to turn tinkly. Camelot and culture subsided into staid rote as rhetoric fell to realism and Alexander the Great appeared to change into Demosthenes. Historians will find it difficult to trace the true lineaments of the Kennedy administration performance as an incomplete art form. In the heavy wash of the post-Dallas hagiography, Kennedy was all but canonized. Legends accumulate around the dead President like a halo. This writer has met persons who whisper the belief that President Kennedy is "still alive," but "paralyzed and they don't let anybody see him."

To many on-lookers, Kennedy gave the appearance of acting a role, the role of President of the United States, and acting it with grand flair and dash. It was not Franklin Roosevelt being completely at home in the Presidency as if he and it were made for each other and were, in fact, one and the same thing. Kennedy, in contrast, gave the appearance of a temporary passage across the stage, leaving the effulgent afterglow of a great actor. Insufficient elucidation comes from the memorialists of the Kennedy court, the alter egos of power. Between the elegy and the *apologia pro vita sua,* the ancient observation re-emerges that kings are never criticized, but only fallible advisers and cronies. As with every presidential administration when it settles down, power magnifies the vices and dilutes the virtues. Kennedy, upon becoming President, inevitably had to consider his presence on a global stage. He more than once remarked that a domestic failure could be harmful to the country but that a foreign policy failure could be fatal.

In the foreword to *Decision-Making in the White House,* by his aide, Theodore C. Sorensen, Kennedy recalled a remark of President Franklin Roosevelt that President Lincoln "was a sad man because he couldn't get it all at once. And nobody can." President Kennedy continued, "Every President must endure a gap between what he would like and what is possible." Kennedy wrote further: "The loneliness of a President is another well-established truism. . . . No one in the country is more assailed by divergent advice and clamorous counsel. . . . [A] wise President therefore gathers friends, strength, and insight from the nation. Still, in the end, he is alone. There stands the decision—and there stands the President."

Kennedy started out his administration by determining to be his own Secretary of State and by finding a man for the titular position who would work in complete consonance with his ideas and never be a rival in this crucial field. Kennedy set up his White House staff under McGeorge Bundy with the patent intent to call the signals in foreign policy. This delusion was finally shredded because not enough advance attention had been paid to the operating machinery which would execute the ideas of the brilliant galaxy of braintrusters gathered in the White House. Streamlining top-level foreign policy decision-making was also impelled by the desire that all major action-oriented decisions in foreign policy should be directly attributable to the President himself as the prime instigator, and thus enhance his stature and prestige and give evidence of his personal greatness. The OCB, or Operations Coordination Board, was eliminated and the NSC, or National Security Council, was downgraded. Both these cumbersome organizations unnecessarily delayed and impeded the speed of the presidential progress. Their wool padding dampened and deadened the effect of presidential spontaneity of command in foreign policy acts and pronouncements, detracting from the uniqueness of the President's individual role.

Kennedy's illusion in thinking that he could physically be his own Secretary of State immediately produced a further miscalculation. The President and his associates did not appear to attach sufficient importance to the continuity of policy in foreign affairs. Kennedy was irritated about the problems he had inherited from the past. There seemed an innocent pipedream in the Kennedy circle that the world had been born afresh, with a clean slate, just because their favorite candidate had been elected President of the United States. The lapse in apprehending the necessity of continuity appeared less obvious at first. In 1958, the U.S. Senate Foreign Relations Committee under the Democratic majority had authorized and published a fat volume of authoritative studies, analyzing in detail the shortcomings and shortfalls of the Eisenhower Republican administration. In 1960, after the electoral victory, a series of Kennedy task forces gathered facts and pointed up solutions to current problems. When President Kennedy and his team did take over in January 1961, it was not quite the same thing at all. In essence, the three years' critique of the past was already out of date. The world had kept on whirling. Events had subtly, drastically, or suddenly changed, as the Kennedy men found to their dismay. It had looked different from the outside; it was not the same as being on the inside. President Kennedy's own wry wit summed it up best: "When we got into office, the thing that surprised me most was to find that things were just as bad as we'd been saying they were."

There was the case of having prepared for the Laos crisis a month before the inauguration but of not having realized the importance of Vietnam until a month later. There was the passionate desire of the President to immerse himself in all the details, titillating lowly bureaucrats in the State Department with personal calls at all hours of the day and night for particular views. But the President had not yet had time to develop a scope and a spectrum to position individual views in their proper context and weight. There was JFK's service as a virtual desk officer for Latin America in the spring of 1962. Kennedy associates wanted to support left-wing, or left-of-center, political groupings in Latin America without knowing or realizing that the non-Communist left everywhere in the world was ill-organized, impotent, or inept as a base from which to launch a revolution. To make a revolution one had to be a thoroughgoing uprooting radical. There was a desperate search for bright expediters and action men, men who had both ideas and capacity for action. There was disillusionment. When Ralph Dungan, the principal Kennnedy bureaucracy watcher, sounded out a crack trouble-shooter in the State Department for possible service in the White House, he asked whether the elite technician had any new ideas for the President. The technocrat replied, "What does he need? What does the President want me to do?" The expectation seemed to be that an idea and a policy, like Siamese twins, would fly out, ready to function, from Zeus' head. There was the love affair with the British, notably Harold Macmillan, whose sonorous double-talk and circumlocutions, like those of a watered-down Churchill, fascinated the President, though history in Britain had marked Macmillan as "Mr. Ambiguity," the man who fuzzed things over until you couldn't tell the difference and fudged things up so it didn't make any difference. This was an art which President Kennedy, as a practicing politician, must have been inordinately envious of.

There were outbursts against the press over leaks in policies about Europe and anti-Diem coverage in Vietnam. Though his complaints were not as public and plaintive as those of his successor, President Johnson, Kennedy was just as vigorous in expression. Kennedy was as adept in the salty language of a sailor as LBJ is in a ranch hand's vocabulary. President Kennedy could say, like many politicians, but with some justification, "I used to be a newspaperman myself." He was, actually, for International News Service, after World War II for some months in a specialized head-line-celebrity capacity, a mode which the Hearst organization was skilled at in its heyday. This background gave Kennedy a feel for the routine of the newspaper business. He was an expert Monday-morning quarterback at reading news copy, despite his unfair advantage of knowing slightly more of the inside than the poor reporter could find out on the outside. President Eisenhower also liked to blue-pencil copy on stories which he had given favored correspondents and which he had demanded to see and "correct" before publication, when he was Commander-in-Chief at SHAPE in Paris.

Kennedy appeared to be a man of conservative instincts, despite the der-ring-do of some of his intellectual paladins. The constraint of caution tightened perhaps into traumatic hesitation as a result of his narrow, 100,000, majority in the 1960 election. Illustrative is the recollection of this writer who covered both Kennedy and his Republican opponent, Vice President Richard M. Nixon. In the very last two weeks before the election, Nixon was beginning to slope upwards, and in the two weeks before that Kennedy was beginning to coast slightly downwards. But Kennedy had enough of a lead, from the two years in which he had been running fast, to flash across the finish line first. Kennedy took his victory with a cool insouciance, as if the events were happening to somebody else.

Unlike Winston Churchill, who used to say he needed only a majority of one to act as if he had a majority of a hundred, Kennedy seemed to allow this thin edge of victory to weave him between underaction and overreaction. There was the underaction of not putting the machinery of government exhaustively through the wringer after the Bay of Pigs affair. This was compensated for by overreaction in the Berlin crisis, when his senior subordinates in Europe felt that he had "overinsured" the situation by calling up the reserves and pledging the dispatch of six divisions for the defense of Berlin and NATO. Eventually he sent over 37,000 troops. Historians may speculate on whether the heightening of the Berlin crisis led to the counter overreaction by Soviet Premier Khrushchev in trying to implant nuclear missiles in Cuba in the fall of 1962. There was apparent underaction in Kennedy's acceptance of the military analysis made by General Maxwell D. Taylor in South Vietnam in October 1961. Taylor had recommended that the Korean-style standup army, bugles, and banners, stationed against the North Vietnamese potential enemy at the 17th parallel, be redeployed to meet the Communist insurgency. This Taylor succeeded eventually in having partially done, but only on the style of the Greek army's static defense in fixed position in cities in the early stages of the Greek war in 1947, instead of restructuring the South Vietnamese army into mobile battalions and constabulary that would fan out and root out the Viet Cong before they multiplied like dragon teeth.

The apogee of the Kennedy foreign affairs renown in the military-diplomatic victory of the Cuban nuclear missile crisis might also be analyzed as a mixed bag of properly balanced action, underaction, and overaction. This was indicated in a crisis post-mortem by Walt Rostow and Paul Nitze in February 1963. Kennedy recalled the difficulty of spotting the S.S. *Santa María* in 1961, with a Portuguese rebel leader aboard, and the inability of the Brazilian Air Force to find the vessel. Whereupon Kennedy ordered the U.S. fleet units to be doubled for the blockade that was being organized against Cuba. The possible charge of overreaction in mobilizing a tremendous array of U.S. armed might, topped by a public threat of nuclear action against the Soviets, is based on the premise that the Soviets would not risk World War III for territorial or political gain in a place so far from their home bases and because of the obvious vulnerability of their supply lines. Hence, diplomatic means might have been effective in calling Khrushchev's bluff. The charge of underaction is based on the fact that the number of Soviet troops in Cuba, estimated at 22,000, was never brought publicly into dispute. In fact, news of the Russian forces in Cuba transpired almost a month later. The crisis did not affect the power of Castro in Cuba, which may point the moral that there are no victories in "ultimate" confrontations. In short, the post-mortem brought home the lesson that the nation's defense had need of a wider run of conventional-forces options, so that such early recourse to the nuclear threat could be avoided, hopefully, in the future. Also instructive were the points that U.S. intentions should have been made clearer, to the Russians, which, in turn, led to the conclusion that an immediate communications capability had to be established. The Moscow-Washington teletype "hot line" was one consequence.

The greatest disappointment of the Kennedy foreign policy was without question Vietnam. As Arthur Schlesinger, Jr., said in *A Thousand Days,* "No doubt, he [Kennedy] realized that Vietnam was his great failure in foreign policy, and that he had never really given it his full attention."

Kennedy was virtually a helpless Cassandra about Vietnam, particularly in his insight into the Laos question and the control of the eastern part of that country by the Pathet Lao under the tutelage of the North Vietnamese. He knew that the use of the Ho Chi Minh trail by the North Vietnamese would be the path of escalation for increasing United States forces in South Vietnam. He realized that inevitable failure or delay in stemming the tide down the Ho Chi Minh trail would prompt demand for bombing of North Vietnam. In other words, infiltration was a built-in ladder of rationales for greater United States involvement, as Roger Hilsman said. On the Vietnam issue, Kennedy discarded the counsel of two of his favorite intellectuals concerning the Presidency. Richard E. Neustadt's counsel was to use power to gain or enhance presidential popularity. That of Sidney Hyman was to plunge into the thick of the issue and expend presidential popularity in order to resolve issues of vital purport.

Kennedy was always conscious of the possible eventual necessity of taking military action in South Vietnam. He was prepared to strike at North Vietnam in March 1963, when the Pathet Lao were on the Plaine de Jarres and 3,000 American troops were on the alert to move in if the Pathet Lao persisted to the Mekong River. However, he did not want to get locked into a land war in Laos because of the long overground communications and arms supply. He would have preferred in the end to take military action from the sea side of the peninsula, that is, Vietnam. Again, in August 1963, three months before his death, Kennedy told Graham Martin, later to become Ambassador to Thailand, that he was prepared to use U.S. military forces to contain the Viet Cong and the North Vietnamese threat in South Vietnam. But he seemed to feel that he could pull it off with minimum force, being assured by Defense Secretary McNamara that it could be so done. The "advisory" forces grew from 600-plus in 1961 to 11,000 in 1962, to 16,000 in 1963. The advisers were authorized in 1963 to fire back at an enemy if fired upon. The McNamara assurances that the war in Vietnam could be contained were based on the high repute of McNamara as a "can-do" man who could deliver on his word. As late as October 1963, McNamara maintained his optimistic predictions about the Vietnam war. He asserted that by the end of 1964 and the beginning of 1965 at least 1,000 U.S. military forces could begin to be withdrawn from South Vietnam, though William H. Sullivan, presently Ambassador to Laos, tried to dissuade him from making the statement.

Kennedy's frustration over Vietnam was also a consequence of the Kennedy ambivalence about McNamara, a man of personal sweetness and private culture, his dour public mien and forbidding official competence notwithstanding. McNamara was hard to overrule, particularly when he embarked on a steamroller flight down a runway of facts and inexorably logical conclusions. McNamara's insistence that the Vietnam problem required a military solution was buttressed by the Joint Chiefs of Staff and by the acquiescence of Secretary Rusk who, not specifically allocated primary responsibility for the Vietnam problem, deferred to the judgment of the competent military minds who held the responsibility. Kennedy's almost sole bureaucratic ally for his own doubts concerning the McNamara approach was Roger Hilsman, Assistant Secretary for Far Eastern Affairs. Hilsman insisted that the only effective solution to the Vietnam war was an American–South Vietnamese investment in counterinsurgency. The British, after their experience in Malaya, agreed with Hilsman on the technique of counterinsurgency against the Viet Cong. The difficulty with the Hilsman approach was in the lack of the political backstopping necessary for the success of a counterinsurgency movement. That lay in the inadequacy of the Diem Government to provide either an efficient authoritarian apparatus or a grass-root emotional motivation to create the impetus and atmosphere only within which counterinsurgency could be a success.

Amid proposals and counterproposals, President Kennedy became a Hamlet, whose

> . . . native hue of resolution
> Is sicklied o'er with the pale cast of thought;
> And enterprises of great pitch and moment,
> With this regard, their currents turn awry
> And lose the name of action.

It was a time of despondency, seen in retrospect and even noted at the time, for President Kennedy, as the weeks and days inexorably ticked by toward his assassination. It was the time, in September 1963, when this writer asked Sorensen at the White House about the criticism concerning the President, ironic after the brief and high euphoria of the nuclear test ban treaty accord six weeks before: "When is the President going to do something about the ankle-snappers?"—the critics who were pinpricking Kennedy. Sorensen answered that he and the President had been discussing precisely that situation and the necessity of meeting the criticism that very morning. A week later, Kennedy made a notable speech at the University of Washington in which he spoke of United States leadership by example, of cultivating the American garden at home, of the problems of the Negroes, poverty, jobs, and education. This was the period when civil rights leaders in New York grieved to the writer that President Kennedy appeared to be stagnating in a strange mood of inertia and ineffectiveness, that he seemed to lack the will to put out his hand and grasp the handle which opened the door to action—and fame. Only 37 out of his 405 legislative requests to Congress had been approved. His rating in the Gallup poll had slipped to 55 per cent. It was in those same days that the gathering atmosphere impelled the writer, upon an irrational impulse, to jot down in a file being kept on President Kennedy:

> He will become great—or be assassinated.

On November 2, 1963, President Diem of South Vietnam died in the
coup which the Americans knew was coming, could not predict the outcome
of, and did nothing to prevent. There was no evidence at that time of the
possibility being canvassed that Diem's disappearance from South Vietnam
would remove the one symbol of national unity and authority which, for
better or worse, held that nation together against Communist insurgency.
Captured Communist documents tell of Communist glee that the Americans
had allowed this to happen, to have had thus removed in one rattle
of gunfire their principal antagonist and rival for allegiance of the Vietnamese people. With the passing of Diem, the infrastructure that he and his
brother, Nu, had built up no longer had a base or nutriment. It eroded,
crumbled, and disappeared, and into the vacuum moved the Viet Cong.
Hanoi accelerated its infiltration of North Vietnamese cadres and then of
regular troops to take over. South Vietnam, like an overripe apple, was
ready to fall into Communist hands with a moderately good shaking.

Almost three weeks later, on November 22, gunfire ended President Kennedy's life. It was unbearable pathos and ironic tragedy. The difference between the pathetic and the tragic may be defined as the degree of expend-
ability of the human being so weighed. In the heartless and callous world
of government, Kennedy may well have been expendable. But in the hearts
of men engraved with the legend of the golden prince in the fairy tale, he
who has nobility of aspiration is never expendable and the death of dreams
in human souls is forever tragic and irreplaceable. Prince Hal never became
Henry the Fifth.

The apotheosis of President Kennedy, whose trailing nimbus lingered on
into the public ambiance of 1968, necessarily made it a hard act for President Johnson to follow. Invidious comparisons between JFK and LBJ have
resulted in greater vilification of Johnson than of any President since FDR
drew down surly snarls from the Union Clubs and Harvard Clubs of the
nation a generation ago. If the Kennedy adulators tended to lift JFK into
Butler's *Lives of the Saints,* the Johnson denigrators were inclined to dump
LBJ into Suetonius' *Lives of the Caesars.* What both Presidents shared
in foreign policy was a time of history that had progressed beyond the
choice of a good life, as in the past, to the necessity of survival as a nation.
The advent of the atomic age created new definitions of power for the
American President. President Truman had been described as having experienced for the first time the new dimensions of power; President Eisenhower as one who made reluctant use of power; President Kennedy as one
who experimented with the limitations of power; and President Johnson as
one who is experimenting with responsible extensions of power.

The fact that the silvery litheness of the Kennedy stance, almost like a bas-relief sculpture, has given way to the dusty posture of the workaday world under Johnson only underscores the inextricable closeness of the Kennedy-Johnson succession. President Johnson freely dwells on the Kennedy myth for rationalizing and supporting his own necessities of behavior. He said in Los Angeles in June 1967, "John Kennedy promised to get America moving again—and he did it." Kennedy is cited as a precedent for the Vietnam commitment. In June 1967, the Kennedy statement about supporting Israel from an attack by the Arabs, made in May 1963, was cited by Johnson aides in support of presidential policies in the Middle East. The Kennedy acolytes tended to disparage Johnson attainments. The Johnson entourage stressed the similarities between Kennedy's and Johnson's working styles and operational premises: Both were strong men. Both were highly political. Both took keen personal interest and responsibility in detail. Both were voracious readers of memoranda. Johnson is not a book reader; Kennedy was. Kennedy devoured half a dozen newspapers and a couple dozen magazines; President Johnson reads only the *Washington Post,* the *New York Times,* and the *Baltimore Sun* regularly, with a scattering sample of clippings from other newspapers, and *Time* and *Newsweek.* One publication he reads every day without fail is the *Congressional Record,* a habit formed in his years in Congress. Both Presidents consulted many individuals outside official channels as a corrective to views of the official establishment, even in the foreign affairs field. Both men instinctively shared a common viewpoint of the nation's necessities because only Kennedy and Johnson together were strong enough as a team to have gotten elected on the Democratic ticket in 1960, as was evident even before the political conventions in the summer of that year.

Johnson no longer boiled over as publicly as he used to at cracks about the LBJ "eucalyptus rub" or the "Byzantine atmosphere" in the White House, though he retained a deep distrust of the press. He still growled occasionally at the reappearance of old canards, declaring that although certain tales were old, they were not necessarily true. In nearly four years, President Johnson has become disillusioned and philosophical about, if not acquiescent to, the vagaries and aberrations of the press, as had Kennedy in three. Kennedy once asked a veteran wire service correspondent at the White House why had his off-the-record confidences, given in good faith to the White House circle of supposedly trusted correspondents, landed in various newspapers nonetheless. The old-time reporter told Kennedy that in Washington, among the press and others, an individual's importance was rated by many on his presumed proximity and ostensible friendship with the President. Therefore, whenever the Chief Executive did give out confidences about world affairs, most correspondents would immediately and dutifully write a confidential memorandum to their publishers. For some, the purpose was to let the bosses know how closely they were "in" with Kennedy. This enhanced their prestige and justified their expense accounts. The sophisticated Kennedy was slightly shocked to hear this press shoptalk.

If Kennedy was to the manner born, Johnson has to the purple grown. For thirty years Johnson trained himself in the observation and use of power as exercised in the halls of Congress. Secretary Rusk remarked after Johnson's accession to the Presidency: "Now you will see a man who really knows how to use power." A feeling for the gut issues of power was a hidden but very real trait in Rusk himself. It is no idle comparison to liken Johnson to the imperial Caesars of Rome in his style of wielding power, his attitude of command, and the ease with which he takes it and enjoys it. Even Johnson's constant reading of public opinion polls might be said to resemble the reading of entrails in ancient Rome for auguries of the future. And as every schoolboy used to know from the study of history, imperial Rome also laid heavy emphasis on image-building as the public façade of the Emperor and his action for the good of the state. In short, the need for consensus and for the good opinion of the citizenry to enhance and enforce the prestige and power of the President in his direction of affairs is as old as Rome. Eisenhower had the aura of consensus by nature, and by training as an Army Commander, not to overlook the expert tailoring provided by Press Secretary James Hagerty. Kennedy won consensus by personal magnetism and by the artful ministrations of adept image makers. Johnson attempted to gain consensus by bona fide achievements, by force of will and maneuver, and by a ceaseless effort to capitalize on popular aspirations for prosperity, order, and the freedom to enjoy the fruits thereof. The same desires characterized citizens in the age of the Caesars, which, like the mid-twentieth century, was also a time of urbanization, administration, and bureaucracy.

The political character that permeates President Johnson's foreign policy emanates from no spelled-out philosophy, but from deeply intense personal experiences. He adulated and emulated his two political heroes, President Franklin Delano Roosevelt and Speaker of the House Sam Rayburn, Johnson's almost paternal mentor. This writer recalls, at the 1960 Los Angeles Democratic Convention, watching Rayburn treat Johnson almost like a little boy. When the band played the national anthem and the dignitaries attending the candidate-designate, John F. Kennedy, turned to face the American flag to the rear of the platform, everybody about-faced except Johnson. Rayburn, almost three feet shorter, spun the rangy Johnson around to face the right way. Also leaving an impression on Johnson's behavior was James F. Byrnes, the "Assistant President" for domestic affairs under President Roosevelt during World War II and later Secretary of State. A former Senator, like Johnson, Byrnes had a remarkable talent for compromise.

Byrnes used to say, "Where there is politics, there's got to be a compromise."

Johnson observed four Presidents at close hand: Roosevelt, Truman, Eisenhower, and Kennedy. Much of his knowledge was the sediment of careful listening and inductive reasoning for his own use and application. No student of the forces of history and the errors of kings and parliaments, Johnson soaked up contemporary events that he knew at first hand, the inside stories of what the notables in authority really did and why they did it, and why it failed or succeeded. He relished folklore of public life and Texas court trial stories like that of the witness who was the "bottle-scarred veteran of a thousand drunks." In postwar Congresses, Johnson participated in the first major innovation in United States foreign policy since the founding of the republic, namely, the commitment of United States resources to the implementation of foreign policy. He had had contact with foreign policy and its administrative ramifications through the appropriations process much longer than had most previous Presidents before they took office.

Johnson liked to take the measure of the foreign politicians and diplomats as well as the local ones he met, screwing up his eyes to figure out what made the new acquaintance tick, what was his price, his real desire in life, how he would fit into the Johnsonian scheme of things. Foreign visitors said that Johnson had a quick "feel" for his visiting fellow Presidents' political problems and sought to find out what issues fenced them in and prevented the cooperation which they might otherwise deliver. As Vice President, Johnson had visited thirty-four countries. He met representatives of ninety-two countries at the funeral of President Kennedy. Between the summer of 1966 and that of 1967 he held talks with sixty-five foreign chiefs and ministers and seventy-four foreign ambassadors. He had a politician's photographic memory for names, places, and context. He carried on extensive correspondence with chiefs of state and heads of government all over the world, including writing 70 letters to Russian leaders and having a total of 192 exchanges with British Prime Minister Harold Wilson. The President received 350,000 letters and other messages on Vietnam between February 1965, the start of the bombing of North Vietnam, and February 1967, two years later.

A characteristically major transformation effected under President Johnson has been the transmutation of foreign policy into foreign politics, a shift in emphasis, tactics, and style, which was both decried and misunderstood in the early days of the Johnson administration. Johnson reiterated this deep conviction about the politics of foreign policy so frequently that it is now accepted and even comprehended as a further development in the evolution of foreign policy. He said at various times:

"One thing people forget—and I'm seeing to it that my staff and my Cabinet don't forget it—the platform, the policy of this administration is simple: our foreign policy abroad is our domestic policy at home. When we hit a problem of disease, ignorance, and poverty at home, we are attacking the same things all around the world."

"As long as we are living in a world with 122 nations, we have to realize we have got to have 122 foreign policies."

Johnson fervently believed that the Great Society was an essential element of his foreign policy and that the United States could deal with the world only if the world conceded that the United States was dealing successfully with its own ills. The axiom that domestic policy affects, interferes with, or impedes the President's handling of foreign policy had been projected one step further into recognizing that the internal politics of other countries are just as important a factor in the United States resolution of a problem. In brief, LBJ desired prosperity and health, a better standard of living and housing, and human dignity for everybody, Americans and foreigners alike.

All this, it might be added, did not mean that so-called traditional foreign policy was either superseded or dead. It meant that an extra dimension had been added to the old-fashioned way of dealing between governments and governments in formalized and too often arid methods of communication. It meant, further, a melding of classic political theory—what is the good life—with new international theory—how to survive as a nation—and one more step from abstractions to actualities.

A bitter example of this mixture of domestic and foreign politics is the Vietnam war, which President Johnson inherited and which he deliberately intensified in the saving hope of making a virtue out of necessity. His only other choice was to have to give up Vietnam entirely. It was by the greatest effort of will and determination that Johnson, between presidential authority, timing, a rhinoceros skin, and frequent recourse to his favorite injunction from Isaiah, "Come now, and let us reason together," succeeded in bringing or dragging, if you will, the nation through the Vietnam war during almost three years of steadily intensified commitment. Johnson risked the same danger that President Jefferson faced in the embargo of 1808, when a policy short of war became too injurious to too many people. Even Jefferson could not sustain it and had to give up the embargo. Johnson had been consistent in his views on Vietnam since his first visit there as Vice President in May 1961. He was fully cognizant of the creeping involvement during the Kennedy administration. He recalled during his visit to Thailand on the 1961 trip being told that peace in Southeast Asia was "indivisible," and that a successful Communist rebellion in South Vietnam would seriously endanger the rest of that rich, fertile, and strategic area, not in the domino-theory sense necessarily but simultaneously in across-the-peninsula internal upheavals.

The Johnson views on Vietnam and the Communists were further stiffened later in 1961, when President Kennedy sent his Vice President to Berlin in August, after the erection of the Berlin Wall and the mounting tension of Khrushchev's threat of an imminent showdown over Berlin. Johnson remembered Kennedy's parting words, "I hope you get back," on that occasion. But even more vividly he recalled Kennedy's quoting Khrushchev as having said during the Vienna meeting in June, "If we got to have a war, we might as well have it this year." Johnson had had his stint of on-the-job training for Vietnam.

What is commonly fluffed over in analyses of the Vietnam war is what Johnson did or did not do in 1964, in the period of his so-called interregnum, that is, after he had become legally President by succession but had not yet been elected under his own popular mandate. In September 1964, a national intelligence estimate rated the Saigon situation as "the worst since 1955." As Johnson said in a 1967 speech, the United States would have been forced to choose between "major commitments for the defense of South Vietnam, or retreat, the evacuation of more than 25,000 of our troops, the collapse of the Republic of Vietnam by subversion and external assault." The Viet Cong were in point of fact about to take over South Vietnam within weeks or months at the end of 1964. Johnson sent American combat troops in strength to South Vietnam in June 1965, four months after the February beginning of the bombing of North Vietnam. He put in 100,000 men in 120 days. The United States commitment was taken up in earnest, but almost too late.

During 1964 President Johnson kept the Vietnam war more or less at arm's length. It was run by the State Department bureaucracy and the Pentagon military with a slow meandering motion. No verifiable word has ever been allowed to transpire of what was the President's personal evaluation of the matter in those months before he took personal charge. In the months after the murder of Diem, South Vietnam was disintegrating economically, politically, and militarily. Yet Johnson did not act, except for the burst of patriotic anger at the Gulf of Tonkin incident in August 1964. In the most profound sense, the President must have believed that he needed the mandate of the people before he risked launching his policy in South Vietnam. The Kennedy mystique was still as heavy as glue in Washington. Radical innovations in Southeast Asia would have been immediately construed as criticism of Kennedy policies in Vietnam, which kept on sliding down the slippery slope.

The President straddled the dilemma of moving forthwith to stem the collapse in Saigon or risking loss of the November elections by a major early commitment of United States armed forces and consequent casualties in South Vietnam. The decision narrowed to what was more important to Johnson as a leader—the war or a victory at the polls and an opportunity to complete the New Deal reforms which had been his exhilarating introduction to political life as a young Congressman. The Johnson dreams were embodied in such memories as the LCRA. Nobody but a few New Dealers could recall what the initials stood for. They refer to the Lower Colorado River Authority. The LCRA had made the desert hills of West Texas bloom and brought at least a subsistence prosperity to the bleak and desolate region where Johnson friends and relatives had eked a living out of the flinty soil. In the same area of Texas, it was Johnson's deep sense of outrage at the utter poverty of his Mexican neighbors and constituents that compelled him as a freshman Congressman to muster up the temerity to beard President Franklin Delano Roosevelt and complain that the new seeds available from the AAA (Agricultural Adjustment Administration) were being denied his Mexican friends.

Johnson's native habitat was the old frontier of the American Southwest. His election as President was a new transfusion into the bloodstream of the Republic. The Texas breakthrough into political first rank uncovered a further layer of Americans without a voice, the Spanish Americans, whose grievances have yet to be heard, and in the process of which yet another ethnic-racial crisis will be started, from Texas right across to New Mexico, Arizona, and southern California. The New Deal had begun, but never finished, its mission to launch the nation on the road to social justice and welfare. In Johnson was a burning desire to brand new and necessary progress in 1964 with his own initials. To do so, he had to have unquestioned power as symbolized by the greatest possible popular victory in the elections. To be effective, one had to be powerful. Nothing could be allowed to interfere with that true accession to power, not even the Vietnam war and the American commitment there. It was a classic example of intermittent presidential necessity to safeguard political power by sacrificing an otherwise crucial foreign policy for the time being. So Johnson took the gamble. He was still gambling of necessity all the way through 1967, to the 1968 presidential elections. During the 1964 campaign, he dissimulated as Franklin Roosevelt had done before Pearl Harbor, with the pledge that no American boys would fight in Europe. Johnson similarly declared that "no United States boys should ever get bogged down in the swamps of Asia." Johnson's intentions about Vietnam were his own personal secret. During off-the-record meetings with Washington bureau chiefs in the second-floor White House living quarters before the 1964 campaign, Johnson cut off questions about the relevance of foreign policy as an election issue with a low rumble of denial. His strategem, as events proved, gave him a landslide and unassailable prestige. It allowed the massive Great Society program to pour through the Eighty-ninth Congress in 1965. His bombing of North Vietnam in February 1965 accomplished a triple objective—it shocked the American people as to the gravity of United States commitment, it steadied the tottering Saigon regime, and it warned the North Vietnamese that their otherwise imminent victory in South Vietnam could not be obtained gratis.

With his twin Great Society and Vietnam decisions, President Johnson did that which President Kennedy was never quite willing to attempt, namely, to carry out the Neustadt thesis of building up power and the Hyman thesis of expending it with known risks to his popularity in the prosecution of a foreign cause. He won great credit on the Great Society and spent it on Vietnam. The risks are still there to be mortgaged off— newspaper criticism, the bleeding of the doves and the shrieks of the hawks on Capitol Hill, the surge of anti-Vietnam demonstrations and teach-ins, draft-card burnings, hunger strikes, and revolt in the academic community.

By late 1967, the Johnson betting on his foreign affairs stakes, if patently not yet paying off conclusively, at least was reaching a standoff. The lack of public appreciation in the United States for the improvement in South Vietnam over the near-chaos of early 1965 mystified and irritated the President beyond the capacity of his own words to encapsulate his abraded feelings. He carried in his pocket a little yellow dog-eared card with re- marks by President Lincoln, who is said to have handed out a similar card to visitors. (The Blondin referred to is a legendary acrobat of Civil War times.) LBJ also showed his card to visitors. It said:

Gentlemen, suppose all the property you were worth was in gold, and you had put it in the hands of Blondin to carry across the Niagara Falls on a rope Would you shake the cable, or keep shouting out to him, "Blondin, stoop a little more—go a little faster—lean a little more to the north—lean a little more to the south"? No! you would hold your breath as well as your tongue, and keep your hands off until he was safe over. The Government is carrying an immense weight. Untold treasures are in their hands. They are doing the very best they can. Don't badger them. Keep silence, and we'll get you safe across.

The Vietnam acid, which had unquestionably eaten away at the ac- ceptance of Johnson as an undeniably strong and possibly truly great Presi- dent of the United States, had tarnished or deflected his worthwhile initia- tives in Latin America, Africa, and Europe. How well a President succeeds or fails in keeping four other continents in global view depends on what use he, the President, makes of his key associates and immediate staff. Three rules appear to be in order: The President must perforce work with those individuals he has available. He can work only with persons in whose personal loyalty and integrity he has complete faith as agents of his will.

He must set the pattern of his personal working habits and set priorities for whatever subjects he ranks as primary duties. His White House staff, therefore, has to be practically hand-tailored to fit the President's most intimate characteristics and daily life, starting when he gets up in the morning, through his afternoon nap, to when he goes to bed at night. President Johnson, for instance, spends from 11 P.M. to 1 A.M. in his Oval Office from time to time. Further factors are whether a President likes oral presentations or prefers to receive everything in writing. Kennedy, for example, could read faster than most people could talk. Such details determine the eventual pace and pitch of a President's working effectiveness.

An instrument for this round-the-clock servicing of the President's needs is the White House Situation Room, located in the rear of the basement. Maps of crisis areas—the Far East and Middle East in 1967—show the disposition of all U.S. armed forces and the current state of alert in all six military commands. The theaters of operations are CINCLANT (Atlantic), CINCEUR (Europe), CINCSAC (Strategic Air Command), CINCPAC (Pacific), CINCAL (Alaska), and CINCSOUTH (Mediterranean). The alert designations or defense readiness positions range from five to one. The bottom is normal peacetime and standard precautions. The next is an alert of keep your eyes open, if conditions are restless. Real alerts start with No. 3, which is preparation to react and ushers in a stand-by stage, as is customary in most of East Asia in recent years. No. 2 signifies danger of imminent attack. No. 1 is nuclear war or its threat, as the time of the Cuban missile crisis. Four large clocks show the time in Saigon, GMT (Greenwich Mean Time), Washington, D.C., time, and the time at whatever place the President himself happens to be, on the road or in the White House.

Since it is clear that the President cannot control the results of his actions in the foreign field by law, fiat, or quick agreement, as he usually can in domestic crises, it follows that the importance of an alert and fast-off-the-mark White House staff rises in direct ratio to the incidence of foreign crises. The Arab-Israeli conflict, to illustrate, made President Johnson devote nearly 80 per cent of his time to the Middle East, from the moment he was awakened with the news of the hostilities at 4:30 A.M. on Monday, June 5.

Indicating the pace of the presidential activity was his schedule a few days before, on June 1, 1967:

7:28 A.M.	Called Leonard Marks, Director of the USIA.
8:00 A.M.	Marvin Watson, Appointment Secretary, to the President's bedroom.
8:57 A.M.	Called Farris Bryant, Director of Office of Emergency Planning.
9:40 A.M.	Was called by Walt Rostow, Special Assistant.
9:55 A.M.	Was called by Joe Califano, Domestic Affairs Aide.

10:00 A.M.	George Christian and Tom Johnson, Press Secretaries, to the President's bedroom.
10:18 A.M.	Called by Walt Rostow.
10:27 A.M.	Called by Richard Helms, Director of CIA.
11:00 A.M.	Christian and Tom Johnson out.
11:17 A.M.	Called Marvin Watson.
11:18 A.M.	Called Marvin Watson.
11:25 A.M.	President and Mrs. Johnson went to the diplomatic entrance on the South Grounds to greet Prime Minister and Mrs. Harold Holt of Australia.
12:00 noon	President and Prime Minister met privately in the Oval Office.
12:43 P.M.	The President called Henry Wilson, House liaison.
12:44 P.M.	The President called Barefoot Sanders, House liaison.
12:45 P.M.	The President called Joe Califano.
12:50 P.M.	The President called Mike Manatos, Senate liaison.
1:20 P.M.	Called George Christian.
1:21 P.M.	The President went to Marvin Watson's office and talked to George Christian and Lincoln Gordon, retiring Assistant Secretary of State for Inter-American Affairs.
1:35 P.M.	The President and Australian Prime Minister Holt returned to the President's office.
1:43 P.M.	The President and the Prime Minister went to the second floor of the Mansion.
2:00 to 2:30 P.M.	The President had lunch with Holt, Christian, and Tony Eggleton, Holt's press man, Edward Clark, Ambassador to Australia, John Keith Waller, Ambassador to the U.S.A. During the luncheon, he talked to Francis Bator twice by telephone to get information on trade questions he was discussing with the Prime Minister.
4:10 to 5:18 P.M.	The President napped.
5:18 P.M.	Called George Christian.
5:27 P.M.	Called Joe Califano.
5:40 P.M.	Called George Christian.
5:50 P.M.	Called Bess Abell, Social Secretary.
5:51 P.M.	Called by Secretary McNamara.
6:00 P.M.	Returned to his office.
6:05 P.M.	Called Secretary McNamara.
6:10 P.M.	Met with Admiral Thomas H. Moorer, Chief of Naval Operations.
6:37 P.M.	Met with magazine writer. The President discussed with him the functions of the National Security Council staff and his high opinion of Walt Rostow.
7:02 to 7:25 P.M.	Met with Secretary Rusk, Eugene R. Rostow, and Walt Rostow concerning Foreign Minister Adan Pachachi of Iraq.
7:26 to 8:00 P.M.	The President met with Pachachi and Iraqi Ambassador

	Nasir Hani, Walt Rostow, and Robert Houghton, State Department Country Director of Iraq, on the mounting tensions in the Middle East.
8:02 P.M.	The President went to the Mansion to change clothes for State Department dinner for Prime Minister Holt.
8:15 P.M.	The President and Mrs. Johnson went to the North Portico to greet the Prime Minister and his wife, then returned to the second floor with the Holts and the official party, and for about twenty minutes talked with the party.
8:41 P.M.	To the East Room to receive guests for the State Dinner.
10:20 P.M.	Toasts.
10:45 P.M.	Coffee in the parlor.
11:05 to midnight	Entertainment in the East Room.
	About 1 A.M. the President returned to the second floor, went over his night reading, and retired at 2:05 A.M.

Equally evident, it is a necessity to have on the White House staff men who are on the President's wave length, who can read his mind, or at least accurately anticipate the direction of his interests and eventual focus. No President, however, is ever very easy to read. Franklin Delano Roosevelt rarely gave instructions or indicated specifically what he had in mind, since he had the habit of making it up at the last minute. Truman might have been very clear about what he wanted, but he had to spend an inordinate amount of time trying to persuade subordinates to do what they ought to have done in the first place. Presidents vary in their personal loyalty to their staff subordinates. Truman was fiercely defensive about his associates. Johnson is equally vehement on their behalf, especially if they are under political attack. FDR showed little sense of attachment to his underlings, feeling the Presidency was too important to have to worry about individuals.

Close physically though the White House staff may be to the President, it naturally takes second place to the high barons of the bureaucracy in great decisions of state. After President Kennedy's death, the importance of the White House staff was somewhat downgraded as President Johnson shifted his chief reliance to the statutory and responsible departments. Thus, all major decisions on the Vietnam war were taken to the very top of the Government, at regular Tuesday luncheon meetings attended by the President, Secretary Rusk, Defense Secretary McNamara, Special Assistant Walt Rostow, and Presidential Press Secretary George Christian, the last two primarily as channels of communications rather than full partners in the decision-making, though the Rostow voice grew steadily during his tenure.

Much of the Tuesday luncheon discussions was devoted to the task of picking which of 5,000 possible targets to bomb in North Vietnam. The final decision was always up to the President, who by late 1967 had approved over 300 targets. The White House staff, for example, had favored bombing power and oil complexes but had originally argued against bombing the transportation network in northern Vietnam, where the U.S. planes had been forbidden to bomb within thirty miles of the Chinese border. Lieutenant General William W. Momyer, Commander of the U.S. Seventh Air Force and deputy to General Westmoreland for air operations, with the aid of new secret electronic devices and refined, fresh tactics, in the summer of 1967 demonstrated that the North Vietnam distribution system could be damaged more effectively. A proof of Momyer's success came from reconnaisance photos of the pile-up of unloaded shipping in Haiphong port and the scattering of Communist supply ships into inadequate harbors up and down the North Vietnamese coast. In August 1967, bombing of the hitherto inviolate staging areas and railroad marshaling yards near China was authorized. It brought added strain to the North Vietnamese network.

President Johnson went outside government channels for advice and counsel, as had President Wilson with Colonel House and Felix Frankfurter, and FDR with Harry Hopkins. President Johnson often consulted Supreme Court Justice Abe Fortas; Clark Clifford, who became McNamara's successor and who had also been a Truman aide; and James H. Rowe, Jr., who used to be President Roosevelt's administrative assistant; these three were LBJ's top general advisers. But as Rowe remarked, in foreign policy any counsel a trusted outsider may give can't have much relevance unless the adviser has also read the incoming cables and thus has facts upon which to base his analysis and advice. The President's outside consultants on foreign policy included Dean Acheson, Eugene Black (on Asian bank matters), David Lilienthal (on economic development), Arthur Dean (on armaments), George Ball, Robert Anderson (on Middle East and Latin America), John McCloy, McGeorge Bundy, Herschel Newson (President of the National Grange, on agricultural matters), and Dwight Eisenhower.

From the Tuesday Vietnam luncheons invariably eleven or twelve decisions eventuated, Rostow getting on the phone afterward to brief Benjamin H. Read, the Executive Secretary of the State Department, who passed on pertinent information to responsible operating officers. McNamara informed his immediate colleagues in the Pentagon and General Earle Wheeler, Chairman of the Joint Chiefs of Staff. Information about the Tuesday meetings was held extremely close. Lateral indications transpired that the President placed tremendous confidence in Rusk for his counsel, thereby vastly enhancing Rusk's power in Government councils. Rusk was described as "very tough indeed" and as "a slugger" in the Tuesday decision-making which was marked by much debate as a matter of course. In contrast with his usual mild public demeanor, Rusk sometimes made McNamara's eyes snap wide in surprise at a sudden vehemence of argumentation. President Johnson repeatedly expressed his surprise that Rusk and McNamara could still operate so smoothly in their intimately entwined spheres without a blowup.

President Johnson made a further innovation in his White House foreign policy techniques through twice-monthly Cabinet meetings, a procedure suggested by his former Secretary of the Cabinet, Robert Kintner. At those meetings, Johnson required Rusk and McNamara to tell the rest of the Cabinet exactly what they had done and proposed to do, in their respective fields. Rusk dominated the foreign field without question, as McNamara did the military field. Once a month, all twelve departments, including State and Defense, prepared memoranda covering their current problems and issues, for circulation to each other. This Cabinet technique was effective in informing the top executives of the Government on across-the-board problems, particularly in the foreign affairs community, so that every agency knew the relevant policy and plans at the White House level. With so many departments now directly operating in, or heavily concerned with, foreign affairs, the Cabinet cross-communication became a further tool for the President, as chief administrator, in trying to make programs work, insofar as common understanding at the topmost echelon could help.

The need for substantially enlarged White House staff support for the President was apparent since the Brownlow Commission had so recommended in 1936. It had been a continuously increasing need, whether the White House had an absolute President like FDR, a ruling President like Truman, a reigning President like Eisenhower, a developing President like Kennedy, or an operating President like Johnson. J. I. Coffey and Vincent P. Rock said in the 1960 National Planning Association study *The Presidential Staff:*

> The action the President takes [or doesn't take] to ameliorate racial discrimination reflects upon the prestige of the office at home and abroad, while the decisions with respect to military strategy and force-levels unavoidably affect the economy as well as the foreign policy of the United States. Thus, the Presidency is really a web, in which no move can be made without shaking and stirring the remotest fibers and tendrils.

The White House staff is not a gadfly to goad the steed of state. It is a channel to get presidential decisions into the administrative machinery. In the process of so doing, it has the duty to pull the threads together for the President in those proposals which come up from the bureaucracy. At the crossroads of conflict which the White House is, the staff has the high responsibility for insuring with all possible fairness that the total national-interest contribution is clearly defined and outlined for the consideration of the President. This particularly applies to those domestic issues which are specifically relevant to foreign policy, whether from Agriculture, Interior, Commerce, or another department. The President does not preside as chief magistrate in order to decide theoretical problems. All Presidents are hesitant about hooking on to great generalities without taking a look at the fine print. Therefore, a significant delegated function of the White House staff is to act as executioner of "ideas that won't fly," as well as expediter in execution of ideas, programs, and policies adjudged worthy of undertaking. The White House staff under President Johnson developed a closer relationship with the executive departments and agencies than had been done under Presidents Eisenhower or Kennedy.

The difference between the great departments and the White House lies in the contrast between that which it is easy to propose and that which it is difficult to reduce to substance. The State Department bureaucracy, for instance, gives an invaluable negative service to the White House staff. State's bureaucracy carries the institutional memory of the Government in foreign affairs. It has the obligation and habit of looking at the semicolons, reviewing all precedents, flushing out all the angles, recalling what was similar and dissimilar, and what went right or wrong in previous instances. It is, in short, an indispensable insurance agency.

The foreign policy contingent of the White House staff operates also as part of the National Security Council staff. The NSC apparatus was virtually disregarded by President Kennedy. President Johnson convoked it every two weeks, more or less, for purely formal meetings, more in keeping with possible legal requirements than as an operations instrument.

More closely impinging on the oblique upon the White House foreign affairs staff is the Bureau of the Budget, a financial and managerial arm of the President. The Bureau liked to portray itself to the State Department in particular as the interpreter of the President's "wishes," in the light of its statutory responsibilities for Government organization, preparation of the national budget, and cost-effectiveness of programs. The State Department tended to resist this rather self-anointed role of the Bureau of the Budget. The Department demands direct access to the President and that its views not be interpreted by another organization. State frequently felt that the Budget Bureau tried to mix into policy matters by slashing funds in areas where it was competent to judge neither the needs nor the results. The Budget Bureau described the Department as incredibly crusty and conservative, and responsible neither to the President's nor to Congress' desires.

Needless to say, White House–State Department relationships are a complicated matter. Some Foreign Service officers feel that the White House uses the Department as the "fall guy" when something goes wrong, disregarding embarrassments the Department may suffer in consequence. The Department's Foreign Service officer corps is vexed that criticism of its performance comes often from fellow Foreign Service officers who have been posted to duty in the White House and invariably adopt White House attitudes, to the discomfiture of their erstwhile brethren in the Department. White House–State Department relationships at least are far better than in the days of Secretary Dulles, who instructed his officers to pay no attention to the White House staff and only to direct presidential orders.

Despite improved relations of the latter years, the State Department remains the target of White House criticism, if for no other reason than that the Department acts as a brake on an activist President who may want to go too far too fast. The White House analysis maintains that the State Department response to presidential needs is far too slow, that papers are far too long—for instance, thirty-six-page papers, single-spaced, where eight pages, double-spaced, would have done much better—and that State uses stilted and extremely complicated language. State Department memoranda are in no shape to be read in their original format by the President. This imposes on the White House staff the need to break memos down to usable form. A State memo of twenty pages might end up as a one-page summary. But the State Department is learning. The Executive Secretariat now sends over daily summaries of activities which are a tight one–two pages in length and regular weekly summaries which run only from twelve to fifteen pages.

State is regarded as the most difficult department in the Government to do business with, because of its monolithic character and the tendency of its officers to dwell too much on past methods and over-long processes. State Department documentation too frequently is devoid of the political factors which will have to be considered at the White House level. This deficiency Under Secretary Katzenbach is endeavoring to correct by having the Department's geographical bureaus do their homework for the domestic side after they have made their foreign policy analyses and recommendations. The State Department does not take the White House criticism lying down. Foreign Service officers pan the White House staff not infrequently as technically incompetent in the field of diplomatic expertise, as not operationally responsible, as too casual in the treatment of what the diplomats may consider the prime issues, and as too addicted to misleading verbiage for purposes of public presentation.

Despite the frictions ensuing from such intimate cohabitation, White House functionaries are constantly on the prowl in State Department corridors, circulating to pick up new ideas from brainy bureaucrats. The State Department is keenly aware that the White House appetite for new ideas is immense and demanding. Speeches are one sure way of obtaining recognition and action for foreign policy ideas by the ambitious within the faceless bureaucracy, particularly those who do not have political power or the good fortune to be able successfully to funnel their ideas through normal channels from downstairs up to the seventh floor. George F. Kennan, former State Department policy planner, said years ago that speeches are "not an inconsiderable means of influencing what goes on in the world." Bill D. Moyers, Johnson's former Presidential Press Secretary, agreed: "Policy in major speeches is very important as means to start things going." If the public is indifferent to an issue, it is imperative that the President mobilize public support by means of a major speech before action can be initiated. If a presidential speech is to kick off a major campaign, there must be a decision that the game is worth the effort.

Before the 1962 Trade Expansion Act, President Kennedy's advisers were torn between asking for a one- or two-year extension of the Reciprocal Trade Agreement Act. The nut of the issue was to prepare the United States with a long-enough grant of authority to negotiate successfully with the steadily stronger European Common Market. Kennedy cut short the arguments. He said: "Let's not have a fight over nothing." Knowing that he would have a real battle over the tariffs anyhow, Kennedy ordered as a goal a five-year authorization to make the fight worthwhile. If the public is interested and involved, it is difficult to maintain a policy of restraint in order to make the best of a situation without a public intervention through a speech or a series of speeches. These thus become instruments of foreign policy, the most recent series of such examples being the speeches on the Vietnam issue.

Not that major speeches can always be successfully organized in advance, or even come out as planned. The famous Marshall Plan speech was preorganized in 1947. The historic reference to Point IV (for technical assistance to underdeveloped countries) in the inaugural speech of President Truman in 1949 was not. Under Secretary of State Robert Lovett was horrified at the idea of Point IV and instructed the Department's Counselor, Charles E. Bohlen, to cut it out. President Truman reinserted the proposal when the draft came back to the White House. Another speech that was a major instrument of United States foreign policy was that of President Eisenhower before the United Nations in September 1958. Therein he proposed a UN force as a permanent body in the Middle East, an Arab Development Bank, and arms control for the Middle East, prescient proposals in light of the 1967 Arab-Israeli war.

Technical details behind major speeches have ironical sidelights. The Eisenhower Middle East speech was the work of Gerard Smith, Chairman of the Policy Planning Council of the State Department. Smith had to overcome Secretary Dulles' opposition before Eisenhower could deliver it.

President Kennedy's famous speech on Atlantic interdependence at Philadelphia on July 4, 1962, aimed at European ears, had little echo because
most of Europe was distracted with other matters at the moment. JFK
was somewhat bitter at the lack of response. A speech by President Johnson
in May 1966, ushering in a new United States policy on Africa, was the
product substantially of Deputy Assistant Secretary of African Affairs
Wayne Fredericks and of Presidential Aide Bill D. Moyers, though Fredericks rated low on the totem pole of the power hierarchy. The April 1965
speech of President Johnson at Baltimore on Vietnam was, in essence, the
result of three years of work on the concept of regionalism as applied to
Asia. Presidential foreign policy speeches sometimes come in series: an
introduction at one point, as in August 1966, on Latin American integration; and a later climax, as at the summit of American Presidents at Punta
del Este in April 1967, when the idea of a Latin American common market
became a practicality to consider.

President Johnson in May 1964, at Lexington, Virginia, took President
Kennedy's American University speech of June 1963 one step further and
stressed "building bridges to the East." Johnson early in 1966 demanded
"new initiatives" from his staff. After six months of gestation there came
forth the President's October 1966 speech on East-West relationships and
"peaceful engagement" between the two Europes and their mutually dependent destinies. This speech was the result of at least ten helping hands.
Dean Acheson was the highly effective conveyor of pressures to persuade
Johnson to make the speech. The first draft came from Zbigniew Brzezinski,
a member of, and Henry Owen, chairman of, the Department's Policy Planning Council. Along the way there were State contributions from Secretary
Rusk, Under Secretary Ball, Assistant Secretary John Leddy; and in the
White House, from McGeorge Bundy, Walt Rostow, his successor, plus
Francis Bator, the White House staff's specialist in foreign economic policy
and European affairs, and his assistant, Lawrence Eagleburger. At least 50
per cent of the final product was still in Brzezinski's words. The western
European part had been beefed up by the other contributors.

Other speeches are spur-of-the-moment exploitation of handy audiences
or happenstance suggestions. President Johnson made a major defense of
his Vietnam policy in September 1967 before the National Legislative Conference at San Antonio, Texas. No speech had been planned. But a few
days before, Johnson had as a guest at a private luncheon the former
Australian Prime Minister, Sir Robert Menzies, whose rough-hewn bluffness
appeals to the President. Menzies suggested that the President take advantage of his proposed weekend rest trip to the LBJ ranch to talk to the legislators. Johnson said that he had already spoken about Vietnam three or four
times that week. Menzies replied with a tale of his old political mentor

in Australia who had made a series of seventy-three speeches all on the same subject and had arranged to make still another on the same topic. When this fact was pointed out to him, Menzies recalled, the old pro said, "Ah yes, but they were seventy-three different audiences." In the San Antonio case, Johnson felt he got a multiplier dividend; the legislators came from fifty states to which they could take back the message.

Indicative of the variations in the character of the White House staff was the electric change in 1961, when the measured orderliness of the Eisenhower White House, where the staff work was complete and the chain of command worked most of the time, gave way to the heady confusion of the early Kennedy White House, where everybody seemed to want to get into the act, and often did. This spatter of apparently unorganized effort prompted pointed criticism of the Kennedy White House staff by the State Department. The State pros hinted that brain power notwithstanding, many Kennedy intellectuals were individualistic and had no gift for the making of policy, specifically the transmutation of ideas into workable patterns of government operations. Neither was President Johnson, for that matter, an organization man. A phenomenally intense individual, Johnson, like Kennedy and like many dynamic executives who try to do their own chores, instead of spending time to delegate them, always had to resist the tendency to do the job himself. Johnson was, and is, virtually insatiable in his demands for information and for action. He drove his staff at a terrific pace, a trait mitigated only by the fact that he drove himself even harder.

The White House staff had to move a lot faster than the officers of the State Department. White House memoranda were shorter, brisker, more pointed. The aim was to give the President what he wanted by the end of the day. When a red-hot issue was sizzling on the griddle, the staff instinct was to try to give the answer instanter, which, of course, was usually impossible. President Johnson liked four- or five-paragraph letters. But if the need for completeness of presentation were cogent, he would sign a four-page letter. The White House staff prepared between seventy and eighty items for Johnson's night reading, about half on foreign affairs. If a fifty-page briefing book were handed to him, appended thereto had to be a short memorandum summarizing its gist. The President not infrequently finished reading the rest of his overnight memos at 6:30 in the morning. These had better be clear and concise, and preferably half a page in length, if possible, and never the long, intricate memoranda that originally came from the State Department. Staff face-to-face contacts with the President were invariably quick and to-the-point, unless he requested longer verbal explanations. Besides his predilections for telephoning an enormous range of friends for their opinions about varied matters, the President apparently liked philosophical discussions of issues on the telephone rather than in his office.

Each aide had a direct phone to speak only to the President. It would ring loudly and insistently at the aide's desk without the call going through any secretary.

On a normal day the President would awaken between 6 and 6:30 A.M., go over his morning Vietnam reports and other intelligence data, read the early diplomatic cables, and then call Secretary McNamara about 7 or 7:30 A.M. The President often commented that Secretary McNamara was the only man in the Government on duty that early in the day. By 8:30 A.M. he had usually talked to Walt Rostow and possibly to Secretary Rusk or Under Secretary Katzenbach. Before the President went to his office at 10:30 or 11 A.M., he had again talked on the phone to Rostow two or more times on pending foreign policy decisions.

In an average week, between January 1 to June 30, 1967, McNamara was called seven times, Rusk four, Katzenbach two, and CIA Director Richard Helms once. On June 5, the first day of the Middle East War, the President talked to Rusk and McNamara three times each by telephone, in addition to holding a series of meetings with them during the day. When a real crisis was popping, Rusk and McNamara would usually be at the White House. On that June 5, the President talked to Walt Rostow fifteen times and to George Christian eleven times.

The White House staff function is not so much to change an item coming from the State Department as to shape it. In other words, the medium is the massage the White House staff gives it. The staff, in effect, pushes buttons, pulls levers, lubricates the machinery. It endeavors to flag issues in advance, to identify areas where action may be necessary, though it has to depend on the State Department and other agencies with overseas responsibilities for subsequent action. It metes out scepticism to that which it receives and attempts to maintain a decent humility about that which it itself proposes. The responsibility for spotting, defining, and refining issues for the President gives the Chief Executive the extra imperative ingredients of forethought and anticipatory preparation for crisis and reaction. The staff is supposed not only to identify views but also to find the blank spaces where views have not been expressed.

Though foreign affairs in the Johnson White House had been the primary responsibility of, first, Bundy and, later, Rostow, other aides got into the action in specialized provinces. Before he left to join the John F. Kennedy Institute of Politics at Harvard University, Francis Bator was a sort of éminence grise in the field of foreign economic policy and European affairs. Bator handled these fields for the President, with copies of memoranda to Rostow, though only in later days did Bator finally achieve the supreme accolade of direct access to the President, on an occasional basis. Bator had authority to receive foreign ambassadors in Washington on matters of foreign economic policy, and also visiting foreign ministers on the same subject. Bator was a one-man operating agency in his field at the White House, making involuted deals with the major agencies with Hungarian flourish and circumlocution, busily negotiating for his points of view, and generally creating his own system of floating tactical alliances within the bureaucracy. Though this at times might have been construed as an invasion of the responsibility of the operating agencies, the bureaucrats knew the value of easy access to a presidential assistant who could become a powerful ally. Bator's interests included international monetary reforms, the offset issue on German payments for the cost of United States forces in West Germany, and the Kennedy Round of tariff negotiations, on which Bator became a walking encyclopedia in 1967.

Half of Johnson's daily appointments related to foreign matters, as did nearly two thirds of his press conferences and background interviews. The heavy concentration on foreign policy in the White House was reflected by the 400 telephone calls a day the Press Office used to receive under Pierre Salinger, President Kennedy's Press Secretary. The calls were not all from the press; there were also internal calls from the State Department, Defense, USIA, Treasury, and CIA, in connection with events which were breaking into the public domain, or might so break, and upon which the official facts and position had to be ascertained in advance.

Telephone calls from the bureaucracy were tricky matters, however, especially if the call was a critical warning signal. The State Department functionary would be happy if he could have gotten rid of the hot potato he had just discovered by the simple device of passing the buck over the phone to the all-powerful White House. Handling the hot item became a question, in the bureaucratic lingo, of "who takes the rap." The White House staff, therefore, would have to insist that a properly authenticated and approved memorandum be swiftly sent over. This meant it had been worked out efficiently enough so it could get past the discerning eye of Secretary Rusk, who could spot instantly whatever significance the situation had for possible presidential action and give relevant advice about it. A case in point occurred in August 1967. Communist Rumania, which the United States was cultivating as an Eastern European maverick, asked permission to sail through the Great Lakes and land a Communist ship at Chicago, a restricted port, off limits to Communist shipping. The touchy question was the reaction of U.S. labor unions in the Chicago port. Would they unload the cargo or raise a stench, offensive in the nostrils of developing diplomatic relations? It took a heated telephone discussion to get the Department official to get off the dime and act. The written memo request was forcing him to take the rap. He took it. The denouement was instructive. The Rumanian ship was eventually diverted on its own orders to Mobile, Alabama. A possible incident had been averted by masterly White House in-action.

Vitally important on the White House staff is the presence of at least one voice who will stand up to the President and say, "No," and even argue with him, risking the President's annoyance. Such a role in the early days of the Johnson administration fell to Bill Moyers, who also served the highly useful purpose of passing on to the President views and facts which might have escaped the narrower channels of the establishment. Moyers thus was a corrective to the frequently lopsided views prevalent in the hot-house atmosphere of the nation's capital. President Johnson did not appreciate aides who had axes to grind. In his sceptical caution, Johnson systematically insisted that aides act as devil's advocates to argue against positions which they themselves might have indicated they preferred. Before his departure, Moyers was accused by critics of having become too much of an advocate, eroding his usefulness to the President. Johnson began to keep personal secrets from Moyers. He did not confide in Moyers at the 1966 Manila Conference that he, Johnson, faced surgery on his return to the United States, though Dean Rusk, Marvin Watson, his Appointment Secretary and political confidante, and George Christian were told about it.

In contrast to the Moyers type of aide, from the political world, was Robert Komer, a professional bureaucrat who came from the CIA. He worked first in the Kennedy White House. He rose in power, prestige, and effectiveness under Johnson as the President's Special Assistant for Civilian Affairs in Vietnam. Komer's intense drive, sharp intelligence, and devil-take-the-hindmost attitude gave him a reputation as an *enfant terrible,* a "blowtorch," and the Government's number one expediter. Komer's method was simple in the extreme. He worked closely with the agencies—the State Department, the Defense Department, and the Agency for International Development—to formulate the bureaucracy's recommendations in a form and style which would be acceptable to the White House.

Komer was the sole White House staff aide in the foreign field who shared command authority with the bureaucracy. His success was due to intimate knowledge of the machinery, fearlessness in tackling problems head-on, and an earnest persuasiveness in sorting matters out with the bureaucrats about how to put the programs into operation. To illustrate: Komer sent at least thirty-five memoranda of ideas to McNamara without a single response. When approached for not having acted on Komer's memos, McNamara asked, "What is it you want me to do?" In short, Komer discovered that his memos had been too vague. If the matter was feasible, McNamara would promptly honor any concrete request. As a consequence, Komer succeeded in obtaining swiftly from McNamara a ceiling on the expenditure of Vietnamese piasters by U.S. Armed Forces in South Vietnam and an agreement to allow one fourth of the port of Saigon to be turned over to AID civilian import shipments, which had been barred for lack of landing facilities. Komer asked for, and received from McNamara, a guarantee of 1,800 tons a month of military airlift for internal civilian shipments of AID supplies. Another time, AID told Komer that South Vietnam desperately needed American agricultural experts to serve as county agents in Vietnamese provinces and that none were available in the United States domestic economy. Komer asked McNamara urgently to find twenty U.S. Army officers with agricultural degrees and immediately to post them to AID for this basic rural development operation. McNamara did it.

No aspect of foreign policy becomes more important to the President than when it cuts deeply into domestic policy, as with trade and aid. The White House staff responsibility here rested with Joseph Califano, who inherited Bill Moyer's original assignment for preparing the President's legislative program to the Congress. Califano got into food exports; textile imports; copper prices, which had to be kept from rising in the United States but still kept acceptable to foreign copper-producing nations; and asphalt prices, which in 1967 also rose, affecting crude oil imports from friendly nations like Venezuela, which, in turn, had been damaged by privileged overland oil imports into the United States from Canada. On the perpetually embattled foreign aid bill, a key instrument of United States foreign policy, Califano had at least ten sessions with AID bureaucrats, sessions that lasted at least two or three hours each, to shape the foreign aid program for Congress.

Califano had Defense Department visual-aid technicians prepare eighty-page charts for the 1967 program. Items for which the administration needed legislation were marked with a red dot, and items on which the administration could act by executive decree were marked with a blue dot. Drawing up the President's legislative program for Congress entailed the most penetrating look at the specifics of all programs. This particularly applied to foreign policy programs, which had to be presented for authorization and appropriations to Congress, and for execution by the machinery of the governmental departments, above all, as related to overlapping overseas operations.

A good many White House aides were involved in foreign affairs in one way or another. Those whose involvement was a daily routine were Rostow, Christian, and Harry C. McPherson, Jr. Others came in on specific matters, such as John P. Roche on presidential statements and Douglass Cater on international education. McPherson, tough-minded but diffident and slow to speech, served as an objective or independent observer and commentator on many foreign policy questions, especially Vietnam.

From formal programs to individual actions of foreign policy, the President operates under five limitations, as Sorensen said in his *Decision-Making in the White House*. First are the limits of permissibility, that is, what the President can get away with in the light of the prevailing atmosphere and general constraints at the time of action. Second are the limits of available resources, that is, when issues are truly urgent and time literally presses during a crisis. Next are the limits of available information, that is, the difficulty of verifying information from distant foreign lands, a difficulty multiplied X times when a foreign land is hostile. Last are the limitations of previous commitments which inhibit, limit, or denounce past precedents and obligations. Sorensen pointed out that in a specific policy there must first be agreement on the over-all objective. In sequence then come precise definition of a problem and canvassing all possible solutions and all possible consequences, before the final selection of alternatives and the lines of execution. The White House staff responsibility for both domestic and foreign affairs is to provide the President with a creative mix of coherence and coordination. As a presidential decision is ushered into the public domain, there arises the necessity of its presentation. A press conference, as one means of publicity, may highlight a decision or camouflage the lack of decision. It may stimulate follow-up decisions from the bureaucracy or smother conflicting decisions from rival pressure group. It may deliberately escalate a decision into a chain of future consequences. The end product is a presidential orchestration of the cacophonies as well as the melodies of the immediate problem and the tonal atmospherics of the moment.

The White House likewise uses a foreign policy check list, but one much more specific than the wide and necessarily ambiguous type of analysis made by the State Department. The first question White House staffers ask is, "Why is the proposed policy necessary?" Second is, "What is it specifically expected to do?" Third is, "How is it to be technically put into effect? By means of United States agencies and/or those of what other countries and international instrumentalities?" Fourth is, "How much of it will the Congress stand for, and accept?" Fifth is, "What are the budgetary considerations, the dollar cost?" Sixth is, "What are the consequences in the execution of the proposed policy?" Finally, there is a seventh, "What effect will this have on the President's image?" The White House staff, in brief, is expected to translate a policy into a program.

But a dry run through these rubrics is only the start of the exercise. The key question arises: "What are the alternatives or options or choices that the President can exercise in fashioning this potential program into the most practical instrument that can do the job, with the least resistance from the circumambient political atmosphere?" The President may have a very good personal and instinctive reason for not wishing to take on as much of a program as has been proposed or to go as far as it recommended. He may desire to do it in a different manner. Therefore, he demands alternatives or, in other words, suggests that there may be more than one way to skin a cat. Theoretically, the White House staff should have a close sense of the President's mind on the matter so as to be able to select the alternatives in advance and present the President with his "options," a word the Kennedy administration made fashionable. The White House staff method under President Eisenhower had been criticized as "all teeth and no meat," that is, never sufficient details for close analysis and debate of alternatives. The State Department is criticized as giving no alternatives at all, but only basic recommendations, with little or no consideration of the possible consequence and costs. The trouble with the "keeping the options open" theory was that it became in practice a series of multiple train rides along different routes. Options were never arriving at real destinations. It was often a process of floating on a sea of unchosen choices, an encouragement of ingenuity in techniques of accommodations, and at times a process, as Thomas L. Hughes, Director of Intelligence and Research in the State Department, said, of "purposeless surface manipulation."

A foreign policy crisis theoretically should produce the most effective choices of actions under the spur of the old proverb that "necessity is the mother of invention." Not frequently, however, as the philosopher Alfred North Whitehead wrote, "Necessity is the mother of futile dodges." Not showing your hand, of course, is temporarily as effective in foreign policy as in poker. The need of keeping options open, or seeming to do so, keeps alive the possibility of changing a course. Ambiguity can be an effective political instrument to keep certain political publics in hopeful suspense, since presidential foreign policy affects both domestic audiences in the United States and multiple foreign publics abroad. There is nothing new about not revealing one's path of action prematurely, as a tactical measure under a cloud cover of apparent indecisiveness. Yet no government in history has been able consistently and permanently to be all things to all men. Concerning this doctrine of diplomatic casuistry, Hughes wrote in the *Foreign Affairs Quarterly* of July 1967:

If prolonged, the attempt to keep all options open prevents the persistent pursuit of any of them. At some point the doctrine of preserving all options becomes a policy of perpetually reserving judgment. Ultimately the effort to do so erodes all feeling for commitment and consistency, for priorities and perseverance. A foreign policy whose chief characteristic is a plethora of unclosed options is not much of a foreign policy at all. Essential consistency is a virtue necessary to any policy worthy of the name; it goes to the heart of what policy is all about. A government whose behavior represents all policies at once in actuality has not resolved on a policy. Never really in search of a policy, it is doomed never to find one. Policies in perpetual motion become policies in suspense. Dozens of daily decisions contradicting themselves means that no decision has been made. Partial policies competing with one another means that policy itself is undone.

Naturally this critique was not an indictment of the option theory, or a plea for its elimination, but rather a yellow light against persistent confusion of the means for the ends. Alternate plans of attack and variations in patterns of approach always have to be considered. But, though there were at least twenty-one proposals to solve the Berlin crisis in 1959, the Berlin problem remains unsolved despite the large number of options.

The high priest of the options game in the Kennedy administration was McGeorge Bundy, the President's Special Assistant for National Security Affairs. The "preserving the President's options" slogan, originating in part from the RAND war games strategists on contract to the U.S. Air Force, was a particular addiction of Defense Secretary McNamara. It quickly became S.O.P., or standard operating procedure, for both Presidents Kennedy and Johnson. Bundy made it work, as far as any formula or tactic could work. Bundy's apparent conviction was that, if nothing else, options and more options were the best insurance the President could have to keep the door open to the future, the process in process, and possibly progressing in the right direction, so that stasis and inertia would not intervene to stall or deflect the forward thrust of the American nation, or to allow a foreign enemy or potential enemy to intervene with counterprocesses of his own.

The unique talent of Bundy as the holder of the reins on the nexus of military, diplomatic, and intelligence policy, and as White House staff catalyst and top expediter in the foreign affairs for the President, lay basically in running just fast enough on the treadmill to stay on top of events, most of the time. Bundy was the prime exponent of Neustadt's theory of decision-making as an action-forcing process, in which concrete issues that could be acted upon were at least set in motion. As an expert winnower of the chaff from the grain in the conglomerate chaos which poured into the White House, Bundy was an epitome of the cool, the deft, and the cautious. He helped figure out the odds, laid the bets, and waited for the pay-off, taut, tart, tranquil. Nigh unfathomable to friends and strangers alike, Bundy in his almost six years in the White House had been tagged as a particularist-pragmatist, a professor-in-power, an engineer of practical priorities, and a White House nonpareil. He sparked response from the bureaucracy as well as gained its respect on account of his impeccable flair for systematic and equitable allocation and evaluation of technical responsibilities. Crack bureaucrats sighed with relieved pleasure as Bundy masterfully dealt out the chores like a sharp house dealer at Las Vegas. Despite the Washington smog, Bundy was always able to keep a White House window open and let the real air of the outside world in. This was fortunate, since the big Bundy drawback lay in the white-hot cerebration and the fluid articulation with which he swamped his interlocutors. He had the genius of Protagoras for justifying practically any position under attack, regardless of the so-called truth, a word that for Bundy had unseemly overtones of epistemology. Institutional engineering expertise was his penchant. Both Bundy and his later deputy, Carl Kaysen, Harvard-certified eggheads, were absorbed by the operational problems of the present, instead of concepts, principles, and the long view, as intellectuals are supposed to be.

The State Department, with a Bundy next to a President, could enjoy the luxury of a narrow foreign policy because the highest echelon was pondering the wider spectrum. The State Department could be an irresponsible advocate of its views with greater conviction because Bundy at the White House would sort out the right priorities and recommend how the job be done. Without a character like Bundy in the White House, the State Department would face the overwhelming task of rising above its past attitudes to matters of vital national interest, which were for the most part beyond its scope and ken, in view of its limited previous experience in total responsibility.

Bundy was a "how-to" man par excellence. He dismissed the "theologians" of the MLF with a derisive snort. Rather, he appreciated those functionaries in the State Department and on his staff who cut to the marrow of an issue, or could splint fractures among policy-making groups. He cooled off the emotionally aroused with the query, "Why the heat?" Bundy took a shine to Charles ("Chip") Bohlen, the Russian expert, for his superlative flair at sensing tactical moves by the Soviet power players. Bundy admired Bromley Smith, Executive Secretary of the National Security Council, for his sophisticated feel in knowing "how to spot the scatter rugs on the polished floor of Government." These were the tricky and slippery areas of bureaucracy which could give trouble in coordinating joint agency actions in overseas operations. In White House self-defense, there sprung up the key word, "by-pass," like a signal in a basketball game to get around a pat, or set, defense. The White House play was to short-circuit or go around or over normal, lethargic channels, when celerity was the most urgent consideration to get the fact, analysis, and recommendation to the President in the shortest possible time.

As dean of the Faculty of Arts and Sciences at Harvard University, Bundy had plenty of experience in handling bureaucracies, since the academic world so much resembled the government world in its crablike guerrilla harassments. In his government course at Harvard, Bundy could refer with donnish aplomb to the "liberum veto" of the Polish Sejm, or Diet, in the eighteenth century and its reckless misuse of the powers of democracy. In Washington he rapidly realized and overcame his innocence of actual big-league experience when he saw at first hand, and shook his head with amazement at, the political ploys that President Kennedy had to manipulate in handling foreign affairs issues before the Congress and citizenry. Bundy was an early convert to the Siamese-twin realities of foreign policy and military power. He was largely instrumental in creation of the political-military affairs office in the State Department, where a direct liaison between the State and Defense Departments was organized for the first time, on a formal and continuing basis.

Not one to suffer stupidity with a smile, Bundy was all business, brusque and impatient. These traits prompted Washington to label Bundy arrogant and patronizing, an impression which he did little to dissipate by lecturing press visitors as if they were sophomores in his college class. James Deakin of the *St. Louis Post-Dispatch,* beginning an interview with Bundy, after a few minutes' conversation, heard Bundy tell him, "This is very boring." Deakin, without another word, got up and left. Bundy, in a sense, had more disciples than friends. Outside the intense pressures of his work, he deigned an astringent compassion toward lesser mortals and, after a drink or two, even a convivial warmth, whose initial manifestation to some may have appeared a forced or nervous gaiety. Further acquaintance, however, unveiled a gay companion. Bundy danced, sang, mimicked, with gusto. Rare in the political world of the capital, he was a widely cultured man at ease in literature, history, and philosophy, as well as in the arcane technicalities of helping to run a vast enterprise like United States foreign affairs. Bundy, like most people, at first seemed rather taken in by the portentous mystique of the intelligence community and foremost the CIA. He did not challenge the assertions and analyses that led to the Bay of Pigs misfortune, which, afterwards, he was a bit quick on the trigger to dismiss as only "a brick through the window." Later, as the White House member of the special group (CI) on counterinsurgency activities, Bundy had constant occasion to ride herd on the CIA. He seemed to take a sort of diluted morbid pleasure in having the bright zombies of CIA flock around him and make up to him, like a grand duke beseiged by courtiers at a levee.

Bundy, as was inevitable, left deflated egos and lacerated scalps all over the shrubbery as he knifed in a detached and surgical manner through the red tape and pet projects of organized bureaucracy. A principal victim was former Under Secretary Ball, one of the most amiable human dynamos to hit the capital in decades. Bundy embalmed the MLF, or multilateral nuclear force, the love of Ball's life, with clinical dispassion and Pharaonic phlegm. Defeated, depressed, and disgusted, Ball quit several months later, in September 1966. Before that, in February 1966, Bundy himself had left the White House to become President of the Ford Foundation. But he was kept on tap by President Johnson for confidential high-level chores on occasion. Among these was Bundy's membership on the Heineman Committee, a Presidential task force, one of fifty groups the President had appointed and never announced, to do special jobs for him. The Heineman Committee, organized in October 1966, had the mission of investigating the practicabilities for reorganization of the executive branch of the United States Government, particularly in the field of foreign affairs. The hope was to bring some semblance of order and logic into the vaulting growth and complexity among the multiple United States agencies involved in foreign operations.

Ironically, the two old friendly enemies, Bundy and Ball, almost worked and fought together again when the Arab-Israeli war exploded on June 5, 1967. The President ordered a call put out immediately for both Bundy and Ball. Bundy came, but Ball was in Chicago and could not be reached. Bundy was appointed Executive Secretary of a Special Committee of the National Security Council for the Middle East crisis, an "Ex-com" group like that for the Cuban nuclear missile crisis. Bundy's deft touch and sure-footed procedure amid the confusion of administrative and diplomatic actions imperative in those first days of war and through interminable attempts at a cease-fire in the United Nations once again demonstrated the calm reliability and effortless dispatch that were Bundy's metier. The Middle East crisis clearly was going to be a protracted affair, and not a sharp in-up-and-out business like Cuba in 1962.

Symbolic of the stature of Bundy as a junior elder statesman, still in his forties, was his appearance to speak before the TV cameras outside the Press Lobby of the White House after President Johnson's announcement of his appointment for the Arab-Israeli crisis, though he had secretly been on board several days. One noted that the high occasion called for a certain orotundity in the Bundy cheeks and precisely pursed lips, the properly frocked phrase from the tribune, and a hint of a glint of the feline behind the eyeglasses. The invisible mantle of a possible future of Secretary of State nobly draped upon his shoulders, Bundy retained an astral air of the pedagogue. It is a mark of occupation shared in degree by President Johnson and Secretary Rusk, both former teachers.

Among the many accomplishments of Bundy & Co. during the Kennedy administration was the rich and multicolored vernacular brought into play or adapted to describe, with cogent metaphor and nice evocation, the nuances in complications and the fleeting convolutions of diplomacy. The verbal sparklers delighted foreign diplomats who understood English well enough to appreciate such spectacular departures from the dead and dull jargon of traditional diplomatic exchanges. But the Bundy et al. elliptical figures of speech confounded in despair foreign diplomats whose knowledge of English was stiff, schoolbookish, and obtuse.

Among such phrases was "smoke is coming out of the basement." It could be translated as something stirring in the field of diplomatic interest, but not yet jelled. Or, "noises on the stairs, but no one has come into the room yet," meaning just a lot of rumors, but possibly prefiguring some action, and said to be a translation from a Chinese proverb. Or, "pull the plug," meaning to liquidate an operation and let it go down the drain. Or, "show the clout," meaning to throw the weight of the President's name and office around. Or, "get on the horn," that is, take to the telephone to pass the word. Or, "put in the wiring," that is, to install the circuit of common understanding among the agencies through adequate directives and arrangements. Or the ironic phrase, "We are in a state of creative tension." To the beleaguered White House staff, this meant there was a multiplicity of advisers competing for the President's attention.

Or the revealing phrase, "Crises make the plumbing show." This referred to the myriad details that have to be checked, coordinated, and collected when sudden eruptions like war shatter the normal channels and daily routine of standing operating procedures. In the immediate wake of initial hostilities between the Israelis and the Arabs, the Bundy Committee had to plunge into half a dozen·matters at once—setting priorities, organizing the follow-through, and getting set for the long, drawn-out denouement: C-130 planes to be flown down from Germany to Athens, Greece, with water, if needed, for the straggling Egyptian soldiers in the Sinai Desert; AID supply arrangements to cancel, divert, or reschedule to a score of countries when the shipments, including grain to hungry India, had been obstructed by the closing of the Suez Canal; emergency plans for evacuation of American civilians, estimated at 40,000, by airlift from fourteen Arab countries. There was the enormous and tragic problem of over 200,000 more new refugees, piled onto the bitter embers of the million old ones from the Palestine war of 1948. Scurrying and hurrying and lobbying and questing for votes by remote control in the corridors of the United Nations in New York. Positioning of agents and instrumentalities for intelligence in key places. In short, when a war demolishes a superstructure above ground, all the pipes and drains and sewers of the plumbing underground have to be taken care of, and immediately.

Finally, there was the phrase: "Drop the china and blow." It meant that when matters pressed too heavily, just forget everything and go away. It might have applied at Harvard, but not in the White House.

One of the few lasting satisfactions in Washington is the appreciation, by osmosis if not by direct participation, of the enthralling, subtly cruel, and amusing spectacle of human beings at, or near, the peak of power. Concerning the actual behavior of such characters, it is manifestly almost impossible to render equity with compassion because of the outsider's pure ignorance. The April 1966 transition in the White House from Bundy to Walt Rostow in the post of Special Assistant to the President for National Security Affairs points up the quicksands of comparative judgments. In one sense, Bundy was anemic, and Rostow had too much cholesterol. Bundy was a Puritan product of the knotted constringencies of New England; a latest-model machine tool of fine tolerances turning over at incredible velocity; an heir of the organic culture of the Massachusetts high gentry epitomized by Henry James, the ultrarefined novelist, and William James, his brother, the original American pragmatist. Rostow is a product of Jewish-Slavic heritage and American birth. Bundy's inherent contempt for generalizations bequeathed no single concept of United States foreign policy with which his name could be associated as an originator. His future career may remedy this omission as he elucidates his own rationalizations and his place in the destiny of the nation. Generalizations were Rostow's forte. With them, Rostow was prodigality itself, throwing seed with a sweeping hand across the horizon. The seed was not always quite certifiable by U.S. Department of Agriculture standards. One could not know immediately whether the harvest would be flowers, weeds, or sturdy trees. Yet the Rostow yield more often than not confounded the captious.

A fellow officer of some consequence who worked closely with both Bundy and Rostow described Bundy as a man who sees things in black and white, a positive, sharp, crisp, incisive, decisive, cutting, humorous, scintillating man, more of an advocate who would try to get the President to go Bundy's way. Rostow was analyzed as philosophical, subject to error, an outliner of the pros and cons of an issue with precise judgment, an ideal staff man who does not shove in his own opinions, not combative or competitive, one who does not try to win all the arguments and lose the sale, fair, erudite, and a none-better all-round man.

Rostow was an idea-man for Presidents Kennedy and Johnson, and, earlier, for President Eisenhower. He coined one of the New Frontier's most effective campaign phrases, "Let's get this country moving again." He was one of the authors of Eisenhower's "open skies" proposal at the 1955 Geneva summit conference. Rostow ranks with President Johnson and Secretary Rusk as a leading victim of vilification in the envenomed animosities exhaled by the Vietnam war. His former Kennedy administration colleagues praised Rostow for "unusual inventiveness of mind and copiousness of expression" and "inexhaustible capacity for meeting every crisis with a plan" and for "force and fertility of thought." The impassioned foes of the

Johnson Vietnam policy attacked Rostow for having too many ideas, which are too thin and mostly unworkable at that; for being "sycophantic" toward President Johnson, telling him only what LBJ wanted to hear; for a supposedly intransigent position on the bombing of North Vietnam, which, his former associates charged, was in reality an attempt to justify Rostow's preconceptions in theories of bombing, born out of his service in the U.S. Strategic Bombing Survey of Germany during World War II. His critics speculated on whether Rostow's intensity of conviction perhaps shrouded some need for "over-compensation" in his make-up. He was derided as the author of "Panaceas out of Bomb Bays." The critical chorus declared that, like a lot of academic types, Rostow liked to "play general," a poke at Rostow's long-time acquaintance with generals of the Pentagon and the Joint Chiefs of Staff.

It was easier to satirize Rostow, who instinctively and enthusiastically led with his chin, than to find nicks and flaws in the suave and seamless Bundy as ringmaster of the White House team of intellectual gymnasts. The canards, the slings and arrows of outraged and outrageous critics, not to mention the occasional spray of merde that came his way from quondam pals, left Rostow apparently undismayed and serene, unfailingly decent, sympathetic, and affable. The criticism in no whit detracted from the sense of spaciousness with which Rostow contemplated the universe and his steady but zigzag course to near the center of the operating power structure in the United States. It was a path he had traversed with a certain guileless innocence and a smiling instinct for survival.

Rostow is a transliteration of Rostov, a city in southeast Russia. Rostow's father, Victor Aaron, fled the Bolshevik Revolution from north of Odessa to the United States at eighteen. He became a metallurgical chemist, graduating from Pratt Institute in Brooklyn. He had three sons, Walt Whitman, the second youngest; Eugene Victor Debs, the eldest, former Dean of the Yale University Law School and now Under Secretary for Political Affairs in the Department of State; and the youngest, Ralph, owner of a ladies garment emporium in Ann Arbor, Michigan. The father advised the boys not to expect too much from life, so that they would not be so surprised if matters did not work out, but if things did work out, to take it as so much to the good. This sense of inner security nourished by the close unity of a loving family compares with that of the affectionately bristling Bundy family. Its brilliant members in the Kennedy-Johnson administrations, McGeorge and William, the latter a veteran of CIA and the Defense Department, and now Assistant Secretary of State for East Asian and Pacific Affairs, were enjoined by their father, Harvey, himself a distinguished senior bureaucrat, never in any way to allow personal rivalry in public life to invade by even an infinitesimal fraction the personal loyalty they owed to each other as blood brothers.

Rostow came to join the Kennedy administration in 1961, with an unstrained faith in his own capacities, an unhurried posture as to how he would put them into practice, and three books, the classic *Democracy in America,* by Alexis de Tocqueville; *The Green Curve Omnibus,* by Major General Sir Ernest Swinton, a volume of short stories written before World War I by an eccentric genius and professor at Oxford, whose revolutionary foresight in the art of strategy had made a lasting impression on Rostow as a Rhodes scholar at Oxford before the war; and *Microcosmographia Academia—A Guide for the Young Academic Politician,* by F. M. Cornford, an essay written by a Cambridge University professor of philosophy some fifty years ago, a volume Rostow dipped into like a breviary when the bureaucratic hounds bayed.

Tennis was an escape, solace, and discipline for the travails in the power jungle. As many of the New Frontier crowd did, Rostow played at the St. Albans School for Boys tennis courts, rarely missing a game except for reasons of high crisis, arriving and leaving on the dot, and practicing faithfully. Like many middle-class players who learned to play on public courts in boyhood, Rostow was a plodder at tennis, hitting the balls with a heavy top spin, a residue of the days when one could not afford to buy new balls often and had to hit the balls, old and light, just right to keep them in the court. He played an extremely tenacious game, and heady, not neglecting the drop shot, also a heritage of a youthful Machiavelli on the courts. His best feature was his forehand, which went direct to the spot of his choice. His serve was somewhat that of a windmill, but it had enough drive. He never stopped running, and he scrambled all over the courts. His backhand was none too strong: he usually ran around it. Rostow was dovish when in trouble and resorted to lobs to protect weakness. His double partners' assessment was uniform: good man to have on your side.

Rostow was one of the three men in the Johnson administration, the others being Rusk and McNamara, who had been dealing with Vietnam from the very first, with Rostow taking precedence because McNamara did not get into Vietnam in depth until 1962, and Rusk not until 1964. Rostow headed a task force on Vietnam in February 1961 in the White House for Kennedy, having the watch on Laos and Vietnam while Bundy looked after Europe, Berlin, and Cuba. In 1958, Rostow began his official concern with the theme of counterinsurgency resulting from Communist "wars of liberation," when he helped write President Eisenhower's speech on the Middle East before the United Nations. Rostow had gone into the subject of guerrilla warfare in the 1950's, when he was a professor at the

Massachusetts Institute of Technology. Secretary Dulles in 1958 felt that the main topic should have been "indirect aggression," the term used for guerrilla infiltration in that day. This theme Rostow and his fellow speech writer, C. D. Jackson, helped enunciate as American policy for the first time.

Rostow was transferred from the White House to the post of Chairman of the Policy Planning Council in the State Department in late 1961. He had originally been assigned the job by Kennedy, but had not been able to take it because Secretary Rusk had demurred. Characteristically, Rostow looked upon his duties at State as an opportunity for pumping new blood into the heart of the bureaucracy. He developed contingency plans for the bombing of North Vietnam which became so well known that even the Communists referred to Rostow's "War Plan No. 5." Rostow used to fret later that it was not his particular plan of bombing that had been put into effect. Being State's number one planner gave Rostow carte blanche to range far and wide. He predicted the slowing down of the rate of Russian economic growth at least six months before the CIA, for its own special political propaganda purposes, did so in an early 1964 unprecedented press background briefing.

Though out of the stream of operational decisions in the State Department, Rostow had been keenly interested in Latin America as a working laboratory of his theories, as exemplified in *The Stages of Economic Growth*. When a sophomore at Yale, Rostow had pledged himself to write "the answer" to Karl Marx's *Das Kapital*. He helped the Latin Americans in May 1964 to organize CIAP, the inter-American steering committee, as a political motor for the Alliance for Progress. The Latinos for the first time started to make their own decisions on the allocation of resources and on the feasibility of plans for their own economic and social improvements. Rostow's activities did not escape the omnivorous eye of President Johnson. It was at this time that Johnson used to mutter: "The only place in the State Department where I ever get any ideas is the Policy Planning Staff."

In the White House post, where the necessity for the wide-angled view of a President is a *sine qua non* of the job, Rostow was a natural. He surprised his denigrators by reversing his field and becoming terse, clear, and to the point in his official business with the President, as the President demanded, while still retaining his loquacious accessibility to the world at large. Rostow quickly arrived at an understanding with the President. He had no political or appointive ambitions; he had only one eventual aim: to write a book on the stages of political growth as a sequel and a capstone of his earlier work on economic growth.

Rostow felt at home in his new role of being the closest staff adviser to the President in foreign affairs because of his deep-seated conviction that all Presidents need planners and that the prime concern of presidential leadership is the shape of a future, the lines of which cannot be organized without plans. Rostow had the good fortune of working with a President who was decisive without question. His job was to invite the President's attention to those matters which were ripe for discussion and decision; to outline impartially all—the emphasis was on "all"—the relevant views from each concerned agency as to what the decision might be. A man who was not impartial wouldn't last one month with Johnson. Rostow further gave his own gloss and criteria as to the weight of the views submitted. He passed the eventual presidential decisions on to the huge foreign affairs bureaucracies in State, Defense, CIA, Agriculture, and other departments, and he followed through to see that decisions were actually carried out as directed. It was all standard procedure.

Despite the closeness of his standing with the President, Rostow was extremely sensitive of the prerogatives of the Secretary of State. He said unequivocally: "A man in this job under no circumstances should consider himself at the Cabinet level. . . . The advice of a White House aide cannot rank with that from a responsible Cabinet official."

While growing adept at action-on-demand, Rostow also shifted gears at times back to his favorite occupation. This was the making of world purviews, in response to the President's insistent demand for "new initiatives" in other world areas, politically to demonstrate that the Johnson administration did have a wider spectrum than the so-called parochial war of Vietnam. Rostow had nurtured the concept of regionalism for three years in the State Department's Policy Planning Council. He hoped this concept of regionalism would become his own modest contribution in the evolution of United States foreign policy. Regionalism was an idea to which Rostow had been faithful from the start, from espousal of continental unity through the western European common market in 1946 to the similarly projected unity in Latin America through the Alliance for Progress in 1967. A bare beginning of the same character for Africa, starting in the Organization of African Unity, had been sketched out. The self-same concept for Asia was developed through, first, the Asian Development Bank and then a series of groupings like ASPAC, ASA, ASEAN, all encouragements to the Far Eastern nations to join together for their own common social and economic improvement. Rostow showed almost a childlike pleasure in playing with these building blocks of the future. In the midst of exacting duties and subject instanter to the beck of an imperious master, he seemed continually to be annotating his own Pilgrim's Progress toward visions which filled his eyes.

Rostow felt that in the long sweep of the centuries the United States was on the crest of the wave and could discern the not-too-distant harbor of peace and surcease of wars; that stout opposition to violent attempts to alter the *status quo* was the best insurance that forward progress would be maintained, so that an era of true serenity and universal prosperity would prevail in the affairs of men, particularly when Communists stopped exploiting and exacerbating the frictions of growth and joined the United States and all aspirant nations to build, if not a global Great Society, at least a system of states self-sufficient unto their needs and enjoying in common the decent respect for human dignity that mankind owed to itself as an absolute minimum.

CHAPTER VIII

THE CONGRESS:
Democracy's Folk Wisdom

LIKE EVERY OTHER DEPART-
ment of the Government, the State Department has an office for management of the legislation which the Department is proposing for passage in furtherance of the President's program. The responsible officer is the Assistant Secretary of State for Congressional Relations. He has a staff of twenty-six and spends over $386,000 a year for braving the big wide world of politics as symbolized by the Congress—the House of Representatives and the Senate—of the United States. As soon as State's officers leave their snug little harbors in the State Department headquarters and head for Capitol Hill, they are immediately out in the open sea, taking the spray of their forward thrusts for enactment of legislation as well as the backwash of the resistance to their proposals.

The Congressional office has one of the most thankless jobs in the State Department. Two veterans sit in a backroom and keep close technical watch on foreign affairs legislation in Congress. The office has lacked infusion of first-class Foreign Service officer blood. Few diplomatic careerists have worked in it. In the past, some of its jobs were pure and simple patronage pay-offs to Congressmen who had "Hill" friends needing safe niches. Its prospective overhaul is long overdue. The aim is to improve the Congressional office in at least two ways. The first would be to make the office like a forward artillery observer's post, apprising the State Department of specific Congressional attitudes in advance, and preparing State for effective presentation of policies in a manner that better satisfies Congressional wishes. The second would be to make the office a message center for the entire State Department, so that officers who tended to think of Congress as another country could be trained and become habituated to the close need of keeping Congressional considerations in mind.

The unhappy part of Foreign Service officers' experience in the Congressional bear pits is that, not being professional politicians (though in theory diplomats are at best only high-class politicians), State Department Congressional staff men are often damned for what they do as well as for what they don't. Worse yet is the fact that since the State Department is the titular head of the foreign affairs community, the Department frequently has to collaborate and work with foreign affairs sister agencies without having complete operational control of the other agencies' endeavors at Congressional lobbying and liaison.

Explaining foreign aid, a major instrument of U.S. foreign policy, is under direction of the Agency for International Development's Congressional Liaison staff, which may or may not be up to par, and not infrequently isn't. Unlike that of other departments of the Government, State's Congressional team cannot form alliance with key Hill committee members, as used to happen in the past between the Department of Health, Education and Welfare and pertinent House committees, because State holds no domestic operational constituency. The Department has the assistance of the White House Congressional Liaison staff, which numbers only five. As Postmaster Lawrence O'Brien pointed out, a small though elite White House staff makes it incumbent upon the State Department, like any other executive department, to be prepared itself to push its programs before Congress. State was blamed for over-zealousness when AID Congressional staffers piled into the corridors of the Capitol, upsetting careful arrangements made by the Senate leadership, the Assistant Secretary of State for Congressional Relations, and White House liaison officers. The influx annoyed the Senators during the 1967 debate on the foreign aid bill. Mansfield was so irked that he complained to President Johnson, urging him to order the AID lobbyists "to keep their distance" from the Senate. State and AID officers did not show their faces for two weeks.

All kinds of collateral influences shape the fate of a piece of legislation. A factor in the AID situation had been the notorious silliness about the confirmation of Rutherford Poats as Deputy Administrator of AID some months earlier. Poats' confirmation had been placed in jeopardy by the objection of Senator Birch Bayh, Democrat of Indiana. AID backers of Poats, unchecked by proper State Department guidance, indulged in the undignified spectacle of exchanging statements and counterstatement with Bayh. No one had told them long before to keep quiet and lie low. The ire of Bayh won sympathy from fellow Senators. The situation frightened AID officials to the point where they were considering withdrawal of the Poats nomination. White House staffers stepped in and pointed out that the prestige of the President of the United States could not be so bandied about as to have a nomination withdrawn on such flimsy grounds. After it was all over, nobody seemed to remember what the original argument between Bayh and Poats had been. It had started out over Bayh's complaint about the purchase of AID-financed Korean steel for use in South Vietnam. This was important to Bayh, since his state had a big steel industry and an upcoming election, to boot. He had to raise the issue as a matter of duty to his constituency. Yet in all the hassle back and forth, this steel interest was never prominently mentioned.

The Senate leadership cooperated with the White House Liaison staff by allowing a "command post" to be set up in Room 104 on the first floor, on the Senate side, of the Capitol. State Department and AID technicians were on hand to be consulted and to give expert information and advice to any Senator who requested them, and even to draft any amendment that a Senator might request. Yet the best laid plans sometimes went kerplunk despite expert preparation. At the very hottest moment of the debate on authorization of the foreign aid bill, a key amendment was being offered on the floor by Senator Henry M. Jackson, Democrat of Washington, to restore the flexibility of the Defense Department's position by retaining the revolving fund for financing arms sales. There had been a hullabaloo about arms sales in 1967, though the arms situation had been getting out of hand for at least three years before the Senate suddenly discovered the so-called scandal. The Senate leadership arranged for a meeting of fifteen key Senators to hear explanations from State, AID, and Defense officials on the arms sales and on any other matters the Senators wished to bring up. As the briefing broke up, Senator Joseph D. Tydings, Maryland Democrat, stopped at the door to ask military liaison officers present about a minor technical matter. The military were unprepared and flubbed the answers, instead of admitting their lack of information. Five votes on the aid bill were lost among the fifteen Senators present right on the spot. The Jackson amendment was rejected by seven votes.

Happily, it was not all high drama and low comedy on Capitol Hill for State's Congressional team. The office had turned in an increasingly substantial performance over the years, learning the hard way and performing yeoman service for individual Senators and Congressman. The office handled an average of about 25,000 items of Congressional correspondence a year. The 1966 breakdown, by subject and number, follows:

Consular Affairs	8,593
Employment	2,363
Educational and Cultural Affairs	1,607
Foreign Policy (General)	1,155
African Affairs	900
Latin American Affairs	1,502
European Affairs	2,213

Far East Affairs (excluding Vietnam)	861
Vietnam and Related Subjects	2,658
Near Eastern and South Asian Affairs	1,055
Foreign Aid	374
United Nations	665
Miscellaneous	378
TOTAL	24,323

The State Department's two Congressional Liaison telephone lines got in 1967 an average of more than 50 calls a day, or roughly 30,000 a year, while another 50-plus calls per day came in on other telephones in the Congressional Liaison offices, making another 30,000, or a total of 60,000 calls a year. Since establishment of the FTS, or Federal Telecommunications System, operated by the General Services Administration, members of the government can dial on the system from anywhere in the United States. Thus, even when Congress is adjourned or Congressmen are on vacation, the State Congressional offices still get an average of thirty-five calls a day. Before FTS, Congressmen who were at home and wanted to call Washington had to do so on their own official allowance funds. Now, with FTS, the State Department is as near as the next telephone.

Consular affairs and passports account for from 40 to 45 per cent of all calls and letters received by the State Congressional offices. They land more often than not in the lap of Eugene L. Krizek, former administrative assistant to Representative Charles A. Vanik, a Cleveland, Ohio, Democrat. A Kennedy administration political appointee, Krizek became, in effect, the unofficial Ombudsman of the State Department. He received pleas from Congressional constituents relayed to him by their representatives, thus putting him on the spot to give top service on behalf of the State Department. In many cases, this entailed jogging State's deliberate-minded bureaucracy into speedier action, reversing actions on visas which had been denied to relatives of Congressmen's constituents, putting in plugs for exceptions in quotas for immigrants, tracing the whereabouts of lost Americans for anxious relatives, in short, what, in newspaper jargon, is called "Action-Line" or "Quick-Line" service to the public. Krizek usually needed four days to get action on a Congressman's request, which, considering the State Department's leisurely sense of time, was somewhat of a miracle. One call from a Congressman might initiate a chain reaction of twelve further calls before satisfaction could be given to the Congressman's constituents, all of which, of course, made the State Department look good and created good will. Krizek, in fact, received 43 per cent of all written inquiries and 50 per cent of all telephone inquiries.

The Congressional Liaison Office, inevitably, was continually propagating the gospel on foreign policy as written by the senior apostles on the sixth and seventh floors. It arranged regular Wednesday briefings for members of the House of Representatives who wished to attend, an average of twenty such briefings being held a Congressional session. Attendance ranged anywhere from 25 to 150 Congressmen, while 30 to 40 Senators sometimes also showed up. At the request of members of Congress on behalf of special guests or prominent constituents, the Congressional office arranged for their attendance at the regular briefings on foreign policy given by the State Department every Tuesday and Friday morning for the public. Besides the Representatives and Senators, the office made a practice of briefing key staff aides of the Congress, having had as many as 400 top legislative functionaries at such briefings.

High on the priority of Congressional Liaison operations was arranging trips overseas for members of Congress and their staffs. In 1965, for example, approximately 832 members of Congress and their staffs voyaged abroad on 282 "CODEL" trips, "CODEL" being Department cablese for Congressional delegations. These advance warnings invariably sent waves of apprehension through most embassies. In recent years, practically half the Congress traveled overseas. Western Europe was the leading attraction and the Far East next, State and Defense picking up the transportation tab. The State Department also brought out a travel guide for the care and feeding of touring Congressmen, the *Handbook for Congressional Foreign Travel*. All Foreign Service posts had a major responsibility for providing VIP treatment to legislators, including a welcome at the airport by the U.S. Ambassador. On arrival, visiting Congressmen were to receive envelopes containing local currency equivalents of five, ten, and twenty dollars for quick pocket money.

The office had become so attuned to the needs of its own public relations that, like any convention and visitors bureau, it put out a card listing its services in detail. Here is the latest sample:

SERVICES PROVIDED BY THE
OFFICE OF CONGRESSIONAL RELATIONS

DEPARTMENT OF STATE

INFORMATION ABOUT FOREIGN POLICY

You can call this office for information—general or specific—about our foreign policy in any area of the world or pending foreign policy legislation.

If your question deals with a particular country or area, for prompt action, we suggest you call the "H" officer who is in charge of that area (see list below).

If you wish general information about foreign policy, please call Government code 182, Ext. 4747 or 4748.

GENERAL FOREIGN AFFAIRS INFORMATION

The Department is always glad to assist you with your constituents' questions on foreign affairs and Department operations, as well as your own. Call Ext. 4747 or 4748.

BRIEFINGS

Members—We will be happy to arrange briefings for you here at Department or in your offices whenever you wish. Call Ext. 4748.

Staff—In order to help your top staff members to be of maximum assistance to you, we will also be pleased to arrange briefings for them. Call Ext. 4748.

Special visitors—Public briefings on the Formulation of Foreign Policy are conducted in the Department Auditorium, at 21st St. and Virginia Avenue, each Tuesday and Friday, at 9:30 A.M., and some of your constituents who are visiting Washington may be interested. For groups of ten or more, we would appreciate your calling us on Ext. 4748. If your group would like to have a specific topic discussed, this can be arranged if we have at least one week's notice.

YOUR CORRESPONDENCE WITH STATE DEPARTMENT

For information regarding your correspondence with the Department, such as questions on past-due replies or follow-ups to interim replies, please call Ext. 4286, 6654, or 7579.

PUBLICATIONS

A wide variety of information material on U.S. foreign policy is available. You can obtain sample copies by calling Ext. 4747 or 4748.

TOURS

(Daily—Monday thru Friday) Tours of the Department of State can be arranged for your constituents by reservation. Call Ext. 6200.

RADIO AND TELEVISION

Department officials, including officers who have recently returned from the field, are available for radio or television interviews with individual Senators and Representatives in the Hill Studios. To make the necessary arrangements, please call Ext. 4748.

SPEAKERS

The Department stands ready, at all times, to assist you in obtaining speakers for meetings and conferences in Washington or your district. Whenever possible, please make requests in writing to this office as far in advance as possible.

OVERSEAS TRAVEL

Our Congressional Travel staff will be happy to assist you in every way possible on your overseas travel, including briefings, advance notification to the posts, arrangements for optimum utilization of your time while abroad, and in any other aspects of your trip. Please call Miss Bunn, Ext. 8195.

LIST OF CONGRESSIONAL RELATIONS OFFICERS

William B. Macomber, Jr., Assistant Secretary	X5395
H. G. Torbert, Jr., Deputy Assistant Secretary: European Affairs	X3276
John P. White, Deputy Assistant Secretary: East Asian Affairs and	
International Organization	X6446

LEGISLATIVE MANAGEMENT OFFICERS

Kathryn Folger: Near East & South Asian; Educational; and
    Protocol Affairs   X5005
Eugene L. Krizek: Consular Affairs (visas, passports, special consular
    services), Personnel Programs, Refugee Matters   X8165
John S. Leahy: Africa, Legal Matters, Security, Fisheries   X3311
Alexander Schnee: Economic and Latin American Affairs   X3644
John Gonella: Scientific Affairs; Public Affairs   X6460
Edith Waskewich: Legislative Reports   X2258
George Winnett: Correspondence   X4286, 6654, 7579
    Travel: Jacqueline Bunn   X8195
    Briefings, Publications, and General Information:
      Mae Sykes   X4747, 4748
    Transcripts: Peggy Proctor   X3594
State Department Code: 182

The Department opened a new chapter in its endeavor to improve relations with Congress by assigning two junior Foreign Service officers in 1966 to serve for eight months as personal aides to Congressmen. They did exclusively Congressional chores, from answering constituents' mail to preparing technical material for the Congressmen's committee hearings.

As Larry O'Brien said, it was about time the State Department pulled its weight in working with Congress. It was also one of Under Secretary Katzenbach's first ideas to work in this field when he went over to State from the Justice Department. The State Department's need for public support of its policies meant intensive involvement of all responsible State Department personnel in dealing with the press for the education of public opinion and with Congress for the efficacy of its desired legislation. Katzenbach felt that State could not expect to continue to call upon the President to sell two-bit issues, on the one hand, or to make desperate appeals through the President at the last minute just when an issue was going down the drain, thus wasting the President's credit. Katzenbach's needle even produced a rah-rah spirit, as indicated in a memorandum describing "the mission of the Congressional Liaison Office," which called for "both offense and defense tactics," as in a football game.

In 1967 the eager lobbyists of foreign affairs produced a rack of ready-to-be-delivered speeches for Senators and Congressmen. Eight were from State on the proposed Panama Canal Zone Treaty revision, while two had been prepared by the U.S. Arms Control and Disarmament Agency, an autonomous subsidiary of the State Department, on the very day that a convention signed by the United States and Russia on the nonproliferation of nuclear weapons had been tabled in the Senate. Some Senators who received the speeches resented being what they termed "State's

Charley McCarthys." As one said, "The least they could have done was to send me a memorandum with the information, and I could have decided what to do with it if I wanted to."

Top-drawer Foreign Service officers fully realize what the new diplomacy entailed politically, particularly with Congress. As one officer brought to Washington from Saigon said: "I always suspected there was a lot of pressure back here at headquarters. In Saigon all we had to do was to carry out the policies, or advise how they could be improved. Back here, we devise the policies well enough, but the big worry is on the play and the presentation."

The plurality of the Foreign Service, however, seemed to shudder with distaste at the necessity of Congressional involvement, and it firmly believed that great issues of state were not settled by riotous public debates. Assistant Secretaries for Congressional Relations tended to have more trouble inside the State Department than they had with Congress. Douglas MacArthur II found himself wrestling 80 per cent of the time with his colleagues concerning issues which had to be presented to Congress, and his successor, William B. Macomber, Jr., at least 55 per cent of the time. Macomber had the advantage of having been Assistant Secretary for Congressional Relations under Secretary Dulles. Formerly, in turn, he had been a U.S. Marine, a Central Intelligence Agency official, Ambassador to Jordan, and Assistant AID Administrator for the Near East. Macomber was called back to the job by Secretary Rusk in 1967. He is rated as the best man in that post in the last decade.

Competence notwithstanding, Macomber or any other Assistant Secretary for Congressional Relations under present conditions operates with two strikes on him because of repeated Congressional criticism. Congressmen believe that candor on the part of State officials would be highly useful but is a rare commodity. They are particularly irritated by State's handling of their correspondence, charging lack of responsiveness, tardy replies, and stiff and offensive style, characteristics which State's higher echelons recognize and despair of correcting, despite perennial crusades for better writing. The Congressmen would like to hear in person from individual desk officers in charge of dealing directly with foreign country matters, and not from the big names alone. They accuse State of denying the legislators access to the junior technicians on the grounds that the officers are always too busy on the front lines of crises. Congressmen's hackles rise when a State Congressional Liaison functionary, obviously under the rather fatuous impression he is doing a smooth selling job, asks: "You're not going to say 'no' to the President, are you?" As practically every Congressman says, "That's one sure way of losing my vote." The faulty tactic violated a cardinal rule of the pros: Don't crowd a man more than the issue is worth.

Most Congressmen can only grumble about their frustrations with State. But the House Appropriations Subcommittee on the State Department, under Congressman John J. Rooney, Democrat of New York and Chairman of the Subcommittee (for the past several centuries, State Department officials groan), doesn't have to take any backtalk from State. The Rooney Committee, moreover, will not deign to talk to any representative of the office of the Assistant Secretary of State for Congressional Relations on matters before the Committee. Nor will it accept any letters concerning its agenda from the Office of Congressional Relations. The Committee's members do their business only with the administrative branch of the State Department, that is, the office of Deputy Under Secretary of State for Administration, Idar Rimestad. Rooney is in undisputed charge, and State Department officials are punctilious with their "yes, sir," "thank you, sir," and "if you please, sir." The Department has permission to review the subcommittee's transcript, but it cannot cut out even one word without permission of the subcommittee, which sometimes even reverses its off-the-record rulings, deciding that the so-called confidential information of State should be in the public domain and on the record. Given the subcommittee's hound-dog instincts for tracking down dollars and cents of waste or dubious expenses in State Department budgets, not to mention Congressman Rooney's fearsome reputation for cutting bureaucrats down to size, State Department officials at times feel they have come through trial-by-torture after they have escaped from Rooney's chambers.

A moment of titillation in the subcommittee's inquisition regularly occurs during the examination of the proposed budget for the State Department's Office of Security. Congressmen are let in on the secrets: the history and cost of debugging the embassies in Eastern Europe and Russia during the last two years. In the March 1967 hearings for the fiscal 1968 budget, Rooney's eye was caught by an item for $513,400. Deputy Assistant Secretary of State for Security Affairs G. Marvin Gentile explained that it was for equipment for the secure acoustic room program in embassies in unfriendly territory. There had been thirty-nine such bug-free rooms installed and now in use. Rooney wanted to know whether any more electronic devices had been discovered in U.S. posts abroad during the year past. Gentile said he would not like to talk about it on the record, but in off-the-record discussion he revealed that electronic, or bugging, devices have also been found in so-called friendly countries in Western Europe.

Every year without fail, Rooney asks, "What is your report this year with regard to security risks?"

The 1967 subcommittee hearings report continued:

Mr. Gentile: "This year we had a total of 19, Mr. Chairman."

Mr. Rooney: "Made up of what sort of risks?"

Mr. Gentile: "Seventeen were for homosexual activities and two were in the area of immoral conduct."

Mr. Rooney: "What was the highest grade in the Foreign Service of those among those 19?"

Mr. Gentile: "The highest grade in the Foreign Service among those 19 was a Foreign Service Office Class 3."

Mr. Rooney: "How long had he or she been in the Foreign Service?"

Mr. Gentile: "Twenty years."

Mr. Rooney: "When he was confronted, he resigned, didn't he?"

Mr. Gentile: "Yes, sir."

Mr. Rooney: "Married?"

Mr. Gentile: "Yes, sir."

This standard catechism also occurred in February 1966, when Congressman John M. Slack, Jr., Democrat of West Virginia, was the point man. Gentile again was in the straight-man role. He explained that in 1965 State had dismissed thirty people, who had left under the category of security risks. Gentile added: "Two were non-homosexual types, dismissed for things such as excessive drinking, bad debts, and excessive use of leave, and 28 for homosexual reasons."

Former Deputy Under Secretary for Administration William J. Crockett attended the 1966 hearings and interpolated:

"We are trying very hard, more than ever, to do what we call preventive security. It is my feeling it might be easier to find the n in advance than afterwards. We are having a direct confrontation before employment, and after investigation by the Security Officers.

"We personally interview the applicant and it is surprising how many admissions we get to direct questions that we would never find out without the direct questioning because the evidence and referrals just has not produced it. But when we ask the questions directly, they tell us and we are screening quite a number out of the applicant files.

"This will not have any effect on our statistics, I do not think, for some time to come, but I think it is a worthwhile program and one which hopefully will get the embarrassing statistics down a little bit."

Mr. Rooney: "It would seem to me, Mr. Crockett, under your administration you have increased the animus of the Mattachine society, the organization composed of homosexuals, to the extent that it picketed the State Department here in Washington. Is that a fact?"

Mr. Crockett: "Yes. They wrote us two letters. They wrote saying that we were denying Americans the right of employment, that this was unconstitutional, and they wanted a chance to come in and talk to us about this policy."

Mr. Rooney: "About this time each year, I get a number of letters from these poor sick people."

Mr. Crockett: "And they said if we did not talk to them, they would picket us. We did not talk to them and they did picket us. It was surprising, both sexes were there."

Mr. Rooney: "How many of the 28 were males, and how many were females?"

Mr. Gentile: "Out of the group of 28, 26 were males and two were females."

Obviously, this low-level sociology did not enshrine Congressman Rooney in the hearts of State Department officials. The feared Congressman's raspy tongue and the odds for getting mired in this hurly-burly of crass politics feed the resentment of many diplomatic officers against their treatment in Congress. Even ranking officials of the Department often feel they are treated in a cavalier manner by Congressional committees, almost to the point of humiliation. They are intensely grilled by men who know far less about the subject matter than the officials do and who seem to delight in snide ways in venting their frustrations at the Department's expense. Senior officials complain that 20 or 25 per cent or more of their time is taken up with appearances on Capitol Hill, an unconscionable imposition on their harried calendars. The officials argue that policy makers just can't concentrate on politics, particularly Foreign Service officers who have been overseas for four or five years. They have been purposefully disciplined to be detached about the concrete application of the so-called U.S. national interest, which, to their bewilderment, they see in a totally different context and in chaotic creation when they get back to Washington.

State Department officers instinctively resist the release of information to Congressional committees in even supposedly secret sessions. Senior officials declare that during crises the Department in all sincerity cannot disclose to Congress its full mind because of the necessities of operational secrecy. Officials are convinced that practically all executive committee sessions, with the single exception of the disciplined Joint Committee on Atomic Energy, despite oaths of secrecy, produce leaks or distorted versions. These filter to the press and may injuriously affect the diplomatic posture the United States desires to present to its potential adversaries. Officials fully agree that Congress should concern itself with broad lines of foreign policy, but they point out that Congressmen unfailingly wish to pry into details of operations and raise arguments about specifics, creating vexing problems for the Department. Senators and Congressmen, on the other hand, assert that State Department officials much too frequently allow themselves to be bullied and do not put on a vigorous enough defense of their own positions in front of Congressional inquisitors.

In the view of the more sophisticated diplomats, there is a widespread failure on the part of Foreign Service officers to understand the needs of the President, whose arm they are; the officers even profess disdain for the lowly "political" considerations that a President must continually keep in mind. The old-type professional Foreign Service officer declaims with passion, "This is what he ought to do. I don't want to listen to all this political nonsense." Many officers simply have no idea of the realities of the domestic political obstacles in the United States and so disregard them and the democratic process by which the President tries to get done that which he has to do.

The command appearance of senior Department officers before Congress demands appearances at at least four hearings, two authorizations, House and Senate, and two appropriations, House and Senate. For example, in 1964, senior Departmental officers testified at 169 formal hearings. The great brunt of State Department representation before Congress inevitably falls on the Secretary of State. Secretary Dulles made over a hundred appearances in two years, Secretary Acheson over two hundred in four years. Acheson said he spent one sixth of his total time on the Hill as a matter of course. During two months in 1951, at the hearings on the dismissal of General Douglas MacArthur by President Truman, Acheson recalled, he spent half his time on the Hill. He did not have harmonious Congressional relations because of his overlordly manners, intellectual impatience with mediocrity, and aristocrat's contempt for the mean by-ways of alley politics. He epitomized his attitude toward Congress by the statement, "The understanding of relevance continues to elude the gentlemen on Capitol Hill."

During seven years in the administration of Presidents Kennedy and Johnson, Secretary Rusk appeared before Congressional committees some 200 times, 22 times in the first six months of 1967. This was the equivalent of over 500 hours of physical presence. Rusk actually met far more often with Congressmen and Senators away from the Hill at breakfasts, luncheon, special briefings, and working meetings in the State Department or at the White House, a total running to at least 400 meetings in seven years, 44 in the first six months of 1967. On the Hill itself, Rusk sometimes dropped into the offices of key Senators and Congressmen to chat with them. During crises like the Arab-Israeli war in June 1967, Rusk went up to the Hill practically every day, and sometimes twice a day, to keep important Senators and Representatives informed. On one such occasion he briefed sixty-one Senators.

About the only cavil voiced in connection with Rusk's indefatigable collaboration with Congress concerned situations of close votes on crucial foreign policy legislation. At such times Rusk was advised of the urgency but failed to call key Senators or Representatives in time, as other Cabinet officers were in the habit of doing to obtain needed votes on vital legislation. Rusk's practice had been to pass on the word and delegate the chore to a lesser functionary. In retrospect, the fault might be laid to the White House staffers who made the original request to Rusk. They did not spell out precisely why Rusk's personal assistance was urgently needed in the concrete parliamentary situation. Lacking precise data and reluctant to act on ambiguous information, Rusk obviously preferred not to spend his credit, just as the President did not spend his own, unless the matter were one of the highest urgency.

Rusk's assiduous visits to Capitol Hill and numberless statements on Vietnam, China, nuclear disarmament, foreign aid, and security commitments were a substitute, in a sense, for the British parliamentary system, in which the members of the House of Commons question the Prime Minister in writing on specific issues of foreign policy. The Secretary of State appeared on the floor of the Senate in the early days of the Republic, as Secretary of State Thomas Jefferson did. The custom died with desuetude, and when Secretary of State Charles Evans Hughes desired to appear before Congress to explain his foreign policies, he was refused permission. Rusk has never complained about interference of Congress in foreign affairs or asserted, as Secretary of State Edward Livingston did in the 1830's, "that constant infringement by Congress produced a feeling of futility in the performance of [Livingston's] arduous duties." Rusk had a deep respect for the Congress as the equivalent in responsibilities to the executive branch. However, Rusk confessed to intimates that he "bites his tongue" when under pressure and temptation to utter sharp rejoinders.

Sharp words from other Secretaries of State to the Congress have not been lacking. Secretary Thomas F. Bayard, in the 1880's during the administration of President Grover Cleveland, said: "I weary so over the tone of men high in public councils who propose to deal with the vast issues of war and peace in the spirit of prize fighters and boot-blacks. It has been a pitiable sight to witness the conduct of the Senate Committee on Foreign Relations for the past four years."

In and out of the limelight, politics have always been an integral, indeed inescapable, quotient of foreign policy, despite pious protestations on behalf of bipartisanship by all administrations and the anguished screams of opposition parties that any regime in power plays football with the nation's secrets. When foreign policy issues get to the top level of the Secretary of State and the President of the United States, most State Department functionaries more or less automatically relapse into being mere onlookers and plain citizens, giving their own discreet or candid opinions on issues, without too much, if any, private knowledge of the angles and considerations being examined by the President and his top advisers. It is only on the seventh, executive, floor of the State Department that the domestic-political contribution is cranked into the foreign policy equation which will be presented by the Secretary to the President.

As a right arm of the President, State automatically falls into the role of a foil to Congress. Rusk believes that the Secretary of State in front of Congress must be independent but not detached, that he must cooperate with Congress but not be subservient to it. Rusk is fatalistic in the knowledge that practically every Secretary of State eventually becomes controversial no matter what his personality. He has pointed out that the State Department is "in very close contact with the Congress, not only its leaders but with its back bench members who themselves are in touch with their own states and their own constituencies and, after all, they are under a Constitution elected for the purpose of representing the people of their states or their districts so that we have a pretty good idea most of the time of what public opinion would be with respect to particular policies."

But Rusk added that "there are people who have problems about one or another aspect of our foreign policy and they sometimes generalize these into objections to foreign policy as a whole." In these taped remarks from a Northwestern University radio program, Rusk concluded: "We're not inclined to negotiate with a newspaperman or with Senators or with others who might want to discuss a point in the abstract because it is something we ought to talk about to somebody with whom it makes a difference."

Rusk had been taking an increasingly active political role since 1966 and allowed himself occasional remarks which, in a man of his mild public temperament, might even be characterized as "acidulous." He remarked in April 1967, as Arab threats against Israel mounted, "The doves are growing claws." Or when told by a flatterer that Rusk was popular on "the Hill," the Secretary replied, "I would prefer a little less popularity and a few more votes."

Typical of Rusk's composure under political strain was his "calm eye of the hurricane" posture in late August 1967, when a crescendo of criticism arose in the U.S. Senate concerning the fairness of the September third presidential elections in South Vietnam. It was the kind of political storm that makes some Foreign Service officers quiver. If not exactly fearful, there was an air of solemn anxiety in the group of senior advisers who had gathered outside Rusk's office late one afternoon, waiting to consult with him upon the State Department's stand on the charges about the Vietnamese elections being rigged. The upshot of the Rusk decision was: Let the critics have all the facts, and they will be in the same position to judge as we are. This tack took the heat off the issue.

Rusk regarded the exposition of foreign policy as a very important part of his job. Aides continually remonstrated with him because he committed himself to more public meetings than he should, when he could have well refused them on grounds of press of business. Congressmen were persistently after Rusk to appear with them on taped TV interviews. Rusk made himself available on the telephone to any important legislator or committee, or subcommittee, chairman, coming to the phone within seconds.

Rusk's accession to political prominence as a formidable figure in his own right occurred some two years ago, in the famous televised 1966 hearings before the Senate Foreign Relations Committee, when Rusk and Senator J. William Fulbright, Chairman of the Committee, debated eyeball to eyeball before a national audience. It was a unique confrontation in the annals of the Republic as Rusk of Georgia, speaking for the Johnson administration's right-of-center position on the Vietnam war, and Fulbright of Arkansas, attacking for the opposition, exchanged verbal blows under the klieg lights. Senators Richard B. Russell of Georgia and John Stennis of Mississippi, the prime hawks of the Senate Armed Services Committee, watched from the wings. Downtown, President Lyndon B. Johnson of Texas devoured the spectacle on his triple-TV set. It was the South's resurgence, echoes of the days of Henry Clay of Kentucky and John Calhoun of South Carolina before the War between the States, all Southerners, all Democrats, all nationalists, in high debate about the destiny of the nation, and symbolizing in the five personalities the South's command responsibility for the conduct of foreign affairs in A.D. 1966.

The Secretary of State's stout defense and massive counterattack against the barbs and arrows of the probing Senators, in a hearing room packed with an unfriendly audience, were a reflection of the Rusk character which had expressed itself in an article he had written fifteen years before:

"There are few fields of human endeavor where wishful thinking and self-delusions are as common, or as dangerous, as foreign policy. We demand simple answers to the most complex questions confronting human intelligence. We expect consistency in policy, though the facts themselves are full of contradictions. We should like an easy way to carry the heavy burden, an agreeable way to perform disagreeable tasks, a cheap way to bring about an expensive result."

After the officers of the State Department and its leader, the Secretary of State, get through for the instant with foreign affairs in Congress and the public domain, the next word is up to the President. Since there are no fixed formulas of presidential style, there is no predictable pattern of the way in which the issues will devolve. In the case of President Johnson, critics denounced him as an involuted, conspiratorial, and disingenuous sinner. Friends averred that Johnson was an uncomplicated man, whose own criterion of his place in history will be, he told his intimates, "what the grandchildren will think of me." By mid-1967, Johnson felt his rating had lost twenty points on Vietnam and ten points on the Negro riots.

The contrast between the public image and the private aspect of President Johnson was relevant to his effectiveness in putting across to Congress his foreign policy message. Johnson's admirers believed that the President looked like John Wayne in a Western movie, conveying attractive manliness and force. His detractors derided Johnson's face on TV as sanctimonious. Johnson confessed that he was uncomfortable psychologically with TV. He recalled that the late U.S. Senator Walter George, Democrat of Georgia and former Chairman of the Senate Foreign Relations Committee, never forgave President Franklin Delano Roosevelt for an indiscreet remark at the time of Roosevelt's attack on the Supreme Court. Senator George, Johnson never forgot, forever after consistently and implacably opposed anything that FDR ever wanted and that George was in a position to deny him. Johnson was thus constantly self-conscious that one little flub he might make in an unguarded moment on TV could do irreparable damage to American foreign policy interests, something that French President de Gaulle might never forgive or the West Germans might always remember. Those who had seen Johnson testified that in small private gatherings the President displayed warmth and directness as he poured out anecdotes, reminiscences, projections, plans, and musings in a compulsive volubility of the shoptalk which was the lifeblood of his being.

The intense political character of the President and his need to know the inner core of his companion, antagonist, or adversary were best exemplified on the occasions of visits to the White House by foreign heads of government or chiefs of state. The very first thing that President Johnson did was take the visiting notable aside in private and engage him in a thorough discussion of the domestic political situations in their respective countries. The two leaders exchanged views in a mutual confession of the limitations imposed by political considerations on the course of foreign policies.

Such exchanges of inside views on politics are rarely shared by the visitor with his own foreign minister, and by President Johnson with few others, with one possible exception, Vice President Hubert H. Humphrey. The Vice President's role as the chosen and beholden aide of the President, and his legal successor in the event of the President's death, imposed upon the Vice President not only complete loyalty and obedience but utter discretion. In 1967 the President leaned more and more upon the Vice President, calling him at all hours to hold private conversations that lasted from one to three hours and utilizing the fruits of Humphrey's expertise in foreign affairs and disarmament from his days as a fellow Senator with the President.

President Johnson was fascinated by the experience of other Presidents in foreign affairs. He had a continuous preoccupation with the public's view of his own role in conducting foreign affairs. He recalled that President Kennedy had also had to resist "hard-line" advocates in 1962, during the Laos crisis, when bombing of rail marshaling yards in Hanoi and bombardment of the North Vietnam coast by the U.S. Seventh Fleet were being proposed. Johnson recalled also an era when President Roosevelt, in his inaugural address on March 4, 1937, devoted only 54 of 1,800 words to foreign policy. Johnson read with absorption an article entitled, "President, Press, Dissent and War," by J. R. Wiggins, editor of the *Washington Post*. Wiggins wrote, in part:

The President from the outset displeased much of the press at home and abroad. A leading French newspaper was one of the first to isolate as one fact of discontent the lack of candor. The same newspaper bluntly criticized him for putting men in the field, "that much blood was being spilled and immense sums expended only to achieve in the end a negative result."

The President's character as a politician also annoyed the French press. The French papers said: "Once more he has allowed himself to be led astray by the sad habit of the conflict of parties, a native second nature to him, and which consists in bringing to the government the same expedients for keeping equilibrium as fights in the management of an electoral campaign."

It did not suit the British press any better. The *London Times,* annoyed at the President's stubborn pursuit of military objectives, said, "This helpless and blind pertinacity would be excusable and harmless in him personally but is inexcusable and disastrous for the President of the United States. It makes him useless, and worse than useless, for that which ought to be his great purpose, the guiding, controlling of vast forces of passion and interest and ideas which sway the unsettled nation he presides over."

The President's efforts to obtain peace were almost as much criticized as his management of the war. The *Richmond Sentinel* spoke for many when it said, "He demanded terms that he knew to be uttterly inadmissible and were intended to be so."

There is no doubt that comment of this kind reflected a long-standing and profound unhappiness for the President. The country and its press, from the start, found fault with the war he directed, with the way he directed it, with his domestic programs, with the style of his public papers, the manner of his speech, his ungainly appearance and his frequent disregard of proprieties, hitherto respected in public conduct.

The Wiggins article consisted of quotations entirely about President Abraham Lincoln from 1861 to 1865.

Historical allusions dropped by Walt Rostow, Johnson's principal foreign affairs staff aide, during long telephone conversations with the President, inspired Johnson to ask that a study be made of the way other Presidents fared with the public during American wars. Rostow commissioned Henry B. Owen, Chairman of the State Department's Policy Planning Council, to do a paper on the subject. Johnson read excerpts to everybody, friends and visitors, to illustrate the continuity of presidential travail during moments of national agony.

Owen reported that American wars had given rise consistently to two types of issues on the home front: criticism of, first, the war itself and, second, of domestic problems that had been accentuated by the wars in question. Owen wrote: "Supported only by one-half of the population in the colonies, the rest being neutral or loyal to Britain, few American wars have been less popular than the American Revolutionary war."

Nor were opponents of the Revolution men of no importance. Anglican churchmen led the pack, and, as the war stretched into seemingly endless stalemate, economic problems mounted on the home front. The general picture was one of turmoil, a war that was not popular and that many thought could not be won.

In the War of 1812, Owen continued, domestic opposition was open from the start. Of 160 members of both Houses of Congress, 52 voted against the declaration of war. In a speech so vehement that its publication was suppressed for nearly a century, Daniel Webster denounced the Government as "more tyrannical, more arbitrary, more dangerous, more allied to blood and murder, more full of every form of mischief, more productive of every sort and degree of misery than has been exercised by any civilized government, with a single exception in modern times."

The *Boston Sentinel* said: "The tyrannical oppression of those who at present disturb the powers of the Constitution is beyond endurance. And we will resist."

The Mexican War of 1846–1848, Owen went on, was popular at the start, but the public mood changed dramatically as the conflict dragged on. Democrats defended it feebly and a great many thought it had been a grave political blunder. Intellectuals took the lead and a Harvard professor was one of the war's milder critics in denouncing it as "maniacal." Whig journals assured Mexico "her cause was just, that a majority of Americans detested the war, that our Treasury could not bear the cost, that our government was incompetent, that our armies could not win the war, and that soon the administration would be rebuked and its policies reversed."

Senator Corwin of Ohio said that if he were a Mexican, he could welcome the Americans to a bloody grave. Herman Melville, the author of *Moby Dick,* compared his countrymen to South Sea cannibals. Henry Clay asserted, "This is no war of defense." Senator John Calhoun gloomily conceded that as Congress had not acted, "there is no war, according to the sense of our Constitution."

In the Civil War the outbreak of hostilities was greeted with enthusiasm, which waned as the conflict wore on. The 1862 Congressional elections went heavily against the Lincoln administration in the Midwest. The Illinois House of Representatives passed an antiwar resolution by a large majority. The Indiana legislature refused appropriations for raising troops.

Economic discontent as well as opposition to the war was reflected in draft riots. Homes and offices were burned to the ground. Negroes were seized, hanged, and shot. Battles were fought between rioters and police. In New York at least 1,000 persons were killed or wounded and $1 million worth of property was destroyed.

In 1864, as General Ulysses Grant's offensive against Richmond brought heavy losses, large peace meetings were held in major cities in the North. Every week seemed to add another newspaper or public figure to the list of Lincoln's opponents. In August 1864, the Chairman of the National Republican Committee told Lincoln, "The tide is heading strongly against us." Later that month, Lincoln recorded his belief that he would be defeated in the election, and that the new President would be forced to suspend the war.

In World War II, Owen pointed out, though the war was supported with rare unanimity, the home front was very troubled with rises in juvenile delinquency and school dropouts; mass Negro migration from the South to the North, bringing changes in the population pattern and new tensions which exploded in the historic Detroit race riots of June 1943; labor disputes involving the loss of more than 36 million mandays; and inflationary pressures making food prices rise 50 per cent.

In the Korean War, Owen concluded, dissatisfaction with the conflict was widespread. It seemed an endless stalemate. The general malaise came to a head when President Truman sacked General Douglas MacArthur. The Gallup Poll showed 29 per cent favoring the President, against 69 per cent for the General. Letters by the tens of thousands poured into the White House, Congressional offices, newspapers, and radio stations to condemn the outrage. Preachers thundered from the pulpits, and Legion posts, service clubs, and PTA's passed angry resolutions. U.S. Senator William E. Jenner, Republican of Indiana, asserted: "Our only choice is to impeach President Truman."

Yet, Truman is regarded today as one of the great Presidents of the United States, a rating reached by Europeans long before a similar American consensus was arrived at.

His forerunners' unhappy experiences with Congress had not dissuaded President Johnson from indefatigable cultivation of Congress in support of his foreign policy, above all, of the Vietnam war. Johnson had had more frequent recourse to Congress in foreign affairs than any other American President. He leaned heavily on his Congressional background for techniques of enlisting support. The first thing he did after being informed by Walt Rostow of the outbreak of Arab-Israeli hostilities at 4:30 A.M. on June 5th, and while still in bed, was to call Secretary Rusk at 5:09 A.M. and instruct him to arrange an early briefing of the key officers of the Congress, which Rusk did within the hour.

In February 1967, hearing that Senator Frank J. Lausche, Democrat of Ohio, was unhappy that he had not seen the President for some time, Johnson made a point of inviting Lausche to the White House for a twenty-minute chat on Vietnam. Six months later, Lausche came out for a protracted stoppage of the bombing in North Vietnam. In August 1967 the President saw 300 freshmen Congressmen in thirty days, including 247 Democrats.

Despite the liberal dove opposition in the Senate, Johnson refused to criticize in any way the leadership of Senator Mansfield, likewise a dove. Johnson pointed out that President Eisenhower had it much worse with Senator William Knowland as Republican leader. He recalled that during the Eisenhower administration he, Johnson, had led the Democrats to vote for Eisenhower's proposals 78 per cent of the time. He deplored the fact that Congress seemed to vote only on Tuesdays, Wednesdays, and Thursdays, and hardly ever on Fridays, while Johnson, as Senate majority leader, had kept the Senate in session at nights and on Saturdays to vote on key legislation.

Mutual recriminations between the executive and legislative notwithstanding, Congress is the modern exemplification of the total national involvement in foreign affairs which all states and peoples in a nuclear age must henceforth be engaged in. As the Marquis of Curzon wrote years ago: "Foreign affairs are really the most domestic of all our affairs, for it is in relation to foreign affairs that every man and woman in a country secures immunity from war, relief from a heavy burden of taxation and prosperity of trade and industry."

Although throughout the postwar period Congress had been more continuously and intensively involved in foreign affairs than at any other time in the history of the Republic, the complaint came like a broken record, "We want to be in on the take-offs, as well as the crash landings." This writer recalls the late U.S. Senator Robert A. Taft's saying so under the Truman Democratic administration in 1950 and Senator Mike Mansfield's uttering the self-same lament under the Eisenhower Republican administration. The Senatorial dignity, moreover, felt it received scant respect from the executive branch by the lack of advance consultation, and that such information as was provided was too often inaccurate, partial, irrelevant, and not timely.

Congress, as an equal branch of the United States Government, believed it gave more continuity to foreign policy than the State Department. There was faster turnover in Department personnel, compared with long-term Congressional tenure wherefrom senior members could recount the experiences of twenty years' dealing with foreign issues in Washington.

Secretary Rusk himself had said: "If you look around the country at people who have had to deal with foreign policy issues year after year, you will find some of the very best in Congress. Many of them have had a continuing experience."

Many eminent Senators had been originators of ideas which became standard U.S. foreign policy programs. Vice President Humphrey, as Senator from Minnesota, fathered the Peace Corps and the Arms Control and Disarmament Agency. Senator Mansfield of Montana gave birth to the Development Loan Fund for long-term assistance to underdeveloped countries. Senator Mike Monroney of Oklahoma authored the International Development Association, an affiliate of the World Bank as an instrument for "soft," or high-risk, loans to emerging nations. Senator Allen J. Ellender of Louisiana created Public Law 480 for the donation or sale of surplus American agricultural commodities to foreign nations. A brain child of Senator Wayne Morse of Oregon was civic action, wherein U.S. military forces or those of friendly nations engaged in engineering and welfare activities sought to help backward areas of nations and so attract the allegiance of neglected populations. Civic action is now a standard counterinsurgency tactic all over the so-called Free World.

However, just as in World War I French Premier Clemenceau thought that war was too dangerous a matter to leave to the generals, Congress has always thought that peace was too precarious an issue to leave to the diplomats. Congressional impatience with and petulance at the executive branch was continuous from the days when the Continental Congress and the Committee of Secret Correspondence handled foreign affairs. Congress had been reluctant and grudging in giving up its functions to the newly established State Department of 1789. Under the Articles of Confederation, the Department of Foreign Affairs in actuality played second fiddle to the Congress. Foreign ministers were received by the Congress and, in fact, every Congressman expected a courtesy call from every accredited minister. Foreign envoys in Washington today still seek out Congressmen and Senators. When the post of Secretary of the Department of Foreign Affairs was vacant for a year during the Confederation, Congress itself answered requests for guidance written from abroad by U.S. diplomatic agents. It did so by passing Congressional resolutions indicating Congressional intent and assessment. Only seventy-five years ago, when the spoils system for diplomatic appointments was still in force, Congress had enough power in the field of foreign affairs to cause the dismissal of 317 U.S. consuls in overseas posts.

The debate between Congress and the President over the power to direct foreign policy arose formally as long ago as 1800. Secretary of State John Marshall, later Chief Justice of the United States, wrote an opinion that the President was the controlling factor in foreign affairs, but that it was incumbent upon him to sense the feeling of the Congress before he took any important action. For the first forty years of the Republic, foreign policy played a crucial part in the affairs of the young nation. Daniel S. Cheever and H. Field Haviland, Jr., said, in *American Foreign Policy and the Separation of Powers:* "Presidents were chosen in large measure because of their competence and experience in international affairs. Four Presidents out of the six in this period (from 1789 to 1829) were former Secretaries of State and, generally speaking, all of them displayed strong leadership in the exercise of the foreign relations power."

The Constitution of the United States, the bible which both the executive and the legislative branches fell back upon as the authority in interpreting the doctrine of separation and/or shared powers in foreign affairs, is full of "buts" and ambiguities, just as is foreign policy itself. To reiterate the words of Edwin S. Corwin, in *The President: Office and Powers:*

The Constitution is an invitation to struggle for the privileges of directing American foreign policy. . . . Actual practices show that the President is usually in a position to propose, the Senate and the Congress are often in a technical position at least to dispose. . . . The power to determine American foreign policy is a divided power with the lion's share falling, usually though by no means always, to the President.

The immemorial debate has far greater significance today because of the vastly expanded backdrop of the nuclear era. The old rules of the game in conventional warfare were debatable enough. Just as gunpowder shattered the laws of chivalry and medieval feudalism seven centuries ago, the atomic bomb fragmented the practicability of old concepts and regulations concerning the exercise of Constitutional power in a modern evolving nation like the United States. Congress, in particular, possessed an outmoded machinery and mentality, which had not even begun to encompass or understand the unraveling of the old diplomacy and the knitting-in process of a new diplomacy.

In rare instances Congress energized itself under forced draft to cope with major emergencies, usually under the spur of presidential leadership. But as constituted today, Congress is continually falling behind in the race for equivalent power and authority in the direction of foreign affairs. Issues have become far too crucial and complicated to be left to antiquarian Congressional devices. Lacking functional expertise, Congress cannot cope with the intricate technicalities of modern foreign affairs and is left with the mere device of changing proposals but never initiating any of its own. It is forced to rely too much on the authoritative testimony of the federal bureaucracy, whose professional loyalties are more toward their two million fellow employees in the Government than to the 200 million Americans in the nation at large. Congress is tempted to take short cuts and cut the Gordian knots of foreign affairs by impetuous recourse to military solutions. Conversely, in a spirit of futile resignation or artificial exaltation in the mood of the moment, it tends to become a rubber stamp for a powerful leader and nourishes the seeds of eventual Caesarism, embracing in a dynamic leader the very qualities it lacks itself.

In its haste to get itself cut in on the big foreign policy deals, Congress becomes a victim of its own confusions and falls steadily behind schedule in its work, with a prospect, now, of year-long Congressional sessions. It goes on fishing expeditions in its investigations, having sound instincts that there is indeed something fishy to investigate but not knowing exactly what it is, or what to do with it after it finds it. It exploits differences within the executive branch with a bit of sadism and a mite of malice. It picks on trivia. It enacts amendments reflecting popular resentments rather than considered cures, amendments which cause more difficulty than they eliminate. It runs after side issues, hunting the needle in the haystack, as in trying to identify low-level action officers in the State Department or authors of ideas or memoranda, whom they would like to cross-examine at first hand, only to be barred by the door of executive privilege, should the President decide to close it. It is full of witticisms, germane and otherwise, at the State Department's expense. Congressman Wayne Hays, Democrat of Ohio, upbraided Foreign Service Association officers who failed to meet him when he arrived for a speech. Hays told them, "How can you expect to run the world when you can't even find space in your garage to park my car?"

Congress, given today's circumstances, is regarded as the weakest of the three branches of the American Government. The action is "downtown," at the White House and in the executive departments. Congressional functions tend to be diffused and dispersed. Congress in recent years developed a new neurosis because of the perplexities, paradoxes, and dilemmas of the Vietnam war. Republicans were not quite ready to make up their minds which way to go. Rank-and-file Democrats, wedded willy-nilly to a war policy of their party's administration, chaffed at the bit but trotted along somehow.

Congress' ambivalent engagement with foreign affairs repeatedly evoked Alexis de Tocqueville's indictment, in his *Democracy in America,* that "It is especially in the conduct of their foreign relations that democracies appear to be decidedly inferior to other governments. A democracy can only, with great difficulty, regulate the details of an important undertaking, persevere in a fixed design and work out its execution in spite of serious obstacles. It cannot combine its measures with secrecy or await their consequences with patience."

In its new and still strange role of participating in foreign policy through the massive allocation of national resources to foreign programs, Congress finds itself immobilized between two polarized forces. One is the political world, which looks toward every next election and toward the accumulation of patronage and power between elections. The other is the world of international society and diplomatic relations, of foreign and alien psychologies, ill at ease with cultures they do not understand and with governments they cannot control. Outraged by enemies, baffled by friends, betwixt and between necessities on both sides, the Congressman cannot but be confused concerning the relevant issues. In self-defense he tends to blur their sharpness, which is another way of avoiding confrontation with reality. Former Congressman Chester Bowles, in a 1959 speech, gave an apt summing up:

Basically the American people look on the election of a Congress and of a President in quite different ways. When we cast our votes for a Senator or a Congressman, it is usually questions that most directly affect social security, wages, prices, employment and profit which presumably carry the greatest weight.

When we choose a President to direct American policy in this troubled, difficult world, it is quite another matter. In four of the last five presidential elections, foreign policy played a dominant role.

In 1960, when foreign affairs again played a key role in the election campaign, President Eisenhower said: "Foreign affairs is today the greatest preoccupation of all people in positions of political responsibility for a very simple reason—foreign affairs in our relations with others affect every other problem we have. It involves our taxes, our inner feelings of confidences or apprehension. It affects our trade."

The nation's continuous concern with foreign policy in critical times finds its natural forum and echo chamber in the Congress. The 1966 legislative record of major Senate accomplishments in the second session of the Eighty-ninth Congress listed 434 actions, of which a good fat fourth, or 133, related to foreign involvements in the diplomatic, military, national security field. Of these, 37 were in general international affairs, 41 in international economic affairs, and 55 in military affairs.

The babel of discord in 1966 and 1967 over the Vietnam war naturally had its impact on diplomacy. Foreign policy in a democracy is a fuzzy product of interacting official and nonofficial publicity. As foreign affairs become a stalking horse for domestic party politics, a nation's foreign policy inescapably becomes less effectual abroad the more it is publicly attacked at home, as in the current classic case of the Vietnam war argumentation in the United States. Still, the Congressional uproar is useful for temporizing with foreign governments, the sound of trouble with Congress serving as a ready-made excuse to rationalize diplomatic inaction or drift.

Whatever State Department officers might be operationally doing with the prosaic nitty-gritty of its problems, nothing hinders the members of Congress from exploiting all possibilities, true or false, of a given crisis for whatever political mileage they can get out of it. The artless or spontaneous demagoguery of an ordinary Congressman is, by the nature of the two beasts, considerably different from the discretion and deviousness with which the State Department frequently must operate among foreigners. Congressmen obviously have a built-in stake in controversy. They believe they can ill afford to be neutral about problems they do not understand. Distortions, half-truths, misleading assertions, and general disingenuousness perforce are often the order of the day. Congressmen seem to have an inherent compulsion to verbal battle and a delight in tensions, which heighten the backdrop against which they can appear in dramatic relief to the voters, no matter what the damage to the State Department image, morale, or operational atmosphere.

Despite the considerably higher level in public understanding of foreign affairs compared with the past, the gap between adequacy and superficiality provides a temptation for political opportunists to say the most outrageous things about the conduct of foreign relations, charges moreover which are very difficult indeed to respond to and which gain a momentum of their own before they can be knocked down, just as retraction in newspapers never quite catch up with the original slanders or misquotations. Foreign affairs are a star vehicle for patriotic perorations, no matter whether the declamations are also full of anachronisms, from the "manifest destiny" of the hawk to the utopian isolationism of the dove, both of which sentiments date back to the nineteenth century. In the mishmash of logic pervading Congressional hustings, there is always available a fallback position of moralisms and even great models to quote from, including two of the greatest but most moralistic Presidents, Thomas Jefferson and Woodrow Wilson.

There is the persistent phenomenon of the lag in Congressional reaction to a situation which has been already met. In early 1966 there was a small outcry at British shipping to Communist North Vietnam. The matter had already engaged the attention of the State Department officially in attempting to prevent supplies from reaching an enemy. U.S. diplomatic efforts had, to a very large extent, succeeded in cutting down entry of so-called Free World shipping to Haiphong harbor, except for freighters registered in the British crown colony of Hong Kong but legally chartered by Chinese Communists, residents of Hong Kong, against whom the British authorities could not act, since Britain itself was not at war with North Vietnam, and had to abide by its duly constituted laws. Later in 1966, the general public awakened belatedly to the shipping issue. Constituents began writing to their Congressmen in protest. Several weeks later the air was filled with Congressional clamor "demanding" that the State Department "take action"—despite the protestations of bewildered officials who had indeed taken action and had so briefed the Congressmen in detail. Naturally, mere facts failed to dampen Congressional "indignation" and the enjoyment of castigating the State Department, all of which provided an exhilarating experience for audiences back home in Peoria and Chillicothe. This good, clean fun, of course, raised no hackles among the partisan adversaries, because it was "just politics," and friendly enemies could laugh together and have a drink over it.

Congressional outbursts were effective if they gained publicity and they normally did in the press, which, despite the holy grail of "objectivity," found a high utility in Congressmen, who are a prime source of certain information normally under the tight control of the diplomatic operators in the State Department. The Congressional interest was to learn as much as possible about what the executive branch was doing, motivated by its sense of coresponsibility for the Government and by its curiosity to discover something supposedly secret, an act helping to enhance one's ego and sense of importance. Congressional talkativeness in consequence had been a constant tribulation to State Department officials fearing leaks of information about projects in train. The press and the Congress, therefore, are natural allies in leaking stories and in joining forces against the secrecy of any administration.

The central relevance of the Congress to foreign policy, despite the anxieties aroused in the State Department, devolves upon the basic fact that Congress symbolizes the nationalism of the American people. This is much the same as the nationalistic impulses daily exemplified in other nations throughout the world, particularly in the new and developing ones. Congress frequently is like a hall of faded or broken mirrors, reflecting distorted, warped, or double visions of American reality, yet, despite the aberrations, a faithful duplicate of both the confused and the pertinent currents of the times. For the State Department, Congress is the antechamber to the realities of the world, only one step removed from the cold plunge into the foreign whirlpool of power tides and undertows, where U.S. policies are strictly on their own and subject to less and less control by their originators.

Congressional activity concerning foreign relations operates under triple-entry bookkeeping. One column represents the trash box of American history, still-born dreams, and elusive illusions carried from the early manhood of politicians, like the populism of Representative Wright Patman, Democrat from Texas and Chairman of the House Banking and Currency Committee, who launched an attack on the Federal Reserve system as a central bank, with scant regard for possible international repercussions on the balance of payments and the international monetary system.

In many respects, American history, particularly in the twentieth century, is a continuation of strains of European history, whose conflicts and concerns still echo over here. There is the case of Senator Lausche of Ohio, whose immigrant parents came from a unique district of pre–World War I Yugoslavia. This area, Gottschee Kocevje, was inhabited by about 700,000 Gottscheer in what is now Slovenia, about sixty miles from Ljublmana, capital of the region. Betwixt Nazi and partisan warfare, most of the Gottscheer disappeared or were exterminated in World War II. This circumstance had been a major factor in Lausche's consistent and determined opposition to anything in U.S. foreign policy that favored Titoist Communist Yugoslavia, despite U.S. policies that differentiated between various types of Communists in order to serve U.S. purposes. Unlike Congressmen of Polish extraction who, while opposing the Polish Communist Government, still kept sympathetic and sentimental ties with the population of their forebears, Lausche continued to resist the blandishments and standing invitation of the Yugoslav Government to visit that country.

Another column of the triple-entry Congressional bookkeeping deals with constituents who, after all, are the voters who placed the Congressmen in office, whose wishes must be catered to, and whose opinions must be solemnly considered and responded to. The ever-present pressure of constituents patently is disruptive, since most constituents have special cases to plead in endeavoring to exploit the Congressman's influence for expeditious action. Constituents want weighted judgments through and by the executive departments, including the State Department, in matters of immigration quotas, travel visas, and economic easements for foreign trade investments and foreign aid contracts.

Vast amounts of mail are directed at Congress as foreign affairs issues hit the public eye and interest shoots up and down like a fever chart. The constituents' letters and the Congressional replies are pure Americana on both sides. In March 1967, Mrs. Carl O. Boucher of Columbus, Ohio, wrote Senator Lausche, complaining about the failure of the United States Government to exercise its responsibility to its taxpayers by collecting the debts owing from foreign nations in World War I. Mrs. Boucher said: "The Senate has the final say in such matters, I believe, as giving or lending. However, people in government are there as representatives of us but that still does not entitle you to give our earnings away right and left."

Lausche, who is an ineffable thespian when he gets wound up, replied: "In the ten years that I have been in the Senate I have been fighting vigorously but frustratingly against extravagant, wrongful, and unjustified public spending of the taxpayers' money. . . . In World War I, I was a member of the Infantry of the military forces of the United States Government . . . and prepared to serve in whatever assignment was given to me, but had nothing to do with incurrence of the loans that were made to our Allies in the war in which we were commonly engaged."

Lausche reported to Mrs. Boucher that the World War I Allied debt to the United States was $14,403,284,560, Great Britain being the largest debtor, with $6,837,699,302, and France next with $4,688,478,840. Though the Allied debt issue had been dead politically since 1933, Mrs. Boucher's query reflected a weird intuition. The U.S. Senate had, in July 1953, ratified the London agreement deferring the problem of governmental claims against Germany arising out of World War I until a final general settlement was reached. The proviso had in mind the huge but unspecified amount of debts claimed against Hitlerite Germany for damages arising out of World War II. The pack of claimants was led by the ravaged countries of Eastern Europe which had suffered most from Nazi oppression. Until the question of German reunification is decided, the over-all settlement of all German reparations problems must remain in abeyance. It would be a condition of the eventual peace with Germany. Therefore, like a good housewife, Mrs. Boucher was reminding her Senator that she still had her eye on what was eventually coming to her as a taxpayer. The Senator got the point right away.

Congressional sensibilities respond like galvanometers to concrete expressions of the voice of the people. Seven million Americans of Eastern European extraction are a vocal group in cities like New York, Buffalo, Cleveland, Detroit, and Chicago. Almost automatically every summer a Congressional resolution for the liberation of the "captive peoples" of Eastern Europe is passed by the Congress, though the indictment from the depths of the Cold War can no longer be justified. It makes no difference to the Congressional denunciators.

Much more to the forefront in latter days has been the threat, real and/or exaggerated, of Fidel Castro's Cuban Communism. This is a serial story without an end concerning subversive activities in the Caribbean for the extremely active Internal Security Subcommittee of the Senate Judiciary Committee, over which U.S. Senator Thomas J. Dodd, Democrat of Connecticut, most frequently presides, backstopped by Senator Strom Thurmond, former Democrat but now Republican of South Carolina. This subcommittee, under the crafty and careful staff work of J. G. Sourwine, chief counsel, also spotlighted the case of the State Department Security supervisor, Otto F. Otepka, into one of the minor notorieties of the last few years. During the four-year inquiry, Otepka received his full pay, retained his official rank and position, but did absolutely no work. Backbenchers in Congress find in the State Department and foreign affairs a fertile field for political dividends. Right-wing groups and disgruntled former State employees supply just enough ammunition to keep up a steady pepper of harassing fire, which the State Department suffers with pained silence and a saintly air.

More of a standard occupational hazard for State's diplomats are American lobbyists registered, under the Foreign Agents Registration Act of 1938, on behalf of foreign principals. The agents work openly for foreign interests, as in the case of China, which has eleven agents active for the cause of the Nationalist Chinese Government on Formosa. Four individuals are listed as agents for Communist China but turn out to be representatives of Peking publishing houses whose publications are of considerable interest to U.S. readers, official and unofficial. Much more pertinent to U.S. foreign policy is the agency listed as the Committee of One Million Against the Admission of Communist China to the United Nations. The Committee of One Million, formed in 1953, was successful enough to obtain in the Eighty-ninth Congress, ending in 1966, supporting signatures of 51 Senators out of 100 and of 283 Representatives out of 435.

Though all lobby groups at different times interest themselves in some aspect or another of the wide foreign affairs spectrum, the most annoying are the high-decibel and well-organized minority lobbies who, as Sorensen, aide of President Kennedy, once said, make so much noise in relation to their numbers that they require a disproportionate amount of time and effort to palliate or neutralize. Among the most prominent of such influence groups is the "Liberty Lobby." Its agents talk directly to Congressmen and testify before Congressional committees on legislation. Its principal sustenance derives from its monthly publication, *Liberty Letter,* boasting a paid circulation of approximately 175,000. Its readers are asked to write letters to members of Congress on behalf of the lobby's views, which are presented almost exclusively through a red lens. The Lobby's activities in 1967 concentrated on the Consular Treaty with the Soviet Union, to which it almost succeeded in attaching a restrictive amendment which would have forced renegotiation of the whole treaty between the United States and Russia.

The third column of the triple-entry bookkeeping Congress maintains on foreign affairs relates to issues officially referred to it by the State Department and the White House, to real-life actions in the outside world which have been set in train by a policy of the State Department, or to foreign events which challenge or call into question the efficacy or wisdom of State Department policies. In these overlapping areas Congress can trill up and down the scale for weeks with charges of malfeasance, misfeasance, and nonfeasance. These, respectively, are charges of legally unjustified wrongdoing, of wrongful and injurious exercise of public authority, and of omission of acts which ought to have been performed.

The proposed new Panama Canal Zone Treaty between the United States and Panama in the summer of 1967 is a case in point. Although the Senate is constitutionally responsible for the ratification of treaties, the loudest opposition came from the House of Representatives, where approximately 150 members expressed reservations about the proposed Treaty and submitted critical resolutions. Sentiments about the Panama Canal were an echo of the days of the Spanish-American War for the liberation of Cuba and the Philippines, the forced creation of Panama by President Theodore Roosevelt, and the dead, gone days of incipient American imperialism, of which the Canal Zone was the last glamorous and complacent enclave under United States jurisdiction, as the Hong Kong crown colony is for Britain today. Similarly evocative of this nostalgia for the comfortable days of the past was the leader of the House opposition, Congressman Daniel J. Flood, Democrat of Pennsylvania, whom, by coincidence, this writer as a boy used to see in Wilkes-Barre, Pennsylvania, when Flood was the town's glittering exemplar of the Scott Fitzgerald era, with gay mustache, raccoon coat, and Stutz roadster, as debonair and dashing as he still looks today, more than forty years later. As in the case of crises in the geographical bureaus of the State Department escalating, because of their importance, to the level of the White House and the seventh floor, similarly the legislative crisis of the Panama Canal Zone Treaty was in process of escalating out of the direct hands of the Department's Office of Congressional Relations into the personal involvement of the Chief Executive and his principal foreign affairs adviser, the Secretary of State.

The most dramatic category of Congressional uproar occurs perforce in Congressional reaction to great events overseas, like wars. The Arab-Israeli shambles of June 1967 is a classic illustration. The urgencies of close liaison with the Congress impelled Secretary Rusk to spend half his time or more, it seemed, in Congressional consultation. Rusk's intervention was all the more urgent after the Senatorial eruption following the gaffe of the State Department's official spokesman about the United States being "neutral in thought, word, and deed," and the powerful complaint, lodged by Senate Minority Leader Everett Dirksen of Illinois, that the Johnson administration was not providing sufficient information about the crisis. The eminent Senatorial voices were raised in anguished protest at the possibility that the American Government might be throwing Israel to the Arab wolves. Senators like Joseph Clark, Democrat of Pennsylvania, one of the leading doves on Vietnam, proclaiming his concern for Israel, cried: "Their cause is our cause. We are not neutral." There was certainly cause for President Johnson and Secretary Rusk to be concerned, for if the Vietnam war could be the cause of defeat for the President in the 1968 election, mishandling of the Middle East crisis would in no uncertain terms lose the President's re-election. The Senators felt even more self-righteous than usual in their indignation because several had given early warnings of the rapidly deteriorating situation in the Middle East. As early as October 1966, Senator Ernest Gruening, Democrat of Alaska, had thundered that "the simmering Middle East once again threatens to boil over in armed conflict between the Arab states and Israel, and once again the Department is to be found with its head in the sand, unwilling to take the stand even where important American economic interests are involved." Prophetic also was Senator Jacob Javits, Republican of New York, who certainly had a right to get into the picture since in New York City are contained almost a million and a half voters of the Jewish persuasion.

In this same critical spring of 1967, there occurred a curious case of melodrama involving Representative Wayne Hays, the Ohio Democrat. From late winter to almost the outbreak of hostilities, Hays had been secretly and repeatedly approached by unofficial emissaries from Cairo entreating him to go posthaste to talk to Gamel Abdel Nasser, on whom Hays' bluff candor and spontaneous kindness to the Egyptian President's little daughter had, on a 1960 visit, made a warm and friendly impression. The Cairo emissaries told Hays that, as one of the few Americans Nasser trusted, he must go at once and talk to Nasser straight from the shoulder, for the sake of Egypt as well as the United States, because the Cairo Foreign Office feared that Nasser was slipping more and more under Soviet influence. Hays kept Secretary Rusk informed of the secret contacts but never took the trip, because by that time matters appeared to have gone much too far to have allowed Nasser to draw back.

The June crisis was a first-class example of a world event escalating like a high-speed elevator right up through the State Department, to the White House, to the Congress, and right out into the national political arena, thanks to the effective role of the nation's nearly six million Jews as strong, generous, and articulate supporters of the Democratic Party. The Jewish voters, moreover, were heavily represented in the big industrial states with sizable electoral votes, states which, by coincidence, were also in a mood of political disaffection with the Johnson administration on account of the Vietnam war and the Negro racial unrest. These states, from west to east, included California, Illinois, Ohio, Pennsylvania, New Jersey, New York, and Massachusetts. Senators and Congressmen up for re-election in 1968 were galvanized into alertness by a flood of letters and telegrams in the week of the war; for example, nearly 25,000 communications arrived at the office of Senator Robert F. Kennedy of New York within ten days.

The widespread pro-Israel sentiment in Congress and the necessity of the Johnson administration to tread most gingerly amid the diplomatic sand traps of the Middle East irked not a few officials in the State Department, who perennially had been accused, at the very least, of being pro-Arab. A number of U.S. diplomats grumbled that it was impossible to conduct foreign policy in an atmosphere "prejudicial to the total vital interests of the United States." Whispers against an official for being allegedly anti-Zionist were immediately translated into being anti-Israel and even anti-Semitic, a process some officers bitterly characterized as a "triumph of inverse propaganda." The secret lament was that in the diplomatic negotiations the United States had no bargaining levers with Israel; that whereas U.S. aid to the Arab nations had been cut off, Israel still had the key to the bottomless philanthropy of American citizens of the Jewish faith who had responded with millions of dollars at the outbreak of the war. There was even the suggestion that potential U.S. leverage on the Israeli could be obtained by removing tax exemptions which permitted charitable donations to Israeli causes. Naturally, one can be sure that this heretical notion never rose above the lower floors of the State Department.

The most constant source of abrasion between the State Department and the Congress arises in the appropriations process, markedly since World War II, when the allocation of resources to the execution of foreign policy programs has been the massive new component of modern U.S. foreign affairs. The power of the pinch-purse provides a wedge for Congress to get into the details of foreign policy. As a result of the backlash foreign policy disagreements, the State Department suffers more than other agencies of the Government in not receiving the appropriations it requests. As far back as 1820, Congress complained that the State Department was costing twice as much as it had in 1800 and tried to introduce a retrenchment program.

The built-in impasse is complicated by the State Department's implicit assumption that Congress need only ratify the diplomatic proposals, while the implicit assumption of Congress is that it shall modify the proposals. The differences in point of view become concrete, in fact may be said sometimes to be set in concrete, by the appropriate Congressional committee report which renders its understanding of the requested legislation and outlines its own Congressional intent in regard to the legislation. This "intent of Congress" is a matter close and dear to its prerogatives, which the State Department and the President tamper with at their peril. The legislative authorization and appropriation sequence becomes still more intricate, like a set of Chinese boxes, one within the other, by Congress' determination not only of the way in which appropriated funds will be used but even of the way in which the funds will be accounted for, as per the Constitution's Article I, Section 9, Paragraph 7, which says: "No money shall be drawn from the Treasury but in consequence of appropriations made by law; and a regular statement and accounts of the receipts and expenditures of the public money shall be published from time to time." In effect, the Appropriations Committee of the House of Representatives and the Senate are powers unto themselves—and virtually a third House of Congress—so that the House Foreign Affairs Committee and the Senate Foreign Relations Committee see their importance eroded, invaded, or threatened in the proportion to which the latter committees' decisions on the monies needed to carry out foreign policies are disregarded.

The House of Representatives, with its large membership of 435 members, feeling the pride of being the most authentic assembly of the peoples, couples its constitutional authority to raise revenue for the general welfare with the conviction that it should have a definite and substantial voice in foreign policy. In August 1962, Representative Frank T. Bow, Republican of Ohio and ranking Minority member of the House Appropriations Committee, gave the most extensive analysis in recent years of the role of the President and of the House in foreign affairs. In a major debate with former Representative Walter Judd, Republican of Minnesota, who was defending the President's role, Bow said:

> It has long been recognized by Presidents, Members of Congress, and political scientists that the appropriating of public money often has a far greater impact on the formation of foreign policies than the substantive decisions coming from the White House.
> The House is at liberty to insert provisos or instructions in appropriations bills. We have the effect of determining or modifying policy. Congress may withhold funds altogether and thus completely cancel an Executive policy. To the extent that funds are withheld, or terms and conditions set for the expenditure of Treasury money, Congress may prescribe its own policy. But this is as it should be.

Bow quoted as the heart of the matter an appropriations bill introduced for implementation of the Jay treaty with Britain in 1796, which guaranteed the young Republic's territorial integrity. Bow cited the companion resolution to the money bill, which said:

> When a treaty stipulates regulations on any of the subjects submitted by the Constitution to the power of Congress, it must depend for its execution, as to such stipulations, on the law or laws to be passed by Congress. And it is the Constitutional right and duty of the House of Representatives in all cases to deliberate on the expediency or inexpediency of carrying such treaty into effect, and to determine and to act thereon as in their judgment, which may be the most conducive to the public's good.

Mindful of the Congress' jealous regard for its own rights, the President and the State Department walk on eggs to placate Congress wherever possible and cater to its crotchets, which include in some members a tendency to treat the executive branch as nothing more than an institution for carrying into effect the will of the Congress, an arrangement that is precisely what some delegates desired during the Constitutional Convention in 1787. President Johnson's well-publicized routine of turning off unnecessary lights at the White House was designed as much to impress economy-minded Congressmen as to satisfy his own personal prejudice against wasted energy. Johnson said that normal electricity for lighting the White House cost $5,000 a month and that alertness in shutting off electric lights from burning to no purpose saved $1,000 a month.

Other Presidents also have had to take radical steps to mollify Congressional opposition to proposed foreign policy legislation that needed money. President Kennedy, in 1962, had to launch a full-scale campaign to pass a compromise United Nations financing bill for $100 million after Harlan Cleveland, former Assistant Secretary of State for International Organizations Affairs, had prematurely unveiled a UN financing proposal at a press conference, not only without consulting the White House in advance but without touching base with ranking members of the Senate Foreign Relations Committee, who, to put it mildly, took umbrage at being ignored.

President Eisenhower and Secretary of State Dulles withdrew the Aswan Dam offer to Egypt because, as Senator Walter George, Democrat of Georgia and Chairman of the Senate Foreign Relations Committee, told this writer in 1956, it was nonsensical to finance a dam that would lead to the growth of cotton in competition with the cotton of the American South, which had enough difficulties in getting its own marketed.

Sometimes a President feels he must go to the mat despite Congressional views, as President Truman did in 1947 with a hostile Congress, when he resisted pressure to increase wool import tariffs. State Department bureaucrats at the time felt that this Truman decision took even greater courage than going to the aid of Greece and Turkey in that same year.

Foreign policy legislation all too frequently becomes a captive of economic interests and domestic politics at home. Agriculture is a perennial. Senator George McGovern, Democrat of South Dakota, attacked the Johnson administration for curtailing food shipments abroad and cutting wheat acreage at home, while people go hungry around the world. Tariffs are another sore. Senator Carl T. Curtis, Republican of Nebraska, bewailed the fact that "total footwear imports were more than 22 per cent of domestic production." Senator Vance Hartke, Democrat of Indiana, wanted to repeal the new international antidumping code negotiated at Geneva in the Kennedy Round. Senator Edward M. Kennedy, Democrat of Massachusetts, plumped for a foreign aid amendment to include a new fish-protein concentrate as a diet supplement for underdeveloped countries. Massachusetts has a big fishing industry, naturally. Government Operations Committees in House and Senate conduct their own guerrilla expeditions in Vietnam, chasing waste. A 1957 foreign aid amendment had a direct bearing on South Vietnamese conditions in the Vietnam war. The Congressional amendment forbade the foreign aid agency from spending funds to teach South Vietnamese peasants to grow and market their rice and grain efficiently, so that, instead, the cereals would have to be imported from the United States surpluses and help make profits in the U.S.A. When the Viet Cong war expanded in South Vietnam, the peasants were not sufficiently trained at increasing rice production; shortages and crises resulted, and rice had to be imported.

By far the Congressional practice most disturbing to the State Department is that of attaching foreign policy riders or amendments to legislation. An amendment by the Senate Minority Leader Everett Dirksen stopped a proposed $50 million loan by the Export-Import Bank for the purchase of American machine tools to be used in an Italian Fiat automobile plant that was to be built in Soviet Russia by the Fiat Company of Italy. This ran full tilt against the Johnson administration's policy of "building bridges to the East." The Vietnam war, symbolizing to many Congressmen a renewed Communist menace, inspired many similar amendments. Senator Harry F. Byrd, Democrat of Virginia, produced a rider to restrict Export-Import Bank loans to any nation whatsoever which furnished goods or supplies to Communist North Vietnam, despite the Johnson administration plea that this restriction would cause the loss of more than $1 billion worth of U.S. export sales, in comparison with the miniscule sum of $13 million worth of exports that U.S. allies were selling yearly to North Vietnam.

A further plain flouting of a U.S. foreign policy commitment by domestic economic interests occurred in the September 1967 passage of the $70 billion Defense appropriation, the largest single such sum in the history of Congress. Congressman John W. Byrnes, Republican of Wisconsin, won an amendment that required all U.S. naval vessels to be built in American shipyards, in the frank hope of getting a Defense Department contract for sixteen mine sweepers to be built in Wisconsin shipyards on Lake Superior. This canceled out a U.S. commitment to Britain to allow bidding on seven wooden mine sweepers for the U.S. Navy. President Johnson said that, to get the business for his home state, Byrnes broke up a deal in which the United States would have spent roughly $400 million in Britain, in return for the British buying $2 billion worth of American military equipment, including fifty new F-111 fighter-bombers.

Congress' action produced its diplomatic fallout reminiscent of the heavy weather caused by the McNamara cancellation of the Skybolt missile in December 1962. The importance of the F-111 lay in the fact that it would function east of Suez, where Britain had made commitments to the United States to help police the vast Indian Ocean area between the Middle East and Australia. British Defense Secretary Dennis Healey said: "If I saw any signs that this was the beginning of the end of the F-111 agreement, it would raise the most serious problems of defense in foreign policy and undermine the whole relationship between Britain and the United States."

One of the most startling consequences of Congress' heightened interest in foreign policy-cum-money arises when it stumbles upon a sensational situation, in the course of whose investigation the lid is lifted for a few moments from the inner workings of the executive branch, and the nuts and bolts, gears and springs, and, some might add, the worms and boll weevils can be seen whirring and sliding around inside the foreign affairs operating agencies, headed by the State and Defense Departments. An almost flawless *succès de scandale* of this sort erupted in the summer of 1967 as enhanced awareness of the Arab-Israeli crisis spotlighted the issue of arms supply.

The uproar began with release of State Department testimony given in March 1967 to the Senate Foreign Relations subcommittee on Near Eastern and South Asian affairs, chaired by Senator Stuart Symington, Missouri Democrat. The din was renewed a few weeks later, when the House Banking and Currency Committee—a new entry into the Congressional foreign affairs field—deliberated renewal of the charter of the Export-Import Bank, whose normal function was to finance American exports to foreign purchasers but which had also financed $2.6 billion worth of arms, $2 billion to industrialized countries and the remainder to so-called underdeveloped countries. The first Congressional reaction was righteous outrage at not having been "informed" of these parlous circumstances by the executive departments. The next shock was the discovery that Defense, using the flexible accounting resources of its multibillion-dollar budget, itself owned nearly a half-billion-dollar revolving fund, from which it issued credit for arms sales, guaranteeing 25 per cent of purchase loans, Senator Eugene J. McCarthy, Minnesota Democrat, said, like "a kind of Federal Reserve Bank for arms sales around the world." In its bewildered chagrin at all this hanky-panky under the very noses of its august Appropriations and Armed Services Committees, Congress never quite realized that what it had uncovered was the residual refuse pit of the Cold War, the spillover from which was spreading all over the world, as the two great superpowers, the United States and the Soviet Union, gave away or sold surplus arms for their own purposes.

Beset as it was by domestic preoccupation and the Vietnam war, Congress never had time to peel back all the ramifications of the surplus arms imbroglio, involving over $11 billion worth of arms, sales, and grants in the five years that ended in 1966. To this day, it is fairly safe to wager, Congress has yet to look into the relevant roles of the Treasury Department, of the Agency for International Development, and of the State Department's Office of Munitions Control. The internal indications reflect actions under necessities, frailties of bureaucratic personalities, and fortuitous neglect, coupled with what-can-we-do-about-it resignation. A high State official sighed later, "We walked into that one."

The first basic ingredient in the arms mix was the almost continuous necessity to modernize the NATO allies, including West Germany, Italy, Greece, and Turkey, and also to provide for Japan and Australia. The second factor was the deficit in the United States balance of payments, which had persisted since 1957. The third item to open the floodgates of arms exports was the accord between President Kennedy and West German Chancellor Adenauer in February 1961 that Germany should, for the first time, meet its just share of NATO defense expenditures.

Treasury Secretary Douglas Dillon, with the principal collaboration of his director of Foreign Assets Control, Charles A. Sullivan, almost desperate to stem the dollar outflow in the balance of payments, the international double-entry bookkeeping of trade and finance between nations, came up with the idea of "offset." This was a device whereby dollars spent for support of the half million U.S. armed forces inside the native German economy could somehow be made to wend their way home. Otherwise, the West Germans would keep on adding to their large stocks of dollars and gold at U.S. expense. The answer was for the Germans to buy U.S. arms, for which chore the Defense Department was the necessary partner. Even better, Dillon and Sullivan hit on the ploy of persuading the Germans to pay for arms in advance, which helped make the balance of payments books look better.

Sullivan, a jovial and supershrewd Irishman and a career professional, first at Treasury and then successively at Defense, State, and again Treasury, pingponged back and forth between Washington and Europe, wheeling and wheedling deals for monies, above all out of the Germans. In six years, Sullivan was responsible for "collecting" almost $3 billion for the U.S. Treasury, for which feat he received a distinguished service award from a grateful Dillon. Sullivan left the Government to go into private business to make some money for himself for a change, early in 1967. Thus, he never figured in the arms sales inquiries by Congress. Sullivan's Defense Department counterpart, Henry J. Kuss, Jr., Deputy Assistant Secretary of Defense for International Logistics Negotiations, took the heat.

The second area unplumbed by Congress was State's Office of Munitions Control, whose rather self-conscious description of itself in a September 1967 *News Letter,* the Department's house organ, said, in part: "The licensing for export of arms, ammunition and implements of war and control of arms traffic is an important instrumentality of U.S. foreign policy. The primary issue is invariably political, and often involves considerations of military security."

In February 1967, Senator McCarthy of Minnesota, with sardonic effect, said: "I can find little evidence that the State Department's Office of Munitions Control has any real control over, or knowledge of, the activities of the largest arms exporter of all, the federal government."

What the Congress never had occasion to learn were the extremely irksome complications encountered by former Deputy Under Secretary of State for Political Affairs U. Alexis Johnson and his chief aide, former Deputy Assistant Secretary of State for Politico-Military Affairs Jeffrey C. Kitchen, in attempting to obtain a firm handhold on the Office of Munitions Control as a lever of power in supervising the movement of arms overseas. The difficulties arose in trying to shift personnel within the built-in safeguards of the Civil Service system which dominated the munitions office.

The third untouched field of inquiry concerned the concept and method of military aid given by the United States to its collective security allies, who, from 1945 to 1963, for example, received over $32 billion worth of weapons and equipment. The key question revolved around who had kept the watch on military aid since 1961. The short answer turned out to be that no over-all watch had been kept on military aid since 1961.

In the closing years of the Eisenhower administration, Dillon, then Under Secretary of State, by presidential delegation personally acted as coordinator of the Mutual Security Program, as foreign aid was then called. With John O. Bell, later Ambassador to Guatemala, as his watchdog, Dillon kept close tabs on military aid, as handled by the Defense Department, in relation to economic aid. When the Kennedy administration took over, there was almost a year's gap in finding a new foreign aid chief, until Fowler Hamilton, a law partner of George Ball, came in and found so much backlog to handle that he "temporarily" put aside the intricate issue of military aid. His successor, David E. Bell, former Budget Bureau Director and a high-class administrator, found himself in the era of aid policy mutation, from free or grant aid to development loan aid, and again never had time properly to focus on the over-all supervision of military aid, its relation to economic aid, and the political implications of the mixture.

It was not until 1966 that, on orders of superiors, the first serious attempt was made by the Kitchen politico-military office to get into the substance of the matter. Thus, for six years military aid went on its smooth and rarely disturbed way within the efficient and, in the nature of things, rigid channels of the Pentagon. Basic to the entire situation was the U.S. practice of updating its equipment every three or four years, which in turn made previous stocks "obsolescent," hence, fit for surplus in aid or sale. There was patently insufficient foreign policy consistency in supervision of military aid except at such times as political events in the overseas field would surface its workings to a crisis and require urgent case-by-case decision. By 1967, the question was how much could the State Department, to compensate for its previous passivity, retrieve of a policy that by then was water over the dam, spilled milk, and cold beans.

The State Department, while it leaves the administration of foreign aid to its subsidiary agency, AID, inescapably has an absorbing interest in the fate of the annual foreign aid bill, since money is a vital oil of diplomacy. An attempt had been made to enhance operational intimacy between State and AID in recent years by "back-to-back" relationships. AID and State work together in integrated offices for Latin American affairs, but scarcity of expert personnel kept the experiment from tryouts in other bureaus. The arrangement would educate AID in political policy considerations, and State in practical economic immediacies.

Secretary Rusk concerned himself with large policy issues as foreign aid escalated to his level, but he also kept a private eye on AID operations through the Inspector General of Foreign Assistance, a relatively new post which was created by Congress and whose first occupant was a veteran "Hill" hand, J. K. Mansfield, former staff director of the Jackson Senate subcommittee on national security problems. Mansfield, a disarmingly affable character, known privately as a foreign sports-car buff, ran a small informal shop with only thirty-nine persons and on only some $700,000 of his $2 million budget, to the not inconsiderable pleasure of his old Congressional friends. These he further delighted in 1966 by making verifiable savings of over $50 million in foreign aid operations. Mansfield's simple expedient was writing highly unbureaucratic commonsense letters to AID officials and Pentagon generals. The communications were follow-ups after constant staff trips all over the globe, looking into foreign aid operations on the spot. Mansfield's pixie advent on the scene with bizarre frequency resulted in odd discoveries. In Antofagasta, Chile, 600,000 sacks of American flour were stacked up in the open, awaiting eventual shipment up to the mountains of Bolivia. Asking why the food was not stored under cover, Mansfield was told that it was safe enough; it had not rained in Antofagasta in forty-seven years. Two days later there was a torrential four-hour downpour. Mansfield wrote AID Administrator William S. Gaud, suggesting "that AID abandon support of cloud-seeding techniques. . . ." Mansfield's casual, clubby approach was frowned upon by the starchy bureaucrats of the General Accounting Office, a post-audit arm of the Congress, which desired more weighty reports.

If the well-vaselined Mansfield needle did not find a responsive vein, somehow U.S. Senator John L. McClellan, Democrat of Arkansas and

Chairman of the Senate Government Operations Committee, might hear about it. AID continued to deposit sums in payment of tractor purchases to a U.S. company's London office, which was a definite convenience to the industrial corporation but which also upset the U.S. balance of payments to the tune of some $40 million a year. The corrective was the Arkansan's raspy, "What's all this about?" Or the case of the $10,000-bottom limit on competitive bidding in the import program to hedge against inflation in South Vietnam, so fixed because policing bids below $10,000 would have involved too much extra paper work. The catch in this under-$10,000 cellar of high-finance-minded AID was that it screened over a bushel of monkeyshines that was breaking apart at the seams and spilling petty but pervasive corruption throughout Saigon. By coincidence, U.S. Senator Frank E. Moss, Utah Democrat on the Commerce Committee, had the same idea about cutting off the $10,000 umbrella for the small-time crooks. AID complied with alacrity—finally.

This was trivia compared to the damage the mastodons of the United States Senate inflict when they start trampling all over the precariously cultivated foreign policy garden. The rampage was more pronounced as the strains, anxieties, and fears of the Vietnam war atmosphere exacerbated tempers, foreclosed judgments, and vented accumulated frustrations on foreign aid, which, after all was the easiest available victim and one whose flow of lifeblood could be cut off in reprisal by the simple act of denying it funds. This is exactly what Congress does in degrees. In 1967, for instance, the Johnson administration request for authorization of $3.4 billion was cut to the lowest foreign aid figure in twenty years, adding insult to injury by tacking on a host of policy riders that spread havoc among carefully laid foreign affairs plans as Congressmen unloaded their grievances on the foreign aid catchall for the sorry state of the world. Brandishing cries of "arsenal diplomacy," the Senate in 1967 proved far more ferocious to foreign aid than the House of Representatives, which in former days had been the more intransigent in wielding the ax on foreign aid. Military aid developed into the prime target, with Senator Wayne Morse, Oregon Democrat, charging that military aid fostered dictatorships in Latin America, Senator McCarthy laying on military aid the blame for the India-Pakistan war of 1966, and Senator Fulbright muttering darkly that the U.S. involvement in the Vietnam war was directly ascribable to military aid.

The executive branch's proposal for fiscal year 1968 military aid, as originally presented to Congress in the spring of 1967, included, roughly, $283 million for the Far East, exclusive of Vietnam and Thailand; $234 million for the Middle East; $6 million for Europe, which had gotten $15 billion in free military grants in the first eighteen years after World War II; $31 million for Africa; and $45 million for Latin America. The country breakdowns, in round figures, were:

FAR EAST

Formosa	$ 90,000,000
Burma	3,000,000
Indonesia	6,000,000
Korea	16,000,000
Philippines	22,000,000

MIDDLE EAST

Turkey	$134,000,000
Greece	65,000,000
Iran	31,000,000
Jordan	1,900,000
Saudi Arabia	1,000,000

EUROPE

Spain	$ 4,700,000
Portugal	1,000,000

AFRICA

Ethiopia	$ 14,000,000
Congo	3,500,000
Libya	3,600,000
Liberia	900,000
Morocco	3,500,000
Tunisia	5,200,000

LATIN AMERICA

Brazil	$ 8,100,000
Argentina	7,000,000
Colombia	5,100,000
Chile	3,300,000
Bolivia	2,400,000
Dominican Republic	3,000,000
Ecuador	2,800,000
El Salvador	700,000
Guatemala	1,200,000
Honduras	1,100,000
Nicaragua	1,300,000
Peru	4,000,000
Venezuela	1,300,000
Uruguay	1,400,000
Paraguay	1,100,000
Panama	300,000

State Department geographical area Assistant Secretaries, AID area Assistant Administrators, Defense Department International Security Affairs

officials, and generals of the Joint Chiefs of Staff all get into the act of justifying the requests, explaining and arguing to the point of exhaustion to the
distinguished Senators and the honorable Representatives of the double
foreign affairs committees, double appropriations committees, and double
armed services committees at what precise point economic aid stopped
and military aid began, or where they shaded into each other under the
term of "supporting assistance," such as the $20 million recommended in
this latter category for the Dominican Republic, almost half its total proposed economic aid for fiscal 1968.

The explanations get more and more involved and tricky in comparing
why India should receive a proposed $412 million and Pakistan $172 million, both almost all in development loans. Neither would get military aid.
Or why Indonesia would be allotted $23 million for a development loan,
while a tidy sum was also set aside in the contingency of trouble in that
potentially rich and volatile island nation. The need for South Korea's
$96 million in economic aid was quickly rationalized: half for develop-
ment and almost the same sum for support of the big army defending the
fifteen-year-old truce line against Communist North Korea. The military
factor was even more apparent in Laos: four fifths of the proposed $56
million in so-called economic aid was to support the nonstop hostilities
against the North Vietnam–backed Pathet Lao.

It was difficult to fault the Congress, punch-drunk with demands for aid
since 1945, which in the first twenty years had run over $100 billion, from
the days of GARIOA (Government and Relief in Occupied Areas) and
UNRRA (United Nations Relief and Rehabilitation) to ERA (European
Recovery Administration) to FOA (Foreign Operations Administration)
to MSA (Mutual Security Administration) to ICA (International Cooperation Administration) to today's AID (Agency for International Development), acronyms which in sequence reveal the ups and downs of foreign
relations since 1945.

Amid the crash of breaking U.S. embassy and USIA library window-
panes by sticks and stones and bullets of foreign mobs, it was in no wise
strange that there should have arisen a Savonarola to denounce the "evils"
of foreign aid, Representative Otto E. Passman, Democrat from the
bayous of Louisiana. Though not as fearsome as he had been in his salad
days of ten years ago, when the late Clarence Cannon, long-time Chairman of the House Appropriations Committee, had mischievously allowed
him full throttle, Passman was still a redoubtable antagonist of Presidents,
Secretaries of State, and AID administrators in hamstringing U.S. efforts
to succor the heathen.

Benighted as the Passman exegesis might appear to the harassed officers of State, the paradox transpired that Passman had been frequently

right for the wrong reasons or wrong for the right reasons, depending on which foot he was standing on, or how he manipulated the figures. Passman performed an educational service in helping identify the very scope and arithmetic of the foreign policy base and spectrum of overseas operations.

In a four-page mimeographed statement which he updated every year and passed out to all who sought his words of wisdom, Passman said:

The AID Agency, this year [1967], agrees with my definition of foreign aid. I quote their definition verbatim:
"Broadly speaking, foreign assistance is any aid—military or economic—which is extended by one country to another as loans or grants. This definition includes assistance rendered through the various international agencies—such as the United Nations—as well as that which is on a strictly bilateral basis. Used in this context, foreign aid includes not only those programs carried out by the Agency for International Development, but also a number of other programs authorized by Congress. . . ."

In the following compilation of requests for foreign aid funds, Passman pointed out that only the first item on the list was usually referred to as "foreign aid," though all items related to financing of foreign policy.

NEW FOREIGN AID FUNDS REQUESTED
FIRST SEVEN MONTHS OF 1967: CATEGORY I

Foreign Assistance Request (Mutual Security)	$3,226,420,000
Receipts & Recoveries from Previous Credits	266,356,000
Military Assistance Advisory Groups (MAAG)	42,000,000
Export-Import Bank (Long-term Credits)	2,295,000,000
Public Law 480 (Agricultural Commodities)	1,772,500,000
Inter-American Development Bank (Latin America)	300,000,000
International Development Association (IDA)	104,000,000
Peace Corps	118,700,000
Total—Category I	$8,124,976,000

OTHER FOREIGN AID REQUESTS: CATEGORY II

Export-Import Bank (Regular Operations)	$ 555,000,000
Permanent Construction Overseas (Military)	331,900,000
Contributions to International Organizations	109,362,000
Educational (Foreign and Other Students)	54,800,000
Ryukyu Islands	14,956,000
Migrants and Refugees	5,660,000
Atomic Energy Commission (Euratom)	2,500,000
Inter-American Highway	7,000,000
Total—Category II	$1,081,178,000
Over-all Total—New Foreign Aid Requests	$9,206,154,000

This untidy spread of the foreign affairs spectrum was a constant irritant to Congress because there was evidently no single place that offered a handle to get hold of it. Conversely, the absence of a logically organized Congressional system to process the foreign affairs chores according to constitutional requirements made Congress look like an amusement park's crazy-house labyrinth. In effect, Congress duplicated the executive branch's own confusions and split personalities and dead ends. The foreign affairs federal departments, with their interagency rivalries and power conscious bureaucracies, were copies of the Congressional side of the coin. There was a parallel dispersion of authority in the proliferation of the competitive committee system and its jealously defended prerogatives. This was the alley of thorns that the State Department had constantly to traverse in a great time-wasting procedure of repetitious explanations, which tended to attenuate as they spread out to more and more committees that demanded to be informed and consulted.

Although in the executive branch there was one point of final decision in the person of the President, in the Congress there was none. The uncertain pace and attitude of Congressional committees made it difficult for the President and the State Department to prepare in advance a program whose size and scope could rarely be predicted with confidence and which, instead, might be expanded, mutilated, or redirected. The end result was to splinter and aggravate the innately provisional nature of presidential and State Department foreign policies. In short, the Congressional system, as constituted, made every executive foreign policy initiative a gamble and placed stability of policy on a rolling and shifting base.

The problem had not been ignored by the responsible leaders of Congress. They had long seen the urgent necessity to cope with the growing issue of the separation and sharing of powers with the President and his several built-in advantages of responsibility to the nation as a whole, leadership of his political party, and storehouse of assets in experts, information, and possibilities of coordination. In July 1966 a Joint Committee on the Organization of the Congress, in its final report, said:

The Congress of the United States is the only branch of the Federal Government regularly and entirely accountable to the American people. Indeed, it is the people's branch. Our constitutional system is based on the principle that Congress must effectively bring to bear the will of the people on all phases of the formulation and execution of public policy.

However, it is becoming more and more difficult for any collective decision-making entity like Congress to meet its responsibilities. A global foreign policy in an age of nuclear confrontation requires a timely and cohesive national response. Moreover, an increasingly complex society produces social, economic, and technological problems of staggering complexity.

Many contend that Congress no longer is capable of exercising initiative in the solution of modern problems. A fundamental reason for this loss of initiative is the lack of organizational effectiveness. Under the pressure of modern circumstances, the Congress has tended to delegate authority to the executive branch of the government. While Congress has not abdicated its role, it has permitted that role to become diluted.

A year later, in 1967, U.S. Senator A. S. Mike Monroney, Democrat of Oklahoma, who had coauthored the bill that had last remodeled the Congress, in 1946, faced heavy seas in attempting to steer a new bill through the Senate as policies and reform brought out traditional antipathies, despite the rallying cry that the proposed legislation would reassert Congress as the "First Branch" of government and halt erosion of its powers to the President. The Congress' difficulty in meeting the problem, in large measure, lay in the atmosphere created by the intertwined relationships, cross-purposed policies, and wrangling committees that mirrored the jurisdictional overlaps and tangled lines of authority, a hodgepodge that resembled the jumble of wires tightly packed into a space rocket, but, unfortunately, without clearly identifiable markings.

The joint committee, cochaired by Monroney and Representative Ray J. Madden, New Jersey Democrat, in analyzing the record of the Eighty-eighth Congress (1963–1964), noted several startling facts. The members had worked through the medium of 535 committees of all types, including boards and commissions, 245 in the House and 157 in the Senate, and including 24 joint committees and 75 conferences committees to iron out differences on bills.

The Senate had eighteen full committees, of which sixteen were standing committees, while the House had twenty-two, of which twenty were standing. This was an improvement over 1946, when the number of standing committees had been reduced from eighty-one to thirty-four. But with the vast amount of referrals from the State Department and its multiplied global involvements, there was still an inordinate amount of running around to do, since foreign affairs considerations touched, centrally or importantly, on the domains of at least thirteen of the standing committees in the House and Senate. Among these were foreign relations, agriculture, armed services, education and labor, government operations, interstate and foreign commerce, finance, judiciary, banking and currency, space and aeronautical sciences, not to mention appropriations, which got into everything because nine tenths of the work of Congress dealt with spending-money issues.

The subcommittees had sprouted like weeds. The report listed 139 in the Senate and 223 in the House, including temporary ones. The main point was that the standing subcommittees of both Houses totaled 221, or more than 40 per cent of all bodies upon which members of the eighty-eight had served. They held two thirds of the more than 8,000 committee meetings of all types. The back-breaking strain on members was plain, conflicts in meeting dates being the rule rather than the exception, forcing members to scurry frantically and to spread themselves too thin in more than 5,000 member assignments. As a consequence, the members were not very responsive to the serious, complicated, and sensitive briefings or testimony which the State Department offered in rationalization of its foreign policy proposals. To top the cake, Congress in recent years had been tending to concentrate its workload from Tuesday to Thursday, averaging 2,000 meetings a day on those three days, thus imposing on the State Department and other foreign affairs agencies the necessity of frantic efforts to pursue its pressing interests within foreshortened time limits.

The Monroney-Madden report contained several pertinent recommendations, included as given below but not approved as the consensus of the majority:

"Establish a Joint Committee on National Security Operations to furnish greater coordination in foreign policy, national defense and other security matters [which] should replace the present armed services and foreign relations committees of both Houses." But no one expected a chairman of prestigious committees to give up his seat of power.

"Establish a Joint Committee on Intelligence Operations to provide better supervision of CIA." Senator Russell & Co. had already defeated such an attempt led by Senators McCarthy, Fulbright, and Mansfield in 1966.

"Establish a question period before Congress for high officials, particularly those involved in foreign policy."

"Provide that treaties shall be with the advice and consent of both Houses of Congress by majority vote, rather than by two-thirds vote of the Senate." This would recognize the House's claim that its primary control over the purse should allow it to get in on the ground floor of foreign affairs.

"Review the war-making power to determine the congressional role in the area of undeclared wars and 'police actions.'" Here, the scalpel of analysis was cutting close to the biggest bone of contention between the legislative and the executive, namely, what was the mete and legitimate ratio of responsibility in foreign policy between the Congress and the President.

Finally, as an umbrella rationalization of the whole Congressional dilemma, there was a plaintive and belated realization that the semantic monstrosity of legislative "oversight" should be renamed "review," so that there would be "greater public awareness" of this congressional responsibility to oversee performance of the laws and in particular the efficacy or ineffectiveness of foreign policies, their execution and their consonance with the "intent" of Congress.

The "oversight" function had become simple oversight, an admission which rankled in the breast of Congress. Legislative oversight, after the united legislative-executive front of the Truman Doctrine–Marshall Plan–

NATO days in the first flash of the Communist challenge twenty years earlier, had become incidental, spasmodic, capricious, or atrophied, in the face of assertive, implied, or overreaching presidential powers in the nuclear years. During most of the past century before World War II, Congress had been out to lunch as the slow but ineluctable involvements of foreign policy spun their web about the nation. Since 1939 the Congress had sat steadily at the table of foreign affairs, eating what was placed before it, not having to do any of the cooking, let alone having the opportunity of dictating the menu. As legislators, the members were stultified by the practical impossibility of personal participation because of the labyrinthine complexity of the Congressional organism. Every Senator and Congressman had a vital stake in foreign affairs. But few had a voice loud enough to rise above the ubiquitous chorus demanding to be heard, thus compounding the frustration of most. As representatives of their constituents, they heard in the voices of America coming to them weariness and impatience at the fact that the tried-and-true methods of the past, continued today with one million troops overseas, military training missions in thirty-eight countries, and major bases in twenty, were no longer efficacious in the new and unstable era of emerging countries and the bloody spectacle of North Vietnam holding at bay the United States, the greatest power on earth.

Even Congressmen eager to snatch a free headline by off-the-lip comments on foreign affairs were beginning dimly to comprehend what President-and-Secretary of State John Quincy Adams meant when he decried the penchant of politicians to broad, abstract principles which vitiated the all-essential factor of precision in foreign policy formulation. Exactitude was all the more imperative in a world as complex and fissionable as today's, when the mixed equation of creeping or adventitious involvement, peripheral strategic interest, and marginal application of U.S. power was almost impossible to determine, let alone to control in advance.

Belated second thoughts, misgivings, and doubts concerning the diffusion of U.S. power and its undefined limits began to burgeon in 1966, after a year of bombing escalation and massive reinforcements of U.S. troops in South Vietnam. Ironically, it was not the Senate doves or anti-involvement aviary which sang out the first shrill trills against the global overextension of U.S. objectives and overcommitment of U.S. resources. It was U.S. Senator John Stennis, Mississippi Democrat, the protégé of Senator Russell and Chairman of the Senate Armed Services Preparedness Subcommittee. Stennis was a character not unlike Senator Robert A. Taft of Ohio, "Mr. Conservative" and "Mr. Republican" of the first postwar decade. Taft had led the assault fifteen years before, in 1951, against the dispatch of four U.S. divisions to Europe for NATO. In the same month of August 1966 that Stennis voiced his fears of stretching U.S. military manpower too thin too far away in Asia, Senator Mike Mansfield, the Majority leader, concurrently was demanding "substantial reduction of U.S. forces permanently stationed in Europe."

There was not much that State Department officers could do as agents of the President but ride out the growing disgruntlement. The defense had to be placed on the level of Secretary Rusk. The Secretary reminded the Senators that the collective security system now under attack was the self-same mechanism, based on Senate Resolution 239 of June 11, 1948, by Senator Arthur Vandenberg, Republican of Michigan, that had forestalled World War III in the late 1940's and early 1950's. The Stennis hearings proved to be but a dress rehearsal for 1967 as worry about overcommitment coalesced with the issue of executive-legislative consultation in foreign policy. The storm gathered speed, almost month by month through 1967. In March, President Johnson asked Congress for a resolution to support a Latin American common market and to pledge $1.5 billion for the next five years for the Alliance for Progress, whose summit meeting of Presidents LBJ was to attend at Punta del Este in April. The House bought the proposition, but the Senate balked. Senator Fulbright, already leery of blank-check authorizations because of Vietnam, persuaded a like-minded Senate to his view.

A similar expression of displeasure, with the fear of overcommitment the overriding factor, led hawks and doves to unite under Senator Russell to scuttle for the first time in ten years a Defense Department hardware proposal. This was to build FDL, or "fast deployment logistics," ships, seven for a start, with which Secretary McNamara had planned a new mobile strategy of rapid global movement of supplies to distant reaches of the globe, in the event of "new Vietnams." Mansfield, backed in 1967 with forty-three senatorial cosponsors, raised again the issue of reducing U.S. forces in Europe. His long campaign succeeded in part, the administration announcing in May that U.S. forces in Germany would be cut by 35,000, the first reduction in sixteen years. The sudden outbreak of the Arab-Israeli war in June focused even sharper attention on the issue of overinvolvement, the universal anxiety, despite pro-Israel popular sentiments, being not to get sucked into still another war in the Middle East unless Israel were actually in imminent peril of destruction.

Still more fuel was added to the fire in July, when, at the outbreak of revolt, the United States dispatched three C-130 cargo planes and 100 paratroopers to the Congo. This move aroused instant and violent Senate protests. Russell again led the chorus with the cry: "It is immoral to send even one American boy into a country where we have no commitments and where we have no vital interests." Russell had not labored, he said, to help build up the strength of the United States armed forces in order to scatter them "all over the world."

The nettled air was further poisoned by arms sales disclosures of sleight-of-hand dealings among American allies like West Germany, Iran, and Turkey to transfer planes and equipment to Pakistan despite State Department bans against such shipments without U.S. consent. U.S. bombing within ten miles of the Communist Chinese border in North Vietnam re-animated the fear, never dormant, of Peking intervention in the Vietnam war.

The Senate barrage was causing international repercussions, not merely generalized anxiety among friends or malicious hope among enemies. In Britain, Prime Minister Harold Wilson repeated his pledge to the United States of continuing the costly East of Suez defense involvement. Absurdly enough, it was again a question of birds, not hawks and doves this time, but the pink-footed booby, the flightless rail, last surviving descendant of the now-extinct dodo, and the ibis, rare and sacred to the ancient Egyptian gods. The British and Americans in 1963 had thought up the idea of a chain of stripped-down way stations in the Indian Ocean, to be used by aircraft dispatched from Britain or the United States, thus avoiding the sensitive issues of overflying other nations' sovereign space. Two uninhabited islands had been picked and restructured governmentally into the BIOT, the British Indian Ocean Territories, possessions of the Crown and therefore not under the control of British colonial regimes which might become independent and deny the islands' use to the Anglo-American allies. The islands were Aldabra, north-northeast of Madagascar, and Diego Garcia, due south of Ceylon and the Maldives. On Aldabra were rare species of birds, preserved and flourishing because of the perfect ecology. The Royal Society in Britain had taken up arms against use of the strategic outpost because of danger to the birds, which had been described by Charles Darwin in his *Voyage of the Beagle*. The National Academy of Sciences and the Smithsonian Institution in Washington, both para-statal organizations supported financially by the United States Government, joined forces with the Royal Society to "save" the birds.

The bird lovers demanded that an alternate site be found for the airstrip, namely, on the Farquhar Islands, some 300 miles farther to the east-southeast. Whereupon a snag developed at once. The normal route from the first hopping stone, Ascension Island, east of Africa, in the Atlantic, finds its natural landfall at Aldabra. But to have to fly another 300 miles would have presented a military problem of jet fuel versus bomb load versus tactical mission. In brief, the effectiveness of a contingent allied defense counteraction to possible Communist-exploited insurgency in the volatile African continent would be in a substantial degree compromised even before it started.

To meet the bird crisis, the State Department pulled the original negotiator of the island deal, former Deputy Assistant Secretary Kitchen, out of the Foreign Service Institute senior seminar, the top governmental training course in foreign policy given by the U.S. Government to its elite personnel, and sent him winging to London. In national security parlance, a tactical problem had arisen inside a strategic situation. The mission was to ascertain the British side of the bird crises and to prepare State for the worst in Congress if Senators like Frank Church, Idaho Democrat, who had vowed not to vote another penny for any new U.S. commitment anywhere, rose to denounce the project.

It was in this thunderhead climate that Senator Fulbright in August 1967 introduced Senate resolution No. 151, "Relative to U.S. Commitments to Foreign Powers," and launched hearings on the proper roles of Congress and the President in the direction of foreign policy. The prologue to the opening drama had overtones of the Senate of ancient Rome defending the prerogatives of the Republic against the encroachments of the Princeps-Imperator-Caesar. The conflict of interest on the two sides, equally sincere and selfish, had been implicit even in the minds of the Founding Fathers, as the powerful pamphleteering of *The Federalist* papers indicates. James Madison, regarded by scholars as the largest single contributor to the Constitution of the United States, and later Thomas Jefferson's Secretary of State and his successor as President, in Federalist Letter Number 41, wrote: ". . . the liberties of Rome proved the final victim to her military triumphs; and the liberties of Europe . . . have, with few exceptions, been the price of her military establishments."

The Federalist was full of examples from Greek and Roman history, a reflection of the publication of Edward Gibbon's first volume of the *Decline and Fall of the Roman Empire* in 1776, the year of the Declaration of Independence by the American colonies, which still imported their intellectual pabulum from London. Gibbon, also a favorite browsing pastime of Senator Fulbright, said in Chapter II, "On the Constitution of the Roman Empire in the Age of Antonines," with evocative pertinence in the light of 1967:

The choice of the enemies of Rome was regularly decided by the legislative authority. The most important resolutions of peace and war were seriously debated in the Senate and solemnly ratified by the people. But when the arms of the legions were carried to a great distance from Italy, the generals assumed the liberty of directing them against whatever people, and in whatever manner, they judged most advantageous for the public service.

A few pages later, Gibbon, again with the touch of the seer, added: ". . . but whenever the senate empowered the first magistrate to consult the safety of the commonwealth, he was raised by that degree above the laws, and exercised, in the defense of liberty, a temporary despotism."

Earlier, in describing that tumultuous era of transition from republic to empire, Gibbon had also delved into the Roman executive-legislative confrontation. He wrote: "It would require the pen of a Tacitus . . . to describe the various emotions of the senate; those that were suppressed, and those that were affected. It was dangerous to trust the sincerity of Augustus; to seem to distrust it was still more dangerous."

The drama between the chief magistrate and the senators of the American Republic, developing in 1966 through 1967 to the election year of 1968, never quite rose to the heights of the grand inquiry of Gibbon. Gibbon had held that the crisis of Rome had been that of a nation selling its soul for the wealth of Asia, while Michael Ivanovich Rostovtzeff, the late, great modern scholar of Roman history, believed Rome's fall had been basically a failure of nerve.

The State Department versus the Foreign Relations Committee scene in the Capitol was rather a low-camp bowdlerization of an epic of imperial purple and flashing republican daggers of liberty. Fulbright was neither an implacable Cato nor quite a Cicero of the Philippics, though he did evoke the image of a dedicated Roman senator in the last days of the republic, sage, stoic, and sardonic. President Johnson certainly was no Catiline, though possibly faintly a precursor of Caesars to come. The play on Fulbright's resolution of July 31, 1967, unfolded as if two sovereign states were in full diplomatic parley, as Woodrow Wilson had already observed in his *Congressional Government* of 1885. Fulbright wrote the State Department requesting, with polite punctilio, answers to four questions. Assistant Secretary for Congressional Relations Macomber replied, with equally courteous consideration, appending seventy-one pages of references listing official statements and agreements that showed the nature of U.S. commitments.

The key Fulbright question was No. 1:

Of the 42 countries with which the United States has bilateral treaties or multilateral agreements for collective defense, in how many instances would the Executive Branch view as automatic the American commitment as one upon which the United States would act unilaterally—meaning that we view the obligations not only as collective but individual, as the Department has interpreted the SEATO treaty?

For example, should one of the members of the 1947 Inter-American treaty of reciprocal assistance be attacked by subversion or from an external source, to what extent, if any, would there be a commitment for the United States on its own to supply men or material to respond to such attack? We would like to have such nations listed, not only in the American Republics, but elsewhere.

The State Department's answer, as conveyed by Macomber:

Under each of our multilateral treaties, the commitment to extend assistance in the event of an armed attack is individual and requires no collective finding or decision by a multilateral organization. . . . Under each of these treaties there is an individual obligation independent of any collective action.

Macomber cited supporting chapters and verses in the Rio treaty for Latin America, the North Atlantic (NATO) treaty for Europe, the Southeast Asia collective defense treaty (SEATO), and the Anzus Security Treaty for Australia and New Zealand, adding "the same is true of the bilateral treaties with the Philippines, Korea, Republic of China (Formosa) and Japan."

In reply to the Fulbright query on commitments via subversion, Macomber wrote: "All of our defense treaties call for consultation in the event of a threat other than armed attack—such as externally supported subversion."

The Fulbright-Macomber exchange of letters was the first thrust and parry of the duel between Congress and the President. Fulbright called for testimony to support his proposal to allow Congress to read the President's fine print in advance but also permit it to write in its own, too, as necessary, on the specifics of commitment.

The voluminous Macomber file, however, did not include the personal interpretations of the technical diplomatists who had their own pragmatic concepts of what all these treaties meant. First and foremost, the network of treaties was regarded more as insurance options, operationally, rather than as binding contracts, as the eminent senator-politicians appeared to regard the so-called commitments. Second and significantly, the pacts consistently included the phrase that the eventual action possibly contemplated for each nation, including the United States, would be "within the framework of its constitutional processes." In short, the United States and any other country could slip, slide, squeeze, or bug out of its seemingly clear commitment if and when the situation became too politically distasteful, or plainly counter to its sovereign will and interpretation of its vital national interests, in a showdown.

This was, as the operating Machiavellis saw it, a large gray area for tactical maneuver within the legally binding treaty complex. The difficulty on both bureaucratic and Congressional sides was the temptation to hedge the insurance bet by investing funds. There was a tendency on the part of the military to overelaborate an incipient or reserve beachhead. The political legislators, puffed with alarm and/or unquestioning patriotism, inclined to "give the boys what they need." Furthermore, in a body traditionally heavy with lawyers, adept in putting off the hearing of a case, there was always someone to remember Alexander Hamilton's definition of treaties as "contracts with foreign nations" in Letter Number 75 of *The Federalist*. Additionally, there was the shrewd gloss supplied thereon by that formidable attorney-at-law, Calvinistic hair-splitter, and Secretary of State, the late John Foster Dulles, who said, "Contracts are binding only so long as the relevant facts and circumstances remain basically the same." John Jay, in Letter Number 64 of *The Federalist*, in 1788, spoke to both sides of the question:

Others . . . are averse to [treaties] being the supreme law of the land. They insist, and profess to believe, that treaties, like acts of assembly, should be repealable at pleasure. This idea seems to be new and peculiar to this country, but new errors, as well as new truths, often appear. These gentlemen would do well to reflect that a treaty is only another name for a bargain, and that it would be impossible to find a nation who would make any bargain with us, which should be binding on them absolutely, but on us only so long and so far as we may think proper to be bound by it. They who make laws say, without doubt, amend or repeal them; and it will not be disputed that they who make treaties may alter or cancel them; but still let us not forget that treaties are made, not only by one of the contracting parties, but by both; and consequently, that as the consent of both was essential to their formation at first, so must it ever afterwards be to alter or cancel them. The proposed Constitution, therefore, has not in the least extended the obligation of treaties. They are just as binding and just as far beyond the lawful reach of legislative acts now, as they will be at any future period, or under any form of government.

Hamilton, in the aforementioned Letter 75, stated the proposition in modern terms in speaking of the "constitutional agency of the President in the conduct of foreign negotiations" when he said:

The qualities . . . indispensable in the management of foreign negotiations, point out the Executive as the most fit agent in those transactions, while the vast importance of the trust, and the operations of treaties as laws, plead strongly for the participation of the whole or a portion of the legislative body in the office of making them.

The august organization which was to all intents and purposes challenging the authority of the President was formally known as "The Committee on Foreign Relations of the Senate of the United States," a sonorous roll upon the ear. It was established in 1816 and listed first in the naming of standing committees at that time. To its juniors, it preferred to be known simply as "The Committee." Others in the capital city preferred to refer to it as "those guys." Above the entrance to its conference room, S-116, was a wall mural of Fulton and the steamboat. It had been suggested that more appropriately SPQR, the abbreviation for the senate and people of Rome, should have been emblazoned above its portals. Nineteen members—thirteen Democrats and six Republicans— meet punctually at 10 A.M. every Tuesday, with remarkably few absentees. The committee in the Eighty-eighth Congress held nearly 200 full committee meetings, a total considerably in excess of any other committee in Congress, and a pace maintained through 1967.

Although, as Henry Adams said in his *Education,* "the Senate is much given to admiring in its members a superiority less obvious or quite invisible to outsiders," members of the Foreign Relations Committee, its quintessential Senatorial nature notwithstanding, are singularly free of airs. Meetings under Chairman Fulbright tend to run with a loose rein. There is no unitary feeling of loyalty in belonging to a unique body. There is no evidence of Senatorial vindictiveness against the executive such as impelled Secretary of State John Hay to say: "The thing that has aged and broken me up has been the attitude of the minority of the Senate which brings to naught all the work the State Department can do."

Fulbright is too easy-going and is not as strong a chairman as, in the recent past, Senators Arthur H. Vandenburg of Michigan, Tom Connally of Texas, and Walter F. George of Georgia were. Connally and George in their times showed little patience with Fulbright. In its present incarnation the committee is full of strong personalities, or vocal ones at any rate. Congressman Wayne Hays of Ohio, no drooping lily himself, said, apropos, to Senator Wayne Morse of Oregon, "What you need is a chairman who can handle you like Doc Morgan handles me." Hays is on the House Foreign Affairs Committee, headed by Representative Thomas E. Morgan of Pennsylvania. Part of the cause of confused legislative-executive relationships in recent years had been the simultaneous disappearance of strong committee chairmen with whom presidential administrations could make sensible deals. The chairmen could apply enough discipline to keep their committee from wandering afield and to arrive at responsible decisions.

A floating majority of eleven has been against the Vietnam war, and eight have been for it. The more individualistic the Senator, the more his reasons appear tailored to his special cloth. Senator Frank Church of Idaho appeared to be emulating his isolationist predecessor, Senator William E. Borah, and espousing withdrawal from commitments overseas. Senator Morse, whom Senator Mansfield, the Majority leader, described as "the greatest intellect in the Senate," at times sounded like one of the I.W.W., or "wobblies," of the post–World War I era on the West Coast. An incorrigible iconoclast, Morse was one of the few anti-Vietnam Senators consistent enough to demand rejection of military appropriations for the Vietnam war. At one time in 1966, the White House discussed sending

Morse to Hanoi to present the U.S. case for a cease-fire and peace conference.

On the prowar side, Senator Bourke B. Hickenlooper of Iowa, ranking Republican member of the committee, is pure American Gothic from Grant Wood and plows his furrow straight on the line of nationalism. Hickenlooper did not wish to waste time talking about what might have been, but wanted to go on to win the war. He was asked from time to time to lecture to Foreign Service officers and had been given delicate missions abroad by the State Department. One such was his 1962 confidential embassy to King Faisal of Saudi Arabia. Hickenlooper informed the King that the U.S. Senate approved of United States recognition of the new Yemen Government because Nasser of Egypt had "guaranteed" removal of his 30,000 troops from Yemen. Nasser began moving them out five years later, after Egyptian troop strength in Yemen had risen to 70,000.

The third member, with Fulbright and Morse, of the Senatorial anti-Vietnam top triad, Mansfield of Montana, is perhaps the most difficult of all to pin into a category. Tall and ascetic-looking, like a grand inquisitor, his nostrils pinched in distaste at the senselessness and the evil forces abroad in the world, Mansfield has been consistent, responsible, and foresighted in his foreign policy views. He endeavors to couple his criticisms with constructive remedies. He saw opportunity for reducing unnecessary U.S. troop commitments in Europe long before the State Department took action. He advocated closer relations with Eastern Europe, as a means of loosening its ties with Soviet Russia, well before official policy to that end was enunciated. He was extremely sensitive to changes in the world scene, years earlier having pointed like a Cassandra to Southeast Asia and Vietnam as danger areas. In late 1967 Mansfield circulated to all 100 Senators a seven-page letter outlining his determination to seek all means to utilize the United Nations as an avenue for settlement of the Vietnam war. He foresaw a crisis with Japan, which was steadily rising as a Pacific power and with whom renewal of the mutual security treaty with the United States must be planned for in 1969, a year before it expires.

Treaties, in point of fact, are one of the Foreign Relations Committee's principal stocks in trade, by virtue of its authority under the Constitution, Article II, Section 2, Paragraph 2. One of the Senate's early actions, in 1789, was ratification of the first U.S. consular convention, that with France. Up to forty years ago the Senate ratified treaties in executive session. Only Senators were permitted to be present, and perhaps six staff members. Until June 1952, treaties were often, if not usually, passed with few members present. A minor rumble of publicity changed the practice when consular conventions to Ireland and Britain were consented to with only two Senators present. One of the Senators did not vote, and the other, who did, did so from his presiding chair. The next month Senator William Knowland of California, the Republican Majority leader, announced that thereafter all votes on treaties would be made roll-call votes as a matter of practice, though there is still no Senate rule requiring a roll-call vote on treaties.

Since 1947, the Senate has approved 268 treaties, including 26 in the Ninetieth Congress up to late 1967, practically all of them by unanimous vote. Virtually all were additions or amendments to existing bodies of international agreements, mostly commercial. The only debate was over the consular convention with the Soviet Union, which received the required two-thirds vote almost exactly, 66 to 28. In actual experience, as is evident, the Senate did not frequently get into action on a major treaty which involved high principles of coresponsibility with the executive in major decisions on major matters of foreign policy.

The envoy of the President to the domain of the Committee on Foreign Relations, and the first witness to testify on Fulbright's resolution, was the former Attorney General and now Under Secretary of State, Nicholas Katzenbach. The issue was joined on who, President or Congress, had the greater political muscle. Neither took a bite at the bullet really on the table, namely, to reduce or not to reduce the nation's global commitments. Katzenbach, stoutly, even truculently, defended the President's prerogatives in foreign policy, prompting irritated Senators to comment afterward: "He told us to mind our own business." The short tempers rose in exchanges over the Tonkin Gulf Congressional resolution of August 1964, passed after North Vietnamese torpedo boats had attacked the destroyer, the U.S.S. *Maddox*. With the 1955 Formosa and the 1958 Middle East resolutions in mind, President Johnson, in consultation with Congressional leaders, had asked for and obtained the authority of Congress to "repel any armed attack against the forces of the United States," and, in addition, at his request, authorization "to prevent further aggression," including a key operative phrase, "as the President determines."

In the self-conscious chagrin of hindsight the Senators felt they had been played for suckers, imposed upon, outfoxed, and duped by the President. He, they charged, had used the Tonkin Resolution as carte blanche for intensification and expansion of the Vietnam war. Fulbright had floor-managed the resolution in the Senate in 1964. He now insisted he had "misinterpreted" it. Some light, however, did get through the heat. Katzenbach, for the first time on the behalf of any presidential administration, asseverated that "the function"—not "power," be it noted

—of the Congress to declare war was "outmoded phraseology." He relentlessly laid it on the line that the "gut issue" in a national crisis was the duty of the Congress to give the President political support for the prosecution of the foreign policy objectives which the President, as the duly empowered constitutional leader, had already decided upon. The grievances of the Senate and the justifications of the Under Secretary of State began to sound like a broken record as the engagement ended in the draw it had been fated to be. Fulbright summed it up: "It is incumbent upon the Congress hereafter to consider in detail and precision the grant of authority involved in its action."

Fulbright, junior Senator from Arkansas, a world figure for his opposition to the Vietnam war, deeply ambitious to write his name indelibly in the annals of history, had made his point, as usual. He did so with an insouciant and mildly masked superciliousness worthy of a Rhodes scholar who had been honed to a nice sharpness by the lessons he had learned from the nimble wit and rolling barrages of the prize debaters at the Oxford University Union in England in the late 1920's. In introducing his resolution, Fulbright had utilized the malaise of the country over the Vietnam war to capitalize on the institutional loyalty of the Senate to its own self-defined perquisites, prerogatives, and powers. It was no concern of Fulbright's that the acidulous atmosphere of political harassment in which the State Department found itself immersed had become an occupational hazard. Its magnitude not only corroded United States diplomatic influence overseas among friends and neutrals but was a security factor of undefinable proportions exploitable by unfriendly powers in Moscow, Peking, and Hanoi. This was the classic dilemma of American diplomacy. Fulbright, in any event, was thoroughly consistent; he had been making points for a long time and on the same theme, the proper role of the United States in the modern world.

The Fulbright who had become the hero of the anti-Vietnam war movement in the United States was one of the most remarkable personalities ever to sit in the Senate of the United States, brilliant, erratic, moody, his shining armor slightly encased in rust. Despite the shyness of his natural disposition, he has been virtually enshrined as the grand panjandrum of liberalism in foreign affairs by shoals of adulating admirers, academics, and newspapermen who found him a natural ally in their own critical impatience for a perfectionist world which never seemed to arrive. Fulbright was both a Don Quixote, tilting against the windmills of the higher globalisms, and a Sancho Panza, who seemed to stumble into a bagful of political pesetas when he apparently least planned for it. He was a reluctant dissenter, who seemed to have slid by degrees into his role of opposition. He was a paradox of a cultivated eighteenth-century mind stylized by the ante-bellum South and of the Arkansas Traveler, taking saturnine pleasure in mimicking a hill-billy philosopher from the Ozarks. He was full of parlor patter, this thing wrong and that thing wrong, uttering clichés as if he were bored with the subject, which undoubtedly he often was, and suddenly displaying prismatic penetration into involuted subjects, lighting up the horizon and eliciting sheer admiration even from State Department senior and middle-grade officers for his mental acuity.

Back in the 1950's, Secretary of State Dulles and Fulbright, not yet Chairman of the Committee on Foreign Relations of the United States Senate, had developed a mutual detestation of each other. Dulles grumbled that Fulbright was a "spoiler" and "negative," whereupon a Dulles colleague assured the Secretary that he need not worry too much because Fulbright's fundamental character would give the Democrats much more trouble in the end than he would ever give the Republicans. Fulbright had a proclivity for picking on eminent or glittering subjects like lightning seeking the tallest tree. In his maiden speech as a freshman Congressman in 1943, he picked, of all people, on the glamorous and fork-tongued Clare Boothe Luce, Republican of Connecticut, in a speech in which he said: "Our Representatives should begin negotiations at once with our allies to formulate a specific and concrete system of alliances for collective security of the nations of the world." This was a full ten years before Dulles came to power and began putting into effect the "pactomania" which Fulbright was later to attack.

Few politicians in Congress have ever risen faster in public acclaim than Fulbright. Though a freshman in 1943, he introduced in Congress what is now known as the Fulbright Resolution. It called on the House of Representatives to express itself on behalf of "the creation of appropriate international machinery, with power adequate to establish and maintain and adjust a lasting peace among the nations of the world." It was a precursor of the United Nations. In 1946, his proposal for using foreign funds accumulated by sale of surplus U.S. war goods abroad for the exchange of American and foreign students became a byword of twentieth-century culture in the Fulbright Fellowships. R. B. McCallum, Master of Pembroke College at Oxford University, wrote in 1963: "Fulbright is responsible for the greatest movement of scholars across the face of the earth since the fall of Constantinople in 1453."

A muller-over of an idea, rolling it back and forth across the palate of his mind like a caramel, Fulbright acted in his own good time through the medium of scholarly speeches, reminiscent of the high era of oratory in the Webster-Haynes debates before the Civil War. His powerful and lofty prose at times contrasted astoundingly with his loose verbalizing and slipshod syntax during crowded moments at the Committee hearings over which he presided like a weary ringmaster. He was an artist of the sugared sarcasm and a nonpareil at triple implications, a one-man orchestra of overtones, undertones, and lateral affects, few of which ever proved to be complimentary to his interlocutors. No more sadistic sight was to be seen in Washington than Fulbright, with courtly and barely disguised venom, goading the irascible maverick, Senator Lausche of Ohio, into a rage, like a picador slinging banderillas into a bull.

The slow-motion scintillation of Fulbright in public performance not infrequently relapsed into deep brooding in private, when he seemed sad, abstracted, and, to outsiders, too lazy to attend to his duties. In reality he was merely underscoring De Tocqueville, another favorite author. Fulbright at such times was sunk in virtual despair at the shoddiness, pretentiousness, and superficiality of American representative government as it tried, with apparent futility, to meet the vital and vexing problems of the world. He was disdainful both of Congressional ineptitudes and of the cynical abuse of power by Presidents.

Fulbright had tangled with Presidents before, though not always on purpose. In 1946 he suggested that President Truman resign after the Republican overturn in the Eightieth Congress, whereupon Truman called Fulbright "that over-educated Oxford s.o.b." Fulbright admired the British parliamentary system of government in which the Prime Minister and Cabinet in power do resign when the party majority is definitively overthrown in the House of Commons. Years later, in 1966, a senior official of the State Department suggested to President Johnson that, since Fulbright praised the British system so much, he, the senior official should write a public letter, demanding that, if Fulbright was so sincere about the British way of politics, he should resign his post as Chairman of the Senate Foreign Relations Committee and allow someone more cooperative to take his place. Johnson said, now you let Bill alone, and you all try to get along with Bill.

Johnson was Senate Majority leader in 1959, when Fulbright became Chairman of the Senate Foreign Relations Committee. Johnson kept Fulbright on a short leash. Fulbright, in fact, had been rather a faint star in the Johnson Senate planetarium. He was recommended, after the 1960 elections, by Vice President–elect Johnson as a candidate for Secretary of State. The failure of the Fulbright candidacy was ascribed to his segregationist and anti–civil rights views, necessary politically in Arkansas but unacceptable nationally. More powerful still was the enmity of the Jewish establishment, which had been greatly displeased at Fulbright's opposition to the amendment offered in 1960 by former Senator Paul Douglas, Democrat of Illinois, to the Mutual Security bill. Douglas had urged the President to cut off aid to the United Arab Republic unless it opened the Suez Canal to Israeli shipping. Fulbright is still rated as anti-Israel by American friends of Israel.

State Department resentment against Fulbright for attacking Vietnam policy was marked by a feeling almost of injury, as if Fulbright were an apostate, because of his support of the Vietnam policy from 1961 through 1964. Whatever Fulbright's earlier doubts about Vietnam, he broke with the Johnson administration, characteristically, over a collateral issue, the intervention in the Dominican Republic in April 1965. This first break with official Democratic administration policy was followed by his first severe criticism of the Vietnam war in June 1965. The climax of Fulbright's 1966 full-scale revolt against the Johnson-Rusk foreign policy came with his delivery of the Christian A. Herter Lectures before The Johns Hopkins School of Advanced International Studies on "The Arrogance of Power." The new attack, blazoned in headlines, rubbed White House and State Department sensibilities raw. In 1967, Fulbright advanced from forensic assault to legislative mayhem, fighting the President at every turn. He and the whole entourage of his liberal cohorts on the Senate Foreign Relations Committee by this time had become highly emotional on the Vietnam issue.

The war had become almost a personal matter on both sides. The President was a very personal man himself. An incident in the winter of 1965 was taken as an affront to the Senator, by Fulbright's friends at least, and marked the start of the break with the White House. Fulbright and a delegation of Senators were scheduled to attend a British Commonwealth parliamentary meeting in New Zealand. A presidential jet had been earmarked. So the Fulbright aides thought. Senator Mansfield and another party desired to go on a round-the-world "fact-finding" tour. The Mansfield party got the only "available" extra presidential jet. Fulbright and his party had to fly in a "slow" DC-7 on the long journey across the Pacific. By this time, Fulbright was also fed up to the eyeballs with hearing the same old lectures on the necessity of foreign aid, the American commitment to the Free World, and so forth, the same old rote he had been hearing for years in turn from each new set of newly appointed State and AID officials. As far as Fulbright was concerned, they had nothing to teach him; he had heard it all before. As for Secretary Rusk, Fulbright had been a Senator and suffered through eight years of foreign policy hearings and activities, an exposure which Rusk was not receiving in the same manner at the Rockefeller Foundation in the same period. Fulbright did not pay too much mind to gossip circulating back to him from downtown. Statements of former years, in support of fuller presidential control of foreign policy, which Fulbright had made in a lecture at Cornell University in 1961, were now thrown back at him. Of late, he had exercised the privilege of changing his mind, because, he freely admitted, he had been mistaken at the earlier time.

Fulbright fell back on his original philosophy, the one which motivated him two decades ago. In God's good time the natural and normal exchange of cultures would temper and transmute the aggressiveness of insecure peoples into civilized intercourse, as it already had done for the Russians and was bound to do for the Chinese Communists in years to come. As for the Vietnam war, he did not propose for the United States to slink away, but he did want the war to end soonest. He believed profoundly that the United States was great enough to be magnanimous enough to end it by itself, and powerful enough not to suffer overmuch from a theoretical loss of prestige in accepting whatever verdict even the General Assembly of the United Nations should give. To make peace, someone had to begin, even with giving safe-conduct passes to the Viet Cong and the National Liberation Front and having them come to Saigon to discuss peace terms. There was no reason to get excited about the Russians or the Chinese and threats of wars. The turbid stream of life settled itself in time. There was no sense to causing still more unnecessary pain and futile death. It was America's duty to humanity to rise above geopolitics.

Fulbright had got used to being in the White House doghouse since 1966 and no longer an insider. He felt there was a large life outside, too, and he was beginning to enjoy it in a sad sort of way. Fulbright was profoundly convinced he was firmly in the right. He vowed never to yield on Vietnam. At moments he toyed morosely with the idea of honorably withdrawing from the battle by not seeking re-election in 1968, despite the fact that his Arkansas voters, "on balance," as Fulbright liked to say, seemed to approve his Vietnam stand. He saw no end to the awful stew the country and the Congress had gotten into over Vietnam. Yet, Fulbright notwithstanding, the Vietnam war would one day grind its miserable way to a halt. And the United States involvement in the world would continue. There was no other place to go.

CHAPTER IX

DOMESTIC–FOREIGN INTERFACE: Backfires of Self-Interest

THE STATE DEPARTMENT AND Congress, in short, were stuck in the same glue pot, a sticky mixture of domestic and foreign interests which were the obverse and reverse of every question, making national policy an indivisible unity of both. For an ever-increasing number of Americans, the world was now in their midst, late and soon, too much for some, but fated to be so more and more for everybody from now on.

United States foreign policy was demonstrating that it was a projection of United States national and sectional interest beyond the national frontiers. Foreign policy was the balance between foreign needs and the price that a national administration desired to pay on the domestic scene. President Eisenhower apropos told Sherman Adams that he had become "completely convinced that every important decision of the Government, no matter what field it was in, had a direct effect upon our relations with other nations."

An Associated Press dispatch quoted a political leader as saying that "the nation's growing industrial might will mean better living standards," but warning that "foreign crises could jeopardize benefits." The leader was Soviet Premier Alexei N. Kosygin in Moscow, proving not for the first time in the Soviet Union that internal affairs had a greater effect on Russian foreign policy than events in the outside world. It was another demonstration of the axiom that a nation's foreign policy is an outward manifestation of its character and of the circumstances within its own territory.

Moreover, America's fat was getting thinner, and foreign policy demands on finite, though enormous, U.S. resources were leaving less for domestic needs and domestic pressure was being put on foreign policies to trim and modify them, as in one aspect of the Vietnam war agitation. As Neustadt said, in *Presidential Power,* regarding the competing claims between domestic and foreign interests, "the intensity of pressure may make foreign policy controversial . . . and more critical." The theorem was proven all through 1967, as U.S. self-interest in the foreign world created backfires and Baudelaire's "rubble of humankind" grew to be much more than a mote in the American eye: it was a whole dust storm. The nation seemed driven by a dozen causes and distracted by scores of conflicting demands for attention. "If we could lick the Americans, we could lick the world," an exasperated official said half-whimsically.

There was no surcease in sight. The American society and the economy were bubbling like lava in a live volcano. The gross national product had jumped from 355.2 constant dollars in 1945 to 664.6 constant dollars in 1967, with the GNP in current dollars being recorded at $775.3 billion. The swift pace of change in the nation's 200 million population generated the illusion of nigh-revolutionary expectations, heightened by the mobility and expansion of the new middle classes and the refusal of a large minority like the Negroes, one tenth of the nation, to be barred from enjoying the fruits of the evolving and flowering American civilization.

A special presidential (and never-announced) task force, chaired by Ben Heinemann, Chairman of the Board of the Chicago and North-western Railroad, studied for a year the reorganization of the executive branch. In September 1967 it gave the President its secret report, to the effect, in part, that the foreign affairs community of the U.S. Government was not in such bad shape but that the domestic side was in rather a mess. The President, for example, had hoped to combine the Department of Commerce and the Department of Labor into a new Department of Economic Development, but he received no encouragement. Yet the Heinemann Commission found that, in eight years of static domestic administration under President Eisenhower and two years more under President Kennedy, that is, from 1952 to 1962, hardly anything of major significance had been done for the welfare and progress of the United States itself.

In sum, the United States also was a backward and underdeveloped country in many respects. No longer adequate was the Anglo-Saxon liberal gradualism of the past, which in an almost painless way had provided for the eradication of social evils by seducing the nation into virtue. The experiments of foreigners, according to the Americans' austere ethic, were much too radical and drastic. In this American paradise, the shock of discovery that millions of children still lacked decent medical care; that one out of every six Americans lived in the slums; that pollution dirtied up the air, the rivers, and the lakes; that millions still had less than seventy-five cents a day to spend for food; and that crime ran like a rat through the streets led to the realization that the United States was not too unlike many of the rebellious societies which it had been trying to aid abroad. U.S. experience in foreign aid offered belated lessons and germinated new insights into its own problems. For example, a basic criterion of U.S. foreign aid to other nations was the degree to which the recipient nation could absorb the aid given. An American parallel lay in the housing and urban development assistance to the fifty states and their bulging and wracked cities. There it was also a question of the capability of the American municipal and state governments to digest, or absorb, efficiently the funds coming from programs like model cities. America, as it long had been supposed to be, was turning out again to be a laboratory experiment for the world. For example, despite the once-feared displeasure of the American Catholic Church, President Kennedy, gingerly as the innovator, and President Johnson, finally, introduced birth control as part of foreign aid assistance to the population-spurting nations of Latin America and to India.

The world was arriving every day in a flow of international mail. Fiscal year 1966 saw 170.8 million pounds coming into the United States and 178.6 million pounds going out. Incoming mail more than doubled that which had come from overseas in 1956 and quadrupled that of forty years ago.

The people of the United States were staking out personal interests abroad, like next-door neighbors. Thirty-two American states made themselves partners and advisers to a like number of states in Latin America. Fraternal and civic organizations—the Rotary Clubs, the Lions, the American Legion, the U.S. Chamber of Commerce, the American Federation of Women's Clubs—opened branches in many foreign countries.

The once-distant outside world, which had given the United States 43 million immigrants since 1820 and provided nearly 9 million immigrants in the first decade of this century and nearly 10 million in the next two, was still bringing living testimonials from the foreign scene. Five million immigrants and refugees came in the twenty-five years from the start of World War II to 1967, while almost three and a half million aliens found it comfortable and profitable to reside in the United States. The new arrivals joined the nearly 35 million persons of foreign stock in the United States, who, according to the 1960 census, accounted for 19 per cent of that year's U.S. population of nearly 180 million. Nine states had over a million inhabitants of foreign stock—California, Illinois, Massachusetts, Michigan, New Jersey, New York, Ohio, Pennsylvania, and Texas. The manners and outlook of non-Anglo-Saxon stocks—five million of Italian origin; nearly three million of Polish origin; nearly a million of Czechoslovak origin; others, like Hungarians, whose presence in Cleveland made it the largest Hungarian city outside of Budapest at one time; refugees from Castro's Cuba—all gave new color and vibrancy to the American atmosphere. By 1968, the full impact of the 1965 immigration law would be felt and southern Europeans and Asians would add to the wave of still newer immigrants.

The descendants of the mid-nineteenth-century immigrants, the Irish and Germans, had been long established in, and even dominated, the Congress. They were by 1967 not quite as chauvinistic with regard to their former fatherlands as they had been during the late nineteenth century, when Secretary of State John Hay, in rebellion at Irish-German pressure against a proposed Anglo-American treaty said, "That we should be compelled to refuse the assistance of the greatest power in the world [Britain] because all Irishmen are Democrats and some Germans are fools, is enough to drive a man mad." Since World War II, the Italians and the Poles had achieved political respectability, seventeen Italians and eleven Poles being members of the Ninetieth Congress. In 1967 a new minority group began to develop political muscle, the Greeks, with three Congressmen.

The new Americans, both older and more recent arrivals, consistently managed to give the State Department trouble. Greek sympathizers were outraged at the arrest and imprisonment of Andreas Papandreou, son of the former Premier of Greece and a former American citizen and professor before he returned to Greece in 1964 to join his father in Greek politics. The Greek community and friends agitated while the State Department sympathized but looked on helplessly as the Greek colonels' junta began to try to propagandize the American Greeks through newspaper ads and Greek fraternal organizations. These, the junta apparently hoped, could influence the State Department in the direction of a more amicable attitude toward the military dictatorship.

Also vexing for the State Department was the boycott that anti-Communist Yugoslav groups in the United States organized against American cigarette manufacturers using Yugoslav tobacco. A similar boycott of Polish hams distressed the Department and undercut its policy of encouraging Communist nations to be independent of Soviet Russia. Another anti-Communist citizens' campaign forced the Firestone Rubber Company to give up a profitable contract with Communist Rumania, a country which the State Department especially was trying to woo. Patriotic protectionism was impeding the State Department's efforts "to build bridges to the East," as President Johnson desired.

The world was arriving in the United States in even more unpleasant fashion in the guise of exotic diseases. Joining Calcutta and Cairo, Washington was becoming a crossroads of the world's germs, given the constant to-and-fro of military, diplomatic, and business travelers from all parts of the earth. Vietnam was bringing rare ailments, including virulent malaria and drug-resistant venereal disease. State Department officers posted to fast trips abroad and back frequently found themselves stricken with one-day fevers. Unidentified "bugs" ran through the nation's capital from time to time, incapacitating hundreds but never quite causing epidemics because of strict American hygienic standards and public health controls. These were so efficacious that few Americans ever had a chance to build any immunity to the world's dirt and ailments. The too-clean American way of life did not travel well.

Foreign governments were arriving on U.S. shores almost en masse. Japanese Cabinet economic ministers met with U.S. Cabinet counterparts, as did the joint United States–Canadian Cabinet Committee on Trade and Economic Affairs. Relations with the neighbors to the north and south, Canada and Mexico, were becoming ever closer and more intertwined. Canada furnished the State Department plenty of business. There was always the delicate political fear of American domination of its neighbor, over 60 per cent of Canada's productive capacity being controlled by U.S. citizens. There was common Canadian-American concern at the Soviet fishing fleets just outside their territorial limits on the high seas. There was keen rivalry for world export markets in wheat, Canada having, in 1967, a vast supply of over a billion bushels. There was the official diplomatic displeasure over Canada's tolerant relations with, though not recognition of, Communist China and of Canadian trade with Communist Cuba. In a practical sense, the State Department looked the other way, since the Canadian posture was highly useful in maintaining reliable and extra contacts with the Peking Chinese, if and when necessary, and in Cuba the Canadian Embassy was a first-class pair of eyes and ears for an inside intelligence look at that paradoxical land.

Foreign relations with Mexico were improving, but not without domestic American repercussions. There was a large and steady influx of American tourists into Mexico. The 1,600-mile border between Mexico and the American states of Texas, New Mexico, Arizona, and California was a cause for friendship and for friction, as fences always are. President Johnson had had a life-long connection with, and affection for, Mexicans, many of whom, as American citizens, were his loyal supporters in Texas. Mexico had more U.S. diplomatic outposts—sixteen—than any other nation in the world, and more U.S. Government missions visited Mexico City than any other capital. The long border provided sharp reactions on both sides in 1965, when the U.S. Customs Bureau cut the tax-free liquor imports from one gallon to one quart and the Treasury Department, also attempting to hold down the foreign dollar drain, reduced the duty-free limit for returning American tourists from two hundred to one hundred dollars. Mexican border towns bitterly complained of the drop in

American business, which resulted in unemployment and anti-American resentment.

For a nation fizzing with anxiety over its foreign commitments, it was clear that there were a lot of unanswered questions in the American mind besides the official issues, executive responsibility for which intersected with that of Congress in the American political process. It was therefore incumbent upon the State Department to make a direct approach to the general U.S. citizenry. This was all the more imperative because of the multiple, overlapping, and contradictory fragmentation in the kaleidoscope of news from overseas, which alternately bewildered and dazzled the reader, the listener, and the viewer of the mass media. The State Department's point had been expressed by Frederick W. Maitland, the British historian: "The essential matter of history is not what happened, but what people thought and said about it." The gloss might be added—what people thought had happened—which produced further corollaries of misunderstanding. George Allen, a noted professional of the Foreign Service and former Director of the U.S. Information Agency, stated the position succinctly: "The Department of State has the responsibility not only for keeping the public informed on foreign affairs, but for seeking public support and assistance in the formulation of foreign policy."

There was the recurrent hope that the technical resources of the USIA could be utilized profitably by the American people as well as by foreigners. Dr. Frank Stanton, President of Columbia Broadcasting System and Chairman of the United States Advisory Commission, proposed in 1967 to permit the agency's materials to be made available to Americans and foreigners alike. He said:

It has to do with the people's right to know—in this case, their right to know what the Government is telling the rest of the world about us. While no efforts [should] be made to distribute USIA materials in this country, they [should] be made available for appropriate inspection and specific requests by parties with a legitimate interest—their own and the public's.

The new idea died a-borning because of frowns in Congress, which still adhered to the sense of the Dworshak Amendment to Public Law 82-400, the Mutual Security Act of 1952, which forbade use of aid funds to publicize U.S. foreign programs within the United States. Though this Amendment was repealed by the 1961 International Development Act, Congressmen still feared that any administration in power could use the channel and instruments of USIA to conduct political propaganda in its own favor, as Goebbels did in Nazi Germany, as Mussolini did in Fascist Italy, and as the Soviet Politburo does in Russia.

The State Department managed to do very well all by itself. It kept in touch with more than 200 organizations of all kinds which had either a direct or marginal interest in foreign affairs—veterans', labor, church, women's clubs—and were estimated to represent between 80 and 90 million citizens. The task was how to reach them most effectively and how to funnel the mass of material available so that citizens could stop, read, and ponder. In short, it was the organization of the constituency the State Department had long said it lacked.

The first notable step was, for the Department, the revolutionary one of organizing foreign policy conferences both in Washington and in the major metropolitan areas of the nation's regions—from Boston to San Francisco, Chicago to New Orleans and Houston. The influential opinion-molders en masse—newspaper columnists, radio and TV commentators, educators, businessmen, labor leaders—were invited to Washington, where the top brains and personalities of the Department could personally address them and answer their questions in background, nonattributable conferences. The regional meetings, aimed at important civic leaders of the areas, would bring within the reach of cities remote from Washington as many of the illustrious officials of the Department as could be spared.

The exploiter of this fecund idea of face-to-face meetings between the citizens and the State Department in 1961 was former Assistant Secretary of State for Public Affairs Robert W. Manning, now editor of *The Atlantic Monthly*. In the five-year period between 1963 and 1967, over twenty-five regional conferences, sponsored by local groups, were held for a total audience of nearly 40,000. Twelve national foreign policy conferences were held in Washington, for total audiences of more than 7,000. Weekly or special briefings in the last three years, from 1965 to 1967, totalled nearly 1,300, for audiences approximating 75,000—tourists, students, members of civic organizations, church groups, and even those of the 40,000 persons who, in 1966, visited the State Department building.

To the State Department speakers, both in Washington and in the countryside, it was an education to listen at first hand to the citizens' questions, which were shrewd, naïve, germane, and irrelevant. The bi-weekly sessions at State itself included odd-ball questions: Why did the State Department not coordinate policies for all fifty American states? Why couldn't the Indians practice birth control for their sacred cattle so the beasts would not multiply so much and eat all the U.S.-supplied grain? Had U.S. sailors in a foreign port ever gotten drunken Foreign Service officers out of jail? This was a twist on the normal duty of young Foreign Service officers serving as consuls in foreign ports to rescue misbehaving Americans from the clutches of the local gendarmes.

A virtual State Department sales saturation campaign resulted in a program of nation-wide community meetings on foreign policy. Three- or four-man teams of Foreign Service officers visited a state or a general area for a week at a time, speaking in five or six different cities. From 1963 to 1967, thirty-one such teams reached estimated audiences of 340,000 persons.

Individual State Department officers, from Secretary Rusk on down, gave nearly 8,000 speeches by special invitation in a five-year period. In testimony before Congressman Rooney's Appropriations Subcommittee, Assistant Secretary of State for Public Affairs Dixon Donnelley listed 431 trips to make 941 speeches in fiscal year 1966, that is, from July 1, 1966, to June 30, 1967, at the end of which report Congressman Rooney asked Donnelley: "Of course, you know how I feel about the Bureau of Public Affairs, do you not?"

Donnelley answered, respectfully, "Yes, sir."

Whereupon Rooney perorated: "While I have great respect for you, I thought it [the Bureau of Public Affairs] should have been abolished before it ever got started. I think it does more harm to the image of the Department and to the Foreign Service than any part of the salaries and expenses operation. However, that is only my opinion."

There was much more that the State Department was doing for its so-called image. Besides running its lecture bureau, it was operating, figuratively, a circulating library, a direct-mail advertising company, an extension-course university, a corporate public relations firm, and a convention and visitors service center. The Department bureacracy was taking its mission of personal democracy seriously. It filed a report with John W. Macy, Jr., Chairman of the U.S. Civil Service Commission, entitled *Improvements of Communications and Contact with Public.* Macy had been charged by President Johnson to make a continuing survey of the way in which the U.S. Government could provide individual citizens with better services. Deputy Under Secretary for Adminstration Idar Rimestad related that the American Consulate General in Palermo, Sicily, was now sending a "welcome letter" and information sheet to every American who stopped at hotels in that Italian city. Three embassies, in India, Israel, and Egypt, even sold surplus local currency to U.S. tourists. The acme of bureaucratic involvement was reached with the announcement that a special "public duty officer manual" was under preparation. The American Telephone and Telegraph Company produced a film to show State Department employees, among others, how to take the needed "extra step" in order to provide the best possible service to the public.

There was still more. By the end of 1967, over a million publications had been distributed by the Department. On request, 10,000 poster exhibits, nearly 3,000 film prints, and 13,000 tape recordings were distributed.

Sales of the State Department's *Background Notes,* leaflets on the countries of the world, including brief summaries of their history, geography, politics, and economy, passed the half-million mark in sales by the Superintendent of Documents in the Government Printing Office.

The Department tapped the annual cycle of debates organized by high schools and colleges. In 1967 all the high school national debates concentrated on foreign policy questions. The State Department was inundated with requests for help from students and teachers. Approximately 130,000 students were involved in these spring high school debates. In 900 colleges and universities, another 10,000 students were engrossed in debating foreign policy. The topic chosen for debate: "That the United States should substantially reduce its foreign policy commitments." The discussion question, separate from the debate proposition, asked, "What should U.S. policy be toward Communist China?"

Then there was always the public mail. Nearly 200,000 letters, postcards, and telegrams were received each year by the State Department, necessitating the creation of a Correspondence Center as part of the Bureau of Public Affairs. White House mail referred to the State Department got top priority. It had to be answered within forty-eight hours. The Department's mail run began to get heavy in 1962, before the Cuban missile crisis, breaking all records with nearly 260,000 letters, nearly seven times the mail influx of 1958. The volume of the mail fluctuated widely, with the rise and fall of critical news. In one "heavy" week of February 1967, 6,000 items of correspondence arrived in the Department from the citizenry. In late September and early October 1967, following the marriage of Miss Margaret Elizabeth Rusk, daughter of the Secretary, to Guy Gibson Smith, a Negro, a torrent of letters descended upon the Department. Many were scurrilous ones from right-wing Southern bigots.

There were some raised eyebrows in the Foreign Service officer corps at such intrusions into the traditional private preserves of diplomacy, but for the most part the Foreign Service welcomed with zest its happy rediscovery of America.

In its new reincarnation, the State Department also was decorously inching its way into national politics through the medium of a new office, that of Special Assistant to the Secretary of State for Liaison with the Governors of the Fifty American States. This apparent return of the State Department to domestic interests assigned it in the early days of the Republic had a curious history. In December 1966, after the Congressional election GOP upturn, there had been a so-called rebellion of Democratic Party Governors against the Johnson administration, the political unrest in part due to the ferment of the Vietnam war, a white backlash against Negro civil rights, and the lag in urban development. At that time, the President instructed Farris Bryant, Director of the Office of Emergency Planning, to make expeditions to all parts of the nation in an effort to help the state Governors straighten out and more efficiently utilize their relations with the Federal Government. In March 1967, Secretary Rusk suggested to the President that it might be useful, too, if the Department had a small office which could keep the Governors informed of foreign policy developments and serve as a channel for any assistance that the State Department might give them in the foreign field. Former Ambassador to Korea Winthrop G. Brown was appointed Special Assistant. He took office in June 1967, a month after the President had announced the program at the Conference of the New England Governors. In the first four months, Brown and his deputy, Abram E. Manell, another veteran Foreign Service officer, visited twenty-one Governors, in the Northwest, in the Northeast, and in the Midwest, discussing, for instance, fishery problems with the New Englanders and Canadian problems with the Northwesterners.

The witticism that the State Department needed a diplomatic embassy in the United States to find out how the natives lived was fast becoming outdated. For some years, the Department had had a program of Senior Fellows whereby Foreign Service officers were detailed as foreign policy advisers and representatives to communities at universities around the country. In the process, they imparted a knowledge of foreign affairs to the students and civic groups and, in turn, exposed themselves directly to American citizens. Eric Kocher, an officer stationed at the University of Texas in Austin, said: "Reacquainting oneself with America is not as simple as it sounds. After being abroad for many continuous years, the Foreign Service officer tends to lose contact with his country. I don't mean roads and bridges and supermarkets, but more a sense of thinking and being and the development of America and all its aspects."

Perhaps most significant of all was the emergence of the Senior Seminar of the State Department's Foreign Service Institute as a dynamic vehicle for carrying senior Foreign Service officers of high talent deep into the American scene. The Senior Seminar is rated as the most advanced educational program of studies in international relations and foreign policy offered by any agency of the United States Government. It lasts ten months, from August to June, and is limited to an honor group of about twenty-five senior officers, half from the Foreign Service and half from the armed forces and other Government departments, and all slated for top positions in their organizations.

The new aspect of the Senior Seminar, intensively developed by a veteran Foreign Service officer, G. Lewis Jones, Jr., a former Assistant Secretary of State for the Middle East, was to couple vigorous inquiries into the complexities of foreign policy with the mushrooming intricacies of U.S. domestic problems. Under Jones' energetic guidance, the officers delved into every phase of American life, traveled to locales where the ferment of the American people was in motion, in order to meet and discuss off the record the problems of America with more than 450 leading figures in science, art, communications, space, atomic energy, industry, commerce, agriculture, labor, education, transportation, the poverty program, the Peace Corps, race relations, city-state relationships, automation, computers, and systems and functional analysis. These ranking officers, already sophisticated, were highly motivated in meeting face to face American leaders on federal, state, and municipal levels and in private enterprise. In 1967, the Senior Seminar in a group went to Pittsburgh, Detroit, and Chicago. The members spent intensive hours with steel industry leaders in Pittsburgh. In Detroit they discussed the 1967 summer riots and urban renewal with Mayor J. P. Cavanaugh and labor problems with Victor Reuther of the United Automobile Workers. In Chicago they spent equal time in close quarters with Mayor Richard J. Daley and saw the detailed operations of a great metropolis, where all the urgent problems of the times come up every day.

The State Department's working officers, as well as the Senior Seminar's temporary students, were discovering that, as the Italian proverb says, *"Tutto il mondo è paese"* (the whole world is like your village). The messy problems confronting the United States were the same as the problems overseas, for example, the crisis of urbanization. Every American knew about urban problems in New York, Washington, Cleveland, Detroit, Chicago, and Los Angeles. Few knew that the same problems of slums, jobs, water, health, and housing faced the citizens of Bombay, London, Paris, Rome, Calcutta, Tokyo, Rio de Janeiro, and Lagos. The racial riots and congestion in America were paralleled by the uncontrolled growth of cities overseas, and foreign demands for urban reforms abroad were of such magnitude as to disrupt the orderly development of national economies. The world population was expected to increase by 50 per cent by the end of the twentieth century, but the urban population by 240 per cent.

Yet, despite the growing urbanization in industrial countries, the pace of urban growth was even faster in the underdeveloped countries. Over 50 per cent of the urban population of the world resided not in the so-called advanced countries but in the underdeveloped or developing countries— the Congo, Ghana, Egypt, India, Pakistan, Venezuela, Brazil. Though the future world will be 80 to 90 per cent urban, in the present expectation, no nation, including the United States, had adequate urban development plans to meet the deeply rooted difficulties of decaying central districts, unbelievable traffic snarls, and housing, school, and hospital deficiencies. This was the compost that fertilized political unrest, even before the fundamental problem of the allocation of resources, that is, determining how to meet the conflicting demands of society, was faced. In effect, the germs of the urban problems now discerned in the United States and already impinging upon foreign claims had their counterparts abroad. In the total global picture, these elements were new additions to the critical issues which the modern Foreign Service officer of the State Department had to be trained to understand as he juggled the foreign-domestic, domestic-foreign interface.

The traditional Foreign Service officer, preening himself on his expertise in political analysis, tended to look down his nose at this "brown area" of urban complexities, their potential for political explosion notwithstanding. The question asked a bit disdainfully was, whoever saw an urban specialist become an ambassador? The relevance of labor specialization was considered somewhat more admissible, given the power and status of the labor unions in the United States and in western Europe and their growing importance in the underdeveloped countries, where trade unions are also avenues to political exploitation.

American labor affairs, with nearly 17 million union members representing 22 per cent of the labor force, almost automatically became foreign labor affairs in the early days of the Marshall Plan, when Irving Brown of the American Federation of Labor was practically an official U.S. ambassador without portfolio. He was followed belatedly by Victor Reuther of the Congress of Industrial Organizations in grafting American ideas about collective bargaining onto the old-fashioned craft guild outlook of European unions, with immediate effects on national political situations in Europe and North Africa.

The question of whether a labor specialist could ever aspire to be an ambassador had already been answered by Samuel D. Berger, Deputy Assistant Secretary of State for East Asian and Pacific Affairs and former Ambassador to Korea. Berger had started out as a lowly welfare and labor attaché in the American Embassy in Britain, but because of his close acquaintance with the leaders of the British Labor Party he created his own springboard to swift advance in the Foreign Service.

It was also a long time since 1951, when Victor Reuther used to complain to this writer that the State Department had "not been properly aware of the role which European laboring masses could play on the side of democracy." Fifteen years later, Reuther and the CIO were taking one side of the Dominican Republic's labor front, while the AFL was taking another, the more conservative, under the masterminding of Jay Lovestone, quondam founder and official of the American Communist Party and now rigidly anti-Communist.

The U.S. labor interest was a direct factor in the formulation of the U.S.-Canadian trade agreement on automotive products in January 1965. This pact allowed adjustment assistance if, in the process of free and reciprocal trade, jobs were lost. Compensation was mandatory if the workings of the agreement were held to be the cause of the labor dislocation. Increased American investment in Canada carried on its back the problem of parity wages. If U.S. investment eliminated differences in prices charged in the United States and Canada for the same product, it was clear to U.S. labor leaders that the lower-paid Canadian workers, branch members of the American Union, now had a right to claim the same wages as those paid in the United States. This was a first-class example of the foreign-domestic mix working back and forth across frontiers to provide diplomatic problems for diplomacy in the State Department.

The State Department's Foreign Service Institute in 1966 announced that "in order to meet the increasing need for an appreciation of the role played by labor, political, and social developments in the world today," the Institute, in cooperation with the Department of Labor, was offering a course in international labor affairs. The announcement was down to earth in stressing that instruction would be "pragmatic rather than academic." The series of lectures was studded with distinguished names of American labor, besides the technical specialists of Government departments and agencies like Labor, AID, State, and Health, Education and Welfare. The arrival of American labor at top status in U.S. foreign policy was symbolized by the appointment of a Special Assistant to the Secretary of State.

A still more pervasive embodiment of the American people's interest in the outside world is the Bureau of Educational and Cultural Affairs in the State Department. Mrs. Katie Louchheim, Deputy Assistant Secretary of State in the Bureau, epitomized the Department's view in this new and rapidly growing field of operations when she told a Dallas audience: "We are a person-centered culture and progress still depends upon relationships between individuals. As Edward R. Murrow once said, 'The most effective communication still takes place at a distance of three feet.' "

Mrs. Louchheim baptized the twentieth century as "the first truly international century [because] most of the world's people know, however vaguely, that they are now part of a world environment, and deeply affected by it and capable of doing something about that environment and the way it affects them and other people all over the world.

"It is the first century," she said, "of formal, structured, international, intellectual, and cultural projects in an extensive sense—of UNESCO, foundations operating internationally, Fulbright Scholarships, Rhodes Scholarships, a century in which the international flow of movies, books, machinery, magazines, tourism, and advertising has been so great as to stamp common cultural patterns on large parts of the globe."

Mrs. Louchheim's remarks were a simplified version of the thesis that cultural and educational matters have been *The Neglected Aspect of Foreign Affairs,* the title of a book authored by former Assistant Secretary for Educational and Cultural Affairs Charles Frankel, who transferred from being a professor of philosophy at Columbia University to being a professor of culture in the State Department—and then back again at the end of 1967.

The Cultural Affairs Bureau, organized only in 1961, though there had been a Division of Cultural Relations in the Department as long as thirty years ago, was already one of the largest in the State Department and, given its universal scope of education and culture, had nowhere to go bureaucratically but up. The Bureau, moreover, had the largest single slice of the State Department budget, consistently near the $50 million mark. For 1968, Frankel had aspired to a $58 million budget, but he was cut first by the Department's own budget officers to $50 million and then by the Budget Bureau reviewers to $49 million, arriving before Congressman Rooney's Appropriations Subcommittee with a request for appropriations of $46,817,000, with the expectation of further cuts as a result of presidential budget tightening up and down the line. During the 1967 springtime ordeal of testifying before the Rooney group, Frankel looked like the figure of a martyr on a Byzantine ikon, complete with halo, the result of the cyanide-bath reducing treatment and Chinese torture of a "thousand little cuts" undergone on Capitol Hill.

Its Congressional sufferings notwithstanding, the Bureau could look forward to a happy future of empire-building for the good and substantial reason of its participation in the workings of the International Education Act of 1966. Although action responsibility within the Government was vested in the Secretary of Health, Education and Welfare, the Bureau had a large role in the ultimate disposition of matters through its chairmanship of the Inter-Agency Council in International Education and Cultural Affairs, which includes about twenty-five agencies of the Federal Government involved in some degree in international educational and cultural exchanges and research abroad. From this group was formed the IRG, or Interdepartmental Regional Group, for supervision, coordination, and direction of activities among agencies operating overseas in the same field, under the presidential authority for over-all Government supervision of foreign policy programs carried by the Secretary of State.

Indicative of the microscopic scrutiny given the Bureau's activities by the Rooney Subcommittee is the fact that almost one third of the 785-page hearings report is devoted to it alone. The central part of the Bureau's operations, as might be expected, had to do with supervision of the famous cultural exchange, or Fulbright-Hays, program. In 1968, this program was budgeted for $36,583,000 and had scheduled a total of 9,655 grants to individuals, 7,203 for citizens of more than 130 countries coming to America to study and 2,452 for Americans going to almost 100 countries. Of the total, 1,432 related to Africa, 2,391 to Latin America, 2,904 to western Europe, 513 to eastern Europe, 1,164 to the Far East, and 1,251 to the Middle East and south Asia. Since 1949, over 100,-000 students, two thirds of them foreign, had been exchanged. The actual selection of the lucky students was handled by an elaborate system, topped by the Board of Foreign Scholarships, in which the U.S. academic community was heavily represented, as if in protection of its vested interests, and in which it had a major say concerning which academics could go abroad. Cynical Foreign Service officers in the poltical field remarked that if the Federal Government ever interfered in this academic fiefdom, the resultant fracas would make the dispute over the Vietnam war sound like a sewing circle temper tantrum.

The twenty years of the Fulbright program had stimulated a multiplied expansion of student travel by private means. In 1967, there were some 90,000 foreign students in the United States, the proportion of U.S. Government-sponsored ones being roughly 10 per cent. A new development of student exchange was the appearance of foreign teen-agers across the American landscape, living with American families and attending American schools, mostly by private means, the Bureau indirectly assisting more than 4,000 a year. The Bureau also aided American private schools abroad—50 in Africa, 43 in Latin America, 14 in Europe, 11 in the Far East, and 18 in the Middle East—at a cost of over $2 million.

The heightened interest in international education had been first sparked by the national consternation over the Soviet Sputnik in 1957 and the chagrined realization that the Soviets had apparently transformed education into a weapon of national and foreign policy. There was the further example of France, which even in the Fourth Republic, before Charles de Gaulle, was spending $100 million a year on cultural and educational activities affecting more than 40,000 persons under a huge official establishment.

In his 1966 Message to Congress on the international education proposal, President Johnson said, "Education lies at the heart of every nation's hopes and purposes. It must be at the heart of our international relations."

In effect, the American educational system, from grade schools to universities, would be asked to take on a vastly increased role of educating students in the basics of international relations, so that American citizens could know enough about the background and rationale of foreign policy to render the ultimate judgments necessary at the polls. The cry for educational training for world citizenship, which the President had voiced, challenged the ingrown nationalistic system of education and parochial-minded textbooks upon which American history and the relations of the United States to the rest of the world were based. In the past, these anachronistic texts had helped form narrow and even isolationist attitudes ingrained in citizens from childhood.

Assistant Secretary Frankel, speaking before the National Congress of Parents and Teachers in Minneapolis, said: "Events will force the adults of the future to recognize that foreign affairs are domestic affairs, that political boundaries insulate no country, and least of all our own, from the commotions, revolutions, frustrations, and aspirations of the people in other parts of the world."

Dr. John T. Robinson of the University of Michigan Survey Research Center, summarizing surveys made since 1957, reported that one third of the United States population, or that portion with less than a high school education and with an annual income of less than $7,500, knew little about world affairs and was insulated from information concerning the foreign scene. Robinson said that this stratum of American society rarely read printed materials or even picture magazines dealing with international affairs. He was pessimistic about the expectation that information on world affairs would filter down from the better-educated and more affluent classes to the less-educated and poorer ones through the medium of so-called opinion-makers.

The International Education Act was, at the point of departure, primarily directed at the United States itself: Americans would have to educate themselves before they could attempt to educate others. Yet, despite all the high-minded tribute to the necessities implied in that bill, the Congressional Conference Committee on Appropriations for the Departments of Labor and of Health, Education and Welfare and related agencies, for fiscal 1968, in October 1967 denied funds to support the International Education Act. The $45 million proposed for the Act's funding were caught in the meat grinder during the conflict between the Congress and the President over cutting expenditures and imposing a tax increase in the latter part of that year. American educators hailed the Act as the most significant step ever taken in international education. The entire federal bureaucracy had been stimulated by the scope of the Act and the opportunities it offered for practically every department to enter into this glittering new field of foreign affairs.

International education, moreover, was the President's private and cherished project, one upon which he had set his heart. In his speech before representatives of nearly fifty countries at the Conference of World Education at Williamsburg, Virginia, in October 1967, Johnson said:

As a former school teacher of a small rural school, I have had the feeling that if we could help the people of the world to maintain a good sound body and if we could provide them with proper education, with a good mind and a good body they could build their own steel mills.

Despite the Congressional setback, the President was planning ahead for 1968. He called upon the United Nations to make 1968 an International Education Year. The President proposed to found a global university with the best teachers in the world from both the United States and overseas to teach basic subjects—English, mathematics, sciences—through television by relay from communications satellites.

He proposed at least to start a pilot project by 1968, in collaboration with UNESCO, the foundations, COMSAT (the American Satellite Communications Corporation), and the resources of the U.S. Agency for International Development and the Department of Health, Education and Welfare. He set up a working committee of HEW Secretary John Gardner, McGeorge Bundy, President of the Ford Foundation, and Leonard Marks, the Director of USIA. He consulted William Benton, the U.S. representative at UNESCO, and called upon his "scholars," as he called them, Secretaries Rusk and McNamara and Special Assistant Rostow, to help iron out the wrinkles.

International education affairs in the State Department were focused on the future, but passport matters were very much in the present, and to an even greater extent in the future, as more and more Americans travel abroad and, as year after year, the Passport Office breaks its previous records. In 1965, for example, 2.6 million Americans traveled overseas; in 1966, 2.975 million. The expectation was that 1968 would be a year to top all others, with a record number of 1,800,000 passport issuances anticipated. The Passport Office, with 439 officers and staff and operating on a budget of $4,879,000, including salaries and material costs, produced revenues of $12,230,000, or nearly $8 million profit for the U.S. Treasury, in 1967. There had been a 166 per cent increase in demand for passports in the ten years from 1956 to 1966. Branch passport agencies had been opened in ten cities—New York, Chicago, Boston, Los Angeles, San Francisco, New Orleans, Miami, Seattle, Honolulu, and Philadelphia, with two more, Detroit and Houston, possibly in the offing.

The Passport Office was the only "face-to-face" regular service that the

State Department offered all the time to American citizens. The American passport in foreign lands is the symbol and documentary proof of U.S. citizenship. The concrete significance of what it means to be an American was dramatically illustrated during the 1967 Middle East crisis, when, in the first days of the Arab-Israeli war, the Passport Office received over 90,000 telephone calls, three times its normal volume, and nearly 4,000 letters, not to mention 2,200 urgent Congressional inquiries relayed from constituents. The callers wanted to know whether it was true that they couldn't go to such and such a place, or they asked anxious questions about relatives in the affected areas. In short, to many citizens the Passport Office was the most recognizable embodiment of the U.S. Government at that moment.

The Director of the Passport Office since 1955, Miss Frances G. Knight, is one of the most decorative, one of the most combative, and one the most efficient officers in the entire State Department, feared by the incompetents, approached rather apprehensively by her superiors, and widely respected for her professionalism. By 1967, she had triumphantly survived almost six years of constant embroilment with higher bureaucratic echelons. In the early Kennedy administration she was a prime target of liberals as a relic of Scott McLeod, who had been Administrator of the Bureau of Security and Consular Affairs during the McCarthy witch-hunting era, for her stubborn refusal to issue passports to persons with alleged Communist records without a written order, despite the ruling of the Supreme Court of the United States that passports could not be denied even to Communists. On the more practical plane, Miss Knight, despite her great personal charm, when she wished to turn it on, was anathema to Congressman Rooney, who, as has been noted, was the constant bugbear of the State Department because of his power over its appropriations. Former Under Secretary for Administration William Crockett encouraged the policy of placating Rooney. Crockett was beholden to Rooney for having been recommended to President Kennedy for the post.

Rooney did not like Miss Knight because she had fired a woman in the New York Passport Office whom she considered inadequate. This employee had a nephew who worked in the office of the late Francis Cardinal Spellman in New York. As a good Irish Catholic, Congressman Rooney was given the word to get the dismissed employee back on the job. Miss Knight fought the case all the way up to the U.S. Civil Service Commission—and made the dismissal stick. The next round came after the appointment of Abba Schwartz, an expert on refugee matters, a protégé of Eleanor Roosevelt, and a noted liberal, to whom Miss Knight represented the abominations of the McCarthy years. It was Miss Knight who stayed while Abba Schwartz left.

For several years now Miss Knight has refused to appear before the Rooney House Subcommittee, remarking: "Let Rooney cut the appropriation—and then wait for the screams," that is, the clamor of the American public if it did not get its passports on time. Miss Knight's office was one of the rare exceptions to Congress' 1967 budget-cutting, thanks to her wit and political connections. The House had cut the State Department's appropriation by some $2 million. State's budget office, in turn, had cut the Passport Office by $320,000, which had been earmarked for seventy new permanent employees, the need for which, in view of the tremendously increased workload, was self-evident. When Miss Knight got through testifying, members of the powerful Senate Appropriations Subcommittee, Republicans and Democrats alike—John L. McClellan of Arkansas, Spessard L. Holland of Florida, Allen J. Ellender of Louisiana, Mike Mansfield of Montana, Margaret K. Smith of Maine, Milton R. Young of North Dakota—vied in being solicitous and complimentary to Miss Knight, particularly in recognition of the "instant service," or practically push-button speed which she had regularly provided Congressmen and Senators over the years in meeting their own passport requirements and in dealing with emergencies of their constituents.

For example, a prominent businessman and constituent of one Congressman had to rush to Paris because his wife had become seriously ill. Miss Knight instantly cleared his departure on an airline without a passport and arranged for the Paris Embassy passport officer to meet him with a new one. In the meantime, because of bad weather, the plane was diverted to Brussels. Miss Knight had the passport delivered to the passenger at the Brussels airport. It was understandable why Miss Knight's favorite witticism was, "A Congressman is a girl's best friend," and why she said at a press interview in 1967: "I'm very happy. I've got my personnel, got my budget, and we were able to process an all-time high in passports. Everybody has been nice to me. People smile in the halls, instead of ducking into the men's room when I come along."

It was no surprise either that Miss Knight had gilt-edged allies on her flanks also. She devised a smooth system of giving passports to dependents of U.S. armed forces overseas, in 1966 nearly 76,000 such passports being issued. Bureaucrats on Government business receive official passports, of which nearly 100,000 were issued in 1966. Only bona fide diplomats on actual Foreign Service duty are supposed to get diplomatic passports, of which there are now 22,000 outstanding. Regular passports have a light blue cover, official ones maroon, diplomatic ones black. There is a special category of courtesy diplomatic passports issued to eminent American personages and to persons in the White House political range, though the President of the United States personally does not require a passport. As the wife of a President, Mrs. Jacqueline Kennedy had a diplomatic passport. It was canceled in July 1964 and a courtesy diplomatic passport issued to her as the widow of a former U.S. President; she still holds it. There have been 216 courtesy diplomatic passports issued up to 1967. Starting in 1954, issuances at first were comparatively rare, only one or two a year through 1962. In 1963, fifty were issued; in 1964, seventy-five; in 1965, thirty-six; in 1966, twenty-seven; in 1967, thirteen.

Besides Pentagon officials and her political friends, who include Senator Fulbright of Arkansas, Senator James Eastland of Mississippi, and Vice President Humphrey, Miss Knight is well connected, to say the least, with the Federal Bureau of Investigation, because of the constant liaison necessitated by the Passport Office "Look-out" file. The Passport Office has a 22 million card index, half of which had been microfilmed by late 1967. Cards noting refusals to issue passports for various reasons made up the "Look-out" file proper. In 1958, under Miss Knight's vigorous broom, the file was swept down to 700,000, and by 1967 to 245,000 cards. This was done by eliminating references to applicants of ninety years ago, innumerable World War II censorship violations, and notations of persons with Nazi connections in those days.

About 90 per cent of the modern "Look-out" file deals with lost citizenship cases, dating from 1906; because passports are regarded as valid legal documents in courts of law, one of the few public documents so still held, these are retained as reference archives in case of need. There are about 9,000 cases of American citizens who had once been repatriated from abroad after having been loaned U.S. funds for the passage and who had not repaid these official loans. If any of them applies for a passport again, the Government first asks for its money. Every month about fifty persons who still owe $50 or more for unpaid repatriation loans show up, applying for new passports. Another class relates to persons who are subject to court orders in child custody cases. Five or ten passport applicants in this category appear each month. A further classification relates to persons who repeatedly "lose" their passports and to mental or psychiatric cases for whom it is considered dangerous to travel alone; five to ten such cases also appear each month. The remainder, less than 10 per cent, have to do with known criminals and other persons wanted by the police, espionage agents, hard-core Communist organizers on the FBI list, and Americans who have renounced their U.S. citizenship and therefore are no longer eligible to receive passports.

The rate of passport issuances, starting with over a million in 1964, has been jumping every year since by at least 200,000. It is a dramatic statistic demonstrating the difference between the space age of today and the sedate and peaceful world of the beginning of the century, 14,554 passports having been issued in 1901 and 24,064 in 1910. Before 1914 most travelers went abroad without passports, but once World War I broke out, no one did. The work of the Division of Citizenship, as the Passport Office was then called, quadrupled. By 1926, the Passport Division was already the second largest division in the State Department. It was getting into the headlines, just as in current times, by revoking passports of foreign Communists or by refusing to issue passports to ladies suspected of moral turpitude.

In 1930 the Passport Office had 78 employees; in 1941, 121; and in 1945, 239, this number remaining fairly static until 1955, by which time the issuance of passports had been speeded up to six weeks. Today the average time is one week and, if applied for in Washington, only three days. In a real emergency a passport can be, and has been, issued in fifteen minutes flat. The transition from quieter times to the eve of the new era was symbolized by Mrs. Ruth Shipley, who reigned over the Passport Office for twenty-seven years. She hand-picked Miss Knight as her successor. The color of the ordinary passport went from red to green and now is blue. It is valid for three years, and for two years more if renewed, for a fee of ten dollars. A proposal is now being prepared for Congress to extend the life of a passport to five years.

The Passport Office has had a 77 per cent increase in productivity per man-year since 1956. Electronic scanning of the "Look-out" file can clear thirty names in twenty-four seconds, allowing production of from 6,000 to 7,000 passports a day. The new teletypewriter network that links the Washington headquarters of the Passport Office with its ten field offices will be converted to computer handling by 1968, so that the field agencies can likewise clear names with dispatch. Electronic embossing machines place the State Department seal on the photographs and passports, an improvement over the cast-steel screw press used from 1884 until 1929. The glue pots and brushes used to paste the photographs onto the passports prior to 1956 have been replaced by electric gluing machines. Just one procedure has not changed: hand flatirons are still used to seal the photographs to the passports.

The Passport Office has had a tradition of personal hospitality to visitors ever since Mrs. Shipley used to serve tea to VIP's seeking passports. In recent years, it has had the reputation of putting up the most artistic Christmas decorations, providing the tastiest home-made buffets and cookies, and in the holiday season throwing the happiest family parties of any office in the State Department. Its only regret is that it has never personally been visited by a Secretary of State within living memory, save for a fleeting in-and-out of Secretary Christian A. Herter in 1958. In October 1967, the Passport Office moved from the State Department headquarters proper to a brand-new federal building in downtown Washington, at 17th and H Streets, Northwest, to be "where the action was," Miss Knight said.

By 1967 the Passport Office was faced with an extraordinary peak period lasting from January to June and beyond, that is, it was operating practically at a seven-month maximum capacity, necessitating extra temporary staff, who pushed the top employment figure to nearly 600; this situation is similar to the Post Office rush at Christmas time, but it is measured in months instead of weeks.

Visitors from forty-five governments since 1960 examined at first hand the U.S. passport operation. Both the foreigners and the Americans were facing a formidable new problem: the travel explosion of the 1970's. U.S. overseas travelers were increasingly using air transportation, 93 per cent in 1966. More and more use of air travel was expected. In 1967, international carriers serving the Atlantic, Caribbean, and Pacific raised scheduled trips to 1,769 a week, compared with 1,556 in 1966, a record number of 234,840 seats thus being made available. The number of round-the-world passengers jumped from 6,000 in 1962 to 70,000 in 1965. Miss Knight was attempting to anticipate the problems that would arise in the next decade with the giant supersonic transports, several of which could land within minutes in metropolitan airports on the Atlantic and Pacific coasts, disgorging up to 5,000 passengers, to crowd into jam-packed terminals. By 1974, according to projections, some 3.6 million passports will be issued and 600,000 renewed, bringing the total to 4.2 million. One collateral easement will be to facilitate the numbering of the passports by using Social Security numbers as the basic identification. Another idea under investigation is the issuance of travel cards, good for one trip to one country or for one group of passangers traveling together to western Europe, for instance.

The principal concern of Miss Knight and the senior officers of the Department was the integrity of the U.S. passport. Its unique standing as a legal document can affect cases in the courts of law fifty years hence in matters of wills, property, and custody of children in divorce cases, situations in which mere travel cards or other abbreviated documents would not have comparable relevance and authority. In a report on the approaching problem of the processing of travelers in the mass air transportation of the supersonic age, Miss Knight stated that the five Government agencies interested in travelers had one principal question: Where is the traveler FROM? This question interested the Customs Service, the Public Health Service, the Agricultural Quarantine Service, the Immigration Service, and the Security Police. With the swift back-and-forth of travelers from all over the world and the danger of epidemic disease, it was all the more urgent to be able to identify a traveler's route through clearly identi-

fiable and authoritative documents like passports. For instance, in mid-
1967 a traveler who had been in a plague area in the Middle East arrived
in Los Angeles, a fact discovered after he had disappeared in the bustle
and confusion of the L.A. airport. There was no way to trace him in order
to question him except through the Passport Office. Identified within ten
minutes, he was located at the Travis Air Force Base in California a few
hours later.

The cliché about the American tourist being an unofficial ambassador of
the United States abroad was becoming literally true, and with ramifications. Whatever his intentions or personal disposition, the American was
creating impressions upon the foreigners he was visiting, building up, by
his bodily presence, the foreigners' fragmentary or instinctive visions,
judgments, and anticipations of American behavior. In turn, the American
traveler was receiving impressions and making his own judgments, whether
considered or off the hip, of the people and situations in the midst of
which he was enjoying himself and concerning which he could not help
making some political determinations. In brief, foreign policy was becoming alive, going and coming, by the mere presence of the American on
foreign soil.

The principal destination of the American traveler in the first six
months of 1967 was Europe, eighty-three out of a hundred passport
recipients listing that area as their goal. Only seven of the hundred were
going to the Far East, four to other parts of the Americas, three to the
Middle East, two to Australia and the Southwest Pacific Islands, and one
to Africa. How Americans were fanning out all over the globe is indicated
by the specific countries planned to be visited between April and June
1967, according to a Passport Office survey of over 700,000 passport
applicants:

EUROPE

Italy	299,970	Norway	26,450
France	258,760	Luxembourg	18,620
Switzerland	209,070	Monaco	18,550
United Kingdom	189,220	Yugoslavia	12,520
Germany	187,910	U.S.S.R.	10,950
Netherlands	165,810	Finland	6,880
Ireland	123,170	Poland	6,310
Austria	117,090	Czechoslovakia	6,300
Belgium	110,730	Hungary	4,440
Sweden	76,390	Iceland	2,300
Spain	74,690	Rumania	1,960
Denmark	54,000	Gibraltar	1,060
Greece	48,970	Bulgaria	700
Portugal	33,310		

AMERICAS

Mexico	7,880	Colombia	2,620
Brazil	6,770	Canada	2,280
Peru	5,890	Chile	1,990
Panama	3,840	Jamaica	1,560
Argentina	3,720	Guatemala	1,350
Venezuela	3,270	Bolivia	1,220

FAR EAST

Japan	34,490	India	3,770
Thailand	15,440	Korea	3,610
Hong Kong	14,220	Pakistan	3,380
Taiwan	6,320	Malaya	430
Vietnam	4,720		

AUSTRALIA AND OCEANIA

Philippines	11,400	New Zealand	3,360
Australia	5,300	Indonesia	3,160
Okinawa	3,750		

MIDDLE EAST

Israel	26,940	Iraq-Iran	5,150
Turkey	10,970	Lebanon	5,030
Egypt	7,090	Syria	3,180
Jordan	5,530	Saudi Arabia	1,150

AFRICA

Africa	2,930	South Africa	680
Morocco	2,750	Libya	560
Ethiopia	1,040		

The Passport Office statistics shed light on the Americans who were entering foreign scenes. Fifty-eight per cent of the passport recipients resided in twenty-eight metropolitan areas of the United States—including 22 per cent in the New York area, 7 per cent in the Los Angeles area, 5 per cent in the Chicago area, 4 per cent each in the Boston and San Francisco areas, and 3 per cent each in the Detroit and Washington areas. Out of a hundred travelers, eighty were going abroad for personal reasons or pleasure, seven for business reasons, five for education, and seven on official business, and one was listed as miscellaneous. All ages were traveling abroad. Thirty-two out of a hundred were over forty, and thirty-four were from twenty to thirty-nine years of age. Most trips' duration was less than two months, though seventy-six out of a hundred travelers expected to travel again within two years. Whole cross sections of American society were on the move overseas.

But not everywhere. The State Department may apply a travel ban to a specific country in only three situations: when that country is at war with the United States, when armed hostilities are in progress there, or when travel must be restricted in the national interest because it would seriously impair the conduct of United States foreign relations. The United States maintains passport restrictions on travel by American citizens to five areas: Albania, Cuba, Communist China, North Korea, and North Vietnam. During the Middle East crisis, passports were invalidated for practically all the Arab countries, several of those restrictions having been lifted by late 1967. The only exceptions to the rule are made for certain professional and occupational classes entitled to obtain special validation of their passports when the purpose of their travel is directly related to their professional responsibilities, such as newsmen, doctors and scientists in public health, scholars, and American Red Cross representatives. The Department can issue individual "discretionary" exceptions to persons in cultural, athletic, commercial, educational, and public affairs activities, the latter group including even travelers who are not professional journalists. Newsmen may travel to Communist North Vietnam and Communist China if they can get in, and scholars and doctors likewise may visit Communist China, again if the Communist Chinese will grant them a visa.

The event that from time to time rears into public headlines is the trip to restricted countries without proper passport validation or even without a passport, as in travel to Communist Cuba for reasons of political protest or for adventurous curiosity. Infractions of the regulations have been grounds for the State Department to revoke or cancel the violator's passport and are punishable under federal law. But lately, State's authority is under court challenge. Before a new passport is issued, the Secretary of State must receive formal assurance that the owner of the canceled passport will not again violate travel restrictions. Official justification for these restrictions is that they help to assure that the ordinary American citizen will not become an innocent victim of hostile policies of foreign powers in areas where the U.S. Government can offer little protection.

Besides travel to Communist Cuba, the most publicized violations of the passport law have been unauthorized visits to North Vietnam. The matter of such technically illegal trips to North Vietnam, like that of Stokely Carmichael, the Negro "Black Power" leader, goes to the heart of the passport's significance, involving allegiance of the passport owner to the country which has issued the passport, namely, the United States. Carmichael's passport was revoked upon his return to the United States. From the early days of the nation, when Benjamin Franklin used to issue passports in Paris, and from July 8, 1796, the date of the first passport in the State Department files, to October 20, 1966, the U.S. passport served not only as a symbol of sovereignty of the government issuing it but also as a free testimonial by the citizen who received it. By implication, in the act of asking the national authority for a passport, the citizen signified the choice of that country as his country and as his protector when he ventured into an alien and foreign world.

Until 1966, the oath of allegiance in application for a passport was based on Sections 211-A and 212 of Title 22 of the United States Code, Section 212 providing: "No passport shall be granted or issued to, or verified for, any other person than those owing allegiance, whether citizens or not, to the United States."

One way of determining whether a person was entitled to a passport was the requirement of the oath of allegiance. This oath has no connection with the so-called Loyalty Oath, which has been struck down by the courts as being essentially negative in character and, generally speaking, a declaimer of membership in certain organizations considered subversive by the governmental body requiring the oath.

The Department felt that the oath of allegiance contained in the passport application was an affirmative statement of allegiance to the United States. But matters like the Vietnam war and the protests against it intervened. An American applicant for a renewal of a passport in the U.S. Embassy in Athens, Greece, protested that the Consul had no right to require an oath of allegiance. Contemporaneously, two employees of the New York Passport Agency refused to administer the oath of allegiance to two passport applicants. The latter two got their passports eventually, and the two (temporary) employees got the sack.

In consequence, the Department issued a new instruction on November 14, 1966, telling all Foreign Service posts overseas to delete the oath of allegiance on passport and registration forms. Characteristically, on December 27, 1966, a second instruction was sent to all the Foreign Service posts advising them that the Department, on further consultation, had decided not to delete the oath of allegiance from passport and registration forms. The cable went on to inform the consuls that the Department had no legal authority to deny a passport to a citizen for refusal to execute the oath of allegiance and that, if a refusal were voiced, the oath of allegiance might be deleted in the application by lining it out. By late 1967 the Department had not yet officially incorporated the new oath of allegiance instructions into its Foreign Affairs Manuals. The oath of allegiance in connection with a passport application has never been ruled on by the U.S. courts, and when it is brought up, as eventually it probably will be, it will no doubt go up to the U.S. Supreme Court.

The Passport Office was seized with variations of the same problem of the significance of the passport and to whom it may be issued in May 1967, when the U.S. Supreme Court ruled that Congress lacked the constitutional authority to pass laws that stripped American citizens of their nationality without their consent. Though the U.S. Code indicated that passports would be issued to persons owing allegiance, whether citizens or not, to the United States, in practical effect the passport was issued only to those persons who proved that they were citizens, a normal requirement in the passport application today.

The Supreme Court 5–4 decision declaring unconstitutional the Federal National Act of 1940, which deprived citizens of their nationality if they voted in a foreign election, uncovered hundreds of cases of former American citizens living abroad who had lost their citizenship and, consequently, their passports by violating various American laws. These were principally laws which assumed that those nonresident American citizens no longer were interested in obeying the laws of the country to which they had once given allegiance. The citizen in the Supreme Court case at issue was a seventy-three-year-old artist, Beys Afroyim, born in Poland and nationalized in America in 1926. He had voted in an Israeli parliamentary election in 1951, after moving to Israel in 1950. When he tried to return to the United States in 1960, State Department officials discovered that he had voted in the election for the Knesset, or parliament, and revoked his citizenship.

Thousands of former U.S. citizens in Europe, particularly in Italy, Greece, and Israel can now reclaim their American citizenships and, in particular, their passports. In practical effect, they will have double nationality, since most of them will continue living abroad. The Supreme Court decision theoretically reopened the case of Andreas Papandreou, who became a naturalized U.S. citizen in 1944 but who lost his citizenship twenty years later, under the now-unconstitutional law, by becoming a Minister in the Greek Government, headed by his father, George Papandreou. State Department legal advisers and Justice Department attorneys mulled over the problem in late 1967 as a step in persuading the Greek military junta to free Papandreou from jail in Greece, which it finally did.

The Supreme Court decision opened up fascinating possibilities of, and opportunities for, double nationalities, major and minor allegiance, giving legal cognizance to the ineradicable diversity of mankind. Perhaps, in the world of the future, whose boundaries are constantly being foreshortened by the speed of travel and the interchange of cultures, it will be feasible for the citizens of every country to vote in each other's countries, thus giving the moral weight of their personal choice to the eventual unity of the world and expressing their opinions of other governments' behavior, *en passant,* in a sort of global Gallup Poll.

The Passport Office also means Negroes, who make up two fifths of its staff. The Pulitzer Prize winning foreign correspondent of the *Chicago Daily News,* George Weller, on a return trip to this country a few years ago, found himself in the basement of the State Department, where the passports used to be processed, and said, "I thought I was back in the Congo." In any event, the Passport Office has the largest single concentration of Negroes in the State Department. Under the vigorous enforcement of the Government's Equal Employment Opportunity Program, the Department has made valiant efforts to enlist Negroes in its ranks. In 1961, there were only 17 Negro Foreign Service officers out of a Departmental total of about 3,500; in 1967, there were 25. In 1961, there were only 3 Negro Foreign Service Reserve officers; in 1967, there were 65 out of nearly 1,900. The percentage of Negro officers was 2.8, in line with that of the Federal Government as a whole, while the proportion of Negroes in the total nonofficer manpower in the State Department was 18 per cent, 1 per cent higher than the federal average.

On the lower levels, the influx of Negroes into the State Department was a stream of raw life, seeping in under the door jamb. On the higher levels, the educated Negroes contributed an instinctive human understanding and a scope of adaptability in handling the nationalities of the underdeveloped countries, though the fact was that in truly black Africa an American Negro had often been dismissed as "virtually a white man." Having Negroes on the staff of the various bureaus became a social and political "must." As one young Negro woman told a friend, "I am the Secretariat's new status symbol." For many Negroes, employment in the State Department lent a certain cachet to their social life. Negroes who entered the State Department's service in the early 1960's with practically a log on their shoulders over civil rights found they were accepted, trained, and promoted without too much strain into middle-class placidity. In fact, the old and settled Negro employees of the State Department are among the most middle-class citizens of Washington, sedate, responsible, and self-composed, like the elevator operators at the Twenty-first Street and Virginia Avenue entrance of the old State Department building who operate their cars with the decorum and stylized hand motions of Balinese dancers.

Under the suave and agile prodding of Eddie N. Williams, a Negro special assistant to the Deputy Under Secretary for Administration, the Department has experimented with innumerable ways to attract Negroes.

Careers are offered as Foreign Service staff officers, whose salaries start at around $8,000 a year, plus housing and other allowances for overseas tours of duty; as diplomatic couriers, with a starting salary of nearly $6,000, to roam the world from the three courier headquarters, in Frankfurt, Manila, and Washington; or as Foreign Service nurses, again at almost $8,000 a year for a start. A foreign affairs program was launched. It consists of two summers of intern work at the State Department and associated agencies, plus two years of graduate study, financed by a $600,-000 grant from the Ford Foundation. Forty scholars have been selected annually since 1963 in national competitions, providing 120 students as possible candidates for the Foreign Service. Recruiting drives are advertised in Negro and Spanish-American publications, Spanish Americans also being considered a minority group which should be offered equal opportunities for advancement and entrance into the mainstream of American society. Besides Negroes and Spanish Americans, special attention is paid to enlisting American Indians.

The difficulty has been that, despite these best efforts, not enough qualified educated young Negroes have been found to seize the opportunities offered by the State Department. Between 1961 and 1966, approximately 26 per cent of all applicants for the Foreign Service passed the competitive Foreign Service officer examination, but only 38, or 3.5 per cent, of all Negro applicants passed it. The rate of failure among the Negroes continued to be so high that the Department had no hope of obtaining any sizable number through regular channels. In 1967, a new Junior Foreign Service Officer Program was initiated whereby Negroes up to thirty-one years of age, and with only general educational qualifications, were allowed to by-pass the written examination and take only the oral one. A noted Negro psychologist, Dr. Kenneth B. Clark, was given a State Department contract to study the Foreign Service officer examination with the mission of making it more adaptable to the varying standards of preparation of the Negro applicants.

The Department encountered still more trouble. A large number of the Negro applicants were simply unwilling to work overseas. The Department could not compete with the increased number of federal jobs on the staffs of the Office of Economic Opportunity, Peace Corps, and Equal Employment Opportunity programs, which were offering higher salaries in place of career status and tenure, so that the brighter of the so-called minority candidates priced themselves out of the State Department market.

While stymied at the moment in its efforts to obtain an influx of Negro blood, the Department goes a long way toward getting established Americans of the Negro race to participate in its activities. It gives every possible advantage for advancement to Negroes in the Department. The number of Negroes in the middle echelon of the Department rose from 1.6 per cent in 1961 to 7.5 per cent in 1967. Negroes have been appointed to the State Department Promotion Boards, as public members of Foreign Service inspection teams, and to the Board of Examiners for the Foreign Service. Prominent Negro leaders are selected to go overseas on cultural tours. Several Negroes are labor advisers in Washington or labor attachés abroad. One is the country director for Malaysia and Singapore, another a deputy chief of mission in the Republic of Togo in Africa. Five Negroes, including one woman, are ambassadors. Two, again one of them a woman, are Deputy Assistant Secretaries of State. The highest ranking woman in the State Department is a Negro, Miss Barbara Watson, Acting Administrator of the Bureau of Security and Consular Affairs.

It was not the Negroes inside the State Department but rather those outside, in the streets of America, who gave the Foreign Service corps anxious thoughts as violent riots erupted in the United States in August 1967. The diplomats were absorbed by the parallel between the rising expectations for civil rights accelerating into violence in the United States in the same way that agitation for independence in the African nations had exploded into violence when new states emerged from the old colonies of Africa. There was amazement that the Negroes of Detroit, relatively advanced politically and with a not unsubstantial stake in society, should riot.

The Foreign Service officers, however, recalled analogous experiences in France and Italy, where the well-off peasantry voted Communist as both a protest and as a goad to swifter action by lethargic authorities to remedy social inequities. As had been noted overseas, frequently the most sensitive and potentially dangerous situations arose after a nation had made its economic take-off and was from one fourth to one half of its way to development. It then began to have serious political troubles as the various factions started to fight for their particular long-run stakes in the ultimate society. The beginnings of improvement in the Negro situation in the United States had only slightly opened the door to the sight of still greener pastures and whetted the hunger and the desire to get there faster. U.S. diplomats, in brief, did not have to go overseas to study the psychology of underdeveloped peoples. The ghettos of Newark and of Hough in Cleveland and of Watts in Los Angeles and of Detroit were burning brothers to the slums of Rio de Janeiro, Caracas, Cairo, and Calcutta.

There was also a *Lumpenproletariat* of the bottom layer of society among the 5 million American Negroes who had never even made the census count. Karl Marx's theories of class warfare not only were out-moded but paled beside the reality of the passions the American diplo-mats had been familiar with in the explosions they had witnessed in Asia, the Middle East, and Africa. They now rediscovered violence as a native ingredient of the U.S. frontier atmosphere and almost a surface tendency in the American psyche, putting historical flesh to the metaphor of H. Rap Brown, leader of the curiously named Student Nonviolent Coordinating Committee (SNCC), who had said, "Violence is as Ameri-can as cherry pie."

The fiery scene of the 1967 summer illuminated for the State Depart-ment the operating truths that race and equitable access to opportunity were a flaming issue all around the world; that aid in underdeveloped countries had its close parallel in the United States, when Whitney Young of the Urban League could call for a Marshall Plan and when Negro churchmen could demand a national economic development bank like the Asian development, or inter-American, banks. American Negro unrest in the United States had direct and collateral foreign policy conse-quences. In 1967, more than 7,000 African students were enrolled in American universities to help meet their countries' urgent need for trained manpower in government, education, agriculture, and industries. Nearly 600 American colleges, universities, foundations, religious groups, business firms, and social welfare groups were listed as being specifically interested in doing something about African problems.

Immediate protests rose when the U.S. aircraft carrier *Franklin Delano Roosevelt* was scheduled to make a fuel stop in Capetown, South Africa, though a previous aircraft carrier visit had been canceled in 1965, when South Africa had raised the issue of the segregation of the mixed Ameri-can crew, a question which the Americans had refused to entertain. It was only after a liberal coalition of Congressmen and Negro leaders had got through to Marvin Watson, President Johnson's Appointment Secre-tary, that Watson was able to get the Defense Department, at the Presi-dent's order, to cancel the visit of the *FDR,* whose crew had planned to go ashore in segregated groups, the only way acceptable to the South African's principles of apartheid but plainly not to be tolerated by anti-segregationist Americans. The United States had become a laboratory study in foreign-domestic interaction of the race question, from which the Foreign Service officers could profit when they reported on race issues in their overseas assignments.

Apartheid was surfacing in the United States among the Negroes, though with little prospect of a division of territory among whites and blacks, obviously. There was also a severe white backlash, that is, resent-ment and fear among white people against the blacks because of excesses of violence and because of the abuses and pretensions of unqualified Negroes seeking immediate economic equality, with a bonus to boot, as some demanded; their reaction was similar to the outraged feelings of the French *colons* against the Arabs and Berbers of North Africa in the 1950's. There was even a loose and pernicious comparison with the times of the rise of the Nazis in Germany when Negro groups began to demonstrate an anti-Israel viewpoint bred by Negro resentment against a few shopkeepers of the Jewish faith in the Negro slums and ghettos who had been accused of overpricing their goods and profiting on Negro misery. Rap Brown of SNCC said, "We are not anti-Jewish, we are not anti-Semitic, but we don't think Zionist leaders in Israel have a right to that land." In short, another pressure group in foreign policy was born.

The world's mesmerized attention had been fixed upon arson, pillage, and bitterness in the United States, reactions which the State Department duly had to take into account.

The Munich, Germany, *Sueddeutsche Zeitung* said, "One gets a fore-taste of coming disputes which smack more of civil war than civil rights." The *London Daily Telegraph* said, "Each successive outbreak surpasses its predecessors in some aspect of mad violence, as if fumbling elemental forces are finding the weak joints behind the magnificent façade of the American social structure." Brussels' *Le Peuple* headlined: "USA: The Blacks in Revolt." Moscow's *Pravda,* the Soviet Communist Party newspaper, said, "America is living through alarming days."

The page-one banners around the world were mild compared with the self-righteous gloating of the Communist radios. The Yugoslav Ljubljana radio quoted Belgrade's Borba: "Negro riots in the United States are the perfect reflection of a growing gap between the living and working conditions of an average American and the socioeconomic status of a second-class U.S. citizen." This was tepid stuff compared with a Peking international broadcast, which said: "Negro youths for the first time machine-gunned the Fascist troops and police. The U.S. ruling clique has been thrown into panic." Radio Warsaw told its listeners, who, after all, found the report believable, their history being replete with Cossack pogroms in the past: "Some 5,000 paratroopers today began the brutal massacre of the Negro population." The East Berlin Communist radio, with Teutonic pedanticism, labored the subject: "The Negroes are fighting for democracy in the United States, and for the United States. From the very beginning, the ruling circles were engaged in a despicable and, at the same time, shrewd game. They not only exploited the millions of Negroes to their last penny, but until today they have simultaneously used them to impress white workers too." Radio

Moscow was patronizing: "America has never seen the likes of it before, and America is, after all, accustomed to racial disturbances."

The most malicious exultation at American expense was voiced by the United States' two most personal enemies, Communist North Vietnam and Communist Cuba. To put the frosting on the cake, Havana fulsomely welcomed Stokely Carmichael, former president of SNCC, who had gone to Havana without a validated passport, as an observer-delegate to the first Latin American Solidarity Organization Conference of radical revolutionary Communists from all over Latin America. Carmichael called for guerrilla warfare by the Negroes against the United States. He told the conference that the American black power movement was ready to help the Communist revolution in Latin America from "Tierra del Fuego to Alaska," in order, Carmichael said, to "change the power basis of the world." Radio Hanoi reported to southeast Asia that Carmichael believed that "the only solution for America's racial problem is the destruction of the capitalist system and North American imperialism, which is accompanied by racial discrimination and exploitation everywhere" and that he had described the American Government as "the most Fascist regime in the world."

The Communist call for "more Vietnams," echoed by Carmichael, revived fears among some American groups that the danger was a real possibility in Rhodesia, South Africa, Mozambique, and Angola, with overtones of antiblack, and prowhite, feelings. In the State Department itself the fear was that if peaceful change did not occur in Rhodesia, if the white minority government there did not peacefully allow majority rule to come into force, the situation would indeed deteriorate and give African extremism its opening to prevail, and thus confront the United States with still another dilemma of intervening or not intervening in an insurgency and/or civil war—but this time a more bitter and explosive one, a racial war between whites and blacks. The developing situation in southeast Africa was beginning to draw its array of support and opposition in the United States. American civil rights leaders journeyed to Kitwe, in Zambia, for a conference on interrelated political problems. In Washington fifty-eight Congressmen sent the State Department a letter protesting U.S. policy regarding Rhodesia. The issue of Africa, in fact, was becoming economic. There were heavy investments in South Africa. But in all the six southernmost countries of the continent, where apartheid was a policy, U.S. assets were only somewhat over half a billion dollars, whereas they were over a billion dollars in the rest of the continent.

As often happens in the State Department, the issues were getting down to dollars and cents. It was, as in every nation, a question of the allocation of resources, not only among the various sectors of private and public need and interest in the economy, but between that which should be done inside a nation and that which might have to be done beyond its shores. In short, the domestic-foreign interface was rubbing itself raw on multiple fronts among the passions and the policies of a time of Cold War, in-between animosities, and not-quite-definable hot war.

CHAPTER X

INTERDEPENDENCE: Global Shrinkage

THE STATE DEPARTMENT perforce had to be interested in the outside world, not only because of national security, plain idealism, or platonic good will, but foremost because of its material interest in helping obtain from other nations the goods and services which even the fabulously rich United States could not afford to do without. The old cliché was never quite true that trade follows the flag. More realistically, the flag follows trade. And trade is the most characteristic activity of international relations. It represents the overlapping of different domestic interests whose principal concern is to make money no matter what the locale or, if it has a good thing going domestically, to pyramid its profits by transposing the operation to foreign shores and taking advantage of American initiative before the foreigners catch on to its tricks.

Economics was the capillary network that tied the world together into enforced unity. The United States had a direct and absorbing interest in the health of every part of the world, and no part of the world was without a comparable keen concern over the fate of the United States economy, either to share in its profits or to take unfriendly advantage of it by denying it profits.

As Congress' Joint Economic Committee said in 1966: "The world is in trouble—deep trouble—in at least five different areas of economic negotiations and policy: trade; aid to less developed countries; attaining a balance in international payments; international monetary reform; and maintenance of stable price levels in economies marked by full employment and rapid economic growth."

The American nation's specific interest was enforced by the fact that, though the United States had only 6 per cent of the world's population and occupied only 7 per cent of its land surface, it produced 33 per cent of all the goods and services in the world, held nearly one third of the free world's gold, and accounted for 15 per cent of the world's international trade.

State Department diplomats began to engage themselves in trade matters in a regular fashion for the first time only fifty years ago. Consuls had done this supposedly lower-class work in earlier times, stimulating $171 million worth of business in 1833, for instance. The difference between the pre-World War I era and today is a large-scale invasion of diplomacy by economic problems. In the nineteenth century most commerce was free trade. It was only as the twentieth century was about to open that the United States began to erect tariff barriers at a time when autocratic or later totalitarian states, like Germany, Russia, Italy, and Japan, in the interests of creating autarchic or self-sufficient economies, instituted the intervention of government bureaucracies into economic affairs.

Illustrative of permanent intrusion of economic interests into the diplomatic field is the case of Britain, where one third of the work of the Foreign Office became preponderantly economic, commercial, and financial. The British Plowden Report of a few years ago made cogent observations that now apply to many, if not most, of the countries of the world, including the United States. It said:

The problem of earning our [British] living has become more difficult, and is the major preoccupation which influences all our international actions and attitudes. An alert and efficient diplomacy can exercise an influence disproportionate to physical strength, but it cannot operate effectively on the basis of prolonged economic weakness. The survival of Britain, let alone her influence, depends on trade. Economic and political motives intertwine throughout our foreign policy, and have always done so.

In the economic field, as in all others, the State Department is responsible for the totality of American interests and takes no special responsibility for the interests of any particular group. Its instrument is the Bureau of Economic Affairs, whose mission is to defend the international economic interests of the United States, not only against competing foreign interests, but also against local American parochial, narrow, or protectionist interests, which may injure or erode the over-all national self-interest. Its constant mission, therefore, is to arrive at the right mix of domestic and foreign interests of the United States, which may appease or deny citizens' immediate demands, but hopefully will prove most effective and profitable in the long run for all citizens.

The Economic Bureau's functions carry it into practically every phase of State Department operations, abroad and at home. It has its finger in every pie, since there is always money involved. In its diplomatic function, it is constantly on call, because it has been estimated that 80 per cent of the friction points with other countries arise over economic matters. As a result, the Economic Bureau probably accounts for at least half of the day-to-day decisions in the State Department.

The Bureau had been headed since 1965 by Anthony M. Solomon, an effective operator whose background includes U.S. Government service at home and in Iran, a profitable private business career in Mexico, teaching at the Harvard Graduate School of Business Administration, and duty as a former Deputy Assistant Secretary of State for Latin America. The Bureau's 234 officers operated on a budget (for fiscal year 1968) of $3,354,500. Its appropriations since 1964 also covered support for the Kennedy Round negotiating team, at a cost of $2,767,000, including an emergency appropriation of $180,000 in 1967 to complete the cliff-hanger finale of tariff negotiations at Geneva up to the last minute of June 30, 1967.

Indicative of its wide-ranging importance is the fact that the Economic Bureau has five Deputy Assistant Secretaries of State—for international trade, commercial affairs, monetary affairs, international resources, and transportation and telecommunications—more than any other bureau in the State Department. It has constant and intimate liaison with the key departments dealing with materials and money—Treasury, Commerce, Agriculture, Defense, AID, and Interior. The Bureau has to keep its weather eye not only on the normal government indices of economic activity in the United States but also on the private boiling of the American economy as it gets overheated by labor-management conflicts and strikes which affect the production of materials slated for export and lead to innumerable questions from foreign embassies on the significance of such labor troubles in terms of the continued strength of the U.S. economy.

While the action responsibility within the U.S. Government in the economic field goes to various departments like Treasury for finance, Interior for oil, Agriculture for farm products, and Commerce for business promotions, the Economic Bureau must keep itself intimately informed of the myriad details in all these vast fields in order to make its foreign policy contribution to the final programs that eventuate.

The Bureau, from time to time, gave the impression of abrasiveness as it challenged weak-founded claims of geographical bureaus in "political reasons" put forth to justify proposed measures. In any event, it had the final diplomatic say-so as the official instrument conducting negotiations of treaties and agreements with other governments in the commercial and related fields of international economic relations.

The kaleidoscopic range of the Bureau's day-to-day problems is unique in the State Department. On a normal working day, Bureau personnel might discuss with Latin American ambassadors the revision of sugar quotas, a big plum since the embargo against Castro's Cuban sugar, with some thirty countries bidding for a cut; negotiate an agreement on radio frequencies for U.S. space communications; explore with other maritime nations international shipping problems and ocean freight rates; or look into the possibilities of negotiating an international cocoa agreement, a perennial issue of commodity prices, the lifeblood of the LDC, or low-developed countries, as the State Department jargon has named them.

Or the Bureau might negotiate bilateral civil aviation agreements, like the Moscow–New York air route, or it might join with textile industry representatives in arranging agreements with textile-producing countries concerning the ceilings of their imports into the United States, like the series of recent cotton accords with the Philippines, India, Portugal, Spain, nationalist China, Pakistan, and Jamaica, amending and extending present arrangements through September 30, 1970, in line with the decision of the cotton-textile committee of the General Agreement on Tariffs and Trade (GATT). Textiles, in particular, are major industries of the emerging countries because of their ease of manufacture and opportunity for individualistic designs, allowing the LDC's to compete in world markets and obtain the precious foreign exchange they need so desperately.

Bureau officers seem perpetually on the go overseas for international conferences on the trade problems of the developing countries, such as the one scheduled at New Delhi in early 1968, the UNTAD. Preparation for the conference was begun in September 1967, and since, as always, the stage will be dominated by the complex and involved problem of commodity prices, the study for it was begun the year before, in September 1966. A day's agenda might include a NATO review of the COCOM list of strategic items embargoed for sale to Communist countries and a decision on whether the list should be modified. Or preparatory meetings for international conferences on world monetary reform, such as were held in Paris and London since 1965 by the Group of Ten of the leading industrialized and financial powers, in preparation for the 1967 Rio de Janeiro Conference. At Rio was created the so-called paper gold of the future, the SDR, or special drawing rights, in order to meet the problem of world trade, which in the previous ten years had doubled, while world money reserves were increasing by only 40 per cent. In short, a case of liquid funds to buy and sell goods. Or the Economic Bureau might consult with the Bureau of East Asian and Pacific Affairs on the projected lines of a study for future trade with Communist China, a study completed and put on the shelf in 1966.

As might be surmised, a field of endeavor so lucrative in the personal satisfactions of being engaged in, and privy to, matters of major moment inevitably has its troubles. Normally, after the ranking officers of the Secretary of State and the Under Secretary of State, the third ranking officer may choose to be Under Secretary of State for Political Affairs or for Economic Affairs. Because political affairs cut across everything else, many new appointees select that field. Political affairs inextricably include economic factors, so the dignitary in charge finds himself drawn into economic affairs anyhow. The style of a particular Under Secretary for Political Affairs affects the atmosphere of the Economic Bureau. Former Under Secretary for Economic Affairs Thomas C. Mann was not an activist, and he allowed the Bureau more or less to carry on its own affairs. The 1967 Under Secretary, Eugene Rostow, brother of the White House Rostow, is of an ebullient personality that leads him into any number of fields, including economics.

On the operating level, the Economic Bureau traditionally has had its problems with personnel. Its officers must be experts, both in wide areas of economics and in specialized technical subjects. They must be able to hold their own against the professional stars of all Government departments. Since those officers have no action responsibility, except at the very end of the process, in the diplomatic field, the Bureau's influence depends, in many respects, on their personal prestige and knowledge. The Bureau has suffered from the widely held belief in the Foreign Service that the highest rewards of career go to officers performing political tasks and its corollary, that economic specialists rarely become ambassadors. As a result, the Bureau has alternated between weakness and strength because of a shortage of qualified personnel, so much so, in fact, that ten years ago former Deputy Under Secretary for Administration Loy Henderson feared that the lack of qualified personnel would eventually lead to a "divestment of responsibility of economic matters by the State Department." Even when experts in special fields were found, it was hard to keep them, because the personnel system did not adequately reward and promote them if they wanted to stay in Washington, while the demands of the Foreign Service led to their inevitable rotation to the field.

While senior officers in the Bureau, like former Deputy Assistant Secretary Edward R. Fried, who was selected to succeed Francis Bator at the White House, are highly rated as foreign economic policy specialists, not all the lower staff members are quite so good as the best in the other agencies with which the Economic Bureau is in constant consultation, hence, they are less able to defend and project the total national viewpoint that the State Department, by definition, must exemplify. In recognition of the dearth of economic officers, the Department's Foreign Service Institute,

in recent years, has done an exceptional job of compressing a whole college course of economics into practically a semester's work. It succeeded
in giving a recognition vocabulary to officers who had known little or
nothing about economics. The course would allow them to do basic
economic reporting. But they would not yet be quite qualified to engage in
intricate economic negotiations, despite the officers' uniformly high grades
in the course's final exam.

Because of its close working relationship with the departments mentioned, and with others like Transportation, Labor, and Justice and agencies like the Civil Aeronautics Board and the Tariff Commission, the
Bureau becomes much more actively involved, in its daily contacts, in the
main ebb and flow of American life than any other area of the State
Department. This involvement not only demands a high level of expertise
and adaptability in dealing with many other rival or dovetailing bureaucracies of the Government, but also requires a considerable degree of political
sophistication in that the Bureau has frequent consultation with American
business, farm, and labor representatives who speak both for grass-roots
interests and for more elaborate concerns of large and politically influential
organizations. These myriad domestic interests must be finely balanced
when the officers of the Bureau, as they must eventually do, go to the
mat with other nations in international conferences. For example, in 1964,
of 540 multilateral meetings, about 360, or two thirds, were principally
concerned with economic matters. The Bureau's senior officers must be
diplomats both at home and abroad in their contacts, on the one hand,
with the Council of Economic Advisers or the Governors of the Federal
Reserve System and, on the other, with the powerful bankers of the nation
who, in 1966, had 244 branches overseas with assets of over $9 billion.

The Economic Bureau has experts whose technical knowledge is unique
among professionals of the State Department. One recondite field is that
of money, its inflow, outflow, and reflow in the economic pipelines of the
world as indicators of political stability at the point of departure. The Bureau's experts must be familiar with the U.S. Federal Reserve System's
"swap" network. This means bilateral agreements with fourteen central banks
of other countries, plus the Bank of International Settlement at Basle, Switzerland, which together provide each other with credit facilities, in case of
need, totalling over $5 billion. Like the operating bankers, the monetary
pros must have sharp eyes and cool nerves to note the exact reach of the
backwash of violent events in the world, like the 1967 outbreak of war
in the Middle East. This sparked a burst of selling the British pound
sterling, a currency which the United States is pledged to defend, like a

tail to the dollar, as a reserve currency in lubricating the channels of trade payments in the world.

Among the ABC's such experts must keep in mind are that the gold value equivalent of one U.S. dollar is 0.888671 grains of fine gold and that the new SDR, or special drawing rights, of the new "reserve currency" will be "gold value guaranteed," but definitely not "redeemable" in gold, when in the next few years the International Monetary Fund arranges for at least a billion of these rights to be made available to world traders, including $245.9 million for the United States. The Bureau must be able to back up Treasury explanations of why the Middle East crisis cost the United States nearly $60 million in gold during the second quarter of 1967 and how it affected the U.S. balance of payments and U.S. gold stocks, which dropped to $13 billion in September 1967, the lowest level since 1938.

The Bureau's officers must be equally adept at clarifying to fairly shrewd Congressmen the reason why the United States does not charge foreign governments at least storage costs for keeping $13 billion worth of gold in vaults five floors below ground level at the New York Federal Reserve Bank in downtown Manhattan, and at framing cables to U.S. embassies regarding what must be explained to economic "illiterates" in the small developing countries about the 40 per cent jump in silver prices in September 1967. This jump would not affect the value of their dollar holdings, their prime worry. The fact that the dollar was exchangeable for gold underlined its universal acceptability in the world. Though gold in the U.S. domestic monetary system had not been used since the 1933 devaluation, all over the world from ancient times until today gold is the insurance commodity that persons in uncertain or insecure situations want to get hold of as a nest egg against the perils of the future. In 1966, for example, for the first time that anybody could recall, all the newly mined gold in the West went into private hands, mostly to satisfy the fears of hoarders.

The U.S. dollar was the only currency acceptable on sight anywhere on earth as a substitute for, or even in preference to, the local currency. In many places it was also used as a cover and backing for the local currency. Thus, it was inevitable that U.S. economic officers constantly had to reassure foreign holders of dollars that the American nation was and would always be in sound enough shape to maintain the value of its currency. The officers' tested answer was to point to the incredible strength of the U.S. economy and to its steady expansion over the decades, as expressed in its gross national product. The GNP, expressed in billions of constant (1958) dollars, tells its own story in the following table:

Year	GNP
1890	$ 54.1
1900	74.5
1910	120.1
1920	140
1930	183.5
1942	297.8
1945	355.2
1955	438
1960	487.7
1965	616.7
1966	652.6
1967	664.6 (*estimated in the second quarter*)

The State Department's economic team over the years, like that of many of the other bureaus, got into most of its trouble with the Treasury Department. Treasury traditionally had the cold banker's eye on the cost of foreign policies. It felt more comfortable dealing with its peers among the great bankers of the Big Ten—the five countries of the European Common Market (France, Germany, Italy, Belgium, and Holland) and the four outside (Britain, Canada, Sweden, and Japan). The Common Market countries will become still more important in the "new gold" money of the SDR arrangements for the new world reserve currency. The Common Market, as a bloc, will control 16 per cent of the votes in the International Monetary Fund, against the United States' 20 per cent. The Economic Bureau frequently faced the problem of mitigating the somewhat callous attitude of the Treasury toward the LDC's, as the low-developed countries were referred to. Their feeble economies from time to time needed a helping hand to meet their international obligations, a hand which the State Department was more willing to extend when it had to for political reasons than was the coldly calculating Treasury Department.

With the overriding necessity imposed on the entire U.S. Government of watching its P's and Q's in expenditures which might further aggravate the unfavorable balance of payments that the United States had suffered heavily since 1958, the Economic Bureau, in particular, was bedeviled by its obligation to help American enterprises abroad through its instructions to U.S. embassies and by the political dilemma arising from the reactions of foreign governments to American business initiatives overseas. The heavy payments deficits of the three years between 1958 and 1960, averaging $3.7 billion a year, had been met by various short-term stratagems which the State Department's attachés abroad had to help put into effect as far as they could. Problems in this field included the flow of dollars from American corporations and banks to their branch offices and affiliates abroad. As for the long-range program to bring the balance of payments within livable limits, the problem, in part, had been political. For example, 94 per cent of U.S. gold losses to foreign central banks from 1964 to 1967 was directly laid to conversion of dollars into gold by the Bank of France, as part of General de Gaulle's political offensive against the United States.

The balance-of-payments strategy looked to stimulating additional repatriated dividends and returns to the United States from the more than $42 billion in new plant, equipment, and working capital invested by Americans abroad since 1960. There was also the diplomatic task of encouraging foreigners to invest long-term funds in United States enterprises rather than keep almost $30 billion in short-term funds for quick and profitable turnover. The U.S. plan included stringent measures to insure that bilateral aid came back to the United States in the form of exports from the United States. This program succeeded in making the percentage of U.S. aid monies to foreign countries actually spent in the United States rise from 42 per cent in 1960 to over 85 per cent in 1967, and it was hoped that it would reach 97 per cent in 1968.

Much more important is the now-permanent export drive to sell U.S. goods overseas. American embassies and their economic staffs were being geared, starting with 1967, to put on the hard sell to potential customers. Commercial fairs were expanded, reaching an estimated 5 million persons in fiscal 1967, compared with only 1.6 million in 1963. The number of U.S. firms participating in these fairs also rose from 147 in 1963 to nearly 1,000 in 1967. Immense new quantities of information on the international trading interests of the 23,000 U.S. corporations were being gathered. Already, 13,000 of the corporations were exporting goods. The problem was to find areas of business opportunities for the remaining 10,000, which would go into export trade if they knew where the business was. While the Commerce Department and its Foreign Commercial Service bore the brunt of such operations, in the end, when it came to dealing with the foreigners, the Economic Bureau had to spur the U.S. embassies to take a more direct hand in smoothing the path for the businessmen, a procedure which traditional diplomats had been loath to undertake until recent years.

For the first time, the U.S. Government went into travel promotion to obtain its share of the $60 billion a year world tourist business, of which about $13 billion represented international tourism. In 1967, overseas visitors to the United States numbered more than 900,000, but the $4 billion spent by Americans in other countries exceeded the tourist revenues the United States received in 1966 by more than $1.8 billion.

U.S. travel abroad was a constant red-ink figure in the international payments books.

There never seemed to be an end to the balance-of-payments deficit, which had persisted every year since 1950 with one exception, 1957, when there was a half-billion dollar surplus. Small potatoes compared with American tourist expenditures, but still an item, was the increased number of American Social Security beneficiaries moving abroad and drawing their benefits there in recent years. In 1967 there were 181,171 beneficiaries living overseas, where their payments bought more retirement, in sixty-five different countries, Italy and Greece, with 35,835 and 14,956, respectively, being the favorite countries of settlement. It cost the payments deficit $150 million. The Veterans Administration accounted for most of the remainder of the $334 million listed in U.S. budget accounts as federal international transactions for the 1968 fiscal year.

The ubiquitous presence of Americans overseas and their apparently unshakable intention to stay in the outer world aroused the occasional suspicion of some political economists in the State Department that the supercautious technicians of Treasury and Commerce, not to mention the politicians of the Congress, had transformed the balance-of-payments problem possibly into a psychological complex. The new fundamental fact of life was that private U.S. entrepreneurs had by 1965 invested $76 billion overseas, $65 billion in long-term investments and $11 billion in short-term. The proposition was put forth that international production—not export trade—had become the most dynamic activity of world business. Overseas production accounted for four dollars of U.S. sales abroad compared with one dollar of U.S. exports, with overseas production rising more rapidly than export sales, to which, however, it was a major stimulant. To ascertain the latest statistics, before proper analysis and intellectual judgment could be made, the Commerce Department, in the latter part of 1967, undertook its first survey in ten years of direct U.S. investments abroad.

Foreign investments in the United States were, in 1965, $57 billion, of which $25 billion were long-term and $32 billion short-term. Of the latter, $18 billion were private investments and $14 billion were foreign government investments. Significantly, 90 per cent of U.S. capital going overseas was in the form of indirectly owned American plant and machinery. The conclusion emerged that American corporations operating personally in many countries of the world were developing a new people-to-people economics and a new diplomacy, in which old nationalistic traditions and insistence on narrow sovereignties of the past were no longer applicable.

The balance of payments, as far as the State Department was concerned, was something like the weather—one could talk about it, but there was not much one could do about it. The question of oil or petroleum was another thing altogether, however. Secretary of Interior Udall had the action responsibility for U.S. oil policy but, being more interested in parks and the wilderness, Interior sometimes had to be politely prodded by the State Department for decisions which would have immediate repercussions on the foreign policy stance of the United States, not only in the Middle East, the great oil source of the world, but also in the Western Hemisphere. This was as oil policy decisions related to Venezuela, Canada, and Mexico, the latter two because of their overland oil deliveries to the United States from contiguous North American terrain. Canadian and Mexican oil production is exempted from control under the U.S. mandatory oil import program, despite average imports of over 2 million barrels a day from Canada and 30,000 barrels a day from Mexico. The politically sensitive and carefully nurtured domestic oil program of the Government makes American consumers pay more for domestic oil than the going world price for foreign oil, which is about $1.25 a barrel cheaper than domestic oil. The Department of Interior, the nation's chief resource management agency, has a special responsibility for insuring that the country at all times has an adequate and secure supply of energy at the lowest possible cost. This includes, above all, oil and gas, which supply three fourths of the total U.S. energy requirements. These are increasing at such a rate that, between 1967 and 1980, at presently projected rates, the United States will use more petroleum energy than it has in the 108-year history of the oil industry.

Interior's oil import administration acts to restrict oil imports at the level at which such foreign imports are found to threaten the national security of the United States. The ambiguous area between protectionism for a necessary resource and actual national security considerations provides an umbrella under which independent oil dealers using U.S. domestic resources can wield considerable influence with Congress. They demanded in late 1967 that the Senate Finance Committee write into law Interior's administrative quota of 12.2 per cent of domestic production allowed for foreign oil imports. The fact that many of the great American oil companies were also major foreign producers, and hence importing their own petroleum, further complicated the domestic producers' difficulties of supply. Domestic producers were obtaining 30 per cent of the total U.S. crude production, or over 2.5 million barrels a day, from secondary operations, and exploration costs in the United States were very expensive, running from $35,000 to $59,000 a month to maintain crews in the fields and to digest their findings.

Because of the great political sensitivity of the oil business, there were at least eight federal departments, plus seven independent agencies and special boards, which all had a hand in oil decisions, not to overlook at least a dozen Congressional committees, with legitimate or professed responsibility for, or interest in, oil. Because he comes from Texas, the great oil state of the nation, President Johnson laid down a deliberate policy of having nothing personally to do with any oil decisions. Therefore, when a touchy case arises between the needs or demands of domestic oil interests and U.S. foreign policy requirements, the matter is quickly lifted out of the Interior Department to White House technicians and to the Office of Emergency Planning in the Executive Office of the President, as in the 1967 case of the price of asphalt, which happens to be an oil product of considerable importance to the vast federally financed highway construction program.

Concurrent international complications snarled the situation. Canadian oil entering the United States through the loophole of the overland clause, that is, oil not subject to import controls because it was traveling on the same contiguous terrain and not being imported from overseas, was being lapped up by independent oil companies which wanted all they could get to process more cheaply in adjacent Great Lakes and upper New York State refineries. Venezuelan imports were dropping because of Canadian competition, though East Coast refineries preferred Venezuelan oil as being less costly in delivery charges than Middle East oil. At the same time asphalt prices began to go up and, as was said, threatened federal highway costs.

An elaborate charade took care of the matter. Joseph Califano, the President's principal special assistant for domestic affairs, made several Solomon-like decisions on the practicalities of the affair. The Office of Emergency Planning unfurled the convenient umbrella of national security. Oil import quotas were relaxed. Canadian overland imports were left undisturbed. Asphalt prices were stabilized. Supplies of crude, or bunker, oil for New England and Florida power plants were eased. Venezuela got back a bit of its lost business. And everybody lived happily until the next time.

Vastly more serious for the Economic Bureau's direct and collateral interest in oil was the foreign policy crisis of the Middle East war and its aftermath in 1967, when the Arab oil companies shut down deliveries to western Europe and the Suez Canal was blocked by the Egyptians. The shutdown of the Canal, through which had passed 167 million tons of oil in 1966, going north from the Persian Gulf to the Mediterranean, coupled with the refusal of the Arab countries, Algeria, Libya, Iraq, and Saudi Arabia, to deliver oil to the West, caused an emergency. It was the duty of the United States to figure out how to meet the needs of its western European allies from alternative sources.

The Arab area provided 45 per cent of the Free World's oil, not only to western Europe but also to the Far East, Japan in particular. The United States had its own direct stake in approximately $1.5 billion a year in repatriated oil profits, and over $900 million in exports to Middle East countries in 1966, while the Arabs themselves gained $2.5 billion in annual income from oil royalty taxes and other revenues from Western markets.

Britain, above all, was severely affected, 72 per cent of her oil coming mainly from Kuwait, Libya, and Iraq. Important as oil was for short-term fuel energy needs to Britain, even more important was the vulnerability of the pound sterling to Arab attack. The most important single holder of sterling in the Middle East, Kuwait, alone held over a billion dollars' worth in the Bank of England. In the postwar period, Britain had had to overcome repeated sterling crises—in 1951, 1957, 1961, and 1964—and any new weakness in the pound at the very least would force Britain, America's closest ally, to take an overcautious line in foreign policy, thereby weakening U.S. diplomatic strength. The calamity of the pound's devaluation finally occurred in November 1967.

The defense of the pound during the Middle East crisis was a test of the resourcefulness of the State Department's Economic Bureau and the Middle East Bureau, coordinated by the Interagency Control Group. The task was to marshal the instrumentalities of the Interior Department and the Treasury Department in relieving Britain's oil needs and in sheltering the pound through the now famous "swap" currency arrangement. It was borrowing from Peter to pay Paul, as a temporary palliative for the pound until the immediate danger was over, for every attack on the pound was also a disguised attack on the U.S. dollar.

The Middle East crisis brought home a number of relevant realities to the oil technicians and economic diplomats of the State Department. Naturally, there was no question of abandoning the vast U.S. investments and profits of American-exploited Arab oil in the Middle East. However, the nations that depended upon Arab oil so exclusively would inevitably have to seek new ways to cushion the potential effects of future crises which seemed fated to recur in the Middle East. The Arab oil embargoes had disclosed that, in the long run, oil was a finite commodity and that the term of indispensable reliance upon that form of energy was no longer absolute. Oil would always be needed as a lubricant, it seemed evident. But a new and alternate source of energy, at least for the United States, was in the offing, namely, power generated by nuclear energy. British Foreign Minister George Brown, apropos, once quoted his great predecessor, Ernest Bevan, as saying: "Give me another ton of coal, and I can make a foreign policy for Britain." Brown was all too cognizant of the fact that the power which economic strength represented in the modern world was the principal raw material which could be translated into effective foreign policy.

The technological development attracting the close attention of U.S. and British diplomats was the report of the U.S. Atomic Energy Commission that, in 1966, almost half, or twenty-one, of the orders for new steam-generating equipment in the United States called for nuclear power. The AEC estimated the cost of the publicly owned TVA's power plant at 2.37 mills per kilowatt hour. On the basis of private financing, the TVA rate would be about 3.5 mills per kwh. In 1967, the Jersey Central nuclear power plant was producing power at approximately 4 mills per kwh. To achieve competitive nuclear power in high-cost areas like New England, the Middle Atlantic states, and California, where the cost of conventional fuel was 35 cents per million BTU, nuclear power would have to be provided at from 6 to 7 mills per kwh. Therefore, nuclear power generation had virtually arrived, with U.S. industry having spent or spending, by the end of 1967, over $4 billion on nuclear power projects. All the projected plants were scheduled for operation before the end of 1973, and by the turn of the century, the Commission predicted, almost all new large generating plants would probably be nuclear-powered. Discounting to some degree any overstatement, it was nevertheless clear that nuclear power as an alternate energy was on the eve of becoming a new weapon in the foreign policy arsenal of the United States.

Modern technology, as a matter of fact, had been a weapon of U.S. world leadership since World War II, because of the astronomical sums invested in research and development both by the Federal Government and by the great business corporations whose size alone allowed them to engage in such vast ventures. The combination of size and technology in Europe was sufficiently threatening to the foreign business community as to become a political problem. In all western Europe, twenty American firms accounted for two thirds of the American investment. Their scale and technology led to American domination of key foreign industries, such as the manufacture of carbon black in Britain and France and of computers in Germany, Britain, and France. Compared with the American giants, the largest European corporations were merely middle-sized. For example, General Motors' sales in 1964 were larger than the gross national product of the Netherlands or of Belgium.

Because of this axiomatic rationale of technology, the senior officers of the State Department's Economic Bureau were intensely interested in patents, particularly international cooperation to bring order out of the chaos of inventions and would-be inventions. In the fall of 1966, the United States asked the United International Bureau for the Protection of Intellectual Property, known among the *cognoscenti* as BIRPI, to make an urgent study of duplications in patent applications. To this end, the United States itself had entered into pilot study agreements with Germany, Switzerland, France, Japan, Austria, and other countries. A proposed patent cooperation treaty was published in mid-1967. In December the executive committee of BIRPI, which is the secretariat for the Convention of Paris for the Protection of Industrial Property, to which the United States and seventy-six other countries adhered, hammered the treaty into final shape in order to be presented to the various parliaments for ratification. A key feature would be a standard format whereby an applicant could file a single international application which could be used by each designated country as a basis for issuing a national patent.

In 1965, the United States alone received 94,632 applications for patents. It was estimated that more than 50 per cent of the 650,000 patent applications filed around the world were duplicates of other applications. In 1972, for example, of the estimated 100,000 patent applications expected to be filed in the United States, 30,000 will originate abroad and be duplicates of foreign applications. In turn, 30,000 of the 70,000 inventions first applied for in the United States will also be filed in an average of five foreign countries, giving rise to 150,000 additional applications world-wide. The multiple filing and examining of applications clogs the dockets of patent offices and causes unnecessary expenses and delays for businessmen engaged in international trade, thereby creating another barrier to the expansion of trade. To be clarified in the process will be the confusion between "first to file" and "first to invent." Seventy-four of the seventy-seven countries belonging to the World Patent Union place priority on a "first to file" basis. Only the United States, Canada, and the Philippines place priority on a "first to invent" basis.

It is difficult to overstate the importance of the relationship between technological change, as represented by patents, and international trade. Decreasing exports and low technology products can be replaced with increasing exports and high-technology products. A recent Commerce Department study illustrated this point concerning U.S. exports of yarn and fabrics. In 1956, $187 million worth of cotton and wool, low-technology items, were exported, compared with only $125 million worth of those products in 1965. But in the same period, the export of high-technology synthetic fibers increased from $158 million to $241 million, resulting in a net gain in exports of U.S. yarn and fabrics of over $20 million during the decade.

Technology is a great boon to the balance-of-payments deficit, stimulating income to the United States for technical know-how, data, licenses and patents, and royalties. The Organization for Economic Cooperation and

Development (OECD) calculated in 1961 that the United States had a favorable balance of $514 million in technology, having received $577 million while paying out only $66 million to other countries for their technological expertise.

The companion field of telecommunications was another major interest of the Economic Bureau, and one that was destined to grow. The Bureau kept a fatherly eye on the operations of Communications Satellite Corporation, or COMSAT, which launched the world's first commercial communications satellite at Cape Kennedy on April 6, 1965, as a first step toward a world-wide network of satellites linking as many nations of the world as possible. COMSAT's first satellite, called the Early Bird, was an eighty-five-pound cylinder jammed with microcircuits and sailing through the heavens in synchronous orbit, 22,300 miles above the equator, at a speed which keeps pace with the rotation of the earth. It handles as routine commercial traffic phone calls, TV, teletype, and other transmissions. As a para-statal commercial organization, whose charter is spelled out by the Congress, COMSAT comes under the constant purview of the Government, including the State Department, as regards its relations with other countries. Thus, the Economic Bureau participated in examining COMSAT agreements with communications entities in other countries to share the ownership and use of the commercial satellite system. Fifty-eight countries of the 124 nations which are members of the International Telecommunications Union, a United Nations specialized agency, had signed the pact by late 1967. The co-signers, in effect, had formed a partnership to own the space segment, but not the ground stations. The organization was to be known as the International Telecommunications Satellite Consortium, or INTELSAT. COMSAT, by the original agreement, would own at least 50.6 per cent of the total stock.

Such Buck Rogers adventures in the sky were a comparatively rare relief for the usually more mundane experiences of the State Department economists in matters relating to land and sea. As for the latter, the maritime and shipbuilding industries have been a perennial headache to the State Department. Private entrepreneurs of the sea seemed to have consistently made the State Department a favorite whipping boy through the years. Since 1965 there has been a major argument between the Government and the shipbuilding industry over the proposal of an inter-agency maritime task force to build U.S. flag merchant vessels in foreign shipyards. This raised a great cry of anguish among American shipbuilders. As the custodian of the nation's international interests, the State Department and the Economic Bureau's Office of Maritime Affairs had a professional interest in the national security and foreign relations aspects of the proposal to build U.S. ships overseas at lower costs, and as a means to give needed business to worthy allies. The shipbuilding industry marshaled its forces in the President's Maritime Advisory Committee, and with Congressional opposition against the export of market and job opportunities for U.S. shipyards and their workers, not to mention the raising of the balance-of-international-payments specter, the Government proposal was, if not defeated, at least greatly retarded. The affair recalled the fracas after World War II, when the Navy League and the maritime labor unions protested against the State Department's attempts to reduce the vast accumulation of wartime surplus shipping in the United States by the cry, "The State Department always wants to give everything away."

Just as in the Vietnam war State and Defense were front-line allies, in the battle for the export market State and Commerce were in the forward echelon. In 1967, U.S. exports were expected to rise to $31 billion, topping the 1966 record high of $29.4 billion, which, in turn, had surpassed the 1965 record of $27 billion. Despite wars and unrest, the world was an expanding market and for 1970 a global trade volume of $250 billion was anticipated, compared with $192 billion in 1966. The United States was the world's largest market and largest trading nation, though exports comprised only 4 per cent of the U.S. gross national product, compared with 11 per cent for France, 12 per cent for Japan, 15 per cent for Britain, and 16 per cent, the top score, for West Germany.

But there was a serious hitch to the export prospects. It concerned inflation and the fact that the rise in prices in the United States was not similarly occurring in the other industrial countries which were America's great competitors. This lent even more urgency to the need to utilize the available instrumentalities to control inflation: on the monetary side, interest rates and liquidity, or readily available funds, and on the fiscal side, budgets and taxes, already in full public debate. As the economists knew better than anyone else, exports and inflation controls had to balance like a well-designed mobile; if one part dipped, another part would have to rise, to compensate.

The U.S. export surpluses since 1964 had amounted to over $15 billion, creating the velvet, or extra cushion, of monies which allowed the United States to engage in foreign ventures, economic aid, and military war. If the 1967 increases in U.S. prices were not halted or rolled back, the year's rise could amount to nearly 6 per cent, almost double the 3 per cent that the economists considered to be verging on real inflation.

The prospect of export battles to come, amid the handicaps of an unsettled domestic scene, was less than exhilarating, particularly after the combat fatigue of four annual sessions of the Kennedy Round Tariff Negotiations, begun in Geneva in May 1964 and ended on June 30, 1967. The talks, which were the largest single trade negotiation in modern times, culminating a thirty-three-year movement in the United States toward freer trade, involved over $28 billion worth of trade in give-and-take by the fifty-five countries concerned. Assistant Secretary of State for Economic Affairs Solomon, who had realistically predicted reductions on only 25 to 30 per cent instead of the full 50 per cent that the U.S. authorization allowed, told a House Committee in the spring of 1967:

> The Kennedy Round is the most difficult negotiation of any the United States has had since World War II. It has been tremendously complicated by the Common Market countries and the compromises that go on between them, before we get to negotiate with them. They do not have a negotiator to bargain. Every time we say something is not good enough, they have to go back, and six governments have to meet to decide on the answer for us, and it is all very difficult.

The U.S. tariff cut was 35 per cent, compared with an equal 35 per cent reciprocity by the Common Market, 38 per cent by Britain, 30 per cent by Japan, and 24 per cent by Canada. For U.S. consumers there were lowered duties on champagnes, Scotch whisky, brandy, perfume, bone chinaware, sewing machines, television sets, record players, motorcycles, automobiles, yachts, binoculars, luggage, handbags, shotguns, and cameras, all grist to the high-consumption U.S. economy. The United States had cut tariffs affecting nearly $8 billion of its industrial and agricultural imports and obtained tariff concessions on a roughly equivalent volume of exports.

In May 1967, Under Secretary of State Rostow said prophetically: "If we fail in Geneva, restrictionism will once again become epidemic. In one sense, the Kennedy Round is a last stage of the process of undoing the damage to the world economy caused by the restrictive policies most of us adopted in response to the great depression of the thirties. It would be a costly setback if these efforts failed."

The U.S. tariff negotiating efforts did not fail. They never reached the jubilant hopes voiced at the time of the 1962 trade extension act, but the show was not yet over. In October 1967, the *Wall Street Journal* reported: "The Johnson administration, less than four months after celebrating the historic reduction of U.S. and foreign trade barriers at the completion of the prolonged tariff bickering in Geneva, is now maneuvering—defensively and almost desperately—to hold back a tide of protectionist legislation."

The newspaper comment pinpointed an extraordinary state of affairs that had developed: an atmosphere compounded of currents motivated by feelings, actual or latent, of anti-Vietnam war, anti-civil rights, anti-administration, sometimes it seemed anti-everything, a generalized anxiety about inflation and the cost of living. There was widespread disorientation in the country. Protectionist forces saw it as a great opportunity to wear down, if not wreck, the liberal trade milestone of 1962 and to return almost to the Smoot-Hawley tariff of the 1930's, putting the nation on the road to isolationist economics and, conceivably, in its wake, to Fortress America foreign and military policies.

The protectionist reaction was no series of isolated drives, but a massive and concerted campaign all across the trade front. Bills were introduced covering products ranging from textiles, lead and zinc, oil, meat, and dairy products to mink skins, strawberries, and baseball gloves. The opposition was led craftily by the Senate Minority Leader Everett M. Dirksen, Republican of Illinois and by Senator Russell B. Long, Senate Minority Whip and Chairman of the powerful Senate Finance Committee. Long introduced legislation to impose a 12.2 per cent quota (of domestic production) on foreign petroleum imports. His bill had been cosponsored by thirty other Senators. Obviously, Long was not particularly free-trade-minded at that moment. Neither was Senate Majority Leader Mike Mansfield, who was always worrying about the copper situation and the miners in his home state of Montana and who followed, with anxious eyes, copper imports from Chile.

Southern textile manufacturers wailed that the new textile import levels would mean the loss of nearly 250,000 jobs. A textile bill introduced by Senator Ernest F. Hollings, Democrat of South Carolina, was cosponsored by 68 Senators. A similar bill in the House had been backed by 135 Representatives, and all 13 Governors of the Southern states supported it.

The steel industry demanded relief, lamenting that steel imports had risen from $162 million worth in 1957 to $1.1 billion worth in 1966 and that 11 per cent of the steel used in the United States was imported, compared with 1 per cent in 1957. In 1950, the steel makers pointed out, there were only thirty-two steel-producing nations in the world. In 1965, there were fifty-five. World exports of steel had risen from 23 million tons in 1955 to 51 million tons in 1965. Twenty per cent of these exports were now entering the United States, which had paradoxically become the world's largest importer of steel.

The steel industry, further, was prosecuting a campaign to prohibit the use of imported steel in any project financed by tax money, state, county, or municipal. Drives were already under way in Pennsylvania, Ohio, California, and Massachusetts challenging the authority of the State Department, which maintained that such action was unconstitutional state intrusion into foreign trade policies over which the national Government had exclusive jurisdiction.

On the chemical front, there was a variant in the impending battle. The Kennedy Round negotiators had made a contingent deal in negotiating duties on chemicals. In a two-phase deal, the United States had agreed to cut duties by an average of 43 per cent on almost all chemicals imported into the United States and in return to receive reductions averaging 26 per cent on $900 million of U.S. chemical exports. The proviso was that the United States had tentatively agreed, subject to approval by Congress, to repeal ASP, or the American selling price duty formula, on certain imports into the United States of benzenoid inorganic chemicals or coal tar, mostly in dyes, pigments, plasticisers, and pharmaceuticals. The issue had proved to be the most controversial in the entire Kennedy Round between the Americans and the foreigners.

The $3 billion benzenoid chemical industry, however, had a major factor in its favor. The other protectionist groups were attempting to introduce barriers. The chemicals, on the other hand, had only to resist repeal of the law which had been favoring them since 1922. Therefore, they were in the favorable position of being the "ins" and found it easier to look to their defenses. For forty-five years, the benzenoid chemicals had been profiting by the protection given to them by Congress as an infant chemical industry. The tariffs were added on to the American wholesale price. This unique protective device applied, and still does, to only three other products, namely, rubber-sole footwear, certain canned clams, and wool knit gloves. The effective rates of duty on the benzenoids are above 100 per cent, sometimes with a peak of 172 per cent.

Such an industrial advantage naturally was highly worthy of defense to its owners, who are gathered in a trade association which includes some of the pre-eminent names in American industry—E. I. duPont de Nemours & Company, Union Carbide Corporation, Monsanto Company, Dow Chemical Company, Allied Chemical Corporation, Owen Mathieson Chemical Corporation, among others. The Europeans had bitterly complained about the highly discriminatory nature of the ASP. American industrialists, in turn, voiced their grievances about European hidden tariffs in the form of border taxes, turnover, or value-added, taxes, and other price-equalizing devices which, in effect, subsidized native exports and made foreign imports costly.

Behind the loud outcries about alleged damage from imports were deeper and more disguised noises, voiced in some sectors of the American business community and discreetly echoed in some sectors of the Government and in Congress. This was the tempting prospect of international cartels in which world markets could be divided through international accords between governments, a practice not unfamiliar to

Europeans in the past. One model for this was the present international "orderly marketing agreement" for cotton textiles and apparel, to which more than twenty countries adhered in rationalizing textile imports and exports. Some steel executives were interested in such arrangements, as were some textile manufacturers who would like to apply stabilization to synthetic fibers and woolens. Senator Mansfield of Montana, it was felt, would not be reluctant to see a similar formula applied to the world copper industry, the better to protect his Montana miners.

As the various sets of tariffs erectors mobilized, Ambassador William M. Roth, the President's special representative for trade negotiations at Geneva, rang the firebell against the rising protectionist fire. He pointed out that the hard-won games at the Kennedy Round appeared to be "an agreement that was successful on paper but that was nullified even before its provisions could take effect." He said that the protectionists' bills pending in Congress would affect $3.6 billion in U.S. imports, causing other nations to undertake reprisals on a commensurate scale and launching a possibly disastrous trade war.

Amid this anarchy of special interests, the role of the State Department Economic Bureau was downgraded to its staff advisory functions, as the domestic-foreign crisis of trade, like diplomatic crises, escalated to the top levels of the State Department's seventh-floor executives and to the White House, where a beleaguered President, already beset by a frustrating war in southeast Asia, was now being attacked on an unexpected flank. Secretary Rusk, like the U.S. Cavalry coming to the rescue, personally volunteered to lead the counteroffensive. He spearheaded a team of five Cabinet members against the flock of import curb bills. Rusk's colleagues were the Secretaries of Commerce, Agriculture, Labor, and Interior. Rusk bit off his words as he vigorously cautioned the Congress that raising U.S. import barriers would not only set off retaliation against American goods by foreign nations, but, "Many foreign governments would be likely to make it as painful as possible for us, hoping thereby to bring us to our senses." These prospects, Rusk said, would be "nothing short of appalling."

Repercussions from the foreigners were not slow in coming as the trade-wind storm threatened to shipwreck so-called Western unity on the shoals of hard cash. Canada and Japan, two of the United States' largest export markets, would be sharply affected by the proposed import bills. The four Scandinavian nations—Denmark, Norway, Finland, and Sweden—jointly expressed their concern over the Congressional proposals as grave-faced ambassadors sought explanations from State Department officials. European, Latin American, and some Asian ministers called to their chancelleries several American ambassadors abroad and raised eyebrows and tapped nervous fingers concerning the threat of American reneging on the Kennedy Round agreements. These covered 6,000 trade items annually imported into the United States.

Japan, already the industrial dynamo of the Far East, was on the road to becoming a future great power and one which the United States was delicately wooing as a possible ally against Communist China and a guarantor of security in the Pacific. Japan was not amused. The Japanese pointed out that they had subscribed to the Kennedy Round, confident that they could meet the freer tariffs because of their own price elasticity; they could still export more in consumer goods than they would have to import in capital goods. Japan accounted for some 60 per cent of U.S. exports to the Far East. In 1966, Japan bought $2.4 billion, and further trade increases were in the offing. In 1967 alone, Japan bought over a billion dollars' worth of feed grain, soy beans, wheat, cotton, rice, livestock products, and tobacco. Moreover, the Japanese had been very cooperative in making "voluntary agreements" not to sell beyond a certain amount of their products in the United States in order not to further arouse protectionist displeasure. These "voluntarily restrained" Japanese imports into the United States included cotton textiles, ceramics, transistor radios ($94 million worth in 1966), sewing machines, tuna fish, stainless-steel flatware, baseball gloves, and silk.

The Latin Americans were aggrieved and so informed the commercial and economic attachés in U.S. embassies overseas and the Economic Bureau and the high officers of the State Department in Washington. Mexico was definitely put out about the prospective import restrictions on her important exports of lead and zinc to the United States. Argentina, Brazil, Paraguay, and Uruguay, exporting mostly canned corned beef and cooked frozen meats to the United States, were alarmed at the proposed U.S. meat import restrictions.

Brazil and the United States, also in late 1967, were having a parallel foreign economic policy argument over coffee, of which Brazil, the world's largest producer, sells more than 40 per cent of the world's exports, while the United States drinks 52 per cent of the coffee sold in the world. The contretemps occurred over soluble, or instant, coffee, from the American popularity of which Brazil had profited by exporting $20 million worth a year to the United States. The fact that coffee entered the United States free of duty irritated American producers of instant coffee, who complained of unfair competition. The problem was left to the Council of the International Coffee Organization, which represents thirty-seven producing and twenty-two importing countries and which regulates allocation of the world surplus of 160 million bags, which weigh 132 pounds each.

The verbal back-and-forth barely disguised one irreducible fact: the United States needed the world even more, perhaps, than the world needed the United States—if the American Republic intended to continue to be what it was, namely, a nation of advanced technology, racing into the twenty-first century. The United States depended exclusively or heavily on imports of some thirty-nine essential metals and minerals, which had to come from overseas sources. The following list shows the percentage of typical key materials from foreign sources:

Aluminum	88	Mica	99
Antimony	95	Molybdenum	0
Asbestos	96	Nickel	91
Beryllium	100	Platinum	97
Cadmium	57	Rhenium	0
Chromite	100	Rutile	91
Cobalt	83	Selenium	23
Columbium	100	Silver	71
Copper	11	Sulfur	0
Fluorspar	74	Tantalum	100
Iron ore	33	Tellurium	11
Lead	53	Tin	100
Magnesium	0	Tungsten	51
Manganese	99	Vanadium	0
Mercury	36	Zinc	52

The whole earth was a provider of raw materials for the gigantic maw of the American economy. Rubber, tin, mica, chrome, and titanium came from the Far East. Latin America supplied copper, lead, tin, zinc, tantalum, and columbium. Africa was the provider of cobalt, industrial diamonds, graphite, manganese, and, again, chrome. The raw materials of fifty nations fed the American industrial machine. For the telephone alone, forty-eight different materials had to be imported from sixteen countries. Forty-four imported materials went into automobiles. The women of America needed lithium as a lubricant in their lipsticks. Fluorspar was brought from abroad to be used in the manufacture of steel furnaces and for insecticides. There were also perishable commodities imported to provide the cream in the American consumption society— coffee, tea, cocoa, bananas, and a large part of the sugar, spices, olives, shellfish, and tuna, not to mention three quarters of the newsprint.

The high value of the imported materials could be noted in their end uses. Manganese went into steel alloys, photographic chemicals, pharmaceuticals, stainless steel, animal and poultry feed, and coloring agents. Asbestos was necessary for clutch facings and brake linings. Cobalt went into jet engines, rocket nozzles, gas turbines, magnetos, and steel alloys. Antimony was a necessary ingredient of storage batteries, plastics, tracer bullets, and smoke generators. Beryllium, of which this country possessed no native deposits, was indispensable to nuclear reactors, gyroscopes, heat shields, rotor blades, solar cells, and optical parts. The United States paid out $21 billion in 1965 and $25.5 billion in 1966 for its total imports.

It was therefore understandable why the United States enacted the Defense Production Act after the Soviet Sputnik in 1957 and directed the General Services Administration to gather a national stockpile of vital and strategic materials. Every attempt was made to find deposits of the critical materials on American soil. The U.S. Government contributed up to 50 per cent of the total allowable costs of exploration for some thirty-six minerals in which it was interested. The list of minerals eligible for Government financial assistance:

Antimony	Mercury
Asbestos	Mica (strategic)
Bauxite	Molybdenum
Beryllium	Monazite
Bismuth	Nickel
Cadmium	Platinum
Chromite	Quartz crystal (piezoelectric)
Cobalt	Rare earths
Columbine	Rutile
Copper	Selenium
Corundum	Silver
Diamond (industrial)	Sulfur
Fluorspar	Talc (black steatite)
Gold	Tantalum
Graphite (crucible flakes)	Tellurium
Iron ore	Thorium
Kyanite (strategic)	Tin
Manganese	Uranium

In May 1967, the total market value of all the materials in the national stockpile kept by the General Services Administration, or GSA, was approximately $6.4 billion. The ninety different materials amounted to 48 million tons, were stored in 150 warehouses, and occupied almost 90 million square feet of space. Of the $6.4 billion, only $3.1 billion was actually stocked under the strategic materials list made up by the Department of Commerce, in consultation with the nation's industries and Government departments such as Defense and NASA. This meant that $3.3 billion worth of materials was in excess for stockpiling needs.

The Economic Bureau of the State Department got into the act in both surpluses and shortages of stockpile materials. In 1967 there was a severe shortage of nickel, U.S. demand exceeding available supply by about 75 million pounds. Copper was also in short supply but seemed to have balanced out, though a disruption of transportation facilities in Zambia, in Africa, might possibly lead to another copper pinch. Obviously, the State Department's economic officers had a job to do in easing these matters. Sticky situations arose when the GSA, after consulting with the Office of Emergency Planning, disposed of surplus stocks on the open market. This procedure invariably went under the personal scrutiny of President Johnson, whose aim was to obtain as much revenue as possible from the sales. The Economic Bureau at times had to step in to restrain the GSA from dumping rubber and tin on the open market, thus upsetting potential sales for the low-developed countries, whose principal dependence for income was on the sale of such raw materials. As an ultimate resort, it had frequent recourse to the President in order to protest such sales or to ease their effect on the LDC's own balance-of-payments problems.

The gray world of the "dismal science" had denizens who could put the most wide-awake interlocutor to sleep with their monotone and singular ability to reduce a description of Sophia Loren to avoirdupois in a container. Though economics is the heavy diet of meat and potatoes for much of the State Department's daily repast, there is also available an endless diplomatic bill of fare with enough spice and sauce to awaken the most jaded palates in the startling diversity of today's modern interdependent world, whose constant variety produces unexpected *plats du jour*. The literal interdependence of the world is a result of the shrinkage of time and space brought about by jet aircraft and electronic communications. In a jet airplane, the flight from Washington, D.C., to Tokyo, Japan, 6,850 statute miles distant, can now be made in 19 hours, whereas in propeller aircraft the trip took 38 hours and 15 minutes, both types of planes making four stops each en route. New Delhi, 8,054 miles from Kennedy Airport in New York, can be reached in 22 hours and 35 minutes in a jet against 40 hours and 15 minutes in a prop plane, both making seven stops. In a jet, it takes 11 hours to cover the 5,676 miles to Tel Aviv from New York, while in a prop it took 25 hours, both planes making one stop. To European destinations, nonstop, the contrast is even sharper, as the following schedule of flights from New York indicates:

To	Miles	Jet	Prop
London	3,456	6 hrs. 40 min.	13 hrs. 40 min.
Paris	3,621	7 hrs.	14 hrs. 30 min.
Rome	4,277	8 hrs.	17 hrs.
Madrid	3,588	6 hrs. 50 min.	14 hrs. 20 min.
Frankfurt	3,858	7 hrs. 30 min.	15 hrs. 35 min.
Geneva	3,862	7 hrs. 25 min.	15 hrs. 35 min.

One consequence of this shrinkage of the globe is that officers of the State Department and other Government agencies with overseas responsibilities in 1967, for example, participated in well over six hundred multilateral conferences, compared with only fourteen in one year two decades ago. Every working day the Department is represented at from fifteen to twenty meetings somewhere in the world.

In another instance of closer ties with foreign lands, it is now possible to dial London and Paris direct on the telephone for some eighty New York subscribers who regularly use such telephone service, like news magazines, broadcasting networks, major oil companies, and banks. The service will be extended gradually to the general citizenry by 1970.

The common needs of men as neighbors on the planet basically prescribe interdependence as a way of life. The United States and Canadian weather bureaus were linked by a high-speed teleprinter circuit capable of carrying 1,050 words a minute, ten times the previous rate. The U.S. weather service supplied Castro's Cuba with hurricane warnings from the Miami Weather Bureau despite mutual antagonisms. It is hoped that a World Weather Watch, a coordinated global system for forecasting weather, will be operational by 1971; it is to be run by the World Meteorological Organization, a United Nations specialized agency.

Through two global wars and a spate of lesser ones, the United States, the Soviet Union, Italy, and Japan have without interruption operated the International Polar Motion Service. Since May 1900, when the service was begun, this organization has measured the wobbles of the earth on its north-south axis by taking sightings four times a night on eighteen pairs of stars through six-foot telescopes, all of the same type. Scientists have been trying to determine whether there is any uniformity to the shimmy of the earth as it circles the geographical North Pole, zigzagging at a maximum spread of seventy-two feet over a fourteen-month period. The five astronomical stations, all near the parallel of 39 degrees 08 minutes north latitude, are at Gaithersburg, Maryland, and Ukiah, California, in the United States; Kitab, near Samarkand in Turkestan, in the Soviet Union; Carloforte, Sardinia, in Italy; and Mizusawa, Iwate-Ken Province, in Japan.

Symbolic of the technological unity of the earth is Radio Station WWV, operated by the National Bureau of Standards of the U.S. Department of Commerce and broadcasting continuously since 1923. Its scientifically exact time and frequency signals are tuned into by listeners on all five continents of the globe—power companies to keep their output at exactly sixty cycles per second, satellites tracking stations to synchronize their clocks, symphony orchestras to tune their instruments, and radio stations to make sure they are at their correct spot on the dial.

The monotonous hit program consists, in essence, of a one-second tick-tick-tick, like a slow-speed metronome, which with proper equipment can be refined down to a thousandth of a second.

The global interdependence emphasized in President Kennedy's 1962 Philadelphia speech was no new notion to American diplomats, however. Secretary of State Elihu Root first stressed the concept in 1906. He said: "No nation can live unto itself alone and continue to live. There is not one of our countries that cannot benefit the others. There is not one that will not gain by the prosperity, the peace, the happiness of all. We wish for no victories but those of peace, for no territory except our own, for no sovereignty except the sovereignty over ourselves."

Though the countries of the world were becoming more interdependent, they did not always recognize it at once because of their own nationalistic blinders and internal needs to insure their sense of independence. Interdependence, nevertheless, added a great new dimension to the labors of diplomacy. A hugely augmented workload arose from the back-and-forth of nations as the demands of other nations affected U.S. policy and, in turn, the United States sought foreign support or the U.S. domestic situation necessitated U.S. initiatives to modify or deflect foreign actions. In the friction of the interplay arose the fission of dissent, and sometimes disgruntlement, as outgoing initiatives from the United States bounced back in repercussions from the nations with which the United States had diplomatic relations, not to mention those like Communist China or, temporarily, some Arab states with which it did not have official relationships.

For the State Department, the intermingling of issues and problems was like playing pingpong on a trampoline. For Americans it was an utterly absorbing spectacle as the imagination played on the images created by the written and spoken word and, above all, by the staccato welter of life thrown at the viewer by the omnipresent television set. The exotic and the familiar were bedfellows. An innocent thing here could turn out to be an abomination there. For the United States, plane disasters all over the world were front-page news, because an American might have been riding on that airplane. Racial disturbances in America singed guilty consciences in Britain, which also had widespread discrimination against human beings with dark skins. Western Europe was irritated at the United States' preoccupation with the Vietnam war, which was a disturbance to the complacent prosperity of the continent. Europe wanted to live and let live, and not be bothered by other people's problems. But the sheer existence or acts of Americans could not be ignored. The British were enraged in 1953 when Secretary of State Dulles presented Egyptian President Gamal Abdel Nasser a pistol as a gift from President Eisenhower. Dulles never thought of the weapon's symbolism as the British and the Egyptians were mounting the road to the Suez crisis.

Western Europeans grumbled at the "brain drain," 100,000 skilled, technical, or professional workers having emigrated to the United States between 1949 and 1966. Between July 1963 and June 1964, the exodus of foreign scientists, engineers, and physicians to the United States numbered 7,728, raising the grumbles to cries of indignation. The rest of the world was no less vocal in its displeasure. In 1965, instead of returning home, 11,000 of 19,000 foreign students in the United States planned to stay on in America for the higher-paying jobs available.

American pressures were still causing political crises in Europe. Similar to U.S. insistence on the formation of the European Defense Community, or EDC, in 1953, which created the greatest internal crisis in France since the days of Munich in 1938, U.S. insistence on military budget contributions at the LBJ ranch in Texas in December 1966 helped overthrow the frustrated West German Government of Ludwig Erhard. It ushered in the Kiessinger Government and a new and more independent attitude in West Germany after twenty years of neurosis as the man in the middle, between Russia and America.

Europe and America had begun to affect each other from World War II onward. The impact of Coca Cola, chewing gum, juke boxes, Kleenex, American movies, blue jeans, comic strips like "Blondie and Dagwood," cigarettes, American automobiles, hamburgers, snack bars, neon lights, gas stations, supermarkets, and drugstores was not to be denied.

American-type political campaigns caught on in Europe. In Germany both Christian Democrats and Social Democrats copied President Kennedy's "New Frontier" style of appealing to the voters, as did British Prime Minister Wilson's Labor Party. French politicians also began to find the direct approach to the voter profitable at the polls. American political campaign management firms opened offices in London and Paris, adapting market research methods to politics. In the 1967 South Vietnamese election as well, candidates who had been educated in the United States campaigned with sound trucks, political pamphlets, bales of campaign posters, and precinct organizations.

There was old-style American politicking also in the foreign countries, bringing shocked surprise to ingenuous Americans. The chicaneries would have been envied by Tammany Hall or the Kansas City Pendergast machine. Italian Communists were extremely clever in challenging voters of the democratic parties at the polling places. South Korea specialized in trick balloting. There was the "sandwich vote," in which a batch of unfriendly votes was placed between "safe" ones and the entire package recorded for the ruling party. The "piano" vote meant smearing inky fingers on suspected unfriendly ballots, rendering them invalid. The "owl" vote was counted at night, after the lights were out.

American managerial expertise was imported into Europe, with professional institutes being set up in Britain, France, Germany, and Italy. Retailers in Europe and particularly in the developing countries discovered the big American department store chains as choice markets in volume for their products, including the hard-grained reality of the Americans' exacting merchandise requirements.

Europeans were grateful for the swift efficiency of the American wire services in providing spot news and photographs on a practically instant basis, thanks to American technical ingenuity. American jazz was universal in appeal, and American-type traffic jams grew as Europe prospered. In the reverse flow, French perfumes and wines, British miniskirts, sports cars and Scotch whisky, German cameras and automobiles, Italian and French styles in clothes and hairdos, French, Italian, Dutch, and Danish cheeses, European antique furniture and artfully fabricated reproductions, old silver, and soccer—a new mass audience game in the United States but the leading spectator sport of Europe—all made massive inroads into America.

As the American nation matured to world responsibilities and power, the attendant vices appeared. Tipping in the United States grew almost as shameless as in Europe. Private business lobbies flourished in Washington as they had for decades in Europe. Social Security charges and fringe benefits in America crept up and up as they had long done in Europe.

What happened in one part of the world had an immediate and intimate reaction in many other places. A locust plague in Cairo made wheat prices rise in Chicago and ultimately cost the American consumers one cent more on a loaf of bread. An American steel strike could cause temporary shortages of steel in European plants making spare parts for NATO armies. World-girdling rumors flourished in the recurrent though fleeting presence of U.S. visitors, planes, and ships in foreign capitals and ports. Grain on a U.S. vessel in Alexandria, Egypt, was being "secretly" transshipped to China, to Russia, to Cuba—starting a chain reaction of garbled reports which eventually the State Department had to unscramble.

U.S. foreign aid food policies became an issue in India's general election in early 1967, as President Johnson imposed stricter requirements before shipping grain. The Indian Government was also perturbed over a New York Greenwich Village play spoofing Prime Minister Indira Gandhi. Indian Embassy officials held owlish conversations with the State Department, which, *bien entendu*, was "most distressed" but helpless. The play,

Indira Gandhi's Daring Device, depicted a tumult of starving untouchables crying for food, whereupon Mrs. Gandhi's aide solved the country's population explosion by freezing the populace. A theater critic described the play as "madness, no doubt about it, but also immensely theatrical and exciting as it is mindless and irrelevant."

A seesaw was in progress in 1967 between Washington and Tokyo. Japan was getting more prosperous by the minute. Tokyo campaigned politely but persistently for the return of Okinawa and the Ryukyu Islands, occupied by the United States as military bases since the end of World War II. Japan's boom was comparable to that of West Germany in the 1950's. Japan had no defense forces to support and hence could invest heavily in economic expansion. U.S. Senator Edmund S. Muskie, Democrat of Maine, in Japan on a visit, openly warned the Japanese that they were dragging their feet in failing to do their share in providing economic aid to the less developed countries. The Japanese Government was sharply divided on the question of Japanese foreign aid, which had a not unfamiliar ring to American ears. It was even more surprising to find in the Soviet Union considerable internal criticism of the Soviet aid program to foreign countries. Russians' objections were published in letters to the editor. Kremlin wall scrawls abused foreign aid, employing the recognizable phrase, "Money going down the drain," and adding a Russian twist, "to a bottomless pit." Soviet foreign aid since 1954 apparently was not quite promoting the Communist-type state capitalism in the emerging countries that the Soviets had expected.

The State Department duly reported foreign items which sounded like transplanted Americana. Two industrial giant aggregations were locked in battle over who should get the rich contract for making 450,000 cars a year in southern Italy, Alfa-Romeo or Fiat. Florida and California fruit and vegetable industries were all ears at the fact that Italy was finally taking a belated but major step toward rationalizing its huge fruit and vegetable trade south of Naples for the northern European market.

Relations between the United States and other nations frequently came to consultations at the summit in Washington. A happy crossroads was the August 1967 visit to President Johnson of Mohammed Reza Shah Pahlavi, the Shahanshah of Iran, in whose country President Truman's Point IV had made its first impact in the years when it was the journalistic procedure to interview the pajama-clad Prime Minister, Mohammed Mossadegh, in bed. Johnson noted that, since he himself had seen Iran in 1962, there had been "very genuine progress," to say the least: an annual growth of about 10 per cent, one of the highest in the world; 20 per cent of the rural population attending 6,500 elementary schools, whereas only 8 per cent had in 1962; and 50 per cent of Iran's rural families now farming their own land, with more than 7,000 cooperatives in operation.

There was the unhappy discovery for the State Department, when it had to explain the matter to virtuous Congressmen, that thieves were an international brotherhood, which included Americans. In wartime cities like Saigon, some Americans and South Vietnamese were frequently happy brethren in arranging profitable briberies of officials and "kickbacks" from American manufacturers and in serving as transfer agents for the flight of black market capital into gold from Saigon to Laos to Paris to Switzerland, where the illegitimate profits were cached. Wars, as America forgot but the natives never, had always been bonanzas for sharp operators. State Department officials were shocked into disbelief when its ally, South Korea, asked exorbitant wages for its civilians to work in Vietnam to relieve the skilled manpower shortage. Korea, Japan, Singapore, Manila, Taiwan, Bangkok, and Hong Kong reaped profits from the war as South Vietnam became a major market for construction materials, food, and textiles and as rest and recuperation centers in nearby countries for U.S. forces on leave from the war brought in U.S. dollars.

The Bonn coalition government was having fiscal and budget problems, aggravating political disputes, a not unheard of refrain in the Washington of 1967. As the old chestnut has it, when the American economy sneezes, the world economy gets influenza. At the Rio de Janeiro meeting of the International Monetary Fund in 1967, the foreigners were concerned about the slowdown in the world economy and the importance for the low-developed countries producing raw materials to have the great industrial countries, led by the United States, get back into full activity. Foreign critics found U.S. inflation excessive, growth of the U.S. import market much too slow, and U.S. foreign aid falling considerably short of what was deemed Washington's fair share.

Every country was intensely interested in how the United States was allocating its own resources. Each nation had a stake in the American economy's continuing to flourish, so that there would be enough resources from which they might themselves be able to obtain some appetizing crumbs or even possibly a slice of cake. To promote their own image in the United States, at least fifteen countries circulated elaborate brochures of local news, exuding good will toward Americans and inviting the same toward themselves. All were duly registered as foreign agencies in the Department of Justice and watched courteously but carefully by the State Department.

For the State Department or even for the wisest of men, this world of perpetual, free-wheeling motion was no easy matter to keep track of and comprehend, let alone to digest. Every day was a new day of surprises as events skidded into view like three-cushioned billiard shots or, better yet, as in French pool, balls caroming off each other into random pockets. Diplomatic gymnastics to handle each problem as it came up were impossible because of the individually tailored nature of situations. Therefore, some line of consistent policy was imperative, flexible enough for "give" but still coherent enough to be recognizable. New nations, which perhaps had not yet found their own identity but sought to express aspirations that were still unorganized instincts and word-of-mouth traditions, were quick enough to make up their minds that at least they did not desire to become American citizens *in absentia*. The new peoples, bemused by enticing phrases like "the tide of rising expectations" and "historical inevitability," saw with bewilderment that the tide did not rise fast enough to make arrival at the haven of their dreams immediately inevitable. Disillusion generated impatience and the decision that the only way for the wished-for event to happen was to make it happen. The backward nations sometimes appeared to make a professional occupation of being "poor and also proud," plunging into ill-considered adventures to further their interests and lashing back in fear when obstructed. Thus, trouble was and is a major characteristic of most international relationships. Trouble persisted even when situations were improved, for, as G. K. Chesterton said, "Progress is the mother of problems."

In earlier decades not many nations in the world cared what United States views were. Since World War II the United States became involved in so many questions all over the globe that everybody cared and wanted to know what the United States thought. It was sometimes difficult for Foreign Service professionals, let alone ordinary citizens, to appreciate how much the United States possessed a world constituency and that U.S. actions and policies dominated the politics of dozens of nations concerned with "openings to the left" or "hardenings on the right." In their earlier innocence or naïvete, Americans tended to think that the only nation with domestic political problems was the United States.

The Department's officials constantly had to keep in mind the domestic political interests of foreign statesmen and politicians who supported the United States and the importance of not undercutting them unnecessarily by some rash statement which could work against them on their home grounds or make them vulnerable to defeat by their opponents. In fact, the most politically sensitive items in testimony of senior officers of the Department before Congressional committees in executive or supposedly secret sessions related to the candid expression of opinions about foreign leaders. They explained why Department officials were so jittery and scandalized when indiscreet Senators or Representatives dropped public hints of such inside U.S. Government views concerning foreign personalities.

Senators and Congressmen who had been exposed to foreign affairs problems a sufficient number of years had grown sophisticated enough to recognize, as the saying goes, that "one international distress signal is a cry of another politician in trouble." American Congressmen, most of whom have to work at getting re-elected every two years, also understood how new regimes in the developing countries so often breed corruption: because too many people in the governing administration want to make money as fast as possible, since they do not know if they would win re-election.

U.S. Senators and Representatives had several unique avenues of becoming acquainted at first hand with the grass-roots politics and problems of colleagues in other lands. Every member of the U.S. Congress was *ipso facto* a member of the Interparliamentary Union. The Union is the oldest formally organized such body in the world, open to all nations since it was established in 1889. U.S. Congressional authority for participation in the Union dates back to 1935. The next oldest group with which the U.S. Congress had been associated is the (British) Commonwealth Parliamentary Association, which was formed in 1911 and which invited members of Congress to some meetings. The newest similar organization is the NATO Parliamentarians' Conference, organized in 1955. Permanent Congressional participation was authorized for the conference's annual meeting in Paris. A Canada–United States Interparliamentary group was formed in 1959, and a Mexico–United States Interparliamentary group in 1960. Congressmen were invited occasionally by the Council of Europe. Others met yearly with a similar group in the British Parliament.

Mature and experienced legislators are fully aware that the hallmark of a trusted State Department officer is a sense of responsibility. The Department often had to function as a generalized alter ego for all parties concerned in a given situation, a situation that the State Department naturally hoped to control in the interests of the United States. Amid the pointillism of events, the recurring problem was choosing among the least of several evils, making adjudgments in flux, hip-shooting by necessity at times, or, at least, attempting to keep the body diplomatique facing in the right direction. In such unsure circumstances, finding a lack of fire and dash to make swift and heroic decisions was not unexpected. The State Department, in consequence, was not infrequently obligated to take the prudent course, retiring behind a lead protective shield against the possibly lethal radioactive emanations from a hostile outside world, while it pondered the long view and tried to stay on course despite the buffets of the outer seas.

The "long view" unfortunately is not indexed among FAM's, that is, the Department's Foreign Affairs Manuals. One such view, entertained by not a few in the middle echelons of the Department, was that voiced by Senator Fulbright: letting nature take its course. Letting varying world cultures work their healing suasion via osmosis on each other. And cultivating, like Candide, our garden in the meantime. There are precedents for the philosophy. The Argentines and Brazilians, who twenty years ago regularly listed each other as Enemy Number One in their imaginary war games, are now more or less amiable rivals. The United States is a close collaborator of West Germany, Italy, and Japan, its Axis enemies of a generation ago. The traditionally antipathetic French and Germans, despite General de Gaulle, are partners in the Common Market, if not yet trusted friends. The Japanese and the South Koreans are inching toward amity. The feuding Greeks and Turks seem headed again in the direction of gingerly reconciliation, despite Cyprus. Even Russia is thawing out imperceptibly but definitely, in the Fulbright conviction. In the long horizon of the years, perhaps the Arabs and the Israelis, the Chinese Communists and the Americans, the Indians and the Pakistanis might find it advisable, tolerable, and even profitable to live in peace and nonhostility, if not cooperation. However, the Fulbright philosophy was slightly out of favor officially in 1967.

There was also what might be interpreted as the "long view" of Secretary Rusk, who also had a policy of doing nothing—but on purpose—when he so deemed it wise; of not seeking out crises prematurely; and of shooting only when "you see the whites of their eyes," as in the cases where "the other side" might attempt too energetically to make "history inevitable" in its own peculiar way, as the North Vietnamese Communists might have thought of doing in South Vietnam.

The normally prevalent situation confronting the State Department was an absence of authentic and verified information about an actual or potential enemy's bona fide intentions, plans, and operations until such hostile thinking became overt by causing damage to U.S. and allied interests. Thus, it was not surprising that State Department officials, at a loss without "hard" facts to operate on and like human beings everywhere, indulged in speculations and searched for explanations in the personal motivations and environment of the unfriendly personalities who had challenged the well-intentioned course of the United States. Excavations were conducted in the *Mein Kampf*'s of the disturbers of the world's peace in order to find not only the map and calendar of their ambitions but, with more longing, some rock upon which the miscreants could stumble to disaster.

Several fascinating conjectures were available. Did Fidel Castro of Communist Cuba aspire to be the new Simón Bolívar of twentieth-century Latin America? His wing feathers seemed to be molting. Did Kwame Nkrumah of Ghana really dream of becoming the Emperor of Black Africa? He tripped and fell into Guinea. Did Ben Bella of Algeria plan to reconstitute the Maghreb and a new empire of northwest Africa, including Algeria, Morocco, and Tunisia? He landed in jail, or worse. Did Sukarno of Indonesia believe he was destined to rule an Archipelago of jeweled isles, from the Indian Ocean to the Pacific Ocean and the Philippines? He did not make it. Did Gamal Abdel Nasser of Egypt envision himself as the new Caliph Haroun al Raschid of the Arab Middle East? As an imperator, Nasser needed new clothes. Did Ho Chi Minh of North Vietnam, in his aged heart, picture himself as the Stalin of all Indo-China? The apparition was shrouded in the gunsmoke of reality in the Vietnam war of 1968.

There were in the world other dynamic leaders for good or ill whose personalities and possibilities always had to be weighed against the future. In this exercise there had to be added the ingredient of a nation's past aspirations and immemorial dreams, which had a more living continuity than could usually be discerned by outsiders. Did Ayub Khan ever entertain the notion of himself as a founder of a new militant Mogul empire that could topple the unwieldy elephant of India and bring majesty, order, and prosperity to the great subcontinent? Ayub Khan certainly was no idle visionary, but he was a man of power, as imperial as the traditions of the British Empire which had raised him. Or did Archbishop Makarios of Cyprus believe that he could parlay his leadership of Cypriot Greeks into the premiership of mainland Greece—like Napoleon going from Corsica to France to find his niche in world history? Makarios taught the children of Cyprus to make a plaything out of terror and turned kindergartens into horror training chambers for EOKA terrorists, firing the young with a literal and burning faith in nineteenth-century rhetoric about "death and glory" and throwing off the "hideous tyrant's yoke" of the British. His feat in the end still left the Greeks of Athens saying, "Cypriots are as stupid as oxen." Makarios also had a long way to swim.

Such speculations would not make many sales in Peoria, let alone in Congress. But for want of practical alternatives, they were not quite as idle as they might sound, especially when, as often happened, unfavorable circumstances locked U.S. policies into a vise of immobility, temporarily at least. However, if the U.S. diplomatic headquarters in Washington had to tread water from time to time, it was decidedly not so in the U.S. embassies abroad; that's where the action was. GHQ calls the signals, but ambassadors carry the ball.

The American ambassador is first and foremost the personal representative of the President of the United States in a foreign country. He is the eyes and ears and, when necessary, the hand and legs of the President as the Chief Executive of foreign affairs. He operates normally, but not always, through the Secretary of State. In the advanced countries his job is, in one sense, easier because the very size and competence of the staff allow an embassy to run itself. In the less advanced countries, the job is harder on the ambassador personally, not only because of the necessity of making judgments on the basis of traditions unknown or unfamiliar to Western civilization but also because there the ambassador has to be an executive and a manager of foreign programs.

In early 1967 the United States maintained diplomatic relations with 116 countries, though figures varied, depending on the number of countries with which relations had been suspended because of the Middle East crisis. Before World War II, the State Department did 80 per cent of its business with 7 or 8 countries in western Europe. By 1952, there were 50 countries to be dealt with. In 1967, more than half the U.S. embassies abroad, or 63, were listed as hardship posts, located in Asia, Africa, Latin America, and eastern Europe. The "hardship" referred to difficulties of plain existence as expressed in living costs, bad climate, endemic disease, primitive conditions, or inimical atmosphere in Communist or belligerently "nonaligned" countries.

The State Department maintained, in 1967, a total of 276 posts around the world, including 61 in Africa, 16 in Latin America, 34 in east Asia and the Pacific, 79 in Europe, and 41 in the Near East and south Asia. Again the arithmetic varied as conditions changed. Four special posts were the United States missions to the United Nations in New York, the Organization of American States in Washington, the International Civil Aviation Organization in Montreal, and the International Atomic Energy Agency in Vienna. The State Department's work force was 25,778. Of the total, 72 per cent, or 18,596, worked overseas, but of these, 10,477 were local nationals of the country in which the embassy was located. The number of Americans abroad was 8,119, and in Washington, 7,182.

The American ambassador abroad was supposed to have supreme primacy over all the officers and staff in his particular embassy. President Kennedy, in May 1961, four months after he had become President, desiring to upgrade as much as possible the individual authority of the ambassador as a means of meeting the problem of field coordination, sent every ambassador a personal letter in which he said, in part:

In regard to your personal authority and responsibility, I shall count on you to oversee and coordinate all the activities of the United States Government in [name of country].

You are in charge of the entire United States diplomatic mission, and I shall expect you to supervise all of its operations. . . . I shall give you full support and backing in carrying out your assignment.

This so-called primacy proved to be a polite fiction, however, because one key verb, "to direct," had been omitted, and still was in late 1967. Moreover, President Kennedy, in the same letter, made a large exception to the ambassador's purview in giving a separate line of authority to the commanders of U.S. military forces in the area. This exempted, in vital effect, the MAG, or military assistance group, generals from the ambassadorial authority. Worse, it gave the military unhindered ingress into government offices of the foreign countries where missions were operating. More often than not, contacts were made with the foreign governments without the ambassador's knowledge.

Ironically, General Maxwell Taylor, as Chairman of the Joint Chiefs of Staff, had supported this exception, as granted to General Paul Harkins, the MAG commander in Saigon, which was the key testing place of the Kennedy attempt to strengthen his ambassadors' hand. But when General Taylor himself became Ambassador to South Vietnam, the first item on his agenda was revocation of the Harkins letter of separate authority and the issuance of another letter to Taylor, bestowing on him whatever command control he wished to assume over the military establishment in Vietnam. Lodge, on his second tour as Ambassador to Saigon, had the same and newer Taylor authority, but never used it.

Kennedy had further thoughts about a year later. Addressing Foreign Service officers in the State Department auditorium in the spring of 1962, he remarked: "Winston Churchill once said that the secret of the survival of the British Empire was that they never trusted the judgment of the man on the spot. I never understood that until recently."

Kennedy's reflections naturally were the product of his then nearly year and a half experience in office. The increased trend toward centralization of government throughout the world made it all the more imperative that foreign affairs should be under the close control of the top executive, a process facilitated by the tremendous increase in the speed of communications. Modern speeds were almost unbelievable compared with those of the early days of the Republic. Secretary of State Thomas Jefferson complained in 1791 to the American chargé in Spain, William Carmichael: "You certainly will not wonder if the receipt of but one letter in two years-and-a-half inspires a considerable degree of impatience."

Diplomatic communications in those days were indeed slow and irregular. No one in the early State Department ever knew how many dispatches were en route or had been intercepted by unfriendly agents. The minimum time for a dispatch to arrive by ship in Europe was six weeks, but it might take six months. U.S. emissaries abroad worked more or less independently, apparently carrying out State Department objectives by mental telepathy if the careful instructions, a practice which Jefferson originated in the Department, had not arrived. It was estimated that one third of the diplomatic dispatches never got to their destinations. At one time, twelve U.S. diplomatic agents had not reported in eleven months. Today, cables to and fro arrive in minutes and, if necessary, ambassadors can be recalled overnight by jet for personal consultation. Though the revolutionary improvement in communications tended to reduce the independent authority of the ambassador on the spot, paradoxically there developed an even greater reliance on him for trustworthy advice to be provided much more quickly. In turn, the celerity of communications made for more consistency and uniformity in expression of policy and kept down the tangle of cross-purposes which distance and dispersion inevitably create. All these factors were multipliers of diplomatic work: more preparation, more messages, more copies to all key officers of the Department in Washington, and more information copies, as many as a hundred, to marginally interested other U.S. posts overseas and to related foreign affairs agencies.

The voluminous cable traffic and the constant incursion of visiting officers from Washington sent to render specialized expertise generated tremendous activity in the great U.S. embassies abroad, such as those in London, Paris, Bonn, and Tokyo. In the main, economic affairs and issuances of visas made up the largest part of embassy work, and, with the increasing appearance of American tourists from home, demands on embassy officers "to do the honors" were growing in this field also.

The ambassador's principal personal concern had to be not to permit himself to get trapped in minutiae and to conserve his energies for truly essential matters—not to make an elephant out of a fly, as the French say, or an ox out of a mosquito, as the Russian saying goes. In short, to preserve his equanimity and power of judgment. This meant, first of all, that the ambassador had to have information of veracity upon which he could exercise his talents or evaluation. He also had to be perforce a professional man about town, attending cocktail parties in order to hear the political rumors, most of which were wild but which nevertheless gave a flavor of the atmosphere and sometimes could be both true and interesting, and which, in any case, one could not afford to ignore. The value of the ambassador's report and evaluation depended on the diversity and range of his contacts. He had to keep in touch with the "points of power" and maintain friendly relations with all levels of the government and party machines in the country to which he was accredited. He had to be known and respected by those in authority while being also aware of feelings, opinions, and reactions at all levels of the population in the capital and in the countryside.

The great constraint on an American ambassador was the self-discipline to be as objective as possible. If he were as sensitive as gold leaf, he could be still more valuable, because a diplomat's real need was to ascertain what the foreigners in whose midst he was living were actually thinking. Even more important was to understand how they thought and the peculiarities of their mental processes, so that an accurate projection could be made of the way in which the native inhabitants would behave in a given situation. As the philosopher Alfred North Whitehead said: "The foundation of foresight is insight." Timely and shrewd reporting, therefore, marked the effective sphere of influence of an ambassador.

When it came to issues in dispute between the United States and his host country, the ambassador had to be able to convey a precise and practical idea of the intricate problems that arose in the course of a possible negotiation. Wise envoys have said that frequently in disputes it is a matter of the one inevitable way in which a matter would be resolved. The trick was to spot this probability far enough in advance and then wait for it with composure. Negotiation, it has also been said, is the art of trying to persuade another sovereign power to one's own point of view—without effective sanctions, that is, with the full knowledge beforehand that the United States, for example, would not be able, for various reasons, to use force. Otherwise, it would not be a negotiation but the serving of an ultimatum. There were numberless stratagems to the art of negotiation, as the classic memorialists from François de Callières to Sir Harold Nicolson describe it. There is a time to get tough, and a time to keep quiet. The point is to make the offer acceptable and palatable.

Averell Harriman, Ambassador-at-Large in the State Department in 1967 and former Under Secretary of State for Political Affairs, once said, "The key to negotiation is understanding the point of view of the other man, and what is essential to him and to his own political and economic pressures." Harriman started learning the art in labor disputes with railroad trainmen when he was chairman of the board of his family-controlled railroad, the Union Pacific, before World War II.

Since success of any foreign policy initiative depends on the response of foreign governments, the ambassador's degree of accuracy and perception in describing conditions abroad should, in theory, account for 60 per cent of any ordinary decision taken by the State Department. A common American misapprehension is that if only the State Department were more efficient, it could deal with foreign affairs as well as other U.S. departments deal with domestic affairs. This illusion crumbles upon the bedrock fact that foreign affairs are a question of persuasion in a field of a country's activities where it does not have sovereignty. As Lord Strang, former head of the British Foreign Office, noted:

It is true to say, as a broad generalization, that whereas the main function of the other British departments of state [meaning other executive agencies] is to carry out prescribed and fully realizable policies, that of the Foreign Office is to achieve as many of our national desiderata as can be made acceptable to other sovereign governments. This does not as a rule call for administrative science, but for diplomacy; and diplomacy, like all other arts, has the disconcerting tendency to elude scientific analysis.

The American ambassador, therefore, is an indispensable element in the State Department's two-way mission: interpreting to the President and to the other American agencies in the foreign affairs field the views of foreign governments which circumscribe the practical limits of particular problems in which the United States is interested; and interpreting, in reverse, the specific intent and content of American policies to foreign governments in such a manner as to make them acceptable. Thus, if the first problem of the ambassador is to ensure the value and utilization of his information, his second task depends on his knowledge and relations with Washington so that his best-considered views and reports are not ignored, distorted, or emasculated.

Modern U.S. ambassadors, in sum, are held on a relatively tight leash. At a meeting of U.S. ambassadors accredited to western Europe a few years ago, some of the assembled envoys complained mildly to Secretary Rusk, who had gone over for the meeting, of ambassadorial unhappiness at not being cut in very often on foreign policy formulations. Whereupon Secretary Rusk informed his legates that they were, so to speak, slightly "out of their minds."

The ambassador's primary channel of effectiveness is in the impact of his reporting, which, if elegant, arresting, and humorous, like the cables of the Ambassador to Great Britain, David K. E. Bruce, would be read with great interest. Former Ambassador to India John K. Galbraith once indicated that embassy cables should be sufficiently blunt to shock the Washington readers into alert attentiveness. Bruce is one of the few grand seigneurs of high style left in the diplomatic trade, as is Averell Harriman. Bruce had also been Ambassador to France and to Germany and he knew everybody in western Europe, while Harriman, now in Washington, had been Ambassador to Moscow and to London and, besides knowing everyone in western Europe, he also knew the diplomats of eastern Europe as well. Bruce was a marquis out of the eighteenth-century French nobility, Harriman an earl from seventeenth-century English feudal ranks. Another working elder statesman of diplomacy is John J. McCloy, former U.S. High Commissioner in West Germany, also with wide acquaintance among western Europeans. In recent years, McCloy was not a member of the senior bureaucracy but was called upon for special missions, such as solving the

German offset problem in 1966 and 1967, consulting on removal of the Soviet nuclear missiles from Cuba in 1962, and reopening the Suez Canal in 1956. All three men had one special characteristic in common: Despite their so-called advanced ages, in the late sixties and early seventies, all three were *au courant* with the latest stratagems and fashions of the modern age and needed no instruction from their juniors.

U.S. ambassadors on the scene also had the right to make recommendations on what U.S. foreign policy in their areas ought to be, which recommendations might or might not be followed in the light of Washington's wider considerations. But an ambassador's objections to instructions that he thought were not adequately designed to fulfill U.S. objectives could not be too frequent or petulant, else he would be put down and discounted as a chronic complainer. The best ambassadors were never ventriloquist dummies or mere relay vehicles for passing on the latest gossip to Washington. Good ambassadors took the initiative to solve what problems they could on their own; otherwise the home office would have been swamped with trivia. The question of judgment developed around whether to take a decision, with the double hazard of being deemed presumptuous or overreaching their authority by Washington, or being charged with having made a wrong judgment. The top professionals were ready to take the blame as buffers and always realized that they were expendable. The most adroit had an efficacious stratagem: they designed their proposals in such a way as to force the State Department back home to prove that the ambassador was wrong, thus avoiding the backfiring approach or trying to prove that the State Department was wrong.

Ambassadors of proven competence and self-assurance never worried overmuch about their authority. George F. Kennan, former Ambassador to Yugoslavia and now permanent professor at the School of Historical Studies at the Institute for Advanced Studies at Princeton, told the U.S. Senate Government Operations Subcommittee on National Security in 1963: "I had the impression that the authority of an ambassador over official American personnel stationed in his country was just about whatever he wants to make it. If he requires them to do things they consider contrary to their general instructions from Washington, or intrinsically unwise to an intolerable degree, their recourse is in Washington."

The patent key to influencing Washington policy from an overseas embassy was to understand how the U.S. policy-making process operated in Washington. This meant the ambassador's having had Washington experience on the policy-making level so that, at a distance, he could remember the customary angles, roadblocks, and curlicues in the bureaucracy as a draft proposal took its winding or zigzag course toward possible eventual

action. Familiarity with the legislative as well as the executive processes in
the United States, and keeping up with the news of their consequences in
the public domain, was a further essential requirement if the ambassador
was to fulfill his duties frankly to comment on the lines of policy already
promulgated and to suggest, from his experience on the scene, what different options might be added to make it more useful and effective.

Foreign policy is made, a State Department truism says, in the cables
sent and received. In July 1966, Harlan Cleveland, former Assistant Secretary for International Organization Affairs and later U.S. Ambassador to
NATO, asked for guidance. To save time, he hopped a plane to Washington
to get the issue settled. In effect, Cleveland wrote out his own instructions
in Washington and sent them to himself in Paris. It illustrated what Foy
D. Kohler, holding in 1967 the top career appointment in the State Department as Deputy Under Secretary of State for Political Affairs, once said:
"A field ambassador has as much authority as he wants to take; he has a
lot more fun and he can write his own ticket." Kohler, who had been U.S.
Ambassador to Moscow, re-emphasized the ambassador's capacity through
his suggestions to write his own instructions in the end. A career ambassador, which is the senior grade in the U.S. Foreign Service, and a man
of gnarled integrity, Kohler represented a grass-roots strain in American
society as the son of an Ohio tenant farmer. A former Assistant Secretary
of State for European Affairs and director of the Berlin Task Force through
the worst of the Berlin crisis in 1961 and 1962, he looked like a retired
satyr and functioned like a junior Socrates.

Despite the intensive traffic between the U.S. embassies abroad and
Washington, plus voluminous dispatches in the newspapers indicating not
only the drift but frequently the clear outlines of present and coming U.S.
policy, foreigners regularly complained about the lack of consultation by
the United States. The lament was a habitual refrain of the NATO allies
and at times had some justification in the normal restrictiveness of American officials' attitudes, particularly at a time when a policy might have
been in the throes of creation. At least by 1967, NATO allies were being
thoroughly advised about U.S. intentions. Harlan Cleveland, whose gift for
articulate discourse was rivaled among public figures only by that of Vice
President Humphrey and former Soviet Premier Khrushchev in his prime,
had been speaking before the Permanent NATO Council literally more
than all the other NATO ambassadors put together.

The fact still remained that United States practice had not changed, nor
was it going to change fundamentally. Allies would be consulted, not in
advance of a specific U.S. decision to take action but almost invariably after
the fact, a procedure which French President Charles de Gaulle pinpointed
for former Secretary Acheson when Acheson went to Paris in 1962 to

convey a message from President Kennedy about the then imminent blockade in the Cuban nuclear missile crisis. De Gaulle asked: "May we be clear before you start, are you consulting or informing me?" Acheson was there, of course, to carry a message and nothing more, and said so, whereupon De Gaulle commented, "I am in favor of independent decisions." He still is, and so is the United States, and, when a crisis of vital national interest arises, so is every other sovereign state.

Communications and exchange of ideas with other nations through diplomatic channels, in fact, were the least of the problem. In 1967, there were, give or take a few temporary absentees, 116 diplomatic missions accredited to the United States in Washington, an assembly of 1,860 diplomats, compared with 55 foreign embassies and legations and 261 diplomats in 1940. At least 36 African countries had established Washington embassies between 1960 and 1966. So messengers to carry the word to García were not the problem. In the close working relationship with the British Foreign Office, the State Department had several avenues of approach: from the White House direct to 10 Downing Street, the Prime Minister's residence, or to Ambassador Bruce in London and on to the Foreign Office, also on Downing Street in Whitehall; or through the British Embassy in Washington, which, since World War II, had become the most important British mission abroad. When Lord Harlech, the former Sir David Ormsby-Gore, was British Ambassador to the United States, he was virtually a member ex officio of the U.S. National Security Council by virtue of his intimate friendship with President Kennedy.

The British Embassy was a key subway stop throughout the diplomatic ups and downs in the abortive attempts at negotiations with Hanoi to end the Vietnam war. The State Department loaded the British Embassy with background information, pointers, and suggestions in preparation for the visit of British Foreign Minister George Brown to Moscow in early 1967. Besides addressing itself either to the Foreign Office or to the British Embassy in Washington, whichever was the faster or more convenient means at the moment, the State Department sent special envoys to London to help Ambassador Bruce clarify high-level considerations from the topmost levels in Washington. At the time of Soviet Premier Alexei Kosygin's visit to London in February 1967 to see British Prime Minister Harold Wilson, Chester L. Cooper was the special messenger. Cooper was a former high Central Intelligence Agency official, a former key staff aide in the White House for the Vietnam war, a special assistant to Ambassador-at-Large Harriman, and a close personal friend of Sir Patrick Dean, the British Ambassador in Washington. He flew to London to transmit to Prime Minister Wilson, on at least three occasions, American proposals to pass on to Kosygin for relay to Hanoi.

As President Kennedy said in the already cited speech to the Foreign Service officers, "With the trans-Atlantic cable tying the hands of an ambassador in Western Europe, he moves in a more traditional way, in one sense [as] an adviser, in another sense, merely a go-between." In the same speech Kennedy also said: "It is a remarkable fact that the most interesting offices—the areas which place the greatest responsibility on an ambassador—are not the traditional ones of Western Europe but Latin America, Africa, and Asia. These areas give the greatest opportunity to a Foreign Service officer to render direct and really unique service."

Materially, the Kennedy comment was self-evident in the proliferation of new states since World War II. Psychologically, the President was extremely concerned about the problem of the way in which American diplomacy could symbolize a common American bond with the new peoples it was meeting for the first time. The problem, in essence, was how to demonstrate and practice the spiritual equality of disproportionate powers.

The usual American attitude was exemplified in an exchange between G. Mennen Williams, the five-time Michigan Governor and former Assistant Secretary of State for African Affairs, at a House appropriations subcommittee hearing in 1966 with Congressman Rooney. Williams, asked why new embassies were necessary in certain African countries, replied:

"We feel that, as these countries achieve independence, they like to have equal dignity with other countries."

Rooney interpolated: "Oh, we are into that dignity stuff again, eh?"

It would have been more fitting for the answer to Rooney to have come from former South Vietnamese Ambassador to the United States, Vu Van Thai, who once told this writer: "Dignity, we value it more than your freedom."

Over the centuries, dignity has been one of the cardinal intangibles of the peoples of Asia and Africa, an accretion of religious traditions and belief in the reality of the soul. Dignity was the spectral aura of past frustrations and future hopes, a dumb posture of forgiveness for lapses into weakness and succumbing to the temptations of evils, a promissory note for the morrow, an awareness of not-yet-complete competence, a display of will to prevail as a human being, and an unspoken apology for failure, should the gods so decree. The astral shell of dignity surrounding the physical presence, compounded of bravado and supplication and an instinctive resistance against being demeaned, symbolized the blood faith that a human being was worthy of his life, if not in this, in his next reincarnation.

To most Americans, this metaphysical dignity was not quite concrete enough to catch hold of with one's fingers. It was one of the missing elements in the incomprehensible attitude of Hanoi toward negotiations. There appeared to be a mutual psychological block: that the United States could appreciate and even admire North Vietnamese resistance, their psychological adeptness at the judo diplomacy of turning America's democratic strength into weakness. But beyond grudging respect for the cleverness of the Communist tactics, there appeared to be little understanding of the Asiatic mystique. The Americans desired to perceive a signal on the part of Hanoi. The North Vietnamese seemed to be looking for a gesture of acknowledgment on the part of America, a bow to the reality of Hanoi's will power, if not an admission of their bitter valor as a foe.

Dignity to most Americans usually signified a sort of decorum or staid social posture approaching a stage-like shadow of protocol. It did not encompass the old-fashioned word, the spirit, which the most miserable beggar in Lagos, Bombay, or Caracas reflected, no matter what his decrepit or untouchable outward appearance. For American ambassadors in these backward, developing, or emerging countries, the essence of the problem lay in the extreme difficulty in sensing and expressing this "feel" of the human condition. It was very elusive indeed to translate such wisps of impressions by the osmosis of words, inclinations, gestures, smells, and the presence of alien concepts into practical suggestions for political programs that could be understood, let alone acted upon, back in Washington.

It was furthermore difficult to comprehend that the human dignity of the so-called natives had been overlaid for a century or more past with many taboos, memories, and ingrained reactions to the myriad insults and injuries swallowed and sustained for many years from foreign conquerors, colonial overlords, and economic exploiters. A veil of "national dishonor" obscured the eyes of many peoples among whom the American ambassadors had to work. Many of these same nations found it hard to grow out of their own national adolescence. They were not only touchy, they had the crass cupidity of youth who reached for the fruits of social and economic maturity in the modern world before he earned them. They mistrusted over-demonstrative friendliness, like the Vietnamese, who, accustomed to the formal politeness of the French, did not comfortably accept the American arms-around-the-shoulders routine.

The relation of religious, philosophical, and psychological considerations to practical politics in crises in the underdeveloped countries was illustrated in a comment made by Professor Hans Morgenthau, a leading academic critic of the Vietnam war:

That principle [self-determination] is an outgrowth of Western individualism, meaningless in the context of the area dominated by Chinese civilization, of which Viet Nam forms a part. For that civilization, political action is the application of supposedly objective moral principles to concrete circumstances, not the result of free individual choice. In a political world governed by immutable objective laws, the individual has no freedom of choice. He can comply with those laws and succeed, or he can deviate from those laws and fail. In consequence, the future of Viet Nam will be determined by the actual distribution of military and political power in a country and not by legal principles transplanted from the West into an alien, moral, political, and social context.

By 1967 the American bureaucracy in command in Vietnam had belatedly but finally realized that "the actual distribution of military and political power in the country" was indeed the basic fact on the road to eventual stability, Vietnamese style. The Americans in South Vietnam were engaged in precinct politics in an unprecedented attempt at promoting results which would be acceptable to the powers in Washington that were financing the war, defensible in front of world public opinion, and tolerable to the South Vietnamese population, which would have to live with the results.

One phenomenon in the new countries which was recognizable to American ambassadors accustomed to the decorum of their guild was the insistence of local dignitaries upon their perquisites and prerogatives in matters of diplomatic protocol. To professional diplomats, protocol was, at heart, a basis of national order. It was an official matter, specifically designed for official functions, and in no wise private snobbery; it was accorded to officials on the basis of their precise rank and seniority in office, and did not apply to private citizens. In mixed diplomatic receptions, the sensitive problem was always to ensure that a representative of each country felt that due honor and proper recognition were accorded in exact degree to his nation.

This is not unlike the concepts of Arab justice in Saudi Arabia in 1951, when this writer visited Dhahran, operating headquarters of ARAMCO, the American oil combine, whose exploitation of huge oil reserves had produced a large body of monied Arabs from the wages they had saved. ARAMCO proposed to the then Crown Prince of Arabia, Saud, brother of the present King Faisal, that these Arabs be helped to become merchants as the beginning of a new middle class in the modernization of the desert kingdom. An ARAMCO officer, William Eltiste of Phillipsburg, Kansas, was put in charge of the project. Such was Eltiste's common sense, efficiency, and fairness that his fame spread to the far reaches of the kingdom. Arabs crossed the desert to consult him and lay their personal problems at his feet—litigation over the donkeys of Hofhof, said to rival those from Cyprus and Missouri as the best in the world, and matters of camel ownership, brides, and dowries.

For several months, amid his other duties, Eltiste would ponder these grave problems, upon which in due course he would have to render the verdict of Solomon. To his great astonishment, both Arab parties to the disputes at this time proceeded to intimidate him, browbeat him, threaten him with personal injury, try to bribe him, seduce him, and bring the most bizarre pressures to bear in order to sway him toward a judgment favorable to them. Eltiste, when he had made up his mind, gave his findings. In his own infinite wisdom, he learned to slice down the equities to the seventh cipher to the right of the decimal point. It was as precise a rendering of justice as could be expected from a mortal hand, whereupon both fiercely rival Arabs praised Eltiste as the most just man on earth, a man thrice blessed by Allah, and a man whose seed should endure unto the twentieth generation.

Among the occupational hazards faced by American ambassadors in these developing areas was the mercurial change in the political climate, which could transform a political backwater into an area of tactical importance overnight. In one respect, the medium-sized states were the most exasperating to handle. They did not have many options among which the United States might possibly find an interest, or they had such built-in disabilities, because of their backwardness, that it would have taken the exclusive use of American billions to bring such a state up to modern and immediate usefulness as a world partner. The job could not be done in a hurry. In nations where the problems were of more interest to the local nationals than they were to the vital interests of the United States, a different operational approach was required of the U.S. ambassador. It called for a sort of amiable slow-motion sympathy toward the larger goals but also keen interest in the concrete items of technical education and training and small-grain economics. What was needed in certain countries was a special type of American ambassador, the safe-and-sound type, who did not cause waves by being either a too-pushing do-gooder or too bright. An energetic and too intelligent ambassador, out of his own boredom, might by mistake instigate a revolution and have hell to pay.

Vexing and baffling to the American ambassadors in the restless zones was the infuriating custom of the many nations to smash diplomatic conventions, to arrest or physically impede the movements of American diplomats, or to encourage anti-American demonstrations leading to the destruction and burning of American installations, particularly USIA libraries. Breaches of supposedly inviolate rules of civilized diplomatic behavior were most annoying to Secretary Rusk, who was adamant in his insistence on secure channels of communication between governments for the mutual protection of their peoples.

The Middle East crisis of 1967 produced several aberrations from the norm in diplomatic intercourse. Seven nations—Iraq, Syria, Egypt, the Sudan, Algeria, Mauritania, and Yemen—broke relations with Washington as a result of the Arab-Israeli war and alleged American aid to Israel. In former times, a rupture of relations meant that the entire personnel of an embassy, from the ambassador on down, left the capital of the other country. Each country asked an embassy of a third country to look after its interest in the capital it was leaving. In 1930, United States interests in eleven foreign countries were being looked after by third-party nations because of some disaffection in diplomatic relations. In 1955, U.S. interests in twenty-six countries were being looked after by other countries. The United States did likewise for at least thirteen nations in 1967.

In the Middle East crisis, however, a new diplomatic development emerged, so-called gray diplomacy. The traditional break of diplomatic relations occurred in the prescribed way in Syria, Yemen, and Mauritania. But in the Sudan, Egypt, and Algeria, American diplomats below the level of ambassador continued to occupy U.S. embassies and to maintain contacts with Washington. Further, to mix up the situation, American officers left the U.S. Embassy in Bagdad, in Iraq, but Iraqi diplomats did not leave Washington. Negotiations followed for a reciprocal exchange of "gray" missions between the United States and Iraq, while, until this was done, Belgium represented U.S. interests in Bagdad. As a "gray" diplomat said in Cairo in late 1967, "Our policy here is a positive nonexistence." In Khartoum, a small corps of American diplomats remained working under the protection of the flag of the Netherlands. U.S. diplomats in Cairo worked under the Spanish flag; those in Algiers, under the flag of Switzerland. The three foreign flags were flown over U.S. embassy buildings, upon which plaques had been affixed describing the respective U.S. Embassy as "United States Interests Section," with the name of the foreign embassy following. An American diplomat commented, "Twilight relations have debased the coinage of diplomacy and dulled the effectiveness of breaking relations as a weapon."

This climate of old rules being broken and new rules in the process of uneasy formulation was a constant accompaniment to the work of American embassies in unsettled parts of the world, where U.S. embassies are much more sparsely manned than those of the traditional areas. Europe in 1966 had 18.5 per cent of the Foreign Service employees, or 1,984. The Middle East, including India, had 11.9 per cent, or 1,273. Latin America had 12.5 per cent, or 1,339. The Far East had 10.9 per cent, or 1,174. And Africa had 9.6 per cent, or 1,032. It was in these latter areas that American diplomats were making their reputations recently. The remaining third of the Foreign Service was assigned to Washington.

When U.S. ambassadors do a first-rate job, there is always the danger of confusing a personal triumph with the success of U.S. official policy. The professionals keep their fingers crossed as good or ill fortune strikes.

Political appointees are more prone to fall into the delusion of confounding success of their personalities with the end results of U.S. policies. High marks are given for ambassadorial judgment in refraining from doing certain things as well as for performing others exceedingly well. For instance, in Guinea, where former Ambassador William Attwood, a Kennedy appointee, made a name for himself, the immediate evidence of his good sense was that he kept the "Voice of America" from crowing about the fact that Sekou Touré had thrown out the Russian mission for its blunders in Soviet foreign aid. Former Ambassador Winthrop C. Brown's negotiation for a status-of-forces agreement for the 50,000 troops in South Korea ranks in the trade as a textbook exercise.

There is also the Foreign Service classic of Marshall Green in South Korea in 1961. His decisive handling of a coup made such a highly favorable impression on President Kennedy that he was brought back to be a Deputy Assistant Secretary of State for the Far East. Green had been awakened at 3 A.M. on May 16, 1961, when the South Korean military moved forces to overthrow the Government. As chargé d'affaires between ambassadors, Green literally made U.S. policy on the spot because events were moving too fast and communications not fast enough between Seoul and Washington at that time. As Kennedy said in the private speech to the Foreign Service corps: "At what point should we recognize a new government? What should be our attitude toward the military during the crucial forty-eight or seventy-two hours?" The key point was to insure that the South Korean military recognized the obligations of the South Korean Government toward the United States, particularly the status-of-forces agreement and other commitments, before the United States accorded recognition. This is exactly what Green did, all on his own. In Washington, Green was responsible for supervising U.S. policy toward Indonesia in the days before the abortive Communist coup of 1965. Later he was ambassador to Djakarta, where he again showed initiative in talking Turkey to the then Indonesian Foreign Minister Subandrio in protest against Communist-inspired anti-American riots. The delicate timing of the Subandrio exercise was to stop the riots before the situation got so bad that diplomatic relations might have to be broken off, with unforeseen consequences.

Among the notable noncareer but highly professional ambassadors in the Bruce-Harriman class was Ellsworth Bunker, who looked like a cardinal of the Roman Curia and was, as a colleague described him, equally smooth, quiet, deft, with no sharp corners, always in fluid motion. Bunker's experience had been almost totally with temperamental or demonstrative peoples—Italians, Indonesians, Arabs, Argentines, Dominicans, and other

Latin Americans. Secretary Rusk originally considered Bunker for Under Secretary of State, but President Johnson felt that he was more needed as Ambassador in South Vietnam.

An ambassador who took literally his designation as "the personal representative of the President of the United States" was Graham Martin, in Thailand from 1963 until 1967. Martin's take-charge posture clashed head-on in jurisdictional disputes with the U.S. Defense Department, which desired a blanket authorization to handle the U.S. defense commitment in Thailand as it saw fit. Martin purposefully took the not inconsiderable political risk of fighting to maintain definitive diplomatic control over all United States activities in Thailand in his appointed role as the overseer of the totality of U.S. interests in that richest of the southeast Asian states. Bangkok, site of the SEATO alliance, was an observation post for nearby South Vietnam. In the turbid events of 1963 that led up to the overthrow of Diem, the interagency confusion and cross-purposes of the Americans in Saigon were highly instructive. The U.S. military missions and the CIA made their own contacts and ran their shows virtually unmolested, with unhappy consequences. The lesson was not lost on Martin. He was determined that U.S. interests and effectiveness would not be similarly dispersed and dissipated in Thailand. In consequence, Martin was involved throughout his tour in a series of running internal skirmishes with then Defense Secretary McNamara, so much so in fact that one of Martin's superiors asked him once whether he, Martin, desired to become known as the foremost antagonist of McNamara in the administration. McNamara's former principal antagonist in the State Department had been Roger Hilsman, former Assistant Secretary of State for the Far East, who had folded his tent and retired in early 1964.

Martin was able to keep his footing on the slippery inclines of the higher political altitudes for two reasons: President Johnson, when he was Vice President, had visited Thailand in 1961, around the time when President Kennedy had sent 5,000 marines into the country as a warning against the Soviets and the North Vietnam-supported Pathet Lao in the Laos crisis. Johnson approved of Thailand's stand in its own self-defense and as the only effective SEATO partner of the U.S. in southeast Asia. Newsreel photographers had filmed the Vice President's Thailand tour at that time.

It was an uneasy time in Bangkok in the early winter of 1963, after President Kennedy had died and Lyndon Johnson had succeeded him. Thailand, though a monarchy, had been more or less a military dictatorship since 1932. The effective ruler, Field Marshal Sarit Khanarat, had died, and General Thanom Kittikachorn had become Prime Minister. Martin found in New York a file of film clips, coverage shot during

Johnson's 1961 visit. These were spliced together into a thirty-minute film and shown in Thailand. The double objective was to display to the Thais the precedent of the smooth transition from Kennedy to Johnson, hopefully to be emulated in Thailand, and to remind the new regime of the new American President's continuing interest in Thailand.

The substance of Martin's defense of long-range U.S. foreign policy in Thailand over short-range U.S. military objectives lay in the prime fact that the Thais, despite their military dictatorship, for ten years previous had allotted their own military only 15 per cent of the Thai budget, while for twelve years in a row the Thai Government had sunk from 60 to 70 per cent of the total internal income of Thailand into social and economic projects. Achieved thereby was a phenomenal 11 per cent annual growth rate, one never before encountered in so-called underdeveloped countries. Unbelieving World Bank examiners took a second audit to convince themselves that the amazing Thai performance was authentic. Martin insisted successfully that the Thais be encouraged to continue long-range investment in the fundamental underpinnnings of the country as the best insurance against possible future disaffection and disruption by the Communists. The U.S. Defense Department argued that the Thais should be made to cut back on internal programs and to raise the military budget to pay for their own defense.

Another major ambassadorial crisis with heavy political overtones involved heated arguments in the U.S. embassy in Tokyo in 1960 over the scheduled visit of President Eisenhower to Japan. The President's invitation to Moscow had been abruptly canceled by Nikita Khrushchev in the collapse of the Big Four Summit conference at Paris after the U-2 affair over the skies of Russia. The Tokyo visit had been arranged as a substitute for Eisenhower, in part to dramatize the Republican Party's 1960 election propaganda theme as the "party of peace." Coincident with the expected visit in that June of 1960 was a violent debate in the Japanese Diet over ratification of a new mutual security treaty with the United States. Japanese Prime Minister Kishi Nobusuke, angered by the Japanese Socialist Party's tactics of procrastination in the Diet, used his parliamentary majority brutally to ram the treaty through the Chamber of Deputies. Kishi's rough tactics aroused the rage of the opposition, abetted by the mass circulation of the Tokyo press and by Japanese university intellectuals, sparking huge and clamorous demonstrations, in the midst of which growing hysteria Soviet Russia sent four threatening notes to the Japanese Government in an attempt to block the treaty's ratification.

Kishi decided to ride out the storm. Under Japanese rules he had to wait at least forty days for the Japanese Senate to make up its mind about ratification. But, if in this forty-day period the Kishi Cabinet fell as a

result of the massive demonstrations, the treaty would have to be submitted all over again. In the long-range interest of U.S. foreign policy, the
main State Department consideration was that the mutual security treaty
should pass. In the American political context, it was desirable that a
famous soldier-hero like President Eisenhower should be able to visit
Japan. Yet, if the violent Tokyo mobs were excacerbated by Eisenhower's
entry into Tokyo, the Kishi Government might indeed fall and the treaty
urgently desired by the United States be lost. Ambassador Douglas Mac-
Arthur II, a nephew of the great General of the Pacific war and de facto
sovereign of Japan during the American occupation, had been Eisenhower's
political counselor at SHAPE in Paris in 1950, when Eisenhower became
commander-in-chief of the new NATO military organization in Europe.
MacArthur, who holds the rank of career ambassador and was appointed
to head the U.S. Embassy in Vienna in 1967, fought strenuously for
Eisenhower's visit to take place, urging Robert D. Murphy, then Under
Secretary of State for Political Affairs and a former envoy to Tokyo, not
to allow the Japanese to intimidate the Americans. As the riots grew in
intensity, with a death and scores of injured, Kishi decided to cancel the
official invitation to President Eisenhower rather than risk the fall of his
Cabinet and the loss of the treaty.

Two political developments transpired in the aftermath of the Tokyo
affair. If the Socialists had not challenged Kishi, if Kishi had not shown
a heavy hand, if the riots had not broken out, a triumphal visit of President
Eisenhower to Tokyo and successful passage of the vital mutual security
treaty by the Japanese Diet, not to mention the magic of the MacArthur
name, would have made an ideal double springboard from which Mac-
Arthur could have vaulted into the running as a dark-horse candidate for
the vice-presidential nomination on the Republican ticket at the GOP convention which was to take place in Chicago in the following month of
July 1960. MacArthur's wife was the politically astute daughter of Alben
W. Barkley, Vice President under President Truman.

The other by-product of Tokyo was the decision of the then U.S. Senate
Majority Leader Lyndon B. Johnson to look into the situation personally—
a cross-examination of Secretary of State Christian Herter in closed sessions of the Senate Appropriations Subcommittee on the State Department,
of which Johnson was chairman. Johnson asked Herter who had made the
"incorrect evaluation concerning the extent of the Japanese rioting," to
which Herter replied: "It was a collective judgment—but you can pin it
on me, if you like." Herter admitted to Johnson that the degree of violence
in the riots had not been anticipated.

Johnson complained that he was "considerably disappointed that no
new plans or policies had been developed after the collapse of the Paris

Summit conference or even during the last few years." The future President upbraided Herter and the Eisenhower administration, charging it with "not enough initiative to adapt to new problems" and "still getting by on ideas of ten years ago." U.S. Senator John F. Kennedy had for some time been making considerable mileage by similar attacks.

Political aspirations for high office, using the State Department as a "Head Start" program, had been dormant for at least a century in American politics. Senior colleagues of former Secretary of State Dean Acheson, for instance, were convinced that Acheson's friends and relatives at one time also had had presidential hopes for him. Acheson's tough individualism, uncommon high style, rather disconcerting aspect of looking like a Junker aristocrat from the German imperial general staff, and his cross-grained relations with the lesser beings of Congress led to the sorrowful conclusion by his admirers that Acheson had been born fifty years too late for presidential ambitions.

In any event, stratospheric visitations overseas, like those of Presidents Eisenhower, Kennedy, and Johnson, had become standard procedure on the highest levels of world diplomacy. An added factor was television. In the United States, TV had made political discussion a town-meeting-of-the-nation. With Telstar and Early Bird, the global communications satellites, the next stage appeared to be a town-meeting-of-the-world, with eventual simultaneous translations into the specific foreign languages of the many-tongued audiences TV would provide, as the United Nations already had done for its multinational meetings. Just as American politicians talked to many audiences of different classes, regions, and local interests, the same problem would be magnified a hundred times and more in the new art form of projecting U.S. personalities and policies to multiple and many-hued world audiences.

U.S. ambassadors in the places on which the President might descend on an overseas tour were automatically called upon to provide an inordinate amount of advice and arrangements, starting with the itinerary and appointments schedule, which countries to visit or avoid, which personalities to concentrate on or to ignore. The presidential tours involved considerable playing of musical chairs in the upper reaches of the Federal Government. The sheer logistics of housekeeping, security, and transportation, including provision for the mass press which accompanied the President like camp followers, were immense and complex. High officials became, in effect, mere clerks and errand boys for a President. For President Johnson's nine-nation tour in the fall of 1966, former Under Secretary of State for Administration William Crockett personally took on the chore of advance-man to insure that all the physical arrangements would be to the President's liking. The cost of moving White House, State Department, and Secret Service staffs was unavoidably high. The trip of President Eisenhower to India and way-stops in 1960 was estimated to have cost some $75,000. The private cost to the mass media press was estimated at from $5,000 to $7,000 a head for air transport alone on such trips.

The meeting of an American President with a foreign chief of state on the latter's home ground created a mishmash of domestic politics in both countries, a confusion in which the U.S. foreign policy overlay sometimes was barely discernible. The self-evident risk of direct negotiations between summit principals, after the experience of the last decade, was the illusion of definitiveness. Though meetings between heads of states may yet revivify the early Renaissance splendor of modern kings meeting on fields of "cloth of gold," as Henry VIII of England and Francis I of France did in 1520, their high symbolism can dissipate like fog under the noonday sun when the klieg lights of publicity disclose ambiguous results. Summit communiqués are not readily understood by the world public, and their elucidation by the jostle of press correspondents attending the President might be too hasty and superficial. For example, at the Manila conference there was a vigorous argument between State Department officials traveling with the President and Bill Moyers, the then Presidential Press Secretary, over inclusion of the phrase "six months" in paragraph 29 of the Joint Statement issued on October 25, 1966. Discussing the withdrawal of allied forces from Vietnam after certain conditions had been met, the key sentence read: "Both forces would be withdrawn as soon as possible and not later than six months after the above conditions had been fulfilled."

Moyers won the point on the ground that specific citation of a finite term for U.S. withdrawal would enhance the sincerity of American good faith, and, incidentally, provide good, hard copy for news headlines. The State Department debating team would have preferred to leave the option open for later exploitation when more profitable.

An American President's personal advent on foreign soil dramatizes not only his figurative role of running for office in a world constituency but even more vividly his impact on hundreds of thousands of foreigners who see him in the flesh, savor his personality, and are forced to realize that the President's presence in their midst has a large significance for themselves and their futures. In this general connection, Harlan Cleveland, testifying before the Senate Foreign Relations Committee, said in 1959:

The content of international affairs is really the internal affairs of other people. No longer is the primary content of international affairs the formal diplomatic relationships between Foreign Offices. We still talk a good deal in this country about "non-interference in the internal affairs of other peoples," but clearly this is an era of reciprocal intervention into each other's affairs.

The question, therefore, is not "if" but "how" the U.S. should inter-fere or intervene in the internal affairs of other nations. A practical guide lay in the words of the Italian love song, "*Si fa, ma non si dice,*" that is, one does it, but one doesn't talk about it, counsel which the lyricist had applied to another type of clandestine operation. The route from diplo-matic interference to open intervention extended from the covert to the hole-in-the-corner to the overt and legal and to the plain, unavoidable, busy-body instinct of everybody climbing onto their neighbor's shoulders.

The American domestic argument concerning U.S. intervention in the affairs of other nations is as old as the history of the Republic, going back to the propensities of Presidents Jefferson and Madison, and shared by President Wilson, to export the principles of American democracy; including the declamations of Henry Clay, sounding like an early Ful-bright, against the United States' interfering in the affairs of other coun-tries; on to Secretary of State Philander C. Knox, in President William H. Taft's administration, whose dithyrambs in favor of foreign aid would have brought shudders to the latter-day Fulbright. Knox said in 1911:

If the American dollar can aid suffering humanity and lift the burden of fi-nancial difficulty from states in which we live in terms of intimate intercourse and earnest friendship, and replaces insecurity and devastation by stability and peaceful self-development, all I can say is that it would be hard to find a better employment.

Knox also said:

The nations that finance the great Chinese railways and other enterprises, will be foremost in the affairs of China, and the participation of American capital in these investments will give voice of the United States more authority in political controversies in that country, which will go far toward guaranteeing the preservation of the administrative entity of China.

Former Greek Foreign Minister Evangelos Averoff-Tozzissa, discussing the reason why Greek students had smashed the U.S. library windows in the 1950's, told the then U.S. Ambassador George V. Allen, "The students feel that the basic decisions in the free world are made in Washington, so they put the pressure on Washington."

More realistically, American diplomats were not so much the leaders and enticers of American involvement with the outside world as the buffers and outriders of the U.S. presence in the world. The United States, by the very energy, wealth, and power of its citizens, created indelible impres-sions in almost all corners of the earth, regardless of its considerations of policy. The presence of Americans on foreign grounds was so widespread that foreign policy problems were made merely by the sheer fact of the

United States' own existence. Thus, in one practical sense, the Department of State could be considered an organ to give some order and purpose to the American presence and American power which already obtained on other people's home grounds, without trampling on the natives or causing unwanted frictions or blundering into costly or explosive confrontations with other foreign visitors in the same place.

The ever-increasing intermingling of the activities of both American and foreign governments and their peoples around the globe made it all the more difficult to differentiate between pressures and counterpressures and to define the legitimacy and allowable extent of countries' playing in each other's backfield. This was the constant piano accompaniment to U.S. Foreign Service operations, both in Washington and overseas. For every nation in the world, the number one objective was to influence United States foreign policy just as it was the United States' aim to try to sway every other nation. It always came back to how it was done. When done discreetly, no one heard about it, though it happened every day. Acceptable no longer were the gunboat-diplomacy methods of British imperial power of a century ago. The modern Greeks, for example, blame the foreign interference of the nineteenth century for many of the domestic irregularities that persist in that country.

The matter of "interference" also involved the famous American activist character. Some Foreign Service officers in the less-developed countries found opportunities plentiful for assistance and/or meddling. Such Americans instinctively tended to interfere more than necessary in a vacuum of activity or to take sides in local conflicts. Certain American types were always "positive" of the "facts" and knew "exactly" how to put a situation to rights. They took a proprietary interest in the development of the country to which they were accredited.

On the traditional side, there was the gambit of "showing the flag," that is, a display of military force for supposedly subtle political objectives. At the time of the Malta elections in March 1966, twenty-five ships of the U.S. Sixth Fleet, mostly small supply craft and destroyers, all sailed the same day into Valletta to point out to the Maltese on which side of the slice of bread their butter lay.

Sometimes downright inability to intervene, when in reality pressure should have been applied, became a convenient excuse for State Department inaction, such as failure to press for early land reform in South Vietnam. Well-meaning U.S. planners said they found it impossible to organize in 1966 and 1967 because of the war. Yet, to Americans at home, it appeared incomprehensible that U.S. power could not be exercised to remedy a situation. For instance, in January 1964, General Nguyen Khanh executed his coup in South Vietnam in complete defiance of the injunction of General Maxwell Taylor, the U.S. Ambassador at the time, not to "dare" to try to change the Government. The crass fact of power was that the United States did not have enough troops on the ground to make Khanh stay his hand. The United States did not have sufficient force until 1967, when, after the September elections, it forced the South Vietnamese Government to release a Saigon politican, Au Truong Phanh, eighteen hours after he had been arrested for questioning about alleged Communist leanings.

The intertwined relationships—personal, human, psychological, economic, cultural, military, and all others that may exist—were represented by invisible ties of international legality that form the network binding the society of nations together. The United States had well over 4,000 treaties and executive agreements with other governments. U.S. treaties with other powers had the effect of law in the United States, equal with the Constitution. Executive agreements, however, did not make new law, to be observed in the United States. Every year the State Department published an inch-thick multigraphed volume entitled *Treaties in Force,* which listed the international agreements in effect as of January 1 of the year of publication.

In the 150 years since 1789 and the formation of the federal Union to 1939 and the outbreak of World War II, the United States executed 1,300 presidential executive agreements which did not have to be ratified by the Senate. Executive agreements usually were of three general types. The first type was extra pacts made pursuant to existing legislation or a treaty which covered their authority. The second type was agreements that did need Congressional approval for their implementation, that is, needed funds. The third type was made in accordance with the President's constitutional power, which, as has been noted, was vast but vague.

Since the abortive attempt to place the Bricker Amendment in the Constitution in the early 1950's, U.S. national administrations, whatever the party, have been much more conservative about treaties and have increasing recourse to executive agreements, a style of operation not particularly to the liking of the United States Senate. Though hundreds of executive agreements were listed in *Treaties in Force,* including forty-eight for the conduct of educational and cultural exchange programs between the United States and other countries, no one seemed to come up with the precise figure of how many presidential executive agreements had been made under the President's own definition of authority for ostensible reasons of national security. In many defense executive agreements there were operational annexes which were not published, again for reasons of military security.

The State Department boasted, with considerable justification, that the United States had an "umblemished record" of observing its treaty obligations, but insisted on reciprocity as the fundamental token of good faith in international relations, a concept which Secretary Rusk was personally and intensely committed to.

For the State Department, and the world as well, however, the ligaments that bound the society of nations together were fragile and tenuous. Considerable dissonance was evident in world discourse as to whether international society was a fiction, an illusion, or mere pragmatics. In this twentieth-century time of troubles, without an infallible compass and a planetary map upon which all peoples could agree, savants and politicians alike would welcome a new Vattel or Grotius as pathfinders in the modern age for an effective and equitable world system of law acceptable to all. Though there were glosses innumerable upon international law and society, in the considered estimate of the experts, there has been no radically significant advance in the principles of international relations since the sixteenth and seventeenth centuries.

The urgency for a legal Virgil in the present era centers on the control of violence as represented in the annihilating force of thermonuclear power and the complexity of maintaining order without recourse to this ultimate weapon. Operating in the universal flux of events that Heraclitus, the ancient Greek philosopher, epitomized in the aphorism, "You cannot step twice in the same river, for other waters are continuing and flowing on," the State Department obviously had no time for theorists but had to stick to practicalities. Yet even the State Department could not avoid theories where they might have practical application, from that of the balance of power, that is, not to allow any one state or group of states, potentially hostile, to become more powerful than an equivalent balancing group of states; or seeking collaboration between the great powers, like the tentative, on-again-off-again *rapprochement* with the Soviet Union. In general practice, U.S. diplomats employed a variation of the balance-of-power thesis, attempting to establish a system of collective security, which, in its turn, fragmented under the sandblasting of time and new generations.

As in all countries, the American national society, through its Government, had the legal monopoly for the use of force to maintain order. But there was no government of an international society which could own and exercise a similar monopoly, the United Nations as a potential world government being at the moment some light-years away from such a point. An idealized equivalent of a world regime could be the universal state, a modern Roman or British empire in the prime of power and even-handed justice. Many Americans feared, and some still do, that Soviet Russian Communism was, and is still, trying to create such world-wide dominion.

But already for a decade, if not more, the Communist monolith had disintegrated into diverse national socialisms. Effective world government with instant police actions would provide order and security at the expense of liberty and individuality, and, without instant police action, would itself be pockmarked by regional civil wars.

There were also those who wondered why the United States did not establish a world empire, or feared that it would, though the question might be asked whether Americans were fit to rule the world when they could not quite rule themselves. The American nation had had several chances at the vaulting stool that might have led to global empire. After the "Manifest Destiny" days of the mid-nineteenth century and the Mexican war, President James K. Polk also wanted to buy or take Cuba. The island of Santo Domingo later sought commonwealth status within the United States. In the iffy realm of historical conjecture, had the Americans decided to conquer Canada, Mexico, and Central America, they could have become the first truly continental power in the history of the world, especially if they had had the foresight to make Spanish a second language in the United States. But most of the American people were too busy plowing up their own forests to hunger after foreign conquests or the subtleties of governing alien populations.

Another opportunity came at the end of World War II, when the United States owned the world's greatest armaments in ships, planes, and armed forces of 14 million, topped by the greatest weapon of all, the atomic bomb. Instead, President Truman demobilized the nation's strength so fast that U.S. might was turned overnight into a shadow of its potential. Even after the demobilization, while America still had the atomic monopoly, the United States might have taken the lead in the formation of a world state. But the U.S. monopoly of the atomic bomb ended when Russia exploded her first nuclear device in 1949. There was still in 1950 a nostalgic feeling among the elite colonels on General Eisenhower's staff at SHAPE, who desultorily talked of recreating American strength in order to bring order and justice to a turbulent world.

The immediate present, however, finds the State Department's philosophy of diplomacy sliding between the raw facts of international anarchy and the wishful pipe dreams of one-world utopias. But even mundane diplomatic bureaucrats need an umbrella of rationale to give a cover of coherence to operations. In substance, the State Department's operating philosophy is the dominant normal pattern of international politics and diplomacy in a world society of states with rights and duties, functioning under an international rule of law as far as it can be applied with reason and suasion, and with the hint of sanctions and force. Behind the ritual and power etiquette of international relations between states, there are implicit in the *modus operandi* of U.S. diplomacy the premise and precedent that at times, as in Vietnam, the principles of international law have to be enforced by individual members by war, to the end that the balance of power can be recomposed and political conflicts settled. War cuts the Gordian knot when the issue is defined as a vital interest and there is need to restore order and nonviolent processes of government.

Such generalizations tend to come as afterthoughts to the main business in day-to-day foreign affairs operations, which in the 1960's was like a continuous basketball game without a recess, wherein an apparently settled pattern of play began to unravel almost at the very moment it had reached its climax. The players paid lip service to moralities but continually sought self-justification or attempted to change the rules to suit their convenience in the middle of the game.

A sanguine school in the Department believed that, with patience, forbearance, and strength, this time of turmoil, too, would pass and international society would get down at last to efforts in collaboration to reshape the world order, on the analogy of the Treaty of Westphalia in 1648 and the Congress of Vienna in 1815. The former settled the Thirty Years' war in Central Europe and the latter ended twenty-six years of upheaval following the French Revolution and the Napoleonic era, both ushering in a sort of peace for a generation at least.

The twentieth century's two world wars ended what had been called the European civil war, partially at least, in 1957, when the European Economic Community, or Common Market, was formed. But its definitive end was still not in sight as long as the division of Germany endured. The Eastern civil war, or the Sino-Soviet conflict, started coincidently in the same year, 1957. Since 1947 there had spluttered or flamed the global civil war of East-West confrontation, more specifically between the United States and Russia. It was still persisting, though with occasional abatements as the two global powers found common interests in mutuality but overlapping and conflicting interests in the Middle East. Both sides of the Communist rivalry, Russia and China, found a focal point of interest-friction in the Vietnam war, which served as a lynch-pin in the interlocking power mechanisms of all three great states—America, Russia, and China. Thus, for fifty-three years, up to 1967, there had been no complete and simultaneous tranquility anywhere, with dark prospects of war, unrest, and cyclical violence still obscuring the view from the eighth-floor terrace of the State Department.

As the world survived and nations settled into normal pursuits, there emerged the faint but eventual probability of a world summit conclave compelled by at least three reasons: sweeping up the war debris of the era in Europe and Asia; recreating a world order, specifically, in the vessel of the United Nations; and, even more impelling for the onrushing future, rationalizing the affairs of the planet to clear elbowroom for new explorations of space and of virgin wealth on the ocean's bottom.

While concentrating on the standard means of international relations in the society of nations, the State Department hedges its bets by placing its secondary reliance on the United Nations. There is a tentative exploring of the concept of coresponsibility and flirting bashfully with that of abridged sovereignty, as a bridge between the diplomatic traditions of the past and the unknown paths of the future. In short, a major part of what is left of new diplomatic initiative is in the field of the United Nations. It is the best that is available for the principal reason that it exists, and persists.

The United Nations is a way station between the nineteenth century and the twenty-first century, created by fifty-one states with breathless popular anticipation in 1945 as the "hope of the world." It is the heir of its immediate predecessor, the League of Nations, and the distant successor of the amphictyonic council of ancient Greece, where diplomats also were chosen for their oratorical prowess to plead mini-city-states' causes in open forum. Unlike its predecessors, the United Nations has not been shattered by war, but it certainly has been shaken to its back teeth by the injection of the Cold War and the measles of decolonialization, which brought sixty-three newly independent states into the organization since 1943. By 1967 the UN was gorged and overweight with 123 members. At least forty-two ministates were listed as subsisting on the globe, nine making noises about independence and entry into the United Nations. Only one, Western Samoa, declined to join the UN for the simple reason that it could not afford the luxury. On one façade, the thirty-nine-story UN glasshouse at Forty-second Street and First Avenue in New York City was an ivory tower, packed with the 3,500 international civil servants from 108 countries, where what has been termed the "evolving common law of mankind" wound its way up a figuratively endless spiral staircase. In the headquarters basement committee rooms, delegates harangued each other at close quarters and marked the progress of a millimeter as a triumph. An early explorer of Manhattan with a far vision named the East River site of the United Nations, appropriately enough, Turtle Bay. The UN has been called an "echo chamber"; the world's "safety valve"; the "Congress of Mankind," where every nation had one vote and made more noise about it the less power it had; an "international cafeteria"; "a face-saving beauty salon"; and the "world's greatest continuous poker game," with most of the 123 players using wild cards.

The public heart of the United Nations is the General Assembly and the Security Council. Wits maintained that the "heart" should be instead the Meditation Room, because the great function of the United Nations was prayer. The Meditation Room is where the late Secretary General of the United Nations, Dag Hammerskjold, used to sit daily for a few moments to commune with Valhalla.

A part of the heart, the General Assembly is where interminable general debate takes place at the beginning of the annual assemblies, usually late in September. Sceptics listed "talk" as the chief occupation and product of the United Nations and preferred to indicate talk's true locale as the Delegates' lounge, facing the East River, where were spun the infinite cobwebs which might or might not solidify some day to become the visible fabric of diplomacy.

The United Nations is the world's new melting pot, where foreigners are becoming Americanized and Americans surrounding them cosmopolitanized, both in degree. The organization is developing traditions and loyalties of its own in the melding of many national psychologies, those working for the United Nations representing both the most efficient and the most laborious of bureaucratic traits, compounded by their having so many bosses. Love bloomed at the United Nations in many intermarriages, while secretaries from Warsaw, Paris, and Belfast, lonely amid the alien corn, received solace and succor from a wise and compassionate Polish woman psychologist. Humor was essaying its uncertain smile as the UN gained self-assurance. At one committee meeting a gay-caballero type flashed a smile at a handsome female delegate while making a point of order, whereupon the lady asked, "Is that smile procedural or substantive?" As had happened with the receding of the United States' guaranteed Latin American majorities of the 1950's, the reputation of the Latinos as the most debonair lady-killers was, under the new order of decolonialization, giving way to Arabs with endless funds and to Africans with perfect diction in English or French.

Diplomatic missions to the United Nations, if ever they could fulfill UN ideals of removing points of friction between individual states, would theoretically reduce the work of national State Departments to mere routine. At best the United Nations was a faint and ragged foretaste of the millennial "parliament of man." At worst, mere cognizance by the United Nations of the existence of disputes usually afforded some measure of influence against the actual outbreak of hostilities, despite UN failure to halt major outbreaks like the Korean war, the Indian-Pakistani war, the Arab-Israeli wars, or the Vietnam war.

The occasionally comic overtones of its formal proceedings and equally solemn attention to momentous or trivial items notwithstanding, the United Nations could not but be taken with the utmost seriousness because of the utter gravity of the issues with which it dealt. Its ceaseless babble, translated simultaneously into English, French, Spanish, Chinese, and Russian, brought forth a new specialization, which UN professionals defined as "how to weigh smoke," that is, determining whether the "smoke" from the words was radioactive, or dangerous; good for curing hams, or utilitarian; or just plain soot, to be ignored.

All member states, great and small, criticized the United Nations from time to time, but no one left, except temporarily, as Indonesia did in 1965, only to come back in 1966. The emerging nations doted upon the United Nations for its stage, upon which the less poised could parade self-importantly, exhibit their national neuroses, and pick up a modicum of aid from the rich members. The Russians used it as a Cold War battleground and, since 1960, as a major springboard into the affections of the so-called third world of new nations. The Soviets appeared to view the United Nations rather as a "necessary evil," where at least they could keep the capitalist world from dominating. But it was also useful to Moscow as a common ground accommodation with the West when this served a purpose, as in the disarmament conference for the nonproliferation of nuclear weapons at Geneva. The Europeans, possibly more sceptical because of past disillusionment in the League of Nations, found the United Nations adequate for the airing of grievances and a handy meeting place for diplomatic contacts. The Americans, shocked into reality the very next year after the UN's founding by the Soviet incursion into Iranian Aserbajian, also turned to using the United Nations as a Cold War battlefield. Nevertheless, the United Nations had a continuing and definite, if not decisive, influence on U.S. foreign policy.

All countries, including Russia and America, were under scrutiny as their representatives marched up to the UN rostrum. All tried to present their best face, applying rouge, lipstick, and powder to make their policies look as presentable as possible. A major impact of the United Nations on the foreign policies of the major powers was that even the Communist nations could not afford to disregard world opinion. The United Nations helped round out the rough edges of both U.S. and Russian foreign policies. But when it came down to the vital national interests of each country, the naked fist showed just the same. The United Nations thereby served as the only world forum where the hard truths of a nation's policies, when put to a public challenge, could not be evaded and had to be stated out loud for all to hear.

The world organization, which cost over $100 million a year, for which the United States was assessed 31.92 per cent in 1967, or some $33 million, was the unique operational field of the State Department's Bureau for International Organizations. Whereas the Department handled its global diplomacy bilaterally with a hundred-plus separate countries, the International Organizations Bureau handled the entire world in one place, at the United Nations.

The Bureau was the State Department symbol of the world's interdependence. It was the only operating bureau where every facet of U.S. foreign policy came under review, for actual or for potential explanation, in the United Nations. It was the "crisis" bureau in the State Department, because if a world situation arrived at crisis, sooner or later it would also arrive at the United Nations. Therefore, it had to pass through the Bureau for International Organizations as the U.S. presenter of the problem to the United Nations. With the universal application of democratic principles of international relations, every state, therefore, had a say and a vote in everything discussed in the chambers of the United Nations. This fact immeasurably complicated the practical conduct of foreign affairs. The International Organizations Bureau, or, to telescope its title, the UN Bureau, seemed to alternate between operating at white heat and treading water, but never backwater, because the next crisis was around the revolving door.

The rest of the State Department was often a bit cynical or patronizing about the UN Bureau. Its colleagues' pinpricking hardly touched the gung-ho group spirit of the Bureau, which looked on itself as a kind of Marine Corps, elite shock troops to assault and establish a beachhead or to make a valiant last-ditch defense of the nation's interest before the assembled sovereign states of the world.

Part of the five geographical bureaus' annoyance at the UN shop arose out of the fact that the UN Bureau regularly infiltrated their domains. Normally, a problem was handled bilaterally, that is, between the United States and one other country. The UN Bureau assumed action responsibility for the other bureau's problem when the scene of major action shifted, as it did so often recently in the vast area of the underdeveloped world particularly, to the United Nations General Assembly and Security Council. There were many examples of this spearhead role of the UN Bureau taking over other bureaus: in Africa, the Congo, and Rhodesia; in the Middle East, the Arab-Israeli war, Cyprus, and the India-Pakistan war; in Latin America, Cuba, atom-free zones, and the role of Latin Americans as a supporting bloc for the United States in UN parliamentary maneuvering. Even the Vietnam war was shifted into the UN Bureau's diplomatic competence when the State Department, prodded by U.S. Senator Mike Mansfield, started a campaign to force the United Nations to take some action, any action, to bring Communist North Vietnam to the conference table through a Security Council order. The problem of South Korea came within the UN Bureau's purview because the Korean war had been fought as a United Nations war. This was a result of the "Uniting for Peace" resolution which the United States engineered in 1950, when the Soviet Union was boycotting the Security Council and hence was not present to use its veto.

The action-responsibility role of the UN Bureau was a special American diplomatic invention. No other Foreign Office in the world handled United Nations matters in this particular way. The UN Bureau also invaded the patrician purlieus of the European Affairs Bureau. A 1967 instance was the relationship between the nonproliferation treaty being negotiated under the auspices of the United Nations at Geneva and its effect on NATO. The point was to review possible conflicts of purpose, that is, whether a nonproliferation treaty would impair or damage the collective security aspects of the North Atlantic Treaty Organization. This was preventive insurance against a flank attack by the Communist bloc on the continuing necessity of NATO, in the light of the "peaceful" provisions of the nonproliferation treaty.

The UN Bureau primarily got into the business of the geographical bureaus because of the constant overlapping of these bureaus with each other. The regional overlapping sooner than later could end up being vented in the United Nations. For example, it was not quite realized by the State Department that the Latin Americans had strong views of their own about colonialism in Africa, which U.S. diplomats had overlooked. As a consequence, the United States was losing traditionally friendly Latin American votes in the United Nations. The Latin nations themselves had once been colonies of Spain, had revolted to gain their independence, and remembered it.

The State Department profited from the lesson. The UN Bureau began a quiet American decolonialization approach to ride the swells, as the Russians had ridden the early surf, of the emerging nations' tide. This had been launched at the famous fifteenth General Assembly of 1960, when Nikita Khrushchev appeared in person and pounded his shoe to throw the assembly session into bedlam. The original historic resolution by the Security Council was No. 1514 (xv): "Declaration on the granting of independence to colonial countries and peoples."

The UN Bureau consulted with the British Embassy in Washington more than any other section of the State Department did, except the European Bureau. So much of the globe had formerly been under imperial British suzerainty, and some part of it systematically popped into the UN crisis zone, for example, South Africa, Egypt, Cyprus, Rhodesia, India, and Pakistan.

Soviet affairs impelled the UN Bureau to be continually closeted with

the European Bureau. When serious issues shot up to crisis at the United
Nations, their destination ultimately was the Security Council as the court
of last resort. Prior to this arrival, all bilateral remedies to settle disputes
had been theoretically exhausted. In the Security Council the Soviet Union,
as one of the five permanent members (the others being France, Britain,
nationalist China, and the United States), had a veto which it could exercise against any proposed resolution, and did so more than any other
Council member. This happened when Russia was not in agreement with
the United States, which was most of the time. Secondary issues might
be shunted off to the speech-makers in the General Assembly, but the
real beefsteak issues were the Security Council's affair. The Soviets were
deeply interested in such serious disputes, not only because of their
security interest in the global balance-of-power equation but also because
they saw them as opportunities to exercise their new tactical flexibility
of recent years to play up to the so-called nonaligned bloc for collateral
propaganda ends.

A further unique feature marked the UN Bureau. So much of its work
was in the open forum of the outer world. Its public presentations in the
General Assembly and at international conferences were open diplomacy
apparently openly arrived at, in a goldfish bowl. When U.S. Ambassador
to the United Nations Arthur J. Goldberg spoke, his voice was the voice
of America speaking to the world through the United Nations. The constant public aspect of its operations necessitated extreme care in the phraseology of its proposals and comments, particularly since the roughly 200
mass media correspondents at the United Nations were a world press
representing Communist and nonaligned countries, as well as so-called
Free World foreigners and Americans. Besides the substantive, or concrete, diplomatic content, the way proposals sounded on the air and looked
in print had to be constantly examined.

From time to time the Bureau had to take up an alert posture of
defense, as during the meetings of United Nations' Special Committee
of 24, appointed to oversee the "end of colonialism," to protect the rights
of all new nations and to make sure that no territory aspiring to nation-
hood would be blocked in its efforts to obtain independence. The committee of 24 was a convenient sounding board for unfriendly nations to
attempt to pinprick the United States, as, for example, when one group
attempted to place the freedom and independence of Puerto Rico on the
agenda, alleging that Puerto Rico had been denied self-government. The
United States mobilized its support to prevent the Committee from considering such an item and would have boycotted the meeting had the item
slipped onto the program. The Americans and British were able to turn
the tables on the Committee of 24 on one occasion. Knowing that the

Committee would have made a propaganda feast out of the information, the British and the Americans for two whole years kept completely secret their investigations and negotiations for the creation of the Indian Ocean airlift way stations during 1963 and 1964. The two allies thus kept the adjacent African nations from impeding the project by propaganda cries of "imperialism."

Two distinctions characterized the State Department's UN Bureau. It served two Cabinet officers, Secretary Rusk and Ambassador Goldberg, and Secretary Rusk himself was a former Assistant Secretary for International Organizations Affairs. Rusk followed the fortunes of the UN closely ever since, both when he was out of the Department and in New York as president of the Rockefeller Foundation and as a professional diplomat. Moreover, Rusk considered the United Nations Charter as virtually the gospel of international relations and was able to quote Article I, Paragraph 1, on the purposes of the UN, almost by heart, citing its clauses with fervent sincerity. As he frequently reiterated, the first part of this key paragraph underlined all the general principles of his diplomatic philosophy: "To maintain international peace and security, and to that end to take effective collective measures for the prevention and removal of threats to the peace; and for the suppression of acts of aggression or other breaches of the peace. . . ."

The United States Mission to the United Nations might be termed a "junior" State Department by virtue of the scope and size of its problems. But it was in no wise a "second" or "substitute" State Department, not as long as there was a strong President like Lyndon Johnson, who was a Cabinet-operating President and who insisted on lines of command going down through regular channels from himself to the Secretary of State. Goldberg's ambassadorial function as the personal representative of the President of the United States, his eminent career as Secretary of Labor and as Justice of the Supreme Court, and his prerogative of attending Cabinet meetings gave him a substantial voice (but still only one voice) in the formulation of U.S. foreign policy. Goldberg plunged into his UN duties in 1965 with the high vigor he invested in every job he ever undertook, until 1968 when he told the President he would resign. Like all ambassadors, he sometimes was accused of "localitis," that is, of overselling his local field of action, the United Nations. In any event, the Goldberg UN Mission was held fairly close to base. When Henry Cabot Lodge was U.S. Ambassador to the UN, he was politically powerful enough and had a certain commanding manner that helped him obtain considerable leeway in the form in which he presented U.S. policies. Further, those were the years of the Cold War at its chilliest, and Lodge had, in a sense, an easier task in working in black and white. Hence, he did not encounter at the UN the fluid complexities of the postcolonial era, which started with the decolonialization drive of 1960.

The task of serving as a relay point between Goldberg and Rusk fell to Assistant Secretary of State for International Organizations Affairs Joseph J. Sisco. As his predecessor, Harlan Cleveland, had been between Adlai Stevenson and Rusk, Sisco was the "man on the flying trapeze" between Goldberg and Rusk. Committed of necessity to hold the confidence of both Rusk and Goldberg, Sisco had the job of interpreting the State Department in Washington to the New York Mission and the New York Mission to Washington. Ninety-eight per cent of the routine contacts between the State Department and this major diplomatic mission were through Sisco. One per cent of the queries or issues rose to Secretary Rusk, personally, and perhaps half a per cent to the White House on "normal" crises. White House contact came much more so in spurts when in late 1967 the President turned to the United Nations as a possible instrumentality for bringing the Vietnam war to the conference table.

Sisco and his staff, in sum, acted as forwarding agents to the New York Mission, processing the material through all the relevant bureaus as the complete thoughts of the State Department as a whole up to that moment on points of issue. The second Sisco function was to serve as a backstop to the New York Mission as it engaged the world on the front lines in the key meetings of the General Assembly and, above all, the Security Council. This closely integrated method of operation, aided by elaborate electronic facsimile communications, was duplicated nowhere else in the State Department's foreign policy establishment. In the process of helping to ensure that the State Department and the New York Mission were both pointing in the same direction of desired U.S. policy, Sisco and his aides used a "squawk box," a six-by-six black loud-speaker, which relayed the actual debate taking place on the UN premises among the American delegation and the other UN members. The "squawk box" device represented a standby reserve reinforcement for intellectual and debating support to the U.S. delegation in New York as it went into its forensic and parliamentary battles to gain the terrain positions called for by the objectives of U.S. policy, or to deny ground to opponents of U.S. policy. To receive quick reactions and send oral guidance to Goldberg and his aides, telephone lines were held open both in the UN Bureau and at the UN Mission for instant conversation, while the telephone numbers in every telephone booth outside the halls where debates were taking place were also on tap, so that practical guidance or suggestions could be volunteered instanter from Washington either over a scrambler line, meaning a telephone device to block possible eavesdropping, or to an official standing near a telephone booth, to whom recommendations could be passed in a guarded manner. The reverse approach from New York to Washington was made as the U.S. delegation needed new instructions, that is, going beyond the agreed battle plans which had been settled in advance of debate but which had had to be changed as the political opposition brought up its own new guns or made surprise attacks.

The backroom quarterbacks in Sisco's office could provide Goldberg and his advisers with practically instantaneous decisions from the top of the Department within five minutes. This was possible because Rusk personally had an intimate knowledge of United Nations workings from the 1948–1949 days when he headed UN affairs in the State Department. Sisco had immediate access to the Secretary on the telephone. Conversing elliptically in verbal cablese, Sisco could get Rusk to give a decision at the end of a three-minute conversation, thanks to Rusk's acquaintance with the parliamentary requirements in the specialized diplomatic arena of the United Nations; why, for instance, certain steps were being taken or modified, getting a resolution watered down, or taking a firmer stand on a crucial point for tactical reasons. Familiar with the backdrop of UN operations, Rusk had a feel for the actual context of a shifting tactical situation, without wasting time in having matters spelled out to him.

Secretary Rusk, in the quick Sisco fill-ins, kept abreast of the fast-moving UN parliamentary diplomacy so as to be able to answer inquiries from the President or the press. In his own time on the UN job in the late 1940's, Rusk had devised the moratorium procedure on the question of Communist Chinese admission to the United Nations. The tactic was for the General Assembly to decide not to deal with the question. This procedure lasted from 1951 until 1964, when a change in tactics was made by the United States in presenting the issue as an "important question," which, under the rules, prescribed a two-thirds majority for admission.

Assistant Secretary Sisco, as the Department's top expert on the United Nations, had made the United Nations his professional career since 1956. He graduated into his current political post on a record of having been a perceptive and shrewd tactician and analyst, studying the United Nations field like a stock market trader figuring out which stocks were going up or down and when to buy long or short, except that in his actual UN work Sisco had increasingly to operate on margin, and a steadily diminishing one at that, as the once safe Latin American majority became engulfed in the rising tide of the emerging countries, which in 1967 made up over half of the United Nations.

Sisco's alternate superior in the UN field, Ambassador Goldberg, was treated as one of the ranking officers in the State Department when he descended upon it, at least one day a week, if he could get away from New York. Symbolic of the top-status treatment Goldberg received in State was having the list of his personal visitors circulated among the senior officers, in the same manner as were the visitors' lists of the four ranking officers of the Department—the Secretary, the Under Secretary, the Under Secretary for Political Affairs, and the Deputy Under Secretary for Political Affairs.

At the United Nations, Goldberg had settled down to being a top-drawer behind-the-scene negotiator. He no longer seemed to entertain, as he might have had reason to once, the belief that international disputes could be settled as easily as those he had negotiated or arbitrated when he was Secretary of Labor or counsel for the trade unions. The fuzz has rubbed off the peach, as far as sanguine expectations were concerned, from the universal frustrations over the Vietnam war and the continued perils of the Middle East. Despite his Jewish faith, Goldberg had been able to present the United States viewpoint dispassionately and without ever having an Arab UN delegate charge him with personal pro-Israel bias. Goldberg's greatest physical travail had been the Arab-Israeli war, when the Security Council met twice a day and often through the night, necessitating terribly long hours for those four or five weeks, with very little sleep. In Washington, Sisco and his immediate staff practically lived in the offices twenty-four hours a day in this period.

No William Jennings Bryan at the rostrum, Goldberg was at his best in private backroom converse. In his first two years at the UN, he held nearly 800 meetings with heads of other delegations and members of the UN Secretariat and attended over 150 of the estimated 700 social events a year that take place in the UN diplomatic milieu. The shock of the Arab-Israeli war and the encroachment of the East-West Cold War into the strategic Arab crossroads, which had started with the 1966 speech of Soviet Premier Kosygin in Cairo calling for the revolutionary unity of the Middle East, were mitigated somewhat for Goldberg when the Russians asked him to collaborate with them in framing a resolution to end the crisis. Goldberg produced a draft from a Latin American prototype, which the Russians accepted. But their political allies, the Arabs, turned it down. The resolution the Russians had accepted in draft would have brought about the withdrawal of the Israeli forces and given the Israelis an end to the state of belligerency which the Arabs had maintained since 1949.

The Department's UN Bureau, in 1967 in particular, operated under the handicap of the unpopularity of the United Nations in the United States because of Secretary General U Thant's withdrawal of United Nations Emergency Forces as a buffer between the Israelis and the Egyp-

tians on the Gaza Strip and the Sinai Peninsula on May 18. The order
was quickly denounced by Israelis, U.S. Senators, and most of the American press as "precipitous." Immediately thereafter, Egyptian President
Nasser launched his "Call-me-if-you-think-I'm bluffing" propaganda campaign by the so-called blockade of the Gulf of Aqaba. This launched the
Middle East crisis almost full force for the United States. Up to the very
outbreak of hostilities on June 5 the UN Bureau was frantically engaged
on a contingency plan, which had passed beyond the theoretical stage and
was in the first stage of rather abortive consultations with fifteen other
countries concerning a means of testing the blockade and calling Nasser's
hand, one way or another, even to the extent of using an armed flotilla
to guarantee the safe passage of merchant vessels to the Israeli port of
Elath, and so re-establish the U.S.-cherished principle of freedom of the
seas and innocent maritime passage.

Exasperation with U Thant's prompt acceptance of the liquidation of
the UNEF was not much lessened by the circumstance that his hand had
been forced by the individual withdrawal of the troops supplied by India
and Yugoslavia, both allies of Egypt in a triumvirate of purported leadership of the supposedly nonaligned world. Sympathy for Israel multiplied
many times after its massive victory. Extreme Arab denunciations of
American policy created a climate in which it was extremely difficult,
if not impossible, for the UN Bureau to propose more balanced recommendations in dealing with both sides on an even-handed basis so that
long-term U.S. foreign policy objectives of being friends with the Arabs
as well as the Israelis could be maintained.

The anti-United Nations mood in the United States was aggravated,
moreover, by the failure of the UN to intervene in the Vietnam war.
There was a profound reason, however, for the UN's attitude, as indicated
by Senator Frank Church, Democrat of Idaho, when he was a member
of the U.S. delegation to the United Nations in 1966, a practice in vogue
since the beginning of the United Nations, with two Senators and two
Representatives appointed by the President as delegates on alternate years.
Church wrote: "But much as we regret the abuse of the veto by the
Soviet Union, it would be a mistake to regard this as a sole reason for
UN inaction. Actually, it was never in the cards for the United Nations
to enforce peace between the great powers. Lions, sporting for a fight,
cannot be separated by a tabby cat, however pure and praiseworthy its
motivation."

Goldberg presented the United States point of view about Vietnam in
speeches at the United Nations in 1966 and in 1967. Both statements
were the fullest, most detailed expressions of U.S. policy made by the
United States for settlement of the Vietnam war. But Secretary General

U Thant declined to think so. His view was that it was first necessary for an unconditional stoppage of the bombing of North Vietnam by the United States. Though U Thant's stand on the bombing halt was popular in many sections of the American community, and unpopular with the Johnson administration, his refusal to take any initiative, despite his proclaimed intent to use his office for mediation, did not sit well with the State Department, provoking irritated comments by American diplomats, among the mildest being that U Thant was "naïve" and "stubborn."

The U.S. appeals to the United Nations, in addition to the February 1966 and the September 1967 attempts to get the Security Council to act on the Vietnam war, were another instance of the UN Bureau's action responsibility, after close consultation with the East Asian and European Bureaus. The strategic intent was to put the Soviet Union to the test of agreeing to, or vetoing, a UN resolution on the war. In September 1967, Johnson urged Senator Mansfield to renew his proposal that the United Nations Security Council take up the Vietnam war, a proposal which Mansfield had been making on and off for the previous ten months, during which time he had received the support of 57 other Senators. Secretary General U Thant, however, still seemed to bear a grudge against the Johnson administration for allegedly having declined to take up what he believed was a bona fide offer from Hanoi to negotiate in September of 1964. For its part, the State Department classified Hanoi's invitation at that time as more an offer to accept an American surrender and dishonorable evacuation of U.S. commitment in South Vietnam. The President fully supported the Mansfield gambit as part of his campaign to explore all approaches to peace, but, always as a minimum, to require some advance indication of the reciprocity which North Vietnam would engage itself to perform in return for the stoppage of the bombing. Hanoi, as the year neared its end, had not budged either.

There was yet another motivation behind the move. U.S. diplomats, envisaging UN action in the name of the world's peoples, could also see a call on the United States to suspend the bombing on its own decision. The UN thereby would be itself in the position of "a friend of the court" and, in good conscience, therefore, obligated to help make the settlement as fair to the United States as to North Vietnam. This potential gambit had obvious political risks on the American domestic scene. It reflected the foreign-domestic interface considerations that the Department's UN Bureau had to take into account in framing proposals for high authority.

The United Nations Bureau's close connection with the Vietnam war was indicated by its membership in the "peace feeler" committee on the top echelon of the State Department. This group systematically was on the lookout for and screened all approaches, from whatever source, which brought, disclosed, or hinted at Hanoi's latest attitude on peace negotiations. The group was headed by Ambassador-at-Large Averell Harriman and included Assistant Secretary Sisco, Assistant Secretary Bundy for the Far East, Benjamin Read, Executive Secretary of the Department, and Chester Cooper, Harriman's special assistant.

Official interdependence did not come cheaply. As the trend increased toward multilateral activity, that is, action involving many nations all at the same time, on top of bilateral, or country-to-country, relations, the work of the State Department was doubled. In consequence, the UN Bureau was responsible for the expenditure of 23 per cent of the entire State Department's budget. Assistant Secretary Sisco spent more time on Capitol Hill, testifying, than any other Assistant Secretary. He was second only to former Assistant Secretary Frankel for Cultural Affairs as the object of Congressman Rooney's sardonic remarks about spending the taxpayers' money.

It was not so much the nearly $2.5 million that the Bureau required in salaries and expenses for its 178 employees, or the $1.6 million for the staff of 128 for Ambassador Goldberg in the U.S. Mission in New York. What galled the Congressman was the sum asked for international organizations. These primarily included the United Nations and eight of its specialized agencies, for which the 1968 budget request asked a sum of $77.1 million, of which $33.6 million was for the United Nations parent organization alone, though the 1967 assessment for the United States had been reduced a fraction, to 31.91 per cent. The total figure for the international organizations, thirty-five of them in all, was $109.3 million. Lastly, there was a request of more than $141 million for voluntary U.S. contributions to such items as the UN development program, technical assistance to the Congo, Palestine refugees, the Children's Fund, and the Cyprus peacekeeping operation. By far the largest contribution was for the UN development program, $75 million worth, a program supervised by Paul Hoffman, the first administrator of the Marshall Plan. Over $19.4 million of the contributions to international organizations were entirely for inter-American groups. Europe, through NATO and the Organization for Economic Cooperation and Development, was due to receive $8 million. Two million dollars were budgeted for expenses of attending international conferences. In nine years, from 1958 to 1967, U.S. contributions for international organizations had risen over $55 million, prompting Representative Elford A. Cederberg, Republican of Michigan, a Rooney colleague, to cry out, "And our share goes up and up."

Sisco tried to explain: "We are in a den of politics in every one of these international organizations. We are negotiating in a very vigorous fashion. We have taken the lead on these budgets, Mr. Chairman, and we are trying to keep them down."

Rooney commented, "The lead must be plenty putrified because the results have been, year after year, additional, additional, additional."

While the world's attention was focused on the loud political debates in the General Assembly, by far the largest part of the United Nations' activities was nonpolitical and went virtually unnoticed. It was the UN Bureau's responsibility to keep its eye on these multifarious activities as well, not only through its major missions in New York and Geneva but also by means of all the U.S. embassies in the world where UN activities were taking place. The word "multifarious" was almost an understatement to describe the tremendous range of operations performed by the United Nations. The United States spent, in all, nearly $300 million a year for the parent organization and the more than fifty international agencies and programs connected with it. Ninety-six members of the United Nations were classified as economically less developed and made miniscule contributions to the regular UN budget.

This meant that economic problems were always backing into the political domain, as, for example, the case of the United Nations Conference on Trade and Development, or UNCTAD, made up, in the very largest part, of poor, or have-not, nations. The conferences conducted themselves like guests in a luxury hotel who were confident that somebody else would pick up the tab. Assistant Secretary Sisco sought sympathy from Rooney, disclosing that the underdeveloped countries had voted to spend from $300,000 to $400,000 for copies of summaries of the voluminous reports issuing from the conference, a printing cost development which Sisco was at a loss to stop.

Besides the Security Council and the General Assembly, the UN Bureau, through its New York Mission, had diplomatic relations with the Secretariat of the United Nations, the officers who supervised the entire organization and carried out U Thant's proposals. In addition, there was the most important general organ of the United Nations, the Economic and Social Council, an umbrella for the many specialized activities. There was also a Trusteeship Council, which, as more and more nations became free, found itself with less and less to do but managed to make considerable clatter about it. Then there was the International Court of Justice, resident in isolated dignity at The Hague.

The United Nations thus had an executive and cabinet department, a congress, and a judiciary, but no army, navy, or air force, as an arm of discipline. This lack was the great issue of debate in the ceaseless disputes about peacekeeping and how to take effective measures against unlawful violence. The following list of the fifteen technical agencies of the United Nations indicates the many worlds of the UN:

UNIT AND HEADQUARTERS

	MEMBER STATES
International Atomic Energy Agency, Vienna	99
International Labor Organization, Geneva	118
Food and Agriculture Organization, Rome	113
United Nations Educational, Scientific, and Cultural Organization, Paris	120
World Health Organization, Geneva	124
International Bank for Reconstruction and Development, Washington	105
International Finance Corporation, Washington	82
International Development Association, Washington	96
International Monetary Fund, Washington	105
International Civil Aviation Organization, Montreal	111
Universal Postal Union, Berne	129
International Telecommunications Union, Geneva	129
World Meteorological Organization, Geneva	129
Inter-Governmental Maritime Consultative Organization, London	64
General Agreement on Tariffs and Trade, Geneva	84

Six functional commissions—Human Rights, Narcotics, Population, Social Development, Statistical, and Status of Women—were the sites of fierce forensics and anthropological merriment as the world cultures attempted to find a common denominator on the highest supportable level. The United States UN representatives had not a little discomfiture in some of these commissions. For example, a Human Rights convention was passed in 1948, but the United States Senate has yet to ratify it because of resistance to civil rights, though every President in the last twenty years has exhorted the Congress to do its duty.

Congressional nonaction on human rights and piecemeal harassment over U.S. contributions to the UN international organizations reflected residual resentment against U.S. foreign involvements. American politicians' indignation at the foreigners, in the light of the huge sums spent by the United States in foreign aid, found a ready scapegoat in the poor nations' behavior in the United Nations when it came to votes in which the American benefactor was interested. U.S. Senator Karl Mundt, Republican of South Dakota, drew up a list of twenty-one nations which had received substantial aid from the United States, "taking," as Mundt said,

"U.S. millions while opposing the United States on vital votes." The list follows:

Country	U.S. Aid through 1963 (millions of dollars)	Votes with U.S.	Votes with Russia
Algeria	94.6	3	9
Burma	117.1	4	8
Cambodia	366.4	4	8
Ceylon	84.3	6	8
Ethiopia	201.6	5	8
Ghana	159.2	6	8
Guinea	30.6	4	7
India	4,692.9	8	8
Iraq	68.3	3	7
Jordan	412.2	3	6
Laos	328.4	3	7
Mali	1.9	2	9
Nepal	67.5	6	7
Nigeria	83.1	6	6
Somali Republic	36.4	5	6
Sudan	74.5	5	8
Syrian Arab Republic	83.5	4	7
Tunisia	355.2	7	8
Uganda	12.1	3	7
United Arab Republic	802.4	3	8
Yemen	29.0	1	7

The United Nations had at least ten continuing special programs, like the Children's Fund, or UNICEF; funds for refugees, both East-West and Arab categories; plus a whole flock of subsidiary, or affiliated, units like UNIDO, or the United Nations Industrial Development Organization, to help the low-developed countries obtain trained consultants on specific problems; or the International Center for Settlement of Investment Disputes, a boon to the advanced or developed countries, which had to put up the money for financing the emerging countries' development.

The specialized or technical UN agencies had done a modest but effective job. As a result, the United States, since 1954, had been attempting to shift more U.S. foreign aid funds into multilateral organizations, not only to take the heat off itself politically in a measure, but as a means of exercising closer control over the way in which the UN spent funds and selected projects and personnel. UN aid was a new field of rivalry between East and West. Senator Fulbright also had believed that aid funneled to the United Nations would be more efficacious economically and more antiseptic politically. However, in 1967, when the Johnson administration tried to emphasize the multilateral aspects of its foreign aid bill, Fulbright reversed course and objected.

A principal attraction in the UN approach was the UN development program. Under Paul Hoffman's expert guidance, the UN had concentrated on preinvestment assistance, mostly in surveys—727 projects with a total value of over $1.5 billion in 103 countries and technical assistance—90,000 experts—to 130 countries—as a means of fertilizing the ground for standard economic assistance when the countries in question were ready for it. Under Hoffman's Rule No. 1, self-help, the program's $520 million for 120 nations, of which the United States contributed more than 40 per cent, generated investments of over $920 million by 92 of the same countries for projects of direct benefit to themselves.

The commentary, light or shrewd, said; the good works noted; the value of the assemblies as an annual migration point for from eighty to a hundred foreign ministers, and as a camouflage and cover for clandestine and furtive meetings between public enemies in efforts to wet down smoldering disputes, recorded—in the end the fundamental fact remained that the United Nations was far from capable of carrying out the prime mission for which it had been organized: to keep the peace, to prevent wars, and to stop wars.

The United Nations had a round dozen major peacekeeping operations to its credit, but of a marginal, fragile, and on-sufferance character. This situation could be laid directly to the failure of nations to abridge, give up, or lend temporarily their sovereignty to the United Nations to act in their name. The refusal was symbolized in the veto of United Nations Security Council. Apropos, U.S. Senator Clifford P. Case, Republican of New Jersey, said, in his report as a member of the U.S. delegation to the Twenty-first, or 1966, General Assembly:

So the 21st General Assembly ended as it began, with a chasm of opinion on the peacemaking issue as wide as ever. . . . The United Nations has entered the third decade of its existence with the same fundamental question before it as its beginning: how is the Organization going to put into practice the principle of collective security.

When the peacekeeping operations were organized, the questions of who was to pay for them always cropped up as the main obstacle, afterward as well as before, although it was superabundantly clear, as Ambassador Goldberg wrote President Johnson, that "the simple prevention of open violence is itself an obvious prerequisite to the ultimate negotiated settlement." The refusal to pay hinged ultimately again on the previously cited fundamental issue of sovereignty: if a nation did not agree with the purpose of the peacekeeping operation, it had and exercised the right of refusing to pay for it.

The Soviet Union refused to pay its assessed share of expenses for both the Congo and Middle East operations, in 1967 amounting to over $72 million. France refused to pay a $17 million assessment for the Congo operation, which employed nearly 20,000 United Nations troops from twenty-three countries for almost five years.

Former Assistant Secretary for International Organizations Harlan Cleveland had been determined to "put the Russians' feet to the fire," in forcing them to pay their assessment. A World Court advisory opinion in July 1962, pursuant to a General Assembly request, said that both UNEF in the Middle East and UNOC in the Congo were proper "expenses of the Organization." Therefore, they could be included in a calculation of payments in arrears under Article 19 of the United Nations Charter.

The gravest constitutional crisis in United Nations history, as a result, opened on January 1, 1964, when the Soviet Union became more than two years in arrears in its contributions. For the first time in the history of the UN, a major power was threatened with the loss of its vote. The General Assembly characteristically stalled, delaying its meeting from the usual September opening to December first. But it was not able to resolve the issue or break down the adamant stand by Russia and France. The impasse almost paralyzed the UN for the whole of the 1964 session.

Ambassador Goldberg, appointed to succeed the late Adlai Stevenson, in his first formal appearance before the United Nations in August 1965, broke the deadlock by withdrawing the American threat to bring the issue to a head. For the sake of preserving the United Nations, yet not giving up American adherence to the principle that all states should pay their just debts, Goldberg said that "the United States recognizes, as it simply must, that the General Assembly is not prepared to apply Article 19."

Senator Church spoke for many others when he said in his report: "Looking back on it, though I failed to appreciate it at the time, the American position on the compulsory application of Article 19 always lacked political reality. Unlike governments, the UN has no power to tax; it cannot compel member states to pay for peacekeeping operations with which they disagree."

Had the shoe been on the other foot, Church went on to say: ". . . for example, a UN intervention to keep the peace in the Caribbean from which Castro were to somehow benefit—can any one imagine an American President agreeing to pay our share of the expense, or the Congress ever appropriating the money?"

Thus, the military staff committee authorized under Article 47 of the UN Charter was merely nominal, and it mostly sat around on its gold braid, since the Security Council, which it was supposed to serve, never activated it to take "strategic" direction of its nonexistent UN peacekeeping "army."

Nevertheless, as Goldberg said in a report to President Johnson, "Measured by the probable cost of the wars that did not happen, . . . [peacekeeping] has already paid for the cost of the United Nations many times over."

The preliminary national security interest of the United States in the United Nations was peacekeeping, a major service in smothering brush fires before they could become major conflagrations and, always possibly, a nuclear war. This was the overriding justification for the expenditure of $3 billion in U.S. funds for the United Nations in its twenty-two-year existence up to 1967.

The United Nations would without question persist in attempting to engineer peacekeeping operations when the necessity arose, either through the Security Council as the organ primarily responsible or, failing that, via the General Assembly. There was a further major problem connected with peacekeeping. It concerned the manner in which the peacekeeping forces could be used. There was simply no basis of applicable law upon which to operate them. Brian Urquhart, an official attached to the UN Under Secretary for Special Political Affairs, in an educational TV discussion, pointed out that this lack of a legal doctrine for UN peacekeeping forces made it incumbent upon the UN troops in blue helmets, their distinctive headgear, virtually to operate with a rule book in hand, as to what they could or could not do. The basic rule for a UN military contingent was that force could be used only as a last resort, in self-defense. In the Congo, the rule was liberalized to include insuring the freedom of movement of UN forces. Urquhart added:

If, for example, hostile elements try to take over one of its [UN] positions, or to deprive it of its weapons, obviously it is going to lead very shortly to a situation in which they may have to use a very limited degree of force. But the degree of force is deliberately and very seriously limited because these forces are strictly nonfighting forces. They are not intended in any sense to get into a situation where they may have to engage in a full-scale military battle.

Besides carrying out its fire-brigade function in crises and its spearhead role when U.S. security interests were at stake in United Nations confrontations, the State Department's UN Bureau faced a main task for the future: to explore and exploit practicable opportunities in the modern United Nations system of interrelated organisms, a field of diplomatic endeavor that had been barely scratched.

Harlan Cleveland, as UN Assistant Secretary, significantly broadened this consciousness of new United Nations possibilities for U.S. foreign policy. He stressed utilization of the operational capacities of the United Nations and the patient brick-by-brick process of institution-building as a foundation for nation-building. Cleveland advocated a continuous campaign to widen the area of concern by ordinary citizens and to lead to greater assumption of responsibility on behalf of the United Nations by the intellectuals of the world, so that one day education and enlightened self-interest might lead the united peoples of the world out of their miasma of mistrust.

CHAPTER XI

INTERAGENCY IMBROGLIO:
Matrix of Decision

THE FACTS, ONCE LIGHTLY
over, have been touched on, as have the difficulties. Everyone knew the
problems. Surprisingly, a lot of very smart gentlemen were full of solutions.
But how does one go about it, translating problems into solutions? And
what about the foreigners at whom all this problem-and-solution confusion
is directed? What happens when these foreigners jump the gun and dash all
one's carefully arranged pieces off the board?

In short, the organization, conduct, and administration of foreign policy
in the nuclear space age still remained the gravest and most complex challenge of the President and of the State Department, the presidential arm
delegated to formulate a consistent world policy of constructive and preventive diplomacy, the kind which critics keep on demanding with almost pathetic desperation. The Department was called upon to accomplish this
Herculean mission in a world which has seedbeds of Balkan wars in Latin
America, Africa, the Middle East, and southeast Asia. Attempts to halt
or withdraw from this enforced world involvement were like Canute's
trying to stay the waves of the sea. Retrenchment into a Fortress America
would entail the necessity of becoming bona fide partners with the Latin
Americans and the Canadians, restructuring a new United States of the
Americas, immediately building the Pan-American Highway from the
Bering Straits to the Straits of Magellan, and starting an antipoverty program in Patagonia.

As it is, half the foreign affairs events on which the State Department
renders decisions are controversial enough. Of the barrage of incoming
cables, the Department handles 80 per cent within its own lower levels.
The remaining 20 per cent gravitate to the Department's senior officers
and keep them extremely busy. Under such pressures, it is surprising
that these overburdened executives are not accused more often of scatter-
shooting their decisions. The tyranny of the work is unbelievable. Too
many issues to decide; too many little fires in the in-basket to put out;

the stacked-up piles of paper, everything marked "action-urgent," that must be gotten through. When does one cut off the analysis process and make a judgment? How much time should one realistically spend on sifting the problem before reaching the point of decision take-off? There is precious little time to reflect about delivering decisions of state in orderly, school-book fashion. The constant tug-of-war was between what one must do and what one would like to do. Lucius Battle, the Assistant Secretary for the Middle East, recalling his time almost two decades ago in the State Department as an assistant to Secretary Acheson, pointed out that Acheson had crises, too—but usually one at a time. Today there may be, and often are, three or four crises going on contemporaneously, with another two or three in the immediate offing, bubbling merrily and threatening to boil over.

The life-enhancing opportunities of the new technologies simultaneously have destructive potentialities. Both compete for the impulses of good and evil that breed in the human heart. In the new uncertainties of fathoming how to live with the sudden efflorescence of technical capabilities for good and evil, construction and destruction, war and peace, the first and foremost duty of all nation-states was to stay alive, with self-respect, if possible, but somehow to survive and flourish. When words like "honor," "happiness," "pride," and "glory" appeared, the whirligig of passions took over. By imperative necessity, therefore, leaders of people who held the heavy decisions were always torn between the two factors of risk and/or safety, in formulating foreign policies. The gravity of the responsibility was multiplied many times by the ultimate thermonuclear power that great superstates like the United States and Russia possess, and that China would possess, sooner than later.

The direct significance of the new age for Americans was made clear as an ABC of modern life by U.S. Senator Arthur H. Vandenberg in 1945, when he said, "The oceans no longer guard our ramparts." In the current era, it was not so much a direct fear that the Soviet Union would unleash a deliberate nuclear attack that bothered American leaders. It was the surprised uneasiness of a giant pinpricked by a hundred or more Lilliputians. These other nations were comparatively small and powerless, but capable potentially of acquiring and shooting nuclear weapons. It was as if the once harmless Lilliputians were all suddenly armed with cannons, with which they could blackmail or browbeat either the United States or the Soviet Union into deadly folly. Inexperienced and irresponsible, but avid of power, the smaller states had imbibed the new doctrine of the atomic power formulated by General Pierre Gallois, the French strategist who provided much of the nuclear philosophy behind President Charles de Gaulle's *force de frappe,* or striking force. Gallois asserted that the atomic bomb neutralized armed multitudes, equalized the size of populations, minimized geographical distances, reduced the strategic advantage of states with vast territories, and leveled nations to equality. The Gallois gospel, besides its terrible poetry, had morbid fascination for the nonnuclear nations. Its potential impact was brought down to earth as a factor to consider in all future U.S. foreign policy planning when Defense Secretary McNamara noted, in a 1966 Montreal speech, that 164 "significant resorts to violence" had taken place in the world since 1958, 15 of them military conflicts between two states and 149 of them internal upheavals.

Reorganization of U.S. policy-making machinery was posed against this background. It forced reconsideration of every issue among three constants: technical or economic aid involvement with other developing nations that would give no cause for friction; opting for the side of caution and still more limited and curtailed involvement as the safer course in ambiguous or nuclear situations; and withdrawing or clarifying past involvements, so that the United States need not be dragged into unforeseen crises by the yoke of past commitments around its neck. George Ball, in *The Discipline of Power,* indicating that the international obligations which the United States was currently stuck with had been entered into too hastily and in too ill-organized a manner, said: "The cold war impelled the United States to extend its commitments throughout the world, inducing us to assume responsibilities where our interests were not always clearly apparent."

It was these U.S. commitments, their implication of an open-ended charge upon the future, that gave Senator Fulbright, a Vietnam dove, as well as Senator Russell, a Vietnam hawk, sober pause and·grave concern. The State Department's Office of the Legal Adviser listed exactly 4,599 international pacts which the United States officially regarded as being in force and to be observed in 1967. Of the total, 4,144 were bilateral and 455 multilateral. Actual treaties numbered 852, while executive agreements, which usually need no ratification by the Senate, amounted to 3,747. Of the 660 bilateral treaties, 42 were mutual security defense treaties. Bilateral executive agreements numbered 3,484. There were 192 multilateral treaties and 263 multilateral executive agreements.

The recurring word in analyses of how better to organize the decision-making machinery of the State Department was "coordination." The Senate Foreign Relations Committee, in effect, suggested a recodification and elimination of superfluities in the nation's legally binding international commitments. This would solve a good part of the problem in that there would be that much less to coordinate. Most U.S. pacts on record dealt with the commercial and technical aspects of normal, peaceful relations among nations and would, by and large, be found not only innocuous but useful. The real argument concerned military treaties—which could be safely canceled and which would it be unwise to terminate. The original debates about treaties had usually been between two attitudes—play it safe or take a chance. The State Department was accused of playing it too safe, the Defense Department of taking too many chances.

To the State Department, whose origins go back to the Continental Congress in 1781, the role of being the man in the middle was nothing new. In the period after World War II, when foreign issues began to proliferate like crab grass, as early as 1951 the Brookings Institution stated that the administrative problems of the U.S. Government in the foreign relations field bulked larger and were more difficult than those of the entire Federal Government in the 1930's. The organization of close-meshed operational machinery that could both sieve out the trivia and focus an integrated rationale upon the crucial problems was increasingly recognized as the overriding national requirement, and one that was imperative if the United States was to maintain domestic tranquility and world leadership.

The State Department had to rid itself of the psychological inheritance of the past, when it was content to devise policies and never worried whether or how they were carried out. It had had to fly its kite inside the bureaucratic structure without a ground wire or solid base of authority. But in March 1966 it received its written delegation of presidential authority. As 1967 neared its end, the Department had yet to come up with an organization that could be a flexible tool not only for itself but for the whole panting federal bureaucracy. It had at long last started the job, but there was a long way to go. There were always so many things to do right away that bottlenecks developed in the existing and makeshift machinery. As a result, few matters of high consequence or long-range import were settled. Staving off the mountain of instant necessities was as much as could be accomplished at times. Bureaucratic rivalries had made decisions a process of bargaining rather than one of wise and balanced determinations. Habits of conflict over the use of funds and resources of expertise and manpower, misapprehension of the total national objective in foreign policies, and arguments over grubby little issues were hard to break. Former Under Secretary of State Robert A. Lovett characterized these shortcomings as the "foul-up factor" in Government. He told the Jackson Senate subcommittee on national security operations in 1960: "Whether or not this itch to get into the act is a form of status seeking . . . the idea seems to have got around that just because some decision may affect your activities, you automatically have a right to take part in making it."

More exasperating was the personal element. It was like the limerick about the nice boy from Khartoum: who does what, with which, and to whom. Who was the right person to talk to, about what subject? Who was the person in point of fact responsible for making a decision at his level? Who were the persons who gave advice to the decision-maker? Who should follow through to insure that a decision was in process of actuation? And how should it be done most efficiently? The Operations Coordinating Board, which was supposed to carry out the function inferred from its name as the agent of the National Security Council, in the Eisenhower administration performed this task via a flurry of snowflakes, that is, memo-reminders. These more often than not turned out to be a daisy chain of futility, as reflected in the remark of President Eisenhower, when asked to make a decision on a certain item. He said in surprise: "I thought I decided that." Passing the word down to the troops proved to be a vexation to President Kennedy, too, despite his best efforts to energize the federal machinery into advance action. In the Cuban nuclear missile crisis, Kennedy learned to his dismay that orders that he had given four months earlier to remove the obsolescent Jupiter missiles from Turkey had not been carried out. And in the midst of the tense week of confrontation with the Soviets, he was informed that an American U-2 plane, taking air samplings off the Chokut peninsula in northeastern Siberia, had overflown Soviet air space. Kennedy said: "There is always some s.o.b. who doesn't get the word." Then there was President Johnson, an old pro at knowing where all the bodies were buried, who needed four months to work with sardonic detachment the levers of power in Washington and abroad before he could fashion a new policy about food aid to India and other undernourished nations in late 1966.

Yet it was not always a question of pure subterfuge on the bureaucrats' part to conspire to work their special will, with a result that might be admirable but narrow and not in the total national interest. Or even a question of bureaucratic receptivity to new ideas, despite the rueful remark of President Kennedy, who said: "I love that idea. The question is, is the Government up to it?" The bureaucracy in actuality liked to see issues aired—once a responsible superior had the courage to break the ice and to lead. Too many top officials allowed themselves to be rushed off their feet and get caught up with the ceaseless round of day-to-day problems. They never gave themselves a chance to see the forest for the trees. In the State Department the Under Secretaries tended to usurp the jobs of Assistant Secretaries, often out of sheer boredom, in order to get into something interesting, employ their unused capacities productively, and, incidentally, obtain a bit of public credit. A supervisor's job was to guide, stimulate, or restrain, not to get mixed up in the hurly-burly of the daily grind. The art of the delegation of labor in the Government service appeared more difficult to practice than in private industry. Few asked themselves the two simple and basic questions: What am I doing that is unnecessary? What am I not doing that I ought to be doing?

The hunger of the bureaucracy for the leadership that it was not receiving was similar to that which many nations of the world also expected from the United States and were not receiving as often as they might like. Bureaucrats were keenly interested in registering their points, in achieving coherence for their programs, and in finding out where they fit into the broader scope of multiagency considerations. The quest was always for a combination of partnership and leadership, again the same equation looked for and desired by the United States' foreign allies overseas.

Besides manmade obstacles, there were natural handicaps to overcome, handicaps existing in the very nature of the American system of Government. This was not alone the system of checks and balances, which permeated all branches and levels of administration. It was rather the sense of separateness between the elected chief executive, or President, and the permanent corps of civil servants and Foreign Service officers. Every new President had to figure out how to find and grasp the handles of power, the throttles which made things move in the vast array of manpower at his theoretical disposal. In the confrontation between long-lived permanent officers of the bureaucracy and Presidents, who would be in office only from four to eight years, there was a built-in static. The President, in a very real sense, was much closer to Congress than he was to the State Department bureaucracy. Both the President and the members of Congress were elected to their posts. They were responsible to the electorate, whose wishes, whims, and interests they continually had to balance out. It was the price of American democracy.

The problem of how to break down and eliminate both the climate of alienation and the functional separatism between the President and the bureaucracy remained, however. President Kennedy employed a system of two governments, his personal one in the White House and the regular Federal Government, upon which the White House "government" operated as an energizer, coordinator, or, if need be, direct administrator at times. Sorensen, Kennedy's closest aide, was in a sense a super-Secretary of State and foreign affairs adviser for the total national-domestic interest. Mc-George Bundy was the Under Secretary of State or chief of staff for specifics of foreign affairs involvements. President Johnson broke up the Kennedy system, particularly as it applied to foreign affairs. He returned direct responsibility to the Government departments and held the Cabinet officers accountable as well as responsible.

In sum, how was the United States going to provide leadership if the nation itself did not know what precisely had to be done or how to do it? There had been plenty of advice from the top experts of the Government and other areas of the nation. The monumental files of the Jackson Committee hearings were comparable to the most praiseworthy findings made by the renowned Royal Commissions in England on questions of high national import. Senator Jackson had conducted the inquiry into the nature of national security and foreign policy operations almost continuously from 1959 to 1967. In the *Foreign Affairs* quarterly of April 1960, he said: "Organizational innovations and inventions—like the assembly line . . . have been among America's greatest contributions to economic progress. Good policy demands both good men and good machinery . . . and good men are more effective when they work with good machinery."

Senator Fulbright in the fall of 1961 analyzed "American Foreign Policy in the 20th Century under an 18th Century Constitution" in the *Cornell University Law Quarterly*. He said:

I wonder whether the time has not arrived, or indeed already passed, when we must give the Executive a measure of power in the conduct of our foreign affairs that we have hitherto jealously withheld. The source of an effective foreign policy under our system is Presidential power. This proposition, valid in our own time, is certain to become more, rather than less, compelling in the decades ahead. The pre-eminence of Presidential leadership overrides the most logical and ingenious administrative and organizational schemes.

However much the Fulbright views concerning the President may have changed because the President's name is Johnson, the point was still valid that determinations of policy in foreign affairs were a result of the insertion of presidential leadership into the interagency imbroglio which, handled with vigor and authority, could transform the bureaucracy into the matrix of decisions. In short, what was needed was a *Popular Mechanics* of statecraft, a survival kit, at the minimum, for the remainder of the twentieth century.

Robert W. Tufts, an Oberlin College economics professor, a former member of the State Department policy planning staff, and a Jackson Committee staff member, in 1963 put the problem in focus:

In the era of the atom, the missile and alliances, a President must from time to time take personal command of critical national security operations. . . . [A] President is, and must be, free to pull any matter out of the normal decision-action process. Like a President, a Secretary of State is free to lift matters out of routine and to give them his personal attention; unlike a President, there will be many issues he cannot resolve on his own authority; and, again like a President, he can give his personal attention to only a small proportion of the matters requiring coordinated interdepartmental decisions and actions.

How the State Department runs depends on the style of whoever is the incumbent Secretary of State, in the same way that the White House runs pursuant to the style and mood of whoever may be the President. Some Secretaries look on their job as one of merely overseeing the staff from on high and advising the President if and when issues arise. This is the historical type, more or less above the battle. The other type is the activist, who stirs things up, takes over key policies, and runs with them. Under Secretary Ball, in effect, acted as this kind of "Secretary," with Secretary Rusk's full approval. The avant garde and go-go-go school demand a Secretary of State who is the "manager" of foreign affairs, who "organizes" issues, "assigns" priorities, and "obtains" decisions from the President, in a continuous assembly-line production of foreign policy. The cry from these sideline coaches is: Go out and hit the problem before it hits you. In this context, the first kind of Secretary of State is imbued with the defensive spirit; the second, with the offensive.

The State Department, issuing from the Eisenhower administration into the Kennedy administration in 1961 and on into the Johnson administration in late 1963 and through 1967, was more or less a regular resident of the public doghouse for seven years. The new charges were variations of the old: Morale was low. The State Department needed fumigation, a vacuum cleaning, surgery. The thread of consistency in the renewed attacks on the Department, sharply aggravated by the spites and insecurities of the Vietnam war, was paralleled by the fact that Dean Rusk had been the head of the State Department for the seven critical years in question.

In the popular view, Rusk was more the passivist type than the activist. The actual facts of performance indicated that he was rather a mixture of the two. Rusk loyalists within the Department invariably added a demurrer to their praises. Rusk, said Foreign Service critics, had not "fought" for the Department. Rusk had "allowed" the Department to go "downhill." Rusk, in sum, had not "managed" the State Department. General Marshall, Rusk's ideal high official of modern times, had once pointed out, when he was Secretary of State, that much criticism of the State Department was unjustified as far as formulation of policy was concerned, because it was under control of the President, who assumed the responsibility. But in the execution of foreign policy the State Department was in charge, and if it failed, criticism of it was justified.

The latest assault on Rusk in 1967 charged that he was making the office of the Secretary of State an issue of domestic partisan politics. Rusk was taking an increasing role as the strongest public advocate of President Johnson's Vietnam war policies. No previous Secretary of State had thus descended into the street-level hustings within the memory of living man. With roots deep in American history, Rusk felt no inconsistency whatsoever. In February 1961, he said: "The Secretary must help also to explain to the country what we are trying to do in foreign policy. The Secretary of State's role is to help the President in every way possible." As a matter of fact, in a new self-confidence and relaxed enjoyment of his own powers, liberated by the Johnson trust in him, Rusk seemed to enjoy the political wars as the 1968 presidential election year opened.

Criticism by State Department underlings of Rusk's alleged shortcomings in leadership and managerial reforms was nothing new. Again in February 1961, after having been given the word by President Kennedy, Rusk made a speech to assembled Foreign Service officers in which he dutifully and most sincerely passed on the message that the State Department was to "take charge." It was a felicitous and vigorous speech, which was to be standard with Rusk and even inspirational to the dewy-eyed types. Nothing happened. Rusk testified before the Jackson Committee several times since 1961 with his customary lucidity. He gave a first-class indictment of the "layering" system in the State Department, that is, too many layers of authority and clearances, which slowed down the pace and curbed initiative. In 1964 former Under Secretary for Administration Crockett announced that "Rusk had been given the mandate to coordinate all foreign policy activities of the U.S. Government." In 1966, SIG, the Senior Interdepartmental Group, spluttered into action, at about five miles an hour, and country desk officers became country directors. In 1967 the innovation was the "Open Forum." Rusk said that he would welcome any and all ideas for the improvement of foreign policy and of the Department, giving assurances that the new suggestion-box contents would be examined by the Secretary in person. No trick patents on how to end the war showed up. The device could do little harm and some good, at least as a safety valve. But as far as permanently improving the machinery and operations of the State Department was concerned, there had been little momentous movement. It began to look like the case of the great Hungarian playwright who could never finish the second act. .. . .

Rusk was more amused than annoyed at the vinegarish whispers that occasionally were wafted up to him. Administration apologists fondly admitted that Rusk was "no executive" to take on the entrenched State Department bureaucracy. The trouble at State was that everything, but everything, got bucked up to the Secretary, piling up a fearsome load for any man. It was suggested that the new era virtually required two or three Secretaries of State: a chief one, who would have to travel overseas much more than in the past; a No. 2 "Secretary," who would tend the store at home, but with full authority as alter ego, in the Secretary's absence; and a No. 3 and permanent "Secretary," who could be completely an "inside" man, running State's workaday shop as Presidents and Secretaries came and went, on the lines of the Permanent Under Secretary of the British Foreign Office. It was even daringly suggested that the "perfect" backstop to Rusk would have been McNamara. John

Quincy Adams had thought it no less than his duty to go from President to Congressman for the good of the country.

Perhaps the criticism did get a little under the skin of the phlegmatic Rusk. There was a view, even on the seventh floor, that "nothing" could be done about reshaping the State Department until Rusk had departed. The expected date was January 1969. Rusk was no organization man. But perhaps that was the trouble with the bureaucracy itself—no individuality. Senior officers murmured that they had no authority to act or would not be backed up if they did. Rusk said time and again that he had never "scolded" a colleague for exceeding his authority, that the horizon was there for officers to reach for and occupy. The self-starters faced no danger of being short-circuited.

Others felt that Rusk did not supervise his staff enough. Rusk believed that he had enough to do on his level for the President without having to do the job of his subordinates also. He was charged with being basically unsympathetic with the whole idea of modern management in the State Department. A career professional himself at one time, Rusk did have a congenital scepticism about gimmicks. He would not stand for any wholesale reorganization of the Department in the midst of the Vietnam war. He felt that an overzealous attempt to organize and delegate functions in the Department was trying to divide that which was basically indivisible in foreign affairs, and that the more important an issue, the more it merged into many others. He did not like to be pushed. He was the greatest exponent of passive resistance since Mahatma Gandhi. The Secretary had a suspicion that the Department, if anything, was overmanaged. He felt it was too big, to boot. He used to point out that it took seven persons in the State Department to do what one individual did in the British Foreign Office. The great liability of the Department in making clear-cut decisions was getting too entangled in its own mechanics, neglecting as a result to keep abreast of what was actually going on in the outside world. At the same time Rusk would not tolerate any attempts to destroy or emasculate the United States Foreign Service.

Critics cited the "ideal" administration of Secretary Acheson, who devoted 95 per cent of his attention to affairs of state and needed to give Under Secretary James Webb only 5 per cent of his time for administrative matters. Rusk had no topflight administrators of the class of Webb, who had become head of National Aeronautics and Space Agency. Chester Bowles was rated tops as an idea stimulator but rather less for effective follow-through. Ball liked to get into issues too much to worry about administration. Acheson thought all lawyers were poor administrators anyhow. Asked why the indictment did not apply to himself as a lawyer, Acheson used to say that Secretary Marshall had "knocked it out of me."

Senior officers were disappointed at not cracking the Rusk reserve, at not becoming chummy with the Secretary. At a certain point, it was like the iron shutters coming down on the shops in Europe and the Middle East when word of possible riots was in the air. Rusk was convivial. He was no teetotaler. Sometimes on Saturdays, because it was not officially a "working day" day, he might start at 11 A.M. with a drink of Scotch on the rocks. He drank well and held his liquor even better. Middle-grade officers criticized Rusk on the grounds he did not "communicate" his thoughts to them. There was the wisp of a suspicion that some of the brighter young brains sulked for want of attention, a little pampering, and handholding. Junior officers sniffed the atmosphere and added their youthfully cynical embellishments. The Department at times was worse than a girls' school for gossip. After all, the State Department was a power center. It was a pretty impersonal, even ruthless, sort of place. As for the face-lifting and orthopedic measures the management perfectionists had in mind, it was clearly impossible to freeze the world's trouble areas and the Vietnam war into instant immobility, in order to redo the State Department from scratch. Management philosophy sometimes sounded like an escape mechanism: talking about methodologies of putting out the fire—while the house burned to the ground.

The impetus of the 1960's in reshaping the Department stemmed from President Kennedy's keen desire to run a first-class shop in pursuit of his constant ideal of excellence. A Kennedy task force from a New York management firm made a 250-page study of what ought to be done to modernize the State Department. It provided the specific starting-block motivation for the Kennedy interest immediately after the 1960 election. Edmund A. Gullion, former Ambassador to the Congo and a Kennedy favorite, told the Jackson Committee in 1964:

From the outset of his Presidency, he [Kennedy] wanted to restore the Department of State to its primacy in the conduct of foreign relations. He reversed a tendency to consider the Department as but one of many agencies involved in external affairs. He cut back the undergrowth of interdepartmental committees in the management of foreign policy. He summoned the Department of State to guide the work of other agencies within the framework of that policy.

Secretary Rusk, as is his habit with Presidents, was completely in accord with the Kennedy approach. He cooperated with Congressional committees that were interested in coordination, patently a good way to save money by eliminating overlap and duplication. He was prompt to reply to Senator Fulbright's inquiries with "Dear Bill" salutations and "With warm regards" closings. Rusk kept a pocket diary in which he noted, among other things, the times he had seen or phoned Fulbright. He explained this to President Johnson on one occasion, whereupon the President instructed him to keep on calling Bill.

The Kennedy 1961 letter to the ambassadors upgrading their authority marked a twenty-year record of U.S. administration attempts to insure that the impact of U.S. programs overseas was not frittered away by loose or competing managements. Early experience in Greece in 1947 had developed into acute personal crisis between the U.S. Ambassador, Lincoln MacVeagh, and the director of the U.S. Aid Mission, former Nebraska Governor Dwight P. Griswold. The U.S. ambassador's powers overseas were strengthened progressively—in 1948 by having the Marshall Plan's mission directors keep the ambassador fully informed; by bringing under direct ambassadorial supervision military assistance groups in 1949, USIA teams in 1953, and Atomic Energy Commission attachés in 1956. In February 1960, Acting Secretary of State Dillon reconfirmed ambassadorial powers even more strongly at the behest of President Eisenhower, who was eager that every ambassador actually use his powers, since there was evident a tendency of the so-called country teams bureaucratically to make the real decisions instead of the ambassadors. General Lucius D. Clay had thought up the country-team concept in 1951.

But while one group was knitting the sweater of ambassadorial authority, another group started to unravel it. Later in 1960, the Budget Bureau made a case study of U.S. official representation in Italy. It threw a hefty rock into the machinery. In the quite sensible, strictly by the book and slightly presumptuous manner in which superbureaucrats sometimes operate, the authority of the head man, the President, was called into question. The Budget Bureau report said in part:

> The chief executive or "full power to direct" concept involves giving more power to the Ambassador with respect to agency activities in his country than the President himself has over the parent agencies. . . . The Ambassador cannot legally exercise the statutory authority of agency heads over the performance by their subordinate officers in overseas missions. The Ambassador is too closely identified with the Department of State and with the Mutual Security Program to perform fully the role of the President's representative with respect to other agencies.

Like proconsuls on frontier posts, U.S. ambassadors in the underdeveloped countries, above all, were displaying native American ingenuity in their new role as "corporate managers." Since 1962, in at least nine African countries the ambassador served also as AID administrator. This added a new dimension to his work, since he now also had to view AID matters in terms of the AID administrator's personal accountability for the program. Because it was impossible to find local Africans educated enough to hire as clerks in U.S. embassies, a pool of employees was formed in Paris to take on temporary assignments to French-speaking Africa. Teams of roving administrative specialists were organized to keep the bureaucratic machinery whirring by rotating their services among isolated embassies. There are also revolutionary brewings out in the bush. One embassy recommended that for special task forces, "The Chairman should be best men for the job and not necessarily the most senior nor the most highly paid." Eyebrows all over the Foreign Service shot up like Venetian blinds when that item hit Washington.

The whole question of the State Department's reorganization was an ancient tale at the State Department. It was symbolized in one sense by the fact that the Department had moved its physical location eighteen times in Washington and that its offices had once been scattered in forty-seven different buildings. Its first reorganization was undertaken in 1818 under Secretary John Quincy Adams, who already found that jurisdictional claims formed the "most troublesome and most embarrassing part of the business of my office." Compelled by the great and constant increase in Department business, Secretary of State Louis McLane in 1833 performed the first over-all reorganization of the Department since 1789. Secretary of State Hamilton Fish in 1870 again had to reorganize the Department because of the pressure of added duties. That setup lasted until 1909.

World War II was the State Department's undoing. U.S. war agencies, which mushroomed all over the seven seas, were steered loosely from the White House while the State Department gave innocuous foreign policy "guidance." Foreign affairs agencies like Lend-Lease, the Board of Economic Warfare, and the Maritime Commission knifed each other in internecine disputes and gave the backs of their hands to the State Department if it got in the way. In 1913, before World War I, the Department had twenty-three units; by 1944, in World War II, it had ninety-four units. When the war ended the Departmental table of organization looked like a Saul Steinberg cartoon. The Department fell heir to all the war agencies in 1945. Secretary of State Edward Stettinius tried to regroup the forces and tie up the loose ends while carrying on a vastly expanded program of world contacts. The first step in the regrouping was throwing cognate units together on a functional basis, for example, economic activities under Dean Acheson, who as Assistant Secretary, first began to make his weight felt in Washington. In those years Acheson was not the enthusiast about the State Department that he was to become when the Department became his own fiefdom.

In 1958 Zara S. Seiner, of the Center for International Studies at Princeton University, wrote in *The State Department and the Foreign Service*: "No amount of administrative tinkering is an effective substitute for clearly defined policies. Despite endless surveys and administrative reforms, there has been little improvement in the direction of foreign affairs."

Reform was not ended at the State Department by any manner of means, nor would it ever be, as the world changed and governmental organisms perforce had to adapt, like all other species in the survival of the fittest. In the Kennedy incarnation of the spirit of improvement, Assistant Attorney General William Orrick was sent over from the Justice Department to replace Roger Jones, a veteran civil servant, as Deputy Under Secretary for Administration. Poor Orrick aged six years in six months. William Crockett, who had been Assistant Secretary for Administration, took Orrick's job in 1963. For the next three years he lit fires all over the State Department as he experimented vigorously to develop the new foreign affairs program manager concept. In his willingness to try anything new, as long as it worked, Crockett rejiggered his administrative units into a horizontal layout rather than the traditional vertical one. Thirty separate and independent units reported to him personally, on the theory that "the boss" should be instantly available to program directors.

A friendly extrovert from Kansas, Crockett was a Charles Dickens character, a bit incomprehensible to the somber George Eliots of the Foreign Service. The corridor backflak suggested that he had gone rather slap-happy over management. From his experience as Assistant Secretary of State for budgetary affairs, he knew at first hand how much Congressman Rooney and the rest of the appropriations committees on Capitol Hill valued whatever savings the Department could effectuate in the midst of its constantly growing—and expensive—world responsibilities. The Crockett aim was to shake the Department into recognition of the imperative necessity to modernize attitudes, concepts, and techniques in the conduct of foreign relations. On his own, Crockett had already conceived and put into effect a series of commonsense administrative improvements in the internal workings of the Department, which he proudly publicized in a 109-page brochure.

In 1966, five years after the proposal had first been made, Crockett carried into effect the country-director system as the first line of State Department diplomatic relations with other nations or groups of nations. The post of country desk officer was upgraded, and senior and experienced personnel were assigned. The theory was that the desk officer-country director would be the de facto "U.S. ambassador" in Washington, providing Government-wide service to his counterpart, the U.S. ambassador in the actual foreign country. The new country officers were "thus the essential block on which the Assistant Secretaries, the Interdepartmental Regional Groups (IRG's) and the Senior Interdepartmental Groups (SIG) could build," as Crockett said. In 1967 the country director was still as vital as Crockett had described him to be, though when the new operation went into effect, Crockett had been immediately accused of creating more high-sounding jobs to take care of Foreign Service officers who were walking the halls with nothing to do that befitted their rank and seniority. Several former ambassadors did become country directors. Several country directors made praiseworthy enough records to be selected as ambassadors. As with most jobs, effectiveness was in direct ratio to the country director's personality. Some waited for problem solutions to be delivered on a silver platter. Others went to the heart of the subject and did not allow the higher rank of officers in other departments to overawe them. The best ones seized the opportunity to assume authority and responsibility on behalf of the State Department for the direction of all U.S. nonmilitary activities involving the countries of their assignment, as the original script had hopefully called for. The full usefulness of the country-director system depended ultimately on the success of the foreign management program on the topmost levels of the Department of State.

The moves to get the issue up to the seventh floor composed a three-year drama of silent and ferocious battles behind the screen, in which, if blood did not actually flow, some was painfully extracted from the veins of dedicated bureaucrats by other bureaucrats just as fiercely committed to their own view. It was a medieval morality play of grotesque terminologies like CCPS and FAPS and PPBS and FAIME and EROP and MUST, not to overlook the climactic SIG and IRG, all sounding rather like postprandial eructations. George Ball had tagged SIG a "dog," and Acheson poofed it away as an "Indian rope trick."

Into the shambles walked Nicholas Katzenbach, the new Under Secretary of State, in late 1966. For months Katzenbach, a glazed look on his face, appeared to sleepwalk. Periodically he was the object of White House prodding: When was your last SIG meeting, Nick? The town must not be allowed to get lazy. . . . As 1967 neared its end, Katzenbach was able to stop grinding his teeth. He had at long last found a highly competent Foreign Service officer, Arthur A. Hartman, to serve as SIG's outboard motor. SIG meetings became regular, at least twice a month in Room 7219 at State, and were kept to one hour in length. A cease-fire, truce, and even working alliance had been concluded with the Bureau of the Budget on fund-and-resources identification and analysis. Even the Foreign Service was on board: If it had been found impossible to turn management programmers into diplomatists, at least the diplomats were now ready to learn

to become programmers. It had been a knockdown-carry-'em-out fight, but
the crew, undermanned as usual, was on deck, and SIG began to chug
away toward its next port. The estimated time of arrival was 1970. The
experiment would then be reviewed. By the next presidential administration of 1972, the United States and the State Department might have a
new foreign affairs management system in full operation.

Among the less celebrated heads that rolled in the carnage was that of
Richard W. Barrett, an intense, redheaded idealist. Barrett had been
Crockett's director of management planning. The chorus at the State Department Wailing Wall had tagged him "Crockett's Svengali." In the
mysterious ways of government that passeth all understanding, it was not
inconceivable that Barrett might one day even get a medal of sorts from
a grateful State Department. He has already received high marks from the
Stanford Research Institute, which was assigned to review his three years
on the firing line. The SRI report cited the "pioneering efforts of the
small State Department group who had fought an uphill battle for foreign
affairs programming" and pointed out that later "events vindicated the
vision and actions of the Barrett group . . . which was perhaps ahead of its
time."

Two years of preliminary studies prefaced Barrett's revolutionary irrup-
tion into the State Department's full and irritated attention. This occurred
in June 1965, via a forty-three-page document, No. 081, of 100 copies,
Series C, and originally classified as "secret." Later all but fourteen pages
of crisis management proposals were declassified and twenty-nine pages
made available for public delectation. If not the last word, the new look at
the Department at least shattered traditional stereotypes. Barrett described
his paper as "a first effort" to analyze the Department's operations within
four programmatic categories: supervision, substance, service, and support.

"Supervision" was concerned with the leadership role of the Department
in the foreign affairs community and its utilization of the two broad pro-
grams then under way—global policy planning under Walt Rostow and
Barrett's own CCPS, or Comprehensive Country Programming System.
Approximately 12 per cent of the Department's officer manpower was
devoted to the function of supervision in the field, and 20 per cent in
Washington. The CCPS planning project sought to create an inventory
of information for the allocation of U.S. resources in countries overseas.
Starting with Colombia, the Dominican Republic, and Venezuela in Latin
America, CCPS was installed in thirty countries—five in Africa, ten in
Latin America, eight in western Europe, three in the Far East, and four
in the Middle East. Thirteen of these, in a joint State-Budget Bureau
operation, were later put under the microscope in an "executive review
of overseas programs."

The rubric of "substance" covered the bulk of the programs usually understood by foreign affairs—bilateral, multilateral, and regional relationships. Almost eighty were listed in the latter two categories. Approximately 28 per cent of the Department's officer manpower was engaged in such activities in the field, and 25 per cent in Washington. This section had a paragraph on basic policy of interest to Senator Fulbright. It said:

Given our location and size and the forces hostile or potentially hostile in Europe and Asia, the principal goal of U.S. policy requires that we maintain a favorable military, political, and ideological balance in these regions; avoid major losses in Latin America and Africa; and move forward, with minimum violence necessary, for the protection of vital U.S. security interests, to the building of a democratic and orderly world community, ultimately embracing nations now under the rule of Communist and other totalitarian regimes.

"Service" covered activities not directly related to the pursuit of U.S. foreign policy. These were the normal services expected of traditional embassies in foreign lands, namely, visas, passports, information collection, welfare. Approximately 44 per cent of the State Department's officer manpower was in service in the field, and 33 per cent in Washington. The major difficulty under this heading was the Department's inability to control demands for its services by other agencies like the national intelligence network or the Commerce Department's economic intelligence system.

Under "support" was that which helped or facilitated the so-called substantive activities, including administrative support to the other U.S. foreign affairs agencies overseas. Sixteen per cent of the Department's manpower fell under this category in the field, and 20 per cent in Washington. Decentralization was the leitmotif. Hierarchal layers in the Department were to be reduced for "improving the responsiveness of line officers to the Secretary."

There was not too much to argue with in this sober document. The real rumble started a few months later, when Barrett put out a manifesto, *Management by Objectives and Programs: A Modern Concept of Organization and Management.* A new "Theory Y" was to be tested as a managerial philosophy in Crockett's administrative arm of the Department. The pronouncement listed problems common to most large organizations, like the State Department:

Static organizational structure inflexible to changing priorities, needs and events. Need for faster, more effective response to top management. Rigid organizational framework unadaptable to the different needs and personalities of successive top management incumbents without major organizational upheavals. Top management frustrated; employees dissatisfied. Absence of clear sense of program purpose and direction: No specific goals and objectives.

Failure to follow established policy and directives. Difficulty in pinpointing accountability. Commingled policy planning and operational planning at all levels. Little challenge and less opportunity for bold, imaginative thinking and innovative management. Deeply layered units requiring excessive vertical clearances: delayed communications. Widely sprawled and fragmented operations requiring excessive lateral clearances. Excessive courtesy and information memoranda. Continuing pressures to reduce manpower and operating expenses.

The memorandum cited a 1963 statement of Secretary Rusk that: "Organization seldom stands in the way of good people and seldom converts mediocrity into excellent performance." Except for the insufferable bureaucratese, the manifesto so far was weak tea. But goose pimples ran up and down the flesh of the Foreign Service officers of the Department of State who were next apprised of the positive-thinking virtues of "Theory Y" as lessons of contemporary social psychology applied to management. The precepts:

The average person does not inherently dislike work.

The average person learns, under the proper conditions, not only to accept but to seek responsibility.

Punitive authority is usually not the best means of achieving organizational goals.

Threat of punishment does not mobilize the intellectual potentialities of the average person.

Commitment to objectives is a function of the rewards, not the punishments, associated with the job.

Direction and control is achieved and maintained best through the identification of the individual's goals with the goals of the organization.

The ides of June were fast approaching for Barrett & Co. There was a convenient "villain," the Budget Bureau, the veteran nemesis of executive departments and now the authoritative exponent of a new-fangled notion, PPBS, or Planning-Programming-Budgeting-System. A prestigious advisory committee was appointed to evaluate the Barrett findings and make recommendations to Secretary Rusk. The chairman of the committee was Charles J. Hitch, a RAND original in the theories of cost-effectiveness, budgeting, and systems analysis; former comptroller and Assistant Secretary of Defense, in which post he had put his theories to work for McNamara; and vice president for administration of the University of California. The vast documentation presented to the committee in June 1967 included such arcane facts as these: that CCPS had been rechristened FAPS, or Foreign Affairs Programming System; that the State Department engaged in precisely 466 international activities, by actual count; that computers had been used in Washington to organize FAPS for installation in Mexico and Ethiopia; and that potential savings of $8 million had been identified in thirteen country missions.

The Stanford Research experts reviewed the Barrett record for the Hitch Committee. They cited the following example of what CCPS had come up with in 1964 in attempting to quantify diplomatic apples with foreign affairs program oranges, in terms of common denominators, that is, man-hours put into an activity and dollars spent on it:

COUNTRY	INTER-NATIONAL RELATIONS	INTERNAL DEVELOP-MENT	REPORTS	SPECIAL SERVICES	GENERAL SUPPORT
(percentage of total program dollars)					
Argentina	2.7	91.9	0.6	1.0	3.8
Colombia	7.1	90.8	0.2	0.3	1.6
Guatemala	25.6	57.8	1.5	2.8	12.3
India	0.2	98.7	0.1	0.1	0.9
Mexico	2.2	90.6	0.6	2.2	4.4
(percentage of total program manhours)					
Argentina	23.6	12.2	6.2	12.6	45.4
Colombia	2.4	60.0	2.5	4.6	29.6
Guatemala	6.7	38.4	4.0	6.0	44.9
India	9.4	23.9	4.2	5.5	57.0
Mexico	11.6	1.5	5.0	30.2	51.7

The trouble was that the Barrett system had no "trade-offs," the Stanford experts said. This meant there was no way to transfer funds from one mission to another in cost-cutting operations. This fatal political error proved to be the undoing of CCPS-FAPS. There had been no time to "cross-walk" the data into budget dollars. And budget figures were the first thing the Congressmen on The Hill asked about. In its funeral sermon, the Stanford Institute noted several further matters with melancholy restraint:

The State Department had never issued a clear mandate or directive for the system. Installation of CCPS in a country was always contingent upon an invitation from the ambassador. . . . The absence of an explicit charter was compounded by the lack of any formal organization. Lack of an organizational identification denied it institutional support within the State Department. . . . There was no formal decision-making mechanism for closing the loop. Inevitably CCPS failed to gain widespread acceptance. There was considerable resentment and resistance to CCPS in some countries. The tradition of the Foreign Service argued against the employment of modern management techniques which would inject the discipline of numbers in the decision-making process of foreign affairs. . . . With rare exceptions, no one really made effective use of even the limited data developed under CCPS. . . . In the Department of Defense there was an executive looking for a management system. In

the State Department you had the case of a management system looking for
an executive. . . . There does not exist today an effective system for managing
the totality of the foreign affairs of the U.S. government.

What had put an end to the Barrett experiment was the incursion of the
Budget Bureau on to the scene via a presidential memorandum on budget
planning in October 1965. The B.O.B., as the Bureau of the Budget was
called, demolished Crockett's CCPS gambit in 1966. By 1967, it was a
front-line participant in State Department affairs by virtue of its writ, which
gave it a say-so in management organization of all executive departments.
Charles L. Schultze, the Bureau's director, who resigned in 1968,
testifying before the Jackson Committee in August 1967, said the new
Planning-Programming-Budgeting-System was mandatory for twenty-two
departments and agencies of the Federal Government, including the State
Department, and "encouraged" for seventeen other agencies. He told the
Senators that PPBS was not "the greatest thing since the invention of the
wheel," nor was it "a naïve attempt to quantify and computerize the im-
ponderable, or an arrogant effort on the part of latter-day technocrats to
usurp the decision-making function in a political democracy." It was
simply "a means for helping responsible officials make decisions" on
"effectiveness-for-what" objectives. PPBS, in brief, was an analytical tool
to determine the significant costs and benefits of alternative policies, a sort
of actuarial table in which the risks were racked up against the insurance
premiums. Schultze said in part:

> The key of the operation is forcing federal agencies to back away from the
> particular program they are carrying on at the moment and to look at their
> objectives. What are they really trying to accomplish? Often, the more we
> learn about how to reach an objective, the more clearly we begin to under-
> stand the objective itself.

Schultze gave the committee the most elaborate analysis of PPBS as
applied to foreign affairs extant up to that time. Under Secretary Katzenbach, who ordered several pages of the Schultze testimony to be reprinted
in the State Department's October 1967 *News Letter,* related that he and
Schultze had explained to four geographical Assistant Secretaries (all except that for Europe, which no longer had major aid problems) how
important it was to review for State the other agency programs in their
respective areas, e.g., AID, MAP (military aid), USIA, CU (cultural),
and Peace Corps, in order to get a handle on policy control, as the President
and Rusk wanted. Schultze, in his Congressional discussion, had said:

> There is a striking parallel between the state of Defense management in
> 1961 and that of foreign affairs management at the present time. Just as the

size and complexity of the establishment for Defense has grown enormously in the last 30 years, so has that for foreign affairs. In 1937, we spent $18 million on foreign affairs—all on the traditional diplomatic functions of the State Department. In 1937 we dealt with 61 countries. We now spend $5.6 billion on foreign affairs, exclusive of expenditures on U.S. military forces and intelligence.

Instead of constituting all our spending on foreign affairs as in 1937, diplomatic functions now account for less than 4 per cent. Six major agencies are involved in foreign affairs programs. Of the $5.6 billion that we will spend on foreign affairs this year, the bulk will go for overseas activities and programs —that is, for activities designed with a particular mission in mind as distinguished from the general overhead of foreign affairs.

If one were to summarize the criticisms of the foreign affairs management process most often made at the present time, they might read as follows:

> Each foreign affairs agency conducts its own planning without any systematic means of comparing its programs with those of the other agencies designed to fulfill related missions—i.e., the scope of the planning process is not matched to that of the problems.
> Foreign affairs resource management decisions are not systematically developed and debated in relation to the costs and the effectiveness of alternative means of achieving national objectives.
> The time horizon of the budget tends to be limited to one year.

There is no integrated foreign affairs management information system.

Katzenbach was not safe in harbor yet. But his tactic of ostensibly underreacting in a town full of rushers-in where angels fear to tread had at any rate floated him around the big rocks. The Budget Bureau had to be watched with a sailor's eye. It had put its management hooks into foreign policy as far back as 1943. Katzenbach had the presidential license to put a lot of chips on SIG. If PPBS and Budget Bureau expertise could be made truly complementary, and not competitive, at least 50 per cent of the underbrush could be cleared away and a great day marked in the history of the State Department. The SIG-PPBS tandem would be the mechanics and the tools. The combination would give the Department the span of command and control which the President demanded it take but which Rusk would not accept unless it were authentic and effective. Rusk had no inclination for commanding paper empires. It State could find the way to make its directives stick with the foreign affairs community, excellent. But Rusk had no intention of permitting the Department to walk into a mare's-nest merely to gratify its institutional vanity.

The 1970's would not be like the Truman years, about which Acheson wrote panegyrics lauding President Truman's rare capacity for decision. Rusk, however, was a tie with the past, having served under Acheson and Truman. He had tossed the Hitch Committee report into a desk drawer, and with amiable cynicism handed the wet baby to Katzenbach when he came on board. Rusk had been open-minded and sceptical at the same time. He reflected the attitude of U.S. Senator Robert A. Taft of Ohio in 1952, after the Eisenhower electoral victory, when jubilant Republican businessmen boasted that they would now show the country how to run a really efficient government. Taft shook his head and said: "They'll learn that business is business, and government is government." The thirty or so decision-makers in the Department felt that the right fork in the road had been taken. A real dent had been made on the massive indifference of the Foreign Service to such dry matters as budgets and procedures. Systems analysis and interagency coordination were here to stay. But the name of the game was still foreign affairs.

The Department discovered that it possessed considerably more inter-agency expertise within its own background than it had given itself credit for. Standing back and looking at its own behavior, it saw the logic and illogic coalesce in perspective. For instance, the United Nations Bureau had the responsibility of signing on behalf of the Secretary of State the formal instructions given to every U.S. delegation to every intergovermental con-ference. This established in fact the primacy of the State Department in international arrangements, no matter what the subject matter. State Department officers participated very actively in a whole range of topics, regardless how technical, because there was no separating the technical from the political once one got into an international negotiation. The UN Bureau coordinated at various time with twenty-three agencies of the U.S. Government in relation to fourteen UN bodies. The State Department had, in fact, more experience in interagency coordination than any other single unit in the Government except the White House.

The clearer air on the seventh floor generated new energy on the sixth floor, where the Assistant Secretaries and the Interdepartmental Regional Groups sat. The IRG's now had no impediments to flushing out the issues and pushing them upstairs. Early-warning signals would give the SIG, or Senior Interdepartmental Group, time to reflect on how to avoid a potential crisis. James Clark, director of the Budget Bureau's International Division, in late 1967 was already closeted with country directors, picking apart anticipated five-year programs for each U.S. client country as projected by eight other agencies. The Latin American Bureau had been active in the coordination field since 1962, despite the handicap of frequent change of top Bureau command. The East Asian Bureau, pre-empted from leadership in the Vietnam war by higher echelons, had concentrated strongly on the far-ranging problem of Communist China. On this looming issue of the near-future, it was building a leadership potential. The African Bureau was improving. It was getting hard-boiled about its interests, speaking with more authority inside the bureaucratic shop. The Middle East Bureau was divesting its hitherto dominant Arabist mentality and taking a cooler, more balanced stance, more professionally reassuring to its interdepartmental colleagues. The European Bureau had refined its classicist approach into top-grade expertise on the problems of the Soviet Union and Eastern Europe, and it was universally accepted as the authoritative voice in this field within interbureaucratic councils.

The Bureau of Educational and Cultural Affairs turned out to be the only one in the State Department which was actually quantifying the intangibles and looking at the cost-effectiveness of its operations. In preparation were country and regional program memoranda on the PPBS scale. Cultural affairs had a full-fledged IRG or coordinating council in active operation. State chaired the council for some twenty-five agencies which competed for the use of funds, manpower, equipment, books, and audio-visual aids. Ticklish issues were decided, such as insisting that U.S. colleges first be certified as observing the civil rights act if they wished to enroll foreign students brought over by international exchange programs.

Personnel was the physical exemplification of the interagency problem facing the State Department. In 1965, there were 33,047 permanent American employees attached to State Department overseas posts. The State Department itself had 21 per cent of the total, or 6,795, of whom 2,583 were classified as administrative support. The Peace Corps had 7,901, or 24 per cent; USIA, 1,166, or 4 per cent; and AID, 3,807, or 11 per cent. The Defense Department had 10,983, or 33 per cent, military and civilian, excluding combat personnel. In addition to the 500 or 1 per cent in transit other departments and agencies had 1,895 Americans overseas, or 6 per cent of the total number. These included 37 Americans in Veterans Administration offices in Rome, Manila, and Panama; 15 working overseas for the Public Health Service Division of Foreign Quarantine; 21 engaged in medical research for the National Institutes of Health; 1 in Athens servicing Social Security Administration annuitants; 105 FBI agents serving as legal attachés; 61 persons working for the Immigration and Naturalization Service; 5 serving the National Science Foundation; 3 Department of Interior Bureau of Commercial Fisheries officials serving as fisheries attachés; 12 men from Interior's Bureau of Land Management; 21 from Interior's Bureau of Mines serving as minerals attachés; 73 from Interior's Geological Survey engaged in topography; 47 from Interior's Bureau of Reclamation in water resource development; and 3 from Interior's National Park Service working as technicians in their field. The State Department Medical Division provided services to forty-four different agencies at various times.

The State Department was not guiltless in the proliferation of foreign affairs agencies. In 1942 Secretary Cordell Hull had supported the creation of separate overseas operating agencies in the hope that the Department would have some control over them. The new agencies became Frankenstein's monsters and devoured State's prestige. By 1949 the Department had again lost its monopoly of foreign policy influence, with forty-six other departments and agencies engaged in foreign activities and thirty interdepartmental committees trying to keep in step. By 1952 there were fifty agencies in foreign affairs. In 1951 the first thoughts had begun to be voiced that a new Department of Foreign Affairs, all under one roof, was needed, a huge corporate merger like that of the Defense Department in 1947. By 1960, the Operations Coordinating Board of the National Security Council oversaw forty-five interdepartmental committees.

In 1967 the Budget Bureau listed sixty-five agencies as having a direct interest, major or minor, in foreign affairs, thirty-five of them with overseas representation. Twenty-three units had major and continuing interest in foreign affairs, and another sixteen a steady interest. The State Department, with its four autonomous subsidiaries—the Agency for International Development, with 12,500 employees; the United States Information Agency, with 11,500 employees; the Peace Corps, with 9,300 employees; and the small United States Arms Control and Disarmament Agency, with 230 employees—was at the theoretical heart of the foreign affairs empire. When the SIG, or Senior Interdepartmental Group, was launched in 1966, the wits noted that there were five "State Departments" in Washington: Old State, International Security Affairs at the Pentagon, the CIA, the White House, and, as a tribute to the ebullient involvements of Leonard Marks, its director, also the USIA. In late 1967 the number of interagency committees chaired by State stood at fifty-eight. The Department had eleven public advisory committees and was represented on four mixed public-interagency groups. It also had five intradepartmental committees of its own. The UN Bureau itself was a member of eleven interdepartmental committees.

If the foreign affairs agencies were not fighting about personnel, they were arguing about money. By 1966, two fifths of the State Department's total manpower was involved in providing support and services to other foreign affairs agencies overseas, a growing trend. Of the 10,475 employees listed in 1966, the Department was reimbursed for 4,303, or 17 per cent. It had the trouble of taking care of 22.6 per cent, or 5,425, foreign local nationals who worked for other agencies, which would pay the State Department eventually. Forty per cent of State's overseas services went to other agencies, to twenty-eight, principally. These included AID, USIA, and the Peace Corps as a matter of course, but also the Central Intelligence Agency, its largest customer; the National Security Agency (code and cipher specialists); and the Foreign Broadcast Information Service (monitoring Communist overt and clandestine broadcasts). In a recent year USIA paid $20 million and AID $24 million for State services. State received from all clients over $134 million. It had a direct or indirect policy voice with regard to 1968 international budgets of these agencies amounting to approximately $5.8 billion. Of this sum, $5 billion, or 90 per cent, went to four areas—$2.5 billion for economic aid, $1.8 billion for food aid, $600 million for military assistance, and $100 million for the Peace Corps.

Conflict between Government agencies had been the rule in the past and was not expected to disappear in the future. A good slugging match made for excitement and brought out healthy competition. Charles Hitch, the former Defense comptroller, once observed, "It was much easier to change policy than to change procedures." Policy involved only a small group at the top. Procedures involved hundreds and even thousands who were upset at having the habits and customs of years smashed by innovations, and therefore dug in their heels against change. If issues were left unsolved, a resentful bureaucracy fell back into a swampland of defeatism. Attitudes deteriorated and even organizations disintegrated. Issues were intractable enough, given their complexity. It would take 50 per cent of one's energy merely to get all the clearances and concurrences, the okays necessary for a project, if inertia were allowed to become endemic. The wiser managers of affairs and men believed that it was easier to get measures through the bureaucracy if there was a "fertilizing ferment" or "fructifying friction" in the atmosphere to stimulate the natural juices for action and decision.

The Atomic Energy Commission, as the era of international peaceful nuclear power progressed, was an agency that State had to keep its eyes on. The AEC had a staff of 130 in its international division. State had the authority to make the appointments to the International Atomic Energy Agency in Vienna, but the AEC had the influential aid of the Joint Congressional Committee on Atomic Energy, probably the single most powerful committee in Congress. The Committee had been virtually a law unto itself, so much so that it had been accused of running the AEC, rather than merely advising it. State had to tread on eggs in tackling two such potential antagonists.

Science and space were new mysterious fields in which State had not quite sufficient expertise in cross-agency consideration, though it had an Office for International Scientific and Technological Affairs. Space was fascinating the old diplomatic pros like Deputy Under Secretary Foy Kohler, into whose bailiwick political NASA matters fell. The National Aeronautics and Space Administration had an Assistant Administrator for International Affairs and ninety Americans at twelve stations overseas for visual tracking of satellites. The negotiation for station sights was not much different from that for military base rights. Six manned flight-tracking stations were already set up in Australia. Three were near Canberra-Honeysuckle Creek, Tidbinbilla, and Ororal Valley, plus sites at Toowooba, Carnarvon, and Woomera, the last for deep-space probes.

A typical problem arose in 1967, an argument about whether to put an eighty-five-foot dish antenna costing $35 million on Madagascar, the Malagasy republic. Earth stations were necessary because ships at sea, which might also serve, could stay out only for two months, instead of the six months needed to maintain continuous observations. The precise scientific thinking on the matter has not yet come into the ken of the diplomats. This was the probability that much sooner than later it would be possible to put two synchronous satellites into orbit as permanent observation posts for space flights. It would eliminate ground tracking stations altogether, saving considerable sums.

Old-timers at State used to say they once had an economics attaché who knew more about world agriculture than the entire Department of Agriculture in pre-World War II days. There were no such nonpareils any longer. President Johnson's designation in 1967 of Secretary Rusk as chairman of a new Cabinet-level committee for the $7 billion Food for Freedom Program gave State an added reason to come up with new technical know-how in order to be able to talk to the Agriculture Department and AID as an equal. In the area of State's historic preference, western Europe, agriculture was a deep involvement in all the countries of the Common Market, necessitating expert counseling to the political negotiators. Agriculture's Research Service had 260 specialists at twenty-four foreign posts acting to prevent spread of plant and animal diseases to the United States. Forty-three were engaged abroad on research on insects and on plant and animal diseases. Thirty others from Agriculture worked in thirty-two countries to organized in 1954, maintained eighty-six Americans in fifty-six countries to profit from foreign farm research. The U.S. Foreign Agricultural Service, develop foreign markets for American farm products. The Budget Bureau and AID, State's economic assistance agency, were collaborating with Agriculture for the first time to make an over-all analysis of P.L. 480 on surplus commodity requirements abroad and to improve farm production in the recipient nations. The moves were about ten years overdue.

AID and State, in fact, were growing closer together with the years. The two organizations merged their labor offices in 1967. Besides the joint effort on food programs, water and population policies came in closer parallel. If it were not for the question of personnel, that is, obtaining expert enough specialists at the higher salaries they demanded at AID, it was not unlikely that State and AID would become more and more operationally integrated in the future. An actual integration occurred in early 1967 between State and the Commerce Department. An agreement was reached to merge their respective economic and commercial activities and personnel overseas. This, in effect, meant an eventual lateral entry of Commerce personnel into State's Foreign Service. Effective State-Commerce liaison had been lacking in the last ten years. The issue of East-West trade was a particularly fractious subject. State may have tried to support President Johnson's call for "building bridges to the East," but the Export Control Office of Commerce apparently never got the word. The issue would grow all the more sensitive, since computers and U.S. technological know-how for export were in high demand, and a renewed drive for East-West trade was in the offing, the moment the Vietnam war came to an end.

Of all the State Department's interagency relationships, one of the three most important and troublesome was that with the Treasury Department. In Europe, a Treasury Department was often called the "second Foreign Office." Finance ministers were rated as holding more real power than defense ministers. The salad days of the U.S. Treasury as a powerful influence on U.S. foreign policy in the postwar period were during the tenure of Treasury Secretary George M. Humphrey of Cleveland. His influence on President Eisenhower and his compatability with Secretary Dulles enabled Humphrey to sit tall in the saddle. His successor, Secretary Robert Anderson, also started out by being quite sticky with State. Former Treasury Secretary Dillon recalled:

When I was in the State Department [as Under Secretary], our chief bureaucratic problems by far came from the Treasury Department, which assumed it had the right to clear any and all telegrams in this area, many of which I had to settle directly with Secretary Anderson. As a result, the two of us had to deal with a mass of minutiae which should never have been brought to our attention.

State had Treasury representatives attached to every major U.S. embassy. All these attachés were extremely competent. Twenty-three Americans worked abroad for Internal Revenue Service's Office of International Operations. Eighteen served overseas for Treasury's Bureau of Narcotics. Three were detailed to Manila with Treasury's Bureau of Accounts, Division of Disbursement, to distribute U.S. Government checks to claimants from various Government agencies. The Treasury took the lead in negotiating tax treaties with other nations, under State's aegis, of course. The Foreign Assets Control Office administered the Trading with the Enemy Act and kept track of frozen Cuban and Chinese Communist assets, among others.

Treasury's Customs Bureau checked to see that goods brought to the U.S.A. from Hong Kong were not in reality disguised exports from mainland China. State and Treasury got caught in the same bind occasionally. In 1966 rich Saudi Arabia insisted on purchasing U.S. arms with an Export-Import Bank loan. The Saudis wanted the Export-Import loan to give themselves status. Everybody else was obtaining Ex-Im arms loans, so why not the Saudis.

The most heated disputes between State and Treasury rarely, if ever, broke into the public print. The bitter feuding between former Under Secretary of State George Ball and Treasury Secretary Dillon never hit the front page, though the words exchanged were sharp, the moves ruthless, and after-feelings a mite sour. Ball and Dillon tangled on the issue of offset payments by West Germany, the major factor in the U.S. balance-of-payments deficit. This went on from 1961 till the issue was resolved in early 1967, nine months after Dean Acheson had suggested the multilateral solution which came to pass. The recourse to a top expert like John McCloy as the President's special envoy to solve the difficulty reflected State's basic weakness in handling Treasury. State had few ranking officers smart and strong enough to stand up to Treasury's heavy guns, and win. Treasury scoffed at State's ingenuousness about money. The traditionalist Foreign Service was accused of a tendency to think of money as beneath one's notice and even petty when it came to the point of giving a helping hand to political friends abroad. State was theoretically the primary spokesman on international matters, but it had a diluted role in monetary affairs, again because of lack of top-level competence and aggressiveness. Treasury held that it would have been wiser to loan France the $4 billion she received under the Marshall Plan instead of giving it to her in free grant aid, for instance. It mistrusted State for apparently playing cute games on behalf of favorite client-allies like Britain and Germany at the expense of the U.S. Treasury pocketbook.

The second most aggravating relationship of the State Department with other agencies was with the Central Intelligence Agency. The full facts were, of course, secret, but enough of them broke out into the open when the CIA, by events beyond its control, was forced to uncover its face in public from time to time. State-CIA relations were a stew. CIA sometimes organizationally placed State in an inferior position, despite State's claim to be the arbiter of foreign policy, because the actual decisions on behalf of CIA had been made by higher authority, that is, by the President and the National Security Council. CIA was cut back from whatever free-wheeling it was guilty of after the Bay of Pigs in 1961, and again after the Diem killing in Saigon in 1963. A Special Group (Counterinsurgency) had been appointed to keep CIA under surveillance after the Cuban caper. The "oversight" function had more or less been inherited by the Senior Inter-departmental Group, in theory, though SIG had no staff with which to do any watching. In actuality, the White House had stood watch through McGeorge Bundy, Walt Rostow, and Bromley Smith, the long-term executive secretary of the NSC. At State, former Under Secretary for Political Affairs and Ambassador-at-Large Averell Harriman maintained a no-nonsense look at CIA operations which might get out of hand.

The CIA had organized, as everyone knew, historic coups like the U-2 flights over the Soviet Union, which fell into a startled world's ken in 1960, though its exploits had been whispered in Washington at least a year before, in 1959, as this writer had heard at the time. In the public arena the CIA had pulled routine feats like the Guatemalan Arbenz over-throw in 1954 and more spectacular deeds like the overthrow of Mossadeq in Iran in 1953. The apogee of the CIA influence coincided with the twin rule of John Foster Dulles as Secretary of State and of Allen Dulles, his brother, as director of CIA. Allen Dulles always stoutly maintained that the CIA did not make foreign policy. He did exercise a considerable amount of influence in his official position as the chief of a great agency, even though one of his principal interlocutors happened to be his brother. As late as 1959, for example, he advocated a much stronger line against Soviet Russia's eastern European satellites, as they were then called. The younger Dulles felt that the Russians were attempting to trick the United States out of its advanced positions in Berlin and Germany, whereas the United States was doing nothing about the advanced positions of the Soviet in eastern Europe. The Allen Dulles thesis was rejected by the National Security Council.

The real influence of the CIA on State Department foreign policy, how-ever, was not fundamentally due to CIA's great political weight inside the highest levels of all national administrations, Democratic or Republican. It lay, rather, in that CIA set the premises for policy discussion by the very selection of the facts it presented for consideration. This was somewhat in the same manner that newspaper editors exercised their own judgment on the selection of the facts they wished published. The logic of CIA facts as premises, presented by some of the most intelligent individuals in the Government, gave CIA a built-in advantage in interagency argumentation in its earlier years. This happened despite the so-called National Intelligence Estimate, devised in concert with the intelligence community, or other agencies, which had not yet acquired the sophistication developed later.

In the phrase of President Kennedy about "the long twilight struggle" of the Cold War, it was not realized by later generations how bitterly cold and vividly present was the feeling of enmity during the Cold War of the mid-1950's. Literally anything went, in the silent and relentless struggle to assault enemy positions and ranks on both sides of the Iron Curtain. The public scandal that exploded in early 1967 concerning CIA subsidiaries to a long array of private educational and student organizations and intellectuals was just another fact of life in those days. This writer used to be acquainted with part-time journalists and labor leaders in the 1950's who were all too obviously on somebody's extra payroll, a fact quickly learned by European security organizations at the time. State, which, like everybody else, had been merely acquiescent in the original CIA subsidy scheme, was in the center of the picture in the clean-up after the CIA debacle of 1967. Secretary Rusk was named to preside over a presidential committee which was to decide what to do about future aid to legitimate private organizations working among foreigners in the education and cultural fields. The CIA had spent an estimated $500 million at least on these "educational" activities. The Rusk committee was divided tentatively on two lines. One was to give the subsidy operation to State's Bureau of Educational and Cultural Affairs, as then Assistant Secretary Frankel had proposed. Another was to establish a private-public corporation to be the recipient of Government funds for distribution to meritorious groups—but all done *en plein air,* like the handling of the Fulbright fellowships.

The CIA was loosely indicted as having gone off on its adventures as almost a free agent. Actually, its missions were meticulously cleared in the bureaucratic fashion on the top levels, and blessing was obtained in general, and sometimes in specific, from the Senators on the "CIA watchdog" Appropriations and Armed Services Subcommittee headed by Senator Russell of Georgia. A *nihil obstat* was usually voiced by the State Department to CIA proposals without too much argument. Follow-up details were shrouded in the mystery of clandestine operations, which diplomats normally did not want to get mixed up in. U.S. diplomats on the spot more often than not simply did not know the concrete operational facts, hence could not gauge possible repercussions if the operation blew up. The giving of State's original concurrence was facilitated by what might be called the stage setting and mood music of the affair. Some Foreign Service officers sincerely held to romantic traditions from the silent-movie days about debonair and gallant heroes suffering agonies in silence amid the foe. There was perhaps an itty-bitty Walter Mitty syndrome, in which one gave the knowing smile with a tight mouth and did not ask too many questions, a straight steal out of John Buchan. The Boy Scout routine passed, but the disarming effect of being privy to clandestine operations still had a capability to sap the judgment.

In addition to its assigned job of collecting, collating, and evaluating intelligence from open and secret sources, the Central Intelligence Agency fell heir to all sorts of odd jobs which came up as necessary in the national interest but which no regular Government department was organized to perform. Thus, in one sense, the CIA was actually pushed and invited to get into the dirty-tricks department, partly because of a failure of normal foreign relations. A quick call for a gimmick, last-ditch "saving" operation was the ultimate expedient of policy desperation. On top of its super-American activism, the CIA inherited the let's-try-it derring-do of General "Wild Bill" Donovan from World War II OSS days, and hence had its own tradition of attempting to pull rabbits out of a hat.

Being a higher-class bureaucracy than most of the Government, but not so much higher that it could claim perfection, the CIA in turn was rather hornswoggled into deals of political intervention that might now be categorized in hindsight as simply bad or short-sighted State Department policy. In this class were the events in Laos in 1959 and 1960, when CIA support for the purpose of eliminating the Communist-backed Pathet Lao was given to right-wing General Phoumi Nosavan against neutralist Prince Souvanna Phouma. It was a matter of betting on the wrong horse without looking at the whole racing form. In 1964 the CIA had better luck in Laos, again with the collaboration of State and Defense. Twenty Thai Air Force pilots, put into Royal Laotian Army uniforms, and a Thai artillery company, likewise disguised as Laotian soldiers, were sent into Laos to stop the Pathet Lao cold on the Plaines des Jarres. CIA "private" reconnaissance planes had pinpointed North Vietnamese infiltration into South Vietnam along the Ho Chi Minh trail inside Laos almost a year before the fact of infiltration was elaborately denounced by the U.S. Government in 1965. Target identification provided by native contacts recruited by the CIA brought U.S. plane reaction on target within four minutes flat.

CIA's influence in relation to State began receding under President Kennedy and leveled out under President Johnson. Before Eisenhower became President, the daily intelligence summary given to President Truman had been prepared by the State Department. Though established in 1947, CIA took over this function only in 1953 under Eisenhower. It thus could, if it wished, give a policy inflection to the wording of the night's intelligence summary, and also have a direct channel to the President. CIA Director Richard Helms, a career professional, was kept at the end of a telephone line by the President, in the same manner as other high officials, but he was not substantially important in the Johnson scheme of things. Helms sat in on major reviews of the Vietnam war, particularly to report on intelligence gathered from Communist and neutral sources concerning Hanoi's actual intentions and plans.

Where CIA and State tended to rub each other raw was in the stationing of CIA personnel in U.S. embassies abroad. The CIA station agent, or number one front man for the Agency, used to have much more money at his disposal than the limited funds available to the ambassador, ostensibly his superior. The CIA agent's residence was impressive and his entertainment allowance apparently without limit. CIA head agents were kept on station for longer periods than the normal Foreign Service tours; consequently, they knew more of the native foreigners and often had a better reading of the local politics than did the embassy political section. The locals, for their part, with the not uncustomary foreign penchant for seeking powers behind the throne, often were inclined to treat the CIA chief as more important than the ambassador when matters of special financial interest arose. Friction arose from the natural desire of intelligence men to shape or make decisions. CIA officers pressed their points of view or interpretations into dominating or heavily influencing an ambassador's decision.

More personally, there was the real-life and irksome problem of how to fit the CIA representatives into the American community abroad—apartments, clubs, commissaries, as well as the local society. Until fairly recently, the standard CIA answer to an innocent query of "Who do you work for?" was, "The Government." Nowadays, the CIA contingents reply, with overwhelming candor, "I work for the CIA." But previously, CIA exposure was taboo. Thus, there was the question of "how visible" CIA personnel should be in the diplomatic community in a foreign capital. Questions of title, rank, and perquisites were involved, and they were headaches to State's administrative officers. The basic situation arose in the first place because an estimated 10,000 CIA personnel worked overseas. Some were Americans working part-time and some foreign nationals who had no obvious embassy connections. CIA personnel on embassy staffs, however, were estimated at more than 1,500, including 400 Foreign Service Reserve officers. State paid them and was reimbursed by the CIA in Washington. These employees, including some CIA men in State's headquarters, were carried ostensibly as part of State's own manpower totals on the public records. The announced State Department employment figure of 15,300 Americans in 1966, therefore, was actually closer to 13,000 straight Departmental employees.

The third agency that the State Department had major problems with was the Defense Department. This was not because Defense was shirty about its rights and prerogatives, but far and away because it was the physical carrier of the nation's global commitments, spread literally over the planet. Defense's nearly 3.5 million armed forces included nearly a million in the Pacific and over 300,000 in Europe. They were stationed on 100 bases in 101 nations, islands, and territories. Defense employed in 1966 over 257,000 civilians overseas, including 24,000 Americans. Even more emblematic of America's ubiquitous presence were Defense's 437,652 dependents overseas, 409,000 of them families of armed forces stationed abroad. Like the Colossus of Rhodes in ancient times, the Pentagon was one of the seven wonders of modern times, and, as Shakespeare said, "doth bestride the narrow world like a colossus," while petty men walked under its huge legs and peeped about. The State Department was by no manner of means a petty personage, though the comparative size of the two organizations made it appear that the tail was trying to wag the dog. The Defense Department spent approximately half the world's defense funds. This global total was estimated to be $130 billion by the U.S. Arms Control and Disarmament Agency in 1964. The 1968 U.S. defense budget was approximately $70 billion. Russia and the United States together accounted for two thirds of the 1964 global total of the thermonuclear age. The Defense Department, in brief, was the era's forbidding symbol.

As a consequence of the military atomics that opened with Hiroshima, the concept of defense after World War II became a standard peacetime activity, whereas between wars in the past the military were forgotten, ignored, or derided. Since 1945, military and foreign policy increasingly tended to become interchangeable, with military policy frequently taking the lead because of fears of swift and unwarned attack and the urgencies of sheer survival. Traditional foreign policy slid into a phase of being considered merely one part of national security policy. As the world learned to live with its fears and still breathe the next day, the pendulum slowly started to shift toward center again. Realization that final themonuclear "victory" would be a Pyrrhic one turned thoughts of generals and admirals back toward first principles, that war must have a purpose consonant with the means employed. In short, the game had to be worth the candle, but not if the candle itself got burned up and left everybody in the dark.

Between strategic lucubrations and human agonizings in the military search for certainties, the psychological climate edged back to the point at which the State Department could again assume a more effective lead regarding the measures that the United States should undertake in relation to the outside world. All Defense Secretaries echoed the truism that military policy was the handmaiden of foreign policy, and with little doubt most of them meant it. The practical realities, however, were in the details of what actually was done. Given the massive weight of the military establishment, the State Department found itself frequently in a panting chase to catch up with accomplished, if not irreversible, facts. The power and speed of execution represented by the enormous sums of money, armaments, manpower, efficiency, and secrecy that attended military plans presented the State Department with considerable handicaps before it could discover how to countervail the momentum that the Defense Department generated. The State Department was still attempting to do so in 1967, with some success, limited but slowly increasing.

The State Department, in actuality, had come a long way. It had lost out to the military in World War II for the patent reason that it had not been up to the job because of the sheer size and volume of the tasks. In the aftermath of the war, the military again moved into the vacuum of the tremendously expanded area of U.S. diplomatic responsibilities, again for want of State manpower. General MacArthur, for example, was the U.S. proconsul in Japan and General Clay in Germany, not civilians. Generals changed into civilian clothes in case after case and became diplomats. The military leaders institutionalized their big edge in internal national influence in the 1947 establishment of the unified Defense Department and won a key role in the National Security Council, including independent access of the Joint Chiefs of Staff to the President. The NSC move had also been a reaction against the highly personal wartime rule of President Roosevelt. Military influence with FDR had been at his choice and whim, not at all a matter of legal right.

It was all too evident that at times military considerations would be the spearhead of foreign policy, if only as a temporary expedient. The air force bases in Morocco, for example, were a deliberate "crash" investment in 1952 to provide short-range bases from which to bomb the Soviet Union if the Korean war expanded into a world war. The bases served their purpose; the cost was "incidental." George Kennan's "containment" policy from State had given Defense a virtual blank check for a decade to sink down roots all over the earth. Geopolitical strategic reasons thrust the United States into the Korean war. The post-hostilities period, however, proved possibly more expensive than the earlier combat. Eighteen years after the Korean war had started, the United States still had 50,000 troops in South Korea. In South Vietnam, the hoped-for military projection in early 1967 was that the United States could maintain at least 100,000 troops there for an unspecified number of years. The idea of military assistance to other nations was based on the premise that it would cost the United States only $540 a year to support a foreign soldier in the countries around the rim of the Communist bloc, as against $4,500 a year for an American soldier. In 1968, fifty-three countries would still receive U.S. military assistance, only ten less than in 1967.

The actualities of State-Defense relations had the characteristic personality overtones of rival bureaucracies. Diplomats liked to play general. They enjoyed the perquisites of luxury associated with generals. The British military had learned the trick two centuries ago in India, and the British in World War II were the mentors of Americans in the field. U.S. generals did not really learn to live it up until after the armistices, and then they did it to a turn. The diplomats had the pick of the cream, but the generals ran the show. The military had the habit of command. The authoritarian style of viewing the world was natural to them. There was an innate difference of outlook between soldiers and diplomats at best. The Foreign Service termed military planning mechanistic; the military called the diplomats hunch-players. Generals thought in terms of direct action and military necessity. Ambassadors thought in terms of indirect action and consequences to third-country interests, with which the United States would also have to live. By the time General Eisenhower came to office in 1953, the power of the American military abroad over civilian authority had become a critical issue in the United States Government and somewhat scandalous to foreign publics.

In the nature of things, however, defense establishments fluctuated more than foreign offices. Civilian ministers came and went. Some officers got killed in battle, others were rotated, and still others were retired. The State Department and Foreign Service corps traditions had longevity and continuity, thus outlasting the vigor and thrust of the vibrant personalities of the armed forces. Still, no German Junker military general staff psychosis took root, despite fears of the military-industrial complex. The younger military generation issuing from World War II and the Korean war acquired much faster a larger appreciation of the politics of modern warfare than the older diplomats had. The Berlin and Cuban nuclear missile crises during the Kennedy administration were climacteric years of breakthrough in State Department experience of balancing military power versus political costs. Much of the groundwork had already been laid in the Eisenhower administration. It illustrated nonpartisan continuity of U.S. policy at its best.

U.S. military officers had undergone much more time in training and extra education than most Foreign Service officers of the State Department, a good augury for future understanding. The military were systematically sent to top civilian universities for studies in history, government, and economics. Military staff colleges had a much larger component of social sciences in their curricula than ever before. For example, approximately 85 per cent of regular U.S. Army officers had bachelor of arts degrees and 24 per cent had graduate degrees. Of the more than 300,000 officers on active duty, approximately 200,000 in the four services were considered to be military career professionals. A key to the new context of the military professional was once expressed by a British general who said, "The function of the profession of arms is the ordered application of force to the resolution of a social problem." Indicative of the familiarity of the military with the contour of the modern age's complexities was the title of an article in the *Air Force Magazine* in December 1966 by Colonel Wesley W. Posvar,

head of the Political Science Department and Chairman of the Division of
Social Sciences at the U.S. Air Force Academy. The title was "The
Political Environment for Military Planning." The Posvar theme was related
to the new and extremely intricate problem of "measured violence" and the
necessity of maintaining "direct and continuous political control of strategic
forces, even in war." Posvar's generalizations sounded like what one
normally heard in State Department offices. His schematic rubrics:

Refined Strategic Doctrines: Controlled response; intra-war bargaining; war
termination capability; damage limitation-assured destruction; accident preven-
tion-arms control.
1980 World Projection: West Europe independent of United States; East
Europe opened; Japan ascendant in Far East, controls own defenses; China
as great power, emerging from isolation; Southeast Asia at economic take-off,
tending neutralist; revolution rampant in Africa and Latin America; eight to
ten nuclear powers.
1980 Military Contingencies: Frequent insurgency warfare from ambiguous
sources; large, local wars creating U.S. dilemmas, e.g., to oppose communism
or racism; limited nuclear arms control; problem of deception; threat of covert
nuclear attack; increased use of international military forces; frequent crises
and saturation of U.S. response capability.

A major contribution to an improved climate between State and Defense
was the exchange program between the two departments. The idea had
been worked out by Secretary Herter, Under Secretary Dillon, and his then
special assistant, Graham Martin. Martin had preached the gospel to the
Joint Chiefs of Staff. The Joint Chiefs had always been a favorite State
Department hunting ground, providing terrain for making end-runs around
the Office of the Secretary of Defense in bureaucratic maneuvering. The
State-Defense exchange program went into actual operation in January
1961, with five officers initially assigned from each agency to work for
two-year tours as regular staff officers of the other department. As Rusk
told Senator Jackson: ". . . the intimate interdependence of foreign policy
and military policy required . . . a growing number of officers with a solid
grasp of the responsibilities, problems, procedures, and operations of the
other."

The intermingling principle was expanded by assigning ten Foreign
Service officers to act as political advisers, or POLADS, to the principal
military commands. The practice had originated with the appointment of
former Ambassador Robert D. Murphy as General Eisenhower's adviser in
North Africa in 1942. Others were sent as faculty advisers, and more than
500 as students, to the five military colleges. Five military and five Foreign
Service officers were detailed as watch officers, the former to State's
Operations Center, the latter to the National Military Command Center

operated by the Joint Chiefs. The value set on the exchanges by both departments was reflected in the caliber of the officers chosen. State's men were picked from Class 3, regarded as the start of senior ranks in the Foreign Service. The Defense selections were colonels and navy captains. All were picked for their high potential and nearly all proved it out in later assignments.

Collaboration between State and Defense was not the order of the day when General Marshall became Secretary of State in 1947. The Pentagon, trained by Marshall personally to refer civilian matters to State, maliciously used to badger State with demands, "We want policy guidance," which State was too undermanned to provide adequately. Closer State-Defense ties bred new differences of opinion.

Military aid got to be big business. It provided lucky opportunities to pay off old cronies, good combat leaders but indifferent staff men, as chiefs of military assistance groups in foreign countries. These posts rated the coveted star of a general. They were also temptation for empire-building pint-sized Pentagons in key countries like Turkey and Pakistan. Military aid generated State-Defense rivalry on behalf of hopeful recipients lobbying between the two departments. Preferences in arms sales in 1967 gave State a belated case of heartburn. General Westmoreland in South Vietnam had wanted the new M-16 rifle for the South Korean troops, who always demanded the best equipment. The Thais also put in a bid to Westmoreland. State's munitions control shop had already approved a routine Defense request for sale of the AR-15, a modified model of the M-16, to Singapore. There was a press exposé. State's East Asian Bureau waxed ex post facto indignant. The fact transpired that the Bureau had been duly notified of the Singapore affair in November 1966, and had goofed. Joint State-Defense secretiveness concerning arms aid shipments produced a delayed time-bomb explosion in Congress in 1955. The House rebelled when it learned that oil-rich Saudi Arabia had received free weapons without House committees being informed of any agreements to do so. The "secret" U.S.-Saudi accord had been published in full in the *Umm al Qura,* the official Mecca gazette, in July 1951, in Arabic, naturally.

Military attachés in U.S. embassies were another problem. They had large staffs, and their entertainment allowances, comparable to the CIA's, were sometimes five times the ambassadors'. Almost two decades later a start was made, in Latin America, to trim down the fat of the public largesse. The military attachés when they were very good were very good, and invaluable aides to ambassadors. When Gamal Abdel Nasser made his revolution in Egypt in 1952, the sole Western contact with the "Free Officers" was a canny young Air Force Major, David Evans. The "Free Officers" immediately asked for arms. (The Russians through the Czechs provided the arms in 1955.) Evans' cables to the State Department arrived under the name of Ambassador Jefferson Caffrey. During the tense hours of the 1956 Suez crisis, U.S. Major Robert Mallory was able to give U.S. Ambassador James Moose an eye-witness report on the precise situation in Syria. In the best James Bond tradition, Mallory made swift night surveys of the entire country to verify that no Russian volunteers had been dropped into Syria, as had been feared.

Some State-Defense differences were swept under a rug by mutual consent. For instance, the pricing formula for foreign military arms aid had been raised in 1959. State did not push it because the issue might have created more difficulties among the foreigners than it would have settled among the Americans. The real bantling in the basket was the bookkeeping charged for the arms being donated by mutual security treaty allies. Defense fixed the arms prices at the full American replacement value. On the open domestic market the items would have had a far lower value as mere salvage. But to the arms-hungry foreigners, a tank was a tank was a tank, and how could they tell the difference anyhow. In effect, U.S. arms grant aid to foreign countries speeded up the modernization of the U.S. armed forces. As the old material was given away or sold, U.S. forces were resupplied with the latest new arms.

Intermittent eruption of crises around the globe maintained the State-Defense enforced cohabitation. The military had contingency plans for everything conceivable. The Congo came under intensive study as a possible theater of operations after the Belgians had given it its freedom in 1960 and walked out. A new nation, totally unprepared for so-called freedom, rent by tribal chaos, and with Patrice Lumumba as its first Prime Minister, presented an excellent target of opportunity for the Soviets. State took the issue to the UN and mobilized an international intervention to prevent a feared intervention by Russian proxies. Defense provided logistical support and airlift, an assistance regularly performed for UN peacekeeping missions. The Congo boiled up again in 1964 as left-leaning African nations, led by Ghana, Algeria, and Egypt, encouraged revolt in the northeastern Congo, where Pierre Mulele, a former colleague of Lumumba in Kwilu province, had launched terrorist attacks. U.S. military airlift for the so-called Congolese army was not enough to crush the revolt. Defense and State called in the CIA to organize the extra punch needed. Defense delivered twenty T-28 fighter-trainers and several B-26 bombers. The CIA hired exiled Cuban pilots to fly them. The State Department held its breath. The revolt collapsed.

U.S. base rights in foreign countries were a source of friction, especially when it came to giving up the bases. Defense blocked the return of Okinawa to Japan until the Vietnam war provided a cogent reason to keep it a little while longer in American hands as a staging area. Wheelus Air Base in Libya was another subject of argument. Both State and Defense were split pro and con. Wheelus, in 1967, under negotiation with the Libyans, could be a symbol of security for the aged King Idriss, sitting on an uneasy throne and subject to restless influences from Egypt to the east and Algeria to the west. Giving it up could be an incitement to pro-Nasser forces to close in on the U.S.-exploited oil resources in Libya, the greatest oil finds of the last two decades. Wheelus served as the take-off base for bombing training flights into the Sahara Desert for the U.S. Air Force in West Germany and Britain. The military never liked closing down bases at all. They did not like to have to send their families home, nor did they care to "shorten the tail," that is, the manpower-heavy lines of supply and communications kept in readiness for the if-and-when of war emergencies.

International affairs had become almost fashionable among the Defense Department's military. It was the hallmark of the soldier, sailor, or airman slated for higher things. All three military services had their own foreign policy shops. The U.S. Army had seventeen military and ten civilian officers in the International and Policy Plans Division of its Strategic Plans and Policies Staff. The U.S. Air Force had an International Affairs Division with thirty-five officers and officer-grade civilians, and a brigadier general in charge. A rear admiral headed the Politico-Military Policy Division in the office of the Chief of Naval Operations, with thirty-four officers and twelve clerks to serve the Secretary of the Navy as well. All this was small beer to Defense's "little State Department," the office of the Assistant Secretary of Defense for International Security Affairs, or ISA. The late John T. McNaughton, who held the post, used to say only as a half-joke, "I am the Secretary of State for the Defense Department." ISA had a total of 312 personnel, including 69 officers, 115 professional civilians, and 1 Foreign Service officer from State as Deputy Assistant Secretary for the Middle East. The Joint Chiefs had foreign territorial commands, which brought them into the picture. For example, there was a U.S. Commander-in-Chief, Middle East, Africa South of the Sahara, referred to as "MEAFSA." USCINCMEAFSA was charged with conducting planning to meet likely contingencies or emergencies in the area, war or short-of-war situations; to maintain liaison with the armed forces of the foreign countries in the region; and to supervise all U.S. military assistance programs within his territorial limits.

ISA was the top civilian authority on foreign policy in Defense. It attempted to ride herd on the profusion of foreign affairs interests inside the armed services, arbitrated among them, and mediated between Defense and the State Department. It tried strenuously to keep the channels of command strictly in its own hands, discouraging lateral policy approaches to the State Department, which was encouraging them. At the same time ISA continually "crowded" State with specific propositions, which State characterized as "tails you lose, heads I win" deals. State thought that ISA had no independent judgment and was merely a "tool" of McNamara. ISA thought that State was "inert" and "backward." State was "fighting the problem," Defense "over-selling the solution." State relied on know-how and the short cut to outwit the Defense mastodon. It pushed country directors and Assistant Secretaries to take the lead in interagency coordination at all levels. State's Deputy Under Secretary for Political Affairs and his key aides met at least twice a month with the Joint Chiefs and plugged State's views.

Despite the in-fighting, the routine contacts and on-the-telephone thrashing out of issues had developed and progressed farther and faster than at any other time in the history of State-Defense relations. The hard tests arose when actual crises were in process. In the State Department, crisis situations were first handled in the Operations Center. In Defense, they were "managed" at the National Military Command Center, or NMCC. This served as the operational hub of the other crisis centers, such as operations at State, the Situation Room at the White House, and the Situation Room at the CIA, all part of the national Command-and-Control System. The NMCC operated round-the-clock. Every shift was always under command of a general or flag-rank officer. The center processed information on current military operations for the President, the Secretary of Defense, and the Joint Chiefs in the same manner that State did in political matters. The NMCC commander on the shift, when everybody else was off-duty, had the delegated authority to act as operational commander for any sudden major crisis until the arrival of higher ranks. Five State Department officers on the shifts had to be doubly alert to see that State's principal officers and interests were served in the most timely manner possible, injecting themselves if necessary into the NMCC command structure to insure State's rights to immediate information. They gave warnings of political implications in transpiring events without waiting to be asked, even though the military might have considered the matter to be strictly within their exclusive military province. There were types on both sides who declined to share information with the other agency, but their numbers were getting fewer. Defense chafed at State's caution and charged it with "holding up operations." State's cautionary signals to Defense were translated into the plaint that Defense "doesn't understand the political limitations and dangers of a wider war."

The focus of the State Department's involvement with Defense was the Deputy Under Secretary for Political Affairs, the key "inside" man of the Department and usually a top-notch career officer. State's Foreign Affairs

Manual Circular No. 449, of 19 October 1966, revised, listed among the Deputy Under Secretary's duties:

. . . gives general direction within the Department to politico-military, intelligence and arms control and disarmament matters and to relations with other departments and agencies on such matters; . . . coordinates policies and assures implementation of politico-military decisions which fall within the jurisdiction of two or more bureaus; . . . supervises the activities of the Deputy Assistant Secretary for Politico-Military Affairs; . . . gives guidance to International Scientific and Technological Affairs.

The concept of military-diplomatic relations in the U.S. Government was a comparatively late starter. The Under Secretary of State in World War II had been the liaison with the War and Navy Departments, but mostly as a relay point of information rather than as a policy influence. SWNCC, or the State-War-Navy Coordinating Committee, in 1944 was a foreshadowing of the modern setup. It coordinated the three departments' views and issued policy directives concerning Germany, Austria, and Japan. In 1946 State had an Assistant Secretary of State for Occupied Areas, Major General John H. Hildring, who had headed G-5, or civil affairs, in the War Department. Hildring said: "The need for such a point of contact from which the armed services might get policy decisions, and get them on time, has existed for the past three years. The best testimony to the success of our program is the fact that we have accomplished more in two months than we had planned for four years."

The present organization for systematized relations with Defense was established by Ural Alexis Johnson, to give him his rarely published full name, in April 1961, when he was Deputy Under Secretary. The first Deputy Assistant Secretary in the job was Jeffrey C. Kitchen, who in 1967, after nearly seven years of constant crisis nursing, took off for a sabbatical at the Department's Senior Seminar. In the State Department's alphabet of symbols, the Deputy Under Secretary's office was designated as G and the politico-military office as G/PM. Johnson, a Kansan, had been Deputy Ambassador to Saigon, twice Deputy Under Secretary, the negotiator with Foster Dulles of the Japanese treaty and a Far East expert, coauthor with General Taylor of the SIG/IRG innovation in foreign policy coordination, completely dedicated, steady as the Rock of Gibraltar, a leading light of the classic Foreign Service, and a man with a fine ear for the precise odds on any given situation. Appointed Ambassador to Japan in late 1966, he was also the closest friend in the State Department of Secretary Rusk, for whom he used to work when Rusk was Assistant Secretary for the Far East during the Korean war. Kitchen was an Oregonian, a former special assistant to Dean Acheson and RAND senior associate, a Middle East expert, big, burly, and tough-minded beneath his Far West affability.

As a centralized staff of functional experts for the Secretary of State level, G/PM underwent its first great test in the Cuban missile crisis, when its small but elite staff helped Alexis Johnson serve as coordinator for the Cuban crisis operations. Johnson had a bulletin board in his office where he pinpointed the exact location and assignments of all the principals involved. He wrote the scenario for the events that were to unfold as they were planned by President Kennedy and his EX-COM group. Johnson described some of it later:

> The evacuation of dependents and reinforcement of Guantanamo, the deployment of destroyers and aircraft, the President's speech, our call for meetings of the United Nations Security Council and the Organization of American States, the delivery of messages by our Ambassadors to heads of governments abroad, the interception of the first Soviet vessel, the delivery of a message to the Kremlin, the cancellation of Navy shore leaves, and so on, all had to be worked out and meshed together hour by hour and minute by minute.

The Kitchen shop was the key channel for all official State relations with Defense and the Military Establishment, that is, the armed forces. It regulated all of State's world-wide politico-military relationships. It also had responsibility for coordination of emergency preparedness and foreign disaster relief. The latter function was performed by the office in the 1967 Middle East crisis, when thousands of Americans had to be airlifted out of the war areas.

The office guided the regional officers assigned to politico-military affairs in the five geographical bureaus. The Johnson-Kitchen team was a functional staff agency. It did not operate in the usual sense of the word—the geographical bureaus did that—but it had specialists who could talk the other experts' language. Defense practice was to send up proposals for strategy and tactics in the shape of draft "Presidential Memoranda," in which vital and substantive issues were discussed. The drafts went to State through G/PM for comment. But, as Budget Director Schultze told the Jackson Committee, State would find it "very difficult to have a major input unless it had the staff to participate in the process in depth." Schultze was referring to the fact that G/PM had fifteen officers as compared with the nearly two hundred in Defense's ISA.

G/PM's operations officer had plenty to do. He was the clearinghouse for the daily nuts and bolts of military affairs concerning which State had to be kept informed, for example, U.S. troop movements, bases, status of forces violations, hostile military movements across frontiers anywhere in the world, missile range clearances, special personnel assignments. Another officer, Raymond L. Garthoff, an authority on Soviet military forces and strategy, was consulted frequently by the Pentagon. There was never any dearth of Soviet data to mull over and analyze. For instance, as a British *Economist* headline said, "Bears can't fly, but American eagles can. Russia is discovering what strategic mobility means." The Soviets in the mid-1960's had begun to place emphasis on amphibious and air-borne troops for the first time. The Soviet Union had started to develop a modest airlift capability with a giant transportation plane. Moscow re-created a Marine Corps, which it had abolished in the 1950's. Russian military leaders were copying the McNamara thesis of "flexible response." The news indicated that the Soviets, too, would create a spectrum of alternative conventional weapons to meet degrees of war contingencies. But, at best, the Soviet capability for distant limited warfare or "police actions" was very low. The Russians had neither global bases on allied territories nor fleets of cargo planes and the logistics that supported them.

The Soviets were also moving on to the high seas. The Russian navy was already the second largest in the world and arriving at global strategic strength. The Middle East crisis had been a disaster for Soviet arms "sold" to Egypt and expropriated by the Israeli, but a windfall for Soviet naval vessels in the Mediterranean. They were beginning to sail the Sea as if they owned it. The dream of the warm seas had always been an impelling force for Russia. Soviet vessels were showing the flag and wagging it like a muscle. The U.S. Sixth Fleet in the Mediterranean observed the Russians with a cold and quizzical eye. In the week of war in June 1967 the U.S. Navy had had a momentary alarm in the first minutes of the Israeli air-sea attack on a U.S. communications ship. It had been feared that it was an Egyptian ruse to make it look like a Russian attack. The Russian flotilla in the Mediterranean dogged the U.S. fleet like a puppy. When several U.S. destroyers anchored at Malta in early 1967, a covey of Soviet minesweepers stood close by, observing every movement through binoculars. A young U.S. destroyer officer, a bit fed up with the attention, put on his skin-diver's suit, ducked under the shower, and came on deck streaming wet, in full view of the Russians, as if he had just surfaced from a frogman's reconnaissance under the nearby Soviet vessel. The Russians went into general quarters, stationed sentries on deck, and wallowed off to a safe distance.

The politico-military team at State was given the further function of previewing the annual Defense budget and analyzing from the foreign policy viewpoint the five-year force goals, that is, the number and kinds of troops and weapons represented in the Defense budget. The State staff also included a systems-analysis expert in an attempt to keep up with the analysts from Defense. State's basic posture was the necessity to project realistically the kind of world which trained diplomats foresaw in the five-year projected time span. Logically there should follow a sounder indication of what kind of force-structure goals would be most useful to the United States foreign policy objectives in the term under review. State's thesis was that armed forces were strictly a tool of foreign policy and had no reason to exist otherwise. If State's diplomats were to abdicate to Defense's scientists and mathematicians and refrain from challenging Defense's assumptions, they felt they would be culpable of disservice to the President as staff officers concerned with the totality of U.S. interests which the President of the United States represented. The President would be stuck with what he had been handed to use instead of having larger political options to maneuver with. State thus contributed a qualitative ingredient to choice of weapon systems, whether they might be short-legged, that is, dependent on overseas bases, or long-legged, home-based in the United States.

The points to be matched between State and Defense were these: State could cite the possible danger areas of vital U.S. interest. Defense could determine the physical feasibility of arriving there with a predetermined degree of force. Defense's review of planning levels was virtually a continuous updating process, though yearly administrative budget submission requirements set the public terminal calendar. The State commentary was based also on an overlapping appreciation of the Joint Chiefs of Staff Strategic Objectives Plan, which ran from five to eight years. The extreme complexities of weapons system choices lay in the long lead time, or period of gestation. New weapons had to be invented, researched, developed, tested, made operational, mass-produced, distributed, and emplaced. This process could stretch from five to ten years.

The State staff possessed a specialist on atomic energy and aeronautical aerospace matters. Philip J. Farley, Kitchen's successor as Deputy Assistant Secretary, had been an expert on nuclear matters under Secretary Dulles when the nuclear test ban treaty was first broached seriously in 1958, at the first meetings of technical experts. In a nuclear world, it was imperative that force as an instrument of foreign policy be of measured and highly limited use. Famous consultants to the Defense Department like Herman Kahn had lectured at State, had deeply impressed the sophisticated audience, but had not made wholesale conversions. The debate between the mathematical theologians of infinite precision and the worldly operators of human judgment and intuition continued, like the never-ending arguments in the Reformation between the value of salvation by works or by faith. The Foreign Service was not quite ready to let diplomacy give way to eschatology, the doctrine of final matters, death, and the future state.

On the pragmatic level of here-now-and-tomorrow, there were ironical twists to the nuclear problem, with uneasy, if not alarming, consequences.

The United States and the Soviet Union, the world's two super-nuclear powers, had in 1967 at long last produced a draft treaty on the nonproliferation of nuclear weapons at Geneva. They were slowly persuading members of the seventeen-nation disarmament conference that the rights of the non-nuclear powers to the peaceful exploitation of atomic power would not be denied them. The obvious fear of the great powers centered on the new circumstance that knowledge of the atomic art could be acquired with comparative ease and that economic costs of manufacturing simple but still deadly nuclear weapons had decreased considerably. Ten countries were estimated as being fully capable of producing nuclear bombs. India, for example, was advanced enough to go into production in possibly one year. Another nine countries could do so sooner than later with rather more effort.

The wry fact was that nuclear proliferation was almost impossible to prevent. The so-called peaceful reactors, which the United States Atomic Energy Commission and the State Department had generously been supplying around the world, were one of the reasons. The "peaceful" reactors produced plutonium, the raw material of bombs, every day they operated. The total of a year's daily operation could provide enough plutonium to make at least one atomic bomb. Fifty-one countries of the world owned peaceful-uses nuclear reactors. The list included, of course, the five states—United States, Britain, Russia, France, and Mainland China—which actually were producing military nuclear devices. Abroad, in 1966, there were an estimated sixty-one peaceful reactors in operation, eight in stages of being built, and three planned. The United States had for export to other nations fifty-nine reactors; ten were being built and three being planned. The anxiety of the Geneva conference over safeguards and inspection of peaceful reactors was self-evident. Thomas C. Schelling of Harvard University, noted academic strategist and consultant to both the State and Defense Departments, illuminated the seemingly unavoidable possibilities in a national educational television discussion in 1967. Schelling said:

It's perfectly possible that within ten or fifteen years, nuclear weapons can be acquired by theft, revolt, political trade, foreign aid. Governments will have them. Military services can split off from governments in case of a rebellion or a coup of some sort. Nuclear weapons may remain in the hands of a political grouping, a dissident military service, a fled dictator. We could eventually run into something with nuclear weapons that could be a little reminiscent of opium, white slavery, and gun running. In the United States, we don't worry about which military service has nuclear weapons every time we change Presidents. But there must be many countries in the world in which ordinary orderly succession is not going to be the typical way the government changes. And when governments change, there may well always be the question of to whom is that military force loyal that possesses the nuclear weapons.

Even if there isn't any actual or threatened use of nuclear weapons domestically, I would suggest that this is going to become a severe preoccupation for the people who rule Indonesia or Cuba even in years to come.

If poor countries, less stable countries, the opposed dictators, and so forth, get nuclear weapons, I would expect that they would be attracted to unconventional, perhaps very mundane, means of delivery. Probably the most important is that they [would] keep their weapons in the places [where], if they wanted to create a fright, they could detonate them when they wanted to. Poor countries, mischievous countries, countries that have nothing but a kind of extortion or blackmail to rely on, won't really be interested primarily in military use of these weapons. It will be terroristic use. Whereas it would make no sense to the Soviet government [or] the American government to try to smuggle a few weapons on to enemy territory ahead of time, it's precisely what could appeal to, let's say, a Castro who had been driven out, who carried away, instead of as in the old days the crown jewels, a few nuclear weapons. His interest would be in smuggling a few into some place which would scare the wits out of Americans, Englishmen, or whoever it was he wanted to frighten.

The antiballistic missile, or ABM, began figuring seriously in State-Defense discussions in early 1966. Word of a purported Soviet ABM system in the so-called Kalininn complex of western Russia for forward defense of Moscow and Leningrad began to transpire and was verified more or less by U.S. observer satellites in space. In the nature of the closed Russian system, an on-the-ground direct scrutiny was impossible; therefore a first-class evaluation was out of the question, a disadvantage unavoidably associated with foreign secrets. The situation began to look like the start of another arms race. Montesquieu had described rivalry in armaments in the eighteenth century. Pre-World War I Germany had engaged in a naval shipbuilding race with Britain. Pre-World War II Japan had been in naval competition with the United States. Russia and America were rivals in the same lethal arena since the Cold War began.

Defense research and development technicians were concerned over the slow pace of ABM progress for lack of huge sums required to reach optimum operational effectiveness, sums which had been deflected in part by the unexpected costs of the Vietnam war but more so by the deliberate higher command decision to let well enough alone and not to disturb the politically fragile Soviet-American strategic balance. State conversations with Britain indicated that a U.S. decision to invest in an ABM system would have a destabilizing influence on the European allies. The Americans did not agree. There was the further impression that the Soviets likewise did not believe that the installation of the ABM would necessarily rattle the eggs in everybody's security basket. Europe once again feared a neoisolationist United States withdrawing into a supposedly safe Fortress America cocoon, leaving the allies exposed, defenseless, and nervous. The United

States was confident that it still had the decisive strategic bulge on the Soviet Union in the number of ICBM's, delivery systems, and penetration devices, including multiple warhead Poseidon missiles to replace the Polaris. More than $1 billion had been spent to perfect the new penetration weapons in recent years.

The Americans felt, moreover, that if the Russians believed in the efficacy of their ABM as a means of restoring their own self-confidence and of lessening chronic Russian insecurity, it would do the United States no harm and might even serve a basically useful purpose. A less tense Soviet state of mind could help create a new appearance of a new world balance between the two great world powers. It could promote stability and give time to solve, in common if possible, the crises being manufactured almost daily by the rampaging third-country elements on the world scene. The consensus of State's evaluation, as reflected by its two most recent ambassadors to Moscow, Llewellyn E. Thompson and Foy Kohler, was that the Soviet decision, on balance, was a minimum first step, impelled by the vast increase in U.S. defense expenditures occasioned by the Berlin crisis and the Vietnam war. The assumed Russian effort looked relatively weak and experimental, to placate Soviet military circles. In short, the Soviet ABM was not a wide deployment and not a real commitment to spend huge funds otherwise needed urgently for domestic Russian investments. This interpretation became the official Johnson administration policy for the time being, avoiding the necessity of spending an estimated $40 billion for an anti-Russian ABM defense and deciding, instead, to spend from $5 billion to $8 billion on a "thin" system as insurance against a Communist Chinese ICBM threat that might appear in the 1970's, but possibly considerably sooner.

The ABM issue was a top-level example of the politico-military mix both in Russia and in the United States. Diplomatic struggles were traditionally a continuation of war by other means and, by intrinsic definition, meant a multiple-front operation. The Americans thus had a two-front problem on their hands: the Russians and the European allies. As to the allies, the view was that talks should ensue sooner than later on the issue of ABM defenses for Europe also. The full circle had come around once again. The nuclear monkey had climbed back on the shoulders of the West. The first act in the play had been the Soviet threat of 711 IBM, or intermediate ballistic missiles, poised in 1966 on western European targets. The estimated 329 Soviet ICBM's were for Chinese and U.S. targets. The second act had been the multilateral force, or MLF, a double device to provide nuclear control-sharing and protection at the same time. The MLF had been buried until the moment of resurrection of a European Defense Community in the uncertain future. The third act was the ABM. In it once again the nuclear problem was posed, since the utility of the ABM's was their nuclear defensive capability to destroy offensive nuclear missiles. When the U.S. decision to proceed with the ABM was made at the December 1966 budget reviews by President Johnson, the allies grumbled as always that they had been "informed" but not "consulted." By this time the tired phrase was getting to be like the man's asking for a slice of pie before the cook had even baked it.

The political atmospherics, in fact, indicated that the ABM issue was approaching the stage of tactics. In their stratospheric ivory towers, the perfectionists of the Pentagon, profoundly sunk in the enormous intricacies of the ABM technical problem, did not quite realize that the ABM was a first-class candidate as a domestic partisan political issue. The Democrats had played heavily the so-called missile gap in the 1960 presidential campaign, though postinauguration inquiry disclosed that no such gap had existed. The little deficiency in truth had not made it any less a forceful issue. All the Johnson administration needed, pummeled as it was all over the ring by the anti-Vietnam war battlers, was to hand the Republicans the crowd-confusing cry of an "anti-missile-missile gap." This possible portent had not yet made a megaton impact on the Defense Department in mid-1966. In any event, in early 1967 Congress came to the rescue, as it had so often done in the past, with action-forcing speeches. U.S. Senator John O. Pastore, Democrat of Rhode Island and chairman of the vitally concerned Joint Congressional Committee on Atomic Energy, came out for the ABM in a literally ringing demand. The small-framed Pastore possessed one of the high-decibel sets of vocal chords in Congress.

The ball was now in play in the American court. The game might still be avoided altogether if the Soviet Union was reasonable. In the same fashion that major issues developed between the great powers because of their involvements with third-party interests, the ABM was an example of a major issue being infiltrated or exploited by third-party interests for their own special stakes. The ABM issue became mixed up in the question of whether the United States should ask to talk detailed ABM realities to the Soviets. The State Department's suggested approach in early 1967 was to present the appearance of actually having undertaken to establish an American ABM system. From this stratagem the Russians in theory would infer that they had better come to the conference table and negotiate a mutual abnegation of the costly ABM business.

There was more than theory in the State proposal, however. It was founded on the hope that the Russians could be delayed in starting their ABM system. The key political point, in State's eyes, was the ABM's effect on the underdeveloped nations, and particularly on those of the Middle East, if the Soviets first established credibility in an impregnable defense against the Americans. Soviet sympathizers and exploiters of Soviet power believed that there had been an excessive reliance by Moscow on the theory of deterrence via ICBM's. The equivalence of the Soviet-American threat resulted invariably in a stand-off, frustrating the designs of the small and mid-size Soviet followers. The ABM would give the Soviet Union the umbrella under which the little fry could with impunity really dare to kick the muscle-bound United States in the nose. In post-mortems after the Arab-Israeli war, State analysts came to the conclusion that this nuance of power tactics had indeed been an element in the contumacious behavior of the Arabs on the eve of the conflict. In State's opinion, Defense had delayed overlong in agreeing to talk to the Russians. This gave the Russians the tactical advantage of playing it either way, in their own good time. The final rebuff to talks was voiced by Soviet Premier Kosygin to Defense Secretary McNamara, face to face, at the Glassboro summit dinner table in late June 1967.

The State Department's politico-military affairs office had a specialist for over-all contingency planning. Spot coordination was done by operational working groups like the Berlin task force or that on Vietnam. With the latter, the politico-military shop actually had little to do. The contingency planning staff officers operated rather as a superplanning counselor on everybody else's plans. The main point to be kept in mind about contingency planning was that it concerned employment of the actual physical resources on hand at the moment an uncertain but dimly foreseen event or unexpected emergency actually came to pass. The drill was: If it happened, one did this-and-this-and-this right away. The long-range strategic plans, with which the State planning specialist was also concerned, were much more hypothetical. The trouble with contingency plans, however, was that they never happened exactly the way they were provisioned. But they were excellent mind-stretchers and positive exercises in constructive imagination. They familiarized operating officers with the contours of the practicably possible.

The contingency work involved considerable consultation with the Joint Staff of 400 or so officers who did the planning for the Joint Chiefs. In the Berlin crisis, for instance, there were at least thirty contingency plans. The Joint Chiefs had from fifteen to twenty master war plans, which required close State-Defense consultation on the order of priorities of action. Physical force or direct military action was consistently at the bottom of the priority list as a fundamental principle of U.S. policy. Continuous contingency planning covered all critical areas in the world, existent and potential. These included the Congo, Cuba, Kuwait, Berlin, Haiti, Taiwan, Korea, India, Pakistan, the Middle East, Laos, and, of course, Vietnam. Since 1966 the

Joint Chiefs had addressed themselves to the problem of precisely what problems would be encountered in a cease-fire in Vietnam and a possible truce to follow: standstills and ways to enforce agreements not to make creeping advances, an old guerrilla trick, and one at which the Israelis had been adroit in the 1949 Palestine armistice.

The southeast Asia front had been a particular nightmare to the military planners because of the lack of clear-cut battle lines. Strategically, there was little question that it was a southeast Asia war. Tactically, it was a medley of frustrations: military action constrained to South Vietnam on the ground; forbidden in neighboring Cambodia, which had no war of its own but which served as a temporary safe-passage sanctuary for the enemy at will; and masked in Laos, which had a war of its own, and was, for the most part, a no-man's land. Farthest west on the peninsula, Thailand had been a silent but active ally of the United States since 1961, and it had become a vocal one by 1967. U.S. air power in Thailand, which was pounding North Vietnam from at least eight U.S.-built bases, was heavier than the total air strength of the United States in the Pacific in World War II. The confused requirements of an unprecedented limited war were a constant temptation to the generals to press for the opening of a second front in Laos from Vietnam and in particular from Thailand. General Westmoreland, besides his role as commander-in-chief of U.S. armed forces in South Vietnam and Commanding General, Military Assistance Group, Vietnam—COMMAGVEE—was also COMMAGTHAI, that is, also responsible for Thailand's military assistance guidance in 1964. The second-front lure encouraged interservice rivalries behind the scenes in earlier days of the Vietnam war after they had practically disappeared from the Washington scene in consequence of Secretary McNamara's stern domination.

U.S. troop strength in Thailand quietly had nearly doubled every year for three years, from approximately 12,000 in 1965 to 25,000 in 1966 and approaching 50,000 in 1967. The Senate Foreign Relations Committee became concerned about the U.S. build-up in Thailand. It feared another U.S. involvement, on the heels of Vietnam, to "protect" the U.S. aid investment in Thailand. The use of the U Taphao air base at Sattahip, south of Bangkok on the Gulf of Siam, by giant B-52 U.S. bombers for the first time in April 1967 was almost in the nature of a final flourish and seal to the fact that Thailand had become a major U.S. ally in Asia. Thailand was strategically the heart of southeast Asia. It maintained a United Nations troop presence, along with the United States, in South Korea, and in late 1967 began sending sizable contingents to Vietnam. Thailand was a member of SEATO, the only treaty to which she subscribed. There were nearly 1,000 miles of border with unsettled Laos and Burma. Thailand was only 100 miles from Communist China, which was always present, while the United

States was 15,000 miles away. The Thai faced the dilemma of maintaining a careful independence or prudently acquiescing to stay neutralist in order to appease China. They were, however, not about to discard their hereditary caution and climb up the mountain only to walk down again. The Thai had always been free, had never been a colony, and had no intention of being occupied by anyone, Chinese or American.

This was the backdrop against which three major battles, with a series of intervening skirmishes, took place between State and Defense in the period from 1963 to 1967. At critical junctures the sharp but silent bureaucratic policy struggles behind the screen necessitated the direct intervention of President Johnson, who, personally impressed with the Thai, ruled more in favor of State. The first engagement was over the utility of Thailand as an ally. The initial, quick U.S. military impression had been that Thailand was comparatively negligible for big league consideration, almost a musical operetta country of the "King of Siam and I." A U.S. investment in rural constabulary might be useful, but if Thailand got into big trouble with China, it could call on the United States to come in and take care of the situation. The Thai's reaction indicated that this U.S. approach was rather whimsical for their tastes. The next State-Defense campaign was joined on the issue of aid. As was noted, the Defense proposal that Thailand cut down its internal economic investments and increase its military budget proportionately had been rejected. Further irritations came up. The Thai were thrifty and used their equipment until it practically fell apart. Defense cost-effectiveness inspectors did not approve of Thai maintenance practices. To the Thai a broken-down truck was better than no truck at all, in case the Americans went away. Between 1950 and 1963, the country had received $500 million in U.S. economic aid. In recent years the Thai economy pulsated with activity, owing to the policy of continuous capital investment from domestic revenues. Thailand thus needed U.S. economic aid no longer. The decision was to pick up the Thai check for military aid, which would be comparatively small.

After his vice-presidential visit in 1961, Johnson persuaded President Kennedy to give the Thai a military aid program of between $50 million and $81 million. Still unconvinced of the value of the Thai commitment, Defense proposed between $25 million and $35 million for 1965. But in 1966 President Johnson intervened again and put the Thai military aid figure up to $66 million for 1967. For 1968, the proposals were nearer the $90 million level. Thai military assistance, however, was very small potatoes in comparison with the direct United States military investment in Thailand after the bombing of North Vietnam was begun in 1965. The very first requirement of the air war had been safe and secure air fields, and South Vietnam, infested with Viet Cong, was not quite the place. In the arrangements that were worked out, Thailand donated the ground space under its obligation as a loyal SEATO ally. It owned the bases, but charged nothing for their use. The complex of air bases, the network of military roads, the latest modern communications system, and the modernization of supply ports were entirely American military expenditures. Depending on the accordion span of the Defense budget, the U.S. direct cost in Thailand was estimated at nearly $2 billion.

The differences between State and Defense in this phase of U.S.–Thai relations had not been exactly a pillow fight. It had involved Secretary McNamara, as the top Defense official, who made the final determination on the shape of the Defense budget and on the allocation of funds in it. The State interlocutor had been the United States Ambassador on the scene, Graham Martin, an intense, self-possessed, positive, assertive, fearless career diplomat who sought and gave no quarter within the Marquis of Queensbury rules for diplomatic in-fighting. The next and final State-Defense engagement in Thailand involved the Joint Chiefs of Staff. The thesis in dispute this time centered largely on the tactics to be employed in enlisting Thai cooperation for U.S. military requirements. Practically, it devolved on the jurisdictional issue of who controlled the activities of the U.S. military in Thailand and, more important, their access to the organs of the Thai Government. The argumentation became so finely drawn once or twice that recommendations, tantamount to orders, from one of the Joint Chiefs' representatives were met with the response that the proposals were not consonant with United States over-all foreign policy objectives in Thailand and would not be executed unless on the direct instruction of the President.

The nub of the dispute was that the U.S. military authorities wanted full and unquestioned permission from the Thai Government to conduct blanket operations in that country. This the Thai, extremely sensitive to the merest hint of foreign domination, would never have agreed to, in Martin's view. They insisted that the American presence in Thailand be as muted as possible. In comparison with other areas where GI's were on the scene, the American presence in Thailand was kept remarkably unobtrusive as a result. The last Bangkok-Washington skirmishing occurred over the scope and manner of U.S. assistance to the Thai for their fight against the minor, but potentially serious, insurgency in northeast Thailand, where six provinces in the Phuban Mountains had become disaffected through neglect of the rural population. The insurgents were banded in the United Thailand Patriotic Front and abetted by Chinese Communist radio broadcasts and Pathet Lao rebels from Laos. The Thai accepted logistical support for the counterinsurgency efforts but permitted no American participation in counterguerrilla operations. The Thai preferred to fight their own internal battles. They were clearly twice as shy about so-called Americanization of their affairs after what they had been observing in Vietnam. The U.S. military had been eager to introduce Special Force, or Green Beret, units into the fighting areas, which McNamara himself forbade. The Thai were highly impressed with American helicopters for a fast airlift of their troops to the insurgent areas. Martin borrowed ten machines from the Seventh Air Force in 1966 until Defense provided a full squadron in 1967. The craft were flown by unarmed U.S. pilots until Thai crews were trained to take over.

The Thai imposed further conditions for U.S. use of Thai territory and for accepting U.S. military aid. This was reversing the pattern that sometimes accompanied U.S. foreign aid in other countries, that is, the imposition of U.S. conditions. The Thai demanded and received the right to approve the United States target lists for the bombing of North Vietnam. The target lists periodically had been selected or approved at the Tuesday White House luncheon meetings of Johnson, McNamara, Rusk, and Rostow. McNamara relayed the word to the Joint Chiefs, who cabled orders down a distribution list which included CINCPAC, the U.S. admiral in command of the Pacific theater, the Seventh Tactical Air Force in Thailand, and Ambassador Martin in Bangkok. In theory, Martin had to receive Thai Government advance permission before U.S. bombers took off on their missions over North Vietnam. In practice, he conveyed the target lists to the Thai only after the U.S. aircraft had taken off and returned from the raids. The diplomatic niceties had been observed in the oblique Oriental fashion.

Martin, the activist who had stirred dust-ups inside the bureaucracy in order to preserve United States long-range diplomatic objectives in Thailand and still satisfy U.S. military necessities at the same time, was rotated home in late 1967. He was succeeded by a solid, sober, and shrewd diplomatic practitioner, Leonard Unger, who had performed a highly delicate holding operation in the quicksands of Laos after the 1962 Geneva accords on that country. Operating diplomatic missions in key countries at crucial times was a matter of choosing the right men for the right jobs in the right order at the right times. After all, as Dean Acheson liked to say as he escalated to a glorious rage, "The State Department is people."

CHAPTER XII

PERSONNEL: Knights of the Round Table

IN THE END, DIPLOMACY AND foreign policy, the management of overseas programs and organizational coherence, came down to the point of individual persons. The State Department, however, had not yet devised a Q clearance of the human psyche and its operative motivations. Washington was full of brainy characters. The proportion of college-educated inhabitants was higher than in any other city in the country. Nor did the narrow imperatives of making a living put too many constraints on effective functioning; more than 700,000 households reported annual incomes of nearly $11,000. Despite the supply of superior minds, there was an occasional absence of character to lend integrity to the intelligence. Some diplomats were impelled by ambition to grasp the levers of power, others drawn by dreams to put flesh on ideals. The majority had their little insecurities and incapacities and traveled in the wake of positive personalities. The greatest single occupational hazard to Foreign Service career advancement was the shifting and complex character of archetypical colleagues—architects of progress, peers of the *status quo*, or eunuchs of power who preferred the perquisites of office to the actual wielding of responsibility.

The determination of policies and the execution of decisions were ceaselessly subject to pressures that could deflect continuity of purpose or modify direction of specific programs. Self-proclaimed originators of policy, influence wielders, opinion molders, and other fashionable fakers of the times were nuisances. Wary eyes had to be kept on politicians and journalists who conducted their education in public and added to the confusion while fighting private battles in the name of the common weal. A quick size-up had to be made of the latest public aspect of the leading players on the stage as they gracefully turned their better profile toward the audience. The sensitivities of policy operators demanded a rhinoceros skin to ward off infectious malaise of the town where despondency, malice, and fatigue ran in periodic epidemics.

Washington was the town of the painless shaft. Its thrust was preceded by the intonation, "He is a nice guy, but——." Part of the game was learning patiently to wait in the anterooms of the great, the near-great, and the would-be-great. The quick learners found that the best defense was a well-insulated, seamless exterior to the circling angle-players in the forest of petrified faces. There were no Caligulas in the State Department, but more than a few Elbert Hubbards, who wearied the ear with sententious counsel. There was the mystifying phenomenon of the officer who was never, never surprised at the latest news,· which he had not heard, but who nonetheless nodded sagely, and responded, "Yes, I know." There was the phrase-stealer from the White House speech writers. He purloined gems in chance conversations and jotted them down in his notebook. There was also the donnish wit, rather low in vitamins, who uttered elegant little epigrams, which Proust once described as "tricks to show that what seems so wonderful is only a little something struck off at random, when it is in fact only a little something struck off at random."

As a company town, Washington was full of the faintly poisonous gossip that families nonchalantly disclose about their members. The confluence of influences, problems, crises, and frustrations promoted excruciating self-examinations and searchings of conscience. It brought on psychological blocks, culture-shocks, and traumas of stress, which necessitated the employment of psychiatrists for consultation by officers of the State Department, the United States Information Agency, and the Central Intelligence Agency. The daily pressures of Western civilization were in few other areas as vividly present as in the foreign affairs field. Increased studies of psychosomatic illness in recent years disclosed multiple effects of runaway, suppressed, or unsublimated emotions on the mental stability of otherwise highly intelligent persons. Prudent Foreign Service officers were forewarned to pay heed to Plutarch's dictum, "Moderation is best," and "avoid all extremes." It was the best insurance against diseases, which were also organic reactions to emotional stress, such as high blood pressure, angina, asthma, ulcers, overactive colon, arthritis, and low back pain.

In the Washington air, sharp interests developed beveled edges. Diplomats appreciated the low-key tribute of their guild epitaph, "He drafted easily, reasoned cogently, served creditably. R.I.P." It was enough for many officers to share in dilute or minute doses the wine of power quaffed by the highest civil servants of permanent tenure and by the senior Senators and Congressmen of important committees that outlived presidential administrations. There was no stimulation from long-standing centers of influence and substance represented by heavy industry, high finance, or commerce in great metropoles like New York and Chicago. For Foreign Service officers, official expatriates that they were, there was no tradition of vital concern in their headquarters city of Washington, where the inhabitants had no national representation or ever exploded in revolt to gain their right to it. Washington, unlike London, Paris, or Rome, had had no blood on the barricades. It had no Faubourg St. Germain or Mayfair of permanently vested aristocrats or solid burghers. Television news programs drew twice as well as in the rest of the country, since government shoptalk was the capital's daily grist. Nationally, Washington decisions made the news. New York, the technological fountainhead of mass media services, shaped the news of the decisions. There, sudden-death demolition of power figures in corporate structures could happen between one day and the next. In Washington, a bureaucrat shorn of power could wait around for years like a zombie.

Washington was a textbook example of what Rudolph Geiger, the German microclimatologist, defined, in *The Climate Near the Ground,* as "eddy diffusion": Turbulences in the air transported all kinds of elements, but they eventually disappeared and merged into a new environment. Washington was the city of psychosomatic weather par excellence. In the summer the heavy air on the street resembled Cairo's; it was like wet cotton. In the spring the air was like Paris'; in the autumn, like Rome's. From the eighth-floor terrace of the State Department, the new year could be observed, unfurling like a banner. By March, the air spangled like sunshot silk. The morning light was a pure gray-violet. The pearl-pink pastels were a painter's delight. The early morning sun gilded the Capitol, the Washington Monument, the Lincoln Memorial, below, with an evanescent reddish paleness. The red glint signified water particles in the air and the precondensation of clouds to come. The morning breeze blew steady at about ten miles an hour, eddying in from the continental mass to the southwest. Fine dust rode the great global air currents flowing in from Texas, Arizona, California, from across the Pacific in Asia. The dust molecules scattered the white light into a yellow hue, which briefly stained the blue.

As the day wore on, thousands of metropolitan Washington's automobiles emptied exhaust gases into the sky. The sun's ultraviolet rays turned the acid gases into noxious ozone. Haze sifted in to veil the clear colors of the morning. Washington air normally had 100,000 submicroscopic particles per cubic centimeter. The polluted light flicked through the colors of the spectrum. Greens in trees and bushes slipped through an arpeggio of differentiation, from yellow-green to gray-blue-green. A thin wash of neuter seeped the depth out of browns and blacks. Sharp outlines began to fuzz. The smog bite in the air became a blur to the look. In the morning it was early Gauguin, in the afternoon Monet and Manet. As the afternoon drooped into twilight in the soft, dreamy air, colors shaded and faded and slid into the next tint. Textures stood out, like muscles with the skin removed. The mauve light rounded out the stone rims of the monuments. Washington floated on a cloud of lavender mist. Clarity and 20–20 vision returned with the northwest wind from the Arctic and north polar wastes. Optical illusions could be brushed away, though man-made atmospherics survived. The landscape stood out distinct and clean-cut, near enough to touch, in solid colors, impressive and stately, in a sweep of vista from Capitol Hill, across the Potomac, to the Eternal Flame of Arlington Cemetery.

The Foreign Service officer was a modern morality play in himself. His many roles included being a perpetual tourist, a legionnaire on the frontier, a martyr, an eremite, a Knight Templar, a demisocialite, even an Elk, and sometimes an Odd Fellow. By 1967 the Foreign Service had been bleeding at the veins for almost a decade. Investigated, cross-examined, reorganized, pinpricked, assaulted or ignored, Foreign Service officers, senior and junior, gloomily agreed that the corps faced the greatest crisis of its existence. There was despondency at the low ebb in its fortunes and doubts as to its adequacy to meet the accelerating complexities of the technological, nuclear world. Arguments and recriminations concerning the effectiveness of the Foreign Service officers as revolution managers, bureaucratic bumblers, or executors of the estate had many connotations. Concern about the Foreign Service shrouded the fact that a very large part of the criticism heaped upon the State Department was in fact laid at the feet of the service. Its officers, reserves, and staff together amounted to almost three fifths of the Department's 13,000 personnel.

As an elite bureaucracy, the self-absorbed Foreign Service at times overlooked the fact that bureaucracies were also under attack elsewhere in the world, in particular within the evolving Communist societies. The Soviet news organs *Trud* and *Pravda* in 1966 attacked petty tyrannies of officials who appeared to be beyond the law. In Communist China, Mao Tse-tung's Great Proletarian Cultural Revolution was directed against the Chinese party bureaucracy, which had moth-balled reform by means of endless committee meetings. In Communist Cuba, Fidel Castro launched a drastic "revolution against the bureaucracy," threatening to redeploy recalcitrant bureaucrats to the farms in the same manner that Mao had sent bureaucrats to dig ditches in China. There had been diabolical suggestions to reduce or eliminate no-longer useful elements in the U.S. Foreign Service by taking advantage of a rarely used regulation. A senior officer could be named ambassador to, say, the Republic of Chad in West Africa, allowed to remain some weeks, then relieved and not given any new appointment whatsoever for six months. At the end of this period it would be mandatory that he retire. This would be a mass walking-the-plank seriatim.

Perennially the butt of popular folklore, diplomats were never abused merely once but over and over again, with the same brickbats and old shoes, and all the more so when in trouble. Duplicity, dubious, double-faced, double-dyed, were standard bequests to diplomacy from the eighteenth century. Louis XI of France in the fifteenth century contributed the tarnish of disrepute to the profession as he corrupted Europe for the sake of absolute power. Diplomacy was a means of waging war without bloodshed and expense, rather than a humanitarian method of preventing war. Louis XI placed "reasons of state" above private morality. Diplomatic agents have carried the stigma ever since. Thirteen centuries earlier the Byzantine Empire organized the first foreign office tailored to conduct professional negotiations. Its involuted artifices grew into what, in a pejorative sense, the word "Byzantine" sometimes connotes today.

In the centuries of being put upon, exploited, and discarded, diplomats developed a self-protective sense of priesthood, a continuity of tradition, and a cabalistic abracadabra to keep the ignorant at bay. They nurtured secret idealisms of a world ruled by reason, where the arts of accommodation and persuasion would forbid the crass imposition of narrow national interests upon international ambiguities and would expose warfare as a wasteful exercise of talent. The self-esteem of chosen merit was early evident in American diplomacy. In 1834 Secretary of State Louis McLane, asking the Congress for more funds to raise salaries, pointed out that the duties of State Department personnel were "of a very delicate nature, requiring not only great fidelity, but talent and education of a high order, general information and an accurate knowledge of public officers both foreign and domestic, not necessarily required in other inferior officers of the Executive Government." The word "inferior" in the sense then used meant "junior," not lesser in quality.

The State Department did not obtain the opportunity to become a sanctuary of the select until the twentieth century, however. It was a target for envy from almost the first years, and it became a major source of patronage after Secretary of State (and later President) Martin Van Buren initiated the spoils system of wholesale political appointments, when the United States had diplomatic relations with only sixteen countries and the State Department had only 22 employees in Washington and 184 diplomatic attachés abroad. In 1877, when William E. Evarts was Secretary of State under President Rutherford B. Hayes, the demand for foreign service jobs was so intense that there were 7,000 applicants for one consular position. In 1885, when Thomas F. Bayard was Secretary of State under President Grover Cleveland, foreign appointments were much sought after, thirty deserving Democrats applying for the post of Minister to Belgium and a hundred for that of Consul-General in Paris.

But the upward swing was on the way. Secretary of State Richard Olney, in 1895, during the second Grover Cleveland administration, took the first steps to remove the foreign service from politics. He improved the consular service and gave promotions on merit alone. In 1905 President Theodore Roosevelt and Secretary of State Elihu Root placed the diplomatic and consular services under civil service. Examinations were required for entry into the Foreign Service. The first exams, in 1907, were so strict that only thirteen of thirty-eight candidates passed. By 1915 the merit system and the career concept were solidly established. Representative John Jacob Rogers of Massachusetts, between 1919 and 1924, from drafts submitted by Secretary of State Charles Evans Hughes, finally produced the Rogers Act, the magna carta of the Foreign Service. The act established the Foreign Service corps by name and amalgamated the diplomatic and consular services, which had been separate since the birth of the Republic.

Almost immediately the newly ensconced Foreign Service got itself involved in the intramural politics which periodically beset it and for which it accumulated large arrears of interest, to be repaid painfully in later years in Congressional distrust. Investigation showed that the 214 promotions in the first two and a half years of the new service represented 63 per cent of all diplomatic personnel, but only 37 per cent of the consular personnel. Exclusiveness was cultivated, breeding later resentments. Between 1924 and 1941, less than 5 per cent of the persons who applied to take the written examination were eventually commissioned.

But the lean years were not long in coming, as if in castigation of the overly proud. President Franklin D. Roosevelt's devaluation of the dollar in 1933 immediately and effectively slashed U.S. diplomats' dollar income overseas by 50 per cent. The administration imposed a 15 per cent cut in salaries and a 65 per cent cut in rental allowances. It was a distressing period of personal suffering, not equaled until 1953 and 1954, when Treasury Secretary George M. Humphrey in the Eisenhower administration decreed a 21 per cent reduction in personnel, the notorious RIF. One of its effects was to eliminate many economic analysts at the very moment when the Marshall Plan had started to produce effects on western

Europe's economy. The woefully inadequate U.S. reporting staffs were unable to gauge in time the course of European recovery and therefore unable to advise in advance on the feasibility of closing out U.S. aid, thus prolonging the possibly unnecessary expenditure of U.S. funds.

It took almost a generation from the Rogers Act of 1924 before the Foreign Service obtained its constitution, in 1946. The statutory codification of its perquisites, salaries, and retirement rights was a direct outgrowth of World War II. In the period between the two world wars, the Department had grown slowly—714 employees in 1921, 753 in 1936, and 971 in 1941. In 1946 there were 820 career officers, but 976 Foreign Service auxiliaries from wartime agency transfers. Already in 1944 the senior officers had begun studying the shape of the service for the new and expanded world role the United States would play after the war. The Foreign Service did not enjoy in the United States the public prestige accorded to diplomats in Europe. But it had a strong *esprit de corps,* a cohesive loyalty among the members, almost like that of a feudal nobility in which everybody was somebody else's cousin, in order to compensate for the poor pay, slow promotion, and inability to obtain the top ambassadorial posts, which still went to leading figures of politics and wealth.

Both the 1924 and the 1946 Foreign Service laws were political acts, a banding together against political encroachments in order to establish a new political organism capable of defending itself, fortified by statutory safeguards. But in fighting fire with fire, the Foreign Service took on politics as an inescapable attribute when it showed its face in the Congressional arena, its record of selfless service overseas notwithstanding. The necessary consolidation of the Foreign Service in 1946 left considerable scar tissue in the Federal Government. Its charter was enacted despite basically unresolved controversy, with defects in conception still stressed and recalled over twenty years later. This was the consequence, above all, of the bitter dispute over the law between the Bureau of the Budget and the State Department. It left the Budget Bureau frustrated, resentful, and suspecting that it had been outfoxed by the smooth intriguers of diplomacy. This famous battle of the bureaucracy was described blow by blow in the classic 1952 case study *Public Administration and Policy Development,* edited by Harold Stein.

Evidence that the Foreign Service Act of 1946 was only the start, and by no means the end, of debate about the future of American diplomats and their role in the nation's service was soon apparent. By 1949 the role of the Director General of the Foreign Service was modified by Congress. Political attitudes were indicated by the pros and cons concerning the change. Opponents charged that the Director General had already become a sort of "Black Pope" of the Jesuits, keeping his domain under rigorous sway and away from control of the Secretary of State. Friends of the service complained that the Director General had been "stripped" of powers to benefit the service.

The magisterial Hoover Commission on government organization in 1949 recommended changes in the State Department. The fact that there was quite a bit still to be done prompted the creation of a special group chaired by James H. Rowe, Jr., a former aide to FDR, on means of integrating the noncongruent systems of the State Department and the Foreign Service. The 1950 Rowe committee found that junior officers were not being recruited adequately; that midcareer lateral entry, that is, entrance from the outside on the basis of proven competence and experience, was largely unused. What slowly transpired was that the 1946 law had frozen into more or less vested interests the attitudes that had prevailed in the 1924 Foreign Service. The basic concept remained, that of the Foreign Service generalist as the patrician peak of diplomatic excellency, slighting or excluding the specialists, who were more and more needed. Between 1946 and 1953, only twenty-five new diplomats had been accepted through lateral appointment. The Foreign Service seemed to be killing the goose that laid the golden eggs.

A report by Dr. Henry M. Wriston, president of Brown University, broke down the doors, in 1951, for an integration of the non-Foreign Service and Government career specialists working in the State Department into the purist ranks of the Foreign Service officers. The Wriston report generated considerable ill will, which lingered for years. Those integrated felt they were accepted with poor grace and cast into the lot of "second-class citizens." The Foreign Service officers felt that the quality of the service was being drastically lowered. The post-Wriston record did not help alleviate resentments on both sides. The 1955 Selection Boards, in rating 1,833 Foreign Service officers and 509 Wristonees, found 1,155 FSO's and 51 newly integrated officers from the Wriston program eligible for promotion. Of the total, 718 FSO's and 2 Wristonees were actually promoted. By 1967, the Wristonees had finally been absorbed and digested, after a span of about ten years.

The Wristonees, in fact, were part of the problem of 1967. This was the log jam at the top—too many senior officers without respectable jobs, or priority jobs that too many senior officers were not quite competent enough to handle at crisis pitch. There was no mystery about the eventual emergence of this and other problems in 1962, when still another committee was organized. This one was under former Secretary of State Christian Herter. Its mission was to examine the dual personnel system of the State Department and to design some method whereby the most qualified person would be placed in the correct slot to function most effectively for the nation. The Herter group consulted more than 1,000 officers and experts. It published its findings in six volumes. The problems were still there in 1967: that Foreign Service officers must retire at sixty, but civil service officers could stay on until seventy; that the Foreign Service could not provide all the specialists who had to be permanently on hand to accumulate the expertise their complex specialties demanded; that continuity of exposure to the American political system was not possible for Foreign Service officers, who served tours of rotation for thirty years in various countries, of which the United States was only one. In brief, the problems were still the same old ones, and only the solutions seemed still as far away, though there was just enough movement to give some hope for further progress sooner than later.

Its grave problems notwithstanding, the Department of State was an amusing place. One of the best-edited house organs in the Federal Government, the State Department monthly *News Letter* provided fascinating oddments of useful data, respectful reprintings of authoritative pronouncements, obituaries of departed worthies, chitchat of bureau activities, and numerous photographs of solid citizens with fixed or nervous smiles no different from those seen daily in the *Peoria Gazette*. The homey flavor of the American provinces had been captured by the editor, Gerson H. Lush, formerly of the *Philadelphia Inquirer*. There were any number of recipients of twenty-five-, thirty-, and forty-year certificates of length of service, happily portrayed with their high-ranking bosses. There was the proud announcement: "State topped all Executive Departments in the recent Red Cross Blood Drive—and attained 128 per cent of its quota, the best record for State during the last ten years."

Notices of changes in the Foreign Affairs Manuals were a must for State readers. The FAM's came in a series of twelve volumes. Volumes VIII and IX were classified. Ten of the volumes were 28 inches wide and had more than 300 pages per volume. State had its heroes, for example, Frank J. Mrkva of the Passport Office. In 1966, Mrkva uncovered the machinations of two Czech diplomats attempting to use Mrkva to plant electronic devices in the office of former Under Secretary George Ball. It was a perfect Good Soldier Schweik plot all around.

State liked to boast, modestly, of course, about its devotion to duty. Whereas most government parking lots were empty on Saturdays, there were numerous autos in evidence on weekends at State. The clerical levels racked up $2.9 million in paid overtime during fiscal year 1967. Uncompensated, or voluntary, overtime was unusually high. A sample survey of Foreign Service officers showed that nonpaid overtime averaged more than thirty-one work days a year per man. Working day and night, sleeping on cots and grabbing sandwiches out of automatic dispensers was standard operating procedure during crises. Nobody made anything of it. More praiseworthy were employee turnouts during Washington's occasional blizzards. The storm of January 29–31, 1966, locked the town down tight. State officers and clerks in crucial areas worked as long as thirty-two hours without stopping. Many mushed miles on foot to work. As a precaution for winter emergencies, the Department modified two four-wheel-drive jeep station wagons, the front-wheel drives kept connected at all times, for crisis transportation.

A daily problem was getting to work from the far-flung Washington suburbs. Hundreds had to rise as early as 6 A.M. to make it in time for the 8:45 A.M. opening hour. There were scores who rose even earlier to attend prework studies at the Foreign Service Institute, where special classes started at 7:30 A.M. Parking permits in the Department's basement garage were prizes of deadly intrigues and marks of status. State personnel lucky enough to have a car handy could use it on official business at ten cents a mile. As the *News Letter* announced:

The distances specified in this table below will be shown on all reimbursement vouchers (SF-1164, Claim for Reimbursement for Expenditures on Official Business) covering transportation between the Department and the places indicated in lieu of actual odometer readings. The General Accounting Office will not require odometer readings for these trips and all Imprest Fund Cashiers shall process claims in accordance with this mileage guide.

This supersedes Budget and Finance Memorandum No. 65-21, dated August 28, 1964. The mileage given covers one way between the Department and destination.

Destination	Mileage
Agricultural Station, Beltsville, Md.	15
Andrews Air Force Base, Md.	11
Bethesda Naval Hospital, Md.	15
Commerce Department	1
Dulles International Airport, Va.	25
Federal Trade Commission	2
Foreign Service Institute, Va.	2
Fort George C. Meade, Md.	27
Friendship International Airport, Md.	35
GSA Federal Records Center, Franconia, Va.	12
Justice Department	2
CIA, Langley, Va.	10
Library of Congress	3
National Institutes of Health, Md.	15
National Security Agency, 3801 Nebraska Ave.	5
Post Office Department	2
Treasury Department	1
Union Station	3
U.S. Capitol	3
Washington National Airport	4
White House	1

The State Department had an unofficial poet laureate, Mrs. Katie Louchheim, Deputy Assistant Secretary for Educational and Cultural Affairs, an extroverted dynamo and former director of the women's division of the Democratic National Committee. An appropriate *capolavoro* of the Louchheim muse was "The Bureaucrat":

> ONE SELDOM SEES A BUREAUCRAT
> WITHOUT A PIPE OR WITH A HAT,
> HIS HABITAT IS CORRIDORS,
> HE TAKES HIS EXERCISE INDOORS,
> HE IS ALWAYS SOMEWHERE IN BETWEEN
> TWO MEETINGS WHERE HE SHOULD HAVE BEEN.
> HIS FAVORITE WORDS ARE ACTIVATE,
> COORDINATE, EVALUATE.
> HE CAN'T AFFORD TO BE PRECISE,
> INDIGNANT, ADAMANT, CONCISE;
> AGENDAS HE WILL IMPLEMENT
> MUST BE EXPLORED AS TO INTENT;
> A MODICUM OF WELL-PHRASED DOUBT
> HIS EXPERTISE WILL IRON OUT
> ATTESTS TO HIS PRODIGIOUS CRAFT;
> HE CLARIFIES THE FINAL DRAFT.
> A BUREAUCRAT IS SELDOM SEEN
> WITHOUT A PEN——OR WITH A DREAM.

Men outnumbered women, about two to one, in the State Department; more so in the Foreign Service, where in 1966 males accounted for 71 per cent of the staff and females 29 per cent. The key support cogs were the Foreign Service staff secretaries, a group of 825 women stationed around the world. Paris had 28; Rome, 26; Saigon, 24; and Washington, some 200. The turnover was roughly fifteen a month. The female staff served a normal two-year duty tour overseas, though only eighteen months in hardship posts. Their only special requirement was a willingness to go anywhere on earth. Most of the women in the Department at home were civil service personnel. Women were no recent influx, the first woman having been hired in 1874. The Department was meticulously protective of its single women, maintaining utter discretion concerning occasional indiscretions, the first ones, that is. Second-time pregnancies in unmarried females were not tolerated.

Of more concern to State's security officers were the temptations brought into the dignified precincts of the Department by devotees of the numbers game. Blue-collar and lower clerical ranks were solemnly warned not to accept calls concerning the lucky numbers of the day or to telephone out their selections. Security officers thrummed like plucked guitar strings every time they recalled the affair at the security-conscious Pentagon in the late 1950's, when Defense Department messengers were discovered operating a numbers collecting agency in the washrooms.

The State Department's college interns had a high time playing diplomat every summer. The unawed collegians formed cliques and importuned for mass interviews with high officers of the Department. The latter, of course, were always happy to give up their limited time on behalf of questing youth. The youths were initially astonished at the language of bureaucracy. It became a game. Groups collated new terms picked up every day. There were the usual sludge words like "viable," charismatic," "meaningful," "implement," "finalize," "innovative," "integrate," "decision-oriented," "spin-off," "interlock," "input," and "converge." A mysterious phrase was "the conventional wisdom"; the antonym was hard to find. There were new vernaculars like "dicey," the American equivalent of the British "sticky," applied to tough and sensitive situations.

The operational meat grinder seemed to turn out bureaucratic hamburger, despite the fact that new Foreign Service officers were given the classic guides to good English, from Fowler to Gowers to Strunk. The putative diplomats-to-be learned to "put a needle down through the overlay" and to "return the *status quo* as it is" while "keeping an in with the outs," in the course of which one "touched base" with the right people, and, if struck by a bright idea, to "maximize it to the utmost, extenuating the negative, intensifying the alternative" in order to "crank it into the system" so as to "have a frank exchange of views" and "keep the ball in play," at the same time being prompt to ask a colleague to "sit down and let me pick your brains for a moment," never failing to flash a brave smile when the boss said, "Scrub it." The young were fast to find out that writing departmental memos was a knack, like taking examinations in college. The results were sometimes similar: no correlation between grades received and knowledge possessed, or between ideas expressed and impressions made. The little trade secrets were not very secret after the youngsters spent a few weeks in the Department. Routine reactions to new ideas were full of hedges and verbal shrubbery obscuring the landscape of understanding.

Two bits of arcana were consistently baffling to innocent laymen from the outside world. One was the fact that hardly anything in the State Department was ever written by the person who signed a memorandum. A typical bureaucrat, in brief, signed something written by someone else and wrote something for someone else to sign. Another "in-shop" practice was "documentation." Secretaries were directed to listen in on telephone conversations, though the practice was officially frowned upon. In the end, "documentation" was a means of "sticking the next guy with the problem." The record became an instrument for catching the other fellow out when he slipped, especially if he had no "documentation" of his own.

There was some self-complacency about their use of the King's English, but Foreign Service officers, in the main, were no Shakespeares. Douglas

MacArthur, a close Dulles colleague, once mildly but properly ticked off this writer for perpetrating the execrable bromide of "unleashing Chiang Kai-shek." This referred to the first major foreign policy decision of the Eisenhower administration in 1953. President Eisenhower, Winston Churchill, and Dulles met in New York after Christmas in 1952 and, among other matters, discussed allowing Chiang on Formosa to attack the Communist Chinese island of Hainan, as a threat that might help relieve Chinese pressure in the Korean war. Dulles returned to Washington and briefed Robert A. Taft of Ohio, Senate Majority Leader in the Eighty-third Congress. Taft briefed the writer, who happened to be visiting him. Dulles had told Taft that the U.S. Seventh Fleet was to be instructed to stop protecting Communist China from Chinese Nationalist attacks, such as the projected one on Hainan. MacArthur suggested that the correct phrase to have used was not "unleashing Chiang Kai-shek," but "equalizing the situation."

Matters of protocol, precedence, and formality were an even greater mystery to the uninitiated. The diplomatic authorities tried to keep it that way. FAM 300 gave detailed instructions through sixty-two numbers and twenty pages, like a high-grade Emily Post or Amy Vanderbilt, but mostly about precedence overseas. The real lowdown was the list of precedence for officers of the State Department and Foreign Service on duty in Washington. This document, classified "confidential," was never published. It was held more closely than the latest nonpeace offer from Hanoi. The precedence list was the official pecking order of who was more important than whom, familiar enough in all large organizations. The rulings were as intricate as Japanese flower arrangements. The list made egos shrink or swell in counterpoint.

Former Chief of Protocol Lloyd Hand won a minor immortality at State by solving one precedence argument. He arranged the names of officers on wall direction maps in alphabetical order, thus canceling an imminent battle as to who was senior to whom. The listing of names looked like a variation of the American practice of Kremlinology. U.S. experts in Soviet affairs tried to deduce the current standings of Moscow leaders according to the rank in which they were placed in photographs, wall posters, and lists in *Pravda*.

The list of precedence was easy enough for the top names; the griping began below the salt. The first five were always the high officers of the Department, in order: the Secretary of State, the Under Secretary, the Under Secretary for Political Affairs, the Deputy Under Secretary for Political Affairs, and the Deputy Under Secretary for Administration. Next followed ambassadors-at-large, invariably very senior and eminent. The basic criteria were presidential appointments that had confirmation by the

U.S. Senate, in order of their date of appointment and confirmation. Assistant Secretaries in charge of geographical bureaus rated next. On one recent list, this took care of at least eleven dignitaries. Thereafter followed the Director General of the Foreign Service, the Inspector General of the Foreign Service, the Inspector General of Foreign Assistance, the Deputy Inspector General of Foreign Assistance, the Director of Intelligence, the Assistant Secretary for Educational and Cultural Affairs, the Executive Secretary of the Department, and the Chief of Protocol. The last named was the officer who had to tiptoe in between rank, merit, seniority, and sensitivities to make up the list. He himself ranked at the bottom of the top pile. The diplomatic list of precedence for foreign diplomats was simpler. Seniority was based on the date of presidential acceptance of an ambassador's credentials.

This folderol was necessary and of specific utility in the workings of diplomacy. It applied strictly to official functions. In Washington society, however, complications ensued. Hostesses adopted the official rankings. Status-sensitive ambassadors felt their importance warranted private honors. Some retired or inactive American ambassadors were also rank-conscious. Once an ambassador, always an ambassador. They carried their ranks like generals. Ambassadors between jobs might possibly be excused their insistence on signal deference. Overseas they commanded an entire embassy and panoply of staff, car, plane, fine residence, and servants. Returned to the Department after a tour as envoy overseas, they often found themselves in boondoggling assignments and inhabiting dusty cubby-holes, a travesty of their former splendor. The Foreign Service had certain hair-shirt aspects.

Diplomatic socializing was a business matter rather than entertainment. Invitations to the French and British embassies were rated tops for prestige. Arab missions were favored for color. Latin missions led the field for sheer *brio*. Lower-ranking diplomats mumbled in their beards from time to time at being left out of White House festivities for visiting notables. Deputy Assistant Secretaries were usually called upon the next day to follow through and clean up the deals made at the high echelons. They complained that a memorandum of conversation between the top dignitaries was never adequate guidance to the nuances probably expressed but not disclosed. Junior Foreign Service officers quickly discovered that the cutoff point for guests invited to foreign embassy receptions usually fell at about FSO-5, a midcareer grade. The juniors organized their own diplomatic social affairs. There were also "coffees" in the various bureaus on festive occasions. Assistant Secretaries of State "poured" for the help, like English gentry who shared a drink with the household servants on family occasions.

In general, diplomatic formalities of the past had eased along with the looser mores of the times. Even the Russians were getting human as they began to lose their fears. They used less stilted language. They relaxed enough to exchange heavy-handed pleasantries with Americans, though the Soviets still defined an "unfriendly" diplomat as one who placed the interests of his own country ahead of those of the Soviet Union.

All this, however, was chiffchaff. The only real news inside the State Department that gave everybody serious concern was of two kinds. The worst was war. In the week of the Cuban nuclear missile crisis in 1962, solemn, dead silence gripped the Department. There were no greetings in the elevators or passing the latest scuttlebutt in the halls, cafeterias, or restrooms. Everybody was grim and nailed to his desk, waiting to do whatever he was ordered to do if hell broke loose.

The other major internal news of the State Department was personnel reorganization. In the months, weeks, and days preceding a major reshuffling of the personnel system, employees were watchful, nervous, impatient, anxious. One never knew what shape the organization would take. Everybody mistrusted the official reasons given to justify the changes. A new crowd in personnel could be a serious threat to the carefully nurtured career ambitions of officers and staff alike. Foreign Service dreams of Eden could be changed overnight to Siberia.

The first seven years of the 1960's saw five shifts in the high personnel command of the State Department, from Loy Henderson to Roger Jones to William Orrick to William Crockett to Idar Rimestad. The personnel office seemed to be in constant throes of reorganization. It was fated: people were the State Department's first and final asset. It was not at all a question of whether the State Department people were good enough. It was a question of how to use them at their best. The fact that State and Foreign Service officers had won nearly fifty of the top six Government-wide awards since 1953 bespoke the high caliber of the Department's leading diplomatic practitioners. The fuss was about the ranks below the peak performers.

Testimonials about the Foreign Service included roses as well as cabbages. President Johnson said, "I consider the Foreign Service to be a necessary part of the effective defense of our country." The nearly forty public or civilian members of the Foreign Service inspection teams who had examined U.S. missions abroad in latter years uniformly rated the Foreign Service as a surprisingly high-class organization. No other department of Government inspected its personnel on such a regular basis to ascertain whether the overseas staffs were indeed carrying out the missions with which they had been entrusted. There were critics in the Senate and in the press who believed the Foreign Service was an anachronism, its usefulness lapsed, and ready for burial. Representative Frank Bow of Ohio, the ranking Minority member, who would be chairman of the House Appropriations Committee in a Republican Congress, admitted that he had developed a "great respect" for the Foreign Service in the field and remarked "how hard they worked and took their beatings without a word of complaint." Bow, for that matter, also grew to admire Adlai Stevenson, though he did not declaim about it at GOP meetings. The elders of the Foreign Service agreed that the Service could be improved, but that as an organization it had no peer in the Federal Government. Except for combat, not even the military took the rough and the smooth in their stride as the FSO's did or served in overseas posts of which 40 per cent were in the hardship category. The Foreign Service boasted that it was the only trade union in the world which pledged itself to make the careers of its members a guaranteed success.

The men and women who were the objects of such persistent praise and blame, according to official State Department records of August 31, 1967, numbered 3,522 Foreign Service officers of career, 1,739 Foreign Service Reserve officers of limited or indefinite tenure, mostly specialists; and 6,130 Foreign Service staff, in technical or clerical support capacities, some of whom were "Foreign Service domestic" and never served abroad. Of 105 chiefs of missions, only 34 were noncareer envoys. The detailed Foreign Service list by class:

Chiefs of Mission	ABROAD	U.S.A.	TOTAL
Career Ambassador	5		5
Career Minister	27		27
FSO-1	38		38
FSO-2	1		1
Total	71		71

Other Ranks			
Career Ambassador	—	3	3
Career Minister	7	21	28
FSO-1	139	156	295
FSO-2	250	211	461
FSO-3	382	284	666
FSO-4	394	268	662
FSO-5	322	214	536
FSO-6	228	150	378
FSO-7	188	75	263
FSO-8	127	32	159
Total	2,037	1,414	3,451

FSR-1	29	100	129
FSR-2	77	181	258
FSR-3	152	222	374
FSR-4	200	146	346
FSR-5	132	116	248
FSR-6	86	72	158
FSR-7	54	119	173
FSR-8	11	42	53
Total	741	998	1,739
FSS-1	58	54	112
FSS-2	161	103	264
FSS-3	227	87	314
FSS-4	300	122	422
FSS-5	410	136	546
FSS-6	728	183	911
FSS-7	766	235	1,001
FSS-8	903	161	1,064
FSS-9	585	333	918
FSS-10	143	435	578
Total	4,281	1,849	6,130
Grand Total	7,130	4,261	11,391

Jaundiced glances continually raked the Foreign Service rolls. Secretary Rusk thought the size allowed too much slack. William Attwood, a former Ambassador and now editor in chief of the Cowles Publications, recommended a slash of 25 per cent. The swollen Foreign Service Reserve officer figures were a special item of curiosity. The Kennedy administration had discovered the loophole whereby deserving and high-toned friends of the New Frontier could easily be given proper jobs through Reserve Officer contracts without the bother of civil service requirements or possible prickly difficulties with the Senate Foreign Relations Committee. One of the first things the White House asked the State Department to do the day after the JFK inauguration in 1961 was to speed up security clearances for the FSR's waiting to be taken aboard.

U.S. Senator Allen J. Ellender, Louisiana Democrat, was very much annoyed about the State Department's apparent overload. He said:

In South America and not only South and Central America, but all over the world, my reports would show that you are overloaded with people in the political section. For instance, in London, I found as many as 20 in one section where maybe five or six would do, just there walking around and warming their seats.

State's cross seemed destined to grow heavier in 1968. The Senate appropriations committee said in its 1967 report:

It is also understood that there are many highly paid Foreign Service officers who are assigned to miscellaneous duties in the United States for unduly long periods of time. Both of these conditions would seem to indicate an excess of personnel in the State Department. It is therefore requested, with a view to eliminating surplus personnel, that the State Department furnish the committee by February 1, 1968, with (1) the total number of junior officers on overseas assignments, setting forth those who are doing the work and filling the post of a Regular officer, and (2), a detailed personnel status report reflecting the Washington-overseas rotational system, the number overseas, the number on regular rotational assignment in Washington, those on (a) extended, (b) temporary, or (c) transient assignment, and those on home leave. The information furnished should reflect the situation as of June 30, 1967, and as of January 1, 1968. It is suggested that this information also be furnished to the Senate Committee on Foreign Relations.

In the eventful past decade, Secretaries of State were too busy with crises to have any time to tinker with the State Department's machinery or to unscramble the works and put them together better. Crockett had come closest to tearing the State Department apart. Rimestad's job was to consolidate the positive lessons of the Crockett experiments. In December 1967 he announced re-establishment of a centralized personnel office. A cautious, low-posture traditionalist from North Dakota, Rimestad could not turn the clock back. But he did intend to restore the confidence of both the Foreign Service and the civil service in the equities and integrity of their respective job systems. The Foreign Service operated within the rank-in-the-man structure, the civil service within the grade-in-the-job framework. Where Crockett was expansive and effusive, Rimestad tended to be flinty and hard-eyed, as well he might, considering the budget economies visited upon State by a Congress supersensitive to the costs of the Vietnam war. Rimestad benefited from the Crockett planning. For the first time in State Department history a central inventory of manpower was made. The executives would actually know who was on board and where, and what Mr. X was doing. A computer tab run was started to list the skills of the Foreign Service and to find out, also for the first time, exactly what all officers were capable of, on the basis of their training and experience. The State Department was finally doing what most major U.S. corporations had been doing for years.

The computer manpower inventory, a Herter Committee recommendation and an elementary tool in modern management, was long overdue. Previous manual surveys were systematically out of date and data always in arrears, incomplete so as to hide sensitive issues and arouse widely conflicting interpretations. Sufficient indications transpired from the constant undressing of the facts, however, to disclose that the Foreign Service had become a microcosm of American society. It had its generation gaps, a growing increment of senior citizens, worries about retirement pay, an element of Spartan callousness and of indifference to the wastage of human resources, and sometimes bitter disillusionment that the modest pot of geraniums at the end of the road had turned out to be a tin can full of wilted weeds.

The pile-up at the top was frankly embarrassing. In latter years there were some 350 Class 1 and 489 Class 2 officers. Half the original 1,500 Wristonees integrated into the Service in the 1950's were still on board. The last decade's reform symbol had become the next decade's rear guard residue. The diplomatic structure had become inflated and the gilt-edged assets of the Foreign Service had accumulated watered stock. About 230 officers were detailed to other Government departments and organizations. In 1966, there were 815 senior-grade officers on duty in the United States. The Foreign Service had the equivalent of civil service supergrades, that is, above GS-15, in the top four grades from Class 2 to Career Ambassador. Other executive departments did not appreciate becoming terminal pastures for State's unusable FSO's, thus losing their own allotment of supergrades as a result.

A further complication was the assignment of USIA officers to State, an arrangement which took up precious positions and provoked resentment that State had become an incidental dumping ground for ineffective USIA seniors. The other major foreign affairs sister agency, AID, could not take many older officers because they lacked technical qualifications. There was a move to place the "oldsters" in outside organizations—foundations and international business companies. American colleges and universities were awakened to the desirability of having "Diplomats-in-Residence," and eighty-five applied for them in 1967. Life on the campus —lecturing, consulting, and social-lionizing—kept some senior officers out of the doldrums for a year at least.

Naturally, most wanted a good job in the field or headquarters. The changeover in ambassadors affected only a few dozen a year, despite the 115-plus posts theoretically available. Not too many of the older men cared to undertake the hardships of places like Africa. Smart seniors took lower-ranking spots like consulates-general. WPA-type work, featherbedding, and chairmanships of "special committees" proliferated. Lower-ranking jobs were upgraded artificially. So were roles of special assistants to major line officers, Assistant Secretaries and up. At one point in 1966, there were seventy-seven special and staff assistants to the brass at State. Secretary Rusk had seven, of whom only two were his immediate aides. Former Assistant Secretary Frankel of Educational and Cultural Affairs also used to have seven. According to one rigorous estimate, there were 600 unneeded jobs. Many seniors had reached their plateaus of personal efficiency. But they were hanging on grimly to obtain their five years in grade at the highest salary legally due them, so they could take advantage of the 1964 pay raise and retire with a decent pension at the end of the five-year term. The top ranks had become overcrowded because of too rapid promotions in the Class 5 stratum a decade ago, those promotions having been hastened because of the undue lag the decade before. A similar speed-up in promotions in 1966 and 1967 was creating a future bottleneck at the Class 4 level. But that was the next generation's worry.

The stacked-up top classes were threatening to go right through the roof. After a few years of characteristically bureaucratic hemming and hawing, a new set of time-in-grade limits was posted. If the officer had not been promoted within the prescribed time period, he would have to retire. For Classes 1 and 2 and Career Minister, this was particularly serious. Time-in-grade was cut from fifteen to twelve years in Class 1, from twelve to ten years in Classes 2 and 3, from ten to eight years in Classes 4 and 5, and from ten to four years in Classes 6 and 7. The new ceilings would not affect the rolls until 1968, when only forty-three officers were slated to retire. Many FSO's had retired around their old stamping grounds of the State Department—238 in Washington, 111 in adjacent Virginia, and 88 in Maryland. One hundred and four settled in California and 83 in Florida.

Despite all the makeshifts for slicing down the senior job totals, there was still an estimated 25 per cent surplus in the Foreign Service. Secretary Rusk used to say, with more implied impatience than he showed about most things, that he had cut down his own UN shop in the State Department in 1946 from a staff of 225 to 160, and had got a lot more work out of them. The only sure way to hasten attrition was by the selection-out process of forced resignations or firing. The annual selection-out rate ran officially at about 2 per cent, or seventy a year, in the race of so-called competitive excellence. The suspicion was that the rate should have been closer to 4 per cent.

The U.S. military seemed to handle matters more equitably, with less fuss and recriminations. Nonselection for permanent promotion for both the military and Foreign Service was based on statutory authority. But the military's system had a positive psychology, it was evident. Officers were selected *into* the next higher echelon or else rotated out automatically. The Foreign Service made it appear that the rejected officer had been thrown out, bag and baggage, with rather dishonorable overtones. In any event, the military officers who could not jump to the next plateau did not appear to develop a persecution complex.

Promotion or selection-out criteria in the Foreign Service were based on efficiency reports from the officers' immediate organizational superiors. If the FSO ranked in the lowest 10 per cent of his class for more than one year, he was politely asked to leave. Some resigned before they were asked. In the Class of 1947, for instance, of 222 original members, 130 remained in 1967. Only nineteen made Class 1. The turnover rates were deceptive. The gross rate ran to nearly 9 per cent. The actual facts of why officers had left often were buried discreetly. Selection-out figures had been comparatively low in past years; 56 in 1954 and 46 in 1960. The total went up to 96 in 1966. In an official report on the ages of 3,541 FSO's, as of July 1, 1966, 38 were from sixty to sixty-five; 745 from fifty to fifty-nine; 1,183 from forty to forty-nine; 1,094 from thirty to thirty-nine; and 481 from twenty-two to twenty-nine. The figures gave some notion of why officers in their forties were restless at the roadblock of the fifties in front of them.

The path up the terraces of promotion was no garden stroll. Beside the official panels, there was the influence of one's reputation in the guild: the man-to-man impression made on fellow officers, sense of practical judgment, ease of personality, and purposeful energy. Officers watched each other's behavior carefully. It was not alone that you did something well, but how you did it. The FSO's were severe judges of themselves, of their associates, and of their superiors. The standards set were very high. The precepts of guidelines issued for the 1967 Selection Boards described qualifications for career ministers that resembled those of a paragon. There were some absolutely first-rate and superlative men among the career ministers, but one was not overwhelmed. The precept said:

The Career Minister is expected to have a high sense of public service, complete integrity, mature and disciplined judgment, good presence and personality, a first-rate mind, and a driving desire for accomplishment. Typically, he will have demonstrated unusual leadership and command talent, a penetrating insight into the foreign affairs process, an outstanding policy sense, a high degree of executive proficiency, superior competence in planning and conducting negotiations, and well-developed skill in oral and written expression.

For officers still struggling from Class 8 upward to Class 1, the twenty-five factors listed in Form FS-315, or Performance Rating Report, were rough teeth in the fine comb of selection. Up to a few years ago officers did not see their performance ratings, but they do now. Besides performance ratings, the selection panels used Form FS-315-A, or the Development Appraisal Report (DAR). The DAR, however, was never shown to the officer unless he was about to be fired and demanded to know why. Rating officers were asked to mark the twenty-five factors within five gradations of worst to best. The factors to be noted, and the bottom and top possible evaluations:

Knowledge of work	Lacks kind of knowledge required for satisfactory performance.	Has exceptionally commanding knowledge of and insights into all aspects of work.
Productivity	Useful output of volume of work is generally inadequate.	Work output is phenomenal.
Accuracy	Error of commission or omission, or lack of precision, is frequent or serious.	Invariably turns out work outstanding in accuracy and competence.
Initiative	Does not take independent action.	Invariably sees opportunities, acts promptly and independently even in most difficult or important situations.
Resourcefulness	Goes strictly "by the book." Does not produce original ideas or adaptations.	Develops and applies original solutions to most difficult problems with exceptional success.
Dependability	Fails to follow instructions, or to observe commitments, or to complete work on time.	Regardless of own inconvenience, invariably meets most difficult commitments and deadlines. Certain to follow through even in absence of instructions.
Decisiveness	Cannot make up his mind, or vacillates.	Officer's decisiveness, even under acute pressure, is outstanding in speed and success.
Analytical Ability	Generally misjudges or fails to realize causes or significance of problems, facts, or events.	Exceptionally effective in reaching the heart of difficult problem, evaluating elements and interrelationships and true significance.

Ability to Anticipate	Short-sighted. Tries to solve today's problem without regard to other problems or tomorrow's needs.	Exceptionally sensitive to ultimate consequences of action. Invariably examines particular item as part of total stream of events. Whole decision-making process is integrated.
Judgment	Unreliable judgment. Overlooks pertinent considerations or has little sense of proportion.	Displays excellent judgment, timing, and insight, even in most difficult and sensitive situations. Judgment unimpaired by work pressures.
Perspective	Has a poor understanding of the goals of job.	Remarkable grasp of relationship of job to total picture and of currents which might affect this relationship.
Attitude Toward Job	Indifferent attitude. Shows little interest in work.	Exceptionally high degree of interest, willingness, and dedication. Job invariably comes first.
Acceptance of Responsibility	Generally seeks to avoid responsibility for past or future actions.	Invariably regards himself as fully accountable for his actions and those of subordinates, if any. Does not hesitate to act in interests of organization.
Written Communication	Does not get ideas across clearly on paper.	Composition has all qualities of excellence: clarity, precision, conciseness, good organization, persuasiveness, and style.
Oral Communication	Has great difficulty in conveying ideas orally.	Outstandingly articulate in choice of words, clarity, conciseness, and persuasiveness. Holds listeners' interest even under adverse conditions.

Adaptability	Resists change or new approaches; is upset by new or different environmental situations.	Immediately grasps new approaches, ideas. Exceptionally able to blend old and new, and adapt own interests and enthusiasms. Takes difficult environmental situations in stride.
Relations with Americans	Officer's relations at work or socially are generally marked by friction.	Exceptionally effective in personal relations at all levels. Has deep understanding of human nature. Highly respected and sought after. Leader in community affairs.
Relations with Non-Americans	Insensitive to and lacks understanding of local people and customs. Creates problems.	Exceptionally successful in developing good personal relations. He is sincerely respected, sought after, and responsive.
Language Improvement	Makes no or virtually no effort to learn local language even when demands of job leave time for study.	Neglects no opportunity to master local language, giving it all the attention his other duties permit, even at some personal inconvenience.
Official Representation	Makes poor impression as representative of United States.	Makes excellent use, for the U.S., of extraordinary range of local contacts. Performs effectively at any social or official function.
Negotiating Ability	Not effective as negotiator. Lacks force or ability to think clearly in negotiations.	Excellent negotiator who holds up under pressure. Rarely if ever caught off guard. Knows subject thoroughly. Obtains desired results.
Effectiveness as a Supervisor	Unsuccessful as supervisor.	Plans and organizes work to meet all contingencies. Takes positive steps to develop staff capabili-

		ties. Subordinates give maximum performance and excel in morale.
Effectiveness as an Executive	Ineffective as an executive.	Superb planner, organizer, and leader. Accomplishment as exexutive outstanding.
Effectiveness as a Rating Officer	Evaluations generally are not objective, candid, thorough, or substantive, or frequently either are not submitted or are so delinquent as not to serve the purpose.	Evaluations are comprehensive, objective, and candid, clearly depicting true value of rated officers.
Technical Advice	Seriously deficient as technician or advisor.	Outstandingly competent advisor. His analysis of conditions penetrating. Understands implications of his advice. Inspires action.

The confidential Development Appraisal Report asked the rating officer for "comprehensive comments" on:

PERSONAL CHARACTERISTICS:
Appearance—Neatness, propriety in dress, general impression.
Bearing—Degree of maturity, composure under varying circumstances, facility in personal contact.
Personality—Discuss fully personality traits of officer, e.g., bright, sparkling, extrovert, dull, abrasive, introvert, pleasant, spontaneous, sharp, witty, good sense of humor, heavy, obsequious, sarcastic, biting.
Range of Interests—Languages, arts, reading, avocations, hobbies, and where appropriate membership in political science, economic, technical, social and other professional institutions or societies.
Other—Matters of special significance not covered above, e.g., acceptance of responsibilities (community or otherwise), willingness to admit error, attitudes toward superiors and subordinates, personal integrity.
FAMILY:
Comment on family, particularly the wife. Is family source of strength or weakness to officer in his performance on this or future assignments? Include, where applicable, comments on: What is family's attitude toward host country and people? What is wife's representational ability? To what extent does family mix with nationals of host country and attempt to learn their language? Does wife participate in local community organizations? Does family entertain and visit with local people in addition to Americans at the post? Does wife participate in U.S. program activities where appropriate, e.g., English language seminars? Does family travel about country?

LIMITING FACTORS:

Health, conduct, over-indulgence (excessive use of alcohol, etc.), suitability, and other factors relating to both officer and family.

LEADERSHIP AND EXECUTIVE CAPABILITIES:

Capacity to plan, direct, organize, analyze perceptively, make decisions, delegate authority, train and supervise subordinates, negotiate effectively, and insure efficient accomplishment of objectives. (Particularly thorough coverage of this factor is essential in reports on officers of Class 4 and above.)

GROWTH CAPACITY:

Officer's strengths and weaknesses related to his work capacity, energy, intellectual abilities and knowledge, versatility, creativity, and other factors pertinent to officer's potential to assume broader or higher responsibility. After making thorough analysis of officer's growth capacity, rating officer shall comment in specific terms on assignments and further training which would be most appropriate for realization of officer's capacity.

ADVANCEMENT POTENTIAL:

Consider officer from overall viewpoint, including evaluations in this appraisal and in performance evaluation. State which of following best expresses your evaluation of officer's advancement potential:

"Not suitable for further advancement"

"Suitable for advancement of possibly not more than one rank"

"Suitable for advancement of more than one rank"

"Suitable for advancement to highest rank"

Support your selection and comment specifically on rapidity with which officer is capable of advancing.

An ancillary paradox to these demands for superior qualifications was the fact that the FSO was continually on the move, this mobility being about the only fixed attribute of his career. The semimilitary control over the Foreign Service personnel was symbolized by the rotation policy, established to guarantee interchangeability of assignments and Washington's capability to staff undesirable posts which would otherwise be avoided. The common complaint was that tours of duty abroad were too short. In 1960 the average stay overseas was 32.8 months. By 1965, it was 34.3 months. By 1966, 58 per cent of the overseas staff spent three or four years on one tour and 42 per cent considerably less than three years. Europe gave the best breaks on length of stay, averaging 39.5 months. Ellis O. Briggs, the epitome of the highly polished American ambassador, who retired a few years ago, fumed in Congressional testimony about having served in four posts in little over four years—Korea, Peru, Brazil, and Greece. Briggs did not quite realize that he was being paid a high compliment as a first-class ambassador in being called upon as a pinchhitter in delicate operations, after he had been *persona non grata* in South Korea.

The best of the classic Foreign Service in the postwar period were great generalists like Briggs. Secretary Dulles called upon former Deputy

Under Secretary Loy W. Henderson to provide a director for the United States Information Agency to replace erratic administrators. Henderson came up with George V. Allen, a top professional. Former Under Secretary Dillon also called on Henderson for a seasoned FSO of top caliber to take over the International Cooperation Administration when it fell on bad days in the late 1950's. Henderson gave him James W. Riddleberger, another top-grade pro and a career ambassador later.

Studies in 1966 and 1967 dwelled on the likelihood that FSO's henceforth would spend much more time in Washington on policy making than on diplomatic representation abroad. A survey of 197 officers a few years ago disclosed that 45 had served in Washington only two years out of twenty. Their life of exile had made them virtual strangers to the United States. Junior officers were kept overseas for seven years, too long a delay before starting specialized training. Midcareer officers should have an opportunity to stay in one place for four or five years to exploit their trained capacities. In short, the State Department personnel policies were not getting full value out of the manpower. The increasingly centralized control of foreign affairs by the President and the Secretary of State made it all the more necessary that officers fully competent overseas learn also the intricacies of American interests at firsthand in their own country, the better to advise on the execution of policies overseas.

It followed, therefore, that much more time would have to be spent on training constantly to develop the full potential of promising officers. In recent years FSO's spent only 5 per cent of their time in training, and only 3.3 per cent in 1966. USIA and AID spent even less, 2 per cent each. Military officers, on the other hand, spent 12 per cent of their time in training schools. The Herter Committee recommended 10 per cent for State. The question that arose was: Training for what? There were large gaps between needs and skills. A survey of a hundred officers showed that only fourteen had served in all four basic areas of foreign service work—service, support, supervision, and substantive, and only thirty-five in three of the four fields. The Herter Committee found shortages of practical planning economists, social scientists for the underdeveloped countries, management specialists, politico-military experts, intelligence analysts, and functional specialists as a whole, specialists whose field was now global.

There was a lack of awareness of the real-life machinery of the modern technological world as well as political naïveté about cross-currents of American politics and social movements. A sabbatical year for a senior officer to immerse himself in the everyday life of ordinary Americans could be revitalizing and fructifying for the officer's basic human capital, himself. Junior officers were caustic about the seniors' lack of contemporaneous information. The older men had undoubtedly been bright students in their day, but many obviously had not kept up with the dramatic advances of knowledge. The recent graduates who entered the Foreign Service possessed new knowledge which was alien to many elders, thereby increasing the psychological gap between the generations. The juniors learned, in due course, that like the seniors, once on the job, they found it extremely difficult to find time to read nonshop literature, and so they, too, in time might miss the ferment of the raw outside world.

A new and growing field for training was multilateral diplomacy, which had come to stay, however distasteful it was to the classic diplomatist. International organization diplomats were a rare breed; they had to be technical experts, political analysts, and good debaters at the same time. Both greater continuity and adaptability in depth were required simultaneously to cope with a hundred rival diplomats. The UN Bureau was continually starting all over again every four years to train new officers as they lost operational officers to the field. Unlike the geographical bureaus, the UN Bureau had no reserve bull pen to draw on.

The realization finally sank in throughout the Foreign Service by the mid-1960's that former neglect of tailored training in preparation for the complexities of modern diplomacy had seriously handicapped effective management of U.S. foreign affairs. There had been more lip service than understanding of the value of education concurrent with a career. Too many officers had resisted breaking off their careers and chances for advancement to take training assignments. Old-fashioned types believed that on-the-job training was much better than classrooms and books. Events proved otherwise: there was no time to bone up on coming situations while in the clutches of constant crises. By 1966 the course was clear; John M. Steeves, Director General of the Foreign Service, pledged "every effort to see that training requirements receive the same attention as operational assignments." An order to report for training was just as much of an order as to advance into battle.

The fully acknowledged need for a systematic process of continuing adult education shot electricity into the State Department's Foreign Service Institute. The FSI was little known but surprisingly impressive. In 1967 it was under the down-to-earth command of George V. Allen, a career ambassador and diplomatic veteran of Iran, Greece, and the Suez crisis. The intensive correlation of training operations and career development turned the Foreign Service Institute into one of the biggest vocational schools in the world. Annual enrollment had almost quadrupled from over 5,000 to nearly 20,000 since 1956. The temporary teacher-diplomats who ran the school under Allen even developed an undiplomatic college team spirit, dubbing the organization a "super-graduate school with a million-dollar faculty." The reference was to the 400 or 500 top academicians who came to lecture. The FSI had a new twelve-story building across the Potomac River, in Arlington, above Key Bridge, with 120 classrooms and half a dozen auditoriums. Students came from over forty government agencies, besides the State Department, and made up half of the ever changing student body.

Training in the Foreign Service was no entirely new thing. The first formal courses were begun in 1907, when State gave seven new consuls a thirty-day course. The Rogers Act of 1924 created a Foreign Service School, and the 1946 Foreign Service Act gave FSI its present name. In 1967 the Institute was organized virtually like a university. There were postgraduate seminars like the prestigious Senior Seminar in Foreign Policy, FSI's ten-month top course. The National Interdepartmental Seminar took four weeks. AID, USIA, Defense, and State problems encountered in a U.S. embassy overseas were exhaustively reviewed. The School of Professional Studies gave courses on economics, international Communism, science and foreign affairs, and internal defense, or counter-insurgency. Teachers were officers from State, Defense, and CIA.

The Center for Area and Country Studies provided fast courses for officers going off to new assignments. Junior officers were required to take basic orientation courses both before they went abroad and after they returned. Wives were a prime target of the Foreign Service educators; an officer's career could be helped or blasted (and often was) by a wife who did not cut the mustard. In 1966, some 900 wives from thirteen agencies who were accompanying their husbands to over 175 overseas posts were trained.

A Vietnam Training Center for officers of all agencies assigned to the Office of Civil Operations in Saigon, which supported the South Vietnam Government's rural reconstruction program, gave a crammed six-week course. Through the Institute, midcareer officers in particular were sent to major universities for special studies as well as to armed forces colleges. More than seventy were attending such other schools in 1967. The Institute encouraged all State Department and Foreign Service personnel to take university after-hours studies or correspondence courses, the Department picking up the tab for tuition costs for up to three courses.

The most notable achievement, in many ways, of the Foreign Service Institute was its amazing record of language training. Besides operating an assembly-line production in some sixty tongues in Washington, FSI language programs were carried out at three overseas branches—Yokohama for Japanese, Taichung on Formosa for Chinese, and Beirut for Arabic —and to more than 8,000 Americans at more than 200 posts all over the world. So-called world languages—French, Spanish, German, Italian, and Portuguese—were figuratively becoming a snap. Thirty-two "hard" languages, rather more difficult to learn, were also successfully taught. These were:

Amharic	Korean
Arabic	Lao
Bengali	Malay
Bulgarian	Nepali
Burmese	Persian
Cambodian	Polish
Chinese	Rumanian
Czech	Russian
Finnish	Serbo-Croatian
Greek	Singhalese
Hebrew	Swahili
Hindi	Tamil
Hungarian	Thai
Icelandic	Turkish
Indonesian	Urdu
Japanese	Vietnamese

The State Department in earlier years had some remarkable linguists, including the legendary Wilfred Stevens, who knew thirty languages. Official language training was begun in 1895, when student interpreters were assigned to U.S. legations in Persia, Korea, and Siam. In 1902 ten were assigned to Peking. Between 1936 and World War II, fifty-five officers took special language courses, Russian especially.

In 1956 the conclusion was reached in the upper echelons that languages were an indispensable tool for confronting the nation's burgeoning global responsibilties. A survey of language capacities was undertaken, the rating being made by self-appraisal, a notoriously optimistic method. Nonetheless, the survey showed that less than half the Foreign Service officers possessed a good enough command of any foreign language to be able to do official business in it. A Departmental policy was laid down that all officers should acquire a "useful" knowledge of two foreign languages and be able to handle simple street-hotel-restaurant requirements in whatever language was spoken at the post at which they served. Proficiency in a foreign language was made a requirement for promotion. Key slots in U.S. missions abroad were designated "language-essential" positions. Scientifically tested proficiency ratings were established. They were:

S/1 (Speaking)—R/1 (Reading)—Elementary proficiency.
S/2-R/2—Limited working proficiency.

S/3-R/3—Minimum professional proficiency.
S/4-R/4—Full professional proficiency.
S/5-R/5—Proficiency equal to that of an educated native.

Minimum professional efficiency was the ability to participate in general conversation and to discuss particular interests with ease, control of grammar and adequate vocabulary, and comprehension of normal native rates of speed of speech. In 1966, 2,215, or 63.8 per cent, of 3,470 FSO's were tested as S/3. Of 1,045 language-designated positions, 725, or 69 per cent, were filled by S/3-capable linguists, although the total S/3 capability of the Foreign Service in French, Spanish, German, Italian, or Portuguese included 3,246 officers.

Junior officers entering the Foreign Service more and more frequently had an immediately useful language skill. In one recent class, 114 knew French, 67 Spanish, 44 German, 18 Russian, 13 Italian, 8 Portuguese, and 5 Greek, and 19 knew thirteen other tongues. One of the 1966 newcomers, Eric Ronhovde, the son of a Foreign Service family, was the outstanding linguist of his class. He tested at S/3-R/3 in German, Norwegian, and Swedish; S/2-R/3 in Dutch and French; and S/2-R/2 in Russian; and he had a smattering of Polish. The western European languages took four months of intensive application to learn. In 1967 more students (723) attended FSI language classes than at any other time in the Institute's history.

The major feat of FSI, however, was its success at teaching hard languages, which normally took two years or more. Since 1955, nearly 700 officers had been so trained. In American embassies language-designated positions in the hard languages numbered 292 in 1967, 54 per cent filled by 158 officers with S/3 ratings or better. To be allowed to take a hard language, an officer had to be under thirty-six and score at least 62 on the language aptitude test. The FSI would like to have officers under thirty when possible; they learn faster. Congressmen who had been sceptical of senior officers' language abilities were pleased to learn in late 1966 that 47 FSO-1's and 112 FSO-2's rated S/3 or better in twenty-seven hard languages, ranging from both eastern and western Arabic to Urdu. Twenty additional teachers were brought over in 1967 to teach Vietnamese to 165 students. The Institute had already taught Vietnamese to 398 Foreign Service and military officers. It also offered courses in ten of the more important African languages.

The impressive languages were Russian, Arabic, Japanese, and Chinese, not only because of their difficulty but also because of the political importance of the areas involved. The U.S. embassy in Moscow designated eighteen of its twenty-three officer positions as "language essential." Chiefs of the political, economic, and cultural affairs sections rated S/4-R/4, or full proficiency. Star U.S. ambassadors to Russia like George F. Kennan, Charles E. Bohlen, Foy D. Kohler, and Llewellyn E. Thompson had all been fluent in Russian. Arabists were also prized. Fifty-six positions were designated for Arabic; in 1967, twenty-nine Arabic-speaking officers held such posts, although the Service as a whole had eighty-eight. Japanese had forty-three language-designated slots, twenty-three of them filled with officers in Japan. The total Service contingent of Japanese-speaking officers was only fifty-three. Career Ambassador U. Alexis Johnson, the U.S. envoy in Tokyo in 1967, had started his Foreign Service career as a Japanese language officer in Japan in 1935. Chinese language posts numbered twenty-eight in 1967; seventeen Chinese linguists held such positions, even though the Service had sixty-six rated at S/3-R/3.

The world reputation of the Institute's language school was founded in 1946 by Henry Lee Smith, Jr., also one of the organizers of the Army Language School at Monterey, California. Smith developed the FSI staff to its current strength of forty-two scientific linguists, a platoon of native teachers, an array of audio-lingual devices, and one of the largest libraries of textbooks for teaching 130 languages. Concentrated courses took up to six hours in classes of between four and six students at most, language laboratory work, and home study, which emphasized constant repetition until habit patterns were formed in the new language. The basic approach centered on uttering the sounds of the foreign language after hearing them. Learning to read came after learning to speak. Fundamental to grasping the psychology of the foreign language was the use of native instructors, who spoke from the beginning of the course at the native rate of speed and used everyday idiomatic phraseology to reflect the style and context of the particular language.

Hidden cultural assumptions of foreign languages were recurrently the cause of public misunderstandings in diplomatic relations. The Russians had a running argument with the United States throughout the Cold War over the phrase "situation of strength." As used in standard Communist propaganda, the Russian translation of the phrase was *"s pozitsii sily."* The Soviet inference was that the United States threatened an offensive against the Soviet Union. In vain did American diplomats attempt to explain that nothing of the sort at all was intended. For Americans, a situation of strength implied a strictly defensive posture, merely a capability to defend the American nation. In the context in which Russians often placed American locutions, many American statements appeared to be instinctively misinterpreted as menacing, owing to the dynamic nature of the American language.

Analogous Russian statements ran into similar blind spots in American psychology. One such was Nikita Khrushchev's remark, "We will bury you," which raised blood pressures in the United States. Edmund S. Glenn, a professional interpreter in the Language Services Division of the State Department and a lecturer at the Foreign Service Institute, averred that Khrushchev's phrase was jocular in intent, was not offensive as used among Russians, and might conceivably even be considered a compliment to Americans.

The Chinese Communists also had a bone to pick with the United States over the use of the word "containment," as in the "policy of containment of China." The Chinese drew the inference of "confinement" from the American "containment." The Russians saw the word "containment," as applied to themselves, as implying violence and forced constraint to keep them in place. There were differences between English and American, leading to misunderstandings in newspaper headlines. When the British "tabled" a bill in Parliament, that was the beginning of the legislative process. When a bill was "tabled" in Congress, it meant that the measure had been effectively killed. Educated Indians had a fundamental miscomprehension of, hence a natural distaste for, the word "freedom," as used by Americans. In the United States it meant no hindrances to the pursuit of one's personal desires. To Hindus true freedom meant liberation from all desire.

Glenn, who had served Presidents Truman, Eisenhower, Kennedy, and Johnson, said that interpreters constantly ran into two types of difficulties: immediately apparent meanings of words and long-range meanings built in the culture of the foreign language. President Kennedy once corrected Glenn on the latter's translation of the French word "administration" as "government." Glenn explained that French usage was the opposite of the American. In French, the word for American "administration" was *"le gouvernement,"* as the temporary political regime. The French word for the American "government" was *"l'administration,"* denoting the permanent management of public affairs.

Press translation of French words ruffled diplomatic feelings between the two countries, particularly when State Department spokesmen jumped the gun before the professionals had had a chance to read the foreign text in the original. A French general a few years ago caused a minor furor by "demanding understanding," whereas he was only politely requesting it. General de Gaulle's remark about the Vietnam war was reported in the American press as being a "dirty affair," a literal translation. The General had said, *"une sale affaire,"* used in the normal French sense of "a nasty business or situation," with no particular implications. Another time, De Gaulle got into hot water with the Americans via a press report indicating that France was trying to be a "free mediator" in the

Vietnam war. Classically educated in the French tradition of Descartes and Pascal, the General had used the phrase *"libre arbitre."* This meant simply philosophical free will. In brief, France would choose her course about the Vietnam war of her own free will. As John Livingston Lowes said at Harvard years ago, "Words mean what they are intended to mean, and words mean what they are taken to mean."

Cultural glaucomas of diplomatic relations in the modern world were outlined in an extraordinary collection of apothegms on diplomacy compiled, edited, and privately printed by Lieutenant Colonel Victor S. M. de Guinzbourg, former liaison officer to the Military Staff Committee of the United Nations and Permanent Secretary of the Paroemiological Society, which was a gaggle of proverb buffs. Two examples illustrated the difficulty in fathoming the native context of words and possible motivations in using them. Monsignor Alberto Giovannetti, Permanent Observer of the Holy See to the UN, wrote: *"Dai da bere al prete perche il chierichetto ha sete."* (Give the priest something to drink because the altar boy is thirsty.) The monsignor explained, "This proverb can mean many things. One of these is: Sometimes one can become involved pursuing an end with means that apparently are in contradiction with the same end." A classic Roman curlicue. The other proverb, without explication of the way it was to be taken, came from G. Coleridge-Taylor, the first secretary of the Permanent Mission of Sierra Leone to the United Nations. Coleridge-Taylor wrote in Krio, an African dialect: "Cotton tree foddom so bay, be high pass grass." He translated it thus: "However low a giant cotton tree might fall, it would still be taller than the grass."

In any event, the Foreign Service of the United States in the mid-1960's still stood taller than its critics, though the grass was slippery. The narcissism that enveloped much Foreign Service guild thinking did not abate appreciably, despite the sniping, which also did not abate. Cases of diplomatic shell shock arose. Self-conscious officers tried to stay above the battle and look dignified, but not starchy, when Congressman Rooney casually referred to them to their faces as "striped pantsers" and "gooney-birds."

Clever chaps, putting on a front of being bored with their own brilliance, looked around to find political patrons within the Deparmental hierarchy. Not-so-clever chaps, who had been getting mileage on out-of-date credit cards, found themselves vulnerable and sank back into the woodwork. Dedicated souls of old-fashioned antecedents retreated to their Gracián, seeking solace and guidance in it almost as if it were a missal. Cultured diplomats of a previous generation used to bestow the gift of Gracián on young friends. The little book's full title is *A Truth-telling Manual and the*

Art of Worldly Wisdom: Being a Collection of the Aphorisms Which Appear in the Works of Fr. Baltasar Gracián, S.J." Gracián was a Spanish monk of the seventeenth century, who penned bite-sized morsels of sagacity, which provided nutriment even for the competitive coexistence of the twentieth century. In the uncertain, if not hostile, environment of the times, the Foreign Service offices started to close ranks like Chinese Mandarins reverting to Confucian fundamentals of authority, loyalty, morality, unanimity, and self-criticism within the family, attributes not unfamiliar to the Chinese Communist bureaucracy in Peking.

Sympathetic onlookers, both in Congress and the White House, felt that Foreign Service officers should not be penalized for honest mistakes in decisions which depended, in the final analysis, on a flip of the coin. Diplomats were invaluable for their professional use of sterilized contacts and sanitized channels. At their best, they acted with utmost precision and therefore tended to fall back on safe and reliable routines while waiting for decisive moments of action. As George E. Reedy, President Johnson's former long-time aide and Press Secretary, said, "If diplomats did not exist, we would have to invent them as a necessary device in a mad world." Under Secretary Katzenbach had been realistic about it in 1966. He said: "I am acutely sensitive of the old saw that Under Secretaries come and Under Secretaries go but the Foreign Service goes on forever. It's all too true. The Service has endured for forty-two years. In the same period, there have now been nineteen of us Under Secretaries." Katzenbach, in the same speech before the American Foreign Service Association, attempted with oblique delicacy and epigrammatic counsel, to stir the Service out of the doldrums.

Other senior officers were less patient. One recalled that he had reviewed literally hundreds of FSO records to establish the Arms Control and Disarmament Agency a few years ago. Far too many records indicated narrow mentalities and lack of initiative. George Kennan, when he wrote the policy planning paper which was to become the Marshall Plan, said that he had not recommended a study of the problem in advance because he knew all too well that the instinctive bureaucratic gambit would have been to request "further study." A new seventh-floor executive, after having been briefed on detailed matters involved in his responsibilities, shook his head in bafflement and said: "I don't know if I've been had." He was referring to the expert manipulative technique and soft "con" approach indicative of masterly Foreign Service presentation. Career Ambassador Foy Kohler, who in 1951 stood up to U.S. Senator Joseph McCarthy, had a standard answer for diffident officers who sought his advice about problems. Kohler asked: "What do YOU think I should do about it?" Convoking meetings even on minor matters was a bureaucratic penchant that surprised new officials in the Department. Sol Linowitz, the U.S. Ambassador to the Organization of American States, one day made a casual inquiry about Paraguay. The next he knew he had twelve officers in his office briefing him fully about Paraguay. Linowitz learned to drop in on desk officers and pick up whatever specific information he wanted on the spot.

An exceedingly curious aspect of bureaucratic behavior was bureaucratic explanations. For a very large part of the time, reasons were advanced for failures to act. In short, the negative was accentuated. Caution was the key word. Too much attention was paid to the written record; little to who wrote the contents. Between the rewards and sanctions of the Service, the safest course was not to suffer unnecessary risks. There was a trace of sanctimoniousness, of "They also serve who stand and wait." There was false modesty hiding inflated egos. There was plain fear of Congress and the press. Family responsibilities counseled prudence. The Foreign Service officer, habituated to bargain, negotiate, and outsmart foreigners overseas, found it difficult not to handle his colleagues at home the same way. The mentality at times appeared to be that of insurance agents. Everybody analyzed everything to death, and did nothing about it, or very little. The emphasis on emotional stability and control of temper tended to emasculate the spirited. The drilled-in habit of obeying orders inhibited imagination and daring. The artificiality of bureaucratic procedures often created problems where none had existed before. A disproportionate amount of energy was expended to win tenths of points.

A falsified ethos prevailed that all jobs were equally important and should be performed with equal devotion and dedication. The reality was that many jobs were secondary and relegated to the lesser breeds. The public vaunt was, all careers open to talent and every Foreign Service officer a future ambassador. The private admonition was that not all officers actually could become ambassadors and that some officers should consider themselves lucky to be kept on long enough to rate retirement benefits. The principle of protective coloration also obtained. If the humanistic values of one of Sir Charles Snow's "two cultures" were in decline, patently, the thing to do was to jump into the other stream, the scientific. In the end, it seemed that too much learning how to play the game progressed into thinking that was the way the game ought to be played.

The emotional maceration heightened the basic feeling of defensiveness inherent in the Foreign Service attitude. The citizenry of the nation it represented had, as Americans, a folk faith that no problem was really insoluble. Yet the experience of Foreign Service officers overseas constantly emphasized the fact that no solutions were to be found to insoluble problems, at least no solutions satisfactory to an impatient U.S. public and politician. This was the original dilemma, the impossible expectations.

By no manner whatsoever was the State Department entirely made up of gray-flannel-mouthed homunculi. Officers of integrity and acuity held firm values and defended them fearlessly. Heroes of dissent persisted, both public and private, although in the nature of the closed traditions of the Foreign Service more of the latter prevailed. There were characters out of the tapestry of history, like Loy W. Henderson. In 1967, Henderson, at seventy-five, received the accolade of "Mr. Foreign Service" to crown a distinguished career of thirty-nine years of active service and, in the citation of his colleagues, a decade as an "elder statesman of unexcelled eminence and respect." There was the faintly Mephistophelian John Paton Davies, Jr., who was expendable to an indifferent Secretary Foster Dulles because Davies had done no more, and no less, than predict the Communist conquest of China.

A dissenter who survived was a career minister with the fine feudal name of Outerbridge Horsey, from an old Cavalier family in Maryland. The Horsey affair occurred in Rome, where Horsey was U.S. deputy chief of mission. Italian Prime Minister Alcide de Gasperi had ejected from his cabinet the Communists and Socialists in 1947. For years, as Italy struggled to modernize her ancient regime, there had been recurrent but groundless rumors of an "opening to the left" with the Socialists, a far larger party than that of the Democratic Socialists, who had seceded under Giuseppe Saragat in 1947. Pietro Nenni, the Socialist leader, however, continued his loose alliance with the Communists. The Hungarian revolution of 1956 widely disillusioned Italian leftists. The Socialists began to drift away on their own. By 1958 Amintore Fanfani was able to organize a somewhat-left-of-center government. But Nenni, still coy, refused to play except at the price of real reforms. When JFK became President in 1961, Italy was ambling along in her usual teeter-totter way.

The bright young zealots in the White House were eager to promote the New Frontier gospel across the seas and to inspire non-Communist-left governments to launch truly democratic "revolutions." Italy thus was an ideal laboratory case. The Italian social situation was the debris of centuries. The Socialists were non-Communists and the Fanfani wing of the Christian Democrats was Christian Socialist. The White House aim was to obtain a united United States embassy front, on the basis of which the United States could exercise its considerable weight to influence the recalcitrants in the Italian Government to accept the "opening to the left." Horsey said nay. As a result there was a high-decibel uproar behind the scenes. The Horsey analysis maintained that there was no necessity for the United States to assume the risks of, in effect, creating a government in another country and of being saddled with the responsibility of picking up the pieces if it collapsed. Horsey was made Ambassador to Czechoslovakia in 1962. The first full-scale left-of-center government was not formed until December 4, 1963, by Prime Minister Aldo Moro, with Pietro Nenni as Vice Premier. By 1967 Moro had formed his third cabinet on the same basis. The Moro regimes had been weak, and Italy had undergone an economic slowdown. A forced change as early as 1961 might or might not have precipitated some confusion. Horsey, in any case, had done his duty, and had stuck by it.

The urge to meddle in Italian politics sometimes was a minor American mania. It was based on a real fear of the large, powerful, and highly efficient Communist party and the possibility of its winning legal access to power. Ambassador Clare Boothe Luce was therefore considerably exercised at the prospect of the election to the presidency of the Italian republic of left-of-center Giovanni Gronchi in 1955. She sat in the diplomatic box in the Italian Chamber of Deputies, listening to the electoral speeches, regal and distant like a Hapsburg empress, but not neglecting to tilt her lovely blond head slightly to the right to present her alabaster profile. The Italian legislators ate her with their eyes, not giving a fig for her rank, as they nudged each other and murmured, *"Che bellissima donna!"*

Mrs. Luce became more serene about Gronchi in consequence of an odd happenstance. Scheduled one day for an appointment with the Prime Minister, she jumped into her embassy limousine and said to the driver, *"alla presidenza,"* and then buried herself in the official documents she would have to discuss. But instead of *"la presidenza deglo consiglio,"* or presidency of the Council of Ministers, the chauffeur thought that "La Luce" had meant *"la presidenza della reppublica,"* or the presidency of the republic. When Mrs. Luce looked up from her papers, the car door was open and she was at the Quirinale, the great palace of the former kings of Italy and the residence of the detested Gronchi. Undaunted by the confusion her completely unexpected arrival had caused, Mrs. Luce proceeded to have a tête-à-tête with Gronchi. She discovered that the Italian President was a charming, small-town lawyer, who talked big, but not as big as a Trojan Horse.

The dialogue between the activists and the passivists, between the let-it-alone and the stir-it-up schools, was bound to continue in the State Department and the Foreign Service as long as human beings were involved, with their peculiarities, strengths, and weaknesses, as in all other organizations of men. The essential was to have a "feel" for the business, which came from God or one's ancestors, or possibly might be developed by training. Averell Harriman related that he had gone to Russia after the Bolshevik Revolution to look into some investments which his companies had there. After conversations with the Communist leaders, Harriman "felt" that Stalin, who was rising steadily in power, would ditch Lenin's NEP, or "New Economic Policy." Harriman succeeded in playing his hunch and got his money out.

But in the mundane affairs of state, it was the expression and manner of translating "feel" and ideas into agreements and action that counted from day to day. As was indicated, there existed styles which obstructed or obscured effective communication toward joint solution of problems. Deputy Under Secretary Crockett, as a result, in 1966 tossed the ACORD program, or "Action for Organizational Development," at the startled Foreign Service. The objective was to improve "the ability of personnel to work effectively together . . . to increase openness with one another, . . . to look at the ways in which conflict can be used creatively." The Crockett prospectus went on to say:

> Much of the work of the Department necessarily is carried on through committees, task forces, teams, and meetings, where the need is to achieve an environment encouraging creative decisions to which people can be highly committed. ACORD will highlight the forces operating in groups that impede or facilitate effective decision-making. Executive team-building will be a major goal of the program.

Senior officers in Classes 1 and 2 were gathered together in "teams" of approximately twenty participants in nearby resorts for six-day sessions. They were instructed to have a go at each other, to bore for the weak spots in each other's personalities until the object "leveled" with what truly made him act that way. The project was termed "sensitivity training." It had been used with some degree of success in a number of large industrial organizations under auspices of the behavioral scientists of the National Training Laboratories, a division of the National Education Association. Over 200 officers, including many brought home expressly from overseas, responded, like good soldiers, but with raised eyebrows. Reactions ranged from derisive snorts to reluctant acknowledgment that the tourneys had been a bit "unpleasant but useful."

In January 1967, as he was about to retire from the Department, Crockett authorized publication of a brochure, *Some Causes of Organizational Ineffectiveness within the Department of State*, by Dr. Chris Argyris, professor of organizational behavior, chairman of the Department of Administrative Sciences at Yale University, and one of the organizers of ACORD. The press, as might be expected, had a ball with the report, which could not help feeding popular prejudices about diplomats. The *Washington Star* headlined, "How to Succeed at State—Don't Rock the Boat." The *New York Times* said: "State Department

Study Finds Diplomats Avoid Policy Debates." Scores of letters poured into the *Foreign Service Journal*, the monthly organ of the American Foreign Service Association.

The Argyris report punched holes in the cellophane cover of the Foreign Service's all too human pretensions. But Argyris was neither Spinoza nor Jonathan Swift. The failings outlined were all true enough some of the time, but certainly not true all the time. Argyris prefaced his scathing analysis by reporting, "Secretary Rusk has told his Business Advisory Council that one of his biggest problems is getting people to accept and enlarge their responsibility."

Argyris made tape recordings at three sessions of the group therapies. But his conception of "The Norms of the Living System of the Foreign Service" was already an anachronism. The practical exigencies of modern diplomatic life had already broken the mold of the past. The ACORD sessions were definitely helpful in one respect at least: they made the Foreign Service mad, particularly at being laughed at in public. Four years of Crockett's sermonizing concerning the cardinal importance of management and modern techniques in foreign affairs programs had been more or less tolerated, if not ignored, until ACORD and the Argyris report. Thereafter, the professionals began to embrace the management philosophy. An executive development seminar was organized at the Foreign Service Institute. Crockett ideas that had been resisted were revived, reshaped, stabilized, examined for their practical application to the Foreign Service of tomorrow. But real life in fields overseas had already begun to transform the body and spirit of the old Foreign Service. It was happening above all in Vietnam, where war, as it always had, brought out the noble, enterprising, and selfless in man, in the midst of death, destruction, and suffering.

Vietnam was no place for the diplomat with Sir Ernest Satow's *Guide to Diplomatic Practice* in his attaché case. Vietnam was very literally a challenge and an opportunity, and possibly death. History was, as Pieter Geyl said, not all made in foreign offices. In Vietnam it was made in the provinces among the people. In 1964 the State Department initiated an experiment by detailing twenty young FSO's to work with AID in the field, away from the top-heavy Saigon headquarters. By 1967 the Department had earmarked 126 junior officers for Vietnam; 75 had received assignments and 35 were already working on the spot. A Vietnam Training Center was organized at the Foreign Service Institute, with seventy-eight students, from all the foreign affairs agencies, in the first class. The big difficulty was the language. Only four officers in the service had been tested at S/4 proficiency. The newcomers had to undergo forty-two weeks of training to obtain a working knowledge of Vietnamese.

For FSO–6 Frederick C. Ashley of Ohio, it was a "fantastic adventure." In 1964, Ashley, one of the original FSO's included in the experiment, was sent to Tuyen Duc province, 180 miles north of Saigon. He was twenty-nine. He worked there until 1967, when he returned to Washington. "We had the most exciting experiences I might not have been able to get in another ten or fifteen years in the service," he said. Ashley had previously served at Tananarive, in the Malagasy Republic, the former Madagascar, where U.S. aid amounted to $900,000 a year. In Tuyen Duc province, Ashley oversaw an annual budget of $1 million and helped supervise a staff of forty-five in his role as acting provincial representative and adviser to Vietnamese officials, most of them old enough to be his father.

Ashley was a front-line participant in the so-called other war, that of demonstrating practical concern for the peasants caught in the middle between the Viet Cong and the Saigon Government. The ruling traditions for centuries had been to ignore the countryside except as a source of food and taxes. Ashley's area, around Dalat, the summer capital of Vietnam, consisted of 3 districts, 30 villages, 200 hamlets, and a population of 160,000, including the Montagnards, tribal inhabitants similar to the North American Indians. All through months of political upheaval and coups in Saigon, the effective presence of the provincial governments, with backstops like Ashley, gave an indispensable continuity to the South Vietnamese regime. Ashley looked on the "new diplomacy" as "getting out and working with people." He was convinced that the future leaders of Vietnam would be labor leaders and farmers and no longer the lawyers and the professors from the cities.

Ashley pushed cement instead of cookies. Robert W. Komer, President Johnson's special overseer for all South Vietnamese civilian affairs, on a flying inspection trip to Vietnam, once gave Ashley an argument about cement. The high-powered Komer took a look around Tuyen Duc and decreed that what the natives needed was fertilizer. Ashley said cement. Komer said fertilizer. Ashley had a hazy idea that Komer was somehow connected with the White House. Waxing earnest, Ashley persisted: "Cement." Ashley wanted cement for schools, warehouses, markets, culvert bridges, rice-drying floors. Komer left without another word. He sent back instructions that he wanted Ashley to become provincial representative in a larger province, a clear promotion. Ashley thought he had better stay where he was and help finish the projects on hand. These included putting a dam on a little river called the "Vietnam Pedernales." It would bring electricity to the high backlands for the first time in the same way that the Marshall Plan had brought light and the telephone to villages in the Italian Apennines in 1951. President Johnson was personally interested in the Tuyen Duc project, remembering rural electrification in Texas thirty years ago.

Back in the United States in 1967, Ashley made a speech in Salt Lake City in which he remarked upon the close similarities between the Dran, or High Donnai Valley, in which he had served in the Central Highlands of South Vietnam, and the mountain valley running south from Salt Lake to the American Fork in Utah. Over 100 years ago guerrilla war had also sprung "like running grass fires" in Utah as the Mormons harassed the punitive federal troops; riding down from the high country, hiding in the rocks and tall grasses, burning the supply wagons, and fighting like wasps. Mormons of those days, if they could see South Vietnam today, would note the same sudden attacks in the night, farms set burning, harvests confiscated, families set wandering, and farmers shot down in the fields. Ashley was intensely convinced that one had to identify one's self with the people to win their trust, but that one could do so effectively only if the people actually did attempt to help themselves. There was a restriction on the way to do it, however, Ashley said. A Vietnamese said it at Tuyen Duc: "Help us, but don't overwhelm us."

The "managerial revolution" in the State Department was sputtering and backfiring. The real revolution was being helped by the young Foreign Service officers on the ground in Vietnam. FSO–6 George C. Nettles of Alabama was blown up in his quarters at Lam Dong in the II Corps area and FSO–7 Richard C. Brown of Oklahoma was mortared once, ambushed once, and sniped at six times in Quang Tri in the I Corps area farther north. Both survived. Down in the IV Corps area at Can Tho in the Mekong River delta, an FSO–1, Sterling J. Cottrell of Illinois, also was finding a new experience. Cottrell supervised 758 Americans from all agencies in sixteen provinces and eighty-seven districts of the delta. He wrote to John Steeves, the Foreign Service's Director General, about his life in Vietnam, saying, in part:

Now that I know a bit about what we are doing in Viet Nam, I'm brooding about the fact that there aren't more FSO's around here. I think the reason is that they just don't realize how important the problem is, what it involves, and how much we need the finest talent we can get. If they did, I think we would have more volunteers than we could handle from the upper as well as the lower ranks of the Foreign Service.

Personally, in my ignorance and because I had a soft job in Caracas, I would never have volunteered. I came without objections only because I'm proud to be an FSO.

Knowing what I do now, I'm sorry I didn't volunteer a year or two ago because this is the most important foreign problem the U.S. has; the reputation of the U.S. is at stake; we must solve this problem or lose face, reputation, and respect all over the world; and failure will mean we will just have to fight the same problem in some other place in the near future.

I see a crying need here for generalists from the Foreign Service of all ranks to mix with the specialists from AID, USIA, CIA, Defense, etc. In IV Corps (the Delta), we have 16 Provinces and only two FSO's as Senior Provincial Advisors. They are excellent officers and I am sure I will be able to point to them as shining examples of what FSO's can do here.

Many FSO jobs are going by default to the military and to AID. If we in the Foreign Service regard ourselves as an elite corps—and we do—then we damn well have to prove it when the going gets tough, or step down. The Army and AID are carrying the flag here in IV Corps, and in a way that fills me with nothing but admiration. Those guys are down at village level doing every conceivable civilian job, as well as helping repel the Viet Cong.

These jobs are nation-building in the midst of a war, and call for executive talents which we have among FSO's. This is the finest crucible I know for training FSO's, who should be lining up begging for these jobs in their own career interest as well as in the national interest.

The whole machinery from Washington to Saigon to Corps Headquarters to provincial level has to get results at the district level, where you finally meet the 14,000,000 Vietnamese people on the ground, in hamlets, villages and district towns. This is where most of the Vietnamese programs are carried out—in the mud along the banks of the canals. Our Public Works program, for example, is expressed in helping to build small foot bridges across the canals so that villagers can get their pigs to market, or building schoolhouses in the mud with AID cement and rebar. This is where the Public Health Program translates into a tin roof over a 3-room shack, with a Medical Advisor, dispensary and a few cots. This is where the Agricultural Program, designed in Washington, finally filters down to a pair of pigs in a cement sty designed by the Agriculture Advisor to keep them alive until they have piglets, which are distributed to other villagers, etc. etc. This is where the Communist infrastructure in a hamlet and in a village is laboriously rooted out by one Army Intelligence Lieutenant with a card file, assisting the Vietnamese at village level. This is where the Public Safety Program helps train a few ragged villagers to maintain law and order, and here is where the battle for the Delta will be won or lost, and here is where FSO's should be.

In contrast (and the Delta is full of contrasts) I coptered in for lunch the other day in Long Xuyen. My Americans there have a mess and a bar in an old Foreign Legion post. Beautiful, romantic and equipped with two attractive Australian nurses (also well equipped). There leaning against the bar (not the nurses) was my old friend, Tom Martin, ex-USIS Labor Information Officer in Caracas. After two dry martinis on the rocks, and a couple of New York cut steaks (medium-rare), I informed Tom that this soft life in Long Xuyen (where they have hardly heard a shot fired in anger for over a year) was too good for him, and I was going to transfer him to Bac Lieu. Tom thrives on trouble.

I'll probably ruin my one-man recruiting drive if I dwell only on the hairy spots! I live in a 12-unit prefab compound. Mud all around us, but inside the compound it's spotless. We planted palm trees, grass and brick walkways. I have a big fat cook named Tuba, and a rail-skinny maid named Hi, both for a total of $35 a month. It's no Caracas Country Club, but I've named it Palm Springs. Others live in apartment buildings and small houses around town. The food is excellent. Wonderful fruits and vegetables, fish, shrimp and lobster. Nobody goes hungry in the Delta, not even the poorest peasant. This area has a great future.

I coptered up to Chau Doc to attend the 28th anniversary of the Hoa Hao religious sect (2 million members in IV Corps). It was the damndest sight I ever saw! A combination of the Rio Carnival, the New Orleans Mardi-Gras and the Tournament of Roses. Every truck in town was decorated with flowers as a float and moved down the main street between carnival throngs, Then we "reviewed the fleet" at 8:00 p.m. A line of battleships moved slowly up the river and passed in review. They were really big rice barges, but with super structures built like pagodas. All lit up like Christmas and swarming with costumed people. One barge was built like a turtle, with a big, bobbing head and flippers. Some crazy character with a .30 caliber machine gun was shooting tracers off the stern. There were fireworks and fire water in abundance. Then when we left the gaiety and flew home, we passed over a fire fight on the ground. The Viet Cong attacking a village not ten miles from the big festive occasion we just left! What a people, and what a country!

Its own manpower commitments all over the world, including Vietnam, were causing the State Department possibly even more anxiety than the proliferation of U.S. military commitments was causing the United States Senate. The tail was not only wagging but threatening to shake the dog. The total of U.S. Government permanent American employees present in State Department posts overseas, as of April 30, 1967, rose to 46,779, exactly 1,111 more than the 1966 total. There were also 34,898 foreign locals employed. State officers engaged in substantive or political policy work accounted for only 9 per cent of the total, or 4,404 persons. An additional 2,661 persons, or 6 per cent of State personnel, gave administrative support and services to the remainder of the overseas Americans. Of the 85 per cent in the other agencies, 43 per cent, or 19,522, were from the Defense Department; 4,885, or 10 per cent, were from AID; 1,365, or 3 per cent, from USIA; 26 per cent, or 12,477, were from the Peace Corps; and others made up 3 per cent, or 1,465. State, in sum, was only one seventh of the U.S. community abroad. Yet two fifths of State's total manpower was engaged in acting as butler, valet, chauffeur, and clerk to the other Americans.

To cap the anomaly, there was indignity: Congress, the press, and the public ninety-nine times out of a hundred blamed the overload on State. State ordered a 2 per cent cut in employment ceilings in early 1967. It would eliminate 273 jobs. The Associated Press report said that the order was "aimed . . . at curbing what critics contend is overstaffing in the big foreign affairs agency." No mention of the big sinners, the other agencies. In December 1967 a similar nonevent was reported in the *New York Times:* "U.S. Seeks to Cut Missions Abroad; State Department Is Moving to Reduce Personnel."

Ambassadors on the ground could declare anyone on their staffs *persona non grata*, but they could not quite toss personnel of other departments out of the country wholesale. Ambassador Robert H. McBride in the Congo tried to get rid of a hundred military attachés, superfluous in his opinion. It was not easy. Nor did the State Department at home quite dare to lay down the law. The SIG, or Senior Interdepartmental Group, almost never got into personnel matters. Bodies, after all, were the big nub of the argument between agencies: who would control them. When State poor-mouthed that it had no funds, the other agencies were more than happy to pick up the tab. They had access to friendlier committees in Congress, which did not put the screws on them in the same manner as the State had to suffer.

State's money relations with the Congressional appropriations committees in the 1960's had not been happy. Crockett had put practically all of State's eggs in Congressman Rooney's basket. State had no reliable friends in the Senate to balance out Rooney in the conference compromises on final sums. President Johnson, it happened, had inadvertently helped build up Rooney's power. When the President was Senate Majority leader, he was also chairman of the Appropriations Subcommittee on State Department funds. He needed Rooney to corral as many Irish votes as possible against the runaway candidacy of John Kennedy for the Democratic presidential nomination. In the Senate-House conferences, Johnson tried to do what he could for the Department, but he could not afford to offend Rooney. So the Rooney cuts in State funds usually set the ceiling.

Backing up the nearly 40,000 non-State Department Americans attached to embassies overseas were fifty-two Washington agencies interested in foreign affairs. Their personnel numbered approximately 80,000, or five times the State Department's total American personnel. The official overseas Americans were under the theoretical control of State's five geographical bureaus. African Affairs oversaw 7,075; Inter-American, 8,452; East Asian and Pacific, 13,755; European, 7,092; and Near Eastern and South Asian, 10,405.

Eleven countries had U.S. embassies with more than 1,000 Americans: one each in Europe, Latin America, and Africa; three in the Middle East; and five in the Far East. In explanation, Belgium had the Brussels NATO headquarters. Athens in Greece housed U.S. military for contingencies in NATO, Cyprus, and the Middle East. Nigeria, Brazil, and India were big Peace Corps demonstration countries. Seoul, in South Korea, had 50,000 U.S. troops to serve for liaison. Taipei staffs on Taiwan kept Chiang Kai-shek's army up to snuff against Chinese Communist threats. Vietnam had put an unprecedented AID effort out in the provinces. In Thailand, the big military staff was liaison for the U.S. bombing of

North Vietnam. Bangkok was the biggest U.S. embassy in the world. The detailed spread:

COUNTRIES	STATE DEPARTMENT			USIA	AID	DE-FENSE	PEACE CORPS	U.S. OTHER	TOTAL
	Em-bassy	Other Posts	Sup-port						
Nigeria	22	16	44	17	213	13	747	18	1,090
Brazil	34	76	63	44	156	229	659	25	1,286
Belgium	68	4	26	8	1	1,645	—	44	1,796
Korea	64	—	23	18	154	1,348	98	1	1,706
Philippines	176	3	45	56	71	312	714	63	1,440
Taiwan	30	—	14	12	9	2,340	—	8	2,413
Thailand	62	8	62	66	239	2,462	298	99	3,296
Vietnam	129	—	71	116	1,506	675	—	6	2,503
Greece	32	6	114	35	7	3,674	—	22	3,890
India	77	52	56	66	117	100	1,289	18	1,775
Iran	47	10	55	22	45	810	331	13	1,333

The relevance of the numbers game lay in the fact that it overburdened or shrouded the much more complex problem of quality control in the State Department. Esthetically, the form and content of State Department administration presented a unity of high camp. In the evolutionary time scale, the management was post-Paleozoic. Administratively, State was shuffling along, two steps forward, half a step backward. Neanderthals and avant garde were just getting on speaking terms. There was thought and action in fits and starts. One FSO and one businessman would exchange jobs, each hopefully to profit from the new ambient. Inspector General Fraser Wilkins came up with the revolutionary proposal of assigning officers on a regional, rather than a country, basis. It ran into immediate opposition from the geographical bureaus, to whom control of personnel had been decentralized—others used the verb "abandoned"— by Deputy Under Secretary Crockett. The geographical bureaus hoarded their good men, short-changing other areas desperate for first-class officers.

FSO's spoke wistfully of the possibility of using the authority of the 1946 Foreign Service Act, about half of which was still operative, to effectuate reforms without new legislation, and thus eliminate the ordeal of a Congressional inquisition. In mid-1967, Senator Fulbright, waking up for a moment from his brown study over Vietnam, mused that a Plowden Commission, "a high-level, blue-ribbon Presidential Committee," was needed to do the same thorough job for re-creation of the U.S. Foreign Service that the Plowden group had done for the British diplomatic service. Fulbright added later:

I would think that the Department would be glad to see such a committee established and would feel a responsibility to its employees to see that the best available minds of the United States were set to work on these organizational problems. It seems to me that these problems, including the problem of the relationship between the personnel systems of the Department of State, AID, and USIA, are so pressing that they will require solutions in the very near future. I would think that the Department would prefer to participate in the process of reaching these solutions than to wait and find these solutions imposed on them.

The handwriting was on the wall. John F. Griner, president of the American Federation of Government Employees, testifying before a Senate Foreign Relations subcommittee, said:

We believe the time is here for a full public discussion of the personnel practices of the State Department, Foreign Service, AID, and USIA. For this reason, we urge the earliest establishment of the Presidential blue-ribbon committee, as proposed by Senator Fulbright, to include representatives from the House of Representatives and the Senate. We request that it include also representatives from Federal employee groups, including one from our own organization, the American Federation of Government Employees.

In the event such a Presidential committee is not established by January 1, 1968, we request that the Senate Foreign Relations Committee itself undertake hearings early in 1968 looking to the reorganization and the personnel reform of the State Department, the Foreign Service, AID, USIA, and such other agencies involved in operations abroad as may be appropriate.

The State Department had adopted some recommendations of the Hoover Commission of 1949 and 1955, but several other prescient ideas were gathering dust. The views of the Herter Commission of 1962 were likewise far from actualization. The first major effort to put one of them into effect was the Hays bill of 1965 to establish an integrated foreign affairs system of State, AID, and USIA, and thus abolish civil service in all three. An attempt to incorporate 700 USIA officers en masse into State's Foreign Service died in the Senate. The Hays bill passed the House, bulled through by Congressman Hays as floor manager. Veterans groups, Government employee trade unions, and last, but certainly far from least, some of the Napoleonic Old Guard of the Foreign Service itself, helped to kill the Hays bill in the Senate Foreign Relations Committee. AID officers did not care to lose the perquisites of their own agency, which gave better allowances for living expenses and for entertainment than State did. USIA was once more trying in late 1967 to persuade the Senate to authorize it to organize its own "compatible" foreign service. The big hitch was the provision of appeals from selection-out, or forced retirement.

Making regulations uniform was a project dear to the heart of bureaucrats. In 1962 a task force was formed to do so. In three years there were nearly a hundred issuances. The accomplishment received the accolade of "significant progress" of a sort. There was also the idea presented by George Allen and James Rowe in their dissent to the Herter Report. Rowe and Allen recommended a permanent Under Secretary of State, appointed from the best of the Foreign Service by the President. He would be No. 3 in the State Department, actually manage it, act as a vessel of continuity between national administrations, and be comparable in function to the Chairman of the Joint Chiefs of Staff in the Defense Department. But then good ideas about the State Department were plentiful, like premature bantlings pickled in alcohol on medical school shelves.

Female members of the Foreign Service periodically groused in ladylike tones or, when necessary, with masculine directness, over sometimes being regarded as second-class citizens. Too many seniors still acted as if a woman's place were in the drawing room, in the kitchen, or in bed. The men deplored the tendency of women to get pregnant. Some seemed to suspect that some women liked to get pregnant, hence, could not be relied upon, in short, were unpredictable. The 199 female FSO's and 189 FSR's included first-class and wise officers like Elizabeth A. Brown in International Organizations Affairs, Ambassador Margaret Tibbetts in Norway, Minister Kay W. Bracken in Athens, and Ambassador Carol C. Laise in Nepal, who is also the wife of Ambassador Bunker in Saigon. But when all was said and done, not too many looked like future ambassadors to Paris, London, or Moscow.

In brief, managerial, administrative, and personnel reform to make the wheels go around better, smoother, and faster was desultory, spasmodic, peripheral, even at times a splotch of the absurd on a patina of the futile. Worse, it was boring. What stirred the chromosomes was power. The thought of power brought a gleam to the eye, deepened the voice, squared the shoulders, and put purpose in the stride down the corridor. To some, power was command of resources to solve problems and move foreign policy from paper theory to live practice. To others, power was moving the levers up and down like a pinball machine and seeing the lights flash on, denoting ostensible results and public acclaim.

Power came from the President of the United States, or his official cousins, palladins, political backers, or parasites, directly or by delegation, propinquity, or thought transference. The President, however, was hemmed in much more than was realized by the checks and balances of the American system. But he could maneuver through tight corners if he so willed. One set of courtiers or theoreticians maintained that the statutory power over the Foreign Service was vested in the Secretary of State and whomever he gave it to, to operate, whereas it should be by explicit law in the hands of the President. The central role for the control and construction of foreign policy was the President's. But, as an instrument, he could not use his own hands except at one remove, as if controlling a fork lift. As constitutional Commander-in-Chief of the armed forces, he could push up or knock down the military through the Chairman of the Joint Chiefs as necessary. For most of the federal establishment, he had John Macy, chairman of the U.S. Civil Service Commission, placed physically in the Executive Offices Building, within summoning distance from the throne. Macy in late 1967 came up with the executive placement plan whereby senior officers could be shifted about the Government to where the need was greatest. The President's decisions affected the disposition of nearly 20,000 key jobs.

Ten thousand attorney appointments and 1,590 Schedule C jobs were exempt from the civil service merit, seniority, and retirement system. So-called supergrades—8,289 of them, a number fixed by the Congress—in GS–16, GS–17, and GS–18 positions were prorated around the departments by the Civil Service Commission. These jobs paid from over $19,000 to over $25,000. The State Department had the equivalent of approximately 800 supergrades in career ambassadors, career ministers, Class 1 and Class 2, more than in any other agency of the Government except the Central Intelligence Agency. But the President did not have a Foreign-Service-Macy by his side. The Director General of the Foreign Service, though he dealt with Macy on presidential appointments, was a unique case. Critics felt that the elite, agile, and shrewd Foreign Service bureaucracy had accumulated enough power to camouflage, deflect, limit, if not thwart, in effect, the President's options for appointments in the foreign field. In 1967, groups in the foreign affairs community, but outside the State Department, met privately to plot pressure campaigns to augment the President's direct controls.

Politically aseptic Government technicians rated President Johnson as unquestionably the greatest administrator in the history of the Presidency. Johnson had been sophisticated by seeing the administrative cogs and wheels at close hand through the appropriation process. He had a phenomenal knowledge of bureaucratic detail, the efficacy of procedures, and the break-even point in the thrust of programs, that is, when and if they were doing what they were supposed to do. In comparison, Kennedy was rated an amateur in administration, but perhaps with more of a flair as an executive in picking, keeping, and inspiring subordinates and delegating tasks to his immediate staff. Johnson delegated responsibility all the way down to the executive departments, but tended to take on to himself more details than necessary. Kennedy appeared to trust the types he could recognize from his own past on the Eastern Seaboard, where there was a fairly good supply of competent men. Johnson seemed to trust persons whose background he could instinctively figure out, which in a sense limited him to Texas, where the supply of competent men was geographically and relatively less plentiful.

The loci of power were thus in strict geometrical relation to wherever the President stood in any given situation. In the State Department five or six top officials had the ear of the President, as part of the direct chain of command or, more infrequently and laterally, as acknowledged experts or sage counselors like Llewellyn Thompson on Russia. Major power centers like Defense, the Joint Chiefs, and Treasury could be courted bureaucratically in the give-and-take of clearances. Penultimate parleys could be attempted with key White House technical aides in bringing influence to bear on the President. Floating alliances were means of gaining leverage that could redound indirectly but ultimately to the benefit of the originator of a complicated ploy. Contacts with the forty or so former Foreign Service officers in the select fiefs of important committee staffs on Capitol Hill were useful, but a little risky. Depending on the nature of the crisis that arose, policy operators in the Department became automatically vested with power. Their number was estimated at between 30 and 300, the former realistically, the latter theoretically. In the entire Foreign Service, including ambassadors, the optimum number of policy operators to whom power organizationally accrued was calculated at perhaps 500 officers, the putative equivalent of army line generals.

Power struggles were waged below the top, executive, floor as lesser but ambitious officers maneuvered toward the seventh-floor elevators and had to remove rivals going in the same direction. Country directors, though still below the salt on the protocol chart, had a built-in advantage. Secretary Rusk liked to use a military simile: Country directors were company commanders, reporting to Assistant Secretaries, who were regimental commanders, reporting to the seventh-floor Under Secretaries, who were divisional commanders.

The place reeked with upmanship. The direct affront was veiled with a hearty smile. When a new idea was proposed, the antiphonal locution was "glad to be reminded of that." Witticisms flourished like weeds. A mild cyanide dosage was the observation that USIA's association with the Bureau of Educational and Cultural Affairs raised the prestige of overseas propaganda programs but depreciated the purity of overseas cultural programs. The interagency overlap regularly provoked similar infighting. A characteristic strategem was simultaneously to attack on the flank, to hide the imminent thorn between two roses, and plunge the argument *ad hominem* right into the jugular.

Real professionals never locked horns with superiors until they had so many facts on all shapes and sizes of Achilles' heels that they knew in advance they were going to win. Operators inevitably tended to shape policy, which was translated into power when the policy was put into effect. Analysts shied away from positive acts like that of making policy; they preferred the exercise of power negatively, like Philadelphia lawyers reading the fine print to obstruct, delay, or obfuscate rivals. There were silent flashes of the stiletto as old scores were paid off by losers in foreign policy battles. Apparent victors did not get to enjoy the spoils; expected promotions were blocked, sidetracked, or shifted to lesser posts by adroitly casual words dropped in the right places. Little Mafia cells protected its members, making it difficult to send old pals to undesirable posts when by rights the old pals should have been retired to pasture. As General Marshall once told Averell Harriman, his hardest job had been "busting old cronies."

Retired senior officers asserted that they loved the escape to "yeasty freedom," in George Ball's phrase. But they kept looking back with lingering glances and cocked ears, as if waiting for a halloo to return. Most former luminaries were careful in post-mortems not to offend the powers they left behind, hopefully insuring themselves for a resurrection in glory. Others burned their bridges and looked eagerly to the future. Roger Hilsman informed Thanat Khoman, Foreign Minister of Thailand, on a Bangkok stop during a world trip, that he was looking into the "foreign policy of the 1970's." Former officials from the State Department and the White House were gathering at the Institute of Politics in the John Fitzgerald Kennedy School of Government at Harvard University. The institution was described variously by Washington witlings as a "shadow government," as a bull pen of expert spit-ball pitchers, and as a rest home for intellectuals glazed with fatigue from their discoveries of political realities.

The best bureaucratic radar was sensitive enough to spot land mines, seismic tremors from afar, and the beating of a butterfly's wings, if it had any bearing on the job or the fate of a cherished program. When McGeorge Bundy was offered the presidency of the Ford Foundation in September 1966, immediately there was the beginning of a falling off of bureaucrats running to Bundy for a decision. Until Bundy left at the end of February 1967, bureaucrats scurried hither and yon trying to find the man who would make up their minds for them. Bundy's six-year accumulation of internal power unraveled under his eyes after the bureaucrats made the determination that the Bundy writ was running out.

Bureaucrats also mended fences and polished up the old image at times, like all good politicians. In early 1967, Henry Owen decided that he had better take a trip to Warsaw to look over the eastern European scene at first hand. The visit would help take some of the discoloration off his image, he said half-jocularly to friends. Owen, chairman of State's Policy Planning Council, had been one of the most ardent advocates of the MLF, or multilateral nuclear force, proposal, which President Johnson had interred.

The Department had its own North-South problem, in a minor way, similar to that of the world outside, with the developed nations of the Northern Hemisphere and the underdeveloped nations of the Southern Hemisphere. The Anglo-Saxons, as De Gaulle would say, behaved at times as if the Latins were a shade too vehement, hence uncouth.

Officers below the Mason-Dixon line of social acceptance tended to snap back that their occasional tormentors had 3.2 beer in their veins instead of blood. Some FSO's had long memories concerning colleagues who had crossed them. The longevity of carefully concealed motivations was reminiscent of a remark made to this writer in Rome years ago by an old widow of a White Russian general. She said: "As we Russians say, if you wait by the bank of the river long enough, you will see the body of your enemy floating by."

Nonetheless, such as it was—and it was much better than it looked—the U.S. Foreign Service corps drew the admiration of other foreign diplomatic bureaucracies. The British considered the State Department very efficient as an organization. The British were returning the compliment, since they were the model for many American Foreign Service officers. Until the advent of the red-brick university types, British diplomats were inclined to be somewhat stuffy, painstaking, thorough, and highly competent. The best were superb, though some nonpareils were rather insufferable in acknowledging their own excellence. The British made shrewd observations about the art: Diplomatic wisdom lay in reducing the impact of accidents of personality, idiosyncrasies of public figures, and irrelevancies of human frailty on relations between nations; they were bad enough to start with. Or, the British Foreign Service supported one political party at a time—the one in office. Old professionals learned to live with public pressures; younger ones were counseled to stay out of the limelight until they knew the score. Sir Patrick Dean, the British Ambassador to Washington, once advised a young officer to figure out what he and his duties must look like to the people who were looking at him. Sir Patrick calculated that this public aspect of the diplomat's work was 40 per cent of the job.

The British and American services had many points in common. The Foreign Office's total manpower in September 1966 was 6,389, almost half that of the State Department. Between 1952 and 1962, 59 per cent of new British diplomats came from Oxford University and 35 per cent from Cambridge University. New entrants were informed that everybody could aspire to the position of counselor or deputy chief of mission in the career, but not necessarily to that of ambassador, which was a special deal. The British also had the problem of placement for senior officers, compounded by the special national vice of "Buggin's turn," that is, jobs by seniority. When the authorities succeeded in persuading a past-his-peak senior to retire, there was trouble from the Treasury. The accountants did not like employees to retire before their normal pension dates; it upset budgets to have to pay retirement benefits to persons who could still work and earn their money. The British had a "minuting" system, analogous to the American "documentation." It was designed to show exactly how questions were dealt with. The "minutes" told who gave what advice to whom on what date and who took final action. Precise evidence was preserved for an inquiry if responsibility had to be fixed. In the State Department the exact facts in time sequence were sometimes buried beneath a mountain of other data when needed in a hurry.

The British Foreign Office likewise had expanded vastly in the course of the turbulent twentieth century. In 1914, when a British Empire still existed, the Foreign Office had only 150 career diplomats and operated H.M.'s diplomacy at an annual cost of one million pounds sterling. In the 1960's, there were 1,163 diplomats and the operation cost 31 million pounds. The British remodeled their Foreign Service as a formally established organization in 1943, on the example of the American Rogers Act. The Foreign Office and the Diplomatic Service had been separate entities until 1920. In February 1964, the Plowden Committee on Representational Services Overseas resulted in amalgamation of the Foreign Service and the Commonwealth Relations Service.

John E. Harr, a staff consultant to the Herter Committee's inquiry into "Personnel for the New Diplomacy" and a leading personnel expert in the State Department, observing the "very slow progress of the major recommendations of the Herter report," examined the results of the British counterpart, in the August 1967 *Foreign Service Journal*. Harr said, in part:

The Plowden Report was implemented almost in its entirety, and needed action was taken swiftly and decisively. Recommendations not susceptible by their nature to quick action appear to be well-established as policy guidance. There are several reasons for this overall success. One was the sponsorship. The Herter Committee was private in character while the Plowden Committee was appointed by the Prime Minister, which does not guarantee success, but certainly helps. The Report was accepted by the government and by all the political parties.

Partly because of the unified representation overseas, information work abroad is a major functional field for the Diplomatic Service, as is development assistance. The British have succeeded in making the commercial field a highly-respected, attractive function for their professional diplomats. It overshadows what we call economic work, which of course the British also do in connection with political analysis and development assistance. Trade promotion is clearly emphasized There has been an administrative effort to reward and legitimize the commercial function for the professional diplomat. It can be said that younger officers have the clear impression that they will not reach the top without having had a good stint of commercial work.

The French, the classic diplomatists of the modern world, also had a grudging respect for the State Department, though they were considerably more critical of individual officers. The French *Diplomatic Directory* listed approximately 1,800, of whom 170 FSO's were graduates of the notable Ecole d'Administration Nationale. An average of nine graduates from the ENA entered the Quai d'Orsay every year. The school trained aspirants for France's higher civil service. The first year was spent in the field, the second at the school, and the third in a private industrial or commercial company. Students chose careers only on the basis of their rankings in the final exams. The most prestigious positions were those of the Cours des Comptes, or inspectors of finance. French Foreign Minister Couve de Murville and Hervé Alphand, former Ambassador to the United States and secretary-general of the French Foreign Ministry, were both finance inspectors. In order of their rating, the next most important posts were those in the Conseil d'Etat, or high administrative council; the Foreign Ministry; as sous-préfet, or assistant governor of a department or province; and lastly, in the central administrations of the government ministries in Paris. For future diplomats, the invaluable part of the ENA was the education it imparted on the workings of the entire French Government. Interagency relationships of foreign policy to domestic interests were quickly made evident.

The French and the British had their problems, too, in recruitment especially, as did the U.S. State Department, all three a reflection of crises of change. In the American Foreign Service the feeling of crisis was one more aspect of the nation's other tribulations, domestic racial conflict and urban renewal, and foreign involvements, as in Vietnam. Senior officers had had their discreet and disillusioned say about the bleak future after a lifetime of service. Junior officers were now to be heard from. The juniors felt disgruntled at discovering the lack of opportunity for rewarding work after their sanguine enlistment. The primary fact remained, however: the junior officers were young. They had the will and the energy to look for constructive ways out of the apparent dead-end they seemed to have stumbled into. After endless talk among themselves, several false starts, and a series of polite confrontations with the top officials of the Department, the Foreign Service's young bloods provided the catalytic agent and the drive which were to spark the start of a quiet revolution in the Foreign Service and the State Department. Many of the youngsters had chosen the Foreign Service career under the inspiration of President Kennedy and the electric charge he sent through the youth of 1960. JFK was the idol of that generation. The youthful diplomats who enlisted under his banner might yet do the job that Kennedy personally failed to do in reshaping the Department of State and become President Kennedy's living memorial.

But as usual in the State Department, the full explanation went much farther back. Publication of *The Ugly American,* by William J. Lederer and Eugene L. Burdick, in 1958 had caused soul-searching about the image of the Foreign Service and the reality behind it, in contrast to the savage satire of the book, which was widely read. Deputy Under Secretary Loy Henderson so testified before the Rooney subcommittee. Harvard, Yale, and Princeton had dominated the new FSO entrants since the war. In 1959 new FSO's came from only twelve states and eighteen universities. Henderson tried to get a geographical spread of America into the service. In 1957 a high-level committee had already come to the conclusion that the Foreign Service needed a "massive transfusion of Main Street into [its] arteries."

By 1967 the junior officer crop was all-American. Young men and women from all fifty states had applied to take the written examination. Successful candidates came from forty-three states. The 218 new FSO's appointed during fiscal 1967 had attended 235 colleges and graduate schools in all parts of the country. More than half, or 121, had graduate degrees. Only twenty had not studied a foreign language. Those who had, knew a flock of exotic tongues, besides the standard ones. The Peace Corps veterans provided high-class candidates. Political science, history, and international relations still led the list of college studies. The Department increased its rate of annual intake to 300 a year in 1968. Classes in 1966 and 1967 were the largest in the history of the Foreign Service.

State's recruitment program had been spotty, but it was improving as senior officers temporarily "at liberty" were sent into the American hinterland to beat the bushes for talent. Compared with the major American corporations or the CIA, State's recruiting "drives" at the start were rather amateurish, mainly for lack of funds. Most of the new entrants' interest in the Foreign Service, moreover, had been self-inspired rather than stimulated by the Department. The selection process was uncoordinated, tardy, and loose in finding, testing, and hiring the best prospects available. The time span averaged ten months, causing a high rate of dropouts. Between an original expression of interest and eventual certification for appointment to the Foreign Service, there was a gap as big as the Atlantic Ocean. In 1965, for example, 10,430 youths made application to take the written entrance examination. Of these, 6,232 actually took the exam. Only 1,552 passed it. (The eight-hour written exam was not, however, as rigorous as those taken for the British and French services.) Only 819 were still interested enough to take the two-hour oral examination before a panel of officers. Only 407 passed the oral. In the end, 359 new FSO's were told they had jobs if they could pass the physical examination and a security investigation.

The new junior officers knew what they wanted. They understood the motivations of the hippies and the draft protesters, but thought, by and large, that it was a lot of waste motion. Like the underdeveloped countries, they were determined to be masters of their own destiny. They took the advice of seniors with insouciant deference, but strictly on a suspended-faith basis for a trial period of "Let's-give-it-a-whirl." They had known no Depression of the 1930's or wartime disciplines of the 1940's, but they were sharper, smarter, better educated than most earlier generations. They looked on the realities of a career with harder eyes and a certain cynicism about professed standards. They had overcome the pressures of the system of competitive grades prevalent at most high-grade colleges, and they were easily confident of their eventual success in federal competition.

Many would give the Foreign Service five years only, and then opt out, if necessary. They made no unconditional surrender to the caste ideals of the Foreign Service and a life of so-called dedication that the elders made such a thing of. This nonchalance of attitude caused some wagging among the graybeards. The reaction did not disturb the new officers because they knew that at their ages, from twenty-five to thirty, they had had many attractive offers from other sources. They believed that they had proven their own idealism by choosing the Foreign Service. They had joined the supposedly élite group because they felt they were élite themselves. They were ebullient, self-confident, and unapologetic. They were fast to pick up the lower-level politics of State Department corridor shuffle. The water-cooler message center quickly circulated the inside word of which jobs were the best, where promotions were faster, which jobs were "dogs," and how not to get stuck in essentially clerical functions with fancy titles. They did not propose to lie down on a bed of Procrustes and be cut down or stretched out to a pattern. They had a suspicion that their superiors did not quite understand the shape of power in the modern world, which the young officers believed themselves to know. They had youth's intellectual perfectionism of wanting to see a job done right the first time, and not in ex post facto patchwork. They were tolerant of dissent, but rough on the dissenter personally unless he could back up his arguments with integrity.

Surveys disclosed a spread of motivations for wishing to join the Foreign Service. In one class, 64 per cent wanted to be useful and effective in the world of today. Fifty per cent wanted to exercise leadership. Forty-four per cent saw themselves as rebellious, impetuous, and not particularly cooperative. Thirty-four per cent described themselves more as outgoing and talkative than as quiet Americans. The newcomers summed themselves up as both sophisticated and idealistic and less middle-brow than their predecessors. A good third were more attracted by the odds of winning high success than by prospects of a safe, moderate, and steady progress toward respectable but undistinguished niches of merit.

The young diplomats had humor, not an intrinsic trait of the old diplomacy. They laughed at themselves as well as at what struck them as out-of-date absurdities. Indicative of the unabashed candor of the new officers toward the Foreign Service and its processes was an article by Lars H. Hydle of Indiana, a Class of 1964 junior officer, published in the Department of Health, Education and Welfare's *American Education* and reprinted in the State Department's *News Letter,* in 1967. Hydle said, in part:

People become interested in the Foreign Service in many ways, and the story of my own involvement is not untypical (note the use of the double negative, a hallmark of American diplomacy). I became fascinated with politics and decided that rather than second-guessing the political decisions of world leaders, I wanted a hand in their making. . . .

Before my final approval, there was a stiff physical examination and a thorough background investigation. The best-known part of the background investigation is the "security check," designed to keep the Foreign Service free of crooks, cranks, Communists, and queers. Identification of the latter group involves searching questions to the applicant and his friends and acquaintances, and is inevitably funny from time to time. Rumor has it that an investigator asked one applicant whether he had ever wrestled with his college roommate, and, if so, whether he had enjoyed it.

Since the best defense is a good offense, evidence of heterosexual activity helps. Boasting, however, is unwise because one of the most valued virtues in the Foreign Service is discretion (ranking higher than a scarcer quality: chastity) and excesses of all kinds are regarded as lack of self-control.

In a general sense, the oral interview and the background investigation are intended to determine an applicant's "suitability" for the Foreign Service. Black Muslims, Klansmen, American Nazis, Communists, Minutemen, and extreme New Left members would probably fall by the wayside if they tried to get into the Foreign Service, but no one within swimming distance of the mainstream would be disqualified on ideological grounds alone.

Basically, the point is to find Foreign Service officers who are able and willing, personally and officially, to represent the United States. One might wonder, then, about differences of opinion. I know I did. At the Foreign Service Institute one of the most frequently asked questions was: "Isn't there room for dissent in the Foreign Service?"

Dissent, our mentors patiently explained to us, is encouraged under certain conditions and discouraged under others. While a policy is under formulation or review, independent and forcefully stated views are desirable, but after it has been established the dissenter must swallow his views and implement that policy, ask for a transfer, or resign.

Entry into active service brought its erosions soon enough for the young hopefuls of the mid-1960's. Resignations in Classes 8, 7, and 6, the junior ranks of the ladder, increased. There was considerable youthful despondency. Slow promotions, the absence of challenging jobs, organizational defects, and the impersonality of relations induced a smoldering resentment. The experience of other bright young men advancing much faster as management interns in other federal agencies provoked further frustration. The young officers were fed up with being overpraised and underutilized. Few junior officers ever got their own post overseas, as in the old days, where they might show what they could do, despite the hardships and loneliness. They sniffed at studies showing that the average time to arrive at Class 1 from Class 8 was twenty-seven years. There was dissatisfaction that the young officers were excluded from any influence or share in the making of foreign policy, the task which they thought they had signed up for. Bright but impatient officers resigned, almost all for better jobs. One joined the Bureau of the Budget. Another became an eminent Senator's aide. A third took a position with Health, Education and Welfare, where he had the responsibility of handling $6 million worth of grants a year. Others began to lose their saving grace of humor. What originally had been amusing crotchets in their superiors became galling irritations.

Professor Chris Argyris of Yale got a sackful of grievances reflecting the mood of the moment in separate and private interviews with junior officers. One said: "One thing people don't realize upstairs is the bind you feel with a dull job." Another said: "One thing too many of us learn early is that to make real changes you may have to be a wave maker and that's dangerous. It could harm your career. If someone is incompetent, he is not fired. He is given an assistant who will do most of the work."

Salaries were not a primary consideration. Many had taken cuts in pay to enter the Foreign Service and could have done far better financially in private industry. Starting salaries at $130 a week were not high; the bigger money would come later, if they lasted that long. The initial annual salaries for each class, as of the December 1967 federal pay raise, were as follows:

FSO-FSR		FSS		Civil Service	
Class 1	$24,944	Class 1	$16,616	GS–18	$25,990
Class 2	20,280	Class 2	13,507	GS–17	23,788
Class 3	16,616	Class 3	11,120	GS–16	20,982
Class 4	13,507	Class 4	9,267	GS–15	18,404
Class 5	11,120	Class 5	8,351	GS–14	15,841
Class 6	9,267	Class 6	7,524	GS–13	13,507
Class 7	7,816	Class 7	6,905	GS–12	11,461
Class 8	6,734	Class 8	6,125	GS–11	9,657
		Class 9	5,575	GS–10	8,821
		Class 10	4,995	GS–9	8,054
				GS–8	7,384
				GS–7	6,734
				GS–6	6,137
				GS–5	5,565
				GS–4	4,995
				GS–3	4,466
				GS–2	4,108
				GS–1	3,776

The situation, in brief, was depressingly familiar. In 1957 the *Foreign Service Journal* had commented: "Junior officers want to know that promotions when they do come will be real promotions in terms of responsibility." The situation, however, was also different. In 1965 a Junior Foreign Service Officers Club was organized. It won social prestige and attention by holding an annual Independence Day reception for junior diplomats from the hundred-odd foreign embassies in Washington, who themselves were left out in the cold for most social activities in town. The JFSOC climaxed its image-building activities by staging an International Junior Diplomats' Ball in the winter. It was a beginning of a respectable façade for politics. Subgroups organized themselves all over State, like cabals in the French Chamber of Deputies during the Fourth Republic. Discussions at lunch hours, in private homes, and in offices ranged over the whole spectrum of foreign policy, the future of the Foreign Service, and the inadequacies of the personnel system. The ferment took form in a memorandum of the club to Under Secretary Crockett on May 4, 1966, in which pointed questions were put and replies requested. The manifesto said, in part:

The Foreign Service must appeal to the excellent. To do this it must offer competitive salaries, responsible jobs, prestige, and the opportunity to develop one's talent. Many junior officers—by all indications a majority—believe that Foreign Service is presently deficient in all these respects.

We have sounded out a number of our colleagues and feel there are definite attitudes and concerns among Junior FSOs, as distinguished from the Foreign

Service as a whole, which have not been adequately brought to your attention.

It is our belief that a strong esprit de corps developed during the first few years of an FSO's career can be and often has been the decisive factor in holding outstanding individuals in the service. In contrast, however, a feeling of professional uneasiness and uncertainty now appears prevalent among Junior FSO's which, justified or not, tends to lower morale and create a climate for resignation.

Crockett responded with unprecedented speed, meeting four days later, on May 8, with the junior officers to "explore" their grievances. Many more meetings followed with Crockett; his successor, Idar Rimestad; Thomas J. Dunnigan, head of the junior officers career development program; and, in particular, Steeves, the Foreign Service's Director General, who had been an educator himself before World War II in India and, in fact, looked like a British brigadier of the old Empire. Some aides saw the juniors' campaign in typical bureaucratic light as a self-serving device to angle pay raises and cushy jobs for the leaders. There were cracks that "lieutenants do not make decisions" and that the juniors "did not know enough to participate in the making of foreign policy decisions." The responsible seniors, however, made no such misreading. They saw that it was not a case of temporary disgruntlement, but one basic to the future manpower intake or the atrophy of the service itself. Rimestad promised "increased responsibilities as early as possible, rapid recognition of proven capacities, rewarded by relatively rapid promotion." The Department started keeping its word. The rate of promotions for the bottom Class 8 had been 45.5 per cent in 1963, 36.8 per cent in 1964, 39 per cent in 1965. In 1966, promotions jumped to 51.6 per cent. The ironic footnote to 1966 was a hold-down on promotions for 1967 because of budget cuts.

Publication of the junior officers' memorandum, the opening of hitherto closed doors, a junior officers' workshop, with the brass there to hear the young men's ideas, all galvanized a reaction not quite anticipated by the senior Department officials. The embers of doubt were fanned into probing arguments all through the great institution. Midcareer officers took up the debate. In November 1966, six of them published in the *Foreign Service Journal* a letter they had sent to Director General Steeves. Its title was, "Are We Obsolete?" The six pointed out that the Foreign Service's functions were being increasingly narrowed by other agencies taking over operations of foreign affairs overseas. They raised the question of whether the Foreign Service would survive the next ten or fifteen years. They called for a revolutionary shift in focus: that the service take over the direction of foreign affairs throughout the Government, without regard to agency boundaries, rather than conduct foreign affairs in the old-fashioned way of mere diplomatic representation.

Simultaneously the juniors returned to the charge for a second assault on the bastions of authority. Promotions alone were not the morale pay-off they were looking for. Impassioned juniors and pragmatic mid-career officers alike believed that the standard diplomatic precepts of Nicolson, Cambon et Cie. had as much relevance to modern nuclear diplomacy as Euclidean geometry to plasma physics. The embattled officers wanted no more the role of the messenger to García. They wanted a piece of the action, much sooner than later, on the clearly understood basis of demonstrated talent.

Liberal-minded seniors began to rally to the cause of the new alliance. The seniors gave the juniors some sound advice: to avoid carping personalities; to resign if they could not stand the system; but if they really meant to improve it, to stick to their guns and improve the service from the inside. There was very little doubt that the junior leaders were among the cream of the nation's youth. They were fully alive to the movements of people and ideas in this country and abroad. As officers of the Department, they performed excellently, by and large. As youthful revolutionaries, they agitated energetically every moment of their spare time. They were touchingly eager to carry on the torch of the new generation of Americans that President Kennedy had so eloquently proclaimed in his inaugural address in 1961. The task was to discipline the power they felt in themselves, above all, to restrain the hotheads. In private sessions, indignant perfectionists demanded that the junior group denounce the rest of the Foreign Service as "supine" for not having fully supported Representative Wayne Hays's 1966 proposal for an integrated and wider-based Foreign Service. Enthusiastic militants demanded that the group's activities be christened "The Revolution." The junior officers, after all, were also budding bureaucrats. The name settled on was "The Movement."

Into the turbid scene in late 1966 walked a new and sizable group of young officers returning from their overseas assignments to Washington for the first time. Initial posts of junior officers kept them abroad anywhere from four to six years. The returnees had gone from training to their first jobs in the first weeks of the Kennedy administration in February 1961 with the words of Secretary Rusk ringing in their ears. Rusk had said, in part: "The State Department is entering a new phase of its existence. We are expected to take charge." The officers were dismayed to note the contrast between the New Frontier exhilaration on their departure and the moody restlessness on their return.

The young juniors, the "veteran" juniors, and the younger midcareer officers formally joined forces. All agreed that the hour had come for a public debate on reorganization of the foreign affairs community. All agreed that a good share of the difficulty in attempting to reshape the Foreign Service for its modern role lay in the Service's own traditions, which were categorized as more hollow than hallowed. In January 1967 the activists distributed fliers throughout the Department calling for a general meeting to discuss reforms. Over 100 jammed a ground-floor conference room normally seating from 30 to 40. Dozens volunteered to work on subcommittees and task forces. More and more Foreign Service officers at all grade levels started to take interest. Many, Class-4 officers, for example, were at the critical watershed stage in their own careers: they soon had to make up their minds whether to stick it out or quit. The Department's senior officials observed the situation quizzically, as "The Movement" began to gain momentum.

The amalgamated group launched a series of intensive studies aimed at working out constructively how the Foreign Service could assume in actual practice the over-all direction of the U.S. Government's foreign affairs. The officers fixed their sights on the SIG, or Senior Interdepartmental Group, which had the authority of NSAM 341 to take charge. But the SIG had no staff. Under Secretary Katzenbach in February 1967 asked the Rooney Subcommittee for seventeen positions to staff the SIG. The costs for the expert personnel would have been $225,179. But the total request for funds was $505,400, which Rooney spotted immediately. Katzenbach's arguments failed to impress the subcommittee.

The "Movement's" leaders concentrated on the issue of SIG manpower. The reform group wanted not only to be the ambassadors of the next decade, but more expressly, to have access to the power system which SIG represented. Analyses were ruthless. They estimated that 20 per cent of the Foreign Service as constituted was not worth its salt, that 20 per cent of the jobs were not worth their presumed importance. They arrived at the general objective that the best talent for foreign affairs inside the State Department and foreign affairs community should be clearly identified, regardless of rank or age, and placed into the most demanding jobs. The group's task forces on their own prepared six SIG personnel restructuring studies, which were six more than the State Department had come up with officially. The Department had had no funds to spend on SIG staffing and could waste no time officially on theoretical exercises. This did not deter the officers from attempting to pin down precisely how many officers a new SIG command system would need, the first time the task had even been essayed. It was estimated that about 5,000 officers in the entire U.S. Government were involved world-wide in the core of foreign affairs management. Of these, only 900 were State Department

Foreign Service officers. Another 1,000 FSO's aided the 900 one way or another. The remainder of the Foreign Service did specialized or traditional work.

As far as State was concerned, SIG would involve a staff of 225—200 in the country-director complex; 15 in staffing the lower-level Interdepartmental Regional Groups, or IRG's, headed by the geographical Assistant Secretaries; and 10 on the senior SIG staff. In the Government outside of State, the projected SIG command estimate was 2,025 officers—1,800 country directors and staffs in the other agencies, 125 in the IRG staffs, and 100 for the interagency share of the SIG staff, for a grand total of 2,250. Further screenings ranged between 400 and 1,800 for an over-all SIG total. The rough consensus settled at between 600 and 700 vital positions for the effective control of all foreign affairs within the huge federal bureaucracy.

Among the documents produced by the task force was *A New Concept in Foreign Affairs Management: Interdepartmental Program Direction.* It said, in part:

THE PROBLEM—It has become increasingly apparent that the Department of State is losing its role of leadership in the management of the country's foreign affairs. The State Department was last reorganized over twenty years ago at a time when the Foreign Service could handle the conduct of foreign relations. But the world and America's role in world affairs have changed radically since 1946 and the Foreign Service as now constituted is unable to meet the challenges and complexities of foreign affairs in the 1960s and 1970s. At many posts abroad, State is only marginally involved in other agency operations although these programs sometimes dwarf the Embassy's output in terms of manpower, money and impact. Foreign Service Officers are reluctant to accept limited tours of duty in other foreign affairs agencies because their achievements will be largely unrecognized by State and may even result in a permanent assignment to do what is considered a dead-end specialization.

As a result, State has proven itself unable to coordinate the legitimate interests of the other foreign affairs agencies. We have not been able to provide trained personnel for the management of many operational areas of foreign affairs, e.g., scientific, economic and technical fields. In addition, State is failing to attract and retain superior officers who would be challenged by broad substantive responsibilities in foreign affairs. All these factors contribute to State's battered image throughout government, foundations, industry and on the college campuses where the Foreign Service is recruited. State needs to create and direct a foreign affairs management system which will effectively assist the Department in exercising its perogatives as *primus inter pares* in the foreign affairs community.

THE OPPORTUNITY—NSAM 341 has given the Secretary of State an unprecedented degree of responsibility for the direction and coordination of foreign affairs. The SIG/IRG Country Director system provides a framework for State leadership. Some of the newer members of the foreign affairs community, e.g., Interior, HEW, are actively encouraging State to exercise decisive leadership.

The White House, the Congress and important private foreign affairs groups all support a take-charge attitude in State. But, NSAM 341 does not treat the vital personnel problem of adequately staffing the organization it creates.

Interest in foreign affairs personnel management is growing again in Washington after the moratorium following the defeat of the Hays Bill. The Civil Service Commission is toying with a plan which would effectively abolish the Foreign Service as we know it and replace it with a federal pool of foreign affairs executives. Senator Fulbright is considering a congressional inquiry into the Foreign Service patterned after the Plowden Commission in England. Various professional groups are studying the problem; and unless State prepares its own recommendations, the Department may well find itself again reorganized from the outside.

THE OPTIONS—If State is to reassert its leadership in foreign affairs, the Department has two basic options: either renovate the existing Foreign Service or create a new Foreign Affairs Management organ. An "in house" reform of the Foreign Service has several advantages: it can be done without extensive interagency consultation or legislation; it would attack the problems of foreign affairs management at the heart of the system—State's Foreign Service; State could serve as a testing-ground and example for similar reforms throughout the foreign affairs community.

Nevertheless, a reorganization limited to the personnel systems and practices of the Department of State will not, in and of itself, reinvigorate State's leadership in the foreign affairs community as a whole. Patchwork on the 1946 Foreign Service Act might succeed in improving the personnel and performance of the Foreign Service. But any "in house" reform of the existing system, no matter how successful it is in making the Foreign Service a happier and more efficient body, would not give the Department the necessary control of all the forces generated by the U.S. Government in its foreign relations activities. Only an agency-wide program of foreign affairs management will prepare State for the broadest possible leadership in the direction of foreign policy.

The energy that had been liberated by the underground explosions of the some 200 junior officers flowed into further meetings with the Department's officials. The authorities had been sympathetic, cordial, fatherly, brotherly, and avuncular. But a hint of the point of diminishing returns became apparent. There was a sense of invisible fingers drumming on the desk tops. A politely unvoiced question was in the back of officials' eyes: Just whom did the group of reformers actually represent? Where was their organized clout, their publicly recognized muscle?

The group got the message. They saw the need for obtaining a permanent core of influence ard continuity to campaign for their objectives when the group leaders had been scattered around the world in the course of their careers. The group took stock. The inner roster of committed activists numbered less than 100—some 50 juniors, 15 midcareers, and 25 seniors. The group had the blessing of none less than the senior career official of the Department, Deputy Under Secretary for Political Affairs Foy Kohler.

On July 3, 1967, the inside leaders—seven juniors, five midcareers, and six seniors—met for the first time, all together, at the same time in Conference Room 7519, down the hall from Secretary Rusk's office and across the hall from the Operations Center. The officers gave themselves a name: "The Group of Eighteen." The meeting was tense. A critical decision was at hand. The American Foreign Service Association, the professional organization of 7,500 active and retired Foreign Service officers, was about to hold its biennial election. The AFSA was long-established and eminently respectable. It was the outside power base the group was looking for. The decision was taken to attempt to capture the leadership of AFSA. The further decision was voted to conduct a blitz campaign, to go for broke, and flat out, before the old guard woke up to what was happening. The "Group of Eighteen" would run as a bloc. It aimed to take over or control the association's electoral college of eighteen, which elected the association's officers.

The "Eighteen" ran into a roadblock right at the start. About 200 candidates had been put up. The reform group had been able to fill four interim vacancies on the AFSA board of directors so as to be able to keep an eye on the machinery. It had posted ten candidates of its own for the election. It wanted to see the full list of candidates and put its other eight on the list. But efficient and alert as the group's officers were, they forgot that bureaucrats bumble sometimes outside as well as inside the shop. The list of candidates was not available ahead of time. The group asked to monitor the count as the ballots came in. This was acceded to. The problem still was how to get the other eight of the "Eighteen" into the election. The only way to get them on the ballot was by a write-in, since the 7,500 ballots had already been mailed out.

There followed what, all sides agreed in retrospect, was the most amazing remote-control election ever held by working officers of the Department of State in their private capacity. It looked like the Daley Chicago machine, the Pendergast steamroller, and the New Frontier network antiseptically rolled into one. There were some entirely new twists added. The "Group of Eighteen" had a campaign slogan: *"Un Peu de Zèle"* (a little zeal), a take-off on Talleyrand's injunction to his diplomatists: *"N'ayez pas de zèle"* (not too much zeal), and a back-flick at the overrestrained Foreign Service types the "Eighteen" deplored.

The group sent out 10,000 pieces of literature. It made three mailings of a campaign flier to all association members in the United States, that is, in the State Department, detached service posts, and the U.S. mission to the UN; and two mailings overseas to all embassies and consulates. It had "Group of Eighteen" agents in 115 posts overseas to drum up votes. The flier read:

Un Peu de Zèle

Are you satisfied that the American Foreign Association is all that it could be? Is it a full-fledged professional association in more than just name? Does it have an effective influence on major administrative decisions? Is its electoral college democratic? Can it be improved?

If you think it can and should be improved, you should consider the following:

Eighteen officers from State (16), AID (one) and USIA (one) have met together and agreed to seek improvement of the Association. They are asking that you elect them to the AFSA electoral college.

They all feel that:

1. The Association can and should function as an effective professional organization; it can and should speak up on matters affecting the professional interests of its membership; it can and should become the focal point of ideas and debate—and perhaps even a new vision of the future of the foreign affairs community.

2. The Association can and should protect and advance the well-being of its membership; it can and should expect to be heard before decisions of major importance in the areas of administration and personnel are made by the agencies of the foreign affairs community; its members should be able to bring their professional grievances and problems to the Association in the expectation of prompt and energetic assistance.

3. The Association can and should take the necessary steps to assure itself an effective and independent voice before the foreign affairs community, the Congress and the American public.

4. The Association can and should accord effective representation in its purposes and among its officials and committees to employees of AID and USIA; they can and should expect equal privileges and protection.

5. The Association, among other possible organizational improvements, should move promptly to establish effective two-way communications with posts abroad by organizing chapters in major missions and encouraging election of AFSA representatives at other posts.

What We Promise

If you elect the eighteen officers listed on the reverse side to the electoral college this summer, they will select the officers and Board of Directors of AFSA for the coming two years from among themselves—thus assuring you at least an approximately direct election as well as a coherent program and active leadership for your Association.

In addition, the group would hope that Ambassador Kohler, the present President of AFSA, would agree to continue his active and aggressive service in that position for another two years.

Do The Following Now

—If you are an active, voting member of AFSA (all dues-paying members who are FSO, FSR, FSCR or FSS) and you have not yet received your ballot, or if it has been lost or destroyed.

—If you have a ballot from the Association, but have not yet voted,

—If you are not a member of the Association, join and

Send in the ballot below, putting a check by each name (X)

Replacement Ballot

(Approved by the Association, if signed)

I hereby cast my vote for the following individuals who are listed on the formal AFSA ballot:

ELIOT, Theodore L.   WALKER, Lannon
McELHINEY, Thomas W.   WILE, Frank S.
DAWSON, Richard S., Jr.   WILLIAMSON, Larry C.
DRAPER, Morris   BASORA, Adrian A.
RUSHING, Charles E.   MICHAUD, Michael

I also cast my votes for the following individuals as "write-ins":

BROWN, L. Dean   BRAY, Charles W.
HABIB, Philip   BLACKBURN, Robert
CURRAN, Robert T.   KIRBY, Harmon
LENNON, Harry K.   NEWBERRY, Daniel

I certify that this is the only ballot I have submitted and that my formal AFSA ballot has been lost, destroyed or never received.

(signature)

Mail this ballot to:
The American Foreign Service Association
c/o Department of State, Washington, D. C.

As the first ballots came in, the group's representatives stood by, analyzed the voting pattern, tried to estimate where the unheard-from voters were, and spot-saturated likely areas of favorable voters. It sent out reports as the votes were tabulated each week. On the first count of July 11, 1967, the projection was that seven of the slate would win, against eleven for the opposition. The July 19 tabulation was reported as follows: "Approximately 12 per cent of the voters are sending in straight tickets for us. It is still too early to show the effect of our new replacement ballot and mailing campaign. As of now there are at least 4,000 ballots still out. WE CAN STILL REACH THOSE VOTERS." The next election data came on July 27: "Some 40 per cent were straight tickets for our slate. The percentage of straight tickets for us out of the grand total has thus risen to 20 per cent. A LITTLE ZEAL PAYS OFF." The August 7 comment: "Some 42 straight tickets for our slate from the latest sample. The total percentage of straight tickets for us has risen to 26 per cent."

It was all over—a month before the balloting officially closed on September 10, 1967. The "peu de zèle" campaign got out four times the usual vote. The "Group of Eighteen" had made a complete sweep of the electoral college by the greatest majorities in association history. The group placed friends in all the key offices. The formal changing of the guard took place at the annual business meeting on September 28, 1967. Two of the eighteen were in their twenties, eleven in their thirties, five in their forties.

Lannon Walker, an FSO-5, at thirty-one, became chairman of the board, the youngest and least senior in AFSA memory. In his official duties, Walker was a line officer of the Executive Secretariat, acting as liaison for the Middle East Bureau and the Secretary of State's office. As happens in the Foreign Service, on the day of the inauguration, Walker was on duty with Secretary Rusk in New York at the opening session of the United Nations General Assembly and missed his own installation. Walker was rated by his peers as the group's politician and organizer par excellence, a junior Jim Farley and Larry O'Brien, who made "The Movement" a success. He was a U.S. Army brat, a veteran of the U.S. Air Force, fluent in French, and an expert Arabic speaker. Despite his youth, he had been married thirteen years.

Indefatigable as a political detail man who mopped up the votes in overlooked precincts was Larry C. Williamson, an FSO-4 and staff assistant to Robert Bowie, counselor of the State Department. Williamson operated on the vacuum-cleaner methodology of Ray Bliss of Ohio, Republican National Committee chairman. If Walker, in a wild analogy, was the "Lenin" of the State Department "revolution," its "Trotsky" was an intense young man of twenty-nine, Adrian A. Basora, of Puerto Rican lineage and gifted with the Latin gift of articulateness. Basora was a pre-med student who intended to become a psychiatrist. In France as a third-year student from Fordham University, he became interested in foreign affairs by studying the differences among individuals and peoples. Basora had been the junior groups' principal propagandist and ideator on behalf of the twenty-six-year-old president of the Junior FSO Club, Anthony H. Wallace, in 1966. Wallace was assigned to Ecuador as his first post in 1967. Basora was getting ready in late 1967 to go to Rumania.

The ice pack in any event had been blasted. The goal of State Department supremacy over all U.S. foreign affairs was clear but distant. The job to be done was still to do: how to construct the saddle of command. In the meantime, there were chores. The "Eighteen" faced the politician's usual problem: putting the platform into practice. A start had been made in persuading the association to go on record before Congress in support of USIA's request for a career service. AFSA had testified in support of the National Federation of Professional Organizations on federal pay scales, pointing out that in 1966 industry had been paying 22.7 per cent higher than Government career service.

The now-dominant group's new motto was: "Ideas won't keep; something must be done about them." They planned to make certain that the voice of the association would be clearly and definitely heard on major public issues and in the right forums, a decided change of pace from the past. The *Foreign Service Journal* was to be spruced up and enlivened;

its past charm had been that of a faded love letter. Awards for creativity in the conduct of foreign affairs were established, as a result of the generosity of Averell Harriman and the estate of the late Ambassador William R. Rivkin. The new muscle began to be recognized; the State Department *News Letter* began printing more AFSA news.

Ideas still had to be marketed. Officers with the innate or trained capacity to make decisions had still to be found in adequate supply. Bureaucrats, as a matter of fact, loved real decision-makers. They took the load off their shoulders, the heat off their brows, the buck off their desks. Not every senior foreign affairs officer could get Bromley Smith on the National Security Council to hold their hands. Smith had played the silent and anonymous Father Joseph to a whole series of Cardinal Richelieus in the White House. He could counsel, but not perform. It was not his job. Desperate bureaucrats therefore fell back upon the theory of the "anticipated reaction." With a crystal ball and a ouija board and their own fears, they fretfully tried to figure out in advance what Mr. Big would or would not stand for. In so doing, they committed the most heinous sin in the White House book: they deprived the President of his options. The presence of true leaders of decision in the Foreign Service would help stop such nonsense.

At long last the U.S. Foreign Service appeared to be of one mind as to what was necessary and desirable. It was expressed with clarity and force in a statement of career principles on behalf of the Foreign Service Association by a representative cross-section of officers headed by Ambassador William Leonhart, a West Virginia child prodigy who had become a career minister and in late 1967 was special assistant to President Johnson for civilian activities in Vietnam. The ever-recurrent problem in any society, foreign affairs or other, was perpetually one of "revitalization," as Warren G. Bennis, professor of management at the Massachusetts Institute of Technology and a State Department consultant, said. Bennis quoted apropos Alfred North Whitehead's summation: "The art of free society consists first in the maintenance of the symbolic code, and secondly, in the fearlessness of revision. . . . Those societies which cannot combine reverence to their symbols with freedom of revision must ultimately decay." The Foreign Service had been warned.

So had the State Department; otherwise it faced stultification. But perhaps, with greater liberty of a political organism, it had taken some baby steps in the right direction. First and last, this had to do with placing top-flight officers in key places; regardless of age or rank. Marshall Green in Indonesia and Leonhart in the White House were only two examples. William H. Sullivan, now ambassador in Laos, had been a Class-3 officer at the Geneva conference on Laos in 1962. Averell Harriman wanted Sullivan as his principal assistant. Several Class-1 and Class-2 officers were senior to Sullivan, the Department pointed out. Harriman suggested that the seniors be sent home and that he would take Sullivan. He did. Sullivan thus jumped about 250 places in rank. Cavendish Cannon also was a Class-3 officer when he was sent to Yugoslavia in 1946 as Ambassador. That also raised an aroma. Cannon also jumped rank. Deputy Under Secretary for Administration Rimestad likewise vaulted about 100 places in the hierarchy from his previous post as administrative counselor at the Paris embassy.

The Department tried conscientiously to push officers of lesser grades into posts normally occupied by officers of higher grades in 1966 and 1967. Two FSO-6's had FSO-2 posts; seven FSO-6's had FSO-3 jobs; two FSO-7's were in FSO-3 slots; thirty-five FSO-6's and five FSO-7's held FSO-4 positions; sixty-eight FSO-6's and thirty FSO-7's filled FSO-5 titles. In late 1967, one of the "Group of Eighteen" high jumped sixty-five places. He was L. Dean Brown, named Ambassador to both Gambia and Senegal. Brown was forty-seven. A forty-six-year-old, Harrison M. Symmes, was named Ambassador to Jordan.

Matters were looking up for the younger men. But the State Department had never done what the United States Navy had done in picking Admiral Arleigh Burke to become Chief of Naval Operations during the Eisenhower regime over some forty senior officers. The United States Army had not been afraid to dig down deep for the best talent. General Westmoreland, commander in Saigon, was the thirteenth-ranking lieutenant general when he was promoted to full general and given the Vietnam command. General Harold K. Johnson, the current Chief of Staff of the Army, was junior to twelve four-star generals and to twenty-nine lieutenant generals when he was made a full general and Chief of Staff. But no veteran of the World War II generation had yet come to occupy the senior career post of Deputy Under Secretary of State. Nor had any officer with significant experience in an underdeveloped country, a principal arena of future diplomacy.

Yet the field of overseas operations was now on the threshold of dramatic change in the activities, status, and, above all, internal politics of the developing countries. Profound changes were stirring and erupting in the inner power structures of the new societies. The urban masses in such cities as Casablanca and Baghdad were undergoing a radical politicization. A quantum jump was clearly imperative on the part of the United States in the attitudes of officers, in methods, and especially in systematic and usable information.

CHAPTER XIII

INTELLIGENCE:
The Raw Material
of Diplomatists

IN THE NORMAL COURSE OF events, State Department officers first hear of a foreign policy happening by means of a message, that is, words on paper. Even when the item is transmitted verbally, the communication has been preceded or is followed by a written document. The notice or account of the foreign affairs event is information, defined as knowledge communicated or received, and for which the usual synonyms are data, facts, intelligence, or advice. The raw piece of knowledge had been lifted, torn, sliced, or extrapolated from the continuous flow of real living as it actually happened. Or it was discovered or realized later, the inert fact accumulating significance in relation to its continuum. The fresh datum was in process of modification or change even as it was emerging as a fact to be considered by the diplomatists. Like a tuft of grass, it carried its sod with it, its original context, when it came into the ken of the observer. The grass-fact, with its dirt-encrusted roots of origin, was the primary fact. Its uniqueness lay in its having transpired in a country of interest to United States foreign policy. But it is a native fact as seen by native eyes. Its importance to the United States, actual or potential, was always secondary, as far as the natives were concerned.

This native content of the original fact too frequently was homogenized, anesthetized, deodorized, or miscomprehended in the transmutation from the primary to the secondary stage. The same original fact normally underwent four or more alterations as it was put to use for intelligence, political, planning, or operational purposes. The fact became a datum of official U.S. intelligence through the inevitable play of the inherent teleological tendency to read purpose into fact. The intelligence evaluator attempted to fathom and organize its significance within a wide range of possibilities of interest to the United States, to uncover the intention of the creator or originator of the fact. The foreign policy operational officer assessed the same original fact in the light of immediate necessities in relation to stated policies and programs, a tighter framework than that of the evaluator.

The same fact received another spin from the high executive, up to the President himself, as he weighed its utility for transmission to the public for both domestic and foreign political motivations. The political effects would be different if the press was used as a release channel or a speech made directly to the citizenry over TV. The form affected the content. The same original fact, by now cloaked in a coat of many colors, was scrutinized by the planner as basis for future policies. These could be contingency plans based on available resources represented by the fact which had come into official, or recognized, existence.

Or the new fact could suggest long-range plans. What might have started out as a sand-smirched pebble of fact ended as a *mille-feuille,* a pastry of philosophy soaked in psychology and glazed by superfine coatings of cultural, political, military, economic accretions. Once the fact became an official fact, it was immediately subject to two basic reservations intellectually. As soon as it was fitted under the rubrics of an organization of society known as a government, it was possible that it would be squeezed into a less-than-lifesize framework, diminishing or discoloring its reality. And since governments were composed of men who, like all other men, were fallible, it was quite possible that the fact in question was not an integral datum, but partial, distorted, or peripheral. The State Department, therefore, as the Government's major consumer of foreign facts, more frequently than not did not have all the information ideally required or did not have it at the moment it was urgently needed. The built-in probability of not having perfect information at all times was the Department's constant occupational hazard.

But short of the perfection not seen on earth, the State Department was the recipient of an unbelievably vast amount of information. The ever-present problem was how to marshal it, how to find it when needed, and how to relay it to the right person at exactly the right time. In sum, handling information was basically the most important problem the State Department continually had to struggle with. Compared with the improvements in information receipt, storage, and retrieval devised by the Defense Department and the Central Intelligence Agency, the Department's record was rather sad, but with extenuating circumstances. State had neither the funds nor the flexibility of Defense or CIA. The budget cuts forced by the Vietnam war victimized the Department's information modernization plans. State's character was such that it would embark on no changes of a permanent nature unless it could be sure in advance that the changes would be wise and irreversible. Consequently, information technology in the State Department was marked by fits and starts.

The global involvement of the United States since World War II was the first cause of State's massive communications and information problem. Officers constantly complained of the enormous amount of paper work increasingly demanded by AID reports and Congressional committees. Imperatives of interagency clearance and joint operations further necessitated many extra cable copies for interested parties. Congressman Rooney recalled to Deputy Under Secretary Rimestad in the 1968 budget hearings that on January 31, 1963, the Department had made 83,646 copies of incoming messages. On January 27, 1967, the count of copies made was 97,468. Rimestad told Rooney: "One of our problems is that we are inundated with paper. It represents constant pressure on the posts and our people. We are asking them not to be so loquacious." He conceded that the Department had not been "too successful" in cutting either the length of the verbiage or the number of communications. In almost ten years the total cost of transmitting and handling information had quintupled. State's information costs rose from $2.7 million in 1959 to $12.5 million in 1968. The largest single segment of the budget went into one aspect or another of information handling: generating reports, transmitting them, processing and reproducing, distributing and delivering, storing and filing, and retrieving or getting the information out of the files. Coding was another special step, since 55 per cent of State's messages were classified.

The multiplier-confusion effect of the data explosion was downright staggering when sample figures were cited. Besides the Central Foreign Policy File, the Department had 150 other major file systems, several data banks, and a computer steadily being loaded. There were 32,000 file cabinets in 1966. The Central File grew by 400 drawers a year. Every day there were nearly 150,000 pieces of paper to file. In 1784, when John Jay started what were to become the Department of State's basic records, the files consisted of five ledgers: a journal of daily transactions, a book of foreign letters sent by the Secretary of State to U.S. representatives abroad, an American letter book of correspondence with foreign emissaries stationed in the United States, a book of reports to Congress, and a book of commissions for envoys and consuls serving overseas.

By 1967 there were over 10 million pieces of paper documents connected with passport work. In visa work, somewhat under 10 million pieces of paper were involved. In 1963 there were 93,000 memoranda of conversations, 199,000 personnel action forms, nearly 1.2 million office memoranda, the same number of reports from other agencies, and 1.3 million foreign publications received. These were all original documents. Unrecorded pouch mail was figured at over 16 million pieces. In 1963 also, there were over 36 million copies of telegrams made, and over 10 million copies of airgrams, or air-mail circulars. In fiscal 1965, over 210,000 cables were received and an average of 75 copies made of each, for a total of nearly 16 million. In calendar year 1966, incoming airgrams numbered 93,767, of which 74 copies were made of each, for a total of nearly 7 million. Here is an example of the distribution list of an AID telegram handled by State, showing the extra number of copies requested:

DEPARTMENT OF STATE

AID CABLE AND AIRGRAM ADDRESS SHEET FOR CIRCULAR MESSAGES

UNCLASSIFIED

Classification

Cable Room: Send to following as:

AIDTO CIRCULAR A 188

AIDTO Circular R	AIDTO Circular F	AIDTO Circular L
4 Abidjan	10 Bangkok	10 Asuncion
8 Accra	13 Djakarta	15 Bogota
7 Addis Ababa	10 Manila	17 Buenos Aires
5 Algiers	10 Phnom Penh	8 Caracas
6 Bamako	5 Rangoon	5 Georgetown
3 Bangui	10 Saigon	9 Guatemala
5 Belgrade	15 Seoul	8 Guatemala Tocap
6 Blantyre	8 Taipei	7 Kingston
6 Bonn	9 Tokyo	10 La Paz
3 Brazzaville	7 Vientiane	13 Lima
5 Conakry		10 Managua
3 Cotonou	AIDTO Circular N	7 Mexico City
5 Dakar		6 Montevideo
8 Dar Es Salaam	7 Amman	15 Panama City
3 Elisabethville	13 Ankara	12 Quito
3 Fort Lamy	10 Athens	10 Recife
3 Freetown	8 Cairo	20 Rio de Janeiro
6 Kampala	5 Damascus	9 San Jose
8 Khartoum	13 Kabul	8 San Salvador
3 Kigali	18 Karachi	14 Santiago
10 Lagos	8 Katmandu	10 Santo Domingo
8 Leopoldville	10 New Delhi	14 Tegucigalpa
8 Libreville	2 Nicosia	
6 Lome	7 Taiz	
5 London	10 Tehran	3 USUN New York
6 Lusaka	2 Tel Aviv	(airgrams only)
7 Mogadiscio		
10 Monrovia		
8 Nairobi		
3 Niamey		
3 Ouagadougou		
16 Paris USRO		
6 Paris MSN		
7 Rabat		
9 Tananarive		
10 Tripoli		
10 Tunis		
3 Usumsura		
4 Yaounde		

The State Department, in sum, had approximately 500 million documents in its files. Even Secretary Rusk and his three top seventh-floor colleagues did not escape the paper flood. The Executive Secretariat in 1966 received 19,378 staff studies, or over 50 a day. Almost all of these were divided among the four principal officers. In testimony before the Jackson committee Rusk stressed the fundamental importance of timely and adequate information. He said: "The ghost that haunts the policy officer, or haunts the man who makes the final decision, is the question as to whether, in fact, he has in mind all of the important elements that ought to bear upon his decision, or whether there is a missing piece that he is not aware of, that could have a decisive effect if it became known."

The highly capable but harassed men who ran the State Department had been aware of the immensity and complexity of the information management problem since 1960, when the first steps toward automation were initiated. What baffled outsiders was the slow pace. The Budget Bureau, in its normal role of the bureaucracy's management gadfly, spurred the Department to move faster. Feasibility studies were made in 1962. Computer tests followed. A program was devised in 1963. By 1964 the Bureau was able to call for bids from information management firms "for modernization of the flow and handling within and among [not only] the Department of State [but also] the Agency for International Development, the United States Information Agency, and the Arms Control and Disarmament Agency," in short, the core of the American foreign affairs community. The project was called FAIME (Foreign Affairs Information Management Effort). It cost $200,000, and it had a shoestring staff and a consultant from the CIA, which, since 1950, had been a Government pioneer in information techniques. The project FAIME breathed for one year, 1965, expired, but was never quite buried. It barely scratched the surface in its exploratory first stage.

A proper research and development effort would cost $5 million to start, and $16 million in five years. A complete new system would cost in the area of $100 million. A thorough revamping of the archaic information system would take ten years. In any event, the recondite FAIME reports were highly useful in exposing to public view a few more square inches of the State Department's exotic skin, revealing hidden beauty marks or blemishes. For one thing, the rapid turnover of events in foreign lands created demands for much more new information than had been regularly provided or even contemplated in the past. The new data needed were sociological and anthropological, above all.

Quantity control of the amount of paper depended in large measure on quality control of the content of paper. This in turn devolved around personalities and value judgments as to the validity of certain subjects. Frequently, there was too much reporting on economic statistics and not enough on biographical details of key figures. The nonstop pressures for putting out fires in the in-basket, that is, the incoming action cables, eventually impaired the effectiveness of officers or dulled their judgment. Too many papers were far too long, or not timely. Papers were difficult to find after being filed away. Striving for a common denominator among the four foreign affairs core agencies repeatedly surfaced the problem of partial duplication, overlap, or gaps in special needs like those of individual country desks or multilateral needs of International Organizations Affairs or Intelligence and Research, which required a wider spectrum of information than that requested by operating geographical offices. Information and intelligence contacts among the foreign affairs agencies on a chart looked more like a chicken's scratchings than properly dovetailed circles of ideal coordination. The simple but basic decision was never made as to how much information should be stored away, to be retrieved or whistled up as necessary, versus the amount and type of information needed under one's hand. The CIA had roughly set down its own rule of thumb: 10 per cent immediately available in hard copy, 30 per cent filed according to other systems, and 60 per cent stored away in a computer.

The FAIME study ratified the obvious, namely, that the foreign affairs community lagged in information technology. Past efforts to solve the information problem—there had been 172 previous studies by State and 167 by foreign aid agencies since 1946—had been piecemeal, peripheral, fragmentary. FAIME itself barely scratched the surface, even though it applied the systems analysis approach and stressed the fullest possible use of electronic equipment. The nature and magnitude of the problem, which was bound to take quantum jumps in the coming years of accelerated change, were at least beginning to be appreciated. Merely identifying real information needs of the future would necessitate inventing new approaches. The situation was not unlike that in U.S. astronautics, where space mathematicians of Bell-Comm advised NASA practical researchers of the existence of problems and their solutions, which the applied scientists did not even know had been thought of.

The Crockett-Barrett-inspired FAIME study, performed mainly by non-Foreign Service types, lifted the lid a fraction on the vast variety of sources which poured information into the State Department. Besides the standard spot reports from overseas posts, there was a Joint WEEKA, or weekly interagency political report, from diplomatic missions; the CERP, or current economic reporting program; and the DIRM, or Defense Intelligence Requirements Manual. The information management analysts were shrewd enough to note the fundamental premise that the information originally received altered by virtue of its use. One report said:

The projection of foreign policy information to the public is a more delicate and exacting task. The Department recognizes a responsibility to describe and interpret events and trends abroad to the American people, and to inform the public of the Government's foreign policy, its rationale, and implications. At the same time the Department acknowledges the constraints which operate in our political system against any Government agency which would attempt to engage in domestic propaganda activities, however helpful they might be to the Government's programs. The Bureau of Public Affairs and the Bureau of Congressional Relations are charged with the responsibility of informing the American people and their elected representatives on foreign affairs subjects fully, but with appropriate restraint and discretion.

The conclusion became evident that the Department's capacity to collect intelligence was outrunning its capacity to process, store, and use information. But like the bureaucrats they unavoidably were, the FAIME analysts proceeded to "solve" the problem on paper by stating that no major expansion of intelligence production was contemplated up to 1970, ignoring the torrent of facts the outside world was generating, like the Sorcerer's Apprentice trying to stop the flood of water. But where did one in point of fact stop? Fifteen per cent of the Department's personnel abroad already devoted its entire time to various kinds of situation and fact reporting. The report went on to say:

The need for information is infinite. Limits can be placed on its collection and dissemination only by the judgmental process of balancing the competing requirements for various kinds of information to fulfill various purposes against available resources and the non-informational activities competing for these resources. Certain kinds of information, such as the location of military installations in unfriendly countries is clearly essential to the national interest. Other data—some of which the U.S. Government is tempted to collect merely to round out a global picture, such as the order of battle for Costa Rica—can be placed at the low end of the scale of utility. The process of program analysis in the information field must place all requirements on this scale and must establish a demarcation line below which the allocation of resources is unwarranted.

The most interesting specific disclosures of FAIME transpired in a 1965 spot check of the document flow comparing the actual number of items in communications centers and the requirements of information actually needed in State, USIA, AID, and ACDA. Though many conclusions had been intuitively suspected, the results showed that much information provided was in fact superfluous and that much information required was in fact not being provided. They explained why busy action officers had to waste time plowing through stacks of paper to find the few but key items of information they needed at once. Old and routine data were mixed with new and vital information. In crises, there was no time to resort to the files; officers operated as best they could, a system which introduced risks of hit-or-miss "seat-of-the-pants" decisions on hasty or insufficient intelligence. The FAIME probe highlighted the crucial and vexing problem of determining precisely what should be the information requirements in relation to the various types of end-users who had to take official action based on the information provided. The spot check disclosed the following illustrative disparities between items actually in the information mill and items theoretically required but not supplied:

Subject	Communications Center Survey		Requirements Study	
	No. of Items	% of Total	No. of Items	% of Total
STATE DEPARTMENT				
Political Affairs & Relations	1,349	24	155	14.4
Defense	220	3.9	110	10.2
Economic Affairs	141	2.5	100	9.3
Science & Technology	98	1.7	51	4.7
International Organizations	85	1.5	73	6.8
Visas	43	.7	167	15.5
Health	31	.5	79	7.3
Public Relations	13	.2	21	2.0
AGENCY FOR INTERNATIONAL DEVELOPMENT				
Procurement & Contracting	824	20.5	114	9.5
Training	752	19	24	2.0
Personnel	553	14	14	1.2
Loans, Guarantees & Private Enterprise	543	13.5	248	20.0
Fiscal, Accounting & Audit	170	4.0	99	8.0
Food for Peace	110	3.0	133	11.0
Program Development	54	1.3	337	27.3
Budget	40	1.0	84	6.8
Legislative & Legal	3	.1	38	3.3
UNITED STATES INFORMATION AGENCY				
Press, Publications & Visuals (USIS)	256	16.0	168	16.6
Cultural Activities (USIS)	241	15.0	63	6.6
Personnel	226	14.0	5	0.5
Motion Pictures (USIS)	209	13.0	32	3.1
Information Activities (General)	176	11.0	366	35.9

Radio (USIS)	145	9.0	105	10.3
Travel & Transportation	91	6.0	4	0.4
Political Affairs & Relations	9	.5	25	2.5
Science & Technology	1	.1	37	3.7

ARMS CONTROL AND DISARMAMENT AGENCY

Relations	161	43.0	31	5.5
United Nations	54	14.5	22	3.8
Administration	35	9.5	70	12.3
Testing and Detection	30	8.0	29	5.1
Regulations	26	7.0	31	5.4
Atomic Energy, Peaceful Purpose	14	4.0	21	3.7
Eighteen Nation Disarmament Conf.	13	3.0	71	12.5
Economics	10	3.0	33	5.8
Conferences	9	2.0	35	6.1
Armament & Armed Forces	7	2.0	58	10.4
Research and Development	5	2.0	83	14.5
Inspection Surveillance & Verifications	3	1.0	23	4.0

The problem of information as the raw material of diplomacy was inextricably intertwined with that of communications. The 1,000-words-a minute influx of messages on State's new computerized communications network would shortly shoot up to be phenomenal speed of 2,400 words a minute, magnifying the gross amount of words to be handled and creating a new problem of information overload. Faster and faster communications made it all the more imperative that the information received and exchanged be precise and timely. The highly effective work of former Deputy Defense Secretary Cyrus Vance, as President Johnson's personal envoy during the Cyprus crisis in November 1967, was rendered feasible by the speed of a six-point communications network arranged among the Greeks in Athens, the Turks in Ankara, Archbishop Makarios in Nicosia, NATO in Brussels, the United Nations in New York, and the State Department in Washington. Vance and Ambassador Goldberg at the U.S. mission to the UN talked directly via a telecommunications screen viewed simultaneously by both thousands of miles apart. Goldberg was so fascinated by the gadget that he pecked out messages with his own fingers and waved all helpers out of the room while he conducted his top-secret conversations with his distant interlocutor.

The new speeds and greater than ever influx of cables predicated a new type of crack officer, an information controller, a sort of top-level message dispatcher, who had the background and the judgment to shunt the flow of messages to sidings and to send the express trains through. Not all ambassadors had the high good sense of the veteran envoy to Italy, G.

Frederick Reinhardt. Shortly before leaving that post after seven years on station, Reinhardt was thrown into the Greek crisis of December 1967, when young King Constantine fled to Rome after the fiasco of his so-called revolt against the military junta in his country. Reinhardt saw the King immediately after his arrival in the early hours of December 13. He filed a FLASH cable of about eight declarative sentences, giving the gist of the situation as described by the King, just enough to let President Johnson know what was up before LBJ went to bed after midnight the same morning. A fuller message with more details was sent in due course. In most crises, ambassadors usually cabled lengthy messages, which took much more time to write and relay, and, the Department complained, made "excessive" use of the FLASH and IMMEDIATE precedence designations.

The Department was caught between pressures from the outside and hesitations on the inside. The Federal Government was deep in modernizing its information technology. In 1951, the Government had one computer. In 1967, it owned or leased over 2,600 and hired 71,000 persons to run them. Social Security records, income tax returns, weather calculations, census findings, FBI reports, and NASA data were all computerized. The Government was spending more than $3 billion a year on automatic data-processing equipment. In 1964 then-U.S. Senator Hubert Humphrey and in 1966 Senator Edward M. Kennedy of Massachusetts proposed a national data bank for federal statistics. There was no central source of fiscal or budgetary data that the Congress, let alone cities and states, could turn to. In 1966 also, President Johnson urged all departments to use computers as much as possible in trying to do better jobs. Private industry had plunged far into computerized information. Nearly 40,000 computers in the United States were being used, for example, for airline reservations, gasoline company credit cards, warehouse inventories, interest charges, petroleum refining, market data, billing, and automatic manufacturing production lines.

The Institute for Applied Technology in the Commerce Department's National Bureau of Standards aided both Government and industry. Its *Automatic Indexing: A State of the Art Report,* by Mary Elizabeth Stevens, analyzed the latest arcane mysteries of cybernetics in search of a standard computer language. The Bureau of the Budget published a computer lexicon. The National Academy of Sciences held seminars in information technology in October 1967. Points of special interest to the State Department were brought out by an eminent behavioral scientist, Herbert A. Simon, professor of computer science and psychology at the Graduate School of Industrial Administration, Carnegie Institute of Technology, and chairman of the Behavioral Sciences Division of the National Research Council. Simon said, in part:

> Potentially, information has four broad classes: as a scorecard; to direct attention; to analyze a system's structure; and to ascertain parameters of its state. A single statistic may serve, at different times, in all four uses.
>
> Planners and policy makers tend to be most aware of their needs for data in the fourth category—for facts and figures they can use for projecting trends and designing actions. Their projections and plans depend critically, however, on how the system operates—on its structure—hence, on the use that fundamental researchers have previously made of information in the third category.
>
> Score cards are the direct links between professional activity and the political process. Some of the information can determine what problems should be at the top of society's agenda—and what it is worth economically or socially to solve them. The operation of the information system may have a great deal to do with whether first things are put first.

Though the attic and basement were stuffed with information and communications problems that needed a lot of sorting out in detail, the State Department found itself, instead, dealing with communications on the broadest possible scale as a result of President Johnson's August 1967 message to Congress on global communications policy. This dealt with the role the United States should play through COMSAT in the International Telecommunications Satellite Consortium, or INTELSAT. Under Secretary for Political Affairs Rostow was given the task of guiding a task force on communications policy, which would take practically half his entire time in 1968. State would have a major voice in world communications policy, but was not making much impact on its own analogous problems. State's reluctance to come to grips with onerous particulars in its own shop was understandable, if not excusable. Organizing itself for the age of information explosion that was coming closer every day would be arduous enough. Integrating the "core" foreign affairs agencies—AID, USIA, and ACDA—into the State information system would be a herculean task. The tie-ins with Defense, CIA, and Agriculture and their vast storehouses of data were impossible to conceive as yet. Problems of interagency security and sensitivity classifications were patent obstacles.

As a political lightning rod in all administrations, the State Department was acutely sensitive to domestic repercussions over any measure it might take in fashioning its information setup. Normally there were at least two types of information systems—intelligence systems and statistical systems. The former generated facts about individuals, the meat and drink of State's operating intelligence philosophy. The latter produced facts about groups or populations in the aggregate, generalizing indices, averages, and percentages, in brief, the backdrop of socioeconomic factors against which spot intelligence would have had to be considered. But already Congress had made self-righteous noises about the issue of personal privacy in debating the creation of a national data center, despite the fact that safeguards had been adequate as far as income tax and FBI records of individuals were concerned. Psychologically, the privacy issue was a contributory factor in making State shy off.

The Jackson committee had also looked askance at so-called computer foreign policy. The United Nations was interested in the computer's effect on human rights. The conservatives in the Foreign Service corps appeared to fear the computer, mostly because so few understood what it could do, or could not do. Under former Deputy Under Secretary Crockett, a State Department Center for International Systems Research had been organized. In November 1966 the CISR published *Occasional Papers,* No. 1, to give personal expression to "significant ideas by foreign affairs professionals," but in no way representing the official position of the Department of State. Issue No. 1 was "The Computer and Foreign Affairs," by Fisher Howe, an FSO-1. Issue No. 2 was the Argyris essay on the behavior of Foreign Service officers. There was no Issue No. 3. When Rimestad took Crockett's job, he abolished CISR and the "Occasional Papers." The Howe brochure had a certain educational impact upon the Department, in any event.

The spectacle of the Department of State facing the Crisis of the Computer had aspects that ranged from the pragmatic to the farcical. Secretary Rusk had made up his own mind long ago. On September 9, 1962, he and his top colleagues had witnessed a demonstration prepared by State's Division of Automated Data Processing by using the computer of the U.S. Air Force Statistical Services Division in the Pentagon. It was established that computers could store and retrieve foreign policy information. This was kid stuff, however, comparable to using a cannon to swat a fly. Information could be extracted from computers, that is, the information put in could be identified and made to come out in its substantially original but more concise form. But this was only a highly efficient file system; it gave no new answers.

The major point of computers was that they gave greater and greater dividends the more they were used to their capacity of stimulating the human intellect in order to provide new answers and not merely repeated information. Information that was arranged to provide answers was transposed to a higher plane of data. But to get data, the computer had to be programmed: rigorously careful alternatives and verified information had to be fed into it in a logically prescribed manner. Arranging material for even visual presentation, let alone computer use, necessitated rethinking of bromides, clichés, and old saws into clearly and finely articulated propositions. It took mental sweat and officers who possessed a high degree of the logical faculty in addition to acknowledged expertise in foreign affairs. The two did not always go together. The programmers were a type of editor; their selection of elements would rest on their judgments. Junior officers were eager to essay the task, but lacked the background. Senior officers had the experience, but did not relish the painstaking concentrated work. Possessing information was power in the bureaucracy, and the computer was almost a rampant symbol of power. The computer could never supplant the decision of a human being. But it was already inspiring a latent struggle for power between the directors and managers of foreign policy and the operators and programmers who would actually operate the computer. The question revolved around whose interest the computer was to work for.

There were other demurrers with regard to the computer. Senior operation officers reacted somewhat like old-fashioned housewives suspicious of a new-fashioned vacuum cleaner. The approach of many was that of a hunter circling the boar in the thicket: don't get too close—or one would have to meet the problem face to face. There was brilliantly argued negativism. At least the Department was gaining yardage out of the wordage. It was not a matter of a dream world where action officers sat at their desks and punched buttons on consoles to pick up random information as needed. It was a matter of practicalities. The State Department did the sensible thing: it began to use the computer as a tool to start fashioning an orderly pattern of control over its information. It concentrated on "massaging" its documents, that is, getting a surface report from them in returned information. The ADP division applied computer techniques to an increasing number of fields, starting with financial accounting and taking in visa and passport files, payrolls, disarmament figures and calculations, international travel statistics, Foreign Service Institute curricula listings, personnel records, and trade facts and factors. In the Kennedy Round negotiations, State went so far as to use the computer for analytical considerations, thus utilizing its higher capabilities.

Billing of sister foreign affairs agencies for State administrative support overseas was made far easier by the computer. Staffing patterns and manpower studies, research bibliographies, and swift updating of publications were child's play for the computer. The slowly but steadily increasing use of the computer allowed the Department to graduate from a second-generation IBM 1401 computer to the third-generation Model 40 of the IBM 360, though, as noted, the 360 was used more as a memory vault than as an electronic brain. Not enough computer professionals and foreign affairs experts in tandem had yet been found to subject themselves to the strict intellectual discipline that the computer demanded. The computer seemed to have its own way of dealing with amateurs. There was a "tilt" element that flashed a red light if some wiseacre tried to shortcut the rules.

But the computer continually amazed its State proprietors with its dispatch. It could read 1,000 punch cards a minute and print them on paper at the rate of 1,100 lines of 132 characters each per minute. It could read and write 120,000 characters from magnetic tape in one second and could flash through the index of 400 million possible characters in a few thousandths of a second. It could read the whole Bible and print it back in approximately twenty minutes. State's computer began to pay dividends in specific operations like visas and passports. The Boston and New York passport agencies and the Toronto consulate in Canada could tune directly into the computer in ten seconds to check records. Soon Mexico City would be able to do the same. The computer screened the 150,000-name visa file and the 250,000-name passport file in accurate "hits," that is, finding the exact names searched for, in two thirds of a second. A computer would shortly be installed in the Paris Embassy to service all U.S. embassies in Europe. The computer was finally taking the drudgery out of State's necessarily voluminous record-keeping.

As 1967 came to a close, virtue seemed to be finding its reward for State's computer adherents. It took a crisis, as ever, to shake the seventh floor into appreciation. The Middle East war, with its lightning moves and perilous uncertainties, had been a near-thing in possible U.S.-Soviet confrontation. U.S. short-run interests had escaped fairly unscathed. But State's executives knew that they had been just plain lucky. The Department might not find it so next time. There had been such a welter of messages pouring in from so many sources, it was sheer happy chance that no greater confusion had resulted. The Middle East brought home the lesson that a real start would have to be made, and soon, on a State information system. State, in short, could no longer afford not to utilize the computer's productive potential. FAIME was tentatively resurrected from its moribund state. The administrative echelon at last seriously pondered making information technology an official Department cause and fighting for budget funds. A request for $500 million and for a programming staff of fifteen was envisioned for the 1969 budget. A pilot system to handle 1.5 million original documents was devised as a demonstration project. State needed all the ammunition it could muster to get past Congressman Rooney and the House appropriations subcommittee. Too often in the past Rooney's withering scorn wilted State witnesses into stultification.

The one particular office in the State Department which clearly stood to benefit substantially from full and adequate use of the computer and automated data processing was the Bureau of Intelligence and Research. The Bureau was the largest in the Department. It employed 359 persons and spent $4.8 million a year. Some 150 professionals read and attempted to analyze approximately 100,000 documents a month. In fiscal 1965, the Bureau received 627,883 separate items and distributed 4,198,625, including copies. It received 327,786 items from U.S. Foreign Service posts overseas; 72,551 from the Central Intelligence Agency; 154,910 from the Department of Defense, including the Defense Intelligence Agency; and 3,657 from miscellaneous intelligence sources, while various State publications and letters included 68,324 items. The Bureau also created its own items or papers; in 1966, it produced 837 Intelligence Notes and 400 Research Memoranda. The Bureau was its own greatest end-user, taking 3,232,870 items and distributing 716,010 items to other offices in the Department; sending 192,051 to other intelligence agencies, including the CIA and DIA, and 57,694 to the Foreign Service posts.

Contact with State's pre-1961 Intelligence Bureau had been like paying a visit to the Kasbah in a demifurtive air of silken curtains and whispered banalities. The Department had formed a Secret Intelligence Bureau in 1916. State's intelligence traditions, in fact, went back to the Committee for Secret Correspondence in the Continental Congress of the American Revolution. The pre-World War II record for State Intelligence was spotty, if not worse. State inherited scores of OSS types from World War II. General Marshall brought over War Department associates in 1947 and tried to modernize the intelligence function. It remained for Roger Hilsman in 1961 to move the Bureau into the 1960's. Policy-oriented intelligence, instead of mulling over the portents for the future or the dead liturgy of the past, became the working principle.

A former West Pointer, a veteran of Burma guerrilla operations, impetuous, tempestuous, vehement, and decisive, Hilsman brought in fresh academic blood, stimulated new studies, and lifted the Bureau to an enhanced effectiveness. When Hilsman became Assistant Secretary for the Far East, his deputy, Thomas L. Hughes, succeeded him as Intelligence director. Hughes brought the Bureau to peak performance, though, compared with the CIA, State's G-2 was rated by White House quarters as only B-plus to A-minus. The White House view was inevitably colored by its being the seat of the National Security Council. The CIA had the legal mandate to brief the President and the NSC; hence, its interpretations inevitably tended to influence, if not dominate, White House intelligence considerations. In any event, there was no argument that both organizations possessed considerable intellectual candlepower. Hughes, a Minnesotan, had been a former political aide to Vice President Humphrey and a Rhodes Scholar. He had imbibed from the Oxford *ambiance* enough of the prevailing linguistic philosophy of Ludwig Wittgenstein to become an adept at slicing words with razor blades.

Like the Economics Bureau, the Intelligence Bureau had had the tag of "graveyard" in the Foreign Service officer corps in the previous era. Aspiring diplomats were counseled to avoid intelligence assignments at all costs. The Bureau had been considered too theoretical and academic, clouded by secrecy and obscurantism, impersonalized by group research, and removed from the actualities of day-to-day operations. But the exacting urgencies of modern diplomacy for speed and accuracy quickly changed the outmoded picture. In point of fact, the former Foreign Service boast that traditional diplomats were the most highly trained intelligence observers no longer fitted modern intelligence requirements, particularly in making subtle discriminations under the goad of deadlines. As a result, a residual mistrust of the Bureau by FSO's persisted. The line geographical bureaus still viewed the Intelligence Bureau with a bit of apprehension.

The Bureau provided "intelligence" to the operating bureaus, over and above that which the line offices received as information from the field embassies. The Vietnam expert, for instance, Deputy Assistant Secretary Philip Habib, read at least 150 cables a day to keep *au courant*. The geographical bureaus in early 1967 had started a weekly report of their own activities. An Assistant Secretary commented, "It lets us know what we have been doing all week." But no one officer or bureau could be expected to keep track of all details, plans, or ideas. The Intelligence Bureau served as a General Services Administration for information, a repository for total information, hence a backstopper for all officers. It was the "official memory" of the Department of State, since it possessed the greatest continuity concerning all incoming information. In the field of the unknown, it was the point man in delimiting the horizons of ignorance. It acted as an uninhibited projector of official policy consequences and as the Department's interpreter of meanings, tasks the operators had no time to get into, especially on such fine points as the differences between an enemy's actions and intentions, and what a foreign statesman said and what he really meant.

The Bureau was also a dealer in obituary futures, keeping an international death watch on every important political leader in the world. It kept a temperature chart and clinical summary on the health of powerful, aged, or politically sensitive personalties whose sudden demise could plunge nations or entire regions into a whirligig. The Bureau had a certain morbid fame for its high batting average concerning the extinction of top figures among the emerging nations, though its dossier on Ho Chi Minh

was rather incomplete. It gave perpetually low actuarial odds on the life
of King Hussein of Jordan because of a prognosis of possible bullet
poisoning.

By presidential designation, the Bureau was the Government's clearinghouse to approve or disapprove U.S. Government-sponsored research
projects in the field of foreign affairs. Over $35 million a year in federal
funds were spent on such studies, including a paltry $125,000 a year for
ten or twelve contracts by the State Department, compared with over $12
million by Defense and nearly $5 million by AID. In 1965 a Foreign
Area Research Coordination Council was formed. Twenty-one agencies
and departments, including the CIA, adopted an interagency treaty for
policing foreign research. By 1966, the Bureau had reviewed nearly 250
projects, 90 per cent of them classified, in order to protect academic
integrity and to prevent "improper" meddling into other nations' affairs.
The new arrangements came about from the fuss raised in 1965 over
Project Camelot, a U.S. Army-sponsored contract to study the conditions
of political instability, and counterinsurgency in Latin America, including
Chile.

The Bureau's External Research Office maintained close liaison with
the production of the academic community, listing speeches, seminars,
articles, and books that threw new light on the foreign scene. The External
Research staff of forty reviewed nearly 40,000 studies, completed or in
progress, from U.S. universities and study centers. The Office ran a
Documentation Center listing 4,500 documents in unpublished or not-yet
published manuscripts and doctoral theses on foreign affairs. Officers in
some twenty Government departments borrowed these files at the rate
of twenty a day in 1965. It was one more channel whereby the State
Department could learn about the views of scholars and profit by new
insights.

Alternately spurred by Hughes's mental agility and restrained from
crotchets by his donnish scepticism, the Intelligence Bureau developed
into a unique organization by traditional State Department standards. It
became a fire-alarm system, a DEW early warning screen, and a seismo-
graph to catch distant tremors, all for its prime function of the timely
alerting of the Department to coming events in the operational world.
The Bureau's basic charter forbade it to express opinions on official
policy, but directed it to make its own independent analysis of the world
situations. Secretary Rusk demanded that Bureau analyses list the alternative courses of action and forecast detailed consequences.

A critique of policy actually could be read between the lines, *verboten*
though it might be officially. The Intelligence Bureau was ironically somewhat in the same position as the CIA: it solemnly proclaimed that it had

nothing to do with making policy. It only provided the facts. Neither said anything concerning the basic premise of intellectual presentation: that the verbal arrangement and sequence of facts created the logical implications within whose frame policy would more or less be influenced.

Hughes had a highly articulate view of the dilemma of the analyst versus the operator. In urbane discourse before private audiences around the country, he seemed to express a wistful desire to be a "pre-policy participant, not a post-policy provider of gloss." He warned analysts not to carry relativism in foreign policy too far by giving "so large a spectrum of variables and choices" which "enables the policy maker to give free rein to what came naturally before—following the path of least resistance along well-worn paths of institutional preference and private intuition," bias armed rather than judgment informed. Hughes' elegant petulance concerning the perfection of the U.S. diplomatic process was no rarity in the senior reaches of the Department. The two-dimensional public façade of the high officials hid multifaceted personalities like Hughes, who evoked the figure of Methodism's John Wesley, in the cloak of a scholastic friar, but from beneath whose capuche at times peeped the wild gleam of a Dylan Thomas.

The Intelligence Bureau, in a unique sense, was the official depositary of the Department's voice of dissent, not that everybody else did not get into the hassle before the top decision-makers laid down the policy line. The Bureau's authorized dissent was vocal, sharp, but always inside the shop. Secretary Rusk noted that the great value of the Bureau's efforts centered in an imperceptible, day-by-day process of educating its Departmental interlocutors. The Bureau was rated faster and more effective than the CIA in making tactical spot interpretations in developing situations. This was possible because of its small size and tailored organization, compared with CIA's massive bureaucracy, and especially because it was much closer to the operating officers who used the Bureau's contributions. State's Bureau, for example, had only three or four experts dealing with internal South Vietnam affairs, whereas the CIA had over a hundred, topped by George Carver, considered the Government's leading authority on Vietnam. The Bureau also gave occasional advice on matters of State's public credibility in order to have statements presented in historically accurate relief, organically consistent with the record. Original errors, lapses, or misconstructions, even in minute proportions, could balloon to silly magnitudes by the time news items hit the mass media if facts were not presented in their correct context.

The No. 1 customer of the Intelligence Bureau was the Secretary of State. All Bureau communications were addressed to him, with copies usually sent everywhere else. Formerly, Bureau papers were addressed to the geographical bureaus, which, however, had the habit of sending them around as their own product, without copyright credit. The Bureau's free rein to dissent in its analyses and its immunity from control or dictation by the line policy makers placed upon the Intelligence Bureau the responsibility to be fully realistic, as logically sound as possible, and completely candid about the authoritativeness of its facts.

The Office of Current Intelligence Indications, with a staff of forty, was responsible for keeping up with the very latest last-minute news. Rotating teams gathered daily at 5 A.M. to cull the overnight traffic in cables, broadcasts, and press dispatches from all over the world, including the CIA and USIA files. The significant highlights were given to Hughes and his top aides at an 8 A.M. staff meeting. Hughes selected and refined the most crucial items and at 8:45 A.M. proceeded to brief Secretary Rusk for fifteen minutes. If Hughes was away, his deputy, George C. Denney, Jr., a Senate Foreign Relations Committee staff alumnus, briefed Rusk. At the same hour, David E. Mark, the Bureau's director for western Europe, briefed Under Secretary Katzenbach.

Hughes usually was the first visitor Rusk had. Rusk listened well, absorbed the briefing quickly. Katzenbach's briefings took longer, straying at times into by-ways as he asked more questions than Rusk did. The bureaucratic benefit of getting first crack at Rusk in the mornings gave the Bureau a clear and unimpeded opportunity to alert the Secretary to events and nuances which the country desk officers customarily had not yet had a chance to learn about. The Bureau's independent line of communications with Rusk helped prevent cobwebs and kept the Department on its toes. It gave Rusk the advantage of being a step or more ahead of the policy operators when they brought their problems to him and also armed him for those sudden calls from the President, the Secretary of Defense, the press, and Congressmen.

If necessary because of new and sensitive intelligence, Hughes saw Rusk more than once a day. Marketing the Bureau's product to the right officers at the right time was consistently the Bureau's toughest task. Normally the papers went forward through prescribed channels. Sometimes a top Intelligence specialist might feel that there were some new points that should be placed at once in Rusk's mental armory. Recourse was then had to out-of-channel bureaucratic politics: knowing the right people who would see to it that the new assessment was placed in the Secretary's in-basket. The coincidence of an Intelligence interpretative being fed to the proper person at exactly the most auspicious time was a matter more haphazard than systematic, however. The result was that decisions were sometimes made under the pressure of time with imperfect information when more complete information was physically available.

Though Bureau area directors regularly briefed the geographical assistant secretaries and attended their staff meetings, the line operators still tended to resent and to resist the Intelligence Bureau's apparent invasion of operating prerogatives by the hard sell of Intelligence interpretations.

In its widest role, the Bureau collected, processed, arranged, varnished, packaged, and presented information, shaping and evaluating it into a pattern if possible. In the process, the information became intelligence. The Bureau's 130 or 140 career analysts, after reading interminable reports, vetted, or screened, the material for essentiality and nuance. The analysts, in fact, were among the very few officers in the Department who could be counted on to read and reflect. The operators were too busy operating.

The Bureau produced two special kinds of items. The first was Intelligence Notes, two- or three-page quickies, double-spaced, on hot news of the moment, or of tomorrow. The second was Research Memoranda, ten to thirty pages long, deeply considered, the highly finished end-products upon whose quality the Bureau rested its reputation for insight and foresight. The Bureau owned no exclusive material, but used everybody else's data. So, more or less, did the other intelligence agencies. Conclusions, however, could be, and were, often different, according to individual viewpoints and the common sense of one's chromosomes. Country desk officers used the Intelligence Notes, especially those relating to Communist activities, as field guidance to embassies abroad. The Notes were in the nature of encapsulated wisdom, a corporate synergism of three or four analysts.

The Research Memoranda contained long thoughts on accurate reconstruction of the immediate past and appraisals in verisimilitude of the immediate or intermediate future, both of patent relevance to the policy operator. The memos were planned and timed to be read just ahead of an imminent decision on policy, as were the notes, for that matter. The memos were long-range looks, hopefully of permanent value; the notes, obviously perishable because of the time element. The stress was always on context and close policy relevance, and if possible a step beyond the conventional wisdom, turning the policy coat inside out, as it were. The aim was to debunk inaccurate information and clarify distorted interpretations; to shrink down to life-size any alarmist implications of sudden events, but at the same time to warn the operating desks concerning the open and the hidden risks and implications in actual or projected actions. An Intelligence Note on Rusk's desk was usually the first considered paper in the Department to outline the significance of a major development that would be the subject of continuing decisions. The Intelligence papers therefore had an indirect but real impact on policy. If a line bureau's stand was x and the Intelligence Bureau's position y, the final decision might be z, reflecting the intelligence factor.

In one two-week period in January 1967, the Intelligence Notes covered subjects as various as the Greek Government crisis, the Nigerian civil war, Malta difficulties, Czechoslovakia on the Vietnam issue, West German Chancellor Kiesinger's views, Goa and India, Soviet-Polish visits, Katanga and the Union Minière, protocol implications at a Rio de Janeiro conference, the harsher Soviet line on Cuba's Castro, Japanese trade with North Vietnam, Peking and Thailand, Nicaraguan elections, Syria and Israel, President Frei and Chile, Kashmir, and Tanzania. These were aimed at the country directors handling relations with their respective areas. In the same period, Research Memoranda covered subjects like Yemen tribal lines, the second phase of the Argentine revolution, Swedish politics, Indian elections, Communists in Uruguayan labor unions, the Sino-Soviet conflict, Britain and the Common Market, Rhodesia, and the Dominican Republic.

Intelligence papers were produced on request, but also self-originated when the Bureau determined that extra analysis was needed. The Bureau consciously strove for diversity and objectivity at the same time. It desired to obtain a name for unpredictability so that its views would not be taken as fixed and "the same old stuff." The precise objective was to strike a net balance between the sensationally actual and the historically pertinent in a free market place of ideas, though never so far, of course, as to become a theatrical devil's advocate.

With the Far East and Europe, particularly De Gaulle and Russia, getting the headlines and the priorities in the Department, the African and Latin American offices in the Intelligence Bureau suffered from the handicaps of their analogous geographical bureaus. Both areas were considered of parochial operational interest, though the former head of the African office, Robert C. Good, was rated so high that he was made Ambassador to Zambia in 1965. The African office, nevertheless, had important regions under surveillance—Algeria, Libya, the Congo, Angola, Rhodesia, Tanzania, Nigeria, Ethiopia, Somaliland, and, always, South Africa. The continent of Africa was still the heart of the underdeveloped world. The thankless grind of keeping careful watch was bound to pay off sooner than later, since Africa indisputably was the future site of rivalry among Russians, Chinese, and Americans.

Latin America, much more critical to United States interests than Africa, was still only a peripheral matter in the global struggle. This was an obvious drawback in obtaining top-level attention for intelligence analysis, unless something spectacular occurred, like the death of Ernesto

"Che" Guevara in Bolivia in late 1967. But the Bureau still maintained a constant check on Communist-supported subversive activities in Venezuela, Colombia, Bolivia, and Guatemala.

Cuba had top priority, though in rather low silhouette. The less said about Castro the better as he floundered in Cuba's growing economic morass. A tip-off on Castro's sense of ineffectuality was his bitter complaint to a Western ambassador that he had been helpless at the time of the Dominican crisis because he could not send troops in safety to help the rebels. The Russians had sold him out by removing the missiles with which he could have neutralized the United States. The conversation in due course was reported to the Bureau.

The major work of the Bureau's Latin American office was the collation of information, particularly articles in the Communist press. These showed a growing split between Cuba and the Soviet Union, and an anti-Castro position in many Latin American Communist parties, including the important ones in Mexico, Bolivia, Colombia, and Venezuela. The leftists fell apart over "correct" revolutionary tactics and the timing of guerrilla activity.

Though it did not receive full seventh-floor attention—the Secretary spent 80 per cent of his time on Vietnam—the Latin American intelligence picture was of high professional importance because intelligence itself provoked the 1962 Cuban crisis, that is, the discovery of the missile sites. In 1961, at the time of the Bay of Pigs disaster, the precise cause of the misadventure had been shifted to the military debacle from the original cause, the political intelligence miscalculation. There had been the assumption that the people of Cuba would rise up against Castro when they heard that an invasion of the exiles was under way. The projected assault had been far too small to overturn Castro without active popular support, which was the original intelligence prediction. The question of a people's uprising in Havana was discussed with Allen Dulles, former Director of CIA, by this writer in January 1961. Dulles did not then believe that such an uprising would take place. Nothing changed in the situation between January and April. It later transpired that the Communist secret police control over the population had been even stronger than realized. Thus, the basic intelligence justification for the affair was lacking from start to finish.

A Bureau area office which frequently skirted delicate situations with the policy operators was that for western Europe, headed by David Mark. Officers of the European Affairs Bureau, packed with classic diplomats, at times felt that, as John Kennedy told Richard Nixon in 1960, they needed "no instruction" from the Intelligence Bureau in their own speciality. Differences of judgment between analysts and operators cropped up from time to time regarding Germany, France, Italy, and, above all, Britain.

In the Intelligence view, for example, operators were oversanguine in expecting West Germany perpetually to follow the American line contrary to its own vital interests in preserving the Franco-German *rapprochement* created by the late Konrad Adenauer. The operators persisted in their view despite cables to the contrary from U.S. Ambassador George McGhee in Bonn that West German Chancellor Kiesinger would stick to his alliance with De Gaulle at the expense of America, an interpretation supported by the Intelligence Bureau. As it turned out, McGhee's shrewd determination proved accurate, despite his occasional reputation as a benzedrined bull in the china shop.

The Intelligence Bureau's flexibility of approach also led into warmish waters on the issue of Charles De Gaulle, who was virtually Public Enemy No. 1 as far as most of the European Bureau was concerned. Its failure to hang De Gaulle in effigy also drew suspicious looks at times from White House circles, but not from the President, whose own deliberate posture toward De Gaulle was one of resigned martyrdom. The Intelligence Bureau naturally was quite concerned over what would happen to France after De Gaulle died or relinquished power. But only seventy-seven in November 1967, De Gaulle, it seemed, would live forever.

The Bureau collected, among its various avocations, jokes about world personalities. De Gaulle's proposed rivalry with Methuselah recalled the story of a visit by the French President to the Paris zoo, where he inspected some rare tortoises. He asked about their ages. Several had an average age of 175, one was 200 years old, and another 250. Whereupon De Gaulle said plaintively, "That's the trouble with pets. As soon as you become attached to them, they go and die on you." De Gaulle not infrequently spoke with Delphic irony of his eventual passage to Valhalla, which prompted another story. De Gaulle asked his aides to find a suitable burial place. The first suggestion was the Invalides, Napoleon's tomb. "What? Me, a marshal of France next to a corporal?" De Gaulle cried. The next idea was the Arc de Triomphe, where France's Unknown Soldier lay. "What? Me, the President of the republic next to a nobody?" Finally Rouen, where Joan of Arc was burned at the stake, was proposed. "Ah bon," said De Gaulle. "The old girl deserves a break." But the next day, De Gaulle changed his mind and asked that diplomatic arrangements be made for his burial in the Holy Sepulcher in Jerusalem. The asking price for the privilege was $1 million, in gold. "Too much," said De Gaulle, "I'll only be there three days."

The serious concern of the Intelligence staff was the emergence of a

Communist-dominated Popular Front in France after De Gaulle. The French Communists won 23 per cent of the vote in the 1967 elections, and they had gained 31 per cent in popular support since 1961 during De Gaulle's reign. A similar preoccupation applied to Italy, where Communist gains amounted to 25 per cent since 1961.

The public theatrics over De Gaulle notwithstanding, the French and U.S. intelligence systems quietly exchanged a certain amount of information. But for Britain the so-called special relationship applied particularly in intelligence matters. The British and the Americans had a gentlemen's agreement not to pry or spy on each other. The State Department habitually informed the British Embassy of almost anything it wanted to know. Though it was fully acknowledged that fundamental principles of administration and staff work decreed that those who made policy should not assess intelligence, the British Foreign Office, the creator of policy, also controlled the British intelligence services because of a virtual veto on intelligence interpretation.

State's Intelligence watchers on Britain consistently warned State's operators that Britain would not be able to support defense forces East of Suez, despite that country's announced intention to do so and the United States' earnest desire that it be done. Before he resigned in 1966, former Under Secretary George Ball with prescience argued for canceling East of Suez plans with Britain in the hope of reducing the special British relationship and conserving British resources for entry into the European Common Market. President Johnson declined to entertain Ball's proposal because the United States needed whatever power Britain could muster in the Far East on the flanks of Vietnam and Communist China. The November 1967 devaluation of the British pound sterling only reconfirmed the Intelligence Bureau's analysis. Though the British promised they would retain forces East of Suez until 1971, the Bureau cited the fact that the British would have to reduce expenses drastically to meet their obligations under the new value of the pound. Reductions would come either in defense spending or in welfare spending. If domestic politics dictated budget slashes in Britain, as it did in other countries, it was evident to the analysts that defense costs would get the ax before welfare costs did. Hence, a further slicing down in the East of Suez British commitment was to be expected, throwing that much of an added burden on the strained resources of the United States in the strategic area between the Middle East and the Far East.

The feel of State Department intelligence about the Middle East, more specifically the Arab Middle East, appeared to be rather ambivalent and ambiguous, as far as one could infer. Middle East intelligence sounded like a multiple personality. Facts seemed to be adequate enough as far as they went, but they did not go far enough. American analysts had long developed a feel for European situations, despite uncertainties and unknowables. They had developed remarkably concerning the Russians, despite the closed Communist society. They were even developing a feel for the Chinese. But U.S. analysts, by and large, and with some notable exceptions, showed little feel for Arabic algebra, which the Arabs invented.

The absence of a clear, conceptual framework of the Arab world multiplied the odds for error in assessing the relationship of Israel to the Arabs, and those of other powers, like the Russians, who intervened in affairs of the region. A series of circumstances obstructed understanding. A state of latent tension, more implicit than explicit, existed between the State Department and the White House because of the explosive potentialities of Israel as an issue in domestic politics. Partisans of Israel—and most Americans were sympathetic to Israel as the underdog—regularly blasted the State Department as anti-Israel and pro-Arab. The Arabists, that is, the Arab specialists, were relatively powerless, if the critics only knew. But resentful of what they considered unjust attacks, the Arabists in defense hinted that a "Zionist lobby" was confusing fact and fiction, hence making it more difficult to sort out the essentials vital to the U.S. national interest. If nothing else, this political overhang appeared to be a definite inhibiting factor in analyzing the entire spectrum of Middle East facts and factors. No great windfalls issued from U.S. embassies in the Middle East, which at best were held at arm's length, somewhat as the Communist nations used to treat Western diplomats during the Cold War.

Several reasons helped account for the incomplete state of U.S. official intelligence about the Middle East. Few of the dignitaries on the top levels of the Government knew much about the Middle East, understood it, or had the time to focus on it, given the demands posed by Vietnam, Russia, and China. There appeared to be considerably more information available in private hands—universities, foundations, business corporations—than in those of Government agencies, including the State Department. But there was a gap, a lag, a missing connection somewhere in translating the accumulation of facts into data usable by foreign affairs operating officers. As William R. Polk, a former State policy planner, Arab expert, and director of the Adlai Stevenson Institute of International Affairs in Chicago, once remarked to this writer: "In the case of most of the observers of the Middle East, there is no matrix into which to fit all the pieces, and however much information one acquires, it all remains in a state of impression, hunch, or confusion."

The precise lack was precise political information. This depended on an accurate and realistic specification of the social forces involved, for what objectives, and how the combination translated into political groupings and, ultimately, into the governing power complexes that ran the Arab states. This original feel of native political motivations apparently was escaping apprehension by too many U.S. diplomats. The mathematics of putting it together looked simple enough on the surface, but internally it ran on the Arabs' own organic and unique modes of calculation, which to most Americans were irrational, emotional, and baffling. In Western eyes, facts could run from a to b, but not necessarily in Arab eyes; a might go to b by way of z. Indicative of the honest puzzlement of Americans in confronting Arab attitudes was Secretary Rusk's question at a staff meeting: "But why does Nasser think we're trying to do him in?"

In essence, the key foreign affairs agencies—State, Defense, and CIA—were inclined to look on the Middle East as a checkerboard on which Russia and America marched their pieces up and down—without quite appreciating that the checkerboard might have a life of its own. The detailed power facts, but not necessarily their roots, arrived in State from the CIA, the U.S. Sixth Fleet in the Mediterranean, the Defense Department's military attachés, and State's political officers in those U.S. embassies that were still allowed to function. These, in January 1968, were in Lebanon, Kuwait, Jordan, and Saudi Arabia. Missions still closed were in Yemen, Iraq, Syria, and Egypt, though a "ghost" team of U.S. diplomats functioned in Cairo.

On one item there was no intelligence dispute whatsoever: The Soviet Union had thoroughly established itself in the Mediterranean and the Middle East as a result of the Arab-Israeli war, despite the huge Soviet armament losses to the victorious Israeli. Even the billion-dollar cost was assessed as tolerable for the Russians in light of their strategic gains. The Russian fleet in the Mediterranean, the Arab open sesame for Soviet economic penetration and technical partnership, and the new access to levers of power were all factors that would have to be continuously weighed in U.S. intelligence evaluations of the future.

What the Russians were up to everywhere—the Middle East, the Far East, Africa, Latin America, southeast Asia, Europe, and, above all, the Soviet Union itself—was under the unblinking scrutiny of the Soviet bloc office in the Intelligence Bureau. Its director was Helmut Sonnenfeldt, a German-born Foreign Service Reserve officer, Class 1. His State associates rated him as one of the very best Soviet affairs career analysts in the trade, including the CIA. The hallmark of the State Soviet intelligence specialists was operational relevance, that is, what a Russian move meant in terms of short- and intermediate-range realities. The key lay in the Soviet Communists' own operating principles. These had been based consistently on tactical flexibility as pronounced by Lenin in his *Left-Wing Communism—An Infantile Disorder*. The Communist party pattern remained rigid and uniform, but the working style differed with targets of opportunity and the "objective realities," which jargon phrase of Marxist dialectics meant, strangely enough, the facts that had to be dealt with if one were to transform them hopefully into Communist assets. The Intelligence Bureau and diplomats dealing with Soviet affairs thus had to discern the internal logic of apparently tortuous Communist moves and couple them with appraisals of Soviet nationalistic self-interest in order to come up with acceptable working hypotheses.

State's Soviet intelligence office, however, had no monopoly on interpretations of Russian actions, trends, or situations, either in the Department or in the Government, or, for that matter, in the nation. The Soviet Union country desk made operational studies of Russian issues, but called them "analyses" instead of "intelligence briefs." A series of outstanding ambassadors—George F. Kennan, Charles E. Bohlen, Llewellyn E. Thompson, Foy D. Kohler—became famous as diplomatic soothsayers on Russia. Kennan was classed as an idealogue, verging on the mystical. Bohlen, Thompson, and Kohler were classified as operators, each with his own style. Bohlen had an uncanny ability to sense the practical turn of events in Soviet affairs through nearly forty years of constant involvement. But, as happens to the best of men, Bohlen had occasional off-days, as when he reported in 1957 that the anti-party group to Khrushchev was solidly entrenched—just before Khrushchev succeeded in breaking it up. Thompson, a meditative type, sensed the flow of Russian events with an instinctive approach, compared with Bohlen's rapier-like thrusts to the heart of the matter. He was the Western diplomat closest to Khrushchev, who had been taken with the American Ambassador's nineteenth-century gentility and integrity. Thompson's association with Khrushchev proved invaluable for psychological insights into the Soviet chieftain. But it also backfired in obscuring the signs which foreshadowed that Khrushchev was riding for a fall in 1964, when he was summarily overthrown. The tip-off had been in Khrushchev's difficulties with his designated successor, the late Frol Kozlov. Soviet specialists from the Intelligence Bureau had only occasional contact with State's executive echelons, whereas the eminent ambassadors who served as advisers to the Secretary of State and the President "cornered the market," as the lower echelons observed with resignation.

The CIA had developed a huge Soviet section; Russia had been the No. 1 enemy since CIA's birth in 1947. The CIA had massive authority in the field of Soviet economic information, and likewise in Communist Chinese economics. American universities had a long, distinguished, and voluminous record of contributions to understanding Soviet Russia. Great centers of Russian studies existed at Harvard, Columbia, Chicago, and Stanford. Exchange of views on Russia between the academic and intelligence communities was continuous and intensive.

Working on the Soviets was tedious and infinitely detailed. The Bureau published *World Strength of the Communist Party Organizations.* Possible gold dust had to be panned from conversations of eastern European diplomats with Soviet comrades and repeated to neutral sources. However, Leonid Brezhnev, Soviet Communist party First Secretary, and Premier Alexi Kosygin never talked off the record, as Khrushchev had done with scores of sources. *Pravda*, the official Communist newspaper, was the Bible, and had to be scrutinized word by word. A *Pravda* editorial stood up; if it outlined a certain Soviet policy, it was invariably so, no matter what conflicting reports transpired. Analyses of principal or neutralist Communist news agencies were screened, for example, ADN (East German), AGERPRES (Rumanian), BTA (Bulgarian), CTK (Czech), INA (Iraqi), KCNA (North Korean), MENA (Middle East), MTI (Hungarian), NCNA (China), PAP (Polish), TASS (Soviet), and VNA (North Vietnam).

Rewarding also, their highly boring content notwithstanding, were accounts of international Communist front organizations. These Lenin termed "transmission belts" and auxiliary units of the Communist party for establishing temporary tactical alliances or coalitions with political rivals or even enemies of Communism. A list of future meetings of the front organizations, which ran the gamut of practically all urban activities, was carefully scanned, from which inferences might be drawn as to imminent Russian political moves. In late November 1967 the front summary reports indicated that there had been "a steady increase of meetings, resolutions, and statements on Vietnam." These heralded a major propaganda campaign to tie the Vietnam war and a "world demand" for a coalition government with the National Liberation Front in South Vietnam. The World Federation of Trade Unions planned an international conference on "Solidarity with Vietnam" for early 1968. Among the Bureau's many tasks was to watch for the orchestration of Communist moves simultaneously in the military, economic, political, propaganda, and diplomatic fields.

Several senior Bureau experts got into the Soviet picture, including David Mark of western Europe, and James F. Leonard, director for strategic and functional intelligence. Evaluations on long-term feasibilities in Soviet measures were always a meticulous affair. In 1962, for instance, the United States had 1,000 ICBM's, about 60 Titan missiles, the Polaris submarine squadrons, and SAC bomber wings as its nuclear arm against Russia. In 1967 concern was voiced in the public prints that the Soviets were making a rapid increase in missile strength. The intelligence community, including State, estimated in 1963 that the Russians had embarked on "crash" programs to catch up with the United States. The research and development effort in Russia, as in the United States, had a comparatively long lead-time. The Russians went through the procedures of developing and testing their missiles, and then finally building silo sites, whose presence was then immediately evident through the U.S. observation satellites.

The political importance of the new power fact to State intelligence was its correlation with other Soviet moves, external and internal. Internal moves would be signaled by changes in the allocation of resources in any significant sense. This would be the strongest indicator of Russia's long-term actual intentions. The Soviet collective leadership was under constant microscopic review. Brezhnev and Kosygin, with Nicolai Podgorny half or three-quarters of a step in the rear, were still skewered on the three basic dilemmas of 1965, when the new leadership reviewed its newly seized responsibilities. The projected economic reforms were still in abeyance; granting more authority to technical managers *ipso facto* would reduce the power of the local Communist cadres, hence undermine the central hold of the party. The intellectuals and the problems of dissent were persistently irksome. Financing their expanding foreign policy involvement as a world superstate was a continuous high-wire act. The Soviets were attempting to achieve high productivity by greater efficiency. A larger pie would give the Soviet consumer a slice perhaps just big enough to keep him mollified while the extra sugar went into North Vietnam and the Middle East. The over-all estimate was that day-to-day U.S.-Soviet relations would remain abrasive, which had been their most lasting characteristic.

The Intelligence Bureau's Far East office had an obvious overlap with that for the Soviet bloc in the matter of the Sino-Soviet conflict. More and more persons, institutions, and agencies were interested in mainland China and professed credentials of varying degrees of validity. Besides CIA and Defense, Agriculture had accumulated a large store of knowledge on Chinese farming, like that already amassed on Russia. Harvard, Columbia, Stanford, and California were academic storehouses. There was a feedback from scholars and cooperative intelligence sources in London, since the British Government maintained diplomatic relations, such as they were, with Peking. Britain still held Hong Kong, the world's principal window on Communist China, where the United States also had a staff of over seventy-five, almost exclusively "China watchers." Reports filtered in as well from the some fifty nations that China had diplomatic relations with. In the State Department itself, there were at least three other groups that kept close track of Chinese affairs. The Far East geographical bureau had a Deputy Assistant Secretary who had China as a principal brief. The line bureau also had an office of Asian Communist Affairs. The seventh-floor executives always had China on their minds.

Finally, there were the face-to-face talks with the Chinese; on September 15, 1958, these were removed to Warsaw from Prague. There had been 134 meetings, as of January 8, 1968, since the meetings had originated at Geneva during the 1955 Indo-Chinese conference. The conversations were the only direct diplomatic contacts that the United States had with Communist China. The exchanges were among the most tightly held secrets of the U.S. Government. Both sides had kept the confidentiality of the talks with a high degree of integrity. In general, the indications reflected no progress. The Chinese repeatedly asked the United States to "get out" of Formosa, while the Americans requested that China commit herself to eschewing the use of force in the solution of international disputes.

Since the Far East intelligence group, given the "Bamboo Curtain," had much less verifiable information about China than was known about Russia, its interpretations about China were subjected to more controversy. This made it difficult to come to a fix concerning the Sino-Soviet dispute. State's intelligence view had been, as early as 1957, that the split was real and irreparable, and subject only to temporary patching up. As a matter of fact, hints of the eventual rupture had been spotted and dwelt upon in Europe. A June 1954 Cleveland *Plain Dealer* report from Paris said: "Systematic inquiry by western analysts reveals a surprisingly large number of specific rubs that could one day weaken or wear away Russo-Chinese Communist bonds." But it was not until late 1961 and early 1962 that the intelligence interpretation of a real split was accepted by the policy operators and made officially public. In 1967 the Sino-Soviet struggle was a constant element in intelligence evaluations. China was considered to be the No. 1 factor in the Soviet foreign policy equation.

The high caliber of the Intelligence Bureau's Far East section had been achieved by Allen S. Whiting, brought in by Roger Hilsman to be the office director in 1961. Whiting had been a forceful arguer against the risks of Chinese intervention in Vietnam, particularly in analyzing among alternative options the hypothetical possibility of invading North

Vietnam. He had been prescient in warning the policy officers concerning the staying power of North Vietnam despite the severity of U.S. bombing attacks. Whiting also had been instrumental in promoting university research on China, which had had a ten-year hiatus since 1952. The federal budget at that time gave almost a hundred times more funds for Russian scholarship than for Chinese. U.S. information about China was full of gaps, however. Greater interest in finding out about China was also stimulated by Vice President Humphrey, who complained that the Government did not have as much information about the power complex in China as it should have.

Whiting's successor, Fred Greene, an academic authority on the Far East but not a China specialist, brought a wider and more detached perspective to the examination of Chinese interpretations. The Hong Kong reports, with a tendency to localitis and overstressing the novel, for example, disorders in China, were fitted into the fuller findings available in Washington. A standard of historical relevance was being created against which to test new and verified information from China. A special guard was put against the errors implicit in the ideological blinders of the Russians and their anti-Chinese propaganda. The increasing sophistication of State's intelligence view of China was evident in interpretation of the upheavals of Mao's cultural revolution. The more facile conclusions had been that China was disintegrating into chaos. This analysis overlooked the slow-motion aerodynamic characteristics of mass populations. The multimillions of China, in effect, acted as shock absorbers to convulsions which in other, less populous nations might well have produced anarchy. Mao had tried to lead a revolution of controlled mayhem against his own government in an attempt to purify Communist institutions and simultaneously give the youth of China an opportunity to experience the thrill of participating in a revolution of their own. The Mao scheme did not quite work out, but at least State's intelligence interpreters did not lose their cool in watching the frantic process. The State Department was becoming mature about China.

The Bureau for Intelligence and Research was the official channel to, and from, the State Department for all matters relating to intelligence. It inevitably had a close relationship with the CIA, though they were not quite brothers under the cloak. State's role was analytical, and its foreign intelligence activities in political reporting plainly overt. By presidential delegation, however, State chaired the Special Group, which had overseen CIA's clandestine activities. The function passed theoretically to SIG, but practically to Under Secretary Katzenbach as chairman of a reconstituted Special Group. By virtue of his function as director of the

State intelligence setup, Hughes had top clearances for all types of classified information, including the sensitive NODIS cables distributed only at the specific direction of the Secretary of State.

Hughes sat on the United States Intelligence Board, which represented the national intelligence community and set the broad directions and priorities of the nation's intelligence efforts. The Bureau participated from the ground up in the weekly formulation of the National Intelligence Estimate, which gave the experts' detailed assessments and projections of the facts, options, and probabilities confronting the United States in the outside world. Hughes sat in on the Board of Estimates' final approval of the draft drawn up by the staff technicians. On behalf of State, he occasionally dissented from the expressed views by taking exception to certain paragraphs, as was the custom for all participants. The Board met usually every Thursday and its considered estimate was published within authorized circles the same day in mimeographed form, and five days later in printed form.

The Board of National Estimates was directed by Abbott Smith, successor to the noted Sherman Kent. Calling the shots and their consequences and implications as it saw them, the Board had opposed the bombing of Haiphong harbor in North Vietnam as unnecessarily risky in view of the secondary military importance of the cargoes arriving there. The Board had also predicted correctly, up to January 1968, that the bombing of North Vietnam would neither result in the surrender of Hanoi nor force the North Vietnamese regime to agree to negotiations. The data that the Board considered were termed intelligence if issuing from official intelligence channels, or simply information if from the open, or overt, world of the press, magazines, technical journals, scholarly publications, and the world's radio networks, which were monitored round the clock by a CIA division, the Federal Broadcast Information Service. The original mass of material also included information bought or stolen via espionage or gathered by supersecret electronic marvels. Ninety per cent of the data under review was not from covert sources. But the integrated product that became "finished intelligence," in the shop term, did include verified information from espionage or electronic sources, if available.

The precision of espionage results at their best necessarily had to deal with documents that were authoritative, approved, and representing operating decisions in actual operating effect, findings which were comparatively rare. State's Intelligence Bureau therefore had more to do with Jack Smith, CIA Deputy Director for Information and Analysis, and little to do with CIA's Plans Division, or covert operations, under CIA Deputy Director Thomas H. Karamessines.

On occasion, when secret espionage information was urgently needed, it was impossible to obtain in time. Such a case was the Berlin Wall on August 13, 1961. The failure of all the intelligence agencies, including State and CIA, to diagnose accurately the intent of the Communists to build the Wall at the moment they did was due to the insuperable obstacle of an airtight security screen thrown between East and West Berlin in the days preceding August 13 by the East German and Soviet intelligence organizations. No agents could get through. No radio contacts came across. Posters proclaiming the Wall's erection were secretly printed, and the printers were locked up for forty-eight hours in their shops until the surprise of the Wall was sprung on the world. CIA's covert side provided the agency with a first-class cover and bureaucratic rationale to obtain a super-large budget free of Congressional harassment for its overt activities, particularly in the research field.

Abstractly, the information sequence proceeded from the raw fact, soggy with reality; to the intelligence datum, evaluated as far as subtle minds could fashion it; to the operational set of facts, where the complex play of total policy considerations overweighted one factor and deliberately disregarded another. In theory, it would be axiomatic that the completeness and integrity of the three stages of the fact process would result in a first-class case of political-press-public facts. Actually, the less-than-perfect state of facts to be presented created a lien which withdrew an equivalent measure of credibility. If the matter of presentation itself was inept, credibility crumbled even faster, though the intrinsic case might be considerably better than it looked.

In the great event of the 1960's, the Vietnam war, the facts and their presentation suffered from every malady that fear and malice, hope and credulity could invite. Any fact, such as it was, once it got into the political-press-public environment, shot up like a runaway missile and, its force spent, hung in space like a mobile, subject to alteration or exploitation by every passing shift of opinion, prejudice, artifice, or wind of doctrine. The national divisions about the Vietnam war, expressed in bitter feelings, demonstrations, passion, and anger, produced a secondary and psychosomatic disease, the failure of credibility. The existence of a conviction on either side, mistaken or correct, became a political fact to be reckoned with.

The original raw-intelligence-operational facts were transformed, as were all facts, indefinably but positively by the field of life into which they were received, like electrons in a magnetic field, or in the same manner that form transmutes content in art. In the case of the facts of the Vietnam war, there was the steamy confluence of a whole series of coincidental factors in the atmosphere: the LSD-for-lunch-bunch at Harvard in 1961; the shock and disillusionment of the Kennedy assassination; the rising civil rights flood tides of the Negro's social and economic liberation; the continuous prosperity bringing new enticements of leisure, luxuries, irresponsibility for basic subsistence, and sexual freedoms; the escapisms and unformulated longings of the beatniks-hippies and emotional extravaganzas of the Beatles; the fake allurements of advertising adjectives on the radio and montages of imitative violence on TV and in the press; the cyclical revolt of the new generation with overwhetted appetites against parents, outmoded mores, and traditional restraints. These all converged on the dominant symbol of President Lyndon Baines Johnson, a dominating creature of protean dynamism who became virtually a hated father figure to hundreds of thousands to curse, denounce, abjure, and misunderstand.

Flaubert once said that masterpieces had *"la mine tranquille comme les productions mêmes de la nature, comme les grands animaux et les montagnes"* (the tranquil mien of productions of nature, of great animals and mountains). History would decide whether Johnson was a masterpiece or not; he had traces of a great animal like a Texas puma, and he was indubitably a fact of nature like a mountain. As the tallest eminence in the American landscape, Johnson inevitably drew on himself all the lightnings and latent electric charges in the turbulent atmosphere epitomized by the Vietnam war. He did not put up a lightning rod early enough to channel and control the chaotic elements in the air. But the confused early explanations of the war, even after more orderly justifications were supplied, remained in the public's memory, like after-images on the retina, to discolor the vision of new facts, perpetuating the mote in the eye of credibility.

The President's failure was as a communicator, until the weight of facts finally made themselves felt. But recognition came at such a slow rate as almost to vitiate appreciation of the magnitude of the Johnson deeds in the process. The original Johnson formula of oversimplification and apparent dissimulation contrasted with the brilliant propagandizing of his predecessor's court, where richly articulate intellectuals like Sorensen, Bundy, Kaysen, Schlesinger, and Rostow (in his New Frontier incarnation) fanned out on order of JFK to blunt the penpricks of criticism. Johnson's highly successful record as Senate Majority leader contributed the myth of consensus as an artificial abstraction which helped impede explication and comprehension of the motivations and circumstances of the Vietnam war. Actually, there had been nothing so easy and naïve as gathering votes by allowing a so-called consensus to soup up like a cloud of permissiveness. Rather, it was slogging, personalized partisanship by

Johnson in his private Senate office as he patiently and arduously pieced together a majority, one by one. The senatorial hallmark of the Johnson operation was secretiveness as he amassed votes individually pledged to him. It was not a policy that translated effectively to the far more open arena of the White House. The impending election was another constraining factor in 1964. In those days of foreign policy review, the President used to lean over the table and say to Secretary Rusk, "And don't tell those guys in your department." Rusk didn't.

If John F. Kennedy was out of "Camelot," all grace and well-staged presence, Johnson came straight from "Bonanza," and more recently "Gunsmoke." He was all wary cordiality with strangers, and earthy intimacy with familiars whom he trusted from a basis of shared experience. Kennedy was a fascinated diagnostician of power, Johnson a surgeon of power absorbed profoundly in the use thereof. Johnson was so busy working close to the details that he never thought to romanticize what he was doing. He acted as if doing a good job spoke for itself. Belated attempts to make up for lost opportunities at proper and normal self-advertisement backfired into canards of news management and contrived publicity. To a man whose veins were instinct with the feeling of power, the Presidency came to Johnson almost too late. He appeared to be in a rush to use the vast powers of the Presidency to turn his dreams into brick and steel, terrifically impatient as if he were endeavoring to drag the future into the present with his two bare hands. However, as Henry Adams said, "power is poison." Few men ever lived who could give themselves homeopathic doses of it as Mithridates, King of Pontus, did with real poison, to insure themselves against power's deleterious excesses. Almost seventy years ago Adams decribed the effect of power on Presidents as "tragic, chiefly as an almost insane excitement at first . . . but also because no mind is so well balanced as to bear the strain of seizing unlimited force without habit or knowledge of it; and finding it disputed with him by hungry packs of wolves and hounds. . . ." The latter phrases in a modern context might be an extreme way of describing U.S. Senators and anti-Vietnam dissenters.

Nonetheless, opposition was no way to bring out lamblike qualities in a patriarchal character of the rock-studded hills of west Texas when the imminent collapse of the South Vietnam war effort in late 1964 and early 1965 impelled the President to do what he felt was his bounden duty to try to save the situation. Johnson was as fierce in private to his own friends and cohorts as he appeared implacable in public to his political enemies or critics. He was rough and almost brutal in aiming at the jugular in discussion, inclining his head to the right so he could hear the better with his left ear, his right being hard of hearing. He glared at his most loyal advisers, daring them to offer counterarguments to his course of action and to answer his insistent question, "What would YOU do?" It was often a trembling hour for interlocutors as the President hammered out searching questions like a fullback trying to find a hole in the scrimmage line. The safest defense was to stick stubbornly to one's candid opinion, after which Johnson sort of subsided, like a receding thunderstorm. Rather than being the "captive of his generals" or a seeker of mere "yes men," Johnson, in his natural role of strong-man, deliberately generated argumentation, making visible his displeasure at what he occasionally heard only by the growing pinkness of his face and the straight rigid line of his mouth.

Essentially, the crisis of credibility had less to do with the competence of reporters and the veracity of officials than it did with the interplay of political and personal psychologies. There were no real villains, and certainly very few heroes of the truth, whatever truth might have been. National feelings were not as bitter about Vietnam as they had been about the War of 1812 or the Mexican War. Emotions about Vietnam were stronger than those about the Korean war, the isolationist dispute before World War II, the China debate of 1949, or the Cuba arguments of 1962. Feelings about Vietnam aroused nothing like the bitterness in Britain over the Spanish Civil War in the 1930's or the Suez disaster in 1956, or that in France over the Algerian war in the late 1950's, let alone the enraged passions of the Dreyfus case in France in 1897–1899. In short, there was a considerable admixture of fabricated hokum in the Vietnam debate, a sort of futile gnashing of teeth, rodomontade, and beating of breasts, masking a mass guilty conscience, a plain neglect of public·duty in not having recognized in time the Vietnam involvement for what it always was, a snake pit, with the corollary duty of deciding what to do about it.

Though by early 1968 the esthetics of the Vietnam war foreshadowed a denouement, much heat and passion had been ill spent during, in Oliver Wendell Holmes's phrase, "the long dead pull" of 1966. The late hour and attendant frustrations created a "credibility gap" almost from the start, disbelief fattening on what former White House Press Secretary Bill D. Moyers termed the "ambiguity, the dilemma, the difficulty, and the complexity of the Vietnam war." The war violated all the precepts of the standard textbooks and daily wrote new chapters for the revisions. In the nuclear-space era, mass information was also a major weapon, triggered by the multiplier of electronic communications. Enemy, hostile, or unfriendly states like North Vietnam cold-bloodedly set out by vociferous propaganda to attempt to overturn the majority rule of a democratic state into a minority. The muscle-bound United States was a fair setup for such a game. Not being able to conceal its internal dissension, it was at a great disadvantage in diplomatic negotiations. The fact that the dispute over Vietnam contained a high ideological quotient greatly complicated what would have been a relatively straightforward problem in other times. The American public in its simplicity and mental laziness expected black-and-white answers and absolute results. But as McGeorge Bundy said in a speech, "Gray is the color of truth."

The concept of a limited war for limited ends by limited means, though limited was pretty bountiful by U.S. superstandards, took a long time to sink in. There was no systematic coordination of Vietnam war information and public philosophy throughout the Government. Scientists recommended a "research effort devoted to understanding the processes of information diffusion, including the ways in which new information becomes credible." Yet for a government which was deeply involved in the most advanced boundaries of scientific technology, information dissemination was curiously antediluvian, like forecasting the weather by lifting a wet finger to the wind. In 1965, Martin C. McGuire, in *Secrecy and the Arms Race*, calculated mathematically that the economic cost of secrecy about heavy armaments was sometimes considerably more than it was worth, and that misinformation also exacted a price in dollars. No supernal brain had yet appeared to make a virtue out of the necessity of concrete candor in a democracy, to demonstrate that the goldfish-bowl world of the modern age was more tolerable and livable than the present mottled shell of half-truths and deceptions based on man's little insecurities. Security officers, however, had the last word on information, not public affairs officials. To question the premises of a security ruling was to raise doubts about one's sanity, or worse, one's credit rating.

In the end, adequate information was almost more a matter of receptivity, of a soul, as Plato said, ready to receive the truth, therefore, of education. Adequate education signified an awareness of past experiences to alert one to the re-emergence of trials, though these would invariably come in new forms since history never really repeated itself. Hence, analogies were no guides, but self-serving rationalizations. Old history was dead and new history in creation offered new forms and challenges. At worst, the past did list cautionary factors obvious to anyone who could read and even remember. However, it was more than evident that the American population was uneducated in the experiences of the world's power areas, current and antecedent. The Republic's political leaders were not far behind in their relative ignorance of world history. Individual members of the trained bureaucracy had a memory of relevant past experiences but not too many. The pertinent facts were somewhere on paper, but not in their heads. The people, therefore, whom President

Johnson ruled over were not the model of an alert and informed citizenry that idealized school textbooks pictured. Rather, the Americans were probably the most fractious subjects of a great power since the ancient Greeks of Athens, likewise a democracy where distinctions between liberty and license and personal self-interest and civic integrity were not always clearly drawn.

Education for the responsible citizen did not entail pondering the brooding evocations of eight centuries of the Roman Empire in Freya Stark's *Rome on the Euphrates,* a book which could profitably stimulate thought on the shortfalls of the Kennan theory of containment so long enshrined in the U.S. foreign policy mystique. But every voter over twenty-five might well recall that in 1958 there were loud and tendentious arguments over the Eisenhower administration's measures to help the Chinese Nationalist regime on Formosa safeguard Quemoy and Matsu, despite the fact that the Congress had passed the Formosa Resolution in 1955 to authorize emergency action in such a contingency. A like situation prevailed concerning the Gulf of Tonkin Resolution in 1964, with the same *mea culpa* senatorial recriminations in 1967. Contingency plans were provisions against the unknown. In the actual event, in a world of instant speeds, there was no time for lengthy parliamentary deliberations. Therefore, consideration of the contingency proposals would have to be undertaken in depth at the time of the original submission. The Senate Foreign Relations Committee finally so decided in 1967.

The record was full of disregarded signposts. The North Vietnamese Communists, as a matter of deliberate tactics, had thrown extraneous considerations into truce talks for twenty-seven months, in order to create a political stalemate favorable to themselves for the 1954 Indo-China accords. The Communists dissimulated their purposes toward the anti-French and non-Communist nationalists in the Viet Minh ranks until 1951, when a common frontier was established with Communist China for supply and sanctuary. Ho Chi Minh then proclaimed openly his Communist aims. Ho, in fact, was one of the Communists world's foremost experts in the creation of "popular front" façades to cover Communist party infiltration and takeover, in the classic manner prescribed by Lenin.

It was not until the summer of 1965 that the CIA began to circulate the first elementary outline of the National Liberation Front of South Vietnam, and not until 1966 that a USIA officer, Douglas Pike, published a detailed work on the NLF, *Vietcong: The Organization and Technique of the National Liberation Front of South Vietnam.* The information on the NLF had been classified, instead of being broadcast early and wide to educate the citizens as to what they were getting into and to anticipate misconceptions which persisted to 1968. Ironically, in late 1964, before Khrushchev's ouster and the resumption of Soviet interest in southeast Asia, the Russians confided in the Americans that they estimated the NLF and Vietcong supporters in South Vietnam to muster only 800,000 votes, all told.

A curious parallelism was visible between the experiences of the Americans in Vietnam and in Greece, the latter the first experiment of the United States in post-war geopolitics on foreign ground. Illustrative were typical headlines from Athens in the Cleveland *Plain Dealer* of March 1947: "Greeks in No Mood for Political Meddling" and "Greek Rebels Wary of Amnesty Proposal." A year later, in March 1948: "Greeks' Problem Is to Bar Guerrillas' Escape Route" and "Sees Greece Sinking in a Sea of Chaos" and "U.S. Officers in Greece Are in War, Can't Hit Back" and "Guerrillas Make 40% of Greece No Man's Land" and "Full Scale War Rages in Greece" and "Sees Dictatorship Dilemma Facing Americans in Greece" and "U.S. Reforms Taking Hold over Greece." September 1949: "Report Greeks Sure Civil War Is Ending." April 1950: "Some American Flaws Are Picked by Greeks" and " 'Get Tough' Policy Tested on Greece" and "U.S. Got Money's Worth in Greek War" and "Greece Seen as Lab of Cold War."

It sounded all too familiar as related to Vietnam, though the calendar of events differed. The Vietnamese had not yet reduced their anti-Communist policy to the simplified Greek rule: "Shoot them, convert them, or sterilize them." The idealistic American press still emphasized the civil liberties aspects of the new battlegrounds, in Vietnam, as it had in Greece, forgetting in the latter case that Greece had been historically noted for its oligarchies and tyrannies in ancient times as well as giving birth to Western democracy. In both cases, there were the perennial difficulties with client-allies, conflicts over dictatorship tendencies, and disputes over treatment of insurgents, that is, safeguarding national security versus healing the wounds of the body politic.

The newspaper headlines recorded lessons that applied to Vietnam in new form, such as one in April 1948, from Rome, which said: "Reform Without Red Grab Is Italy's Need." The headlines about Indo-China echoed with hollow prophecy even before the climactic 1954 Geneva conference which created South Vietnam. September 1950: "French Now Seek U.S. Troop Aid in Indochina." December 1952: "Indochina a Military Mess Worse Than Korea." Paris, May 1953: "Indochina Is Testing Point of U.S. Policy." And for 1968, the headlines from Korea were grimly pertinent. October 1952: "U.S. Facing 'Horrible' Truce Talks Dilemma" and "Fear Truce in Korea Is No Longer Possible."

By 1968, it was seven years since President Kennedy had officially and publicly reinvolved the United States in southeast Asia in March 1961, via Laos and Thailand, and begun edging into the South Vietnam rice paddies; and three years since President Johnson had begun committing major U.S. military power via the bombing of North Vietnam in February 1965, and combat troops some weeks later. The rough but approximate shape of the development of the Vietnam war gradually had come into view. The facts did not emerge nice, tidy, and self-evident. Rather they seeped out, often helter-skelter, out of sequence or out of context, in partially factual or generalized emissions. Authorized U.S. officials gave speeches, interviews, TV broadcasts. There were slabs of backgrounders by State, Defense, and White House sources. Military security safeguards had been consistently invoked by both Kennedy and Johnson to screen U.S. plans from enemy ears. Consequently, administration justifications to the American electorate suffered from considerable restraint. In the Kennedy years, the stress had been more on Laos than Vietnam, which was gingerly kept more or less at arm's length, in the hope of discovering a "political" approach, which never quite came to pass.

The Johnson decision to commit the United States to the Vietnam war in massive force also never quite arrived at general public understanding. Not until casualty lists and draft calls mounted did the realization hit the American public that a real war with U.S. soldiers was going on. The near-rout of the South Vietnamese was never frankly and publicly admitted, though Rusk had painted the "blackest" picture of the war to that date in "strictly secret" testimony before the Senate Foreign Relations Committee on January 5, 1965, as page one newspaper stories reported. Patently, the administration's fear was of creating panic and immediate collapse in Saigon. Almost of equal importance in playing the news close to the official vest was the tension in the bureaucratic ranks as it grew evident that the President would have to make a momentous decision, and war was the ultimate of decisions. In the confused new situation, the Johnson administration was like a new teacher with a new subject preparing the lesson one step ahead of the pupils, in not having sufficient information on hand to brief the American citizenry with confident candor.

Johnson had periodically walked around the subject of Vietnam all through 1964, but had not looked the smoldering crisis right in the eye. Intensive staff studies of the approaching dilemma in Vietnam were begun after the November 1964 elections. By December, State's Far East Bureau had four contingency recommendations on tap: more of the same policy (which procedure would clearly run the affair right into the Mekong River); start planning for U.S. withdrawal from Vietnam; bomb North Vietnam a little, in remonstrance; and bomb North Vietnam a lot, in defiance and as a warning. On Secretary McNamara's recommendation, the President had ordered preparation of a possible list of targets in North Vietnam by the Joint Chiefs of Staff as early as December 1963.

In January 1965, the President took personal charge of the Vietnam war for the first time. Returning from the LBJ Ranch in Texas after the Christmas holidays, he ordered a series of full-dress meetings of his top advisers. Two questions were on the White House table: to bomb or not to bomb; and if to bomb, how to bomb. Bombing would bolster the crumbling Saigon morale, shock the American people into facing the gravity of the crisis, and serve as an ultimatum to North Vietnam to cease and desist abetting the South Vietnamese insurgency. Four years earlier, during the Berlin crisis, Rusk had made an impression on President Kennedy when he recommended a demonstration of force as a "peaceful overture" to big-power diplomacy with the Soviets. Former Under Secretary Ball argued eloquently for withdrawal. Vice President Humphrey listed all the risks and consequences of the heavy U.S. commitment that bombing would preface, but voted to do the necessary. McNamara went along with an air of fatalistic resignation. President Johnson, in his first global league ball game as the newly chosen captain of the team, was not about to strike out the first time he was up at bat. The President indicated in his State of the Union Message that the United States would not withdraw from South Vietnam. But he gave no hint of what drastic action would be necessary to stay there.

Once the decision had been made to bomb, military logic dictated that the impact be effective enough to get political results equivalent to the expenditure of the force used. Therefore, Secretary Rusk, General Wheeler, the Joint Chiefs Chairman, and Treasury Secretary Dillon urged that North Vietnam be hit hard—from the start and for at least three months, and that the harbor of Haiphong be mined, before the Communists knew what hit them, or the Russians had time to help Hanoi build up antiaircraft defenses. McNamara instead favored graduated pressure.

As it turned out, this policy telegraphed U.S. intentions and gave timely warning to Hanoi to set up an air defense system with modern Soviet equipment, particularly radar screens. The President had shied off from initiating a global crisis, with unavoidable nuclear overtones, by a sudden and mighty display of force toward North Vietnam for fear of alarming Russia and Communist China. This argument persuaded Rusk to go along with the President's decision on the McNamara lines. In 1966, Rusk remarked that he had "never thought a year ago [in 1965] that the Russians would let us go as far as we have" in bombing North Vietnam. Three other factors affected the President's decision to attack North Vietnam through the air in stages. These were the lack of sufficient jet airfields, the lack of precision-trained pilots, and inadequate information on target identification. All had to be programmed and provided for in due course. One just did not mash a button electronically and start a war, as the President told visitors later. In any event, the original difficulties attendant upon the bombing were never explained, even after security censorship no longer applied as rigorously. The silence left the inaccurate impression of a fumbling administration.

In the Johnson style, getting on with the job was the first priority, and talking about it came later. News announcements, the press complained, were not in timely fashion, or with facts sufficient to the needs of that particular moment. Public relations were a secondary consideration in the light of Johnson's past habits and mode of thinking. While furiously busy organizing the war, Johnson was first passive, then defensive, with regard to the hostile opinion swelling in the United States as antiwar critics virtually had the field to themselves, in the Senate, on the campuses, and in the shriller press. Working meetings like Honolulu, Manila, and Guam turned into spectacles, despite the sober conviction of the President in the utility of their convocation and the necessity of the United States to find diplomatic allies in the Far East. In the drumfire pace of events, *post facto* explanations or rationalizations were not lacking. Washington, Saigon, Moscow, and Hanoi commentaries were ironical footnotes to a famous saying of Lenin, "The seizure of power is the point of the uprising. Its political task will be clarified afterwards." Power centers talked the same language, no matter what their political philosophy.

Harnessing and riding the multiple horses of bureaucracy was no easy job, even for a knowledgeable and demanding taskmaster like Johnson. The military services, tamed on the surface in the Pentagon by McNamara, engaged in a series of petty frictions in the southeast Asia field over bases, intelligence estimates, task force commands, training missions, and division of labor. In Washington the Joint Chiefs were the only high-level body in the Government to keep verbatim notes of its meetings. These served to inform their service colleagues that they had valiantly defended their respective party lines. In 1965 the job was to get troops and supplies out to Vietnam as fast as possible. Ships left every port in the United States for Saigon, where they waited weeks to unload, Niagara Falls being poured into a thimble. In 1966 intelligence circuits got jammed; reports were slow to reach the White House about the Buddhist crisis, giving morale a sheer drop for days. Precise information and accurate evaluations were in technicians' hands at the State Department all the time, but had not been arriving at proper destinations. The lack of enough Vietnamese-speaking Foreign Service officers raised problems concerning faithful reporting of Vietnamese official attitudes; too many interpreters gave conclusions instead of telling the story verbatim. Endeavoring to piece together the facts for himself, Johnson was like a surgeon trying to tie sutures blind in a valve, before the days of open-heart surgery. Too much was going on everywhere, too much was uncertain or garbled, to know all the facts, let alone to tell the press at the appropriate time.

The distant war came closer to home as State Department officials who had dealt closely with Vietnam returned to Washington after duty tours in Saigon and tried to give the President a lifelike feel of the situation. Ambassador Alexis Johnson reported finding it a shock to confront on the spot "the brutality of the reality." The 1967 climactic wave of opposition to the war in the United States drew ironical cables from the Saigon Embassy to the State Department, stating with mock solemnity, "We understand your problem, and we will support you to the fullest extent of our ability." More informal communications from Vietnam suggested asphalting the whole damned country and paying $300 to every Viet Cong to quit and go home.

To meet the demand for basic facts on the war, the State Department in 1967 started issuing a new series of Department publications entitled "Vietnam Information Notes." Those covered nearly twenty aspects of the Vietnam situation and provided long-needed general information. In the Department the Vietnam war brought to many the thrill and excitement of working on great events. The Chris Argyris interviews with Foreign Service officers elicited a common feeling of participation when working on crisis agenda. Sample comments from various officers:

"I believe that we staff for crises. Once the crisis is over it is hard to cut back. In the organization from which I came, we had three Foreign Service Officers doing one-third of the work, rather than one who could do it all easily. Overstaffing is one of the major problems around here."

"I think all of us are so starved to do something important that we stick around hoping that it will come up. Sometimes, I do not want to go home because others are working."

"What impressed me was the number of people who came around even though they had nothing to do with the crisis."

"We create and enjoy crises. Our office operates with crises. But all of us like them. I know I enjoy them."

"I think that the reason that we create crises is that there are too many people for everyday work and they have little to do. The more the crises, the better they like it. They feel like they're doing something."

"There is a sense of elation that comes with a crisis."

"We're responsive to a name on a memo. The more important the names, the bigger the crises."

Among the contributory developments which helped create the conditions for the rise of the so-called credibility crisis about the Vietnam war was the extensive publicity put out about guerrilla warfare in the early months of the Kennedy administration. To the public, the unexpected change of pace from the theatrical, but not multideath, nature of small-unit combat to more or less conventional war with sizable forces was difficult to adjust to. It was not cowboys and Indians at all. The propaganda build-up about the new U.S. Special Forces organized at President Kennedy's direct intervention had generated false anticipations of comparatively inexpensive exploits. Actually, of course, redressing the situation in Vietnam on the cheap had never been possible, since 1957 at least. By the time the United States sent mass reinforcements to Vietnam in late 1965, it was no longer a question of irregular bands flitting over the landscape, but of standard military operations, though in more open style, with organized forces. It was more like the Pacific island fighting of World War II. Moreover, the North Vietnamese armed units were also massing for more conventional assaults in Phase III of their own General Giap's standard guerrilla strategy. In brief, the U.S. public was taken aback at the change in tactics and suspected the worst, trickery or whatever, hence, was in a mood of disbelief, expecting one thing and seeing another.

The counterinsurgency theme had been promoted by General Max Taylor and Walt Rostow. Taylor later refined and expanded it into the scheme of the Senior Interdepartmental Group, or SIG. Counterinsurgency would apply to the eighty or ninety underdeveloped countries of the world, which comprised four fifths of the United States' diplomatic relations and would be the likely sites for insurgencies. The counterinsurgency idea was no novelty, however. Both Secretaries Dulles and Herter had sought authorization in the National Security Council to organize counterinsurgency units in the U.S. Army in 1958. But President Eisenhower had insisted on keeping his defense budget ceiling, and no moneys were available at the expense of naval ships and big bombers. Kennedy raised the defense ceiling to provide the funds. Counterinsurgency plans were made for five countries in Latin America—Venezuela, Peru, Nicaragua, Colombia, and Bolivia; two in Africa—the Congo and the Sudan; and four in southeast Asia—Vietnam, Laos, Burma, and Thailand. Except for Latin America, the counterinsurgency theory in 1967 cut little ice among the dominant big-war strategists. Its lessons were useful as psychological instruction to troops in a hostile country where an insignificant scarecrow of a peasant could turn out to be the man who killed you, a lesson taken to heart by the Russians, who have a saying, "A thin louse bites hardest."

Roger Hilsman, a third principal counterinsurgency theorist, who in

1964 left the State Department, in 1967 emerged as a special *bête noire* of
the White House. The publication of his book *To Move a Nation,* in
which he gave his own version of the events of Vietnam, irritated his
former colleagues because of what they termed its "I-told-you-so" aspects.
Hilsman wrote in a letter on March 14, 1964, to Secretary Rusk that
U.S. bombing of North Vietnam would "be interpreted by the Communists as an act of desperation, and will, therefore, not be effective in
persuading the North Vietnamese to cease and desist." Johnson blamed
Hilsman for the Diem debacle. The President felt that allowing Diem to
be killed was the big mistake of that era. The Diem death in 1963 indeed
had disoriented and thrown the entire upper echelons of the U.S. Government into disarray for six weeks before the new situation could be rationally reanalyzed.

In any event, the new dangerous situation in Vietnam in January 1965
had not been fully and officially foreseen in Washington, though the sorry
facts had been creeping up faster and faster on the Saigon and Far East
Bureau technicians during the last of 1964. The Washington prognosis,
when it was finally made, looked like an ignominious defeat at worst and
a long, grueling grind at best. No systematic, organized operational plans
existed to meet the imminent crisis. There was not enough accurate
information upon which to base real-life plans for manpower, material,
and strategy. Insufficient and inadequate information, owing to the nature
of the conflict, was to be the hallmark of the Vietnam war, virtually from
the start to finish, not for the mass media alone, but also for the President
and the State and Defense Departments. Vietnam, in brief, was a perfect
intelligence case study.

The Government, in essence, was in not much better position than the
public; it also had to bulldoze down a mountain to unearth a nugget of
fact. The Johnson administration was in a constant struggle to find out
the facts for itself, facts upon which crucial decisions could be based for
the execution of the war. The so-called facts were either missing or consistently warped by controversial interpretations. Secretary McNamara and
the late Assistant Defense Secretary, John McNaughton, in 1967, for
example, received two diametrically opposite briefings in one day from
General Westmoreland's staff in Saigon. The J-2 for intelligence gave a
briefing which was conservative on figures but pessimistic in effect. The
J-3 for operations, using the same set of figures, pictured a need for
more men and resources, but was optimistic in effect. The intelligence
units of the various commands and services differed on statistics, failed
to coordinate or relay findings, or declined to help each other out with
assignment of men and equipment for proposed intelligence missions.
Tacit assumptions of nuclear war strategists precluded entertaining sug-

gestions of ground-war intelligence specialists, missing or delaying opportunities to pinpoint and exploit operational intelligence. Petty bureaucratic spites did not approach the stage of the intelligence shambles the competing U.S. services wreaked upon each other in Berlin in 1953, but inevitably they had negative effects.

The accumulated southeast Asia intelligence from Saigon, Bangkok, Vientiane, and Manila poured into Washington, where the cool-minded and sardonic experts of the Defense Intelligence Agency, the Central Intelligence Agency, and the State Department's Bureau of Intelligence and Research "read all the wash," that is, the incoming cable flood, and renewed the multitugs of war. The occupational hazard of the field intelligence was physically spotting the Communist needle in the Vietnam haystack. That of the Washington intelligence community was overlooking the warning note voiced by raw data as they were refined through abstracts, summaries, abridgments, and précis. The field was perhaps overcautious and unimaginative in making assessments. Headquarters was perhaps overnervous and rigid in continually demanding impossible feats of "hard proof."

The game was arduous enough for the players, even with all the breaks. It was made tense by the demands of the bosses, President Johnson and Secretary McNamara, above all, for more and more information. The President liked visual aids. McNamara breathed statistics from which hopefully could be derived mathematical certainties. Rostow loved charts. But the Vietnam war would not stand still long enough to be tabulated. The voracious American press was pounding on the door for information. The war was a theater of the absurd in which players, audience, and hecklers intermingled on the stage.

The 1967 summer in the Negro ghettos of Newark and Detroit had a lateral repercussion on the Vietnam intelligence snarl. It was noted that many Negroes in the bottom layer of American society had been overlooked. It was estimated that at least five million had not been counted in the 1960 census. A common-sense parallel to the war was evident: South Vietnam had become mysteriously waterlogged with hostile bodies. Their mode of ingress had not been precisely enough identified. Figures showing "enemy strength" showed little basic fluctuation. Yet enough Communists were being killed to have reduced the enemy totals. The disparities began to be more and more apparent as General Westmoreland spread his troops thin on the ground with "go-and-get-them" tactics and broke up long-held Viet Cong bases. G-2 reports, including captured documents, that is, the enemy bureaucracy's files, cascaded into the Saigon intelligence computer center in volume for the first time in 1967.

The problem was getting to be too much information and not enough evaluation. The only place in the U.S. Government where the jigsaw-puzzle-scrabble-Monopoly approach of the intelligence agencies could be pulled together was the White House. By January 1967, the figures had started to look more compatible, but still showed wide variances. By August, the statistics sounded genuinely realistic for the first time, but still far from exact. Robert Komer, first in the White House and then in Saigon, pinpricked the intelligence crowd into re-examining its original premises in an effort to find reliable and agreed units of measure.

In late September 1967, representatives of all the major intelligence units—State Department, Defense Department, Defense Intelligence Agency, CIA, National Security Agency, Air Force, Navy, Army—met in the the White House basement Situation Room in continuous session from 9:30 A.M. until 5:00 P.M. They emerged, still at odds on the correct basis for common interpretation. They were ordered to reconvene and not come out without an accord. They issued at 7:30 P.M. with an agreed formula, again for the first time in the war. The intelligence pact did not last long. The formula was more a party-line papering-over to soothe the White House than a true synthesis. There was a spread of 100,000 in the estimate of enemy forces between the DIA and the CIA. Some austere bureaucrats became huffy and stuffy, like vestal virgins desecrated by a wolf whistle. The offended bureaucracy asseverated that it could not tolerate having its integrity exploited by misconstruing the war statistics for an election year sales pitch. The sewing-circle spat was patched up some weeks later by accepting the higher, or CIA, figures. These referred specifically to the number of Viet Cong political cadres or individuals in South Vietnam. DIA had said 80,000, CIA 180,000.

Contemporaneously, the White House had set up an office of Vietnam war information under Harold Kaplan in the office of Ambassador William Leonhart, the special assistant to the President for Vietnam civilian affairs. Kaplan, a Deputy Assistant Secretary of State and a former principal press official in Saigon, was to help take some of the overload off Walt Rostow and George Christian, the President's Press Secretary, because of the great number of Vietnam background queries. Kaplan also was to help prepare replies to the tremendous inflow of correspondence received by the White House on Vietnam. His most important objective, however, was to recommend how to coordinate all information on Vietnam issuing from the Government in the way of releases, statements, and speeches. Theoretically, the official presentation would gain the virtues of consistency and accuracy, especially in light of conflicting intelligence reports and interpretations. Government statements on Vietnam by 1967 sounded somewhat stale from ingrained habits of previous years and, worst of all, were frequently anachronistic, in that they did not present the case under the changed developments of 1967.

As was not uncommon in the bureaucracy, Kaplan did not have a chance to try reforming the Vietnam presentation; he was assigned to Brussels. In the autocritique of the administration public affairs perfectionists, three basic errors had been allowed to run unchecked. The first had been not fixing an accurate and efficient intelligence rationale. The second had been not establishing a clearinghouse for coordinated and verified Vietnam information. The third, and possibly most important, had been the failure to draw a base line, or zero point, between the time the United States armed forces went into South Vietnam in strength in early 1965 and what had gone on before 1965, as a basis for comparisons.

Psychological ineptness was compounded by bureaucratic inertia. To ordinary Americans, the morbid term "body count" evoked visions of so many corpses lying around to be counted. The true situation was different. Enemy bodies might be left on the field of battle, to be counted by U.S. troops, but not counted actually. Or the enemy carried its dead away. The body count included enemy dead from air strikes and artillery bursts— often calculated unseen. A body in the uniform of a North Vietnamese was clearly a dead enemy. But a body in black pajamas, that of an innocent Vietnamese civilian, was too often automatically a dead VC. Military units customarily made no reports until they had achieved assigned objectives; hence, reports were normally late. Officers new to Vietnam went by the manuals and reported everything in white-and-black absolutes. By the time they had learned to discriminate to gray, their tours were up and the education process had to be redone with the next group.

From 1961 to the end of 1967, the United States had suffered in Vietnam almost 16,000 killed and nearly 100,000 nonfatally wounded. What the war had cost in Vietnamese civilian casualties was unknown. But it had a definite bearing on the rate of VC recruitment, consequently of enemy strength. The contradictions in figures and confusions in definitions added to the political exacerbations in Washington. Typical was a loud altercation between Assistant Secretary Bundy and U.S. Senator Edward Kennedy over civilian casualties in South Vietnam. Both men were arguing from different premises and differing intelligence versions. U.S. military tactics of clear-fire zones and bombing anything in sight that moved in the area regularly resulted in civilian casualties. The local Vietnamese could not be dissuaded to change their habits because of U.S. "military necessity." The problem raised a highly sensitive issue between State and Defense as 1968 opened. Military plans had made no provision for civil affairs officers on combat unit staffs, as had been done successfully in populated areas in World War II. A pile-up of disaffected refugees could grow into a major political liability to the success of the new government of South Vietnam in whose future the United States had a multibillion-dollar stake.

The core of the intelligence problem in Vietnam was the power of Hanoi and its unknown equations: intentions, size and disposition of forces or order of battle, the relationship to the Viet Cong in the South. Essential, also, was knowledge of the nature of the foe—northern Vietnamese customs, Asiatic traditions, and the regime's Marxist mode of thinking. There was little anthropology extant and no Census Bureau on North Vietnam. The French were the source of most information, and they were a bit biased; this in turn led most American officials to downgrade the French experience. The political emotionalism of the Vietnam issue overlooked the fundamental characteristic of the French presence in Indo-China—accommodation with, and cultural coloration of, the ruling native social and power structure. There was no basis of realistic comparison with U.S. military and economic strength and the breaking down and fractionating of native cultures which America's massive power almost blindly encouraged. In the end, it became a matter of applied physics: the centrifugal force of North Vietnam in southeast Asia versus the centrifugal force of the United States in the Pacific. Where the two arcs intersected, war sparked. The confrontation of North Vietnam and the United States evoked images of mighty Rome being lacerated into mad frustration by the Parthians. The contrast spotlighted a major difficulty in the American intelligence perspective: miniaturizing the problem, in order to see the trees instead of the forest. An occupational hazard was the incessant strain to be objective and not to ride wishful impulses.

The deadly blind man's buff of intelligence recoiled on United States military posture and diplomatic strategy. Lack of information as to the intentions of North Vietnam and its commitment of forces had an unforeseen effect on the American economy itself, the source-well of U.S. power. Original administration estimates for the fiscal 1966 budget fell short by $14 billion and the 1967 estimates by $12 billion. U.S. Senator William Proxmire, Democrat of Wisconsin and chairman of the Joint Economic Committee, could not moderate his amazement in learning that the Defense Department, forced by statutory requirements to put itself on record, had built its 1966 budget on the assumption the war would end on June 30, 1967, an assumption which Proxmire said "becomes more fantastic as I think about it."

The cost of the war required preparation of South Vietnam as a supply and staging area for U.S. troops. The total of American manpower in turn depended on the numbers of the enemy they would have to fight. The heavy technology of the American forces and huge weight of ammunition expended drastically reduced the actual number of U.S. combat troops. Combat-maneuver manpower comprised only about 30 per cent of all U.S. forces. General Westmoreland, in late 1967, under prodding by McNamara, raised the percentage of U.S. combat effectives to nearly 40 per cent. He had asked for more than the 525,000 men he was finally allowed and had so told U.S. ambassadors in southeast Asia. The ambassadors reported the meeting to Secretary Rusk. To "demonstrate the historical continuity of the military approach," they quoted Shakespeare's *Henry V*, Act IV, Scene III. In the play, on the eve of the battle of Agincourt in 1415, the Earl of Westmoreland cries out:

> O that we now had here
> But one ten thousand of those men in England. . . .

In December 1967, Westmoreland's staff in Saigon officially estimated Communist strength in South Vietnam as 118,000 main-force troops—54,000 North Vietnamese and 64,000 Viet Cong (some with North Vietnamese fillers); plus 90,000 guerillas, and 40,000 military administrative and logistic personnel, a total of 248,000. Another 80,000 in the Viet Cong political infrastructure were not included in the Saigon total. The Washington intelligence community calculated the VC politicos at 180,000, classed them as equally dangerous, and added them to the total, which thus came to an over-all estimate of over 400,000 enemy forces in South Vietnam. It raised the question of why U.S. intelligence authorities had not realized the magnitude of the enemy presence much earlier. The problem of enemy manpower, however, was not limited to South Vietnam alone, but extended to the whole Indo-China complex.

Westmoreland was very much aware of the issue of North Vietnamese infiltration into South Vietnam by the time of the Honolulu conference in June 1964, a major council of senior U.S. authorities after the death of Diem to consider Vietnam war strategy. McNamara and General Taylor, then Chairman of the Joint Chiefs, had not accepted intelligence indications of mounting infiltration because "hard proof" was lacking. Such "proof" did not transpire until December 1964. In any event, there was no one at Honolulu who was willing to buck City Hall, especially in an election year.

Nearly nine months later, in February 1965, after the bombing of North Vietnam was begun, the State Department issued a White Paper, charging North Vietnam with aggression by infiltration. The problem was not so much the numbers game of how many North Vietnamese did or did not infiltrate into South Vietnam, but stopping them before they entered

South Vietnam. The doors had to be closed; but first they had to be located. The South Vietnamese coast just below the demilitarized zone and above Hue in South Vietnam was an early landfall for Hanoi troops. The western end of the DMZ was an open thoroughfare. The eastern strip of Laos had been virtually a North Vietnam leasehold since before the Geneva accords of 1954. When the bombing of North Vietnam took place, the original military justification held that it placed an undefined—and actually, undefinable—ceiling on the numbers of men and amount of material that Hanoi could effectively send to the South Vietnamese war front. In the retaliatory U.S. bombing of North Vietnam, there was a certain wild justice, like a Sicilian vendetta, as if paying off Hanoi for overweening insolence at daring to challenge the superpower of the United States. Later, the supporting rationale was added that the bombing kept 500,000 North Vietnamese occupied with communications repairs and 178,000 in antiaircraft defenses, a clear drain on the military manpower pool. But, as McNamara testified in 1967, U.S. air attacks in no wise could consistently halt determined infiltration.

The issue between State and Defense and the CIA of finding and killing off the infiltrators from Laos, which was the major wagon-train road, was raised sharply in early 1964. It lay almost smothered for months in bureaucratic cotton padding. Washington intelligence specialists, sensing the weight of a heavier and more organized hostile presence in South Vietnam, insistently queried the Army, Navy, and Air Force for evidence of enemy infiltration. The military services reported that they noted none. But they became more alert and began to look in the right directions. An attempt had been made to organize a systematic intelligence effort in eastern Laos in 1962, to identify Hanoi movements through native road watchers and to relay reports by ground signals like laundry lines and by small hand radios. The proposal never arrived upstairs, to the highest echelons.

The State Department at that time was bending over backwards to observe the Geneva accords of 1962 on Laos, though the North Vietnamese had continually violated them. North Vietnam, from 1954 to 1968, had never officially acknowledged the presence of a single North Vietnamese soldier in Laos, or in South Vietnam for that matter. Leonard Unger, then U.S. Ambassador in Laos, had strict Department instructions to keep matters on an even keel. The United States just did not have enough forces in southeast Asia to stop the North Vietnamese if they did push into Laos. It was feared that any suddenly effective spotting and bombing of North Vietnamese supply columns in southeastern Laos, next to South Vietnam, might frighten the North Vietnamese just enough to make them veer their Pathet Lao-screened attacks toward Luang Prabang, chopsticks." LeDuan predicted that U.S.-Saigon frictions would develop, to the benefit of the VC, which in part also came to pass. He posed the basic American dilemma: "If they oppose our movement inside South Vietnam, they will be unable to stop reinforcements from North Vietnam. If they concentrate their forces to stop the reinforcements, they cannot stand firm on the front in the rear."

In fact, the war in late 1967 was tending to separate in two separate theaters. In the I and II Corps areas in the North, the battle was more or less conventional warfare against the North Vietnamese on the DMZ and in the North Central Highlands. In the III and IV Corps areas, the Southern Highlands, coastal provinces, and the Mekong Delta, the fight was a running war of population control against the Viet Cong.

State's analysis of the documents concluded that Hanoi was using negotiations not as a means of reaching a compromise settlement, but primarily as a means of continuing the fight for domination of South Vietnam. Negotiations were to be carefully coordinated with the military and political struggle, General Vinh citing possible talks as "opening another front." The expectation expressed in the Communist speeches was that fighting would continue and even intensify during negotiations, that is, the North would negotiate, but the South would keep on fighting. The documents emphasized that the battle situation would be decisive in determining the outcome of the talks and that military pressure and political proselytizing would have to be stepped up during negotiations. "We can push the Americans out by coordinating political struggle with diplomacy," and the decision to open talks would be based "upon the actual situation in the South," which would be made only after the fighting had become "indecisive," the documents stated. They cited conditions for negotiations: cessation of attacks against North Vietnam and withdrawal of U.S. and South Vietnamese forces southward, the Americans to the wharves and the South Vietnamese to their barracks. The Intelligence Bureau added its interpretation of an implicit acceptance by the Communists of an American presence in South Vietnam.

The next important document was COSVN 1967 Resolution XIII. Many subsequent references to it were taken down in copious notes by the indoctrinated Communist cadres and later found on their fallen bodies. The emphasis was again on "decisive" victory, but the statements were beginning to point toward a term when the end would be in sight. This would eventuate through a coalition regime in which the National Liberation Front would be represented in a central government, but in which the governmental infrastructure would be in Communist hands. The point was made that "Democracy is instituted in a limited way in keeping with the Front's policy." The State Department had reviewed the role

the capital of Laos. Such a development would have raised an immediate crisis that the United States could not ignore, but was not prepared for.

The concept of close air intelligence faced mental blocks in the high air command accustomed to $4 million nuclear jet bombers, whereas the planes actually needed were small propeller planes with loiter-time, that is, slow enough to be able to look at the ground carefully, and costing only a few hundred thousand dollars. In 1965, some thirty O-1's, or single-engine planes, and later T-28's, World War II craft, were imported. With the help of ground spotters, they did yeoman's work on the Laos supply trails. Previously, the jets returning to Thailand from over Hanoi, with unspent bombs, had orders to jettison their loads on the Ho Chi Minh trail. But without identifiable targets, there resulted a lot of matchwood in the jungle. Compatible radio equipment between ground and air in Laos took two years to obtain. By 1967, the big air-war generals understood that the Vietnam war resembled an eighteenth-century war, where pinpoint specifics counted, and not mass firepower alone. Mishaps dogged efforts to concentrate air power effectively on the Ho Chi Minh trail. Air-tight compartmentalization of air intelligence units prevented data from reaching operations officers. Intelligence passed on to the military command headquarters in Saigon was duly entered on the enemy order of battle, but did not proceed to the Seventh Air Force. Coordination was arriving in early 1968 to where it should have been in 1965. One day, 250 planes attacked the Ho Chi Minh trail, as reported by "informed sources," since the United States, like North Vietnam, never officially admitted its activities in Laos. Laos was where the latest Vietnam war began, and where it might end.

The mission of air power in the Vietnam war had been ideally to isolate the battlefield, that is, to prevent reinforcements from arriving. The air interdiction failure was a failure of intelligence appreciation, with strategic, diplomatic, and political consequences. The cost of the error, in effect, was transferred to the central interdiction of Communist supply lines and depots as well as infiltration routes in North Vietnam. The bombing developed into a systematic pulverization of the North Vietnamese military-industrial complex to such a degree as to arouse world and American opinion and give the Hanoi politburo a sizable propaganda asset, which portrayed the bombings as the principal stumbling block to diplomatic negotiations for an end to the war. The bombing of North Vietnam was an example of the war of attrition the United States had historically waged in three major conflicts—World Wars I and II and Korea. It exposed also the inarticulate American people's raw nerve of complicity in the tragedy of the war. The bombing was not a prime example of the Aristotelian law of "all things in measure." And the war need not have gone on so long if accurate intelligence had been searched for in the early years of the Vietnam crisis.

If having allowed the Ho Chi Minh trail to remain comparatively inviolate had been a failure of intelligence, Cambodia was ultimately a belated triumph of intelligence. Up to two North Vietnamese divisions had been operating out of many installations in Laos for some years. At least one and a half North Vietnamese divisions operating out of Cambodia had been using six staging areas in Cambodia since 1966, if not earlier. The Cambodian issue had broken into the open in late 1967, when U.S. newsmen, usually barred, had been allowed to enter Cambodia to cover the visit of Jacqueline Kennedy. The reporters, all South Vietnam correspondents—George McArthur of the Associated Press, Ray Herndon of the United Press International, and William Touhy of the *Los Angeles Times*—uncovered an actual, but abandoned, Viet Cong base camp, with a log-road running to the Vietnam border. The camp was just where the grid coordinates on the intelligence maps said it would be. It was a major diplomatic news scoop of the Vietnamese war. The reporters' stories confirmed what the U.S. military in Saigon had known for months.

Pressure escalated to Washington to permit on the ground and in the air "hot pursuit" of enemy units which might flee into the Cambodian border areas. Anxiety rose in Washington at the understandable pressure of the military seeking authorization to pursue the enemy across frontiers and risk expansion of the war, with all the international unknowns of Soviet and Communist Chinese reactions. The State Department intervened at this point. Averell Harriman, then Ambassador-at-Large and executive-level staff officer responsible for coordinating the search for, and testing of, Hanoi feelers, resumed his role of elder statesman of the Department. Acting the part of "The Old Crocodile," Harriman showed his teeth to the Joint Chiefs and cooled the "hot pursuit" vehemence.

The breather allowed the Department to undertake diplomatic parleys with Prince Sihanouk, Cambodia's chief of state and the most sensitive weathervane in the Far East. Ambassador to India Chester Bowles, the President's special envoy, handed the Prince a large package of intelligence documentation—photographs, maps with marked locations, and prisoners' of war interrogation records. Sihanouk, whose short name in the Department was "Snooks," was agile enough to seize the opening that might lift the peril from his nation of acting as a helpless sanctuary for the North Vietnamese and their VC allies.

The State Department also was the beneficiary in 1967 of intelligence-by-windfall as the U.S. armed forces penetrated or destroyed forty of the fifty-three hitherto invulnerable Communist base sanctuaries inside South Vietnam and began capturing reams of enemy documents. The Com-

munist papers, which ranged from dead soldiers' diaries and notebo[oks] to military orders, party directives, and resolutions of the COSVN, Central Office for South Vietnam, indicated that the insurgents and infiltrators ran a rather hefty bureaucratic machinery of their own. documents provided a glimpse at the other side of the Looking G[lass] and disclosed that the enemy had motes in his eyes in the same way Americans had some in theirs. By the end of 1967 the documents were [ac]cumulating at the rate of nearly 5,000 a month, and the CIA undertook mammoth task of sorting them out, collating them, and testing their auth[en]ticity. In many cases, events and the passage of time retroactively proved the contents by the time the Americans found them. Sample summaries v[ere] regularly delivered for the fascinated attention of the President. Signifi[cant] document finds were made during January, September, and Novembe[r] 1967, though events referred to had happened several months earlier.

In an analysis made in April 1967 by State's Intelligence Bureau addressed to Rusk, with copies to the White House and fifteen intere[sted] agencies, the Bureau found that the first batch of documents substanti[ated] the conclusions the intelligence community had drawn from diffe[rent] sources, namely, that the Communist effort in South Vietnam was sl[ated] to persist unabated for the then foreseeable future. The first documents been major finds, though the strategy outlined was nearly a year old. [One] was a letter of LeDuan, first secretary of the Lao Dong (Commu[nist] party of North Vietnam to the April 1966 COSVN congress. Two o[f the] documents were copies of speeches made to the same congress by Se[nior] General Nguyen Chi Thanh and Major General Nguyen Van Vinh. [The] former was North Vietnamese commander-in-chief in the South; he [died] later of a "heart attack," believed to be a euphemism for a U.S. air r[aid].

All three Communist chieftains admitted difficulties and were confi[dent] of ultimate victory; however, they called not for "total" victory as bef[ore] but for "decisive" victory, and with no emphasis on "protracted war," the public Hanoi propaganda, echoing Peking, had reiterated. The do[cu]ments frankly admitted that, in 1964 and early 1965, when the C[om]munists had victory in their grasp in South Vietnam, they had not an[tici]pated the scope and speed of the U.S. introduction of forces into [the] battlefield. State's analysis pointed out that the Hanoi-VC forces displayed greater tactical flexibility than the Americans had assumed possible. The Communist reports asserted that the United States did [not] have sufficient troops to execute all its required missions of base defe[nse], sweep operations, pacification, and defense of the DMZ, and that million troops would be needed to do so. This was not far from w[hat] some U.S. generals were also saying at the time. General Vinh said t[hat] VC tactics would be devised so as to make "the Americans eat rice w[ith]

the National Liberation Front might play in a Vietnam settlement as long ago as 1964 and 1965. By January and August 1966, news reports transpired concerning U.S. efforts to split possible nationalist elements from Communist leadership in the NLF.

The third set of key documents all related to a coming climactic winter-spring Communist offensive of 1967–1968, which, in point of fact, began as predicted. The Department was taking a long breath in readiness for eventual negotiations, but was not impatient. Too many unknowns had to come out of the dark before positive plans could be initiated for the specific situation of that moment. The Department authorities approached with extreme caution the latest teaser for negotiations from Hanoi in January 1968. This was the statement of North Vietnamese Foreign Minister Nguyen Van Trinh that Hanoi "will" hold conversations promptly, once the U.S. bombing stopped.

The test would be over two words: resupply or reinforce. The outlook envisaged a concentric circle of negotiations or talks: internal, for South Vietnam as to the fate of the NLF in the political life of that nation; and external, for the United States, South Vietnam, and the rest of the allies with Hanoi, and involving at some point reconvocation of the Geneva conferences for both Indo-China and Laos. Communist China had been a member of the Indo-China conference, and if she showed up again, there was the not unlikely possibility that she would demand a strip of northernmost Laos, in Sam Neua province, to rationalize her frontiers, and as a nuisance price. But there was neither hurry nor delay about a war settlement, however much it was desired. In 1965 alone, there had been at least fifty "peace feelers" initiated or supported by the United States, and by early 1968 the file had become over three feet high and listed nearly 400 reports of all kinds on the elusive subject of peace. As Rusk said, channels for communicating with Hanoi were no problem.

Lastly, and also firstly, as indicated earlier, the press was a source of intelligence to the State Department. It was also a pain to its fundamentals of security operations. The correspondents of the Vietnam war—over 400, and more than half of them Americans—served in the manner once acclaimed by General Marshall as "inspector generals" of the public interest. The standard of reportage since 1967 had greatly improved in quality and, particularly, in volume. Besides satiating or befuddling ordinary readers with saturation coverage, the press was reporting facts or fragments of the situations that more or less consistently went against the grain of the Department and the administration. Controversies in Saigon and reechoing in Washington rose frequently over interpretative stories in which some of the press drew political conclusions at variance with those of the officials. The day-after-day military spot reporting of the wire services, above all, was in the great traditions of war correspondence. As 1968 began, ten correspondents and photographers had been killed and nearly a hundred wounded by virtue of being exactly where the action was.

What alternately baffled or irritated the Department authorities, however, were the conclusions drawn by reporters from official remarks on the record, and the consequent headline play and tag-lines used to describe— the officials would say "distort"—the reports. On October 12, 1967, for example, Rusk held a press conference where, in response to a question from John Finney of the *New York Times,* he said: "Within the next decade or two, there will be a billion Chinese on the mainland, armed with nuclear weapons, with no certainty about what their attitude toward the rest of Asia will be." The news exploded in sensational newspaper headlines that Rusk had invoked "the yellow peril," whereupon indignant anti-Vietnam-policy columnists denounced Rusk, and U.S. Senator Eugene McCarthy, Democrat of Wisconsin, demanded that Rusk resign.

The Rusk press conferences normally ran half an hour, with the senior correspondent present, usually John Hightower of the Associated Press, closing it on the half hour with a "Thank you, Mr. Secretary." On this occasion, Hightower let the conference run on. "He probably saw I was all steamed up and might say something," Rusk said later, with a smile. The explosive question had come after the regular thirty minutes had elapsed. Assistant Secretary Dixon Donnelley had tried in advance to interest the three television networks in live coverage of the press conference, but the TV media declined unless Donnelley could guarantee ahead of time that Rusk would say something sensational. Rusk's news conference had been timely because that week the Congressional critics had been particularly severe. The President naturally was pleased with the vigor of Rusk's counterattack and the word went out that "The Boss wants to crank up the maximum" on Rusk publicity.

After seven years in the grueling office, Rusk apparently had made up his mind that Ortega y Gasset's remark, "After forty, one can no longer live on fictions," was very well taken. Basically, he appeared to have a philosophy about lesser matters of "What difference does it make?," as long as the issues were not in the most sensitive domain that he reserved for himself as the senior cabinet adviser to the President. At such moments Rusk gave away no grace points and was not to be pushed around. Thus, in the heyday of the McNamara prestige, Rusk never chafed at the brighter spotlight accorded the Defense Secretary. McNamara, on his way home, used to drop into Rusk's office for a chat at cocktail time. Rusk often spoke of McNamara's warmhearted humanity. He seemed to treat the Defense Secretary with affectionate tolerance, like a big brother to a younger brother who was terrifically smart but who would get wiser in time.

Rusk's associates, however, chafed at what they termed the upmanship of McNamara's associates in taking advantage of Rusk's laissez-faire nonchalance. The issue that rankled in particular was that McNamara should every year make what amounted to an annual review of foreign policy as the preface to the Defense Department's budget presentation. In 1967, Rusk's cohorts determined to produce a State Department White Paper on the State of the World for Rusk to deliver before Congressional committees. It would outline the foreign policy goals of the United States and their relation to current problems and touch on the major crises of the future, in short, give an account of Rusk's stewardship of U.S. global responsibilities. The brave hope of the faithful was to provide Rusk with a document which would shed some first-class limelight on him, instead of the reflected light Rusk seemed to be satisfied with. McNamara could then take the basic Rusk report and use it to tell Congress how he proposed to implement the Rusk foreign policy outline militarily. As it happened, Defense Department bureaucrats heard of the possible coup and demanded State's foreign policy notes for McNamara's budget presentation before the State officers could hand the finished product to Rusk. So again in 1967 McNamara gave the annual foreign policy review of the world.

Rusk took no notice and could not have cared less. He recalled that in World War II, the U.S. War Department General Staff had made considerable foreign policy by acting faster than State or by stepping into the vacuum created by the absence of the State Department. The "State of the World" issue was too trivial, and Rusk consistently tried to adhere to General Marshall's injunction, "Avoid trivia." Rusk had already made a name in fighting the Defense Department much earlier. In 1949, when he was Deputy Under Secretary of State, he had given Defense Secretary Louis Johnson a hard time because of Johnson's economy-minded attitude about defense preparedness, so much so that Johnson used to complain to Secretary Acheson that Rusk was trying to "take over the Pentagon." Rusk certainly had no such thoughts in the 1960's. When the Vietnam war ended, he would lead the United States delegation into conference for an honorable negotiation and then, his conscience clear, retire for a deeply earned rest and reflection upon the state of the world that he had had so much to do with.

Brooding over the state of the world in relation to the operating foreign policy of the United States was the job of the State Department's Policy Planning Council. Policy planning was one further way in which the original raw datum of information, after passing through the assembly line of intelligence evaluation and operational utilization, served as a building block for the construction of new operational ideas in a global context. The constant purpose of any policy planning was not the examination of ideas per se, but the adaptation of concepts, new, old, neglected, or untried, to the machinery of government within the total framework of U.S. policy. Policy was the commitment of resources to objectives. Policy planning at its best implied filing a "hard brief," bucking the system, shifting the focus, overcoming bureaucratic inertia, in order to change an operational approach or an objective, in the over-all interest of more efficient operations for specifically valid national goals. The operators and the planners were thus natural adversaries, the former wanting to continue doing the same as they had been doing, the latter wanting to try something different. A plan was a hope projected, and possibly articulated within a wide working horizon; a policy was a definite commitment to a line of action to be followed, and possibly consummated in the near or intermediate future.

The Policy Planning Council was in the nature of a testing laboratory for ideas, though to the sceptical directors of policy the problem was not so much new ideas as moving ahead those ideas already in the mill. Many officers regarded the Council as an assignment that looked good on one's record, prestigious but not demanding, a graduate seminar in self-education, where there was even the off-chance that the highest authorities would suddenly become interested in a project and energize one's latent talents. For the basic blue-chip asset of the Policy Planning Council was that its two principal customers were the President and the Secretary of State, who had a vested interest in new and better ideas and approaches in fulfilling what was the President's dominant role as a leader: guiding the nation into the unknown of the future.

The Policy Council's efficacy depended heavily on the style of its immediate superior, the Secretary of State. If not kept effectively busy, it perforce treaded water or spun cobwebs. The first much-heralded postwar policy planning staff of 1947 was that of George Kennan with Secretary Marshall. Under Paul H. Nitze, the planning staff was used closely and systematically as a "kitchen cabinet" by Secretary Acheson. Nitze eventually became Deputy Secretary of Defense in the Johnson administration, but never quite lost the air of a pale conspirator working in a tapestried inner closet of the Acheson ducal palace. His successor, Robert Bowie, ran a more permissive shop, allowing Council members to prosecute their own ideas. Bowie became one of Secretary Dulles' closest confidantes, though he disagreed strenuously with most of Dulles' notions of foreign policy. He was eventually successful in helping Dulles re-educate himself, like a stream of water wearing down a rock. Bowie, in 1967, was back in government as counselor of the Department, gazing on the world out of wise pixie eyes while awaiting summons to the Sultan's council chambers, calls which came not too frequently.

Like Nitze and Bowie, the next policy chief, Gerard C. Smith, was an operator, a most useful high-level bureaucrat. Following Smith came George McGhee, who was strictly a holding operation and a safe anchor for Rusk. McGhee is noted as the only planner who experimentally attempted to translate a foreign policy situation into a mathematical equation so that its elements might possibly be worked out on a computer. The direction of the Policy Planning Council then fell to Walt Rostow, who came from the White House in 1962 and returned to it in 1965. Rostow was the nearest thing to a perpetual-motion machine that the State Department had ever seen, generating ideas, projects, and recommendations like sparks off an emery wheel. Rostow was never very close to Rusk at State, but he had entree everywhere on the top levels of government, including the White House and the Pentagon. Hardly any subject was safe from Rostow's inveterate curiosity. After Rostow, the succession went to Henry Owen, a special breed in government on two counts. He was one of the comparatively few civil service officers who had gone to the top rank as a GS-18 in foreign policy, instead of the technical and administrative side of the Department. He was also a rarity in having been with the policy planning staff continuously since 1955, an unusual continuity of planning expertise. Owen was one of the original MLF, or multinuclear force, zealots and fervently dedicated to the ideals of European unity and Atlantic partnership. His intense drive sometimes aroused friction, hence resistance. But he knew his way around the bases.

Kennan and Rostow had been genuine Grade-A ideologues and intellectuals, respected as the McCoy by the academic world. Owen was scholarly, but too busy in government to write books. Needed was an authentic, high-class intellectual who could introduce some zip, pepper, yeast, and stimulation into Council discussions. The choice was Zbigniew Brzezinski, professor of government at Columbia University and director of its Research Institute on Communist Affairs. In his year on the Council, Brzezinski's effervescent personality and new pragmatism concerning Communist affairs pumped up excitement and debate, if not much action, and brought him swift attention inside government circles. Some admirers already called Brzezinski the "new Kennan." Brzezinski's brisk, crisp, and lucid discourses to the national foreign policy conferences for editorial writers and commentators invariably brought down the house, an uncommon experience for State Department speakers. Kennan adumbrated and lucubrated, sighing profundities like a Delphic oracle breathing words on papyrus. Brzezinski ratiocinated and generated concepts, glosses, generalizations, and comments like a computer spraying electrons on magnetic tape.

Kennan's sense of style was no insignificant element in his early success. State placed a tremendous premium on writing ability, since the product consisted mainly of words. Officers who could write clearly, or who were skilled at deliberate ambiguity, went ahead fast. But at a certain point in literate officers' careers, a language barrier arose. The prose was so good that it interfered with clarity. The words about a problem might have been pungent, but not cogent; replete with the urgency of the moment, but not plain enough about the practicalities of resolution. Acheson used to cite Kennan as a prime example of the author of siren-like prose that seduced the judgment by the chiaroscuro of the diction, so much so, that Acheson used to have Kennan's messages copyread into cablese to obtain their unembellished gist.

Rusk was definitely interested in policy planning. His family friends testified that Rusk personally planned far ahead, and had done so since boyhood. He was especially interested in strengthening advance planning so that foreign policy troubles could be spotted and dealt with before big crises blew up. Rusk said: "The United States must aim at the future if we expect to come on target for the present. Otherwise, we just knock off a few tail feathers of today's fast-flying problems." But Rusk was busy. There was the Vietnam war and there was the imperious President. The Council met with Rusk every three or four weeks, depending on the Secretary's schedule, to discuss a planning paper, which Rusk might have glanced at but not had the time to read. Having Rusk as a captive audience at least was one means of planting ideas in his mind, whence they might germinate into useful reactions at some later date.

Always sensitive to the charge that the State Department did not procreate new ideas, Rusk in mid-1967 asked Owen to "seek out fresh ideas and thinking," even "unorthodox" ones or those "not considered immediately feasible." Rusk desired to encourage response from junior and mid-grade officers. Owen formed an "Open Forum Panel," composed of lower-level officers, who screened some 150 "new ideas" from both the Department at home and overseas posts, including suggestions from clerical employees. Out of all these, the panel culled five or six ideas, mostly of a modest middle-management nature, interesting enough to be sent to Rusk through the Policy Planning Council. Two of these were sent on to the appropriate geographical bureaus for comment. After an initial floodlet, the idea flow petered out to from ten to fifteen a month by early 1968. As the blasé professionals remarked, ideas which were new, workable, and acceptable were the rarest things in government.

Getting ideas or improvements in the machinery was somewhat like rubbing oil into fine furniture. It depended on the right oil and the technique. State's veterans averred that Owen would be better than Rostow at it, Rostow having been a wide-ranging high-flier, while Owen liked to work out details. In any event, in late 1966 the Council produced its first big paper under Owen, an identification of all the major issues which the United States might encounter for the next two years, 1967 and 1968. Rusk sent the policy planning opus back with the comment that the proposals were not controversial enough to challenge the geographical operating bureaus into counterargument. By June 1967 the basic study retooling had been accomplished and exchanges with the operating bureaus undertaken. The list of topics which the Council looked into was nothing if not impressive. How the eventual recommendations would find their way into operating policy was another matter. The Council at any rate fertilized the ground assiduously.

Owen's working philosophy saw crisis as the best time to insert a quotient of a new idea or approach into an issue. In times of crisis, State's senior directors were hungry for options. Work in progress included long-range strategic reconnaissance into control moves after the Soviet-American draft treaty for nonproliferation of nuclear weapons had been approved by the seventeen-nation disarmament conference at Geneva. The treaty essentially pledged good faith on the part of those who adhered; there was no spelling out what came after. The Council for the first time took a real look at the future of U.S. military aid. After seven long years of being lost in the bowels of the Pentagon, U.S. policy for military aid had been quietly taken over by the two top officials below Rusk—Katzenbach and Eugene Rostow. Methods to improve the peace-keeping function of international society were studied, with or without the United Nations, against the backdrop of criticism of the U.S. role of "world policeman" in the wake of the pound sterling's devaluation. In the monetary field, the Council examined the gold question and the balance-of-payments problem in relation to its effects of limiting the scope of U.S. foreign policy in the world.

Methods of international cooperation in handling disasters of nature—floods, hurricanes, and earthquakes—was a new subject on the Policy Planning Council's list. As a sequel to the major planning study on the world food crisis and U.S. policy made by Jerome F. Fried in July 1967, before he moved over to take Francis Bator's job as top foreign economic expert at the White House, the Council was examining the world fertilizer situation. A study of the international exploitation of the resources of the ocean floor beyond the continental shelves was also on the books.

There were continuing stand-by subjects to be assessed periodically and new adjustments to be recommended: the Soviet Union; the European Common Market and British entry; the future of Japan in the Far East and its defense roles; a follow-up study on NATO after proposals of Belgian Foreign Minister Pierre Harmel had been adopted, proposals in which the Policy Planning Council had been consulted; alternative opportunities feasible in southeast Asia, including Vietnam, after the war ended; a short-term study of immediate problems in the Middle East crisis, for example, the problem of refugees, to supplement the high-level study supervised by Under Secretary Rostow; how to supply resources to the underdeveloped countries through private enterprise in supplement to government aid; the relationships of Singapore, Indonesia, and Malaysia to the southwest Pacific; German unification, a central European settlement, and East-West relations; and the defense role of Canada.

Just as new generations fed on the left-overs of the old, the Policy Planning Council had two perennials from its own past regularly in its in-basket. The newer one was regionalism. Even greater emphasis was planned to speed the regional trend developing in Latin America, Africa, and Asia, and possibly a new Pacific Basin grouping. Regionalism had been a pet project of Walt Rostow in 1962. The concept had an effect in helping splinter the so-called Afro-Asian bloc. The older subject was Communist China and Asia. Kennan and Bowie had urged that major emphasis be placed on Japan and India as the two anchors of Free World strength in Asia. Three China studies in the Council files dated from 1961, 1962, and 1966. The interrelation of the nonproliferation treaty and the burgeoning Chinese nuclear capability was of particular importance in a U.S. policy study of India, Pakistan, and south Asia. India, though fully capable of nuclear bomb production, did not desire to undertake the heavy investment involved. Yet she did not welcome U.S. guarantees of nuclear protection.

The Council had two brand-new items on its agenda for 1968. One was an inquiry into U.S. objectives in all of southern Africa, where mixed white-black racial conflicts smoldered, including Rhodesia, the Portuguese colonies, Zambia, and South Africa. The other was a review of U.S. interests in the Caribbean, the Mediterranean of the Americas, where the self-surrender of British influence and the presence of Castro's Cuba were the major factors.

The policy planners had the ancient mariner of all subjects—foreign aid—as a priority project. After twenty years of Congressional buffets, foreign aid was a pretty scrawny creature. Getting funds for foreign aid had become like "kicking the old cow in the ribs to make her give more milk," as Rusk once said. The Council had made a thorough study of the foreign aid issue in 1956, which resulted in the development loan fund approach for long-term aid. Owen had been one of the authors of the study. Bowie, then director of the Policy Planning Council, had felt that the United States had not been devoting enough aid to the less developed countries, and he had been able to bring Dulles around to his viewpoint.

The planners had been involved in aspects of Latin American aid through Rostow in 1964. Earlier, again under Rostow, the Council had taken on the cause of fish flour, which contained 80 per cent protein, as a low-cost food that could be of tremendous use in the protein-deficient underdeveloped areas of the world. More specifically, the championship of fish flour was assumed by Captain William W. Behrens, Jr., a U.S. naval officer assigned for a tour on the Council. Besides making a staff study on the food's potentialities, Behrens personally prosecuted approval of the product through the Washington bureaucracy, where divided opinions had stalled acceptance of the food for human use for several years. Behrens' satisfaction came in early 1967, when the Department of Interior opened its first pilot plant for fish protein concentrate.

Whatever the policy planners would come up with in foreign aid was bound to be of intense interest to President Johnson. The President was looking toward 1970. In talking to many experts in and out of the Government, including Barbara Ward, the British economist, the President was arriving at the conclusion that an entirely new foreign aid framework was imperative, a new world development charter in which all richer countries would give according to their means and all poorer countries would receive according to the degree of self-help they manifested.

The Policy Planning Council of the State Department was keenly interested in exploring dissent, that is, the dissent of the outside academic and communications community. It invited personal argumentation from authors of the articles on "Toward the Year 2000: Work in Progress," in the summer 1967 issue of *Daedalus,* the journal of the American Academy of Arts and Sciences, a top holding company of U.S. intellectuals, on the alleged decadence of American power. Council members even took a careful look at "Black Power" and its significance. The staff read organs of the radical left, such as the *New York Review of Books,* the *New Republic,* and the *New Leader,* in an earnest quest for understanding.

The State Department in 1967 appointed over 125 eminent persons as consultants to its geographical bureaus. The Policy Planning Council did likewise in the fields of food and population, underdeveloped countries, and developed countries. It conscientiously sought out ranking specialists who were in dissent with official modes of thought. It asked experts who had toured overseas to report their findings and send in their ideas, suggestions, and reactions on the operation of U.S. foreign policies overseas.

During fiscal 1967, the Department used the services of a total of 207 consultants, whose normal fee was $100 a day. The average consultant worked fifteen days and was paid an average of $1,053 for his services, excluding travel. The trouble with consultants, brilliant and savvy though some of them were, was they did not stay long enough to meet the payroll, that is, to see the way in which every-day pressures or crises affected originally bright ideas. When possible, which was infrequent, ranking authorities were asked to take a year's leave from their professions to serve on the Council. Even a year was not long enough. Officials concluded that eighteen months as a minimum would have better served both the Department and the experts.

The planning group was admittedly weak in science and its application to foreign policy, as was the whole Department for that matter, despite strenuous efforts to keep abreast of the latest scientific developments. Too many implications between technological progress and military exploitation potentially hazardous to U.S. interests were being picked up tardily. Other nations, for instance, were developing capabilities for shooting communications satellites 72,500 miles into space. The same thrusts could launch missiles.

The Policy Planning Council was thoroughly at home with the military, however. Its founder, in fact, had been a general, George Marshall, in May 1947. It worked closely with the policy planning staff of the Defense Department's Office of International Security Affairs. Almost one third of the Council members dealt with politico-military matters primarily, while all the rest were involved in the same field occasionally. In 1963, for instance, nineteen of thirty-one major studies contained preponderantly military quotients. Council chairmen were regularly in touch with the Joint Chiefs of Staff.

Under Nitze in Acheson's time, the Council was the original architect of top national security policy, as in the now classic case of NSC 68, which correlated the military and economic strength which the United States required to perform the tasks confronting the nation. NSC 68 provided the underpinning for the Korean war. In 1953, before he left office, Nitze executed NSC 114, which provided for another quantum jump to match the needs of the 1950's. Otherwise, Nitze said, a government would face the danger of setting war aims out of line with its capabilities. Nitze was involved with Acheson in nuclear questions and German rearmament. Acheson urged haste with German defense so that by the time the American atomic monopoly had dissipated there could be a countervailing balance of conventional forces in western Europe. Again in the question of building the H-bomb, it was not so much whether to make it or not as planning how to use the increased political weight which Acheson and the policy planners then thought the detonation of the H-bomb would give the United States.

Bowie and Smith, with Dulles, were also heavily engaged with military matters. Bowie recommended in 1954 that NATO be given tactical nuclear weapons, a proposal which surprisingly had few reverberations at the time. Dulles did not get into the issue of tactical nuclears because he felt that his purchase with President Eisenhower rested on Dulles' confining himself to subjects on which Eisenhower would readily acknowledge Dulles' expertise. Dulles said he did not propose to dilute his influence with the President by overextending his leverage. From the start of their relationship, Bowie told Dulles that massive retaliation was nonsense and that a more flexible military posture was necessary. Smith continued Bowie's work. Before Dulles resigned, he admitted that massive retaliation had about run its course, and he told the Joint Chiefs, to no avail, that a new strategy was called for. The last Defense Secretary of the Eisenhower regime, Thomas Gates, began to put into effect many of the ideas which were elaborated later by McNamara in the Kennedy administration.

There was little doubt that the policy planners had consistently kept their eyes on the main arena of events in postwar history. Kennan had been alert to European unity, the British relationship thereto, German unification, the Japanese treaty, the foreign exchange crisis, and the problems of transition between administrations. Disarmament was a continuing theme. Nitze did the first big paper on it for United Nations presentation in 1952. Bowie's single-minded efforts led to the establishment of the first disarmament office in the State Department. He organized the first comprehensive U.S. disarmament plan for the London conference of 1957. Smith and his staff originated many Berlin crisis proposals, the MLF, what was later to become the Alliance for Progress, the "hot line" teleprinter between Washington and Moscow, the substance of the first Western peace plan for German unity, and recommendations for a sea-level Panama Canal.

In the Owen regime the Policy Planning Council met once a week, on Fridays, to discuss projects and papers. Between 1961 and 1966, the Council produced 339 papers, averaging fifty pages in length. In 1962, one series of papers pointed the finger at forty-four potential crises on the horizon. In 1964, the planners had a high-production year, piling up seventy-one studies. A principal manufacture used to be national policy papers. In 1960, the Council wrote thirty national policy papers, identifying 652 courses of action possible. Rostow, when he took over in 1962, started to write a definitive National Security Council policy paper covering the whole range of foreign policy for the new Kennedy administration. But the job was never completed because such a paper did not seem to fit the needs of the new era.

Though Foreign Service Corps inspectors would have preferred a specific national policy paper for each of the 120-odd countries in the world, the decision was made to concentrate, instead, on those countries in which the United States had vital military-economic interests. This limited the list to between twenty-five and thirty-five. By 1965, seven revised national policy papers on key countries had been approved, and thirteen were in the assembly line. The official Department definition said:

Each NPP rests on an analysis of the social, political, economic, and military forces at work in the country in question and of those forces which bear on the country in the international sphere. Alternatives confronting the United States are identified and a U.S. strategy derived for the next three to five years. Regional considerations and the implications of the country's participation in international organizations are taken into account in formulating this strategy. Specific courses of action essential to carrying out the strategy during the next year or two are then set forth.

In theory, the papers purported to outline what the United States would like to see happen in X-country. Sometimes seven different policy positions might have to be rationalized in one paper, but without any effective means of controlling procedures and budgets for the attainment of the goals cited by the over-all national policy paper. Such a situation was precisely what the Senior Interdepartment Group, or SIG, had been established to coordinate. As a result, the Policy Planning Council was brought into the SIG area via regular consultations on the background of the Senior Group's agenda. A new stress was placed on providing papers for specific requirements of the geographical bureaus as the need arose and on stimulating the bureaus to do more systematic operational planning of their own.

The regional bureaus were supposed to keep current statements of policy concerning the countries within their jurisdiction through so-called guideline papers. Generally, the guidelines were rather flabby stuff, such as, "The United States Is Against Communism." Foreign Service officers sniffed at them. Part of the blame for the poor quality was laid on the pressures of work, that is, the lack of time to do a good job and have it approved by the other foreign affairs agencies. There was also the tendency of professionals not to question the assumptions of their own policies, hence, to deprecate the implied scepticism of a policy planning approach.

A measure of confusion existed about what policy planning meant, in relation to other kinds of planning. Basically, a planning paper was a long-term analysis. It could also be a scenario, in which a specific time element was invoked and events were programmed according to the theory of the planner's analysis. Variations were possible in the so-called war-peace game, in which State's officers participated more and more with Defense and CIA in set problems. In addition, there were standard contingency planning for alternative solutions to likely eventualities and straight operational planning for specific actions known in advance. The policy planning staff faced a constant dilemma: If it were removed from operations, it was isolated in an ivory tower of ineffectualness; if it became involved in operations, it was too close to the action to note the long sweep of events. Bowie's answer was that the planners should take part in "selected decisions which were likely to be significant for the future." More conventional bureaucrats held that the essence of policy was predictability; yet they acknowledged that foreign policy had especially a long "lead-time," in which the unknown obscured attempts at focus. System-analysis devotees talked of "structuring uncertainty" and indeterminate strategies, like Boolian mathematicians. The historically minded quoted Freud's remark to Lewis Namier that the mark of a neurotic was his fixation on the past, which, Namier added, was "the normal condition of political societies." There was at least a two-year lag between the time a sound, new policy idea had begun fermenting in the bureaucracy and the time it surfaced to official, let alone public, view. Policy ideas were caught between the hurricane of technological acceleration of events in the outside world and the icepack of anachronisms within the minds of officials and politicians. Between the weight of the future and the suffocation of the past, a policy idea had an extremely breathless time squeezing through the narrow interstice of the present.

It was thus with a sense of pleasurable relief that the policy planning staff from time to time applied to its foreign brethren for stimulation and unofficial suggestions in the arduous business of practical soothsaying about world events and trends. Gerard Smith had initiated a ten-year planning span, principally in connection with the Atlantic Policy Advisors' group. The Council was the U.S. representative to the group. The meetings with foreigners were unofficial and off the record, so everyone could speak freely and not commit his government. Informal planning sessions were held with the Japanese, the West Germans, and the Brazilians. The policy staff aimed at similar relations with the Canadians. The Arabs were out of the question, in the present state of affairs, and the Indians were still too skittish about their neutrality, even in private, to sit down to bilateral planning talks with a world power like the United States. As in so many other fields, the longest-lived planning relations were with the British. The Foreign Office itself had had a planning section only since 1957. The practical British found that it was comparatively easy to agree on forecasts, but difficult to agree on what action should be planned.

The British, as was not unusual, had hit the nail on the head. The consensus was that the Policy Planning Council had produced many original and possibly even profound ideas in the 1960's, but that the ideas were valuable only insofar as they could be moved into the stream of action. The further consensus in the Department was that the great days of the Council had been during the Acheson-Dulles eras, when it had been institutionally employed as a super staff for bringing operations together under specific concepts. Individual planners might become very influential, as Rostow had, or receive generous credit for fire-brigade assignments or helping draft major speeches of the President. How to fructify operationally the talent lying dormant in the Planning Council was a constant preoccupation. Policy planning papers on subjects before the SIG had suggested larger use of the Interagency Planning Group, which had been the heart of the National Security Council system under Eisenhower. After the NSC's Operations Coordinating Board had been abolished, the same members met informally and on a strictly consultative basis every Thursday with State's Policy Planning Council chairman. This already organized group was a tailor-made planning agency, if used, for the SIG. But, as Rusk liked to say, "The last chapter was the hardest to write." At best, there were no easy answers, as Thomas C. Schelling of Harvard, who had delved deeply into the Department, told the Jackson committee in January 1968. Schelling said:

Foreign affairs is a complicated and disorderly business, full of surprises, demanding hard choices that must often be based on judgment rather than analysis, involving relations with more than a hundred countries diverse in their traditions and political institutions—all taking place in a world that changes so rapidly that memory and experience are quickly out of date. Coordination, integration, and rational management are surely desirable; but whether it is humanly possible to meet anything more than the barest minimum standards is a question to which an optimistic answer can be based only on faith.

In sum, planning the fullest employment of its most efficient and wisest officers for a career command staff appeared to be the crux of the problems facing the State Department and the foreign affairs community. Curiously, the Policy Planning Council hardly ever stopped to ponder its own professional environment and the inferences that could be drawn therefrom on the state of the union and the condition of the world. The solution, in the end, was one for the President to propose and for the Congress to authorize. Congress itself needed wholesale reorganization to act rationally concerning the welter of foreign affairs issues and their intimate interconnection with domestic affairs. Considerable reshaping of the foreign affairs community, its methods and objectives, could be accomplished by departmental administrative patchwork and presidential directive, as the bureacracy intimated. But the most solid foundation might best be established by statutory reorganization in which Congress fully participated from the start. The times called for radical decisions like those which created the Defense Department and the CIA in 1947, a new constitution for the conduct and management of the foreign affairs of the nation as the Department of State and the world plunged toward the twenty-first century.

INDEX